Lecture Notes in Computer Science　　10580

Commenced Publication in 1973
Founding and Former Series Editors:
Gerhard Goos, Juris Hartmanis, and Jan van Leeuwen

More information about this series at http://www.springer.com/series/7407

Dang Van Hung · Deepak Kapur (Eds.)

Theoretical Aspects of Computing – ICTAC 2017

14th International Colloquium
Hanoi, Vietnam, October 23–27, 2017
Proceedings

 Springer

Editors
Dang Van Hung
Vietnam National University
Hanoi
Vietnam

Deepak Kapur
University of New Mexico
Albuquerque, NM
USA

ISSN 0302-9743   ISSN 1611-3349 (electronic)
Lecture Notes in Computer Science
ISBN 978-3-319-67728-6   ISBN 978-3-319-67729-3   (eBook)
DOI 10.1007/978-3-319-67729-3

Library of Congress Control Number: 2017953430

LNCS Sublibrary: SL1 – Theoretical Computer Science and General Issues

Printed on acid-free paper

This Springer imprint is published by Springer Nature
The registered company is Springer International Publishing AG
The registered company address is: Gewerbestrasse 11, 6330 Cham, Switzerland

Preface

This volume contains the papers presented at the 14th International Colloquium on Theoretical Aspects of Computing (ICTAC), held in Hanoi, Vietnam, during October 23–27, 2017.

The International Colloquium on Theoretical Aspects of Computing (ICTAC) constitutes a series of annual conferences/schools, initiated in 2003 by the then United Nations University International Institute for Software Technology, to bring together researchers and provide them with an international venue to present their results, exchange ideas, and engage in discussions. There were two additional goals: (i) promote cooperation between participants from emerging and developed regions, and most importantly, (ii) provide an opportunity for students and young researchers to get exposed to topical research directions in theoretical aspects of computing technologies.

ICTAC 2017 received 40 full-paper submissions coauthored by researchers from 20 different countries. Each submission was reviewed by at least three Program Committee (PC) members with the help of reviewers outside the PC. After two weeks of online discussions, the committee decided to accept 17 papers for presentation at the conference.

We would like to express our gratitude to all the researchers who submitted their work to the symposium. We are particularly thankful to all colleagues who served on the Program Committee, as well as the external reviewers, whose hard work in the review process helped us prepare the conference program. The international diversity of the PC as well as the external reviewers is noteworthy as well: PC members and external reviewers have affiliations with institutes in 22 different countries. Special thanks go to the three invited speakers – Jun Andronick from UNSW, Australia; Joose-Pieter Katoen from RWTH Aachen University, Germany; and Ruston Leino from Microsoft Research, Redmond, USA. The abstracts of the invited talks are included in this volume.

Like previous ICTACs, the 14th ICTAC included four tutorials by Jun Andronick, Joose-Pieter Katoen, Ruston Leino, and Zhiming Liu (Southwest University, China). We thank them for agreeing to offer this valuable service.

A number of colleagues have worked very hard to make this conference a success. We wish to express our thanks to the local organizing committee, Hung Pham Ngoc, Hoang Truong Anh, Hieu Vo Dinh, and many student volunteers. The University of Engineering and Technology of the Vietnam National University, Hanoi, the host of the conference, provided support and facilities for organizing the conference and its tutorials. Finally, we enjoyed institutional and financial support from the National Foundation for Science and Technology Development (NAFOSTED) of Vietnam and the HUMAX VINA Company in Hanoi, Vietnam.

The conference program and proceedings were prepared with the help of EasyChair. We thank Springer for continuing to publish the conference proceedings.

October 2017   Dang Van Hung
                                                        Deepak Kapur

Organization

ICTAC 2017 was organized by the University of Engineering and Technology, Vietnam National University (UET-VNU), Hanoi, Vietnam.

Steering Committee

Ana Cavalcanti	University of York, UK
John Fitzgerald	Newcastle University, UK
Martin Leucker	University of Luebeck, Germany
Zhiming Liu	Southwest University, China
Tobias Nipkow	Technical University of Munich, Germany
Augusto Sampaio	Federal University of Pernambuco, Brazil
Natarajan Shankar	SRI International, USA

General Chair

Nguyen Viet Ha	University of Engineering and Technology, VNU, Vietnam

Organizing Committee

Ninh-Thuan Truong (Co-chair)	UET-VNU, Vietnam
Ngoc-Hung Pham (Co-chair)	UET-VNU, Vietnam
Truong Anh Hoang	UET-VNU, Vietnam
Vo Dinh Hieu	UET-VNU, Vietnam
To Van Khanh	UET-VNU, Vietnam
Dang Duc Hanh	UET-VNU, Vietnam
Vu Dieu Huong	UET-VNU, Vietnam

Program Committee

Bernhard K. Aichernig	TU Graz, Austria
Farhad Arbab	CWI and Leiden University, The Netherlands
Ana Cavalcanti	University of York, UK
Wei-Ngan Chin	National University of Singapore, Singapore
Hung Dang-Van (Co-chair)	UET-VNU, Hanoi, Vietnam
Martin Fränzle	Carl von Ossietzky Universität Oldenburg, Germany
Marcelo Frias	Buenos Aires Institute of Technology, Argentina
Dimitar P. Guelev	Bulgarian Academy of Sciences, Bulgaria

Deepak Kapur (Co-chair)	University of New Mexico, USA
Kim Guldstrand Larsen	Aalborg University, Denmark
Martin Leucker	University of Lübeck, Germany
Xuandong Li	Nanjing University, China
Xiaoshan Li	University of Macau, Macao
Zhiming Liu	Southwest University, China
Dominique Mery	Université de Lorraine, LORIA, France
Mohammadreza Mousavi	Halmstad University, Sweden
Thanh-Binh Nguyen	Da Nang University of Technology, Vietnam
Mizuhito Ogawa	JAIST, Japan
Jose Oliveira	Universidade do Minho, Portugal
Catuscia Palamidessi	Inria, France
Minh-Dung Phan	AIT, Thailand
Sanjiva Prasad	Indian Institute of Technology Delhi, India
Thanh-Tho Quan	Hochiminh City University of Technology, Vietnam
António Ravara	Universidade Nova de Lisboa, Portugal
Augusto Sampaio	Federal University of Pernambuco, Brazil
Emil Sekerinski	McMaster University, Canada
Hiroyuki Seki	Nagoya University, Japan
Deepak D'Souza	Indian Institute of Science, Bangalore, India
Hoang Truong-Anh	UET-VNU, Hanoi, Vietnam
Kazunori Ueda	Waseda University, Japan
Farn Wang	National Taiwan University, Taiwan
Jim Woodcock	University of York, UK
Hsu-Chun Yen	National Taiwan University, Taiwan
Naijun Zhan	IoS, Chinese Academy of Sciences, China
Huibiao Zhu	East China Normal University, China
Abdullah Mohd Zin	Universiti Kebangsaan Malaysia, Malaysia

Additional Reviewers

Ana Almeida Matos	Tobias Kapp
Ullas Aparanji	Natallia Kokash
Marius Bozga	Martin Lange
Georgiana Caltais	Xinxin Liu
Pablo Castro	Kamal Lodaya
Ugo Dal Lago	Ben Moszkowski
Duc-Hanh Dang	Matthias Niewerth
Kasper Dokter	Masahiko Sakai
Bertram Felgenhauer	Vinicius Santos
Raul Fervari	Torben Scheffel
Sebastian Gerwinn	Karsten Scheibler
Falk Howar	Malte Schmitz
Huu Hung Huynh	Richard Schumi
Raghavendra K.R.	Xiang Shuangqing

Mani Swaminathan
Martin Tappler
Daniel Thoma
Tinko Tinchev
Ionut Tutu
Mahsa Varshosaz
Hieu Vo
Xuan Tung Vu
Shuling Wang
Karsten Wolf

Zhilin Wu
Xiaoyuan Xie
Yilong Yang
Shoji Yuen
Hengjun Zhao
Jianhua Zhao
Liang Zhao
Quan Zu

Sponsoring Institutions

National Foundation for Science and Technology Development (NAFOSTED) of Vietnam, Hanoi, Vietnam
HUMAX VINA Company in Hanoi, Vietnam
University of Engineering and Technology, Vietnam National University (UET-VNU), Hanoi, Vietnam

Abstract of Invited Talks

From Hoare Logic to Owicki-Gries and Rely-Guarantee for Interruptible eChronos and Multicore seL4 (Extended Abstract)

June Andronick

Data61, CSIRO (formerly NICTA) and UNSW, Sydney, Australia
june.andronick@data61.csiro.au

In this talk we will be exploring the use of foundational proof techniques in the formal verification of real-world operating system (OS) kernels. We will focus on eChronos [2], a small interruptible real-time OS, and seL4 [7, 8], the landmark verified microkernel, currently undergoing verification of its multicore version. Both are deployed in various safety- and security-critical areas, and present challenging complexities due to their performance constraints and concurrency behavior. Foundational techniques have been and are being used for their verification, ranging for standard Hoare logic [5], to concurrency logics like Owicki-Gries [10] and Rely-Guarantee [6]. We will describe their use and combination with theorem proving and automation techniques to achieve impact on large-scale software.

Hoare logic is well known to be the foundation of formal verification for main-stream programs. It is what is taught to university students to prove formally the correctness of programs. Hoare logic can also be the basis of large-scale, real-world software verification, such as the verified seL4 microkernel. seL4 is a very small OS kernel, the core and most critical part of any software system. It provides minimal hardware abstractions and communication mechanisms to applications. seL4 additionally enforces strong access control: applications can be configured to have precise rights to access memory or to communicate, and seL4 guarantees the absence of unauthorised accesses. seL4 has undergone extensive formal verification [7, 8] when running on unicore hardware. The central piece of this verification is the proof of functional correctness: that seL4 source code satisfies its specification. This proof uses Hoare logic at its core, while the top-level theorem is a traditional refinement proof through forward simulation: we show that all behaviors of the source program are contained in the behaviors of the specification. For small programs, Hoare logic can be the central method to prove functional correctness, where the specification is defined as being the description of the state in the postcondition. For larger programs, and in particular for programs where further verification is desired (like seL4's further security proofs), having the specification as a separate standalone artifact saves significant overall effort. In this case a refinement proof links the concrete source code to the abstract specification, and often relies on global invariants to be maintained. In seL4 verification, invariant proofs represent the largest part of the effort [8]. They heavily use

Hoare logic reasoning, combined with important use of automation in the Isabelle/HOL theorem prover [9], both to generate the required invariant statements for each of the hundreds of seL4 functions and to discharge as many as possible without need for human interaction.

Following this verification of a large and complex, but sequential program, we investigated the impact of concurrency in settings where interrupts cannot be avoided (seL4 runs with interrupts mostly disabled), or where running on multiple processors is desired.

Reasoning about interrupt-induced concurrency is motivated by our verification of the eChronos [2] embedded OS. In an eChronos-based system, the kernel runs with interrupts enabled, even during scheduling operations, to be able to satisfy stringent latency requirements. The additional challenge in its concurrency reasoning is that racy access to shared state between the scheduler and interrupt handlers is allowed, and can indeed occur.

The modelling and verification approach we chose for this fine-grained concurrency reasoning is Owicki-Gries [10], the simple extension on Hoare logic with parallel composition and *await* statements for synchronisation. Owicki-Gries provided the low-level of abstraction needed for the high-performance shared-variable system code we were verifying. We could conveniently identify localised Owicki-Gries assertions at the points of the racy accesses, and tune them to enforce the overall correctness invariant of eChronos scheduler. In contrast, the Rely-Guarantee (RG) approach [6] would have required identification of global interference conditions, which was challenging for such racy sharing with no clear interface, unless we made heavier use of auxiliary variables to identify racy sections of code, but this defeats the compositionality of the RG approach, one of its principal purposes. The explosion of verification conditions inherent in the Owicki-Gries approach has been minimized by the controlled nature of the interrupt-induced concurrency, and mitigated by proof-engineering techniques and automation of a modern theorem prover. We were able to develop an abstract model of eChronos scheduling behavior and prove its main scheduling property: that the running task is always the highest-priority runnable task [4, 3]. Our models and proofs are available online [1].

We are currently exploring multicore-induced concurrency for seL4 in a setting where most but not all of the code is running under a big lock. Here we have explored the RG approach, on an abstracted model identifying the allowed interleaving between cores. In this setting, the relies and guarantees can express what shared state the lock is protecting, and what the conditions are under which shared state can be accessed without holding the lock. The main challenge is resource reuse. The kernel runs in privileged mode, and as such has access to everything; it can for instance delete objects on other cores to which critical registers point. This could create a system crash if later on in that core, the kernel code accesses these registers pointing to corrupted memory. Designs to solve this issue include forcing kernel operations on all other cores without holding the lock. The proof that this is sound needs to be expressed via relies and guarantees between cores. We proved, on our abstract model of the multicore seL4-system, that critical registers remain valid at all times.

The main challenge now, for both the eChronos verification and multicore seL4 one, is to transfer the verification down to the source code via refinement.

Acknowledgements. The author would like to thank the people that have worked on the research presented in this paper: Sidney Amani, Maksym Bortin, Gerwin Klein, Corey Lewis, Daniel Matichuk, Carroll Morgan and Christine Rizkallah. The author also thanks Carroll Morgan and Gerwin Klein for their feedback on drafts of this paper.

Parts of the work presented are supported by the Air Force Office of Scientific Research, Asian Office of Aerospace Research and Development (AOARD) and U.S. Army International Technology Center - Pacific under grant FA2386-15-1-4055.

References

1. eChronos model and proofs. https://github.com/echronos/echronos-proofs
2. The eChronos OS. http://echronos.systems
3. Andronick, J., Lewis, C., Matichuk, D., Morgan, C., Rizkallah, C.: Proof of OS scheduling behavior in the presence of interrupt-induced concurrency. In: Blanchette, J.C., Merz, S. (eds.) ITP 2016. LNCS, pp. 52–68. Springer, Cham (2016)
4. Andronick, J., Lewis, C., Morgan, C.: Controlled owicki-gries concurrency: reasoning about the preemptible eChronos embedded operating system. In: van Glabbeek, R.J., Groote J.F., Höfner, P. (eds.) Workshop on Models for Formal Analysis of Real Systems, MARS 2015, pp. 10–24. Suva, Fiji (Nov 2015)
5. Hoare, C.A.R.: An axiomatic basis for computer programming. CACM **12**, 576–580 (1969)
6. Jones, C.B.: Tentative steps towards a development method for interfering programs. ACM Trans. Program. Lang. Syst. **5**(4), 596–619 (1983)
7. Klein, G., Andronick, J., Elphinstone, K., Heiser, G., Cock, D., Derrin, P., Elkaduwe, D., Engelhardt, K., Kolanski, R., Norrish, M., Sewell, T., Tuch, H., Winwood, S.: seL4: Formal verification of an operating-system kernel. CACM **53**(6), 107–115 (2010)
8. Klein, G., Andronick, J., Elphinstone, K., Murray, T., Sewell, T., Kolanski, R., Heiser, G.: Comprehensive formal verification of an OS microkernel. Trans. Comp. Syst. **32**(1), 2:1–2:70 (2014)
9. Nipkow, T., Paulson, L., Wenzel, M.: Isabelle/HOL— A Proof Assistant for Higher-Order Logic. LNCS, vol. 2283, Springer, Heidelberg (2002)
10. Owicki, S., Gries, D.: An axiomatic proof technique for parallel programs. Acta Informatica **6**, 319–340 (1976)

Tweaking the Odds: Parameter Synthesis in Markov Models
(Abstract)

Joost-Pieter Katoen[1,2]

[1] RWTH Aachen University, Germany
[2] University of Twente, The Netherlands

Markov decision processes (MDPs) are the prime model in sequential decision making under uncertainty. Their transition probabilities are fixed. Transitions in *parametric* Markov models are equipped with functions (e.g., polynomials or rational functions) over a finite set of parameters x_1 through x_n, say. Instantiating each variable x_i with a value v_i induces a MDP or a Markov chain (MC) if non-determinism is absent. We present recent advances on the *parameter synthesis problem*: for which parameter values — and for MDPs, for which policy — does the instantiated Markov model satisfy a given objective? For objectives such as reachability probabilities and expected costs we consider (1) an *exact* procedure and (2) an *approximative* technique. Both approaches come with a CEGAR-like procedure to obtain a good coverage of the parameter space indicating which parameter regions satisfy the property and which ones do not.

The exact approach first obtains symbolic representations of the synthesis problem at hand. This can be done using e.g., Gaussian elimination or a technique introduced by Daws at ICTAC 2004 [4] that is based on an automata-to-regular expression conversion. These symbolic representations (in fact, rational functions in x_1 through x_n) can be solved using satisfiability-modulo-theory techniques over non-linear real arithmetic [7]. This technique is applicable to parametric MCs only but extendible to conditional reachability objectives too. Using advanced reduction and implementation techniques [5] it is practically applicable to MCs of up to a few million states and 2–3 parameters.

The approximative approach removes parameter dependencies at the expense of adding new parameters and then replaces them by lower and upper bounds [9]. It reduces parameter synthesis to standard model checking of non-parametric Markov models that have one extra degree of non-determinism. Its beauty is the simplicity and applicability to both MCs and MDPs. It is applicable to models of up to about ten million states and 4–5 parameters.

Finally, we treat parameter synthesis for (3) *multiple objectives* for parametric MDPs. Whereas multi-objectivemodel-checking of MDPs can be cast as a linear programming problem [6], its analogue for parametric MDPs results in a non-linear programming (NLP) problem. An approximate solution of this NLP problem can be obtained in polynomial time using geometric programming [3]. This technique is extendible to richer objectives such as weighted combinations of single objectives.

Initial experiments indicate that this approach seems scalable to models with tens of parameters.

Parameter synthesis has abundant applications. These include *model repair* [2, 8] — how to adapt certain probabilities in a Markov model that refutes a given objective such that the tweaked model satisfies it — and finding *minimal recovery times for randomized self-stabilizing algorithms* [1].

Reference

1. Aflaki, S., Volk, M., Bonakdarpour, B., Katoen, J.-P., Storjohann, A.: Automated fine tuning of probabilistic self-stabilizing algorithms. In: SRDS (2017, to be published)
2. Bartocci, E., Grosu, R., Katsaros, P., Ramakrishnan, C. R., Smolka, S.A.: Model repair for probabilistic systems. In: Abdulla, P.A., Leino, K.R.M. (eds.) TACAS 2011. LNCS, vol. 6605, pp. 326–340. Springer, Heidelberg (2011)
3. Cubuktepe, M., Jansen, N., Junges, S., Katoen, J.-P., Papusha, I., Poonawala, H.A., Topcu, U.: Sequential convex programming for the efficient verification of parametric MDPs. In: Legay, A., Margaria, T. (eds.) TACAS 2017. LNCS, vol.10206, pp. 133–150, Springer, Heidelberg (2017)
4. Daws, C.: Symbolic and parametric model checking of discrete-time markov chains. In: Liu, Z., Araki, K. (eds.) ICTAC 2004. LNCS, vol. 3407, pp. 280–294. Springer, Heidelberg (2004)
5. Dehnert, C., Junges, S., Jansen, N., Corzilius, F., Volk, M., Bruintjes, H., Katoen, J.-P., Ábrahám, E.: Prophesy: A probabilistic parameter synthesis tool. In: Kroening, D., Păsăreanu, C. (eds.) CAV 2015. LNCS, vol. 9206, pp. 214–231. Springer, Cham (2015)
6. Etessami, K., Kwiatkowska, M., Vardi, M.Y., Yannakakis, M.: Multi-objective model checking of Markov decision processes. Log. Methods Comput. Sci. **4**(4), (2008)
7. Jansen, N., Corzilius, F., Volk, M., Wimmer, R., Ábrahám, E., Katoen, J.-P., Becker, B.: Accelerating parametric probabilistic verification. In: Norman, G., Sanders, W. (eds.) QEST 2014. LNCS, Vol. 8657, pp. 404–420. Springer, Cham (2014)
8. Pathak, S., Ábrahám, E., Jansen, N., Tacchella, A., Katoen, J.-P.: A greedy approach for the efficient repair of stochastic models. In: Havelund, K., Holzmann, G., Joshi, R. (eds.) NFM 2015. LNCS, vol. 9058, pp. 295–309. Springer, Cham (2015)
9. Quatmann, T., Dehnert, C., Jansen, N., Junges, S., Katoen, J.-P.: Parameter synthesis for Markov models: faster than ever. In: Artho, C., Legay, A., Peled, D. (eds.) ATVA 2016. LNCS, vol. 9938, pp. 50–67. Springer, Cham (2016)

Directions to and for Verified Software

K. Rustan M. Leino[1,2]

[1] Microsoft Research, Redmond
[2] Imperial College London

Abstract. There are many techniques and tools aimed at creating and main-
taining reliable software. At one extreme of the reliability spectrum is deductive
verification, where software designers write specifications for what the software
is supposed to do and where programs are developed together with proofs that
show that the specifications are met. The journey of research and development
behind deductive verification spans many decades, from early visions of the
idea, through criticism and doubt, through the development of automated
techniques, to education, to experience in using tools in practice, and to the
streamlining of the process.

In this talk, I give a perspective of where this journey of program-verification
research has brought us today, give a demo of a state-of-the-art system for
writing verified programs [1], and discuss directions for what may be possible in
the future.

Reference

1. Leino, K.R.M.: Dafny: an automatic program verifier for functional correctness. In: Clarke, E.
M., Voronkov, A. (eds.) LPAR 2010. LNCS, vol. 6355, pp. 348–370. Springer, Heidelberg
(2010)

Contents

SMT Solvers and Algorithms

Security

Logics

A Formal Proof Generator from Semi-formal Proof Documents

Adrián Riesco[1(✉)] and Kazuhiro Ogata[2,3]

[1] Facultad de Informática, Universidad Complutense de Madrid, Madrid, Spain
ariesco@fdi.ucm.es
[2] School of Information Science, JAIST, Nomi, Japan
ogata@jaist.ac.jp
[3] Research Center for Theoretical Computer Science, JAIST, Nomi, Japan

Abstract. We present the CafeInMaude Proof Assistant (CiMPA) and the CafeInMaude Proof Generator (CiMPG), two complementary extensions of CafeInMaude, a CafeOBJ interpreter implemented in Maude. CiMPA is a proof assistant for inductive properties of CafeOBJ specifications, and CiMPG generates formal proofs that can be fed into CiMPA from semi-formal proof documents called proof scores in CafeOBJ.

1 Introduction

CafeOBJ [17] is a language for writing formal specifications for a wide variety of software and/or hardware systems, and verifying properties of them (see e.g. [4,12,13]). CafeOBJ implements equational logic by rewriting and can be used as a powerful platform for proving properties on systems. More specifically, specifiers can write proof scores to prove properties on their specifications. Proof scores are proof outlines written in an algebraic specification language, such as OBJ [8]. If they are executed by such a language processor and all results are as expected (e.g. `true` is obtained), then the corresponding theorems are proved. Proof scores were developed by Joseph Goguen, and the CafeOBJ team have demonstrated that they are a promising approach to systems verification [5]. An important advantage of this approach to systems verification, also known as "proving as programming" and shared by other paradigms such as the Larch Prover (LP) [7], is its flexibility: the syntax for performing proofs is the same as for specifying systems. However, in the CafeOBJ case this flexibility is obtained by losing formality, since CafeOBJ does not check proof scores in any way. For this reason, in this paper we present an inductive theorem prover that formally proves properties on CafeOBJ specifications and a proof script generator that infers formal proofs from proof scores.

We outline in the next section how to use proof scores to verify CafeOBJ specifications, while Sect. 3 discusses the weaknesses of this approach. Section 4 summarizes the main features of the CafeInMaude Proof Assistant, while Sect. 5 presents the CafeInMaude Proof Generator and somebenchmarks.

© Springer International Publishing AG 2017
D.V. Hung and D. Kapur (Eds.): ICTAC 2017, LNCS 10580, pp. 3–12, 2017.
DOI: 10.1007/978-3-319-67729-3_1

Section 6 briefly discusses related work. Finally, Sect. 7 concludes and outlines some lines of future work. The tool and several case studies are available at https://github.com/ariesco/CafeInMaude.

2 Proof Score Approach to Systems Verification

Let us consider a concrete example: a simple mutual exclusion protocol for two processes specified in CafeOBJ; we will focus on the function introducing the first process into the critical section, while the rest is available at the link given in the previous section.

The module `2P-MUTEX` below is in charge of defining the behavior of the protocol. It first imports the `LABEL` module, which defines the type `Label` and two constants `rs` and `cs` that stand for *remainder section* and *critical section*, respectively. Then, it defines the sort `Sys` and the corresponding constructors; in particular `enter1` indicates that the first process wants to enter the critical section. Moreover, observations on the system are obtained by using `pc1` for the first process and `pc2` for the second one:

```
mod* 2P-MUTEX {pr(LABEL)                        [Sys]
              op enter1: Sys -> Sys {constr}
              ops pc1 pc2: Sys -> Label
```

Note that new functions are defined by the keyword `op`, the function name, the arity, the coarity, and a possibly empty set of attributes, such as `constr` for *constructors*. We will use equations (`eq` and `ceq` for conditional equations) for defining the behavior of non-constructor functions.

We use an auxiliary Boolean function `c-enter1`, which holds if the second process is in the remainder section, to define the behavior for `enter1`: the first equation states that the first process will be in the critical section if `c-enter1` holds; the second equation indicates that the second process is in the remainder section if `c-enter1` holds; and the third equation indicates that `enter1` can be discharged if `c-enter1` does not hold:

```
ceq pc1(enter1(S:Sys)) = cs    if c-enter1(S).
ceq pc2(enter1(S:Sys)) = rs    if c-enter1(S).
ceq enter1(S:Sys)      = S      if not c-enter1(S).
```

Assuming we have defined observations for the rest of states (the initial state, the second process entering the critical section, and both processes leaving the critical section) we state the invariant `inv` that indicates that we cannot observe both the first process and the second one in the critical section at the same time:

```
op inv: Sys -> Bool
eq inv(S:Sys) = not ((pc1(S) = cs) and (pc2(S) = cs)).
```

How can we prove this invariant? We would proceed state by state, starting with enter1. What we want to discharge in this case is written in CafeOBJ as:[1]

```
open 2P-MUTEX.
 op s: -> Sys.
 eq [:nonexec]: inv(s) = true.
 red inv(enter1(s)).
close
```

That is, given the specification in 2P-MUTEX, we add the fresh constant s, that stands for any system, and the equation inv(s) = true (that would stand for the induction hypothesis in a usual induction scheme and cannot be used for simplification purposes thanks to the :nonexec label) and apply the red command, which simplifies by using equations, to the invariant applied to our state. Unfortunately, the term is not reduced to true but to (true xor ((pc2(enter1(s)) = cs) and (pc1(enter1(s)) = cs))). By using this result as a guide, we can enrich the open-close environment above with the equation pc2(s) = cs and use the induction hypothesis as a premise in the red command as inv(s) implies inv(enter1(s)). In this case the term is reduced to true and the invariant holds *under the assumption that pc2(s) = cs holds*. We need to prove that the property also holds for the complementary case, so we would need two open-close environments to discharge this induction case:

```
open 2P-MUTEX.                        open 2P-MUTEX.
 op s: -> Sys.                         op s: -> Sys.
 eq [:nonexec]: inv(s) = true.         eq [:nonexec]: inv(s) = true.
 eq pc2(s) = rs.                       eq (pc2(s) = rs) = false.
 red inv(s)implies inv(enter1(s)).     red inv(s)implies inv(enter1(s)).
close                                 close
```

In this way we obtain the following results, which show that the proof for this case is correct:

```
Opening module 2P-MUTEX:             Opening module 2P-MUTEX:
red inv1(s)implies inv1(enter1(s)).  red inv1(s)implies inv1(enter1(s)).
Result: true: Bool                   Result: true: Bool
```

3   Achilles' Heel and a Possible Remedy

The proof score approach to systems verification, which allows for proving properties in the same language used for specifying the system, is less formal in charge for this flexibility. Since proof scores only require the terms to be reduced to the expected value (in general true) if we skip one of the environments above, if we add extra equations (and more environment are required for checking all cases), or even if we just reduce true we fulfill the requirements and the property would

---

[1] Note that so-called open-close environments allows for adding further objects and equations to existing theories.

be considered proved, although it is not. Hence, if it is permitted to write proof scores at any levels of flexibility, it is unlikely to make the approach really formal: too many equations can be added; non-existent hypothesis can be used; and some cases can be lost, specially if we need to distinguish among many cases. Therefore, specifiers have abandoned extremely flexible ways of writing proof scores. From our experience in many case studies in which the proof score approach has been used to verify that various kinds of systems, protocols, etc. enjoy the desired properties, we have learned that there are mainly four things to be conducted by proof scores: (1) use of structural induction, (2) use of theorem of constants (elimination of universally quantified variables), (3) case splitting based on constructors, and (4) use of the left-hand side l of an equation l = true, where l is ground, appearing in the specification as the premise of the implication (the main idea here is that l stands for the induction hypothesis). Hence, we consider it would be worth implementing an automatic way (1) to formally verify that the proofs carried out by these proof scores is actually correct and, if the proof is wrong, (2) to obtain detailed information on the cases that remain unproved. Although we do not cover all these proofs yet, we set the basis for developing more powerful tools of this kind in the future.

Even though CafeOBJ has an inductive theorem prover, it cannot be used for this purpose because it is implemented in Lisp and hence it cannot access the on-the-fly modules created by proof scores, and it does not provide a data structure that can be manipulated by external sources. For these reasons, we have developed CiMPA and CiMPG, two complementary extensions of CafeInMaude [16], a CafeOBJ interpreter implemented in Maude [1]. In addition to carrying out inductive proofs, CiMPA takes advantage of the metalevel features of Maude to explicitly store the current proof, including the proof tree and the associated modules. On the other hand, CiMPG provides extra annotations for proof scores so it is possible to indicate whether a proof score is related to a specific proof. Once a proof score is annotated, CiMPG can analyze it at the metalevel, put together all those proof scores related to the same proof and try to infer a proof script (that is, a list of commands) for CiMPA.

Soundness in CiMPA is obtained by using the standard inference rules for constructor-based systems (see e.g. [6]); soundness is extended to CiMPG by ensuring a one-to-one correspondence between the leaves of the proof tree and the reduction commands in the original proof scores. We cannot ensure completeness in CiMPG: since our algorithm relies on CiMPA and on some assumptions on the form the proof scores are written, if they require features that are not implemented in CiMPA or follow a different approach CiMPG will fail.

4   The CafeInMaude Proof Assistant

The CafeInMaude Proof Assistant (CiMPA) is an inductive theorem prover for proving properties on CafeOBJ specifications. An important feature of CiMPA is that it takes advantage of the metalevel capabilities of Maude to store the whole proof as a proof tree that can be manipulated by other tools, which is the key of the CiMPG tool described in the next section. In particular, each node in the proof tree stores information about the goal, the list of commands required to reach the node, and the current module, which consists of the initial module enriched with the equations used for case splitting, the fresh constants generated during the process, and possibly the induction hypotheses. CiMPA allows to:

- State a set of equations as initial goal. We consider the goal has been proved if all the equalities stated in the goal can be reduced to `true`.
- Apply simultaneous induction on a variable of the current goal. In this case CiMPA uses the `constr` attribute in the operator declarations to create appropriate ground terms and generate as many new goals as constructors.
- Apply case splitting by equations. This command generates two new goals, distinguishing whether the equation holds or not.
- Apply case splitting by terms. In this case CiMPA adds an equation stating that the term is equal to any ground term built with the constructors defined for the sort of the term. Hence, this command generates as many new goals as constructors defined in the module for the sort.
- Apply the theorem of constants. This command replaces variables by fresh constants and splits the different equations in the goal, hence generating the corresponding new goals.
- Indicate that a given equation (possibly requiring a substitution for binding the free variables) implies the current goal. This command updates the current goal, assuming the equation exists.
- Reduce the current goal. This command checks whether the lefthand side and the righthand side of the equation are equal. If this is the case, then the goal is discharged; otherwise, different commands indicate whether the equations are kept unmodified or reduced.
- Display the current goal, the open goals, and the complete proof tree.

We present here part of the proof script used to prove the invariant in the previous section. First, we introduce the invariant as goal, set `S:Sys` as the variable were induction is applied, and simultaneous induction as:

```
open 2P-MUTEX.
  :goal{eq [inv:nonexec]: inv(S:Sys) = true.}
  :ind on (S:Sys)
  :apply(si)
```

Applying induction on `S` generates 5 new goals, and CiMPA generates them following their alphabetic ordering, so it will try to prove first (the current goal is marked by `>`) the subgoal for `enter1(S#Sys)`, with `S#Sys` a fresh constant; it includes the induction hypothesis as part of the module used for this goal:

```
Current proof:
root  eq [inv:nonexec]: inv(S:Sys) = true.
-- Assumption:
eq [inv:nonexec]: inv(S#Sys) = true.
1. > SI  eq [inv:nonexec]: inv(enter1(S#Sys)) = true.
```

```
-- Assumption:
eq [inv:nonexec]: inv(S#Sys) = true.
2. SI  eq [inv:nonexec]: inv(enter2(S#Sys)) = true.


-- Assumption:
eq [inv:nonexec]: inv(S#Sys) = true.
3. SI  eq [inv:nonexec]: inv(init) = true.


-- Assumption:
eq [inv:nonexec]: inv(S#Sys) = true.
4. SI  eq [inv:nonexec]: inv(leave1(S#Sys)) = true.


-- Assumption:
eq [inv:nonexec]: inv(S#Sys) = true.
5. SI  eq [inv:nonexec]: inv(leave2(S#Sys)) = true.
```

As we saw in the proof scores, we need to use the induction hypothesis as a premise to discharge both cases, so we ask CiMPA to do it by using the command :imp [inv]., where inv is the label of the induction hypothesis. Now we obtain:

```
New goal generated:
imp  eq [inv:nonexec]: true xor cs = pc1(S#Sys) and cs = pc2(S#Sys)
                     implies inv1(enter1(S#Sys)) = true.
```

Now we need to split cases on the equation eq pc2(s) = rs., so we define a macro csb1 and apply it with :apply(csb1).

```
:def csb1 =:ctf {eq pc2(S#Sys) = rs.}
:apply(csb1)
```

hence obtaining the following new goals:

```
-- Assumption:
eq pc2(S#Sys) = rs.
-- Assumption:
eq [inv1:nonexec]: inv1(S#Sys) = true.
1-1. > csb1  eq [inv1:nonexec]: true xor cs = pc1(S#Sys)
and cs = pc2(S#Sys)implies inv1(enter1(S#Sys)) = true.


-- Assumption:
eq pc2(S#Sys)= rs  = false.
-- Assumption:
eq [inv1:nonexec]: inv1(S#Sys) = true.
1-2. csb1   eq [inv1:nonexec]: true xor cs = pc1(S#Sys)
and cs = pc2(S#Sys)implies inv1(enter1(S#Sys)) = true.
```

At this point, the module associated to the current node has enough information to discharge it by using reductions, so we can discharge the goal by means of :apply(rd). Once discharged, the complementary goal (where csb1 does not hold) can be also discharged by reduction, so we apply reduction again by using :apply(rd). The rest of the proof would be carried out in the same way.

5   The CafeInMaude Proof Generator

The CafeInMaude Proof Generator (CiMPG) provides annotations for identifying proof scores defined in open-close environments and generating proof scripts for CiMPA from them. The restrictions imposed to these proof scores are (i) reducing only goal-related terms, (ii) making sure that all environments use the same module expression, and (iii) relying in functionalities that can be simulated by the CiMPA commands presented in the previous section. Restriction (i) ensures that no dummy goals are generated, restriction (ii) is required to make sure that the property is being proved for the same specification, and restriction (iii) ensures that the proof script can be generated. These annotations are of the form `:id(LAB)`, where `LAB` is a label that identifies the proof; the same label must be used in all open-close environments related to the same proof. Then, the command `:proof(LAB)` will generate the proof script from the proof scores labeled with `LAB`. Hence, the modified open-close environments would be:

```
open 2P-MUTEX.                          open 2P-MUTEX.
 :id(2p-mutex)                           :id(2p-mutex)
 op s : -> Sys.                          op s : -> Sys .
 eq [:nonexec]: inv(s) = true.           eq [:nonexec]: inv(s) = true.
 eq pc2(s) = rs.                         eq (pc2(s) = rs) = false.
 red inv(s)implies inv(enter1(s)).       red inv(s)implies inv(enter1(s)).
close                                   close
```

while the final environment would state:

```
open 2P-MUTEX
 :proof(2p-mutex)
close
```

CiMPG stores the metarepresentation of these open-close environments in the CafeInMaude database so it can use them later. Once the user asks CiMPG to generate the proof script, it follows an algorithm for inferring the proof that has been specifically designed for CiMPG. It first infers the goal to be proved by generalizing the reduction commands in the proof scores, hence creating the initial proof tree. Then, it starts a loop that will modify the tree by (i) looking for those proof scores related to the current goal (in the sense the reductions in the proof scores use the same constructors as the goal and the module in the goal contains a subset of the constants and the equations of the module defined in the proof scores) and (ii) enriching the module (by using induction, the theorem of constants, or case splitting) and modifying the goal (by using implications) so they become equal (up to renaming) to one proof score. In this case a reduction is applied and the goal can be discharged. This loop finishes when no more proof scores can be used. Note that these manipulations require to manipulate the proof scores and the proof tree generated by CiMPA at the metalevel, so we can compute and apply substitutions between the terms in the proof scores and the goals and perform reductions in the modules stored in the tree.

In our particular example, the algorithm would work as follows:

1. It infers the goal. Actually, it infers `inv(S)` because it uses not only the proof scores shown in the paper, but also the ones for the rest of cases, that forces the algorithm to generalize the argument (`S` instead of `enter`) and to drop the implication (since it is not used in the base case).
2. It applies simultaneous induction on `S`, since it realizes that all reductions in the proof scores have a constructed term in that place.
3. Apply case splitting, since the proof scores contain an equation and its negation.
4. Apply implication, since the goals have an implication and the premise appears in the current module as induction hypothesis.
5. Once the module in CiMPA and the one in the proof score are equal, reduce.

Note that the obtained proof script is slightly different from the one shown in the previous section, since in this case case splitting is applied before using implication. This proof, as well as the annotated proof scores that generate it, is available at https://github.com/ariesco/CafeInMaude.

How does CiMPG help specifiers? Assume we remove the second proof score in Sect. 2, the proof script generated by CiMPG would contain a `postpone` command, since we did not define all cases for `enter1`, and once introduced in CiMPA the proof score would finish as follows, where the extra information is depicted by using `:desc proof`, which describes the complete proof:

```
Next goal is 1-2: eq [inv :nonexec]: inv(enter1(S#Sys)) = true.
  -- Assumptions:
eq pc2(S#Sys)= rs  = false.
eq [inv:nonexec]: inv(S#Sys) = true.
```

That is, the proof did not finish because the goal for `enter1` was not discharged for the case where `csb1` does not hold. This information would greatly help the user to write the missing proof scores to finish the proof.

The benchmarks performed thus far give us confidence in its applicability. Our main benchmarks are shown in the table below, where LOC is the lines of code of the specification plus the proof scores; Commands is the number of commands in the generated proof script; and Time is the amount of time required by CiMPG. It is worth noting that the benchmark for the cloud protocol allowed us to detect a missing proof score, so the proof contained an error that went unnoticed by experts and that CiMPG found and helped to correct.

Name	LOC	Commands	Time	Comments
2p-mutex	50 + 70	28	470 ms	Mutual exclusion protocol for 2 processes
TAS	50 + 230	76	2130 ms	Spinlock – Mutual exclusion protocol
QLOCK	100 + 400	112	9510 ms	Variant of Dijkstra's binary semaphore
NSLPK	180 + 1100	284	48390 ms	Authentication protocol NSLPK
Cloud	120 + 1700	383	96470 ms	Simplified cloud synchronization protocol

6   Related Work

We briefly present in this section the closest works related to CiMPA and CiMPG. The current CafeOBJ implementation provides a Constructor-based Inductive Theorem Prover. Although it can only be used following the documentation written in Japanese at https://cafeobj.org/files/citp.pdf it is completely functional and provides a set of commands very similar to the ones described here for CiMPA. However, this prover was not suitable for our purposes because it is implemented in Lisp and hence we could not combine it with the information written in the proof scores. Other theorem provers, such as Isabelle [11,15] and PVS [14], present the same drawback and, in addition, are further from CafeOBJ, hence requiring extra transformations.

From the Maude side we also have other theorem provers, such as the ITP [2] and CITP [6]. Since both of them are implemented in Full Maude they were good candidates for a theorem prover that could carry out the proofs inferred from proof scores. However, these tools rely on Maude annotations that are not available in CafeOBJ: we can either add these annotations in CafeInMaude, hence preventing older CafeOBJ specifications to work with CiMPG, or provide intermediate translations that would impair the proof process, since the user will not understand the source of part of the goals to be discarded. Moreover, Maude ITP has a set of commands that does correspond exactly with the mechanisms underlying CafeOBJ proof scores, so we would also need to extend its commands, hence tampering the theoretical basis of ITP.

We think that nowadays software systems have a heterogeneous nature and hence different paradigms should be applied to formal verification of their different parts. CafeOBJ is especially suitable for dealing with complex data structures, such as associative and/or commutative ones, in an abstract way and for representing state machines (or state transition systems) by means of equations, while other frameworks are more appropriate for other tasks (e.g. Dafny for verification of the actual code [9], Frama-C [3] for static analysis, etc.). Therefore, in our opinion it is worth developing different frameworks and utilizing them all during the software development cycle.

7   Concluding Remarks and Ongoing Work

In this paper we have presented two tools that combine different approaches to theorem proving in CafeOBJ. This combination is sound and, even though it is not complete, the examples used thus far give us confidence in the technique.

Although other approaches for heterogeneous verification have been developed in the last years, they basically rely on translation between logic to take advantage of the tools available for each one, like in the Hets system [10]. The translation between proofs described here provides a new approach that can be farther extended by taking into account more complex proofs, e.g. those requiring searches or unification.

Currently, we are working in more commands for performing different kinds of case splitting when dealing with sequences. Once they are proved sound and added to CiMPA we plan to include them into the CiMPG inference algorithm.

References

1. Clavel, M., Durán, F., Eker, S., Lincoln, P., Martí-Oliet, N., Meseguer, J., Talcott, C.: All About Maude - A High-Performance Logical Framework. LNCS, vol. 4350. Springer, Heidelberg (2007). doi:10.1007/978-3-540-71999-1
2. Clavel, M., Palomino, M., Riesco, A.: Introducing the ITP tool: a tutorial. J. Univ. Comput. Sci. **12**(11), 1618–1650 (2006). Programming and Languages. Special Issue with Extended Versions of Selected Papers from PROLE 2005: The 5th Spanish Conference on Programming and Languages
3. Cuoq, P., Kirchner, F., Kosmatov, N., Prevosto, V., Signoles, J., Yakobowski, B.: Frama-C: a software analysis perspective. In: Eleftherakis, G., Hinchey, M., Holcombe, M. (eds.) SEFM 2012. LNCS, vol. 7504, pp. 233–247. Springer, Heidelberg (2012). doi:10.1007/978-3-642-33826-7_16
4. Futatsugi, K.: Generate & check method for verifying transition systems in CafeOBJ. In: De Nicola, R., Hennicker, R. (eds.) Software, Services, and Systems. LNCS, vol. 8950, pp. 171–192. Springer, Cham (2015). doi:10.1007/978-3-319-15545-6_13
5. Futatsugi, K., Gâinâ, D., Ogata, K.: Principles of proof scores in CafeOBJ. Theoret. Comput. Sci. **464**, 90–112 (2012)
6. Gâinâ, D., Zhang, M., Chiba, Y., Arimoto, Y.: Constructor-based inductive theorem prover. In: Heckel, R., Milius, S. (eds.) CALCO 2013. LNCS, vol. 8089, pp. 328–333. Springer, Heidelberg (2013). doi:10.1007/978-3-642-40206-7_26
7. Garland, S.J., Guttag, J.V.: LP, the Larch Prover (Version 3.1). MIT Laboratory for Computer Science (1991)
8. Goguen, J., Winkler, T., Meseguer, J., Futatsugi, K., Jouannaud, J.-P.: Introducing OBJ. Software Engineering with OBJ: Algebraic Specification in Action. Kluwer, Boston (2000)
9. Leino, K.R.M.: Dafny: an automatic program verifier for functional correctness. In: Clarke, E.M., Voronkov, A. (eds.) LPAR 2010. LNCS, vol. 6355, pp. 348–370. Springer, Heidelberg (2010). doi:10.1007/978-3-642-17511-4_20
10. Mossakowski, T., Maeder, C., Codescu, M., Lücke, D.: Hets user guide -version 0.97-. Technical report, DFKI GmbH, Formal Methods for Software Development, February 2011
11. Nipkow, T., Wenzel, M., Paulson, L.C. (eds.): Isabelle/HOL: A Proof Assistant for Higher-Order Logic. LNCS, vol. 2283. Springer, Heidelberg (2002)
12. Ogata, K., Futatsugi, K.: Compositionally writing proof scores of invariants in the OTS/CafeOBJ method. J. UCS **19**(6), 771–804 (2013)
13. Ouranos, I., Ogata, K., Stefaneas, P.S.: TESLA source authentication protocol verification experiment in the timed OTS/CafeOBJ method: experiences and lessons learned. IEICE Trans. **97–D**(5), 1160–1170 (2014)
14. Owre, S., Rushby, J.M., Shankar, N.: PVS: a prototype verification system. In: Kapur, D. (ed.) CADE 1992. LNCS, vol. 607, pp. 748–752. Springer, Heidelberg (1992). doi:10.1007/3-540-55602-8_217
15. Paulson, L.C. (ed.): Isabelle: A Generic Theorem Prover. LNCS, vol. 828. Springer, Heidelberg (1994)
16. Riesco, A., Ogata, K., Futatsugi, K.: A Maude environment for CafeOBJ. Formal Aspects Comput. **29**, 1–26 (2016)
17. Sawada, T., Futatsugi, K., Preining, N.: CafeOBJ Reference Manual (version 1.5.3), February 2015

Institutions for Behavioural Dynamic Logic with Binders

Rolf Hennicker[1] and Alexandre Madeira[2,3(✉)]

[1] Ludwig-Maximilians-Universität München, Munich, Germany
hennicke@pst.ifi.lmu.de
[2] HASLab, INESC TEC, University of Minho, Braga, Portugal
amadeira@inesctec.pt
[3] CIDMA, University of Aveiro, Aveiro, Portugal
madeira@ua.pt

Abstract. Dynamic logic with binders $\mathcal{D}^{\downarrow}$ has been introduced as an institution for the development of reactive systems based on model class semantics. The satisfaction relation of this logic was, however, not abstract enough to enjoy the modal invariance property (bisimilar models should satisfy the same sentences). We recently overcame this problem by proposing an *observational* satisfaction relation where the equality on states is interpreted by bisimilarity of states. This entailed, however, a price to pay - the satisfaction condition required for institutions was lost. This paper works on this limitation by establishing a behavioural semantics for $\mathcal{D}^{\downarrow}$ parametric to *behavioural structures* - families of equivalence relations on the states of each model. Such structures are taken in consideration in the signature category and, in particular, for the definition of signature morphisms. We show that with these changes we get again an institution with a behavioural model class semantics. The framework is instantiated with specific behavioural structures, resulting in the novel Institution of Crucial Actions.

1 Introduction

This paper deals with logical formalisms for the specification and development of reactive systems. Dynamic logic with binders, called $\mathcal{D}^{\downarrow}$-logic, has been introduced in [13] as an institution in the sense of [6] which allows expressing properties of reactive systems, from abstract safety and liveness requirements down to concrete specifications of the (recursive) structure of executable processes. It is therefore well suited for program development by stepwise refinement. $\mathcal{D}^{\downarrow}$-logic combines modalities indexed by regular expressions of actions, as in Dynamic

This work is financed by the ERDF – European Regional Development Fund through the Operational Programme for Competitiveness and Internationalisation - COMPETE 2020 Programme and by National Funds through the Portuguese funding agency, FCT - Fundação para a Ciência e a Tecnologia, within projects POCI-01-0145-FEDER-016692 and UID/MAT/04106/2013, and by the individual grant SFRH/BPD/103004/2014.

D.V. Hung and D. Kapur (Eds.): ICTAC 2017, LNCS 10580, pp. 13–31, 2017.
DOI: 10.1007/978-3-319-67729-3_2

Logic [10], and state variables with binders, as in Hybrid Logic [4]. These motivations are reflected in its semantics. Differently from what is usual in modal logics, whose semantics is given by Kripke structures and satisfaction of formulas is evaluated globally, $\mathcal{D}^{\downarrow}$ models are reachable, labelled transition systems with initial states where satisfaction is evaluated. This reflects our focus on computations, i.e. on effective processes.

1.1   Motivation

The commitment of $\mathcal{D}^{\downarrow}$-logic concerning bisimulation equivalence is, however, not satisfactory: the model class semantics of specifications in $\mathcal{D}^{\downarrow}$ is not closed under bisimulation equivalence; there are $\mathcal{D}^{\downarrow}$-sentences that distinguish bisimulation equivalent models, i.e., $\mathcal{D}^{\downarrow}$ does not enjoy the modal invariance property. As an example consider the two models $\mathcal{N}$ and $\mathcal{M}$ in Fig. 1 and the sentence $\downarrow x.\langle a\rangle x$. This sentence, evaluated in the initial state, expresses that after executing the action a the initial state is reached again. Obviously this is true for $\mathcal{N}$ but not for $\mathcal{M}$ though $\mathcal{N}$ and $\mathcal{M}$ are bisimulation equivalent.

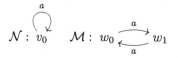

As a way out, we have proposed $\mathcal{D}^{\downarrow}_{\sim}$-logic [12] which relaxes the satisfaction relation such that equality of states is interpreted by bisimilarity of states. We call this observational equality and denote it by $\sim_{\mathcal{M}}$ for each model $\mathcal{M}$. Then the model $\mathcal{M}$ in Fig. 1 satisfies observationally the sentence $\downarrow x.\langle a\rangle x$, denoted by $\mathcal{M} \models_{\sim} \downarrow x.\langle a\rangle x$,

Fig. 1. Bisimilar models

since the two states w_0 and w_1 are observationally equal. Indeed we have shown in [12] that in $\mathcal{D}^{\downarrow}_{\sim}$ the modal invariance property holds. But, unfortunately, with relaxing the satisfaction relation we lost the institution property of $\mathcal{D}^{\downarrow}$ because $\mathcal{D}^{\downarrow}_{\sim}$ does not satisfy the satisfaction condition of an institution. Intuitively the satisfaction condition expresses that *truth is invariant under change of notation* [6]. From the software engineer's perspective it expresses that satisfaction of properties, i.e. sentences, should be preserved when models are put in a larger context. Figure 2 illustrates the problem with $\mathcal{D}^{\downarrow}_{\sim}$.

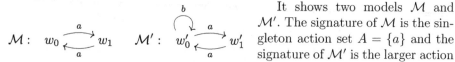

It shows two models $\mathcal{M}$ and $\mathcal{M}'$. The signature of $\mathcal{M}$ is the singleton action set $A = \{a\}$ and the signature of $\mathcal{M}'$ is the larger action set $A' = \{a, b\}$. As a signature morphism we take the inclusion $\sigma : A \to A'$ with $\sigma(a) = a$. Looking at

Fig. 2. Examples of $\{a\}$ and $\{a,b\}$-models

$\mathcal{M}'$ we see that w_0' and w_1' are not observationally equal, since in w_0' the action b is enabled which is not the case in state w_1'. Hence, $\mathcal{M}' \not\models_{\sim} \downarrow x.\langle a\rangle x$. Restricting $\mathcal{M}'$ to A yields the A-model $\mathcal{M}$. As we have seen before $\mathcal{M} \models_{\sim} \downarrow x.\langle a\rangle x$. Hence, observational satisfaction is not preserved in larger contexts and therefore the satisfaction condition does not hold in $\mathcal{D}^{\downarrow}_{\sim}$. In this work, we are looking for possibilities to overcome this deficiency.

1.2   Overview of the Proposal

On the way to solve the problem we found (again) the paper of Misiak [15] who has studied institutions with behavioural semantics in arbitrary logical systems with concrete model categories. Misiak's paper is an abstraction of more concrete institutions that have been studied in the framework of observational algebraic specification where a similar problem to ours was solved by adding restrictions to signature morphisms [5,7] and putting more information into the signatures [3,8,11]. To instantiate Misiak's approach by using labelled transition systems as models, we forget, for the moment, the observational equalities $\sim_M$ and consider instead, for each set of actions A, a family $\approx$ of equivalence relations $\approx_{\mathcal{M}}$, indexed by the models of $\mathcal{D}^{\downarrow}$. A signature is then a pair $(A, \approx)$ and the satisfaction of sentences is defined by interpreting equality of states in terms of $\approx_{\mathcal{M}}$. Misiak's trick is to consider a signature morphism as a mapping $\sigma : A \to A'$ which is compatible with the equivalences of each signature. This means, more formally, that for each A'-model $\mathcal{M}'$ the restriction of $\approx_{\mathcal{M}'}$ to the states of $\mathcal{M}$, denoted by $(\approx_{\mathcal{M}'})|_{\sigma}$, is the same as the equivalence $\approx_{(\mathcal{M}'|_{\sigma})}$ used in $\approx$ for the A-model $\mathcal{M}'|_{\sigma}$, which is the reduct of $\mathcal{M}'$ along σ. This means that we have, for each A'-model $\mathcal{M}'$, the following crucial equation:

$$(\approx_{\mathcal{M}'})|_{\sigma} = \approx_{(\mathcal{M}'|_{\sigma})} \tag{1}$$

Thus the satisfaction condition is enforced by the notion of a signature morphism and we may ask how useful this additional information in signatures, given by the family of equivalences, can be for our problem. In particular, how the family of equivalences can be syntactically presented and how this can be related to the observational equalities $\sim_M$ considered in $\mathcal{D}^{\downarrow}_{\sim}$. To approach this, we first observe that Misiak has reduced the model classes for signatures $(A, \approx)$ to those models $\mathcal{M}$ for which the equivalence $\approx_{\mathcal{M}}$ is a congruence.[1] In our framework of labelled transition systems this makes perfect sense, since the congruence property expresses that equivalence of states must be preserved when an action $a \in A$ is executed. In this way we obtain an institution. We also consider the "black-box" view of each $(A, \approx)$-model $\mathcal{M}$ obtained by its quotient structure $\mathcal{M}/\approx_{\mathcal{M}}$. We show that this construction can be extended to a full and faithfull functor mapping $(A, \approx)$-models to A-models in $\mathcal{D}^{\downarrow}$. This functor preserves and reflects satisfaction of sentences.

Next we are looking for a meaningful syntactic representation of signatures $(A, \approx)$. The idea comes from the observational algebraic specification frameworks [3,8,11] where a distinguished subset of so-called observer operations has been selected for each signature. In our context of labelled transition systems we select, for each action set A, a distinguished subset $C \subseteq A$ of *crucial* actions and consider two states equivalent w.r.t. C if they have the same behaviour under the execution of actions from C. This equivalence is called (A, C)-equality and denoted by $\sim^C_{\mathcal{M}}$ for each labelled transition system $\mathcal{M}$. Following the Misiak's

---

[1] Thus the information in signatures is used to constrain models as in [3]. In contrast, in Hiden Algebra [7] restrictions concern only signature morphisms but not models.

approach we consider only those models $\mathcal{M}$ for which $\sim_{\mathcal{M}}^{C}$ is a congruence, i.e. $\sim_{\mathcal{M}}^{C}$ is preserved by all actions in A. We show that in these models, called (A, C)-models, (A, C)-equality coincides with observational equality, i.e., $\sim_{\mathcal{M}}^{C} = \sim_{\mathcal{M}}$. The model class of $\mathcal{D}^{\downarrow}$ (and of $\mathcal{D}_{\sim}^{\downarrow}$) is therefore restricted to those labelled transition systems for which the set of crucial actions is already sufficient to characterize the observational equality, i.e. bisimilarity of states. This has the side effect that for proving that two states are bisimilar it is sufficient to check transitions with actions from C, a technique which has also been proposed in the selective μ-calculus [2] to reduce verification complexity for modal formulae.

Having signatures as pairs (A, C), it remains to define signature morphisms $\sigma : (A, C) \rightarrow (A', C')$ such that the Eq. (1) from above is valid for each (A', C')-model $\mathcal{M}'$, which now means $(\sim_{\mathcal{M}'})|_{\sigma} = \sim_{(\mathcal{M}'|_{\sigma})}$ (with $\sim$ denoting observational equalities as before in $\mathcal{D}_{\sim}^{\downarrow}$). To achieve this, we require that no new crucial actions are introduced by σ, i.e., $\sigma[C] = C'$. In this way, observational equalities are preserved under change of notation, in particular in larger contexts when the action set A is enlarged to A'. Hence the satisfaction condition holds and we get a concrete institution.

The paper is organized as follows. In Sect. 2, we recall the definitions of $\mathcal{D}^{\downarrow}$-logic and of the observational semantics defined in $\mathcal{D}_{\sim}^{\downarrow}$. Then, in Sect. 3, we apply Misiak's approach to labelled transition systems yielding a behavioural institution with a family of congruence relations on models. We provide the black-box functor in Sect. 4, which maps the behavioural model category to the model category of $\mathcal{D}^{\downarrow}$-logic. In Sect. 5, we consider syntactic representations of signatures and signature morphisms leading to the crucial actions institution. We finish with concluding remarks in Sect. 6.

In order to fix notations, we recall here the institution definition from [6]: An *institution* $\mathcal{I} = \left(\text{Sign}^{\mathcal{I}}, \text{Sen}^{\mathcal{I}}, \text{Mod}^{\mathcal{I}}, (\models_{\Sigma}^{I})_{\Sigma \in |\text{Sign}^{\mathcal{I}}|}\right)$ consists of

- a category $\text{Sign}^{\mathcal{I}}$ whose objects are *signatures* and arrows *signature morphisms*;
- a functor $\text{Sen}^{\mathcal{I}} : \text{Sign}^{\mathcal{I}} \rightarrow \mathbb{S}et$ giving for each signature a set of *sentences*,
- a models functor $\text{Mod}^{\mathcal{I}} : (\text{Sign}^{\mathcal{I}})^{op} \rightarrow \mathbb{C}at$, giving for each signature Σ a category whose objects are Σ-*models*, and arrows are Σ-*(model) homomorphisms*; each arrow $\varphi : \Sigma \rightarrow \Sigma' \in \text{Sign}^{\mathcal{I}}$, (i.e., $\varphi : \Sigma' \rightarrow \Sigma \in (\text{Sign}^{\mathcal{I}})^{op}$) is mapped to a functor $\text{Mod}^{\mathcal{I}}(\varphi) : \text{Mod}^{\mathcal{I}}(\Sigma') \rightarrow \text{Mod}^{\mathcal{I}}(\Sigma)$ called *reduct functor*, whose effect is to cast a model of Σ' as a model of Σ;
- a *satisfaction relation* $\models_{\Sigma}^{I} \subseteq |\text{Mod}^{\mathcal{I}}(\Sigma)| \times \text{Sen}^{\mathcal{I}}(\Sigma)$ for each $\Sigma \in |\text{Sign}^{\mathcal{I}}|$,

such that for each morphism $\varphi : \Sigma \rightarrow \Sigma' \in \text{Sign}^{\mathcal{I}}$, the satisfaction condition

$$M' \models_{\Sigma'}^{I} \text{Sen}^{\mathcal{I}}(\varphi)(\rho) \text{ iff } \text{Mod}^{\mathcal{I}}(\varphi)(M') \models_{\Sigma}^{I} \rho \qquad (2)$$

holds for each $M' \in |\text{Mod}^{\mathcal{I}}(\Sigma')|$ and $\rho \in \text{Sen}^{\mathcal{I}}(\Sigma)$.

2   Dynamic Logics with Binders

This section recalls the underlying definitions and facts of $\mathcal{D}^{\downarrow}$-logic introduced in [13] and its observational variant $\mathcal{D}^{\downarrow}_{\sim}$ introduced in [12]. While $\mathcal{D}^{\downarrow}$ is an institution, $\mathcal{D}^{\downarrow}_{\sim}$ is not as explained before.

2.1 $\mathcal{D}^{\downarrow}$-Logic

Signatures for $\mathcal{D}^{\downarrow}$ are finite sets A of *atomic actions*, and a signature morphism $A \xrightarrow{\sigma} A'$ is a function $\sigma : A \to A'$. Clearly, this entails a category denoted by $\mathrm{Sign}^{\mathcal{D}^{\downarrow}}$.

Definition 1 (Models and model morphisms). *Let A be a finite set of atomic actions. An A-model is triple (W, w_0, R) where W is a set of states, $w_0 \in W$ is the initial state and $R = (R_a \subseteq W \times W)_{a \in A}$ is a family of transition relations such that, for each $w \in W$, there is a finite sequence of transitions $R_{a^k}(w^{k-1}, w^k)$, $1 \leq k \leq n$, with $w^k \in W$, $a^k \in A$, such that $w^0 = w_0$ and $w^n = w$. Given two A-models $\mathcal{M} = (W, w_0, R)$ and $\mathcal{M}' = (W', w'_0, R')$, a model morphism $h : \mathcal{M} \to \mathcal{M}'$ is a function $h : W \to W'$ such that $h(w_0) = w'_0$ and, for each $a \in A$, if $(w_1, w_2) \in R_a$ then $(h(w_1), h(w_2)) \in R'_a$.*

The class of A-models and A-model morphisms define a category denoted by $\mathrm{Mod}^{\mathcal{D}^{\downarrow}}(A)$. The identity morphisms $id_{\mathcal{M}}$ are the identity functions.

Definition 2 (Model reduct). *Let $A \xrightarrow{\sigma} A'$ be a signature morphism and $\mathcal{M}' = (W', w'_0, R')$ an A'-model. The reduct of $\mathcal{M}'$ is the A-model $\mathcal{M}'|_{\sigma} = (W'|_{\sigma}, R'|_{\sigma}, w'_0|_{\sigma})$ where $(w'_0|_{\sigma}) = w'_0$ and $W'|_{\sigma}$ is the largest set with $w'_0 \in W'|_{\sigma}$. For each $v \in W'|_{\sigma}$, either $v = w'_0$ or there is a $w \in W'|_{\sigma}$ such that $(w, v) \in R'_{\sigma(a)}$, for some $a \in A$. For each $a \in A$, $R_a = R'_{\sigma(a)} \cap (W \times W)$.*

The reduct $|_{\sigma}$ induces, for each signature morphism $\sigma : A \to A'$, a functor $\mathrm{Mod}^{\mathcal{D}^{\downarrow}}(\sigma) : \mathrm{Mod}^{\mathcal{D}^{\downarrow}}(A') \to \mathrm{Mod}^{\mathcal{D}^{\downarrow}}(A)$. This functor, named *reduct functor*, maps models as $\mathrm{Mod}^{\mathcal{D}^{\downarrow}}(\mathcal{M}') = \mathcal{M}'|_{\sigma}$ and A'-model morphisms $h : \mathcal{M}' \to \mathcal{N}'$ to A-model morphisms $h|_{\sigma} : \mathcal{M}'|_{\sigma} \to \mathcal{N}'|_{\sigma}$, where $h|_{\sigma}$ is the restriction of h to the scope of $\mathcal{M}'|_{\sigma}$ and $\mathcal{N}'|_{\sigma}$. Finally, we consider the contravariant models functor $\mathrm{Mod}^{\mathcal{D}^{\downarrow}} : (\mathrm{Sign}^{\mathcal{D}^{\downarrow}})^{op} \to \mathbb{C}at$ that maps each signature to its model category and each signature morphism to the respective reduct functor.

Definition 3 (Formulas and sentences). *The set of A-formulas $\mathrm{Fm}^{\mathcal{D}^{\downarrow}}(A)$ is given by*

$$\varphi ::= \mathbf{tt} \mid \mathbf{ff} \mid x \mid \downarrow x.\varphi \mid @_x\varphi \mid \langle\alpha\rangle\varphi \mid [\alpha]\varphi \mid \neg\varphi \mid \varphi \wedge \varphi \mid \varphi \vee \varphi$$

where $x \in X$, for X an infinite set of variables, and actions are composed from atomic actions $a \in A$ by sequential composition choice and iteration:

$$\alpha ::= a \mid \alpha;\alpha \mid \alpha + \alpha \mid \alpha^*$$

An A-formula φ is called an A-sentence if φ contains no free variables. Free variables are defined as usual with $\downarrow$ being the unique operator binding variables. The set of A-sentences is denoted by $\mathrm{Sen}^{\mathcal{D}^{\downarrow}}(A)$.

The binder operator $\downarrow x.\varphi$ assigns to the variable x the current state of evaluation and evaluates φ. The operator $@_x\varphi$ evaluates φ in the state assigned to x.

Each signature morphism $\sigma : A \to A'$ can be extended to a formula translation function $\hat{\sigma} : \mathrm{Fm}^{\mathcal{D}^{\downarrow}}(A) \to \mathrm{Fm}^{\mathcal{D}^{\downarrow}}(A')$, that keeps variables and connectives and replaces each action a by $\sigma(a)$. If we restrict $\hat{\sigma}$ to sentences we get the translation function $\mathrm{Sen}^{\mathcal{D}^{\downarrow}}(\sigma) : \mathrm{Sen}^{\mathcal{D}^{\downarrow}}(A) \to \mathrm{Sen}^{\mathcal{D}^{\downarrow}}(A')$ with $\mathrm{Sen}^{\mathcal{D}^{\downarrow}}(\sigma)(\varphi) = \hat{\sigma}(\varphi)$ for $\varphi \in \mathrm{Sen}^{\mathcal{D}^{\downarrow}}(A)$. Hence we have the *sentence functor* $\mathrm{Sen}^{\mathcal{D}^{\downarrow}} : \mathrm{Sign}^{\mathcal{D}^{\downarrow}} \to \mathbb{S}et$, that maps each signature to the set of its sentences, and each signature morphism to the corresponding translation of sentences.

To define the satisfaction relation formally we need to clarify how composed actions are interpreted in models. Let $\alpha \in \mathrm{Act}(A)$ and $\mathcal{M} \in \mathrm{Mod}^{\mathcal{D}^{\downarrow}}(A)$. The interpretation of an action α in $\mathcal{M}$ extends the interpretation of atomic actions by $R_{\alpha;\alpha'} = R_\alpha \cdot R_{\alpha'}$, $R_{\alpha+\alpha'} = R_\alpha \cup R_{\alpha'}$ and $R_{\alpha^*} = (R_\alpha)^*$, with the operations $\circ$, $\cup$ and $\star$ standing for relational composition, union and reflexive-transitive closure. For a set X of variables and an A-model $\mathcal{M} = (W, w_0, R)$, a *valuation* is a function $g : X \to W$. Given such a valuation g, a variable $x \in X$ and a state $w \in W$, $g[x \mapsto w]$ denotes the valuation with $g[x \mapsto w](x) = w$ and $g[x \mapsto w](y) = g(y)$ for any $y \in X, y \neq x$. Given an A-model $\mathcal{M} = (W, w_0, R)$, $w \in W$ and $g : X \to W$,

- $\mathcal{M}, g, w \models \mathbf{tt}$ is true; $\mathcal{M}, g, w \models \mathbf{ff}$ is false;
- $\mathcal{M}, g, w \models x$ iff $g(x) = w$;
- $\mathcal{M}, g, w \models \downarrow x.\varphi$ iff $\mathcal{M}, g[x \mapsto w], w \models \varphi$;
- $\mathcal{M}, g, w \models @_x\varphi$ iff $\mathcal{M}, g, g(x) \models \varphi$;
- $\mathcal{M}, g, w \models \langle\alpha\rangle\varphi$ iff there is a $v \in W$ with $(w,v) \in R_\alpha$ and $\mathcal{M}, g, v \models \varphi$;
- $\mathcal{M}, g, w \models [\alpha]\varphi$ iff for any $v \in W$ with $(w,v) \in R_\alpha$ it holds $\mathcal{M}, g, v \models \varphi$;
- $\mathcal{M}, g, w \models \neg\varphi$ iff it is false that $\mathcal{M}, g, w \models \varphi$;
- $\mathcal{M}, g, w \models \varphi \wedge \varphi'$ iff $\mathcal{M}, g, w \models \varphi$ and $\mathcal{M}, g, w \models \varphi'$;
- $\mathcal{M}, g, w \models \varphi \vee \varphi'$ iff $\mathcal{M}, g, w \models \varphi$ or $\mathcal{M}, g, w \models \varphi'$.

We write $\mathcal{M}, w \models \varphi$ if, for any valuation $g : X \to W$, we have $\mathcal{M}, g, w \models \varphi$. If φ is an A-sentence, then the valuation is irrelevant, i.e., $\mathcal{M}, g, w \models \varphi$ iff $\mathcal{M}, w \models \varphi$. $\mathcal{M}$ *satisfies* an A-sentence φ, written $\mathcal{M} \models \varphi$, if $\mathcal{M}, w_0 \models \varphi$.

Finally, as shown in [13], the satisfaction condition holds and therefore these ingredients constitute an institution in the sense of Goguen and Burstall [6]:

Theorem 1 (Satisfaction condition). *For any signature morphism $A \xrightarrow{\sigma} A' \in \mathrm{Sign}^{\mathcal{D}^{\downarrow}}$, model $\mathcal{M}' \in \mathrm{Mod}^{\mathcal{D}^{\downarrow}}(A')$ and sentence $\varphi \in \mathrm{Sen}^{\mathcal{D}^{\downarrow}}(A)$, we have*

$$\mathrm{Mod}^{\mathcal{D}^{\downarrow}}(\sigma)(\mathcal{M}') \models \varphi \text{ iff } \mathcal{M}' \models \mathrm{Sen}^{\mathcal{D}^{\downarrow}}(\sigma)(\varphi).$$

2.2 $\mathcal{D}^{\downarrow}_{\sim}$-Logic

In the observational variant of $\mathcal{D}^{\downarrow}$, called $\mathcal{D}^{\downarrow}_{\sim}$ [12], the signature category and the sentences are the same as in $\mathcal{D}^{\downarrow}$. Models are also the same, but model morphisms and the satisfaction relation are different. Both make use of the observational equality of states, denoted by $\sim_{\mathcal{M}}$ for any A-model $\mathcal{M}$. For $\mathcal{M} = (W, w_0, R)$, observational equality $w \sim_{\mathcal{M}} v$ holds for two states $w, v \in W$ if there exists a bisimulation relation $B \subseteq W \times W$ such that $(w, v) \in B$.

Definition 4 (Observational morphisms). *Let* $\mathcal{M} = (W, w_0, R)$ *and* $\mathcal{M}' = (W', w_0', R')$ *be two* A-models. *An* observational morphism $h : \mathcal{M} \to \mathcal{M}'$ *is a relation* $h \subseteq W \times W'$ *containing* (w_0, w_0') *such that the following conditions are satisfied:*

1. *For any* $a \in A$, $w, v \in W$, $w' \in W'$ *such that* $(w, w') \in h$:
   if $(w, v) \in R_a$, *then there is a* $v' \in W'$ *such that* $(w', v') \in R_a'$ *and* $(v, v') \in h$.
2. *For any* $w, v \in W$, $w', v' \in W'$ *such that* $(w, w') \in h$ *and* $(v, v') \in h$:
   if $w \sim_{\mathcal{M}} v$, *then* $w' \sim_{\mathcal{M}'} v'$.
3. *For any* $w, v \in W$, $w' \in W'$ *such that* $(w, w') \in h$:
   if $w \sim_{\mathcal{M}} v$, *then* $(v, w') \in h$.
4. *For any* $w \in W$, $w', v' \in W'$ *such that* $(w, w') \in h$:
   if $w' \sim_{\mathcal{M}'} v'$, *then* $(w, v') \in h$.

A novelty of this model category is that isomorphism corresponds to bisimulation equivalence of models (see [12]). The *observational satisfaction relation* $\mathcal{M}, g, w \models_{\sim} \varphi$ is defined exactly as $\models$ with the exception of the satisfaction for variables which relaxes their interpretation up to observational equality, i.e., for any valuation g and state w,

$$\mathcal{M}, g, w \models_{\sim} x \text{ iff } g(x) \sim_{\mathcal{M}} w \qquad (3)$$

These two adjustments on $\mathcal{D}^{\downarrow}$ ensure that $\mathcal{D}^{\downarrow}_{\sim}$ has the Hennessy-Milner property: Modal invariance holds w.r.t. $\models_{\sim}$ and two image-finite models satisfying w.r.t. $\models_{\sim}$ the same sentences are bisimulation equivalent; see [12]. However, as illustrated in Sect. 1.1, the satisfaction condition does not hold in $\mathcal{D}^{\downarrow}_{\sim}$, i.e. $\mathcal{D}^{\downarrow}_{\sim}$ is not an institution.

3 Behavioural Institution

To get a behavioural institution we use the ideas of Misiak [15] who has studied institutions with behavioural semantics in arbitrary logical systems with concrete model categories. More specifically, our model categories will contain as objects A-models, i.e. transition systems with labels from A. The behavioural semantics introduced in this section is not committed to the observational equality but, following Misiak's idea, to an arbitrary family of equivalence relations, called behavioural structure. It should however be pointed out that, in contrast to Misiak's approach, we can define an explicit satisfaction relation here due to the specific model category of labeled transition systems.

Definition 5. *A behavioural structure for a set of actions A, i.e. $A \in \text{Sign}^{\mathcal{D}^{\downarrow}}$, is a family* $\approx = (\approx_{\mathcal{M}})_{\mathcal{M} \in \text{Mod}^{\mathcal{D}^{\downarrow}}(A)}$ *of equivalence relations* $\approx_{\mathcal{M}} \subseteq W \times W$.

Definition 6 (Behavioural signatures and their morphisms). *A behavioural signature is a pair $(A, \approx)$ where $A \in \text{Sign}^{\mathcal{D}^{\downarrow}}$ is a set of actions and $\approx$ is a behavioural structure for A. Given two behavioural signatures $(A, \approx)$ and $(A', \approx')$, a behavioural signature morphism $(A, \approx) \xrightarrow{\;\sigma\;} (A', \approx')$ is a function $\sigma : A \to A'$ such that for any $\mathcal{M}' \in \text{Mod}^{\mathcal{D}^{\downarrow}}(A')$, we have $\approx_{(\mathcal{M}'|_{\sigma})} = (\approx'_{\mathcal{M}'})|_{\sigma}$.*

Lemma 1. *The behavioural signatures with respective morphisms define a category. This category will be denoted by Sign^B.*

For each behavioural signature $(A, \approx)$, sentences are given by A-sentences as before. The equivalences $\approx_{\mathcal{M}}$ used in a behavioural signature $(A, \approx)$ need not to be congruence relations for all A-models $\mathcal{M}$. Following Misiak's approach, in the new behavioural model category over a signature $(A, \approx)$ only those A-models $\mathcal{M}$ are admitted as $(A, \approx)$-models, for which $\approx_{\mathcal{M}}$ is a congruence relation.

Definition 7 ($(A, \approx)$-Models and their morphisms). *An A-model $\mathcal{M} \in \text{Mod}^{\mathcal{D}^{\downarrow}}(A)$ is an $(A, \approx)$-model if $\approx_{\mathcal{M}}$ is a congruence, in the following sense: for any $a \in A$ and $w, w', v \in W$, if $w \approx_{\mathcal{M}} v$ and $(w, w') \in R_a$, then there is a $v' \in W$ such that $(v, v') \in R_a$ and $w' \approx_{\mathcal{M}} v'$. The morphisms between $(A, \approx)$-models are like observational model morphisms in Definition 4, but observational equalities $\sim_{\mathcal{M}}$ are replaced by the congruences $\approx_{\mathcal{M}}$ for each $(A, \approx)$-model $\mathcal{M}$.*

Lemma 2. *The class of $(A, \approx)$-models with their respective morphisms define a category. This category will be denoted by $\text{Mod}^B(A, \approx)$.*

The next lemma shows that the reduct functor for models in $\text{Mod}^{\mathcal{D}^{\downarrow}}(A)$ leads to a reduct functor for models in $\text{Mod}^B(A, \approx)$. This is important to get an institution. It follows from the definition of behavioural signature morphisms.

Lemma 3. *Let $\sigma : (A, \approx) \to (A', \approx') \in \text{Sign}^B$ be a behavioural signature morphism and $\mathcal{M}'$ an $(A', \approx')$-model. Then, the A-model $\mathcal{M}'|_{\sigma}$ is an $(A, \approx)$-model.*

Proof. We have to prove that $\approx_{(\mathcal{M}'|_{\sigma})}$ is a congruence in $\mathcal{M}'|_{\sigma}$. Let us suppose $w, w', v \in W'|_{\sigma}$ such that $w \approx_{(\mathcal{M}'|_{\sigma})} w'$ and $(w, v) \in (R'|_{\sigma})_a = R'_{\sigma(a)}$. Since σ is a behavioural signature morphism we have that $\approx_{(\mathcal{M}'|_{\sigma})} = (\approx'_{\mathcal{M}'})|_{\sigma}$. Hence, we have

$$
\begin{array}{ccc}
w \overset{\approx'_{\mathcal{M}'}}{\rule{1cm}{0.4pt}} w' & \quad w \overset{\approx'_{\mathcal{M}'}}{\rule{1cm}{0.4pt}} w' & \quad w \overset{\approx_{\mathcal{M}'|_{\sigma}}}{\rule{1cm}{0.4pt}} w' \\
\left.(R'|_{\sigma})_a\right\downarrow \overset{(1)}{\Longrightarrow} \exists v \in W', \; R'_{\sigma(a)} & \left.\right\downarrow R'_{\sigma(a)} \quad \left.\right\downarrow R'_{\sigma(a)} \overset{(2)}{\Longrightarrow} (R'|_{\sigma})_a \left.\right\downarrow \quad \cdot \quad \left.\right\downarrow (R'|_{\sigma})_a \\
v & \quad v \overset{}{\rule{1cm}{0.4pt}} v' \quad v \overset{}{\rule{1cm}{0.4pt}} v' \\
& \quad \overset{\approx'_{\mathcal{M}'}}{} \quad \overset{\approx_{\mathcal{M}'|_{\sigma}}}{}
\end{array}
$$

where (1) holds since $\approx'_{\mathcal{M}'}$ is a congruence in $\mathcal{M}'$ and (2) holds, since $v' \in W'$ is accessible by $R_{\sigma(a)}$, thus $v' \in W'|_{\sigma}$ and by the definition of $R'|_{\sigma}$.

As a consequence of the last lemma, we can use again the construction of reducts $|_\sigma$ to define a models functor $\mathrm{Mod}^B : (\mathrm{Sign}^B)^{op} \to \mathbb{C}at$ similarly as done for $\mathcal{D}^\downarrow$ in Sect. 2.1.

Definition 8 (Behavioural satisfaction $\models_{(A,\approx)}$). *Let $\mathcal{M}$ be an $(A, \approx)$-model, $w \in W$ and $g : X \to W$ a valuation. The* behavioural satisfaction *of an A-formula φ in state w of $\mathcal{M}$ w.r.t. valuation g, denoted by $\mathcal{M}, g, w \models_{(A,\approx)} \varphi$, is defined analogously to the satisfaction relation $\models$ in Sect. 2.1, with the exception of $\mathcal{M}, g, w \models_{(A,\approx)} x$ iff $g(x) \approx_\mathcal{M} w$. For A-sentences φ valuations are irrelevant and we define $\mathcal{M} \models_{(A,\approx)} \varphi$, if $\mathcal{M}, w_0 \models_{(A,\approx)} \varphi$.*

The next theorem is the key to get the satisfaction relation. It relies on the definition of behavioural signature morphisms.

Theorem 2. *Let $\sigma : (A, \approx) \to (A', \approx')$ be a signature morphism and $\mathcal{M}' = (W', w_0', R') \in \mathrm{Mod}^B(A', \approx')$. Then, for any $w \in W'|_\sigma (\subseteq W')$, for any valuation $g : X \to W'|_\sigma$, and for any A-formula φ,*

$$\mathrm{Mod}^B(\sigma)(\mathcal{M}'), g, w \models_{(A,\approx)} \varphi \text{ iff } \mathcal{M}', g, w \models_{(A',\approx')} \hat{\sigma}(\varphi).$$

Proof. The proof is done by induction on the structure of formulas. We consider below atomic formulas x, $\downarrow x.\varphi$ and $\langle \alpha \rangle \varphi$. Actually, cases $\langle \alpha \rangle \varphi$ and $[\alpha] \varphi$ are proved similarly, and the remaining cases are trivial.

In the sequel we denote $\mathrm{Mod}^B(\sigma)(\mathcal{M}')$ by $\mathcal{M}$.

Case x:

$$
\begin{array}{ll}
& \mathcal{M}, g, w \models_{(A,\approx)} x \\
\Leftrightarrow & \{ \models_{(A,\approx)} \text{ def.} \} \\
& w \approx_\mathcal{M} g(x) \\
\Leftrightarrow & \{ \approx_\mathcal{M} = (\approx'_{\mathcal{M}'})|_\sigma \} \\
& w\ (\approx'_{\mathcal{M}'})|_\sigma\ g(x) \\
\Leftrightarrow & \{ w, g(x) \in W'|_\sigma \text{ and by } |_\sigma \text{ def.} \}
\end{array}
\quad \Bigg| \quad
\begin{array}{ll}
& w \approx'_{\mathcal{M}'} g(x) \\
\Leftrightarrow & \{ \models_{(A',\approx')} \text{ def.} \} \\
& \mathcal{M}', g, w \models_{(A',\approx')} x \\
\Leftrightarrow & \{ \hat{\sigma} \text{ def.} \} \\
& \mathcal{M}', g, w \models_{(A',\approx')} \hat{\sigma}(x)
\end{array}
$$

Case $\downarrow x.\varphi$:

$$
\begin{array}{ll}
& \mathcal{M}, g, w \models_{(A,\approx)} \downarrow x.\varphi \\
\Leftrightarrow & \{ \models_{(A,\approx)} \text{ def.} \} \\
& \mathcal{M}, g[x \mapsto w], w \models_{(A,\approx)} \varphi \\
\Leftrightarrow & \{ \text{ I.H.} \} \\
& \mathcal{M}', g[x \mapsto w], w \models_{(A',\approx')} \hat{\sigma}(\varphi)
\end{array}
\quad \Bigg| \quad
\begin{array}{ll}
\Leftrightarrow & \{ \models_{(A',\approx')} \text{ def.} \} \\
& \mathcal{M}', g, w \models_{(A',\approx')} \downarrow x.\hat{\sigma}(\varphi) \\
\Leftrightarrow & \{ \hat{\sigma} \text{ def.} \} \\
& \mathcal{M}', g, w \models_{(A',\approx')} \hat{\sigma}(\downarrow x.\varphi)
\end{array}
$$

Case $\langle\alpha\rangle\varphi$:

$$\mathcal{M}, g, w \models_{(A,\approx)} \langle\alpha\rangle\varphi$$

$\Leftrightarrow$ $\quad\{ \models_{(A,\approx)} \text{ def.}\}$

$\mathcal{M}, g, v \models_{(A,\approx)} \varphi$ for some $v \in W'|_\sigma$
such that $(w,v) \in (R'|_\sigma)_\alpha$ $\qquad\Leftrightarrow\quad \{ \models_{(A',\approx')} \text{ def.}\}$

$\qquad\qquad\qquad\qquad\qquad\qquad\qquad\qquad \mathcal{M}', g, w \models_{(A',\approx')} \langle\sigma(\alpha)\rangle\hat{\sigma}(\varphi)$

$\Leftrightarrow$ $\quad\{ \text{step } (\star) + \text{I.H.}\}$ $\qquad\qquad \Leftrightarrow\quad \{ \hat{\sigma} \text{ def.}\}$

$\mathcal{M}', g, v \models_{(A',\approx')} \hat{\sigma}(\varphi)$ for some $v \in W'$
such that $(w,v) \in R'_{\hat{\sigma}(\alpha)}$ $\qquad\qquad \mathcal{M}', g, w \models_{(A',\approx')} \hat{\sigma}(\langle\alpha\rangle\varphi)$

For the **step** $(\star)$ we just have to observe that for any action $\alpha \in \mathrm{Act}(A)$, $R'|_\alpha = R'_{\hat{\sigma}(\alpha)} \cap (W'|_\sigma)^2$. This can be easily seen by induction on the structure of actions: The property holds by definition for basic actions $a \in A$. We consider below sequential composition of actions $(\alpha; \alpha')$; the remaining cases follow a similar argument. So, we have $R_{\alpha;\alpha'} = R_\alpha \cdot R_{\alpha'} =^{I.H.} (R'_{\hat{\sigma}(\alpha)} \cap (W'|_\sigma)^2) \cdot (R'_{\hat{\sigma}(\alpha)} \cap (W'|_\sigma)^2)$ Hence,

$$(w,v) \in (R'_{\hat{\sigma}(\alpha)} \cap (W'|_\sigma)^2) \cdot (R'_{\hat{\sigma}(\alpha)} \cap (W'|_\sigma)^2)$$

$\Leftrightarrow$ $\quad\{ \cdot \text{ def.}\}$

$$(\exists z)\big((w,z) \in (R'_{\hat{\sigma}(\alpha)} \cap (W'|_\sigma)^2) \wedge (z,v) \in (R'_{\hat{\sigma}(\alpha')} \cap (W'|_\sigma)^2)\big)$$

$\Rightarrow$ $\quad\{ \cdot \text{ def.} + \text{ rewriting }\}$

$$(\exists z)\big((w,z) \in (R'_{\hat{\sigma}(\alpha)} \wedge (z,v) \in R'_{\hat{\sigma}(\alpha')}) \wedge$$
$$(\exists z)\big((w,z) \in (W'|_\sigma)^2 \wedge (z,v) \in (W'|_\sigma)^2)\big)$$

$\Leftrightarrow$ $\quad\{ \cdot \text{ def.} + \text{ rewriting }\}$

$$(w,v) \in (R'_{\hat{\sigma}(\alpha)} \cdot R'_{\hat{\sigma}(\alpha')}) \cap ((W'|_\sigma)^2 \cdot (W'|_\sigma)^2)$$

$\Rightarrow$ $\quad\{ \cap \text{ monotonicity (since } (W'|_\sigma)^2 \cdot (W'|_\sigma)^2 \subseteq (W'|_\sigma)^2) + \bar{\sigma} \text{ def.}\}$

$$(w,v) \in (R'_{\hat{\sigma}(\alpha;\alpha')}) \cap (W'|_\sigma)^2$$

Therefore $R_{\alpha;\alpha'} \subseteq R'_{\hat{\sigma}(\alpha;\alpha')} \cap (W'|_\sigma)^2$. For the converse direction:

$R'_{\hat{\sigma}(\alpha;\alpha')} \cap (W'|_\sigma)^2$

$=$ $\quad\{ \bar{\sigma} \text{ defn} + \text{ actions interpretation}\}$ $\qquad\quad (R_\alpha \cdot R_{\alpha'}) \cap (W'|_\sigma)^2$

$(R'_{\hat{\sigma}(\alpha)} \cdot R'_{\hat{\sigma}(\alpha')}) \cap (W'|_\sigma)^2$ $\qquad\qquad\qquad = \quad \{ R_\alpha, R_{\alpha'} \subseteq (W'|_\sigma)^2\}$

$\subseteq$ $\quad\{ \cdot, \cap \text{ distributivity}\}$ $\qquad\qquad\qquad\qquad R_\alpha \cdot R_{\alpha'}$

$((R'_{\hat{\sigma}(\alpha)} \cap (W'|_\sigma)^2) \cdot (R'_{\hat{\sigma}(\alpha')} \cap (W'|_\sigma)^2)) \cap (W'|_\sigma)^2 = \quad \{ \text{actions int.}\}$

$=$ $\quad\{ \text{I.H.}\}$ $\qquad\qquad\qquad\qquad\qquad\qquad\qquad R_{\alpha;\alpha'}$

Corollary 1 (Satisfaction condition). *Let $\sigma : (A, \approx) \to (A', \approx')$ be a signature morphism and $\mathcal{M}' = (W', w'_0, R') \in \mathrm{Mod}^B(A', \approx')$. Then, for any A-sentence φ, we have $\mathrm{Mod}^B(\sigma)(\mathcal{M}') \models_{(A, \approx)} \varphi$ iff $\mathcal{M}' \models_{(A', \approx')} \mathrm{Sen}^B(\sigma)(\varphi)$*

Proof. This proof follows directly from Theorem 2: the satisfaction of sentences does not depend on the valuations (all the variables are bound and hence, their interpretation is determined by the model). Thus, for any state $w \in W'|_\sigma (\subseteq W')$ we have $\mathrm{Mod}^B(\sigma)(\mathcal{M}'), w \models_{(A, \approx)} \varphi$ iff $\mathcal{M}', w \models_{(A', \approx')} \mathrm{Sen}^B(\sigma)(\varphi)$. Moreover, $w'_0|_\sigma = w'_0$. Hence $\mathrm{Mod}^B(\sigma)(\mathcal{M}'), w'_0|_\sigma \models_{(A, \approx)} \varphi$ iff $\mathcal{M}', w'_0 \models_{(A', \approx')} \mathrm{Sen}^B(\sigma)(\varphi)$, i.e., $\mathrm{Mod}^B(\sigma)(\mathcal{M}') \models_{(A, \approx)} \varphi$ iff $\mathcal{M}' \models_{(A', \approx')} \mathrm{Sen}^B(\sigma)(\varphi)$. $\quad\square$

With the last corollary we have all ingredients to define the *behavioural institution*:

Theorem 3. *The tuple $B = (\mathrm{Sign}^B, \mathrm{Sen}^{\mathcal{D}^\downarrow}, \mathrm{Mod}^B, (\models_{(A, \approx)})_{((A, \approx) \in |\mathrm{Sign}^B|)})$ is an institution.*

4 Black-Box Functor

The black-box view of an $(A, \approx)$-model $\mathcal{M}$ is an A-model that represents the behaviour of $\mathcal{M}$ from the user's point of view. This model that collapses everything that is identified by $\approx_{\mathcal{M}}$, abstracting distinctions between states related by $\approx_{\mathcal{M}}$, is build via quotient construction. In this section we extend this construction to a full and faithful functor that maps each $(A, \approx)$-model into (an A-model representing) its black-box view. Finally we show that this functor preserves and reflects satisfaction of sentences.

Definition 9. *Let $\mathcal{M} = (W, w_0, R)$ be an $(A, \approx)$-model. The quotient of $\mathcal{M}$, denoted by $\mathcal{M}/ \approx_{\mathcal{M}}$, is the A-model $(W/ \approx_{\mathcal{M}}, [w_0]_{\approx_{\mathcal{M}}}, R/ \approx_{\mathcal{M}})$, where $W/\approx_{\mathcal{M}} = \{[w]_{\approx_{\mathcal{M}}} | w \in W\}$ with $[w]_{\approx_{\mathcal{M}}} = \{w' \in W | w \approx_{\mathcal{M}} w'\}$ and $(R/\approx_{\mathcal{M}})_a = \{([w]_{\approx_{\mathcal{M}}}, [v]_{\approx_{\mathcal{M}}}) \mid \text{there exist } w' \in [w]_{\approx_{\mathcal{M}}} \text{ and } v' \in [v]_{\approx_{\mathcal{M}}} \text{ s.t. } (w, v) \in R_a\}$.*

Remark 1. For any $a \in A$ and $w, v \in W$, if $([w]_{\approx_{\mathcal{M}}}, [v]_{\approx_{\mathcal{M}}}) \in (R/\approx_{\mathcal{M}})_a$ then there exists $\hat{v} \in [v]$ such that $(w, \hat{v}) \in R_a$. This follows from the (zig) property of $\sim_{\mathcal{M}}$. This fact can be generalised to composed actions $\alpha \in \mathrm{Act}(A)$.

Definition 10. *The Black Box map is defined as the pair of maps $\mathcal{BB} = (\mathcal{BB}_{obj}, \mathcal{BB}_{hom})$ where $\mathcal{BB}_{obj} : |\mathrm{Mod}^B(A, \approx)| \to |\mathrm{Mod}^{\mathcal{D}^\downarrow}(A)|$ is a function defined for each $\mathcal{M} \in \mathrm{Mod}^B(A, \approx)$ by $\mathcal{BB}_{obj}(\mathcal{M}) = \mathcal{M}/ \approx_{\mathcal{M}}$; and $\mathcal{BB}_{hom} : Hom(\mathcal{M}, \mathcal{M}') \to Hom(\mathcal{BB}(\mathcal{M}), \mathcal{BB}(\mathcal{M}'))$ a function mapping each morphism $h : \mathcal{M} \to \mathcal{M}'$ to the relation $\mathcal{BB} h \subseteq W/\approx_{\mathcal{M}} \times W'/\approx_{\mathcal{M}'}$ defined by $\mathcal{BB} h = \{([w]_{\approx_{\mathcal{M}}}, [w']_{\approx_{\mathcal{M}'}}) | \text{ there are } v \in [w]_{\approx_{\mathcal{M}}}, v' \in [w']_{\approx_{\mathcal{M}}} \text{ such that } (v, v') \in h\}$. As usual, we omit in the sequel the subscripts in $\mathcal{BB}$.*

Theorem 4. *Black box is a functor $\mathcal{BB} : \mathrm{Mod}^B(A, \approx) \to \mathrm{Mod}^{\mathcal{D}^\downarrow}(A)$.*

Proof. Let us firstly observe that $\mathcal{BB}\,h$ is a morphism in $\mathrm{Mod}^{\mathcal{D}^\downarrow}(A)$. According to Definition 1, we have to show that (i) it is a function and (ii) that it preserve transitions. In order to see (i), let us suppose $([w]_{\approx_{\mathcal{M}}}, [w']_{\approx_{\mathcal{M}'}}) \in \mathcal{BB}h$ and $([w]_{\approx_{\mathcal{M}}}, [w'']_{\approx_{\mathcal{M}'}}) \in \mathcal{BB}h$. By $\mathcal{BB}h$ definition we have that $(w, w') \in h$ and $(w, w'') \in h$. Since h is an observational morphism, we have by 2 of Definition 4 that $w' \approx_{\mathcal{M}'} w''$, and hence, $[w']_{\approx_{\mathcal{M}'}} = [w'']_{\approx_{\mathcal{M}'}}$.[2]

In order to see (ii), let us suppose, for a given $[w]_{\approx_{\mathcal{M}}}, [v]_{\approx_{\mathcal{M}}} \in W/\approx_{\mathcal{M}}$, that $([w]_{\approx_{\mathcal{M}}}, [w']_{\approx_{\mathcal{M}'}}) \in \mathcal{BB}h$ and $([w]_{\approx_{\mathcal{M}}}, [v]_{\approx_{\mathcal{M}}}) \in (R/\approx_{\mathcal{M}})_a$. By definition of $\mathcal{BB}h$ and of $R/\approx_{\mathcal{M}}$, we have that $(w, w') \in h$ and $(w, v) \in R_a$. Moreover, since h is a morphism we have by 1 of Definition 4 that there is a $v' \in W'$ such that $(v, v') \in h$ and $(w', v') \in R'_a$. Thus $([w']_{\approx_{\mathcal{M}'}}, [v']_{\approx_{\mathcal{M}'}}) \in (R'/\approx_{\mathcal{M}'})_a$ and $([v]_{\approx_{\mathcal{M}}}, [v']_{\approx_{\mathcal{M}'}}) \in \mathcal{BB}h$.

Then, in order to be a functor we have also to see that, for any two morphisms $\mathcal{M} \xrightarrow{\;h\;} \mathcal{M}' \xrightarrow{\;h'\;} \mathcal{M}''$, $\mathcal{BB}\,h \cdot \mathcal{BB}\,h' = \mathcal{BB}\,h \cdot h'$. Then,

$$([w]_{\approx_{\mathcal{M}}}, [w'']_{\approx_{\mathcal{M}''}}) \in \mathcal{BB}\,h \cdot \mathcal{BB}\,h'$$
$$\Leftrightarrow \quad \{\text{ relational composition}\}$$
$$\exists [w']_{\approx_{\mathcal{M}'}}, ([w]_{\approx_{\mathcal{M}}}, [w']_{\approx_{\mathcal{M}'}}) \in \mathcal{BB}\,h$$
$$\text{and } ([w']_{\approx_{\mathcal{M}'}}, [w'']_{\approx_{\mathcal{M}''}}) \in \mathcal{BB}\,h'$$
$$\Leftrightarrow \quad \{\text{ Step (a)}\}$$

$$\exists w', (w, w') \in h \text{ and } (w', w'') \in h'$$
$$\Leftrightarrow \quad \{\text{ relational composition}\}$$
$$(w, w'') \in h \cdot h'$$
$$\Leftrightarrow \quad \{\text{ Step (b)}\}$$
$$([w]_{\approx_{\mathcal{M}}}, [w'']_{\approx_{\mathcal{M}''}}) \in \mathcal{BB}\,h \cdot h'$$

Step (a): implication $\Rightarrow$: by definition of $\mathcal{BB}$ we have that there are $\bar{w} \in [w]_{\approx_{\mathcal{M}}}, \bar{w}' \in [w']_{\approx_{\mathcal{M}'}}$ and $\bar{w}'' \in [w'']_{\approx_{\mathcal{M}''}}$ such that $(\bar{w}, \bar{w}') \in h$ and $(\bar{w}', \bar{w}'') \in h'$. But we have also that $\bar{w} \approx_{\mathcal{M}} w$, $\bar{w}' \approx_{\mathcal{M}'} w'$ and $\bar{w}'' \approx_{\mathcal{M}''} w''$. The implication follows by 3 and 4 of Definition 4 of the morphism h. Definition of $\mathcal{BB}$ entails the implication $\Leftarrow$. Justification of Step (b) is analogous. Moreover, $\mathcal{BB}\,1_{\mathcal{M}} = \{([w]_{\approx_{\mathcal{M}}}, [v]_{\approx_{\mathcal{M}}}) | (w, v) \in 1_{\mathcal{M}}\} = \{([w]_{\approx_{\mathcal{M}}}, [v]_{\approx_{\mathcal{M}}})) | w \approx_{\mathcal{M}} v\} = 1_{\mathcal{BB}(\mathcal{M})}$.

Given a model $\mathcal{M} \in \mathrm{Mod}^B(A, \approx)$, $\mathcal{BB}(\mathcal{M})$ is called *black box view* of $\mathcal{M}$.

Theorem 5. *The functor $\mathcal{BB}$ is full.*

Proof. Let us prove that $\mathcal{BB}$ is full, i.e. that for any morphism $k : \mathcal{BB}(\mathcal{M}) \to \mathcal{BB}(\mathcal{M}')$ there is an observational morphism $h : \mathcal{M} \to \mathcal{M}'$ such that $k = \mathcal{BB}h$. Let us consider the relation $h \subseteq W \times W' = \{(v, v') | ([w]_{\approx_{\mathcal{M}}}, [w']_{\approx_{\mathcal{M}'}}) \in k, v \in [w]_{1_{\mathcal{M}}}, v' \in [w']_{1_{\mathcal{M}'}}\}$. It is enough to prove that h is an observational morphism. Let us check the conditions of Definition 4: In order to see the condition 1: by assuming $(v, r) \in R_a$ and $(v, v') \in h$, we have by definitions of h and $R/\approx_{\mathcal{M}}$ that

---

[2] For sake of uniformity, we still use along the section the relational notation to present this function, i.e. we use $(w, w') \in \mathcal{BB}h$ to represent $\mathcal{BB}h(w) = w'$.

$$[v]_{\approx_{\mathcal{M}}} \xrightarrow{\;(R \not\approx_{\mathcal{M}})_a\;} [r]_{\approx_{\mathcal{M}}}$$
$$k \downarrow$$
$$[v']_{\approx_{\mathcal{M}'}}$$

k is a morphism $\Longrightarrow$

$$[v]_{\approx_{\mathcal{M}}} \xrightarrow{\;(R \not\approx_{\mathcal{M}})_a\;} [r]_{\approx_{\mathcal{M}}}$$
$$k \downarrow \qquad\qquad \downarrow k$$
$$[v']_{\approx_{\mathcal{M}'}} \xrightarrow{(R \not\approx_{\mathcal{M}})_a} [r']_{\approx_{\mathcal{M}'}}$$

$\forall r' \in [r']$ $\Longrightarrow$

$$v \xrightarrow{\;R_a\;} r$$
$$k \downarrow \qquad \downarrow k$$
$$v' \xrightarrow{R_a} r'$$

Conditions 2, 3 and 4 follow trivially, since $v \approx_{\mathcal{M}} r$ implies that $[v]_{\approx_{\mathcal{M}}} = [r]_{\approx_{\mathcal{M}}}$.

Theorem 6. *The functor $\mathcal{BB}$ is faithful.*

Proof. We have to show that, for any observational morphisms $h, h' : \mathcal{M} \to \mathcal{M}'$, $\mathcal{BB}\, h = \mathcal{BB}\, h'$ implies $h = h'$. In view of contradiction, let us suppose that $\mathcal{BB}\, h = \mathcal{BB}\, h'$ and $h \neq h'$. Then, there is a pair (w, w') such that $(w, w') \in h$ and $(w, w') \notin h'$ (or vice-versa). By $\mathcal{BB}$ definition we have $([w]_{\approx_{\mathcal{M}}}, [w']_{\approx_{\mathcal{M}'}}) \in \mathcal{BB}h'(= \mathcal{BB}h)$. Hence, there is an $r \in [w]_{\approx_{\mathcal{M}}}$ and $r' \in [w']_{\approx_{\mathcal{M}'}}$ such that $(r, r') \in h'$. Since $r \approx_{\mathcal{M}} w$ and h' is a morphism, we have by 3 of Definition 4 that $(w, r') \in h'$. Moreover, since $r' \approx_{\mathcal{M}'} w'$, we have by 4 of Definition 4 that $(w, w') \in h'$, what contradicts our initial assumption. Therefore $h = h'$.

Theorem 7. *Let $\mathcal{M} \in \mathrm{Mod}^B(A, \approx)$ be a model. Then,*

$$\mathcal{M} \text{ iso}_\sim \mathcal{M}' \text{ iff } \mathcal{M}/\approx_{\mathcal{M}} \text{ iso } \mathcal{M}'/\approx_{\mathcal{M}'} .$$

Proof. Implication '$\Rightarrow$' holds since $\mathcal{BB}$ is a functor. Implication '$\Leftarrow$' is entailed because $\mathcal{BB}$ is a full and faithful functor

In the remainder of this section we show that the functor $\mathcal{BB}$ preserves and reflects satisfaction. This result is a simple generalisation of Theorem 5 in [12].

Theorem 8. *For any model $\mathcal{M} \in \mathrm{Mod}^B(A, \approx)$ and for any A-sentence φ,*

$$\mathcal{M} \models_{(A,\approx)} \varphi \text{ iff } \mathcal{M}/\approx_{\mathcal{M}} \models \varphi \tag{4}$$

Proof. For the proof we show, more generally, that for any $w \in W$, valuation $g : X \to W$ and A-formula φ,

$$\mathcal{M}, g, w \models_{(A,\approx)} \varphi \text{ iff } \mathcal{M}/\approx_{\mathcal{M}}, g/\approx_{\mathcal{M}}, [w]_{\approx_{\mathcal{M}}} \models \varphi$$

where $g/\approx_{\mathcal{M}} : X \to W$ is defined by $(g/\approx_{\mathcal{M}})(x) = [g(x)]_{\approx_{\mathcal{M}}}$. The proof can be performed by induction over the structure of A-formulas. For the base formulas $\varphi = x$, we have:

$$\mathcal{M}, g, w \models_{(A,\approx)} x$$
$$\Leftrightarrow \quad \{\models_{(A,\approx)} \text{def.}\}$$
$$g(x) \approx_{\mathcal{M}} w$$
$$\Leftrightarrow \quad \{ \text{ equivalence classes def.}\}$$

$$[g(x)]_{\approx_{\mathcal{M}}} = [w]_{\approx_{\mathcal{M}}}$$
$$\Leftrightarrow \quad \{ [g(x)]_{\approx_{\mathcal{M}}} = (g/\approx_{\mathcal{M}})(x) + \models \text{def.}\}$$
$$\mathcal{M}/\approx_{\mathcal{M}}, g/\approx_{\mathcal{M}}, [w]_{\approx_{\mathcal{M}}} \models x$$

For the case $\varphi = \langle \alpha \rangle \phi$, we have:

$$\mathcal{M}, g, w \models_{(A, \approx)} \langle \alpha \rangle \phi$$

$\Leftrightarrow$ $\{ \models_{(A, \approx)} \text{def.}\}$

      there exists $v \in W$ with $(w, v) \in R_\alpha$ and $\mathcal{M}, g, v \models_{(A, \approx)} \phi$

$\Leftrightarrow$ $\{ \text{ step } \star \}$

      there exists $[v']_{\approx_\mathcal{M}} \in W/{\approx_\mathcal{M}}$ with

      $([w]_{\approx_\mathcal{M}}, [v']_{\approx_\mathcal{M}}) \in (R/{\approx_\mathcal{M}})_\alpha$ and $\mathcal{M}/{\approx_\mathcal{M}}, g/{\approx_\mathcal{M}}, [v']_{\approx_\mathcal{M}} \models \phi$

$\Leftrightarrow$ $\{ \models \text{def.}\}$

$$\mathcal{M}/{\approx_\mathcal{M}}, g/{\approx_\mathcal{M}}, [w]_{\approx_\mathcal{M}} \models \langle \alpha \rangle \phi$$

Step $\star$: The direction "$\Rightarrow$" is trivial using $v' = v$ and the Induction Hypothesis. For the direction "$\Leftarrow$" assume $([w]_{\approx_\mathcal{M}}, [v']_{\approx_\mathcal{M}}) \in (R/{\approx_\mathcal{M}})_\alpha$ for some v'. By Remark 1 we know that there exists $\hat{v} \in [v']_{\approx_\mathcal{M}}$ such that $(w, \hat{v}) \in R_\alpha$. From $\mathcal{M}/{\approx_\mathcal{M}}, g/{\approx_\mathcal{M}}, [v']_{\approx_\mathcal{M}} \models \phi$ it follows that $\mathcal{M}/{\approx_\mathcal{M}}, g/{\approx_\mathcal{M}}, [\hat{v}]_{\approx_\mathcal{M}} \models \phi$ (since $[\hat{v}]_{\approx_\mathcal{M}} = [v']_{\approx_\mathcal{M}}$). By Ind. Hyp. we get $\mathcal{M}, g, \hat{v} \models_{(A, \approx)} \phi$. Since $(w, \hat{v}) \in R_\alpha$, we have $\mathcal{M}, g, w \models_{(A, \approx)} \langle \alpha \rangle \phi$.

The remaining cases are straightforward.

5   Institution of Crucial Actions

This section introduces the "Logic of Crucial Actions". We show that this logic is a specific institution of observational dynamic logic with binders, inheriting the whole theory developed in the previous sections. The crucial idea to do this is to define signatures and signature morphisms syntactically and to relate them to behavioural signatures and behavioural signature morphisms as considered in Sect. 3. An important extra ingredient is that the restriction of A-models to those on which the given equivalences are congruences will yield, in the case of crucial actions signatures, exactly observational equalities. Thus, by applying the results of Sect. 3, we have recovered the satisfaction condition for the satisfaction relation $\models_\sim$ used in $\mathcal{D}^!_\sim$, since signatures with crucial actions have less models than in $\mathcal{D}^!_\sim$.

Definition 11 (Crucial actions signatures and morphisms). *A crucial actions signature is a pair (A, C) where A is a set of actions, and $C \subseteq A$ is a set of crucial actions. Given two crucial actions signatures (A, C) and (A', C'), a crucial actions signature morphism $\sigma : (A, C) \rightarrow (A', C')$ is a function $\sigma : A \rightarrow A'$ such that $\sigma[C] = C'$.*

Lemma 4. *Crucial action signatures with their morphisms define a category. This category will be denoted by Sign^{Cr}.*

Sentences of this logic are the same as in $\mathcal{D}_\sim^\downarrow$ and in $\mathcal{D}^\downarrow$. The sentences functor $\mathrm{Sen}^{Cr} : \mathrm{Sign}^{Cr} \to \mathbb{S}et$ is defined as $\mathrm{Sen}^{\mathcal{D}^\downarrow}$ by forgetting the second component of the signatures. Now, we define a variant of bisimulation on A-models which takes into account only crucial actions in C. In the particular case where $C = A$ we get the usual notion of (strong) bisimulation.

Definition 12 (Crucial actions bisimulation). *Let (A, C) be a crucial actions signature and let $\mathcal{M} = (W, w_0, R)$ be an A-model. An (A, C)-bisimulation on $\mathcal{M} = (W, w_0, R)$ is a relation $B \subseteq W \times W$ such that $(w_0, w_0) \in B$ and*

- *(zig) For any $c \in C$, $w, v, w' \in W$ such that $(w, w') \in B$, if $(w, v) \in R_c$, then there is a $v' \in W$ such that $(w', v') \in R_c$ and $(v, v') \in B$.*
- *(zag) For any $c \in C$, $w, v, v' \in W$ such that $(w, w') \in B$, if $(w', v') \in R'_c$, then there is a $v \in W$ such that $(w, v) \in R_c$ and $(v, v') \in B$.*

Definition 13 ((A,C)-Equality). *Let (A, C) be a crucial actions signature. For any A-model $\mathcal{M}$ the (A, C)-equality on $\mathcal{M}$ is the relation $\sim_{\mathcal{M}}^C \subseteq W \times W$ such that, for any w, w', $w \sim_{\mathcal{M}}^C w'$ iff there is an (A, C)-bisimulation B in $\mathcal{M}$ such that $(w, w') \in B$.*

Lemma 5. *The family $\sim^C = (\sim_{\mathcal{M}}^C)_{\mathcal{M} \in \mathrm{Mod}^{\mathcal{D}^\downarrow}(A)}$ is a behavioural structure.*

Proof. For any A-model $\mathcal{M}$, the (A, C)-equality $\sim_{\mathcal{M}}^C$ is an equivalence relation.

Given a crucial actions signature (A, C), we consider, along the lines of Sect. 3, only those A-models $\mathcal{M}$ as admissible (A, C)-models, for which the (A, C)-equality $\sim_{\mathcal{M}}^C$ is a congruence.

Definition 14 ((A,C)-Models). *A model $\mathcal{M} \in \mathrm{Mod}^{\mathcal{D}^\downarrow}(A)$ is an (A, C)-model if $\sim_{\mathcal{M}}^C$ is a congruence relation on $\mathcal{M}$.*

Example 1. Let $A' = \{a, b\}$ and $C' = \{a\}$. The A'-model $\mathcal{M}'$ of Fig. 2 is not an (A', C')-model since we have $w_0' \sim_{\mathcal{M}'}^{C'} w_1'$ and $(w_0', w_1') \in R_b'$ but action b is not enabled in w_1'. Now, consider the A'-model $\mathcal{M}''$ in Fig. 3. It is obviously an $(\{a, b\}, \{a\})$-model.

The important point to link the current notions to the observational equality $\sim_{\mathcal{M}}$ considered in $\mathcal{D}_\sim^\downarrow$ is given by the next lemma.

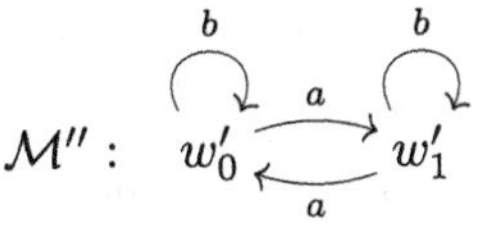

$\mathcal{M}'' : w_0' \rightleftarrows w_1'$ with loops b, a

Fig. 3. $(\{a, b\}, \{a\})$-model

Lemma 6. *Let $\mathcal{M}$ be an A-model. $\mathcal{M}$ is an (A, C)-model if, and only if, the (A, C)-equality on $\mathcal{M}$ coincides with the observational equality $\sim_{\mathcal{M}}$, i.e. $\sim_{\mathcal{M}}^C = \sim_{\mathcal{M}}$.*

Proof. The implication "$\Leftarrow$" is easy since the observational equality $\sim_{\mathcal{M}}$ is trivially a congruence relation and so is $\sim_{\mathcal{M}}^C$ by assumption. For the implication "$\Rightarrow$" we have to prove that $\sim_{\mathcal{M}} = \sim_{\mathcal{M}}^C$. The inclusion $\sim_{\mathcal{M}} \subseteq \sim_{\mathcal{M}}^C$ is obvious - we have the bisimulation properties assured for all actions of A and hence also for all actions of C. For the converse inclusion, we observe that for any congruence $\equiv$ in $\mathcal{M}$, $w_0 \equiv w_0$ (any congruence is an equivalence relation). Moreover, by definition, it satisfies (zig) and, because of its symmetry (any congruence is an equivalence relation), (zag) also holds. Therefore any congruence $\equiv$ in $\mathcal{M}$ is a bisimulation in $\mathcal{M}$. Thus, since $\sim_{\mathcal{M}}^C$ is a congruence and by bisimulation equivalence definition, we have $\sim_{\mathcal{M}}^C \subseteq \sim_{\mathcal{M}}$.

Example 2. Consider again the A'-models $\mathcal{M}'$ and $\mathcal{M}''$ of the previous example. Actually, we have that the observational equality $\sim_{\mathcal{M}'}$ is the identity of states in $\mathcal{M}'$, while the crucial actions equality $\sim_{\mathcal{M}'}^{C'}$ identifies all states of $\mathcal{M}'$. Due to the previous lemma, this shows again that $\mathcal{M}'$ is not an (A', C')-model. Considering $\mathcal{M}''$, however, we have $\sim_{\mathcal{M}''} = \sim_{\mathcal{M}''}^{C'}$ since the execution of action b does not distinguish more elements than distinguished by a.

For each crucial actions signature (A, C) we have the category of models $\mathrm{Mod}^{Cr}(A, C) = \mathrm{Mod}^B(A, \sim^C)$. Next we show that crucial actions signature morphisms are behavioural signature morphisms in the sense of Definition 6.

Lemma 7. *Let $\sigma : (A, C) \to (A', C')$ be a crucial actions signature morphism and $\mathcal{M}'$ be an (A', C')-model. Then, $\sim_{(\mathcal{M}'|_\sigma)}^C = (\sim_{\mathcal{M}'}^{C'})|_\sigma$.*

Proof. Let us suppose $w \sim_{(\mathcal{M}'|_\sigma)}^C w'$. Then, there is an (A, C)-bisimulation $B \subseteq W'|_\sigma \times W'|_\sigma$ such that $(w, w') \in B$. Since for any $c \in C$, $(R'|_\sigma)_c = R'_{\sigma(c)}$, and $\sigma[C] = C'$, the relation B is also an (A', C')-bisimulation and, hence $w \sim_{\mathcal{M}'}^{C'} w'$. Moreover, $(w, w') \in (W|_\sigma)^2$. Hence $w\left(\sim_{\mathcal{M}'}^{C'} \cap (W'|_\sigma)^2 \right)w'$, i.e., $w(\sim_{\mathcal{M}'}^{C'})|_\sigma w'$.

Let us suppose $w\left(\sim_{\mathcal{M}'}^{C'} \cap (W'|_\sigma)^2 \right)w'$. Let $B' \subseteq W' \times W'$ be an (A', C')-bisimulation containing w and w' (its existence is assured by $w \sim_{\mathcal{M}'}^{C'} w'$). Again, since for any $c \in C$, $(R'|_\sigma)_c = R'_{\sigma(c)}$, and $\sigma[C] = C'$, we have that B' satisfies the conditions of (A', C')-bisimulation. We have also that $W'|_\sigma$ is closed by A-actions. Hence, $B' \cap (W'|_\sigma)^2$ is an (A, C)-bisimulation. Therefore $w \sim_{(\mathcal{M}'|_\sigma)}^C w'$.

As a direct consequence of this lemma we have the following result:

Corollary 2. *Let $\sigma : A \to A'$ be a function. If $\sigma : (A, C) \to (A', C')$ is a crucial actions signature morphism, then $\sigma : (A, \sim^C) \to (A', \sim^{C'})$ is a behavioural signature morphism.*

As a consequence of the last corollary and Lemma 3 we get the functor $\mathrm{Mod}^{Cr} : (\mathrm{Sign}^{Cr})^{op} \to \mathbb{C}at$. Next, by taking $\models_{(A,C)}$ as the satisfaction relation $\models_{(A,\sim^C)}$ and instantiating Corollary 1 we have:

Corollary 3 (Satisfaction condition for logic of crucial actions). *Let $\sigma : (A, C) \to (A', C')$ be a crucial actions signature morphism and $\mathcal{M}'$ be an (A', C')-model. Then, for any A-sentence φ, we have*

$$\mathrm{Mod}^{Cr}(\sigma)(\mathcal{M}') \models_{(A,C)} \varphi \ \textit{ iff } \ \mathcal{M}' \models_{(A',C')} \mathrm{Sen}^{Cr}(\sigma)(\varphi)$$

Theorem 9 (Crucial actions institution). *The tuple* $Cr = \big(\mathrm{Sign}^{Cr}, \mathrm{Sen}^{Cr},$ $\mathrm{Mod}^{Cr}, (\models_{(A,C)})_{(A,C)\in|\mathrm{Sign}^{Cr}|}\big)$ *is an institution.*

Remark 2. As a consequence of Lemma 6 the satisfaction relation $\models_{(A,C)}$ coincides with the observational satisfaction relation $\models_\sim$ (see Sect. 2.2) if we use it just for (A, C)-models.

Example 3. Coming back to the example considered in Sect. 1 we want to emphasise that the problem considered there does not apply anymore, if we consider the crucial actions signature morphism $\sigma : (\{a\}, \{a\}) \to (\{a, b\}, \{a\})$ with $\sigma(a) = a$. Then, the structure $\mathcal{M}'$ in Fig. 2 is not an $(\{a, b\}, \{a\})$-model, as explained above, and therefore the reduct w.r.t. σ is not meaningful in the crucial actions institution. The situation is different, however, if we consider the model $\mathcal{M}''$ of Fig. 3 whose reduct w.r.t. σ is just the model $\mathcal{M}$ of Fig. 2. In this case we have $\mathcal{M}'' \models_\sim \downarrow x.\langle a \rangle x$ and $\mathcal{M} \models_\sim \downarrow x.\langle a \rangle x$; see Remark 2.

According to the results of Sect. 4 we get for free the black-box functor mapping (A, C)-models to A-models by constructing quotients w.r.t. the (A, C)-equalities $\sim^C_{\mathcal{M}}$. In particular, we can instantiate Theorem 8:

Corollary 4. *For any (A, C)-model $\mathcal{M}$ and for any A-formula φ,*

$$\mathcal{M} \models_{(A,C)} \varphi \text{ iff } \mathcal{M}/\sim^C_{\mathcal{M}} \models \varphi.$$

6   Conclusion and Future Work

The observational logic with binders $\mathcal{D}^\downarrow$ was suggested in [13] as a suitable formalism to develop reactive systems. This research was pursued in [12] with the introduction of an alternative semantics for $\mathcal{D}^\downarrow$, endowing it with modal invariance. However, with this accommodation, the satisfaction condition was lost, i.e. unlike the original $\mathcal{D}^\downarrow$, this new logic is not an institution. The present paper works on this handicap. As done in the context of the observational semantics (see [15]) we adopted behavioural structures - families of equivalence relations on the states of each model - as behavioural interpretations of the equalities on the states. Then, by adjusting the morphisms of the category of signatures (as done in [3, 7, 15]) the (standard) reduct works properly to assure the satisfaction condition. Under this abstract setting, the black-box functor was defined and the relation between the strict satisfaction of $\mathcal{D}^\downarrow$ and the observational ones of $\mathcal{D}^\downarrow_\sim$ was established. Finally, an interesting instantiation of this generic institution was presented - the Crucial Actions Institution.

These efforts on the parametrization of the logic with generic observational structures (i), as well on the adjustment of $\mathcal{D}^\downarrow_\sim$ to recover the institutional nature of $\mathcal{D}^\downarrow$ (ii) would be worthy explored in the future. Concerning the direction (i), we are looking for a specific observational structure (maybe combined with some slight adaptations of $\mathcal{D}^\downarrow_\sim$) to deal with (internal) τ-transitions (e.g. [9, 14]). Moreover, in analogy with what was done in [3] we intend to define an institutional encoding, in sense of [17], from $\mathcal{D}_{\sim}^{\downarrow}$ to $\mathcal{D}^{\downarrow}$. This could provide useful tool support for $\mathcal{D}_{\sim}^{\downarrow}$ borrowed from $\mathcal{D}^{\downarrow}$ - a calculus for $\mathcal{D}^{\downarrow}$ was already suggested in a journal extended version of [13] (currently in revision process). On the direction (ii), it would be interesting to explore the 'once and for all' techniques and results established for generic institutions. In this view, the use and characterisation of the *Casl-in-the-large* specification constructors [1] in $\mathcal{D}_{\sim}^{\downarrow}$ specifications, as well as the integration of these institutions in HETS [16], could provide appropriate conditions to make $\mathcal{D}_{\sim}^{\downarrow}$ (and $\mathcal{D}^{\downarrow}$) an effective formal method for reactive systems development.

Acknowledgement. We would like to thank the anonymous reviewers of this paper for their careful reviews with many useful comments and suggestions.

References

1. Astesiano, E., Bidoit, M., Kirchner, H., Krieg-Brückner, B., Mosses, P.D., Sannella, D., Tarlecki, A.: CASL: the common algebraic specification language. Theor. Comput. Sci. **286**(2), 153–196 (2002)
2. Barbuti, R., Francesco, N.D., Santone, A., Vaglini, G.: Selective mu-calculus and formula-based equivalence of transition systems. J. Comput. Syst. Sci. **59**(3), 537–556 (1999)
3. Bidoit, M., Hennicker, R.: Constructor-based observational logic. J. Log. Algebr. Program. **67**(1–2), 3–51 (2006)
4. Braüner, T.: Hybrid Logic and Its Proof-Theory. Applied Logic Series. Springer, Dordrecht (2010). doi:10.1007/978-94-007-0002-4
5. Goguen, J.: Types as theories. In: George Michael Reed, A.W.R., Wachter, R.F., (eds.) Topology and Category Theory in Computer Science (1991)
6. Goguen, J.A., Burstall, R.M.: Institutions: abstract model theory for specification and programming. J. ACM **39**(1), 95–146 (1992)
7. Goguen, J.A., Malcolm, G.: A hidden agenda. Theor. Comput. Sci. **245**(1), 55–101 (2000)
8. Goguen, J., Roşu, G.: Hiding more of hidden algebra. In: Wing, J.M., Woodcock, J., Davies, J. (eds.) FM 1999. LNCS, vol. 1709, pp. 1704–1719. Springer, Heidelberg (1999). doi:10.1007/3-540-48118-4_40
9. Groote, J.F., Mousavi, M.R.: Modeling and Analysis of Communicating Systems. MIT Press, Cambridge (2014)
10. Harel, D., Kozen, D., Tiuryn, J.: Dynamic Logic. MIT Press, Cambridge (2000)
11. Hennicker, R., Bidoit, M.: Observational logic. In: Haeberer, A.M. (ed.) AMAST 1999. LNCS, vol. 1548, pp. 263–277. Springer, Heidelberg (1998). doi:10.1007/3-540-49253-4_20
12. Hennicker, R., Madeira, A.: Behavioural semantics for the dynamic logic with binders. In: Roggenbach, M. (ed.) Recent Trends in Algebraic Development Methods - Selected Papers of WADT 2016. Springer (2016, to appear)
13. Madeira, A., Barbosa, L.S., Hennicker, R., Martins, M.A.: Dynamic logic with binders and its application to the development of reactive systems. In: Sampaio, A., Wang, F. (eds.) ICTAC 2016. LNCS, vol. 9965, pp. 422–440. Springer, Cham (2016). doi:10.1007/978-3-319-46750-4_24
14. Milner, R.: Communication and Concurrency. PHI Series in Computer Science. Prentice Hall, Upper Saddle River (1989)

15. Misiak, M.: Behavioural semantics of algebraic specifications in arbitrary logical systems. In: Fiadeiro, J.L., Mosses, P.D., Orejas, F. (eds.) WADT 2004. LNCS, vol. 3423, pp. 144–161. Springer, Heidelberg (2005). doi:10.1007/978-3-540-31959-7_9

16. Mossakowski, T., Maeder, C., Lüttich, K.: The heterogeneous tool set, HETS. In: Grumberg, O., Huth, M. (eds.) TACAS 2007. LNCS, vol. 4424, pp. 519–522. Springer, Heidelberg (2007). doi:10.1007/978-3-540-71209-1_40

17. Tarlecki, A.: Towards heterogeneous specifications. In: Frontiers of Combining Systems (FroCoS 1998). Applied Logic Series, pp. 337–360. Kluwer Academic Publishers (1998)

The Delay Monad and Restriction Categories

Tarmo Uustalu and Niccolò Veltri[(✉)]

Department of Software Science, Tallinn University of Technology,
Akadeemia tee 21B, 12618 Tallinn, Estonia
{tarmo,niccolo}@cs.ioc.ee

Abstract. We continue the study of Capretta's delay monad as a means of introducing non-termination from iteration into Martin-Löf type theory. In particular, we explain in what sense this monad provides a canonical solution. We discuss a class of monads that we call ω-complete pointed classifying monads. These are monads whose Kleisli category is an ω-complete pointed restriction category where pure maps are total. All such monads support non-termination from iteration: this is because restriction categories are a general framework for partiality; the presence of an ω-join operation on homsets equips a restriction category with a uniform iteration operator. We show that the delay monad, when quotiented by weak bisimilarity, is the initial ω-complete pointed classifying monad in our type-theoretic setting. This universal property singles it out from among other examples of such monads.

1 Introduction

The delay datatype was introduced by Capretta [4] in order to facilitate the definition of non-terminating functions in type theory and has been used as such by several authors, see, e.g., Danielsson's work [10] for an application to operational semantics or Benton et al.'s work [2] on domain theory in type theory. Inhabitants of the delay datatype are "delayed values", called computations throughout this paper. They can be non-terminating and not return a value at all. Often, one is only interested in termination of computations and not the exact computation time. Identifying computations that only differ by finite amounts of delay corresponds to quotienting the delay datatype by termination-sensitive weak bisimilarity. In earlier work [5], we showed that the monad structure of the delay datatype is preserved under quotienting by weak bisimilarity in an extension of type theory with inductive-like quotient types à la Hofmann [14], proposition extensionality and the axiom of countable choice.

It is common in the type-theoretic programming community to say that the quotiented delay monad is useful for "modeling partial functions" or "introducing non-termination as an effect" in type theory. In this paper, we explain in what sense exactly this monad meets these aims. To do so, we introduce the notion of ω-complete pointed classifying monad. Such a monad is first of all a "monad for partiality", in that its Kleisli category is a restriction category where pure maps are total. Cockett and Lack [8] have termed such monads classifying monads;

© Springer International Publishing AG 2017
D.V. Hung and D. Kapur (Eds.): ICTAC 2017, LNCS 10580, pp. 32–50, 2017.
DOI: 10.1007/978-3-319-67729-3_3

the restriction categories of Cockett and Lack [7] are an axiomatic approach to partiality where every partial function is required to define a partial endofunction on its domain, the corresponding partial identity function, meeting certain equational conditions. Moreover, an ω-complete pointed classifying monad is a "monad for non-termination", in that its Kleisli category is ω**CPPO**-enriched wrt. the "less defined than" order on homsets induced by the restriction operation. In other words, the Kleisli category is an ω-complete pointed restriction category (in a sense that is analogous to finite-join restriction categories [13]).

We show that the quotiented delay datatype possesses an ω-complete pointed classifying monad structure. To this end, we first prove that the quotiented delay datatype delivers free ω-complete pointed partial orders. From this, we further prove that the quotiented delay datatype is the initial ω-complete pointed classifying monad. Intuitively, this tells us that the Kleisli category of this monad is the minimal setting in Martin-Löf type theory for non-terminating functions.

The initiality result is only interesting, if the category of ω-complete pointed classifying monads contains at least some other interesting examples. We show that the datatype of "values on conditions" also possesses an ω-complete pointed classifying monad structure and observe that it is not isomorphic to the quotiented delay monad.

Throughout the paper, we reason constructively, in type theory. The maybe monad is therefore a classifying monad, but not an ω-complete pointed classifying monad. Classically, both the delay monad and the conditional monad are isomorphic to the maybe monad and thus just complications of something that can be expressed much simpler. But constructively they are very different.

The paper is organized as follows. In Sect. 2, we define ω-complete pointed classifying monads and prove some properties about them. In Sect. 3, we introduce the delay monad and weak bisimilarity. In Sect. 4, we quotient the delay monad by weak bisimilarity and we show that the resulting monad is a classifying monad. In Sect. 5, we construct an alternative monad structure on the delay datatype, which makes it an almost-classifying monad. In Sect. 6, we prove that the quotiented delay datatype is the initial ω-complete pointed classifying monad. In Sect. 7, we present some other examples of ω-complete pointed classifying monads. Finally, in Sect. 8, we draw some conclusions and discuss future work.

Our discussion on ω-complete pointed classifying monads applies to general categories. The discussion of the delay monad is carried out for **Set**; generalizing it is future work. We reiterate that we only accept constructive reasoning.

We have fully formalized the development of the paper in the dependently typed programming language Agda [16]. The code is available at http://cs.ioc.ee/~niccolo/omegacpcm/. It uses Agda version 2.4.2.3 and Agda standard library version 0.9.

The Type-Theoretical Framework. Our work is settled in Martin-Löf type theory extended with the following extensional concepts: function extensionality (pointwise equal functions are equal), proposition extensionality (logically equivalent propositions are equal) and inductive-like quotient types à la Hofmann [14].

Equivalently, we could work in homotopy type theory, where function and proposition extensionality are consequences of the univalence axiom and quotient types are definable as higher inductive types. Remember that a type is a proposition when every two of its inhabitants are equal.

We assume uniqueness of identity proofs, which corresponds to working with 0-truncated types in homotopy type theory. We also assume that strongly bisimilar coinductive data are equal.

We write = for definitional equality and $\equiv$ for propositional equality (the identity type).

We review quotient types. Let X be a type and R an equivalence relation on X. Given another type Y, we say that a function $f : X \to Y$ is R-compatible (or simply compatible, when the equivalence relation is clear from the context) if $x_1 R x_2$ implies $f\, x_1 \equiv f\, x_2$. The notion of R-compatibility extends straightforwardly to dependent functions. The *quotient* of X by R is described by the following data:

(i) a carrier type X/R;
(ii) a R-compatible map $[\_] : X \to X/R$;
(iii) a dependent eliminator: for every family of types $Y : X/R \to \mathcal{U}_k$ and R-compatible function $f : \prod_{x:X} Y[x]$, there exists a function lift $f :$ $\prod_{q:X/R} Y\, q$ such that lift $f\, [x] \equiv f\, x$ for all $x : X$.

We postulate the existence of the above data for all X and R.

2 ω-Complete Pointed Classifying Monads

In this section, we introduce our monads for non-termination. We call them ω-complete pointed classifying monads. Their definition is built on Cockett and Lack's restriction categories and classifying monads [7,8] and Cockett and Guo's finite-join restriction categories [13]. Throughout this section, we work in a fixed base category $\mathbb{C}$.

2.1 Classifying Monads

First, some notation. Given a monad $T = (T, \eta, (-)^*)$, we write $\mathbf{Kl}(T)$ for its Kleisli category. We write $g \diamond f$ for the composition $g^* \circ f$ of g and f in $\mathbf{Kl}(T)$.

Definition 1. We call a monad T an *almost-classifying monad*, if there exists an operation

$$\frac{f : X \to TY}{\overline{f} : X \to TX}$$

called *restriction*, subject to the following conditions:

CM1 $f \diamond \overline{f} \equiv f$, for all $f : X \to TY$
CM2 $\overline{g} \diamond \overline{f} \equiv \overline{f} \diamond \overline{g}$, for all $f : X \to TY$ and $g : X \to TZ$

CM3 $\overline{g} \diamond \overline{f} \equiv \overline{g \diamond \overline{f}}$, for all $f : X \to TY$ and $g : X \to TZ$

CM4 $\overline{g} \diamond f \equiv f \diamond \overline{g \diamond f}$, for all $f : X \to TY$ and $g : Y \to TZ$

CM5 $\overline{\eta_Y \circ f} \equiv \eta_X$, for all $f : X \to Y$.

We call it a *classifying monad*, if it also satisfies

CM6 $\overline{\mathrm{id}_{TX}} \equiv T\eta_X$.

In other words, T is an almost-classifying monad, if its Kleisli category $\mathbf{Kl}(T)$ is a restriction category (conditions CM1–CM4) in which pure maps are total (condition CM5). The restriction of a map $f : X \to TY$ should be thought of as a "partial identity function" on X, a kind of a specification, in the form of a map, of the "domain of definedness" of f (which need not be present in the category as an object). A map $f : X \to TY$ is called *total*, if its restriction is the identity function on X in $\mathbf{Kl}(T)$, i.e., if $\overline{f} \equiv \eta_X$.

The additional condition CM6 of a classifying monad was postulated by Cockett and Lack in order to connect classifying monads and partial map classifiers, or more generally, classified restriction categories and classified $\mathcal{M}$-categories (Theorem 3.6 of [8]), $\mathcal{M}$-categories being Robinson and Rosolini's [17] framework for partiality. While it fulfills this purpose, this condition is very restrictive for other purposes. First of all, it forbids a general monad T from being a classifying monad whose Kleisli category has all maps total. Indeed, define $\overline{f} = \eta_X$, for all $f : X \to TY$. Then conditions CM1–CM5 trivially hold, while condition CM6 is usually false, since generally $\overline{\mathrm{id}_{TX}} \equiv \eta_{TX} \not\equiv T\eta_X$.

Notice that the condition CM1 is a consequence of CM4 and CM5:

$$f \diamond \overline{f} \equiv f \diamond \overline{\eta_Y \circ f} \overset{\mathrm{CM4}}{\equiv} \overline{\eta_Y} \diamond f \overset{\mathrm{CM5}}{\equiv} \eta_Y \diamond f \equiv f$$

Definition 2. A *classifying monad morphism* between classifying monads T and S, with restrictions $\overline{(-)}$ resp. $\widetilde{(-)}$, is a monad morphism σ between the underlying monads such that $\sigma \circ \overline{f} \equiv \widetilde{\sigma \circ f}$, for all $f : X \to TY$.

(Almost) classifying monads and (almost) classifying monad morphisms form categories.

An important class of classifying monads is given by the equational lifting monads of Bucalo et al. [3]. Recall that a strong monad T, with left strength ψ, is called *commutative*, if the following diagram commutes:

$$
\begin{array}{ccc}
TX \times TY & \xrightarrow{\psi_{TX,Y}} & T(TX \times Y) \\
{\scriptstyle \phi_{X,TY}} \downarrow & & \downarrow {\scriptstyle \phi^*_{X,Y}} \\
T(X \times TY) & \xrightarrow{\psi^*_{X,Y}} & T(X \times Y)
\end{array}
$$

Here $\phi = T\mathsf{swap} \circ \psi \circ \mathsf{swap}$ is the right strength.

Definition 3. An *equational lifting monad* is a commutative monad making the following diagram commute:

$$
\begin{array}{ccc}
TX & \xrightarrow{\;\;\Delta\;\;} & TX \times TX \\[2pt]
{\scriptstyle T\Delta}\big\downarrow & & \big\downarrow{\scriptstyle \psi_{TX,X}} \\[2pt]
T(X \times X) & \xrightarrow{\;T(\eta_X \times \mathrm{id}_X)\;} & T(TX \times X)
\end{array}
\qquad (1)
$$

Every equational lifting monad is canonically a classifying monad. Its restriction operation is defined with the aid of the strength:

$$
\overline{f} = X \xrightarrow{\;\langle \mathrm{id}_X, f\rangle\;} X \times TY \xrightarrow{\;\psi_{X,Y}\;} T(X \times Y) \xrightarrow{\;T\mathsf{fst}\;} TX
$$

Notice that, in order to construct an almost-classifying monad, we can relax condition (1) above and consider Cockett and Lack's copy monads [9].

Definition 4. A *copy monad* is a commutative monad making the following diagram commute:

$$
\begin{array}{ccc}
TX & \xrightarrow{\;\;\Delta\;\;} & TX \times TX \\[2pt]
{\scriptstyle T\Delta}\big\downarrow & & \big\downarrow{\scriptstyle \psi_{TX,X}} \\[2pt]
T(X \times X) & \xleftarrow{\;\phi^*_{X,X}\;} & T(TX \times X)
\end{array}
$$

Every equational lifting monad is a copy monad:

$$
\phi^* \circ \psi \circ \Delta \equiv \phi^* \circ T\langle \eta, \mathrm{id}\rangle \equiv (\phi \circ (\eta \times \mathrm{id}) \circ \Delta)^* \equiv (\eta \circ \Delta)^* \equiv T\Delta
$$

Every copy monad is canonically an almost-classifying monad. Its restriction operation is defined as for an equational lifting monad.

2.2 ω-Joins

The Kleisli category of a classifying monad is equipped with a partial order called the *restriction order*: $f \leq g$ if and only if $f \equiv g \circ \overline{f}$. That is, f is less defined than g, if f coincides with g on f's domain of definedness. Notice that, for all $f : X \to TY$, we have $\overline{f} \leq \eta_X$.

Lemma 1. *Given a classifying monad* T:

(i) *the ordering* $\leq$ *makes* $\mathbf{Kl}(T)$ $\mathbf{Poset}$-*enriched, i.e., for all* $h : W \to TX$, $f, g : X \to TY$ *and* $k : Y \to TZ$, *if* $f \leq g$, *then* $k \diamond f \diamond h \leq k \diamond g \diamond h$;

(ii) *if* $f \leq g$, *then* $\overline{f} \leq \overline{g}$, *for all* $f, g : X \to TY$.

Given a stream $s : \mathbb{N} \to (X \to TY)$, we say that s is *increasing* (or a *chain*) with respect to $\leq$, and we write $\mathsf{isIncr}_{\leq} s$, if $s\,n \leq s\,(n+1)$, for all $n : \mathbb{N}$.

Definition 5. A classifying monad T is a *ω-complete pointed classifying monad*, if there exist two operations

$$\frac{}{\bot_{X,Y} : X \to TY} \qquad \frac{s : \mathbb{N} \to (X \to TY) \quad \text{isIncr}_{\leq} \, s}{\bigsqcup s : X \to TY}$$

satisfying the following conditions:

BOT1 $\bot_{X,Y} \leq f$, for all $f : X \to TY$
BOT2 $\bot_{Y,Z} \diamond f \equiv \bot_{X,Z}$, for all $f : X \to TY$
LUB1 $s\, n \leq \bigsqcup s$, for all $n : \mathbb{N}$ and increasing $s : \mathbb{N} \to (X \to TY)$
LUB2 if $s\, n \leq t$ for all $n : \mathbb{N}$, then $\bigsqcup s \leq t$, for all $t : X \to TY$ and increasing $s : \mathbb{N} \to (X \to TY)$
LUB3 $\bigsqcup s \diamond f \equiv \bigsqcup (\lambda n.\, s\, n \diamond f)$, for all $f : X \to TY$ and increasing $s : \mathbb{N} \to (Y \to TZ)$.

Conditions BOT1, LUB1 and LUB2 state that every homset in $\mathbf{Kl}(T)$ is a ω-complete pointed partial order, ωcppo for short. Conditions BOT2 and LUB3 state that precomposition in $\mathbf{Kl}(T)$ is strict and continuous. It is actually possible to prove that $\mathbf{Kl}(T)$ is $\omega\mathbf{CPPO}$-enriched. Moreover, the $\bot$ and $\bigsqcup$ operations interact well with restriction, as stated in the following lemma.

Lemma 2. *Let T be an ω-complete pointed classifying monad. Then the following equalities hold:*

BOT3 $f \diamond \bot_{X,Y} \equiv \bot_{X,Z}$, *for all* $f : Y \to TZ$
BOTR $\overline{\bot_{X,Y}} \equiv \bot_{X,X}$
LUB4 $f \diamond \bigsqcup s \equiv \bigsqcup (\lambda n.\, f \diamond s\, n)$, *for all* $f : Y \to TZ$ *and increasing* $s : \mathbb{N} \to (X \to TY)$
LUBR $\overline{\bigsqcup s} = \bigsqcup (\lambda n.\, \overline{s\, n})$, *for all increasing* $s : \mathbb{N} \to (X \to TY)$.

Notice that the right-hand sides of LUB3, LUB4 and LUBR are well defined, i.e., the streams that the $\bigsqcup$ operation is applied to are chains, thanks to Lemma 1.

Definition 6. A *ω-complete pointed classifying monad morphism* between ω-complete pointed classifying monads T and S is a classifying monad morphism σ between the underlying classifying monads such that $\sigma \circ \bot \equiv \bot$ and $\sigma \circ \bigsqcup s \equiv \bigsqcup (\lambda n.\, \sigma \circ s\, n)$, for all increasing $s : \mathbb{N} \to (X \to TY)$.

In the definition above, the least upper bound $\bigsqcup (\lambda n.\, \sigma \circ s\, n)$ is well-defined, since postcomposition with a classifying monad morphism is a monotone operation. In other words, for all $f, g : X \to TY$ with $f \leq g$, we have $\sigma \circ f \leq \sigma \circ g$. ω-complete pointed classifying monads and ω-complete pointed classifying monad morphisms form a category.

2.3   Uniform Iteration

If a category is ω**CPPO**-enriched, it has an iteration operator that is uniform with respect to all maps. Given a monad T whose Kleisli category is ω**CPPO**-enriched, this means that we have an operation

$$\frac{f : X \to T(Y + X)}{f^\dagger : X \to TY}$$

satisfying the conditions

ITE1 $f^\dagger \equiv [\eta_Y, f^\dagger] \diamond f$, for all $f : X \to T(Y + X)$
ITE2 $g \diamond f^\dagger \equiv ([T\mathsf{inl} \diamond g, T\mathsf{inr} \diamond \eta_X] \diamond f)^\dagger$, for all $f : X \to T(Y+X)$ and $g : Y \to TZ$
ITE3 $(T[\mathsf{id}_{Y+X}, \mathsf{inr}] \circ f)^\dagger \equiv (f^\dagger)^\dagger$, for all $f : X \to T((Y + X) + X)$
ITEU if $f \diamond h \equiv [T\mathsf{inl} \diamond \eta_Y, T\mathsf{inr} \diamond \eta_h] \diamond g$, then $f^\dagger \diamond h \equiv g^\dagger$, for all $f : X \to T(Y+X)$, $g : Z \to T(Y + Z)$ and $h : Z \to TX$.

The standard definition of uniform iteration operator includes the dinaturality axiom. Recently it has been discovered that the latter is derivable from the other laws [11].

Concretely, the operation $(-)^\dagger$ is defined as follows. Let $f : X \to T(Y + X)$. We construct a stream $s : \mathbb{N} \to (X \to TY)$ by

$$s\,0 = \bot_{X,Y} \qquad s\,(n+1) = [\eta_Y, s\,n] \diamond f$$

The stream s is a chain, since the function $\lambda g.\,[\eta_Y, g] \diamond f$ is order-preserving. We define $f^\dagger = \bigsqcup s$. That $(-)^\dagger$ satisfies ITE1 is checked as follows. Clearly, $f^\dagger \le [\eta_Y, f^\dagger] \diamond f$, since $s\,n \le [\eta_Y, f^\dagger] \diamond f$, for all $n : \mathbb{N}$. For the converse inequality $[\eta_Y, f^\dagger] \diamond f \le f^\dagger$, it is enough to notice that $[\eta_Y, \bigsqcup s] \diamond f \equiv \bigsqcup(\lambda n.\,[\eta_Y, s\,n] \diamond f)$ and that $[\eta_Y, s\,n] \diamond f \le f^\dagger$, for all $n : \mathbb{N}$.

3   The Delay Monad

We now introduce Capretta's delay monad, first the unquotiented version D and then the quotient $\mathsf{D}_\approx$.

From this section onward, we do not work with a general base category, but specifically with **Set** only. As before, we only admit type-theoretical constructive reasoning. We use the words 'set' and 'type' interchangeably.

For a given type X, each element of $\mathsf{D}\,X$ is a possibly non-terminating "computation" that returns a value of X, if and when it terminates. We define $\mathsf{D}\,X$ as a coinductive type by the rules

$$\frac{}{\mathsf{now}\,x : \mathsf{D}\,X} \qquad \frac{c : \mathsf{D}\,X}{\mathsf{later}\,c : \mathsf{D}\,X}$$

(Here and in the following, single rule lines refer to an inductive definition, double rule lines to a coinductive definition.) The non-terminating computation never is corecursively defined as $\mathsf{never} = \mathsf{later}\,\mathsf{never}$.

Propositional equality is not suitable for coinductive types. We need different notions of equality, namely strong and weak bisimilarity. *Strong bisimilarity* is coinductively defined by the rules

$$\frac{}{\mathsf{now}\,x \sim \mathsf{now}\,x} \qquad \frac{c_1 \sim c_2}{\mathsf{later}\,c_1 \sim \mathsf{later}\,c_2}$$

One cannot prove that strongly bisimilar computations are equal in intensional Martin-Löf type theory. Therefore we postulate an inhabitant for $c_1 \sim c_2 \to c_1 \equiv c_2$ for all $c_1, c_2 : \mathsf{D}\,X$.

Weak bisimilarity is defined in terms of *convergence*. The latter is a binary relation between $\mathsf{D}\,X$ and X relating terminating computations to their values. It is inductively defined by the rules

$$\frac{}{\mathsf{now}\,x \downarrow x} \qquad \frac{c \downarrow x}{\mathsf{later}\,c \downarrow x}$$

Two computations are considered *weakly bisimilar*, if they differ by a finite number of applications of the constructor later (from where it follows classically that they either converge to equal values or diverge). Weak bisimilarity is defined coinductively by the rules

$$\frac{c_1 \downarrow x \quad c_2 \downarrow x}{c_1 \approx c_2} \qquad \frac{c_1 \approx c_2}{\mathsf{later}\,c_1 \approx \mathsf{later}\,c_2}$$

The delay datatype D is a monad. The unit η is the constructor now, while the Kleisli extension bind is corecursively defined as follows:

$$\mathsf{bind} : (X \to \mathsf{D}\,Y) \to \mathsf{D}\,X \to \mathsf{D}\,Y$$
$$\mathsf{bind}\,f\,(\mathsf{now}\,x) = f\,x$$
$$\mathsf{bind}\,f\,(\mathsf{later}\,c) = \mathsf{later}\,(\mathsf{bind}\,f\,c)$$

We denote by $\mathsf{str} : X \times \mathsf{D}\,Y \to \mathsf{D}\,(X \times Y)$ the strength operation of the monad D (which it has uniquely, as any monad on **Set**).

Theorem 1. *The delay datatype* D *is a commutative monad.*

We do not know how to construct a non-trivial almost-classifying monad structure on D. We believe that such a construction is impossible. In fact, notice that D is not an equational lifting monad. Indeed, consider the computation $c = \mathsf{later}\,(\mathsf{now}\,x)$. We have $\mathsf{str}\,(c, c) \not\sim \mathsf{D}\langle\mathsf{now}, \mathsf{id}\rangle\,c$, since $\mathsf{str}\,(c, c) \sim \mathsf{later}\,(\mathsf{now}\,(c, x))$ and $\mathsf{D}\langle\mathsf{now}, \mathsf{id}\rangle\,c \sim \mathsf{later}\,(\mathsf{now}\,(\mathsf{now}\,x, x))$.

In order to obtain an almost-classifying monad, we work with the following modifications of the functor D.

(i) We identify weak bisimilar computations and work with the delay datatype quotiented by weak bisimilarity, defined as $\mathsf{D}_\approx X = \mathsf{D}\,X/\approx$. $\mathsf{D}_\approx$ does not inherit the monad structure from D straightforwardly. A monad structure is definable assuming the axiom of countable choice [5]. The quotiented delay monad $\mathsf{D}_\approx$ is an equational lifting monad and therefore a classifying monad. We show this in Sect. 4.

(ii) We change the definition of the Kleisli extension. In this way we are able to construct an almost-classifying monad structure on D without the need of quotienting. We show this in Sect. 5.

4   The Quotiented Delay Monad

We know that $D_\approx$ is a functor, since we can define $D_\approx f = \text{lift}\,([\_] \circ D\,f)$. It is easy to show that the function $[\_] \circ D\,f$ is compatible with $\approx$. Unfortunately, in the type theory we are working in, the functor $D_\approx$ does not extend to a monad. It is a pointed endofunctor, since we can define the unit as $[\_] \circ \text{now}$. But we are unable to define the multiplication. In order to overcome this obstacle, we assume the *axiom of countable choice*. In our setting, this principle can be formulated as follows: given a type X and an equivalence relation R on it, the following isomorphism holds:

$$\mathbb{N} \to X/R \cong (\mathbb{N} \to X)/(\mathbb{N} \to R)$$

where $f\,(\mathbb{N} \to R)\,g = \prod_{n:\mathbb{N}} (f\,n)\,R\,(g\,n)$. We refer to [5] for details on how to exploit countable choice in order to construct a monad structure on the $D_\approx$ and for a detailed discussion on why we cannot perform the construction without this additional principle.

Theorem 2. *Assume countable choice. The quotiented delay datatype $D_\approx$ is a monad.*

We call $\eta_\approx$ the unit, $\text{bind}_\approx$ the Kleisli extension and $\text{str}_\approx$ the strength operation of $D_\approx$.

The monad $D_\approx$ is commutative, because D is commutative. Moreover, it is an equational lifting monad.

Theorem 3. *Assume countable choice. The monad $D_\approx$ is an equational lifting monad and therefore a classifying monad.*

Proof. We need to prove $\text{str}_\approx (q, q) \equiv D_\approx \langle \eta_\approx, \text{id} \rangle\,q$ for all $q : D_\approx X$. Using the induction principle of quotients, it is sufficient to show that, for all $c : D\,X$, we have $\text{str}_\approx ([c], [c]) \equiv D_\approx \langle \eta_\approx, \text{id} \rangle\,[c]$. Using the computation rule of quotients, we have that $\text{str}_\approx ([c], [c]) \equiv [\text{str}\,([c], c)]$ and $D_\approx \langle \eta_\approx, \text{id} \rangle\,[c] \equiv [D\langle \eta_\approx, \text{id}\rangle\,c]$. Therefore it is sufficient to show $\text{str}\,([c], c) \sim D\langle \eta_\approx, \text{id}\rangle\,c$ for all $x : D\,X$. We prove this by corecursion on c:

- if $c = \text{now}\,x$, then both terms are equal to $\text{now}\,([\text{now}\,x], x)$;
- if $c = \text{later}\,c'$, we have to show, after an application of the 2nd constructor of strong bisimilarity, that $\text{str}\,([\text{later}\,c'], c') \sim D\langle \eta_\approx, \text{id}\rangle\,c'$. This is true since by corecursion we have $\text{str}\,([c'], c') \sim D\langle \eta_\approx, \text{id}\rangle\,c'$ and we know $[c'] \equiv [\text{later}\,c']$.

$\square$

We continue the construction of an ω-complete pointed classifying monad structure on $D_\approx$ and the proof that it is initial in Sect. 6. In the next section, we show that the datatype D carries a monad structure different from the one presented in Sect. 3. This structure makes D an almost-classifying monad already before quotienting.

5   A Different Monad Structure on D

We show how to endow the type D with a copy monad structure without the need of quotienting by weak bisimilarity. The unit is still now, but we change the Kleisli extension. In order to have an easy description of this construction, it is convenient to give an alternative presentation of the delay datatype. In fact, the type $D\,X$ is isomorphic to the type of increasing streams over $X + 1$ with respect to the ordering $\leq_S$ on $X + 1$ defined by the rules:

$$\overline{\mathsf{inl}\,x \leq_S \mathsf{inl}\,x} \quad \overline{\mathsf{inr}\,* \leq_S \mathsf{inl}\,x}$$

So we define the type $D_S\,X = \sum_{s:\mathbb{N}\to X+1} \prod_{n:\mathbb{N}} s\,n \leq_S s\,(\mathsf{suc}\,n)$. It is not difficult to show that $D_S\,X$ is isomorphic to $D\,X$.

Notice that the stream functor $\mathsf{Stream}\,X = \mathbb{N} \to X$ is a monad. The unit returns a constant stream, while the Kleisli extension on a function $f : X \to \mathsf{Stream}\,Y$ and a stream $s : \mathsf{Stream}\,X$ returns the diagonal of the stream of streams $[f\,(s\,0), f\,(s\,1), f\,(s\,2), \dots]$. The existence of a distributive law $l_X : (\mathsf{Stream}\,X) + 1 \to \mathsf{Stream}\,(X + 1)$ between the stream monad and the maybe monad induces a monad structure on the functor $\mathsf{Stream}_{+1}\,X = \mathsf{Stream}\,(X + 1)$. Concretely, its unit and Kleisli extension can be described as follows:

$\eta_S : X \to \mathsf{Stream}_{+1}\,X$

$\eta_S\,x\,n = \mathsf{inl}\,x$

$\mathsf{bind}_S : (X \to \mathsf{Stream}_{+1}\,Y) \to \mathsf{Stream}_{+1}\,X \to \mathsf{Stream}_{+1}\,Y$

$\mathsf{bind}_S\,f\,s\,n = \mathsf{case}\,s\,n\,\mathsf{of}$

    $\mathsf{inl}\,x \mapsto f\,x\,n$

    $\mathsf{inr}\,* \mapsto \mathsf{inr}\,*$

It is easy to see that $\eta_S\,x$ is increasing wrt. $\leq_S$, for all $x : X$. Moreover, given a function $f : X \to D_S\,Y$ and an increasing stream $s : \mathsf{Stream}_{+1}\,X$, the stream $\mathsf{bind}_S\,(\mathsf{fst} \circ f)\,s$ is also increasing. Thus, D_S inherits the monad structure from Stream_{+1}.

Since the types $D_S\,X$ and $D\,X$ are isomorphic, we also described a monad structure on D. Intuitively, the new Kleisli extension on D, that we call $\mathsf{bind}_\wedge$, acts on a function $f : X \to D\,Y$ and a computation $c : D\,X$ as follows: if $c = \mathsf{never}$, then $\mathsf{bind}_\wedge\,f\,c = \mathsf{never}$; if $c \downarrow x$, then $\mathsf{bind}_\wedge\,f\,c = c \wedge f\,x$, where the operation $\wedge$ is corecursively defined with the help of the auxiliary operation $\wedge'$:

$$\wedge' : D X \to D Y \to D (X \times Y)$$
$$\text{now } x \wedge' \text{now } y = \text{now } (x, y)$$
$$\text{now } x \wedge' \text{later } c_2 = \text{later } (\text{now } x \wedge' c_2)$$
$$\text{later } c_1 \wedge' \text{now } y = \text{later } (c_1 \wedge' \text{now } y)$$
$$\text{later } c_1 \wedge' \text{later } c_2 = \text{later } (c_1 \wedge' c_2)$$

$$\wedge : D X \to D Y \to D Y$$
$$c_1 \wedge c_2 = D \, \text{snd} \, (c_1 \wedge' c_2)$$

When applied to two computations $\text{later}^k (\text{now } x)$ and $\text{later}^n (\text{now } y)$, the operation $\wedge$ returns $\text{later}^{\max(k,n)} (\text{now } y)$. Notice the difference between $\text{bind}_\wedge$ and the operation bind introduced in Sect. 3. Given $c = \text{later}^k (\text{now } x)$ and $f \, x = \text{later}^n (\text{now } y)$, we have:

$$\text{bind}_\wedge \, f \, c = \text{later}^{\max(k,n)} (\text{now } y) \qquad \text{bind} \, f \, c = \text{later}^{k+n} (\text{now } y)$$

After quotienting by weak bisimilarity, the two monad structures on D lift, with the aid of countable choice, to the same monad structure $(D_\approx, \eta_\approx, \text{bind}_\approx)$.

Theorem 4. *The monad* $(D, \text{now}, \text{bind}_\wedge)$ *is a copy monad and therefore an almost-classifying monad.*

Proof. We need to prove that, for all $c : D \, X$, we have $\text{costr}_\wedge^* (\text{str}_\wedge (c, c)) \equiv D \Delta c$, where $\text{str}_\wedge$ and $\text{costr}_\wedge$ are the left and right strength operations associated to the monad $(D, \text{now}, \text{bind}_\wedge)$. It is not difficult to show that the functions $\text{costr}_\wedge \diamond \text{str}_\wedge$ and $D\Delta$ are both propositionally equal to $\wedge'$. □

6 $D_\approx$ Is the Initial ω-Complete Pointed Classifying Monad

We move back to the construction of ω-complete pointed classifying monad structure on $D_\approx$ and initiality. First, we show that $D_\approx X$ is the free ωcppo on X.

6.1 $D_\approx$ Delivers Free ωcppos

Following [4], we introduce the following relation on $D \, X$:

$$\frac{c_1 \downarrow x \quad c_2 \downarrow x}{c_1 \sqsubseteq c_2} \qquad \frac{c_1 \sqsubseteq c_2}{\text{later } c_1 \sqsubseteq \text{later } c_2} \qquad \frac{c_1 \sqsubseteq c_2}{\text{later } c_1 \sqsubseteq c_2}$$

The type $c_1 \sqsubseteq c_2$ is inhabited not only if $c_1 \approx c_2$, but also when c_1 has some (possibly infinitely many) laters more than c_2. The relation $\sqsubseteq$ lifts to a relation $\sqsubseteq_\approx$ on $D_\approx X$, that makes the latter a pointed partial order, with $[\text{never}]$ as least element.

We define a binary operation race on $D X$ that returns the computation with the least number of laters. If two computations c_1 and c_2 converge simultaneously, race $c_1 c_2$ returns c_1.

$$\text{race} : D X \to D X \to D X$$
$$\text{race} (\text{now } x)\, c = \text{now } x$$
$$\text{race} (\text{later } c) (\text{now } x) = \text{now } x$$
$$\text{race} (\text{later } c_1) (\text{later } c_2) = \text{later } (\text{race } c_1 c_2)$$

Notice that generally race $c_1 c_2$ is not an upper bound of c_1 and c_2, since the two computations may converge to different values. The binary operation race can be extended to an ω-operation ωrace. This operation constructs the first converging element of a chain of computations. It is defined using the auxiliary operation ωrace$'$:

$$\omega\text{race}' : (\mathbb{N} \to D X) \to \mathbb{N} \to D X \to D X$$
$$\omega\text{race}'\, s\, n\, (\text{now } x) = \text{now } x$$
$$\omega\text{race}'\, s\, n\, (\text{later } c) = \text{later } (\omega\text{race}'\, s\, (\text{suc } n)\, (\text{race } c\, (s\, n)))$$

The operation ωrace$'$, when applied to a chain $s : \mathbb{N} \to D X$, a number $n : \mathbb{N}$ and a computation $c : D X$, constructs the first converging element of the chain $s' : \mathbb{N} \to D X$, with $s'\,\text{zero} = c$ and $s'\,(\text{suc } k) = s\,(n + k)$. The operation ωrace is constructed by instantiating ωrace$'$ with $n = \text{zero}$ and $c = \text{never}$. In this way we have that the first converging element of s is the first converging element of s', since never diverges.

$$\omega\text{race} : (\mathbb{N} \to D X) \to D X$$
$$\omega\text{race}\, s = \omega\text{race}'\, s\, \text{zero never}$$

Generally ωrace s is not an upper bound of s. But if s is a chain, then ωrace s is the join of s. The operation ωrace, when restricted to chains, lifts, with the aid of countable choice, to an operation ωrace$_\approx$ on $D_\approx X$, which makes the latter a ωcppo.

Theorem 5. *Assume countable choice. The functor* $D_\approx$ *delivers ωcppos.*

Let $(Y, \leq, \perp, \bigsqcup)$ be an ωcppo and $f : X \to Y$ a function. Every computation over X defines a chain in Y.

$$\text{cpt2chain}_f : D X \to \mathbb{N} \to Y$$
$$\text{cpt2chain}_f (\text{now } x)\, n = f\, x$$
$$\text{cpt2chain}_f (\text{later } c)\, \text{zero} = \perp$$
$$\text{cpt2chain}_f (\text{later } c)\, (\text{suc } n) = \text{cpt2chain}_f\, c\, n$$

Given a computation $c = \text{later}^n (\text{now } x)$ (if $n = \omega$, then $c = \text{never}$), the chain $\text{cpt2chain}_f\, c$ looks as follows:

$$\underbrace{\perp \quad \perp \quad \cdots \quad \perp}_{n} \quad f\, x \quad f\, x \quad f\, x \quad \cdots$$

Therefore it is possible to extend the function f to a function $\widehat{f} : D X \to Y$, $\widehat{f} c = \bigsqcup(\mathsf{cpt2chain}_f c)$. The function $\widehat{f}$ is $\approx$-compatible, and therefore it can be lifted to a function of type $D_\approx X \to Y$, that we also name $\widehat{f}$. This function is a ωcppo morphism and it is the unique such morphism making the following diagram commute:

$$
\begin{array}{ccc}
X & \xrightarrow{\;[\_]\circ\mathsf{now}\;} & D_\approx X \\
 & {}_{f}\searrow & \big\downarrow{\widehat{f}} \\
 & & Y
\end{array}
$$

Therefore $D_\approx X$ is the free ωcppo over X.

Theorem 6. *Assume countable choice. The functor* $D_\approx$ *delivers free* ω*cppos.*

Recently, Altenkirch et al. [1] constructed a higher inductive-inductive type that delivers free ωcppos by definition without recourse to the axiom of countable choice. To prove that this datatype is isomorphic to the quotiented delay datatype countable choice is again necessary.

6.2 ω-Complete Pointed Classifying Monad Structure on $D_\approx$ and Initiality

We extend the order $\sqsubseteq_\approx$ to functions in $\mathbf{Kl}(D_\approx)$ in the usual pointwise way. Let $f, g : X \to D_\approx Y$, we say that $f \sqsubseteq_\approx g$ if and only if, for all $x : X$, $f x \sqsubseteq_\approx g x$. (Notice that we use the same notation $\sqsubseteq_\approx$ for functions as well). It is not difficult to show that the order $\sqsubseteq_\approx$ is equivalent to the order associated to the restriction operator that we described in Sect. 2.2.

Lemma 3. *For all* $f, g : X \to D_\approx Y$, *we have* $f \sqsubseteq_\approx g$ *if and only if* $f \leq g$ *(where* $\leq$ *is the restriction order).*

Theorem 7. *Assume countable choice. The monad* $D_\approx$ *is an* ω*-complete pointed classifying monad.*

Proof. Let X and Y be two types. The bottom element of the homset $X \to D_\approx Y$ is the constant map $\lambda\_.\,[\mathsf{never}]$. Let $s : \mathbb{N} \to (X \to D_\approx Y)$ be a chain wrt. $\leq$. We define

$$
\bigsqcup_\approx s : X \to D_\approx Y
$$

$$
\left(\bigsqcup_\approx s\right) x = \omega\mathsf{race}_\approx (\lambda n.\, s\, n\, x)
$$

where the stream $\lambda n.\, s\, n\, x$ is increasing wrt. $\sqsubseteq_\approx$, which is the case thanks to Lemma 3.

One should now verify that conditions BOT1, BOT2 and and LUB1–LUB3 are met. Conditions BOT1, LUB1 and LUB2 follow directly from $D_\approx Y$ being a ωcppo, as described in Sect. 6.1. Conditions BOT2 and LUB3 follow from $\mathsf{bind}_\approx$ being a ωcppo morphism between $X \to D_\approx Y$ and $D_\approx X \to D_\approx Y$. $\qquad\square$

Let T be an ω-complete pointed almost-classifying monad. We already noted that the type $X \to TY$ is an ωcppo, for all types X and Y. In particular, every type $TX \cong 1 \to TX$ is a ωcppo. Explicitly, given $x_1, x_2 : TX$, we define $x_1 \leq x_2$ as $\lambda*. x_1 \leq \lambda*. x_2$. The bottom element of TX is $\bot_{1,X} *$, while the join of a chain $s : \mathbb{N} \to TX$ is $\bigsqcup(\lambda n. \lambda*. s\, n) *$.

We show that there is a unique ω-complete pointed almost-classifying monad morphism between $\mathsf{D}_\approx$ and T. This characterizes the quotiented delay monad as the universal monad of non-termination.

Theorem 8. *Assume countable choice. $\mathsf{D}_\approx$ is the initial ω-complete pointed almost-classifying monad (and therefore also the initial ω-complete pointed classifying monad).*

Proof. Let $T = (T, \eta, \mathsf{bind})$ be a ω-complete pointed almost-classifying monad. Since TX is a ωcppo and we have a map $\eta_X : X \to TX$, there is a unique ωcppo morphism $\widehat{\eta}$ between $\mathsf{D}_\approx X$ and TX such that $\widehat{\eta} \circ \eta_\approx \equiv \eta$. Therefore, we define

$$\sigma : \mathsf{D}_\approx X \to TX$$
$$\sigma = \widehat{\eta}$$

First, we show that σ is a monad morphism:

- $\sigma \circ \eta_\approx \equiv \eta$ by the universal property of the free ωcppo.
- Given $f : X \to \mathsf{D}_\approx Y$, we have $\sigma \circ \mathsf{bind}_\approx f \equiv \mathsf{bind}\,(\sigma \circ f) \circ \sigma$, because both maps are ωcppo morphisms between $\mathsf{D}_\approx X$ and TY and both maps are equal to $\sigma \circ f$ when precomposed with $\eta_\approx$.

Second, we show that σ is an almost-classifying monad morphism. We have to show that $\sigma \circ \overline{f} \equiv \widetilde{\sigma \circ f}$ for all $f : X \to \mathsf{D}_\approx Y$. Notice that, for all $x : 1 \to X$, we have:

$$\sigma \circ \overline{f} \circ x \overset{\text{CM4}}{\equiv} \sigma \circ \mathsf{D}_\approx x \circ \overline{f \circ x} \overset{\text{nat}}{\equiv} Tx \circ \sigma \circ \overline{f \circ x}$$
$$\widetilde{\sigma \circ f} \circ x \overset{\text{CM4}}{\equiv} Tx \circ \sigma \circ \widetilde{f \circ x}$$

Therefore it is sufficient to show $\sigma \circ \overline{c} \equiv \widetilde{\sigma \circ c}$ for all $c : 1 \to \mathsf{D}_\approx X$. The maps $g\, c = \sigma \circ \overline{c}$ and $h\, c = \widetilde{\sigma \circ c}$ are both strict and continuous maps of type $(1 \to \mathsf{D}_\approx X) \to (1 \to T1)$, and the latter type is isomorphic to $\mathsf{D}_\approx X \to T1$. Notice that since $\mathsf{D}_\approx X$ is the free ωcppo over X, we know that there exists only one strict and continuous map between $\mathsf{D}_\approx X$ and $T1$ that sends terminating computations to $\eta *$. Notice that, for all $x : 1 \to X$, we have

$$g\,(\eta_{\approx X} \circ x) = \sigma \circ \overline{\eta_{\approx X} \circ x} \overset{\text{CM5}}{\equiv} \sigma \circ \eta_{\approx 1} \equiv \eta_1$$
$$h\,(\eta_{\approx X} \circ x) = \sigma \circ \widetilde{\eta_{\approx X} \circ x} \equiv \widetilde{\eta_X \circ x} \overset{\text{CM5}}{\equiv} \eta_1$$

This shows that $g \equiv h$, and therefore σ is a classifying monad morphism.

Finally, σ is a ω-complete pointed almost-classifying monad morphism since $\sigma = \widehat{\eta}$ is a ωcppo morphism between $\mathsf{D}_\approx X$ and TX. In particular, it is strict and continuous.

It remains to check that σ is the unique ω-complete pointed almost-classifying monad morphism between $\mathsf{D}_\approx$ and T. Let τ be another ω-complete pointed almost classifying monad morphism between $\mathsf{D}_\approx$ and T. In particular, for all types X, we have that τ is a wcppo morphism between $\mathsf{D}_\approx X$ and TX and also $\tau \circ \eta_\approx \equiv \eta$. Therefore, by the universal property of the free wcppo $\mathsf{D}_\approx$, we have that $\tau \equiv \widehat{\eta} = \sigma$. $\qquad\square$

One might wonder whether $\mathbf{Kl}(\mathsf{D}_\approx)$ could be the free ω-complete pointed restriction category over $\mathbf{Set}$. This is not the case, since the latter has as objects sets and as maps between X and Y elements of $\mathsf{D}_\approx(X \to Y)$. This observation is an adaptation of a construction by Grandis described by Guo [13].

7 Other Monads of Non-termination

In the previous section, we showed that $\mathsf{D}_\approx$ is the initial ω-complete pointed almost-classifying monad and also the initial ω-complete pointed classifying monad. This would not be a significant result, if the categories of ω-complete pointed classifying and almost-classifying monads were lacking other interesting examples. It is immediate that these categories are non-trivial, since at least the monad $\mathsf{Termin}\,X = 1$ is another ω-complete pointed classifying monad. Since Termin is the final object in the category of monads, it is also the final ω-complete pointed almost-classifying monad and the final ω-complete pointed classifying monad. But of course we are looking for more interesting examples.

7.1 A Non-example: Maybe Monad

The maybe monad $\mathsf{Maybe}\,X = X + 1$ is an example of a classifying monad that is not a ω-complete pointed classifying monad.

The maybe monad is a canonical example of equational lifting monad, so it is a classifying monad. But it is not a ω-complete pointed classifying monad: in order to construct the join of a chain $s : \mathbb{N} \to X + 1$, we need to decide whether there exist an element $x : X$ and a number $k : \mathbb{N}$ such that $s\,k = \mathsf{inl}\,x$, or $s\,n = \mathsf{inr}\,*$ for all $n : \mathbb{N}$. This decision requires the limited principle of omniscience $\mathsf{LPO} = \prod_{s:\mathbb{N}\to 2} (\sum_{n:\mathbb{N}} s\,n \equiv 1) + (\prod_{n:\mathbb{N}} s\,n \equiv 0)$.

7.2 Conditional Monad

For a more interesting example, consider the monad C defined by

$$\mathsf{C}\,X = \sum_{P:\mathcal{U}} \mathsf{isProp}\,P \times (P \to X)$$

where $\mathsf{isProp}\,X = \prod_{x_1,x_2:X} x_1 \equiv x_2$.[1] Intuitively, an element of $\mathsf{C}\,X$ is a proposition P together with an element of X for every proof of P (so at most one

---

[1] C is typed $\mathcal{U}_1 \to \mathcal{U}_1$, so it is an endofunctor on $\mathbf{Set}_1$. But as the other examples can be replayed for any $\mathcal{U}_k$, comparing this example to them is unproblematic.

element of X). So a computation produces a condition of its liking and only releases a value of X, if the user can supply a proof; the computation does not give out any hint on how to decide the condition.

The type $\mathsf{C}\,X$ consists of the propositional objects of the slice category of X. The endofunctor C is an equational lifting monad and thus a classifying monad.

The monad C is a ω-complete pointed classifying monad. This is because every type $\mathsf{C}X$ is a ωcppo. To see this, we first define a partial order on $\mathsf{C}\,X$:

$$(P, ip, i) \sqsubseteq (Q, iq, j) = \sum_{f:P \to Q} \prod_{p:P} i\,p \equiv j\,(f\,p)$$

That is, two elements in $\mathsf{C}X$ are related by $\sqsubseteq$, if there exists a morphism in the slice category of X connecting them:

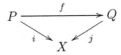

In other words, the poset $(\mathsf{C}X, \sqsubseteq)$ is the full subcategory of the slice category of X in which objects are propositions. Interestingly, this poset is also a ωcppo. The bottom element is the proposition 0 together with the empty function $0 \to X$. Joins of chains are computed as the following colimit:

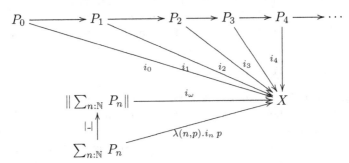

where $\| \sum_{n:\mathbb{N}} P_n \|$ is the propositional truncation of $\sum_{n:\mathbb{N}} P_n$, i.e., the quotient of $\sum_{n:\mathbb{N}} P_n$ by the total equivalence relation (which relates every pair of elements in the type). The function i_ω is obtained as the lifting of $\lambda(n, p).i_n\, p : \sum_{n:\mathbb{N}} P_n \to X$. Notice that the latter function is constant, i.e., $i_n\, p_n \equiv i_m\, p_m$ for all $p_n : P_n$ and $p_m : P_m$. In fact, suppose w.l.o.g. $m \leq n$. Then, since the stream is increasing, there exists a function $f : P_m \to P_n$ such that $i_m\, p_m \equiv i_n\,(f\,p_m)$. The type P_n is a proposition, therefore $f\,p_m \equiv p_n$ and $i_n\, p_n \equiv i_m\, p_m$.

As usual, the order $\sqsubseteq$ extends to function spaces. It is not difficult to show that this is equivalent to the restriction order and that C satisfies the laws of an ω-complete pointed classifying monad.

The types $\mathsf{C}\,X$ and $\mathsf{Maybe}\,X$ are isomorphic if and only if the principle of excluded middle for propositions $\mathsf{LEM}_{\mathsf{Prop}} = \prod_{X:\mathcal{U}} \mathsf{isProp}\,X \to X + \neg X$ holds. Since $\mathsf{D}_{\approx}\,X$ and $\mathsf{Maybe}\,X$ are isomorphic if and only if LPO holds, and since $\mathsf{LEM}_{\mathsf{Prop}}$ is strictly stronger than LPO, $\mathsf{C}\,X$ is generally not isomorphic to $\mathsf{D}_{\approx}\,X$.

The conditional monad C is an instance of a partial map classifier in the sense of [15]. In type theory, partial map classifiers are monads of the form $TX = \sum_{x:D}(x \equiv \top \rightarrow X)$ where D is a dominance in the sense of [18] and $\top : D$ is the truth value corresponding to truthfulness. The conditional monad is the partial map classifier associated to the dominance $D = \sum_{X:\mathcal{U}}$ isProp X with $\top = (1,p)$ where p is the simple proof of 1 being a proposition.

7.3   Countable Powerset Monad

An example of an ω-complete pointed almost-classifying monad that is not a classifying monad (since the condition CM6 is not met), is given by the countable powerset construction. This monad is typically employed to model nondeterministic computations. In type theory, the countable powerset monad can be introduced as follows:

$$\mathcal{P}_\infty X = \mathsf{Stream}\,(X+1)/\mathsf{SameElem}$$

where $\mathsf{SameElem}\,s_1\,s_2 = \prod_{x:X} x \in s_1 \leftrightarrow x \in s_2$ and $x \in s = \sum_{n:\mathbb{N}} s\,n \equiv \mathsf{inl}\,x$. It can be proved that the functor $\mathcal{P}_\infty$ is a monad. This requires the assumption of the axiom of countable choice, because it is defined as a quotient.

Intuitively, the restriction $\overline{f}$ of a map $f : X \rightarrow \mathcal{P}_\infty Y$ is the map that, given $x : X$, returns the singleton $\{x\}$, if $f\,x$ is non-empty, and the empty set otherwise. The restriction order on $\mathcal{P}_\infty X \cong 1 \rightarrow \mathcal{P}_\infty X$ is thus different from set inclusion. In fact, for $s, t : \mathcal{P}_\infty X$, intuitively $s \leq t$ if and only if $s \equiv t$ or $s \equiv \emptyset$.

7.4   State Monad Transformer

New ω-complete pointed almost-classifying monads can be constructed from already constructed ones with the state monad transformer. Recall that the state monad is defined as $\mathsf{State}\,X = S \rightarrow X \times S$, where S is a fixed set of states. Given an ω-complete pointed almost-classifying monad T, the functor $\mathsf{StateT}\,T$ defined by $\mathsf{StateT}\,T\,X = S \rightarrow T(X \times S)$ is another ω-complete pointed almost-classifying monad. All operations of $\mathsf{StateT}\,T$ are defined in terms of the operations of T. For example, restriction is constructed as follows:

$$\widetilde{(\_)} : (X \rightarrow S \rightarrow T(Y \times S)) \rightarrow X \rightarrow S \rightarrow T(X \times S)$$
$$\widetilde{f} = \mathsf{curry}\,(\overline{\mathsf{uncurry}\,f})$$

8   Conclusions

In this paper, we introduced the notion of ω-complete pointed classifying monad. We argued that it explains the idea of "non-termination as an effect". We showed that Capretta's delay monad quotiented by weak bisimilarity is the initial ω-complete pointed classifying monad on **Set** under constructive reasoning and in this sense is the minimal monad for non-termination. We also showed that the class of ω-complete pointed classifying monads is non-trivial, since it also contains the monad C, which is non-isomorphic to the quotiented delay monad.

ω-complete pointed classifying monads are derived from Cockett and Lack's restriction categories. There are two reasons behind this choice over other category-theoretical approaches to partiality such as partial map categories. Restriction categories, being an axiomatic framework for partiality, are conveniently formalizable in a proof assistant like Agda. This is not the case for partial map categories, whose formalization quickly becomes very involved. Moreover, Cockett and Guo [6] proved that every finite-join restriction category is a full subcategory of the partial map category of an adhesive $\mathcal{M}$-category whose gaps are in $\mathcal{M}$. Therefore, one can come up with a complementary notion of a finite-join classifying monad for partial map categories, but this will inevitably be more involved than the simple notion considered here.

As future work, We would like to generalize this work from **Set** to a general base category while still only accepting constructive reasoning. This requires, first of all, generalizing the definition of the delay monad suitably for less structured categories. Also, we would like to understand whether the delay monad could be the initial completely Elgot monad on **Set** constructively under reasonable semi-classical principles (a monad is said to be a completely Elgot monad, if its Kleisli category has an iteration operator uniform for pure maps). Goncharov et al. [12] have proved that the maybe monad is the initial completely Elgot monad on **Set** classically, but the constructive content of this proof has so far remained elusive for us.

Acknowledgements. This research was supported by the Estonian Ministry of Education and Research institutional research grant IUT33-13 and the Estonian Research Council personal research grant PUT763.

References

1. Altenkirch, T., Danielsson, N.A., Kraus, N.: Partiality, revisited: the partiality monad as a quotient inductive-inductive type. In: Esparza, J., Murawski, A.S. (eds.) FoSSaCS 2017. LNCS, vol. 10203, pp. 534–549. Springer, Heidelberg (2017). doi:10.1007/978-3-662-54458-7_31
2. Benton, N., Kennedy, A., Varming, C.: Some domain theory and denotational semantics in Coq. In: Berghofer, S., Nipkow, T., Urban, C., Wenzel, M. (eds.) TPHOLs 2009. LNCS, vol. 5674, pp. 115–130. Springer, Heidelberg (2009). doi:10.1007/978-3-642-03359-9_10
3. Bucalo, A., Führmann, C., Simpson, A.: An equational notion of lifting monad. Theor. Comput. Sci. **294**(1–2), 31–60 (2003)
4. Capretta, V.: General recursion via coinductive types. Log. Methods Comput. Sci. **1**(2), article 1 (2005)
5. Chapman, J., Uustalu, T., Veltri, N.: Quotienting the delay monad by weak bisimilarity. Math. Struct. Comput. Sci. (to appear)
6. Cockett, J.R.B., Guo, X.: Join restriction categories and the importance of being adhesive. Abstract of talk presented at CT 2007 (2007)

7. Cockett, J.R.B., Lack, S.: Restriction categories I: categories of partial maps. Theor. Comput. Sci. **270**(1–2), 223–259 (2002)

8. Cockett, J.R.B., Lack, S.: Restriction categories II: partial map classification. Theor. Comput. Sci. **294**(1–2), 61–102 (2003)

9. Cockett, J.R.B., Lack, S.: Restriction categories III: colimits, partial limits, and extensivity. Math. Struct. Comput. Sci. **17**(4), 775–817 (2007)

10. Danielsson, N.A.: Operational semantics using the partiality monad. In: Proceedings of 17th ACM SIGPLAN International Conference on Functional Programming, ICFP 2012, pp. 127–138. ACM, New York (2012)

11. Ésik, Z., Goncharov, S.: Some remarks on Conway and iteration theories. arXiv preprint arXiv:1603.00838 (2016)

12. Goncharov, S., Rauch, C., Schröder, L.: Unguarded recursion on coinductive resumptions. Electron. Notes Theor. Comput. Sci. **319**, 183–198 (2015)

13. Guo, X.: Products, joins, meets, and ranges in restriction categories. Ph.D. thesis, University of Calgary (2012)

14. Hofmann, M.: Extensional Constructs in Intensional Type Theory. CPHS/BCS Distinguished Dissertations. Springer, London (1997). doi:10.1007/978-1-4471-0963-1

15. Mulry, P.S.: Partial map classifiers and partial cartesian closed categories. Theor. Comput. Sci. **136**(1), 109–123 (1994)

16. Norell, U.: Dependently typed programming in Agda. In: Koopman, P., Plasmeijer, R., Swierstra, D. (eds.) AFP 2008. LNCS, vol. 5832, pp. 230–266. Springer, Heidelberg (2009). doi:10.1007/978-3-642-04652-0_5

17. Robinson, E., Rosolini, G.: Categories of partial maps. Inf. Comput. **79**(2), 95–130 (1988)

18. Rosolini, G.: Continuity and effectiveness in topoi. DPhil. thesis, University of Oxford (1986)

Logical Characterisation of Parameterised Bisimulations

Divyanshu Bagga$^{(\boxtimes)}$ and S. Arun Kumar

Department of Computer Science and Engineering,
Indian Institute of Technology Delhi, Hauz Khas, New Delhi 110 016, India
{divyanshu.bagga,sak}@cse.iitd.ac.in

Abstract. We explore the relationship between bisimulations and logic. The link between them is formed by *logical characterisations*, which have been given for well-known bisimulation equivalences and preorders. Parameterised bisimulations allow us to incorporate notions of abstraction or efficiency into behavioural equivalences. This generalised framework of *parameterised* bisimulations is used to develop a *parameterised* logical characterisation, thereby, unifying the existing logical characterisations as well as paving the way for characterisation of novel bisimulations. Methods for generating distinguishing formulae and characteristic formulae in the parameterised logic are also discussed.

Keywords: Bisimulations · Modal logic · Logical characterisation · Distinguishing formula · Characteristic formula

1 Introduction

Bisimulation checking and model checking are among the two major approaches to the verification of concurrent processes. Both model behaviour using labelled transition systems but differ in specification. Bisimulation checking expresses specification also as a labelled transition system, whereas model checking expresses specification as a collection of logical formulas. Both have their advantages. Model checking allows for partial specifications and its refinements by adding more properties. Bisimulation checking gives us modularity as it is often closed under most of the process constructors [9]. Therefore, both approaches have their own applications.

But there is an interesting connection between them - formalized as logical characterisations - one of the most important being Hennessy-Milner logic (HML) [16], which gives a modal logic characterisation for strong bisimulation. Any two processes are strongly bisimilar if and only if they satisfy the same set of HML formulae[1]. Consequently, for any two non-bisimilar processes, there must exist a *distinguishing formula* which is satisfied by exactly one of the given processes, and can be very useful for debugging.

---

[1] Processes were constrained to be image-finite for finite logical characterisation.

© Springer International Publishing AG 2017
D.V. Hung and D. Kapur (Eds.): ICTAC 2017, LNCS 10580, pp. 51–69, 2017.
DOI: 10.1007/978-3-319-67729-3_4

Sometimes, it is possible to construct a single formula capable of distinguishing a process from every other non-bisimilar process. Known as *characteristic formula*, it facilitates the reduction of bisimulation checking to model checking, which may yield efficient algorithms for deciding behavioural preorders [10]. The existence of a characteristic formula is therefore, central to the study of logical characterisations [14].

The importance of logical characterisations can be gauged from the work done towards showing their existence for many other bisimulation equivalences besides strong bisimulation, e.g., timed bisimulations [19], probabilistic bisimulations and preorders such as prebisimulation preorder [27], efficiency preorders [17], contravariant simulation [1], etc. In this paper, we develop a logical characterisation of *parameterised bisimulations*. As shown in [4], various bisimulation relations can be expressed as instances of parameterised bisimulation. By working in a general framework of parameterised bisimulations, we achieve two goals. Firstly, we unify the results on obtaining the logical characterisations for different bisimulation relations. Secondly, this gives us a systematic way of obtaining a logical characterisation of any novel bisimulation relation, which may be expressed as an instance of parameterised bisimulation. As one would expect, the logical characterisation of the parameterised bisimulations should also depend on the same parameters. Since our logic generalises HML, we refer to it as *parameterised Hennessy-Milner logic*.

The contributions of this paper may be summarized as follows:

- We propose parameterised HML, in Sect. 3, and show that it is a logical characterisation of all bisimulation equivalences and preorders which can be expressed in the framework of parameterised bisimulations.
- We study the conditions required to ensure that the distinguishing formula is always finite. We also give procedures for model checking and generating distinguishing formulae.
- We extend our logical characterisation with fixed point operators, in Sect. 4, which allows us to derive the characteristic formula for any finite-state process, and possibly some infinite-state systems, using suitable abstractions.

2   Background

To model process behaviours, both bisimulation and model checking use labelled transition systems, which is one of the most widely used models of computation.

Definition 1. *A labelled transition system (LTS) $\mathfrak{L}$ is a triple $\langle \mathcal{P}, \mathcal{A}ct, \longrightarrow \rangle$, where $\mathcal{P}$ is a set of process states or processes, $\mathcal{A}ct$ is a set of actions and $\longrightarrow \subseteq \mathcal{P} \times \mathcal{A}ct \times \mathcal{P}$ is the transition relation. We use $p \xrightarrow{a} q$ to denote $(p, a, q) \in \longrightarrow$.*

2.1   Parameterised Bisimulations

The origin of bisimulations can be traced back to logic [24], where it serves an important role in establishing modal logic as a fragment of first order logic

[30]. It was first proposed in [7], as relations which preserve satisfiability of modal logic formulas. Its discovery in computer science and fixed point characterisation is attributed to [23] and is central to Milner's theory of CCS [21]. Being the finest behavioural equivalence [31], its importance in the theory of verification is undeniable.

One can think of interesting behavioural relations, which may relate one process with another behaviourally equivalent but more efficient process. Efficiency need not be only in terms of time, it may also refer to other quantitative measures like probability, energy, etc. One approach to defining these relations is by incorporating efficiency into bisimulation, which is the idea behind efficiency preorder [5] or timed prebisimulation [15]. The key idea behind them is to allow an action to be matched with a functionally equivalent but more efficient one. The same approach is used to incorporate abstraction into bisimulation, e.g. weak bisimulation, where an action can be matched with another non-identical but equivalent under the given abstraction. These bisimulations can be unified under the general framework of parameterised bisimulations, which allow the relations over actions to be parameters in the definition of bisimulation. The parameter relations incorporates the desired notion of efficiency or abstraction.

Definition 2 [4]**.** Let $\mathcal{P}$ be the set of processes and ρ and σ be binary relations on $\mathcal{A}ct$. A binary relation $R \subseteq \mathcal{P} \times \mathcal{P}$ is a (ρ, σ)-*bisimulation* if $p\,R\,q$ implies the following conditions for all $a, b \in \mathcal{A}ct$.

$$p \xrightarrow{a} p' \Rightarrow \exists b, q'[a\,\rho\,b \wedge q \xrightarrow{b} q' \wedge p'\,R\,q'] \tag{1}$$

$$q \xrightarrow{b} q' \Rightarrow \exists a, p'[a\,\sigma\,b \wedge p \xrightarrow{a} p' \wedge p'\,R\,q'] \tag{2}$$

The largest (ρ, σ)-bisimulation, denoted $\sqsubseteq_{(\rho,\sigma)}$, is called (ρ, σ)-*bisimilarity*.

This generalization captures a number of useful bisimulations. Strong bisimulation is obtained by simply setting ρ and σ as identity relation over actions, $\mathcal{I}d_{\mathcal{A}ct}$. Other interesting relations are defined by exploiting semantic relationships between actions. For example, in Timed LTS, a special class of LTS with labels from the set $\mathcal{A}ct \cup \mathbb{R}_{\geq 0}$, one may differ in matching delay actions $d \in \mathbb{R}_{\geq 0}$. We obtain time-abstracted bisimulation [20] by not distinguishing between delay quantities. It is an instance of a parameterised bisimulation where $\rho = \sigma = \mathcal{I}d_{\mathcal{A}ct} \cup (\mathbb{R}_{\geq 0} \times \mathbb{R}_{\geq 0})$. We can also capture delay based efficiency, to define timed prebisimulation [15], where a delay d can be matched by a faster delay $d' \leq d$, by setting $\rho = \sigma = \mathcal{I}d_{\mathcal{A}ct} \cup \leq_{\mathbb{R}}$.

Another class of interesting relations emerge when we model internal actions, in the LTS, as transitions labeled with τ. These τ-actions cannot be observed, and the behavioural equivalence must ignore them. This behavioural equivalence is captured by weak bisimulation [16]. One may also view τ as a measure of internal activity, to define efficiency preorders [5]. These relations can also be expressed as an instance of parameterised bisimulations, which is described in Sect. 5.

We will obtain the logical characterisations for these bisimilarities, by developing results for parameterised bisimilarities. However, we will limit ourselves to parameterised bisimilarities which become preorders (or equivalences), by placing suitable restrictions on the underlying relations over actions.

Fixed Point Characterisation: The fixed point characterisation of (ρ, σ)-bisimilarity, over the complete lattice of binary relations on $\mathcal{P}$ under the $\subseteq$ ordering serves an important role as the starting point for the derivation of characteristic formulae.

Lemma 1. *The relation* $\sqsubseteq_{(\rho,\sigma)}$ *over processes* $\mathcal{P}$ *may be expressed as the greatest fixed point of the monotonic function* $\mathscr{F}_{(\rho,\sigma)} : 2^{\mathcal{P} \times \mathcal{P}} \to 2^{\mathcal{P} \times \mathcal{P}}$, *defined as*

$$\mathscr{F}_{(\rho,\sigma)}(R) = \{(p,q) \mid [\forall a, p' : p \xrightarrow{a} p' \Rightarrow \exists b, q'[a \, \rho \, b \wedge q \xrightarrow{b} q' \wedge p' \, R \, q']] \wedge$$
$$[\forall b, q' : q \xrightarrow{b} q' \Rightarrow \exists a, p'[a \, \sigma \, b \wedge p \xrightarrow{a} p' \wedge p' \, R \, q']]\}$$

One approach to computing the greatest fixed point in a lattice, is to take the top element (the universal relation in our case), and keep on applying the function until it reaches the fixed point. Let $\mathbb{U}$ denote the universal relation, then the ith approximant of (ρ, σ)-bisimilarity is defined as $\sqsubseteq^i_{(\rho,\sigma)} = \mathscr{F}^i_{(\rho,\sigma)}(\mathbb{U})$. In general, the intersection of all the approximants, $\sqsubseteq^\omega_{(\rho,\sigma)} = \bigcap_{i \in \mathbb{N}} \sqsubseteq^i_{(\rho,\sigma)}$, will contain the greatest fixed point, $\sqsubseteq_{(\rho,\sigma)}$, and $\sqsubseteq^\omega_{(\rho,\sigma)} = \sqsubseteq_{(\rho,\sigma)}$ when $\mathscr{F}^i_{(\rho,\sigma)}$ is co-continuous [13].

Lemma 2 [4]. *For any* $i \in \mathbb{N}$, *the i-th approximant,* $\sqsubseteq^i_{(\rho,\sigma)}$, *as well as* $\sqsubseteq^\omega_{(\rho,\sigma)}$ *and* $\sqsubseteq_{(\rho,\sigma)}$ *are preorders iff both* ρ *and* σ *are preorders. Moreover, they become an equivalence iff we also have* $\rho = \sigma^{-1}$. □

The proof for (ρ, σ)-bisimilarity, given in [4], can be generalised for approximants using induction.

Abstracted LTS: The notion of an abstracted LTS allows us to extend our results to some infinite-state systems.

Definition 3. *Given a set* $S \subseteq \mathcal{P}$ *and a preorder* $\leq \subseteq \mathcal{P} \times \mathcal{P}$, *we define an initial set* S^i *and a terminal set* S^t *as*

$$S^i = \{s \in S \mid \not\exists s'[s' \in S \wedge s' < s]\} \qquad S^t = \{s \in S \mid \not\exists s'[s' \in S \wedge s < s']\}$$

where $s < s'$ *iff* $s \leq s'$ *and* $s \neq s'$. *The set* S *is closed if for every* $s \in S$, *there exists an* $s' \in S^i$ *and* $s'' \in S^t$ *such that* $s' \leq s \leq s''$.

Let $p \xrightarrow{a} p_1$ and $p \xrightarrow{b} p_2$ be two transitions such that $a \, \rho \, b$ and $p_1 \sqsubseteq_{(\rho,\sigma)} p_2$. Then matching the transition $p \xrightarrow{b} p_2$ with $q \xrightarrow{c} q'$, where $b \, \rho \, c$ and $p_2 \sqsubseteq_{(\rho,\sigma)} q'$ holds, also matches $p \xrightarrow{a} p_1$ due to transitivity of ρ and $\sqsubseteq_{(\rho,\sigma)}$. Effectively, satisfying the condition (1) in Definition 2 only requires matching transitions to the terminal states under $\sqsubseteq_{(\rho,\sigma)}$ ordering, $\{p' \mid p \xrightarrow{b} p' \wedge a \, \rho \, b\}^t$, provided it is a closed set. Similarly for satisfying the condition (2), i.e. matching a transition of q, it suffices to only look at transitions to the initial states, $\{p' \mid p \xrightarrow{a} p' \wedge a \,\sigma\, b\}^{\mathrm{i}}$. Therefore, we define an abstracted LTS which retains only the relevant states.

Definition 4. *Let $\mathfrak{L} = \langle \mathcal{P}, Act, \longrightarrow \rangle$ be an LTS. For any $p \in \mathcal{P}$ and $a \in Act$, let $a\rho\text{-Succ}(p) = \{p' \mid p \xrightarrow{b} p' \wedge a\,\rho\,b\}$, $\sigma a\text{-Succ}(p) = \{p' \mid p \xrightarrow{b} p' \wedge b\,\sigma\,a\}$ and $TI(p) = \bigcup_{a \in Act}[(a\rho\text{-Succ}(p))^{\mathrm{t}} \cup (\sigma a\text{-Succ}(p))^{\mathrm{i}}]$. Then an LTS abstracted with respect to process $p \in \mathcal{P}$ is defined as $\mathfrak{L}_p^{\dagger} = \langle Reach(p), Act, \longrightarrow_p^{\dagger} \rangle$ where*

$$Reach(p) = \{p\} \cup \bigcup_{p' \in TI(p)} Reach(p')$$

the terminal and initial sets are created with respect to $\sqsubseteq_{(\rho,\sigma)}$ ordering and the transition relation $\longrightarrow_p^{\dagger}$ is the restriction of $\longrightarrow$ to $Reach(p)$.

Since $\mathfrak{L}$ and $\mathfrak{L}_p^{\dagger}$ have common elements, we will subscript the process state with the LTS when there is ambiguity. The following lemma formalizes this intuitive property of preservation of bisimilarity by the abstracted LTS.

Lemma 3. *Let $\mathfrak{L}$ be an LTS such that the sets $\{p' \mid \exists b[p \xrightarrow{b} p' \wedge a\,\rho\,b]\}$ and $\{p' \mid \exists[p \xrightarrow{b} p' \wedge b\,\sigma\,a]\}$ are always closed, for any state p and label a. Then, for any state p, we have $p_{\mathfrak{L}} \sqsubseteq_{(\rho,\sigma)} p_{\mathfrak{L}_p^{\dagger}}$ as well as $p_{\mathfrak{L}_p^{\dagger}} \sqsubseteq_{(\rho,\sigma)} p_{\mathfrak{L}}$.*

Proof. A state q is in $\mathfrak{L}$ is also in $\mathfrak{L}_p^{\dagger}$ iff $q_{\mathfrak{L}} \in Reach(p_{\mathfrak{L}})$. Let $R = \{(q_{\mathfrak{L}}, q'_{\mathfrak{L}_p^{\dagger}}) \mid q_{\mathfrak{L}} \sqsubseteq_{(\rho,\sigma)} q'_{\mathfrak{L}} \wedge q'_{\mathfrak{L}} \in Reach(p_{\mathfrak{L}})\}$.

Claim. The relation R is a (ρ, σ)-bisimulation.

Consider an arbitrary $(q_{\mathfrak{L}}, q'_{\mathfrak{L}_p^{\dagger}}) \in R$. Since $q_{\mathfrak{L}} \sqsubseteq_{(\rho,\sigma)} q'_{\mathfrak{L}}$, if $q_{\mathfrak{L}} \xrightarrow{a} r_{\mathfrak{L}}$, then there must be some b, r' such that $q'_{\mathfrak{L}} \xrightarrow{b} r'_{\mathfrak{L}}$ with $a\,\rho\,b$ and $r_{\mathfrak{L}} \sqsubseteq_{(\rho,\sigma)} r'_{\mathfrak{L}}$. Since the set $\{s \mid q \xrightarrow{b} s \wedge a\,\rho\,b\}$ is closed, there must be some $r''_{\mathfrak{L}} \in \{s \mid q \xrightarrow{b} s \wedge a\,\rho\,b\}^{\mathrm{t}}$ such that $r'_{\mathfrak{L}} \sqsubseteq_{(\rho,\sigma)} r''_{\mathfrak{L}}$. Since $q'_{\mathfrak{L}} \in Reach(p_{\mathfrak{L}})$, by recursive definition of $Reach(p_{\mathfrak{L}})$, we will also have $r''_{\mathfrak{L}} \in Reach(p_{\mathfrak{L}})$. Hence, by definition of R, we will have $(r'_{\mathfrak{L}_p}, r''_{\mathfrak{L}_p^{\dagger}}) \in R$.

Conversely, for any $q'_{\mathfrak{L}_p^{\dagger}} \xrightarrow{b} r'_{\mathfrak{L}_p^{\dagger}}$, since $\mathfrak{L}_p^{\dagger}$ can be embedded into $\mathfrak{L}$, we will also have $q'_{\mathfrak{L}} \xrightarrow{b} r'_{\mathfrak{L}}$. By definition of R, $q_{\mathfrak{L}} \sqsubseteq_{(\rho,\sigma)} q'_{\mathfrak{L}}$, hence there must be some a, r such that $q_{\mathfrak{L}} \xrightarrow{a} r_{\mathfrak{L}}$ with $a\,\sigma\,b$ and $r_{\mathfrak{L}} \sqsubseteq_{(\rho,\sigma)} r'_{\mathfrak{L}}$. Clearly, $r'_{\mathfrak{L}} \in Reach(p_{\mathfrak{L}})$, since it is in $\mathfrak{L}_p^{\dagger}$, and hence $(r_{\mathfrak{L}_p}, r'_{\mathfrak{L}_p^{\dagger}}) \in R$.

By a symmetric argument, we can show that the relation $R' = \{(q'_{\mathfrak{L}_p^{\dagger}}, q_{\mathfrak{L}}) \mid q'_{\mathfrak{L}} \sqsubseteq_{(\rho,\sigma)} q_{\mathfrak{L}} \wedge q'_{\mathfrak{L}} \in Reach(p_{\mathfrak{L}})\}$ is also a (ρ, σ)-bisimulation. Since $p_{\mathfrak{L}} \in Reach(p_{\mathfrak{L}})$ and $p_{\mathfrak{L}} \sqsubseteq_{(\rho,\sigma)} p_{\mathfrak{L}}$, we will have $(r_{\mathfrak{L}_p}, p_{\mathfrak{L}_p^{\dagger}}) \in R$ and $(p_{\mathfrak{L}_p^{\dagger}}, p_{\mathfrak{L}_p}) \in R'$. $\square$

An abstracted LTS may help in reducing an infinite-state system to a finite one. In some cases, it can be obtained without computing the bisimilarity relation. An example would be Timed Prebisimulation in Timed Automata [26].

3   Parameterised Hennessy-Milner Logic

Logical characterisation gives an effective syntax for describing distinguishing behaviour, which differentiates the implementation from the specification with respect to the behavioural preorder, as the distinguishing formula. For strong bisimilarity, Hennessy-Milner Logic (HML) with the possibility modality $\langle a \rangle$ and the necessity modality $[a]$, for every observation $a \in \mathcal{A}ct$, suffice. But when we have a more general notion of functional equivalence, same must also be incorporated in our modalities. For that, we look closely at how these modalities describe distinguishing behaviour.

Suppose distinguishing behaviour arises because the implementation can give an observation a, leading to behaviour described by some formula φ. Since it is not allowed by the specification, there will be no observation b, such that $a \, \rho \, b$, leading to a state satisfying φ. We can describe this using the modality $\langle a \rangle^\rho$.

Conversely, distinguishing behaviour may arise as the specification has an observation a, leading to behaviour described by some formula φ, but there is no functionally equivalent observation in the implementation leading to the matching behaviour. That is, for every b, such that $b \, \sigma \, a$, the implementation does not yield the behaviour φ. This can be described using the modality $[a]^{\sigma^{-1}}$.

Hence, we propose the following as logical characterisation,

Definition 5. *The syntax of the logic $\mathcal{L}_{(\rho,\sigma)}$ is given by the following BNF*

$$\varphi := \top \mid \bot \mid \langle a \rangle^\rho \varphi \mid [a]^{\sigma^{-1}} \varphi \mid \varphi_1 \wedge \varphi_2 \mid \varphi_1 \vee \varphi_2$$

where $a \in \mathcal{A}ct$. The semantics of $\varphi \in \mathcal{L}_{(\rho,\sigma)}$ is inductively defined as

$$\|\top\|^\mathcal{P} = \mathcal{P} \qquad \|\varphi_1 \vee \varphi_2\|^\mathcal{P} = \|\varphi_1\|^\mathcal{P} \cup \|\varphi_2\|^\mathcal{P}$$
$$\|\bot\|^\mathcal{P} = \emptyset \qquad \|\varphi_1 \wedge \varphi_2\|^\mathcal{P} = \|\varphi_1\|^\mathcal{P} \cap \|\varphi_2\|^\mathcal{P}$$

$$\|\langle a \rangle^\rho \varphi\|^\mathcal{P} = \{p \mid \exists b, p'[a\rho b \wedge p \xrightarrow{b} p' \wedge p' \in \|\varphi\|^\mathcal{P}]\}$$
$$\|[a]^{\sigma^{-1}} \varphi\|^\mathcal{P} = \{p \mid \forall b, p'[b\sigma a \wedge p \xrightarrow{b} p' \Rightarrow p' \in \|\varphi\|^\mathcal{P}]\}$$

These definitions can be seen as a natural generalization of those given for HML and observational HML. A process p satisfies a formula $\varphi \in \mathcal{L}_{(\rho,\sigma)}$, denoted $p \vDash \varphi$, iff $p \in \|\varphi\|^\mathcal{P}$. In general, this logic is not closed under complementation. However, when $\rho = \sigma^{-1}$, the two operators $\langle \ \rangle^\rho$ and $[\ ]^{\sigma^{-1}}$ will become dual, making it a modal logic. The satisfiability relation can be used to generate a preorder relation on processes, which brings us to the notion of logical characterisation.

Definition 6. *A logic $\mathcal{L}$ characterises a preorder $\preceq_\mathcal{L}$ over $\mathcal{P}$ if for any $p, q \in \mathcal{P}$, $p \preceq_\mathcal{L} q$ iff $\forall \varphi \in \mathcal{L}[p \vDash \varphi \Rightarrow q \vDash \varphi]$.*

The following lemma justifies $\mathcal{L}_{(\rho,\sigma)}$ by showing its invariance under (ρ, σ)-bisimilarity.

Lemma 4. *If ρ, σ are transitive, then for any processes p, q such that $p \sqsupseteq_{(\rho,\sigma)} q$, we have $p \preceq_{\mathcal{L}_{(\rho,\sigma)}} q$.*

Proof (By structural induction). Conjunction and disjunction being trivial cases, we only sketch the proofs for modal operators. Suppose we are given processes p, q such that $p \sqsubseteq_{(\rho,\sigma)} q$ and $p \vDash \varphi$ holds.

- $\varphi = \langle a \rangle^\rho \varphi'$: There must exist an action b and state p', such that $p \xrightarrow{b} p'$, $a\rho b$, and $p' \vDash \varphi'$. But since $p \sqsubseteq_{(\rho,\sigma)} q$, we must have some action c and state q', such that $q \xrightarrow{c} q'$, $b\rho c$, and $p' \sqsubseteq_{(\rho,\sigma)} q'$. By the induction hypothesis, we will have $q' \vDash \varphi'$. Also since ρ is transitive, we have $a\rho c$. Hence $q \vDash \langle a \rangle^\rho \varphi'$.

- $\varphi = [a]^{\sigma^{-1}} \varphi'$: Consider any transition $q \xrightarrow{b} q'$, such that $b\sigma a$ holds. Since $p \sqsubseteq_{(\rho,\sigma)} q$, there must exist an action c such that $p \xrightarrow{c} p'$, $c\sigma b$, and $p' \sqsubseteq_{(\rho,\sigma)} q'$. By transitivity of σ, we must have $c\sigma a$. If $p' \vDash \varphi'$, by the induction hypothesis, we must have $q' \vDash \varphi'$. This holds for any b such that $b\sigma a$, therefore, $q \vDash [a]^{\sigma^{-1}} \varphi'$. $\qquad\square$

The other direction, that is, if $p \preceq_{\mathcal{L}_{(\rho,\sigma)}} q$ then $p \sqsubseteq_{(\rho,\sigma)} q$, requires additional constraints, one of them being image-finiteness.

3.1 Image-Finiteness

Definition 7. *An LTS $\mathcal{L} = \langle \mathcal{P}, \mathcal{A}ct, \longrightarrow \rangle$ is (ρ, σ)-image-finite iff for any $p \in \mathcal{P}$ and $a \in \mathcal{A}ct$, the sets, $\{q \mid p \xrightarrow{b} q \wedge a\rho b\}$ and $\{q \mid p \xrightarrow{b} q \wedge b\sigma a\}$, are finite. An LTS $\mathcal{L}$ is image-finite upto (ρ, σ)-bisimilarity if $\mathcal{L}_p^\dagger$ is (ρ, σ)-image-finite for every $p \in \mathcal{P}$.*

Image-finiteness enables the decidability of bisimulation by making the bisimulation function co-continuous, which in turn guarantees a finite distinguishing behaviour between non-bisimilar processes.

Theorem 1. *Given an LTS $\mathcal{L}$, if for every $p \in \mathcal{P}$, the sets $\{p' \mid p \xrightarrow{b} p' \wedge a\rho b\}$ and $\{p' \mid a\sigma b \wedge p \xrightarrow{a} p'\}$ are closed and $\mathcal{L}_p^\dagger$ is (ρ, σ)-image-finite, then $\sqsubseteq_{(\rho,\sigma)}^\omega \subseteq \mathcal{F}_{(\rho,\sigma)}(\sqsubseteq_{(\rho,\sigma)}^\omega)$, and hence $\sqsubseteq_{(\rho,\sigma)}^\omega = \sqsubseteq_{(\rho,\sigma)}$.*

Proof. Let $p \sqsubseteq_{(\rho,\sigma)}^\omega q$. Then for any a, p' such that $p \xrightarrow{a} p'$, the set $Q_i = \{q' \mid q \xrightarrow{b} q' \wedge a\rho b \wedge p' \sqsubseteq_{(\rho,\sigma)}^i q'\}$ is non-empty for every i. Since $\sqsubseteq_{(\rho,\sigma)}^i \subseteq \sqsubseteq_{(\rho,\sigma)}^j$, for all $i \geq j$, we would have $Q_i \subseteq Q_j$, which gives us a decreasing sequence of sets. If some q' is common to every Q_i, then $q \xrightarrow{b} q' \wedge a\rho b \wedge p' \sqsubseteq_{(\rho,\sigma)}^\omega q'$ will hold.

We can also show that $Q_i^\dagger \subseteq Q_j^\dagger$, for all $i \geq j$. Suppose not, i.e., $Q_i^\dagger \not\subseteq Q_j^\dagger$ for some i, j with $i \geq j$. Then there must exist some $r \in Q_i^\dagger$ such that $r \notin Q_j^\dagger$. Now we will also have $r \in Q_i$, and hence $r \in Q_j$, since $Q_i \subseteq Q_j$. But since r is not in $Q_j^\dagger$, there must exist some $r' \in Q_j^\dagger$ such that $r \sqsubseteq_{(\rho,\sigma)} r'$ holds. But this would mean that r' must also be in Q_i since $\sqsubseteq_{(\rho,\sigma)} \subseteq \sqsubseteq_{(\rho,\sigma)}^i$, and hence in $Q_i^\dagger$ in place of r by transitivity of $\sqsubseteq_{(\rho,\sigma)}^i$, giving us a contradiction.

By assumption, Q_0 is a closed set, and hence $Q_0^\dagger$ is non-empty. In fact, we can show that for every $i \geq 0$, Q_i is a closed set, making $Q_i^\dagger$ non-empty. Consider any $r \in Q_i$, then r is also in Q_0, and hence there is some $r' \in Q_0^{\mathsf{t}}$ such that $r \sqsubseteq_{(\rho,\sigma)} r'$. But since $\sqsubseteq_{(\rho,\sigma)} \subseteq \sqsubseteq_{(\rho,\sigma)}^i$ and $\sqsubseteq_{(\rho,\sigma)}^i$ is transitive, r' will also be in Q_i and hence in Q_i^{t}.

Now under (ρ,σ)-image-finiteness assumption, Q_0^{t} is a finite set, hence there will be an i_0 such that $Q_{i_0}^{\mathsf{t}} = Q_j^{\mathsf{t}}$ for all $j \geq i_0$. Also $Q_{i_0}^{\mathsf{t}}$ is non-empty, hence any element from $Q_{i_0}^{\mathsf{t}}$ would be common to every Q_i. Similar argument can be made for a transition of q. □

Lemma 5. *If ρ, σ are reflexive and $\mathfrak{L}_p^{\dagger}$ is (ρ,σ)-image-finite for every $p \in \mathcal{P}$, then the preorder $\preceq_{\mathcal{L}_{(\rho,\sigma)}}$ is a (ρ,σ)-bisimulation.*

Proof (Proof by Contradiction). Assume not. Then there must exist processes p, q which are not bisimilar but $p \preceq_{\mathcal{L}_{(\rho,\sigma)}} q$ holds. This can happen only if some transition of p or q cannot be matched, giving us two cases

Case 1: We have $p \preceq_{\mathcal{L}_{(\rho,\sigma)}} q$ and $p \xrightarrow{a} p'$, but there is no action b and state q' with $q \xrightarrow{b} q'$, $a\rho b$, and $p' \preceq_{\mathcal{L}_{(\rho,\sigma)}} q'$. Let $Q = \{q' \mid \exists b[q \xrightarrow{b} q' \wedge a \rho b]\}$. Now Q has a finite terminal set Q^{t}. Moreover, for every $q' \in Q^{\mathsf{t}}$, there must exist a formula $\varphi_{q'}$ such that $p' \vDash \varphi_{q'}$ but $q' \nvDash \varphi_{q'}$. Consider the formula $\varphi = \bigwedge_{q' \in Q^{\mathsf{t}}} \varphi_{q'}$. Clearly $p' \vDash \varphi$, and since ρ is reflexive, we have $p \vDash \langle a \rangle^{\rho} \varphi$. Since $p \preceq_{\mathcal{L}_{(\rho,\sigma)}} q$, q must also satisfy this formula, but this requires some state $q'' \in Q$ to satisfy φ, which in turn requires some $q' \in Q^{\mathsf{t}}$ to satisfy φ, as $q'' \sqsubseteq_{(\rho,\sigma)} q'$ (Lemma 4). But q' cannot satisfy $\varphi_{q'}$, and consequently φ.

Case 2: We have $p \preceq_{\mathcal{L}_{(\rho,\sigma)}} q$ and $q \xrightarrow{b} q'$, but there is no action a and state p' with $p \xrightarrow{a} p'$, $a\sigma b$, and $p' \preceq_{\mathcal{L}_{(\rho,\sigma)}} q'$. Let $P = \{p' \mid \exists a[p \xrightarrow{a} p' \wedge a \sigma b]\}$. Now P has a finite initial set P^i. Moreover, for every $p' \in P$, there must exist a formula $\varphi_{p'}$ such that $p' \vDash \varphi_{p'}$ but $q' \nvDash \varphi_{p'}$. Consider the formula $\varphi = \bigvee_{p' \in P^i} \varphi_{p'}$. For any $p'' \in P$, there will be some $p' \in P^i$ such that $p' \sqsubseteq_{(\rho,\sigma)} p''$, and due to Lemma 4, we will have $p'' \vDash \varphi_{p'}$, consequently $p'' \vDash \varphi$, and hence, $p \vDash [b]^{\sigma^{-1}} \varphi$. Since $p \preceq_{\mathcal{L}_{(\rho,\sigma)}} q$, q must also satisfy this formula. But this is only possible if q' satisfies φ since σ is reflexive. □

Theorem 2 now follows from Lemmas 4 and 5.

Theorem 2. *If ρ, σ are preorders then $\sqsubseteq_{(\rho,\sigma)} = \preceq_{\mathcal{L}_{(\rho,\sigma)}}$, i.e. $\mathcal{L}_{(\rho,\sigma)}$ is a logical characterisation of $\sqsubseteq_{(\rho,\sigma)}$ over (ρ,σ)-image-finite LTS.* □

The proof argument uses image-finiteness to ensure finite conjunctions and disjunctions. If we allow infinite conjunctions and disjunctions in our logic, denoted $\mathcal{L}_{(\rho,\sigma)}^{\infty}$, then we can obtain the logical characterisation result without requiring the constraints of image-finiteness.

Theorem 3. *If ρ, σ are preorders then $\sqsubseteq_{(\rho,\sigma)} = \preceq_{\mathcal{L}_{(\rho,\sigma)}}$, i.e. $\mathcal{L}_{(\rho,\sigma)}^{\infty}$ is a logical characterisation of $\sqsubseteq_{(\rho,\sigma)}$.* □

Procedure. GenerateFormula for generating a distinguishing formula

---

Input: $p, q \in \mathfrak{L} = \langle \mathcal{P}, \mathcal{A}ct, \longrightarrow \rangle$

Assumption: $\mathfrak{L}_r^{\dagger}$ is (ρ, σ)-image-finite for every $r \in \mathcal{P}$. If $p \not\sqsubseteq_{(\rho,\sigma)}^i q$ then
Bisimilar$(p, q) = (a, p')$ s.t. there does not exist any b, q' with
$q \xrightarrow{b} q' \sqsubseteq_{(\rho,\sigma)}^{i-1} p'$ and $a\rho pb$ or Bisimilar$(p, q) = (b, q')$ s.t. there
does not exist any a, p' with $p \xrightarrow{a} p' \sqsubseteq_{(\rho,\sigma)}^{i-1} q'$ and $a\sigma b$

Output: if $p \sqsubseteq_{(\rho,\sigma)} q$ then $f\!\!f$ else φ s.t. $(p \vDash \varphi$ and $q \nvDash \varphi)$ or $(p \nvDash \varphi$ and $q \vDash \varphi)$

GenerateFormula$(p, q) =$ if $p \sqsubseteq_{(\rho,\sigma)} q$ then return $f\!\!f$

else switch Bisimilar(p, q) do

   case (a, p'): do return $\langle a \rangle^\rho \bigwedge_{\{q' \mid q \xrightarrow{b} q' \wedge a\rho pb\}^{\dagger}}$GenerateFormula$(p', q')$

   case (b, q'): do return $[b]^{\sigma^{-1}} \bigvee_{\{p' \mid p \xrightarrow{a} p' \wedge a\sigma b\}^{\dagger}}$GenerateFormula$(p', q')$

Logical characterisation implies the existence of a distinguishing formula, which is satisfied by p but not by q, whenever $p \not\sqsubseteq_{(\rho,\sigma)} q$. The proof of Lemma 5 can be molded into a procedure for generating the distinguishing formula. Procedure GenerateFormula generates a distinguishing formula between the input processes, assuming a bisimulation procedure which not only tells us whether two processes are bisimilar, but also gives us the unmatched transition when they are not. Image-finiteness bounds the number of recursive calls and also the depth of recursion, by guaranteeing an i such that $p \not\sqsubseteq_{(\rho,\sigma)} q$ implies $p \not\sqsubseteq_{(\rho,\sigma)}^i q$ (Theorem 1), and hence ensures the termination of the procedure.

3.2   Testing Preorders Logically

We may also view the parameterised HML formulas as tests. If $p \sqsubseteq_{(\rho,\sigma)} q$, then the $\mathcal{L}_{(\rho,\sigma)}$ formulas satisfied by p, denoted $\mathcal{L}_{(\rho,\sigma)}(p)$, is a subset of the $\mathcal{L}_{(\rho,\sigma)}$ formulas satisfied by q, $\mathcal{L}_{(\rho,\sigma)}(q)$. If q is the specification, then $\mathcal{L}_{(\rho,\sigma)}(q)$ can be seen as the set of allowed behaviours, therefore, $\mathcal{L}_{(\rho,\sigma)}(p) \subseteq \mathcal{L}_{(\rho,\sigma)}(q)$ ensures the correctness of p.

We may define complementation for the parameterised HML. Given a formula $\varphi \in \mathcal{L}_{(\rho,\sigma)}$, its complement, $\varphi^c \in \mathcal{L}_{(\sigma^{-1},\rho^{-1})}$, is defined by following structural induction.

$$\top^c = \bot \qquad (\varphi_1 \vee \varphi_2)^c = \varphi_1{}^c \wedge \varphi_2{}^c \qquad (\langle a \rangle^\rho \varphi)^c = [a]^\rho \varphi^c$$
$$\bot^c = \top \qquad (\varphi_1 \wedge \varphi_2)^c = \varphi_1{}^c \vee \varphi_2{}^c \qquad ([a]^{\sigma^{-1}} \varphi)^c = \langle a \rangle^{\sigma^{-1}} \varphi^c$$

It may be easily seen that $p \vDash \varphi$ iff $p \nvDash \varphi^c$. Therefore, if $\mathcal{L}_{(\rho,\sigma)}(p) \subseteq \mathcal{L}_{(\rho,\sigma)}(q)$, then $\mathcal{L}_{(\sigma^{-1},\rho^{-1})}(q) \subseteq \mathcal{L}_{(\sigma^{-1},\rho^{-1})}(p)$. The specification may be seen as the set of all tests that the correct implementation should pass. Then, an implementation is correct under (ρ, σ)-bisimilarity, iff all the specification's tests, $\mathcal{L}_{(\sigma^{-1},\rho^{-1})}(q)$, are satisfied by the implementation, implying $\mathcal{L}_{(\sigma^{-1},\rho^{-1})}(q) \subseteq \mathcal{L}_{(\sigma^{-1},\rho^{-1})}(p)$, which by logical characterisation result implies $p \sqsubseteq_{(\rho,\sigma)} q$.

Procedure. IsModel for checking satisfiability

Input: $\varphi \in \mathcal{L}_{(\rho,\sigma)}$, $p \in \mathfrak{L} = \langle \mathcal{P}, \mathcal{A}ct, \longrightarrow \rangle$

Assumption: $\mathfrak{L}_p^{\dagger}$ is (ρ, σ)-image-finite

Output: $p \vDash \varphi$

IsModel(tt, p) = true $\qquad\qquad\qquad$ IsModel(ff, p) = false

IsModel($\bigwedge_{i \in I} \varphi_i, p$) = $\qquad\qquad\qquad$ IsModel($\bigvee_{i \in I} \varphi_i, p$) =

$\bigwedge_{i \in I}$IsModel(φ_i, p) $\qquad\qquad\qquad$ $\bigvee_{i \in I}$IsModel(φ_i, p)

IsModel($\langle a \rangle^{\rho} \varphi, p$) = $\bigvee_{q \in \{q \mid p \xrightarrow{b} q \wedge a \rho b\}^{\dagger}}$IsModel($\varphi, q$)

IsModel($[a]^{\sigma^{-1}} \varphi, p$) = $\bigwedge_{q \in \{q \mid p \xrightarrow{b} q \wedge b \sigma a\}^{i}}$IsModel($\varphi, q$)

Procedure IsModel gives a recursive method for deciding whether a formula φ is satisfied by a process p. It is guaranteed to terminate when $\mathfrak{L}_p^{\dagger}$ is (ρ, σ)-image-finite. Note that a finite or algebraic description of the LTS is not necessary. If the LTS is described co-algebraically, then the procedure IsModel gives a co-inductive definition[2]. To evaluate a PHML formula, you only need to look at the current state and its immediate successors, which can be done in a purely observational model. Therefore, we may also view $\preceq_{\mathcal{L}_{(\rho,\sigma)}} = \preceq^{-1}_{\mathcal{L}_{(\sigma^{-1},\rho^{-1})}}$ as the testing equivalence obtained by interpreting formulas of logic $\mathcal{L}_{(\sigma^{-1},\rho^{-1})}$ as the encoding of tests.

4   Extending Parameterised HML with Fixed Point Operators

The parameterised HML can be extended with fixed point operators [18].

Definition 8. *The syntax of the logic $\mathcal{L}^{\mathcal{X}}_{(\rho,\sigma)}$ is given by the following BNF*

$$\varphi := \top \mid \bot \mid X \mid \langle a \rangle^{\rho} \varphi \mid [a]^{\sigma^{-1}} \varphi \mid \varphi_1 \wedge \varphi_2 \mid \varphi_1 \vee \varphi_2 \mid \nu X.\varphi \mid \mu X.\varphi$$

where $a \in \mathcal{A}ct$ and $X \in \mathcal{X}$ ranges over a countable set of variables.

The operators νX and μX denote the greatest fixed point and least fixed point respectively, binding the variable X in its scope. Any variable which is not bound is called a free variable. A closed formula is one without any free variables, and the fragment of closed formulas of the logic will be denoted $cf(\mathcal{L}^{\mathcal{X}}_{(\rho,\sigma)})$. To define the semantics, we need the notion of valuations, which assigns meaning to free variables. Given a countable set of variables $\mathcal{X}$, a valuation $\mathcal{V}$ is essentially a map from $\mathcal{X}$ to $2^{\mathcal{P}}$.

---

[2] It is still inductively defined over $\mathcal{L}_{(\rho,\sigma)}$, but it is co-inductively defined over processes.

Definition 9. *The semantics of the formula* $\varphi \in \mathcal{L}^{\mathcal{X}}_{(\rho,\sigma)}$ *over some process set* $\mathcal{P}$ *is defined inductively as,*

$$
\begin{aligned}
\|X\|^{\mathcal{P}}_{\mathcal{V}} &= \mathcal{V}(X) \\
\|\varphi_1 \vee \varphi_2\|^{\mathcal{P}}_{\mathcal{V}} &= \|\varphi_1\|^{\mathcal{P}}_{\mathcal{V}} \cup \|\varphi_1\|^{\mathcal{P}}_{\mathcal{V}} \\
\|\varphi_1 \wedge \varphi_2\|^{\mathcal{P}}_{\mathcal{V}} &= \|\varphi_1\|^{\mathcal{P}}_{\mathcal{V}} \cap \|\varphi_1\|^{\mathcal{P}}_{\mathcal{V}} \\
\|\langle a \rangle^{\rho} \varphi\|^{\mathcal{P}}_{\mathcal{V}} &= \{p \mid \exists b, p'[a \rho b \wedge p \xrightarrow{b} p' \wedge p' \in \|\varphi\|^{\mathcal{P}}_{\mathcal{V}}]\} \\
\|[a]^{\sigma^{-1}} \varphi\|^{\mathcal{P}}_{\mathcal{V}} &= \{p \mid \forall b, p'[b \sigma a \wedge p \xrightarrow{b} p' \Rightarrow p' \in \|\varphi\|^{\mathcal{P}}_{\mathcal{V}}]\} \\
\|\nu X.\varphi\|^{\mathcal{P}}_{\mathcal{V}} &= \bigcup\{\mathcal{E} \subseteq \mathcal{P} \mid \mathcal{E} \subseteq \|\varphi\|^{\mathcal{P}}_{\mathcal{V}[\mathcal{E}/X]}\} \\
\|\mu X.\varphi\|^{\mathcal{P}}_{\mathcal{V}} &= \bigcap\{\mathcal{E} \subseteq \mathcal{P} \mid \|\varphi\|^{\mathcal{P}}_{\mathcal{V}[\mathcal{E}/X]} \subseteq \mathcal{E}\}
\end{aligned}
$$

where $\mathcal{V}[\mathcal{E}/X](Y) = \mathcal{V}(Y)$ *for all* $Y \neq X$ *and* $\mathcal{V}[\mathcal{E}/X](X) = \mathcal{E}$.

The semantics of any formula depends upon the valuation supplied. Consequently, the satisfaction relation should be redefined.

Definition 10. *A process* p *satisfies a formula* φ *under* $\mathcal{V}$, *denoted* $p \vDash_{\mathcal{V}} \varphi$, *iff* $p \in \|\varphi\|^{\mathcal{P}}_{\mathcal{V}}$. *It satisfies the formula* φ, *denoted* $p \vDash \varphi$, *iff* $p \in \|\varphi\|^{\mathcal{P}}_{\mathcal{V}}$ *for all valuations* $\mathcal{V}$.

A valuation can be seen as an element of $(2^{\mathcal{P}})^{|\mathcal{X}|}$, which is the $|\mathcal{X}|$ fold product of $2^{\mathcal{P}}$. Since powerset forms a complete lattice, and the direct product of a countable collection of complete lattices is also a complete lattice, this must also be a complete lattice under pointwise subset ordering [8]. More formally,

Definition 11. *Let* $\mathcal{V}_1$ *and* $\mathcal{V}_2$ *be any two valuations over* $\mathcal{X}$. *We define a partial order* $\leq$ *on valuations as*

$$\mathcal{V}_1 \leq \mathcal{V}_2 \Leftrightarrow \forall X \in \mathcal{X}[\mathcal{V}_1(X) \subseteq \mathcal{V}_2(X)]$$

The $\leq$ *ordering yields a complete lattice,* $(\mathcal{X} \to 2^{\mathcal{P}}, \leq)$, *over valuations.*

The semantics of any formula is monotonic with respect to this partial order over valuations.

Lemma 6. *Let* $\mathcal{V}_1$ *and* $\mathcal{V}_2$ *be any two valuations over* $\mathcal{X}$ *and* φ *be any formula in* $\mathcal{L}^{\mathcal{X}}_{(\rho,\sigma)}$. *If* $\mathcal{V}_1 \leq \mathcal{V}_2$ *then* $\|\varphi\|^{\mathcal{P}}_{\mathcal{V}_1} \subseteq \|\varphi\|^{\mathcal{P}}_{\mathcal{V}_2}$ *(Refer [25]).* $\qquad\square$

Given a formula φ with a free variable $X \in \mathcal{X}$, the function, $\mathcal{O}_{\varphi}(\mathcal{V}) = \mathcal{V}[\|\varphi\|^{\mathcal{P}}_{\mathcal{V}}/X]$, is monotonic over the complete lattice $(\mathcal{X} \to 2^{\mathcal{P}}, \leq)$. Hence by Tarski's theorem [29], the semantic definition of νX and μX indeed defines the greatest and the least fixed point respectively. It also makes the model checking of $\mathcal{L}^{\mathcal{X}}_{(\rho,\sigma)}$ decidable over finite-state systems. For example, to compute $\|\nu X.\varphi\|^{\mathcal{P}}$, we just need to apply $\mathcal{O}_{\varphi}$ repeatedly, starting from $\mathcal{P}$ (empty set in case of least fixed point), until we reach a fixed point.

Theorem 4. *Given a finite* $\mathfrak{L}^{\dagger}_p$, *for any* $\varphi \in cf(\mathcal{L}^{\mathcal{X}}_{(\rho,\sigma)})$, $p \vDash \varphi$ *is decidable.* $\qquad\square$

4.1   Preservation Under Bisimulations

The characterisation result can be broken into two assertions. Firstly, if q satisfies all the formulae which are satisfied by p, then p is (ρ, σ)-bisimilar to q. Since $\mathcal{L}^{\mathcal{X}}_{(\rho,\sigma)}$ extends $\mathcal{L}_{(\rho,\sigma)}$, this result will continue to hold. Interestingly, the other assertion, i.e. if p is (ρ, σ)-bisimilar to q then q satisfies all formulae which are true for p, also holds for $\mathcal{L}^{\mathcal{X}}_{(\rho,\sigma)}$, despite it being more expressive on account of fixed point operators, provided that the valuation is (ρ, σ)-bisimilarity-closed.

Definition 12. *Given any relation $\mathcal{R}$, a set $\mathcal{E} \subseteq \mathcal{P}$ is $\mathcal{R}$-closed iff for every process p, q, whenever $p \in \mathcal{E}$ and $p\mathcal{R}q$, we have $q \in \mathcal{E}$. Naturally, a valuation $\mathcal{V}$ is $\mathcal{R}$-closed iff $\mathcal{V}(X)$ is $\mathcal{R}$-closed for every variable X.*

For every $p, q \in \mathcal{P}$ with $p \sqsubseteq_{(\rho,\sigma)} q$, $p \in \|\varphi\|^{\mathcal{P}}_{\mathcal{V}}$ implies $q \in \|\varphi\|^{\mathcal{P}}_{\mathcal{V}}$ is equivalent to saying that the set $\|\varphi\|^{\mathcal{P}}_{\mathcal{V}}$ is bisimilarity-closed, i.e., the counterpart of Lemma 4 here will be showing that $\|\varphi\|^{\mathcal{P}}_{\mathcal{V}}$ is bisimilarity-closed. The results given below are a generalization of a corresponding result for strong bisimulation [28].

Definition 13

1. *Given any set $\mathcal{E} \subseteq \mathcal{P}$, its upward (ρ, σ)-bisimilarity closure, $\mathcal{E}^{u}_{(\rho,\sigma)}$, is the set $\{q \in \mathcal{P} \mid \exists p[p \sqsubseteq_{(\rho,\sigma)} q \wedge p \in \mathcal{E}]\}$.*
2. *Given any set $\mathcal{E} \subseteq \mathcal{P}$, its downward (ρ, σ)-bisimilarity closure, $\mathcal{E}^{d}_{(\rho,\sigma)}$, is the set $\{p \in \mathcal{E} \mid \forall q[p \sqsubseteq_{(\rho,\sigma)} q \Rightarrow q \in \mathcal{E}]\}$.*

Lemma 7. *Let $\mathscr{E} = \{\mathcal{E}_i\}_{i \in \mathcal{I}}$ be any collection of (ρ, σ)-bisimilarity-closed sets. Then both $\bigcup_{i \in \mathcal{I}} \mathcal{E}_i$ and $\bigcap_{i \in \mathcal{I}} \mathcal{E}_i$ are also (ρ, σ)-bisimilarity-closed.*   □

Lemma 8. *If ρ, σ are preorders, then for any arbitrary set $\mathcal{E}$,*

1. *$\mathcal{E}^{u}_{(\rho,\sigma)}$ is a (ρ, σ)-bisimilarity-closed set containing $\mathcal{E}$.*
2. *$\mathcal{E}^{d}_{(\rho,\sigma)}$ is a (ρ, σ)-bisimilarity-closed set contained in $\mathcal{E}$ (Refer [25]).*   □

Lemma 9. *Given preorders ρ, σ, (ρ, σ)-image-finite processes in $\mathcal{P}$ and a (ρ, σ)-bisimilarity-closed valuation $\mathcal{V}$, the set $\|\varphi\|^{\mathcal{P}}_{\mathcal{V}}$ is also (ρ, σ)-bisimilarity-closed for any formula $\varphi \in \mathcal{L}^{\mathcal{X}}_{(\rho,\sigma)}$.*

Proof. We extend the inductive argument of Lemma 4, which requires (ρ, σ)-image-finiteness, with the proofs for fixed point operators. The case of the single variable X trivially follows from the fact that the valuation $\mathcal{V}$ is (ρ, σ)-bisimilarity-closed.

– Case $\nu X.\varphi$: For any $\mathcal{E} \subseteq \|\varphi\|^{\mathcal{P}}_{\mathcal{V}[\mathcal{E}/X]}$, we have $\|\varphi\|^{\mathcal{P}}_{\mathcal{V}[\mathcal{E}/X]} \subseteq \|\varphi\|^{\mathcal{P}}_{\mathcal{V}[\mathcal{E}^u/X]}$ (Lemma 6), and hence $\mathcal{E} \subseteq \|\varphi\|^{\mathcal{P}}_{\mathcal{V}[\mathcal{E}^u/X]}$. By the induction hypothesis, $\|\varphi\|^{\mathcal{P}}_{\mathcal{V}[\mathcal{E}^u/X]}$ is (ρ, σ)-bisimilarity-closed. We can show $\mathcal{E}^u \subseteq \|\varphi\|^{\mathcal{P}}_{\mathcal{V}[\mathcal{E}^u/X]}$, as any $q \in \mathcal{E}^u$ will have a $p \in \mathcal{E}$ with $p \sqsubseteq_{(\rho,\sigma)} q$. Since $\mathcal{E} \subseteq \|\varphi\|^{\mathcal{P}}_{\mathcal{V}[\mathcal{E}^u/X]}$, we will have $p \in \|\varphi\|^{\mathcal{P}}_{\mathcal{V}[\mathcal{E}^u/X]}$, and hence $q \in \|\varphi\|^{\mathcal{P}}_{\mathcal{V}[\mathcal{E}^u/X]}$, due to it being (ρ, σ)-bisimilarity-closed. Since $\mathcal{E}^u \cup \mathcal{E} = \mathcal{E}^u$, we can rewrite $\bigcup\{\mathcal{E} \subseteq \mathcal{P} \mid \mathcal{E} \subseteq \|\varphi\|^{\mathcal{P}}_{\mathcal{V}[\mathcal{E}/X]}\}$ as $\bigcup\{\mathcal{E}^u \subseteq \mathcal{P} \mid \mathcal{E}^u \subseteq \|\varphi\|^{\mathcal{P}}_{\mathcal{V}[\mathcal{E}^u/X]}\}$, which is a (ρ, σ)-bisimilarity-closed set by Lemma 7, and hence $\|\nu X.\varphi\|^{\mathcal{P}}_{\mathcal{V}}$ is (ρ, σ)-bisimilarity-closed.

- Case $\mu X.\varphi$: For any $\|\varphi\|^{\mathcal{P}}_{\mathcal{V}[\mathcal{E}/X]} \subseteq \mathcal{E}$, we have $\|\varphi\|^{\mathcal{P}}_{\mathcal{V}[\mathcal{E}^d/X]} \subseteq \|\varphi\|^{\mathcal{P}}_{\mathcal{V}[\mathcal{E}/X]}$ (Lemma 6), and hence $\|\varphi\|^{\mathcal{P}}_{\mathcal{V}[\mathcal{E}^d/X]} \subseteq \mathcal{E}$. By the induction hypothesis, $\|\varphi\|^{\mathcal{P}}_{\mathcal{V}[\mathcal{E}^d/X]}$ is (ρ,σ)-bisimilarity-closed. Therefore, for any p, q with $p \in \|\varphi\|^{\mathcal{P}}_{\mathcal{V}[\mathcal{E}^d/X]}$ and $p \sqsubseteq_{(\rho,\sigma)} q$, we will have $q \in \|\varphi\|^{\mathcal{P}}_{\mathcal{V}[\mathcal{E}^d/X]}$ and hence $q \in \mathcal{E}$. This, however, implies that p must be in $\mathcal{E}^d$, and hence $\|\varphi\|^{\mathcal{P}}_{\mathcal{V}[\mathcal{E}^d/X]} \subseteq \mathcal{E}^d$. Since $\mathcal{E}^d \cap \mathcal{E} = \mathcal{E}^d$, we can rewrite $\bigcap \{\mathcal{E} \subseteq \mathcal{P} \mid \|\varphi\|^{\mathcal{P}}_{\mathcal{V}[\mathcal{E}/X]} \subseteq \mathcal{E}\}$ as $\bigcap \{\mathcal{E}^d \subseteq \mathcal{P} \mid \|\varphi\|^{\mathcal{P}}_{\mathcal{V}[\mathcal{E}^d/X]} \subseteq \mathcal{E}^d\}$, which is a (ρ,σ)-bisimilarity-closed set by Lemma 7, and hence $\|\mu X.\varphi\|^{\mathcal{P}}_{\mathcal{V}}$ is also (ρ,σ)-bisimilarity-closed. $\qquad\square$

If φ is a closed formula, i.e. $\varphi \in cf(\mathcal{L}^{\mathcal{X}}_{(\rho,\sigma)})$, then its meaning is independent of the valuation, and hence is always bisimilarity-closed.

Theorem 5. *Given preorders ρ, σ, for any (ρ,σ)-image-finite processes p, q, $p \sqsubseteq_{(\rho,\sigma)} q$ iff $p \preceq_{cf(\mathcal{L}^{\mathcal{X}}_{(\rho,\sigma)})} q$, i.e., $cf(\mathcal{L}^{\mathcal{X}}_{(\rho,\sigma)})$ is a logical characterisation for $\sqsubseteq_{(\rho,\sigma)}$.*

4.2 Characteristic Formula

Equipped with the fixed point operators, the logic $\mathcal{L}^{\mathcal{X}}_{(\rho,\sigma)}$ is powerful enough to define characteristic formulae. Given a process p, a characteristic formula is satisfied only by the processes which are (ρ,σ)-bisimilar to p. Its existence, therefore, reduces bisimulation checking to model checking. More formally,

Definition 14. *A closed formula $\varphi_p \in \mathcal{L}^{\mathcal{X}}_{(\rho,\sigma)}$ is characteristic of a process p, if for every $q \in \mathcal{P}$, we have $p \sqsubseteq_{(\rho,\sigma)} q$ iff $q \in \|\varphi_p\|^{\mathcal{P}}$.*

Numerous derivations of characteristic formulae share a common underlying structure [2], which encode the fixed point characterisation of the relation as a formula in the logic. We adopt the derivation in [22] for parameterised bisimulations, as it gives a step-by-step conversion of the fixed point characterisation into a characteristic formula.

We will derive an equational system from which the characteristic formula can be obtained using standard techniques [22]. Given some process set $\mathcal{P}$, an equational system $E^{\mathcal{P}}$ is a collection of mutually recursive equations of the form $X_p = \varphi_p$, where $\varphi_p \in \mathcal{L}^{\mathcal{X}}_{(\rho,\sigma)}$ and $p \in \mathcal{P}$. We can also view this equational system as a function over valuations, defined as $(E^{\mathcal{P}}(\mathcal{V}))(X_p) = \|\varphi_p\|^{\mathcal{P}}_{\mathcal{V}}$. By Lemma 6, this defines a monotonic function over the lattice $(\{X_p\}_{p\in\mathcal{P}} \to 2^{\mathcal{P}}, \leq)$, which is isomorphic to the lattice of binary relations over $\mathcal{P}$.

Lemma 10. *The lattice $(\{X_p\}_{p\in\mathcal{P}} \to 2^{\mathcal{P}}, \leq)$ is isomorphic to $(2^{\mathcal{P}\times\mathcal{P}}, \subseteq)$ under the following mapping*

$$\mathbb{I}(\mathcal{V}) = \{(p,q) \mid q \in \mathcal{V}(X_p)\} \qquad \mathbb{I}^{-1}(R) = \{q \in \mathcal{V}(X_p) \mid (p,q) \in R\}$$

The utility of this isomorphism lies in its ability to define a characteristic equational system as $E^{\mathcal{P}} = \mathbb{I}^{-1} \circ \mathscr{F}_{(\rho,\sigma)} \circ \mathbb{I}$, with its greatest fixed point corresponding to (ρ,σ)-bisimilarity. Its encoding in logic follows as

$$
\begin{aligned}
& q \in (\mathbb{I}^{-1} \circ \mathscr{F}_{(\rho,\sigma)} \circ \mathbb{I})(\mathcal{V})(X_p) \\
\Longleftrightarrow\ & (p,q) \in (\mathscr{F}_{(\rho,\sigma)} \circ \mathbb{I})(\mathcal{V}) && \text{[by definition of } \mathbb{I}^{-1}] \\
\Longleftrightarrow\ & (\forall a,p' : p \xrightarrow{a} p' \Rightarrow \exists b, q'[a\rho b \wedge q \xrightarrow{b} q' \wedge q' \in \mathcal{V}(X_{p'})]) \wedge \\
& (\forall b,q' : q \xrightarrow{b} q' \Rightarrow \exists a, p'[a\sigma b \wedge p \xrightarrow{a} p' \wedge q' \in \mathcal{V}(X_{p'})]) && \text{[by definition of } \mathscr{F}_{(\rho,\sigma)}, \mathbb{I}]
\end{aligned}
$$

We can translate the above two conditions to logic in the following manner

$$
\begin{aligned}
(1)\ & \forall a,p' : p \xrightarrow{a} p' \Rightarrow \exists b, q'[a\rho b \wedge q \xrightarrow{b} q' \wedge q' \in \mathcal{V}(X_{p'})] \\
\Longleftrightarrow\ & \forall a,p' : p \xrightarrow{a} p' \Rightarrow q \in \|\langle a\rangle^{\rho} X_{p'}\|_{\mathcal{V}}^{\mathcal{P}} && \text{[by definition of } \langle a\rangle^{\rho}] \\
\Longleftrightarrow\ & q \in \|\bigwedge_{a,p':p\xrightarrow{a}p'} \langle a\rangle^{\rho} X_{p'}\|_{\mathcal{V}}^{\mathcal{P}} && \text{[by definition of } \wedge]
\end{aligned}
$$

$$
\begin{aligned}
(2)\ & \forall b,q' : q \xrightarrow{b} q' \Rightarrow \exists a, p'[a\sigma b \wedge p \xrightarrow{a} p' \wedge q' \in \mathcal{V}(X_{p'})] \\
\Longleftrightarrow\ & \forall b,q' : q \xrightarrow{b} q' \Rightarrow q' \in \|\bigvee_{a,p':a\sigma b \wedge p\xrightarrow{a}p'} X_{p'}\|_{\mathcal{V}}^{\mathcal{P}} && \text{[by definition of } \vee]
\end{aligned}
$$

Assuming ρ, σ are preorders, $\forall b,q' : q \xrightarrow{b} q' \Rightarrow q' \in \|\bigvee_{a,p':a\sigma b \wedge p\xrightarrow{a}p'} X_{p'}\|_{\mathcal{V}}^{\mathcal{P}}$ is equivalent to $\forall b,c,q' : c\sigma b \wedge q \xrightarrow{c} q' \Rightarrow q' \in \|\bigvee_{a,p':a\sigma b \wedge p\xrightarrow{a}p'} X_{p'}\|_{\mathcal{V}}^{\mathcal{P}}$. First implies the second due to transitivity, which makes $\{(a,p') \mid a\sigma c \wedge p \xrightarrow{a} p'\} \subseteq \{(a,p') \mid a\sigma b \wedge p \xrightarrow{a} p'\}$ whenever $c\sigma b$ holds, and hence $q \in \|\bigvee_{a,p':a\sigma b \wedge p\xrightarrow{a}p'} X_{p'}\|_{\mathcal{V}}^{\mathcal{P}}$ is true whenever $q \in \|\bigvee_{a,p':a\sigma c \wedge p\xrightarrow{a}p'} X_{p'}\|_{\mathcal{V}}^{\mathcal{P}}$ is true. Second implies the first due to reflexivity of σ, giving us,

$$
\begin{aligned}
& \forall b,q' : q \xrightarrow{b} q' \Rightarrow q' \in \|\bigvee_{a,p':a\sigma b \wedge p\xrightarrow{a}p'} X_{p'}\|_{\mathcal{V}}^{\mathcal{P}} \\
\Longleftrightarrow\ & \forall b,c,q' : c\sigma b \wedge q \xrightarrow{c} q' \Rightarrow q' \in \|\bigvee_{a,p':a\sigma b \wedge p\xrightarrow{a}p'} X_{p'}\|_{\mathcal{V}}^{\mathcal{P}} && \text{[by ref. and trans. of } \sigma] \\
\Longleftrightarrow\ & \forall b : q \in \|[b]^{\sigma^{-1}} \bigvee_{a,p':a\sigma b \wedge p\xrightarrow{a}p'} X_{p'}\|_{\mathcal{V}}^{\mathcal{P}} && \text{[by definition of } [b]^{\sigma^{-1}}] \\
\Longleftrightarrow\ & q \in \|\bigwedge_b [b]^{\sigma^{-1}} \bigvee_{a,p':a\sigma b \wedge p\xrightarrow{a}p'} X_{p'}\|_{\mathcal{V}}^{\mathcal{P}} && \text{[by definition of } \wedge]
\end{aligned}
$$

Combining the two, the characteristic equational system, $E^{\mathcal{P}'}_{\sqsubseteq_{(\rho,\sigma)}}$, becomes

$$
X_p = (\bigwedge_{a,p':p\xrightarrow{a}p'} \langle a\rangle^{\rho} X_{p'}) \wedge (\bigwedge_b [b]^{\sigma^{-1}} (\bigvee_{a,p':a\sigma b \wedge p\xrightarrow{a}p'} X_{p'}))
$$

Clearly, if $\mathfrak{L}_p^{\dagger}$ is finite, then the equational system will also be finite. Now for any two actions a, b with $a\rho b$, the formula $\langle b\rangle^{\rho}\varphi$ implies $\langle a\rangle^{\rho}\varphi$. Therefore, if every subset of $\mathcal{A}ct$ has finitely many maximal elements under the ordering ρ, then we can always rewrite $\bigwedge_{a,p':p\xrightarrow{a}p'} \langle a\rangle^{\rho} X_{p'}$ as a finite conjunct. Similarly, $[b]^{\sigma^{-1}}\varphi$ implies $[a]^{\sigma^{-1}}\varphi$ if $a\sigma b$ holds, and $\bigvee_{a,p':a\sigma b \wedge p\xrightarrow{a}p'} X_{p'}$ will be finite if we have only finitely many variables. Therefore, if every subset of $\mathcal{A}ct$ has finitely many maximal elements under the ordering σ, then we can always rewrite $\bigwedge_b [b]^{\sigma^{-1}} (\bigvee_{a,p':a\sigma b \wedge p\xrightarrow{a}p'} X_{p'})$ as a finite conjunct. The following theorem captures this idea,

Theorem 6. *A process p has a finite characteristic formula in $\mathcal{L}^{\mathcal{X}}_{(\rho,\sigma)}$, if ρ and σ are preorders with finitely many maximal elements and every action being less than some maximal element, and $\mathfrak{L}^{\dagger}_p$ is finite with $p_{\mathfrak{L}^{\dagger}_p} \sqsubseteq_{(\rho,\sigma)} p_{\mathfrak{L}}$.* $\qquad\square$

By constructing the characteristic formula of p and model checking it for q, we obtain a procedure for deciding parameterised bisimilarity, $p \sqsubseteq_{(\rho,\sigma)} q$ [10]. Though this requires ρ and σ to have finitely many maximal elements, and $\mathfrak{L}^{\dagger}_p$, $\mathfrak{L}^{\dagger}_q$ to be finite, i.e., the set of reachable initial and terminal states from p and q must be finite.

5   Applications

Weak Bisimilarity and Efficiency Preorder. Expressing concrete bisimulations as parameterised bisimulations may involve LTS transformation, for e.g., weak bisimulation requires the transitive closure of the transition relation under τ actions [4], i.e. extending the action set to sequences $\tau^i a \tau^j$, $i, j \geq 0$. Weak bisimulation [16] is a $(\hat{=}, \hat{=})$-bisimulation over this extended action set, where $\hat{=} = \{(\tau^i, \tau^j) \mid i, j \geq 0\} \cup \{(\tau^i a \tau^j, \tau^{i'} a \tau^{j'}) \mid i, j, i', j' \geq 0, a \in \mathcal{A}ct\}$. This gives the logical characterisation $\mathcal{L}_{(\hat{=},\hat{=})}$, which is identical to observational HML [16]. Similarly, efficiency preorders [5] is a $(\preceq, \preceq)$-bisimulation, where $\preceq = \{(\tau^i, \tau^j) \mid 0 \leq i \leq j\} \cup \{(\tau^i a \tau^j, \tau^{i'} a \tau^{j'}) \mid 0 \leq i + j \leq i' + j', i, j, i', j' \geq 0, a \in \mathcal{A}ct\}$. Its logical characterisation $\mathcal{L}_{(\preceq,\preceq)}$, however, differs from the existing one [17].

Covariant-Contravariant Simulation. The classical view of process simulation assumes all actions to be input actions, which the user may trigger. The simulating process must simulate all the input actions of the process being simulated. But in the presence of output actions, this condition is reversed. This forms the intuition for defining covariant-contravariant simulations [11].

Definition 15. *Let $\mathcal{P}$ be the set of process states and $\mathcal{A}ct$ be the set of actions which can be partitioned into the sets $\mathcal{A}ct^r$, $\mathcal{A}ct^l$ and $\mathcal{A}ct^{bi}$. A binary relation $R \subseteq \mathcal{P} \times \mathcal{P}$ is a covariant-contravariant simulation if $p \, R \, q$ implies the following conditions*

$$\forall a \in \mathcal{A}ct^r \cup \mathcal{A}ct^{bi}[p \xrightarrow{a} p' \Rightarrow \exists q'[q \xrightarrow{a} q' \wedge p' \, R \, q']]$$

$$\forall a \in \mathcal{A}ct^l \cup \mathcal{A}ct^{bi}[q \xrightarrow{a} q' \Rightarrow \exists p'[p \xrightarrow{a} p' \wedge p' \, R \, q']$$

We will write $p \lesssim_{CC} q$, if there is a covariant-contravariant simulation R such that $p \, R \, q$.

The covariant-contravariant simulation, defined above, ignores the $\mathcal{A}ct^l$ transitions for p and $\mathcal{A}ct^r$ transitions for q. To specify it as an instance of parameterised bisimulation, we introduce a special state $\mathbf{0}$, such that from every process p there is a transition $p \xrightarrow{!} \mathbf{0}$, and there is only one transition from $\mathbf{0}$, that is to itself as $\mathbf{0} \xrightarrow{*} \mathbf{0}$, where $!, *$ are new action labels. Now covariant-contravariant simulation can be instantiated as parameterised bisimulation by setting $\rho = Id^{\mathcal{A}ct} \cup \{(a, !)|a \in \mathcal{A}ct^l\} \cup \{(a, *)|a \in \mathcal{A}ct\} \cup \{(!, !), (*, *), (*, !\}$ and $\sigma^{-1} = Id^{\mathcal{A}ct} \cup \{(a, !)|a \in \mathcal{A}ct^r\} \cup \{(a, *)|a \in \mathcal{A}ct\} \cup \{(!, !), (*, *), (*, !\}$. All processes will be (ρ, σ)-bisimilar to $\mathbf{0}$. Also, $\mathbf{0}$ satisfies every formula $\psi \in \mathcal{L}_{(\rho, \sigma^{-1})}$. As a consequence, every process p will satisfy any formula of the form $\langle ! \rangle^\rho \psi$, and hence $\langle a \rangle^\rho \psi$ where $a \in \mathcal{A}ct^l$, as well as $\langle * \rangle^\rho \psi$, for any $\psi \in \mathcal{L}_{(\rho, \sigma^{-1})}$. Similar argument also holds for $[!]^{\sigma^{-1}} \psi$, $[*]^{\sigma^{-1}} \psi$ and $[a]^{\sigma^{-1}} \psi$, where $a \in \mathcal{A}ct^r$ and ψ is any formula in $\mathcal{L}_{(\rho, \sigma)}$. If we remove these modalities, we are only left with $\langle a \rangle^\rho$, where $a \in \mathcal{A}ct^r \cup \mathcal{A}ct^{bi}$ and $[a]^{\sigma^{-1}}$, where $a \in \mathcal{A}ct^l \cup \mathcal{A}ct^{bi}$, and ρ, σ are identity relations over these actions. This is exactly the logical characterisation given in [12] for covariant-contravariant simulation.

Time Abstracted Bisimilarity and Timed Prebisimulation. Timed LTS is a special class of LTS, where the label set is of the form $\mathcal{A}ct \cup \mathbb{R}_{\geq 0}$, where the labels in $\mathbb{R}_{\geq 0}$ correspond to delay observations. The strong bisimulation over Timed LTS is also referred as Timed bisimulation. In general, the timed bisimilarity over arbitrary Timed LTS is undecidable, but it becomes decidable when restricted to Timed LTS generated from Timed Automata [3]. The Timed LTS generated from Timed Automata has deterministic delays, that is, there is a unique successor state for every delay transition. This, in turn, implies image-finiteness, and hence the logical characterisation for strong bisimilarity also works for timed bisimilarity.

Time abstracted bisimulation [20], which relaxes the condition of matching a delay transition with any other delay transition, irrespective of the delay amount, is another interesting behavioural equivalence over Timed LTS. As noted in Sect. 3, time abstracted bisimulation [16] is a $(\simeq, \simeq)$-bisimulation, where $\simeq = \mathcal{I}d_{\mathcal{A}ct} \cup (\mathbb{R}_{\geq 0} \times \mathbb{R}_{\geq 0})$. It is also decidable for TLTS generated from timed automata. In fact one can apply zone abstraction [6] to obtain a finite abstracted LTS, as all states in the same zone are time abstracted bisimilar. Since a finite abstracted LTS is always image-finite, we obtain $\mathcal{L}_{(\simeq, \simeq)}$ as the logical characterisation for time abstracted bisimilarity.

Similarly, timed prebisimulation [15] is a $(\gtrsim, \gtrsim)$-bisimulation, where $\gtrsim = Id_{\mathcal{A}ct} \cup \geq_{\mathbb{R}}$. Again we can apply zone abstraction, and use zone endpoints to obtain a finite abstracted LTS for TLTS generated from timed automata. However we require infinitesimal δ-delays, of the form $d + \delta$ or $d - \delta$, to define zone endpoints when zone boundaries are given by strict inequalities. This is also why the decidability result for timed prebisimilarity based on zone abstraction is restricted to one clock timed automata [15]. This technique can only be applied to one clock timed automata, as δ delays for multiple clocks are incomparable. We can remove the δ-delays from our logical characterisation, by noting that $\langle d - \delta \rangle^\geq = \langle d \rangle^\geq$, $\langle d + \delta \rangle^\geq = \langle d \rangle^>$, $[d - \delta]^\leq = [d]^<$, and $[d + \delta]^\leq = [d]^\leq$. Hence we obtain the following as logical characterisation for timed prebisimilarity over TLTS generated from one clock timed automata.

$$\varphi := \langle a \rangle \varphi \mid [a] \varphi \mid \langle d \rangle^\geq \varphi \mid [d]^\leq \varphi \mid \langle d \rangle^> \varphi \mid [d]^< \varphi \mid \varphi_1 \wedge \varphi_2 \mid \varphi_1 \vee \varphi_2$$

where $a \in \mathcal{A}ct$ and $d \in \mathbb{R}_{\geq 0}$. We refer the reader to [26] for detailed proof.

6   Conclusion and Future Work

Parameterised HML, $\mathcal{L}_{(\rho,\sigma)}$, generalises HML as the logical characterisation for parameterised bisimulations. By selecting suitable relations on actions, one readily obtains the existing characterisations of strong and weak bisimulation, covariant-contravariant simulation [12], and novel characterisations for prebisimilarity relations like efficiency preorder [17], timed prebisimulation [15], etc.

The characterisation immediately yields distinguishing formulae between non-bisimilar processes. However it requires (ρ,σ)-image-finiteness upto (ρ,σ)-bisimilarity, in which case non-bisimilar processes have a finite distinguishing behaviour. Consequently, we obtain the algorithm for generating distinguishing formulae when the processes are (ρ,σ)-image-finite and have a decidability procedure for (ρ,σ)-bisimilarity.

The extension of parameterised HML with fixed point operators, $\mathcal{L}^{\mathcal{X}}_{(\rho,\sigma)}$, remains invariant under the corresponding parameterised bisimulation, while increasing its power to allow expressing characteristic formulae for finite-state processes. Model checking of characteristic formula may yield efficient algorithms for deciding behavioural relations [10], and is worth studying in the context of parameterised bisimulations.

Generating distinguishing formula requires image-finiteness; similarly the existence of finite characteristic formula is only guaranteed for finite-state systems. Interestingly, these results may be extended to infinite-state systems through abstracted LTS. Infinite-state systems with quantitative aspects, like time, may offer interesting instantiations of parameterised bisimulations, and can become a good application domain for these results.

The expressive power of parameterised HML is another area worth investigating. This may involve generalizing the correspondence results for modal logic and strong bisimulation [7], and may help in relating this logic to (ρ,σ)-bisimulation invariant fragments of classical logics. This will enable us to compare our logical characterisation with the existing ones, where they differ.

References

1. Aceto, L., Fábregas, I., de Frutos-Escrig, D., Ingólfsdóttir, A., Palomino, M.: Graphical representation of covariant-contravariant modal formulae (2011). arXiv:1108.4464
2. Aceto, L., Ingólfsdóttir, A., et al.: Characteristic formulae for fixed-point semantics. Math. Struct. Comput. Sci. **22**, 125–173 (2012)
3. Alur, R., Dill, D.L.: A theory of timed automata. Theoret. Comput. Sci. **126**, 183–235 (1994)
4. Arun-Kumar, S.: On bisimilarities induced by relations on actions. In: SEFM 2006, pp. 41–49. IEEE (2006)
5. Arun-Kumar, S., Hennessy, M.: An efficiency preorder for processes. Acta Inform. **29**(8), 737–760 (1992)

6. Bengtsson, J., Yi, W.: On clock difference constraints and termination in reachability analysis of timed automata. In: Dong, J.S., Woodcock, J. (eds.) ICFEM 2003. LNCS, vol. 2885, pp. 491–503. Springer, Heidelberg (2003). doi:10.1007/978-3-540-39893-6_28

7. Van Benthem, J.: Modal correspondence theory. Ph.D. thesis, University of Amsterdam (1976)

8. Birkhoff, G.: Lattice Theory, vol. 25. American Mathematical Society, Providence (1967)

9. Boudol, G., Larsen, K.G.: Graphical versus logical specifications. Theoret. Comput. Sci. **106**(1), 3–20 (1992)

10. Cleaveland, R., Steffen, B.: Computing behavioural relations, logically. In: Albert, J.L., Monien, B., Artalejo, M.R. (eds.) ICALP 1991. LNCS, vol. 510, pp. 127–138. Springer, Heidelberg (1991). doi:10.1007/3-540-54233-7_129

11. Fábregas, I., de Frutos Escrig, D., Palomino, M.: Non-strongly stable orders also define interesting simulation relations. In: Kurz, A., Lenisa, M., Tarlecki, A. (eds.) CALCO 2009. LNCS, vol. 5728, pp. 221–235. Springer, Heidelberg (2009). doi:10.1007/978-3-642-03741-2_16

12. Fábregas, I., de Frutos Escrig, D., Palomino, M.: Logics for contravariant simulations. In: Hatcliff, J., Zucca, E. (eds.) FMOODS/FORTE -2010. LNCS, vol. 6117, pp. 224–231. Springer, Heidelberg (2010). doi:10.1007/978-3-642-13464-7_18

13. Gierz, G., Scott, D.S., et al.: Continuous Lattices and Domains, vol. 93. Cambridge University Press, Cambridge (2003)

14. Graf, S., Sifakis, J.: A modal characterization of observational congruence on finite terms of CCS. Inf. Control **68**(1), 125–145 (1986)

15. Guha, S., Narayan, C., Arun-Kumar, S.: On decidability of prebisimulation for timed automata. In: Madhusudan, P., Seshia, S.A. (eds.) CAV 2012. LNCS, vol. 7358, pp. 444–461. Springer, Heidelberg (2012). doi:10.1007/978-3-642-31424-7_33

16. Hennessy, M., Milner, R.: Algebraic laws for nondeterminism and concurrency. J. ACM **32**(1), 137–161 (1985)

17. Korade, N., Arun-Kumar, S.: A logical characterization of efficiency preorders. In: Liu, Z., Araki, K. (eds.) ICTAC 2004. LNCS, vol. 3407, pp. 99–112. Springer, Heidelberg (2005). doi:10.1007/978-3-540-31862-0_9

18. Kozen, D.: Results on the propositional μ-calculus. In: Nielsen, M., Schmidt, E.M. (eds.) ICALP 1982. LNCS, vol. 140, pp. 348–359. Springer, Heidelberg (1982). doi:10.1007/BFb0012782

19. Laroussinie, F., Larsen, K.G., Weise, C.: From timed automata to logic — and back. In: Wiedermann, J., Hájek, P. (eds.) MFCS 1995. LNCS, vol. 969, pp. 529–539. Springer, Heidelberg (1995). doi:10.1007/3-540-60246-1_158

20. Larsen, K.G., Yi, W.: Time abstracted bisimulation: implicit specifications and decidability. In: Brookes, S., Main, M., Melton, A., Mislove, M., Schmidt, D. (eds.) MFPS 1993. LNCS, vol. 802, pp. 160–176. Springer, Heidelberg (1994). doi:10.1007/3-540-58027-1_8

21. Milner, R.: Communication and Concurrency. Prentice-Hall, Inc., Upper Saddle River (1989)

22. Müller-Olm, M.: Derivation of characteristic formulae. Electron. Notes Theoret. Comput. Sci. **18**, 159–170 (1998)

23. Park, D.: Concurrency and automata on infinite sequences. In: Deussen, P. (ed.) GI-TCS 1981. LNCS, vol. 104, pp. 167–183. Springer, Heidelberg (1981). doi:10.1007/BFb0017309

24. Sangiorgi, D.: On the origins of bisimulation and coinduction. ACM Trans. Program. Lang. Syst. **31**(4), 15:1–15:41 (2009)

25. Logical characterisation proofs, July 2017. http://www.cse.iitd.ac.in/~bagga/detailedProofs.pdf

26. Timed bisimulations as parameterised bisimulations, July 2017. http://www.cse.iitd.ac.in/~bagga/TimedBisimulations.pdf

27. Steffen, B., Ingólfsdóttir, A.: Characteristic formulas for processes with divergence. Inf. Comput. **110**(1), 149–163 (1994)

28. Stirling, C.: Modal and temporal logics for processes. In: Moller, F., Birtwistle, G. (eds.) Logics for Concurrency. LNCS, vol. 1043, pp. 149–237. Springer, Heidelberg (1996). doi:10.1007/3-540-60915-6_5

29. Tarski, A., et al.: A lattice-theoretical fixpoint theorem and its applications. Pac. J. Math. **5**(2), 285–309 (1955)

30. Van Benthem, J.: Correspondence theory. In: Gabbay, D., Guenthner, F. (eds.) Handbook of Philosophical Logic. Synthese Library (Studies in Epistemology, Logic, Methodology, and Philosophy of Science), vol. 165, pp. 167–247. Springer, Heidelberg (1984). doi:10.1007/978-94-009-6259-0_4

31. van Glabbeek, R.J.: The linear time - branching time spectrum. In: Baeten, J.C.M., Klop, J.W. (eds.) CONCUR 1990. LNCS, vol. 458, pp. 278–297. Springer, Heidelberg (1990). doi:10.1007/BFb0039066

A Probabilistic Semantics for the Pure λ-Calculus

Alessandra Di Pierro[✉]

Dipartimento di Informatica, Università di Verona, Verona, Italy
alessandra.dipierro@univr.it

Abstract. From a programming language viewpoint, the λ-calculus for-
malises several features of the modern description of computation and
its implementation. We present a denotational semantics for the untyped
calculus that captures a basic feature of probabilistic programming languages, namely probability distributions as both the objects and the
result of a computation.

1 Introduction

Although probabilistic programming is today a well-established discipline, a theory similar to the pure λ-calculus has not yet been fully developed in that setting.
In this paper we address the problem of defining a probabilistic model for the
pure λ-calculus which could serve as a basis for the design of functional programming languages and their semantics. We concentrate here on the denotational
approach which is central for expressing the functional meaning of a program
and is therefore an essential basis for several program analyses.

The idea we intend to develop in this work is that a natural model for probabilistic behaviours can be found in linear algebra and that their analysis is
nothing else than a calculus for finding the solution of linear systems of differ-
ential equations.

It is well known that the choice of a suitable denotational domain for the
pure λ-calculus is problematic due to its type-free character: one has to use
the same domain for denoting both the data and the program. In 1969, Scott
solved the problem for the pure λ-calculus by restricting to cpo's and continuous
functions. We show here that, in analogy to the fundamental results of Scott,
we can identify a solution by considering Hilbert spaces and bounded linear
operators on them. This can be achieved essentially by defining a lifting of the
classical Scott's semantics to a probabilistic interpretation of the pure un-typed
λ-calculus

$$exp ::= var \mid \lambda \, var.exp \mid exp \, exp, \tag{1}$$

and is sufficient to make the pure calculus a foundation for probabilistic (functional) programming. The idea is to define an *environment* as an assignment of
probability distributions to variables. This corresponds to considering the variables of the calculus as *random variables*. Thus the semantic domain could simply
be a set of distributions. However, in order to define a meaning function, $[\![-]\!]$,

D.V. Hung and D. Kapur (Eds.): ICTAC 2017, LNCS 10580, pp. 70–76, 2017.
DOI: 10.1007/978-3-319-67729-3_5

that suitably associates to each λ-expression a probabilistic value, we will define both the environment and the domain as vector spaces and, as a consequence, $\llbracket - \rrbracket$ as a linear operator.

2 Domain Equation

It is well-known that a classical model for the λ-calculus is a reflexive object in the Cartesian Closed Category of complete partial orders (cpo's) and Scott-continuous functions [1]. A set D is a reflexive object if $[D \to D]$, the cpo of all Scott-continuous functions from D to D is a retract of D, i.e. there are continuous maps $F : D \to [D \to D]$ and $G : [D \to D] \to D$ such that $F \cdot G = Id_{[D \to D]}$. In the literature, this kind of models are referred to as continuously complete λ-models (all continuous functions defined on them are representable).

In this section we show how a reflexive domain for the pure λ-calculus can be defined, which supports probabilistic computation. To this purpose we consider *Hilbert spaces* and use their mathematical properties to construct a denotational semantics for the pure λ-calculus as defined by the grammar in Eq. 1.

2.1 The Hilbert Space ℓ^2

A Hilbert space is defined as a complete inner product space [2]. We recall that a inner product space is a vector space V endowed with an *inner product*, i.e. a scalar function $\langle \cdot, \cdot \rangle : V \to \mathbb{C}$ satisfying the following properties:

- $\langle x, y \rangle = \overline{\langle y, x \rangle}$, (where the bar indicates complex conjugation)
- $\langle \alpha x + \beta y, z \rangle = \langle \alpha x, z \rangle + \langle \beta y, z \rangle$,
- $\langle x, y \rangle \geq 0$,
- $\langle x, x \rangle = 0$ implies $x = 0$.

By completeness of an inner product space E, we mean completeness of E as a normed space with the norm defined by the inner product.

A well-known result of the theory of operator algebras states that every separable Hilbert space is isomorphic to the 'standard' Hilbert space of infinite vectors [3, Corollary 2.2.13], [2, Theorem 3.4.27]

$$\ell^2 = \{(x_i)_{i \in \mathbb{N}} \mid x_i \in \mathbb{C} \text{ and } \sum_{i \in \mathbb{N}} |x_i|^2 < \infty\}$$

with standard norm $\|x\|_2 = \|(x_i)_{i \in \mathbb{N}}\|_2 = \sqrt{\sum_{i \in \mathbb{N}} |x_i|^2}$. This is a Hilbert space with respect to the inner product defined by

$$\langle x, y \rangle = \sum_{i \in \mathbb{N}} x_i \bar{y}_i, \tag{2}$$

for $x = (x_1, x_2, x_3, \dots)$ and $y = (y_1, y_2, y_3, \dots)$ sequences of complex numbers in ℓ^2 ($\bar{z}$ stands for the complex conjugate of z).

Moreover, an important result states that every Hilbert space H is a *reflexive domain*; in functional analysis this means that there is an isomorphism between H and its double dual H^{**}, that is the space of all linear bounded functionals on the dual space H^*, which in turn is the space of all linear bounded functionals on H. We will give here this result since it is important in the construction of our probabililistic domain D and in particular of linear functionals $F : D \to [D \to D]$ and $G : [D \to D] \to D$ such that $F \circ G$ is the identity in $[D \to D]$. The proof is based on the following important theorem known as the *Riesz representation theorem* [2, Theorem 3.7.7]

Theorem 1. *Let f be a bounded linear functional on a Hilbert space H. There exists exactly one $x_0 \in H$, called the representer, such that $f(x) = \langle x, x_0 \rangle$ for all $x \in H$. Moreover, we have that $\|f\| = \|x_0\|$.*

We recall that there exists a canonical embedding, $C : H \to H^{**}$, from a Hilbert space H into its double dual H^{**}. This is *natural*, both in the intuitive sense and in the formal sense of natural transformations: it turns an element of a Hilbert space H into a linear functional on linear functions on H as follows. Let x be an element of H and let f be an element of H^*. The action of x on f is simply $f(x)$. That is, x acts on linear functions by letting them act on it or, in other words, by evaluating f at the element x of H.

Theorem 2. *Every Hilbert space H is reflexive.*

Proof. It is sufficient to show that the canonical embedding $C : H \to H^{**}$ is surjective, i.e. $H^{**} = \{g_x \mid x \in H\}$. Since H^* is a Hilbert space, the Riesz representation theorem guarantees that any linear bounded linear functional g on H^* has a unique representer $f_g \in H^*$, i.e. for all $f \in H^*, g(f) = \langle f, f_g \rangle$ with $\|g\| = \|f_g\|$. As f_g is a bounded linear functional on H we can apply again the Riesz representation theorem and obtain that for all $x \in H, f_g(x) = \langle x, x_{f_g} \rangle$ with $\|f_g\| = \|x_{f_g}\|$. This shows that for every $g \in H^{**}$ we can construct a unique $x \in H$ such that $g = g_x$.

2.2   The Probabilistic Domain D

Let $\mathcal{V}$ be the countable set of all possible values that can be assigned to the variables *var* of the λ-calculus in Eq. 1. Then we can define the Hilbert space, $\ell^2(\mathcal{V})$ as the space of all square-summable functions [4]:

$$\ell^2(\mathcal{V}) = \{f : \mathcal{V} \to \mathbb{R} \mid \sum_{v \in \mathcal{V}} |f(v)|^2 \leq \infty\}.$$

This space contains the space $Dist(\mathcal{V})$ of all discrete probability distributions on $\mathcal{V}$, that is the space of sequences $(x_1, x_2, x_3, \dots)$ of real numbers with only a finite number of non-zero terms and such that $\sum_i x_i = 1$. Probability distributions on values are the obvious results of term reduction in the probabilistic interpretation of the λ-calculus. However, although $Dist(\mathcal{V})$ is an inner product space with the inner product defined by Eq. 2, it is not a Hilbert space because it is not complete: there are Cauchy sequences in $Dist(\mathcal{V})$ whose limit is not in $Dist(\mathcal{V})$ (these sequences converge in $\ell^2(\mathcal{V})$, cf. Example 3.3.4 in [2]). Therefore, we will not restrict to this space for the definition of a probabilistic denotational semantics, as it would not allow us to exploit the reflexivity property of Hilbert spaces, but will consider $D = \ell^2(\mathcal{V})$ as our denotational domain.

We now show how to define a retract $[D \to D]$ demonstrating that D is a suitable domain for a denotational semantics of the untyped λ-calculus.

Let $D^* = \ell^2(\mathcal{V})^*$ be the dual space of D, that is the space of all bounded linear functionals on D. A linear operator A is called bounded if there is a number k such that $\|Ax\| \le k\|x\|$ for every x in the domain of A. The norm of A is defined as the infimum of all such numbers k, or equivalently, by $\|A\| = \sup_{\|x\|=1} \|Ax\|$.

It is well known that if H is a Hilbert space then for any $v \in H$, $f_v(x) = \langle v, x \rangle_H$ defines a unique bounded linear functional on H. Similarly, we can apply the Riesz representation theorem and construct a representer x_0 for f_v such that $f_v(x) = \langle x, x_0 \rangle_H$ with $\|f_v\| = \|x_0\|$. In fact, there exists an isometric isomorphism between H and H^* that allows us to identify them. Thus, every vector in our domain D can be dually seen as a functional on D. Intuitively, this means that we can look at vectors $v \in H$ also as linear operators $f_v \in H^*$.

We can now construct a retract for D as the double dual space $D^{**} = [D^* \to D^*]$, that is the space of all bounded linear operators on D^* and define $F : D \to [D^* \to D^*]$ and $G : [D^* \to D^*] \to D$ as below.

For the definition of $F : D \to [D^* \to D^*]$ we can use the canonical embedding of D in D^{**} and construct F as

$$F(z) = g_z, \text{ with } g_z(f(x)) = f(x) \text{ for all } x \in D.$$

In order to define $G : [D^* \to D^*] \to D$, we use the reflexivity of D that guarantees the existence for every $g \in D^{**}$ of an element $x \in D$ such that $g = g_x$.

$$G(g) = z, \text{ with } z \text{ constructed as in the proof of Theorem 2.}$$

We give here a more explicit construction of the element in D associated by G to a functional in D^{**}.

Construction of x_{f_g}. Given an arbitrary $g \in D^{**}$, consider an element f of the space D^* on which g acts. By Theorem 1, we can represent f as

$$f(x) = \langle x, z \rangle, \text{ for some } z \in D. \tag{3}$$

This gives us a map $A : D^* \to D$ by $A(f) = z$. By using this map we can define an inner product on D^* as $\langle f_1, f_2 \rangle = \langle Af_2, Af_1 \rangle$[1]. We know that D^* with this inner product is a Hilbert space, thus we can apply again Theorem 1 and obtain for $g \in [D^* \to D^*]$ the representation $g(f) = \langle f, f_0 \rangle$ for some $f_0 \in D^*$. Now by the definition in 3 we have

---

[1] We can show that this indeed defines a inner product.

$$g(f) = \langle f, f_0 \rangle$$
$$= \langle Af_0, Af \rangle$$
$$= \langle x, z \rangle,$$

and we can take $x_{f_g} = z$. Thus the linear functional G assigns to each $g \in D^{**}$ the representer in D of its argument f, that is effectively $f(x)$.

With these definitions of F and G, it is immediate to see that $G(F(x)) = x$. In fact, we have:

$$G(F(z)(f(x))) = G(g_z(f(x))) = z.$$

Moreover, they are continuous maps since they are bounded[2].

2.3   Semantic Equations

We define $\mathcal{E}nv$ as the set of all functions $\rho : Var \to \ell^2(\mathcal{V})$, where Var denotes the set of all variables. We call these functions *environments*. The semantic function assigning a meaning to the term of the λ-calculus is the map

$$[\![-]\!] : exp \to \rho \to D$$

that we define inductively by:

$[\![c]\!] = c$ if c is a constant

$[\![x]\!] = \rho(x) \in Dist(\mathcal{V})$ (discrete probablity distribution for the random variable x)

$[\![e_1 e_2]\!] = ([\![e_1]\!]\rho)([\![e_2]\!]\rho)$

$[\![\lambda x.e]\!] = G(F(d)([\![e]\!]\rho[x := d]))$

We now present two simple examples demonstrating this semantics. For simplicity we will write terms by using abbreviations containing 'impure' terms that do not belong to the grammar in Eq. 1, such as predefined constants including list of numerals (e.g. b, c) and function identifiers (e.g. f). It is well known that the pure λ-calculus is able to express all of the common constants and functions of arithmetic and list manipulation (see e.g. [5]).

As a first example consider the term $\lambda x. f(x)$, with $f(x) = x + y$. The semantics $[\![\lambda x.f(x)]\!]$ of this term in a given environment ρ such that $\rho(y) = v$ can be evaluated as follows.

$$[\![\lambda x.f(x)]\!]\rho = G(F(d)([\![f(d)]\!]\rho)) = d + v = f(d)$$

Note that the value $d + v$ must be considered in this case as a function in D^*.

As another example, consider $(\lambda x.f(x))(b)$, with $f(x) = x + c$ and $b = (0, 0, 1, 0 \ldots)$ representing the number 3. Suppose that c is a constant representing the distribution $(\frac{1}{3}, \frac{2}{3}, 0, \ldots)$, i.e. the values 1 and 2 with probability $\frac{1}{3}$ and $\frac{2}{3}$, respectively. We have:

$$[\![(\lambda x.f(x))(b)]\!]\rho = ([\![\lambda x.f(x)]\!]\rho)[b]\rho = f(b) = b + (\frac{1}{3}, \frac{2}{3}, 0, \ldots) = (\frac{1}{6}, \frac{1}{3}, \frac{1}{2}, 0, \ldots).$$

---

[2] It can be shown that a linear mapping is continuous if and only if it is bounded. For a proof see Theorem 1.5.7 of [2].

The resulting vector is now a constant representing the values $1, 2, 3$ with probability $\frac{1}{6}$, $\frac{1}{3}$ and $\frac{1}{2}$ respectively. Note that we had to normalise the vector entries in order to get a probability distribution. This assumption would not be necessary in a probabilistic reduction involving only probability distributions.

3   Related and Future Work

We have presented a probabilistic denotational semantics for the untyped λ-calculus which gives a probabilistic interpretation of the classical λ-terms, thus providing a formal basis for probabilistic functional programming.

We are not aware of previous work addressing the problem of defining a probabilistic semantics of the untyped lambda calculus. A recent book by Dirk Draheim [6] contains an extensive review of the various semantics of the probabilistic typed λ-calculus that have been defined up to now. Note that typically the operational semantics for these calculi refers to a λ-calculus that extends the classical one by adding a term for probabilistic choice. Although the syntax is different from the one we adopted in this work, from the semantical viewpoint random choice and random variables are two perfectly equivalent constructs for expressing probabilistic computation. Thus, there are in principle no obstacles in applying our probabilistic interpretation to an untyped version of these calculi.

Chapter 5 of Draheim's book gives a full account of the various approaches to the denotational semantics of the λ-calculus that have been presented in the literature. These approaches all refer to a semantics of types and to the interpretation of probabilistic programs as continuous functions from values to set of probability distributions. The only reference related to the untyped λ-calculus is [7], where a denotational semantics is defined in terms of probabilistic coherent spaces, which is adequate for a probabilistic extension of the classical untyped λ-calculus. Similarly to our approach, this model is based on the construction of a denotational domain as a reflexive object (no powerdomain monad is needed). However, this construction uses morphisms that are power series with non negative real coefficients. This is different from Scott's model D_∞ but is also substantially different from our construction which is based instead on homogeneous functions on probability distributions.

Finally, we would like to mention the work [8], where two alternative approaches to the definition of a probabilistic semantics are introduced in the general setting of programming languages. One of these approaches, called in the paper Semantics 1, is similar in principle to the approach we have followed in our work, in as far as it is based on the assumption that input variables are random variables. This semantics essentially treats probabilistic programs as deterministic ones whose execution refers to an explicit stack where random numbers are kept to allow the execution of random calls. As the author himself argues, this has several limitations especially in applications based on probabilistic semantics such as e.g. program analysis. In such cases a denotational approach like the one of Semantics 2 (the second approach introduced in the paper) would be more appropriate. The denotational semantics we have introduced here for the untyped λ-calculus was inspired by both the approaches in [8] and we believe that its implementation for concrete probabilistic programming languages could enjoy the positive features of Semantics 1 such as the fact of being closer to classical probability theory and therefore more intuitive and operational, and Semantics 2 such as compositionality and therefore suitability for program analysis.

References

1. Barendregt, H.P.: The Lambda Calculus. Studies in Logic and the Foundations of Mathematics, vol. 103. North-Holland, Amsterdam (1991). revised edn
2. Debnath, L., Mikusinski, P.: Introduction to Hilbert Spaces with Applications. 3rd revised edn. Elsevier Science Publishing, San Diego (2005). reprint from Academic Press edition 2005
3. Kadison, R., Ringrose, J.: Fundamentals of the Theory of Operator Algebras: Volume I – Elementary Theory. Graduate Studies in Mathematics, vol. 15. American Mathematical Society, Providence (1997). reprint from Academic Press edition 1983
4. Roman, S.: Advanced Linear Algebra, 2nd edn. Springer, Heidelberg (2005)
5. Slonneger, K., Kurtz, B.: Formal Syntax and Semantics of Programming Languages: A Laboratory Based Approach, 1st edn. Addison-Wesley Longman Publishing Co., Inc., Boston (1995)
6. Draheim, D.: Semantics of the Probabilistic Typed Lambda Calculus - Markov Chain Semantics, Termination Behavior, and Denotational Semantics. Springer, Heidelberg (2017). doi:10.1007/978-3-642-55198-7
7. Ehrhard, T., Pagani, M., Tasson, C.: The computational meaning of probabilistic coherence spaces. In: 2011 IEEE 26th Annual Symposium on Logic in Computer Science, pp. 87–96 (2011)
8. Kozen, D.: Semantics of probabilistic programs. J. Comput. Syst. Sci. **22**(3), 328–350 (1981)

Software Components and Concurrency

Towards a Calculus for Dynamic Architectures

Diego Marmsoler[(✉)]

Technische Universität München, Munich, Germany
`diego.marmsoler@tum.de`

Abstract. The architecture of a system describes the system's overall organization into components and connections between those components. With the emergence of mobile computing, dynamic architectures have become increasingly important. In such architectures, components may appear or disappear, and connections may change over time. The dynamic nature of such architectures makes reasoning about their behavior difficult. Since components can be activated and deactivated over time, their behavioral specifications depend on their state of activation. To address this problem, we introduce a calculus for dynamic architectures in a natural deduction style. Therefore, we provide introduction and elimination rules for several operators traditionally employed to specify component behavior. Finally, we show *soundness* and *relative completeness* of these rules. The calculus can be used to reason about component behavior in a dynamic environment. This is demonstrated by applying it to verify a property of dynamic blackboard architectures.

Keywords: Dynamic architectures · Component calculus · Architecture verification · Configuration traces · Behavior traces

1 Introduction

A system's architecture provides a set of components and connections between their ports. With the emergence of mobile computing, dynamic architectures have become more and more important [2,8,16]. In such architectures, components can appear and disappear, and connections can change, both over time. Dynamic architectures can be modeled in terms of configuration traces [14,15]. Consider, for example, the execution trace of a dynamic architecture depicted in Fig. 1. The figure shows the first three configurations of one possible execution of a dynamic architecture composed of three components c_1, c_2, and c_3. To facilitate the specification of such architectures, they can be separated into behavioral specifications for components, activation specifications, and connection specifications [15]. Thereby, behavior of components is often specified by means of temporal logic formulæ [13] over the components interface. Consider, for example, a component c_3 with output port o_1 whose behavior is given by the temporal specification "$\bigcirc(o_1 = 8)$", meaning that it outputs an 8 on its port o_1 at time point 1 (assuming that time starts at 0).

© Springer International Publishing AG 2017
D.V. Hung and D. Kapur (Eds.): ICTAC 2017, LNCS 10580, pp. 79–99, 2017.
DOI: 10.1007/978-3-319-67729-3_6

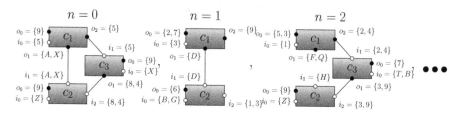

Fig. 1. Execution trace of a dynamic architecture.

For *static* architectures, the original specification of temporal properties of single components remain valid even when deployed to the architecture. The original specification of component c_3, for example, is still valid when deployed to a static architecture, i.e., c_3 will still output an 8 on its port o_1 at time point 1, even if deployed to the architecture. For *dynamic* architectures, on the other hand, the traditional interpretation of temporal specifications of the behavior of components is not valid anymore. For example, it is not clear whether the trace depicted in Fig. 1 actually fulfills the original specification of component c_3, since c_3 is not active at time point 1 ($n = 1$).

So, how can we reason about the behavior of components deployed to dynamic architectures? To answer this question, in the following we provide a calculus for dynamic architectures. It formalizes reasoning about the behavior of a component when it can be activated and deactivated. In the spirit of natural deduction, we provide introduction and elimination rules for each temporal operator. Finally, we show *soundness* and relative *completeness* of the calculus. As a practical implication, our calculus can be used to support the verification of properties for dynamic architectures. This is demonstrated by means of the blackboard pattern for dynamic architectures. To this end, we apply the calculus to verify a characteristic property of the pattern.

The remainder of the paper is structured as follows: First, we introduce our model for dynamic architectures in Sect. 2. In Sect. 3, we then provide the notion of behavior assertions and behavior trace assertions as means to specify the behavior of components. In Sect. 4, we introduce our calculus, which allows us to reason about component behavior in a dynamic context. Sect. 5 then demonstrates the practical usability of the calculus by applying it to verify a property of dynamic blackboard architectures. Finally, we conclude our discussion with a review of related work in Sect. 6 and a brief summary of the major contributions of this paper in Sect. 7.

2   A Model of Dynamic Architectures

In [15], we introduce a model for dynamic architectures based on the notion of configuration traces. Our model is based on Broy's Focus theory [3] and an adaptation of its dynamic extension [4]. In this section, we briefly summarize the main concepts of the model and extend it with the notion of behavior traces to model the behavior of single components.

2.1   Foundations: Ports, Valuations, and Components

In our model, components communicate by exchanging *messages* over *ports*. Thus, we assume the existence of sets M and P containing all messages and ports, respectively.

Port Valuations. Ports can be valuated by messages. Roughly speaking, a valuation for a set of ports is an assignment of messages to each port.

Definition 1 (Port Valuation). *For a set of ports $P \subseteq \mathsf{P}$, we denote by $\overline{P}$ the set of all possible PVs, formally:*

$$\overline{P} \;\overset{def}{=}\; (P \rightarrow \wp(\mathsf{M})).$$

Moreover, we denote by $[p_1, p_2, \dots \mapsto \{m_1\}, \{m_2\}, \dots]$ the valuation of ports $p_1, p_2, \dots$ with sets $\{m_1\}, \{m_2\}, \dots$, respectively. For singleton sets we shall sometimes omit the set parentheses and simply write $[p_1, p_2, \dots \mapsto m_1, m_2, \dots]$.

Note that in our model, ports can be valuated by a *set* of messages, meaning that a component can send/receive no message, a single message, or multiple messages at each point in time.

Components. In our model, the basic unit of computation is a component. It consists of an identifier and a set of input and output ports. Thus, we assume the existence of set C_{id} containing all component identifiers.

Definition 2 (Component). *A component is a triple (id, I, O) consisting of:*

- *a component identifier $id \in \mathsf{C}_{id}$ and*
- *two disjoint sets of input and output ports $I, O \subseteq \mathsf{P}$.*

The set of all components is denoted by $\mathcal{C}$. For a set of components $C \subseteq \mathcal{C}$, we denote by:

- $\mathsf{in}(C) \;\overset{def}{=}\; \bigcup_{(id,I,O)\in C}(\{id\} \times I)$ *the set of component input ports,*
- $\mathsf{out}(C) \;\overset{def}{=}\; \bigcup_{(id,I,O)\in C}(\{id\} \times O)$ *the set of component output ports,*
- $\mathsf{port}(C) \;\overset{def}{=}\; \mathsf{in}(C) \cup \mathsf{out}(C)$ *the set of all component ports, and*
- $\mathsf{id}(C) \;\overset{def}{=}\; \bigcup_{(id,I,O)\in C}\{id\}$ *the set of all component identifiers.*

  A set of components $C \subseteq \mathcal{C}$ is called healthy *iff a component is uniquely determined by its name:*

$$\forall (id, I, O), (id', I', O') \in C \colon id = id' \implies I = I' \wedge O = O'. \tag{1}$$

  Similar to Definition 1, we define the set of all possible component port valuations (CPVs) for a set of component $P \subseteq \mathsf{C}_{id} \times \mathsf{P}$.

2.2   Modeling Component Behavior

A component's behavior is modeled by a set of execution traces over the component's interface. In the following, we denote with $(E)^+$ the set of all finite sequences over elements of a given set E, by $(E)^\infty$ the set of all infinite sequences over E, and by $(E)^*$ the set of all finite and infinite sequences over E.

Definition 3 (Behavior Trace). *A behavior trace for a component (id, I, O) is an infinite sequence $(\overline{I \times O})^\infty$. The set of all BTs for component c is denoted by $\mathcal{B}(c)$.*

Note that a component's behavior is actually modeled as a *set* of behavior traces, rather than just a single trace. This is to handle non-determinism for inputs to, as well as outputs from components.

Example 1 (Behavior Trace). In the following, we provide a possible BT for a component c_3 with two input ports i_0 and i_1, and two output ports o_0 and o_1:
$$[i_0, i_1, o_0, o_1 \mapsto X, 5, 9, \{8, 4\}], [i_0, i_1, o_0, o_1 \mapsto \{T, B\}, \{2, 4\}, 7, \{3, 9\}], \cdots.$$

2.3   Modeling Dynamic Architectures

Dynamic architectures are modeled as sets of *configuration traces* which are sequences over *architecture configurations*.

Architecture Configurations. In our model, an architecture configuration *connects* ports of *active* components.

Definition 4 (Architecture Configuration). *An architecture configuration (AC) over a healthy set of components $C \subseteq \mathcal{C}$ is a triple (C', N, μ), consisting of:*

- *a set of active components $C' \subseteq C$,*
- *a connection $N \colon \mathsf{in}(C') \to \wp(\mathsf{out}(C'))$, and*
- *a CPV $\mu \in \overline{\mathsf{port}(C')}$.*

We require connected ports to be consistent in their valuation, that is, if a component provides messages at its output port, these messages are transferred to the corresponding, connected input ports:

$$\forall p_i \in \mathsf{in}(C') \colon N(p_i) \neq \emptyset \implies \mu(p_i) = \bigcup_{p_o \in N(p_i)} \mu(p_o). \tag{2}$$

The set of all possible ACs over a healthy set of components $C \subseteq \mathcal{C}$ is denoted by $\mathcal{K}(C)$.

Note that connection N is modeled as a set-valued function from component input ports to component output ports, meaning that: (i) input/output ports can be connected to several output/input ports, respectively, and (ii) not every input/output port needs to be connected to an output/input port (in which case the connection returns the empty set).

Configuration Traces. A configuration Traces consists of a series of configuration snapshots of an architecture during system execution.

Definition 5 (Configuration Trace). *A configuration trace (CT) over a healthy set of components $C \subseteq \mathcal{C}$ is an infinite sequence $(\mathcal{K}(C))^\infty$. The set of all CTs over C is denoted by $\mathcal{R}(C)$.*

Example 2 (Configuration Trace). Fig. 1 shows the first three ACs of a possible CT. The first AC, $t(0) = (C', N, \mu)$, e.g., consists of:

- components $C' = \{C_1, C_2, C_3\}$, with $C_1 = (c_1, \{i_0\}, \{o_0, o_1, o_2\})$, $C_2 = (c_2, \{i_0, i_1, i_2\}, \{o_0\})$, and $C_3 = (c_3, \{i_0, i_1\}, \{o_0, o_1\})$;
- connection N, with $N((c_2, i_1)) = \{(c_1, o_1)\}$, $N((c_3, i_1)) = \{(c_1, o_2)\}$, and $N((c_2, i_2)) = \{(c_3, o_1)\}$; and
- valuation $\mu = [(c_1, i_0), (c_1, o_0), (c_2, i_2), \cdots \mapsto 5, 9, \{8, 4\}, \cdots]$.

Note that a dynamic architecture is modeled as a *set* of CTs rather than just one single trace. Again, this allows for non-determinism in inputs to an architecture as well as its reaction. Moreover, note that our notion of architecture is dynamic in the following sense: (i) *components* may appear and disappear over time and (ii) *connections* may change over time.

In the following, we introduce an operator to denote the number of activations of a component in a (possible finite) configuration trace. Thereby, we denote by $[c]^i = c_i$ the i-th component (where $i \geq 1$ and $i \leq n$) of a tuple $c = (c_1, \ldots, c_n)$.

Definition 6 (Number of Activations). *With $\langle c \overset{n}{\#} t \rangle$, we denote the number of activations of component c in a (possibly finite) configuration trace t up to (excluding) point in time n:*

$$\langle c \overset{0}{\#} t \rangle \overset{def}{=} 0,$$

$$c \in [t(n)]^1 \implies \langle c \overset{n+1}{\#} t \rangle \overset{def}{=} \langle c \overset{n}{\#} t \rangle + 1,$$

$$c \notin [t(n)]^1 \implies \langle c \overset{n+1}{\#} t \rangle \overset{def}{=} \langle c \overset{n}{\#} t \rangle.$$

Moreover, we introduce an operator to return the last activation of a component in a configuration trace.

Definition 7 (Last Activation). *With $last(t, c)$, we denote the greatest $i \in \mathbb{N}$, such that $c \in [t(i)]^1$.*

Note that $last(t, c)$ is well-defined iff $\exists i \in \mathbb{N}: c \in [t(i)]^1$ and $\exists n \in \mathbb{N}: \forall n' \geq n: c \notin [t(n')]^1$.

Finally, we introduce an operator which for a given point in time returns the least earlier point in time where a certain component was not yet active.

Definition 8 (Least Not Active). *With $\langle c \overset{n}{\vee} t \rangle$, we denote the least $n' \in \mathbb{N}$, such that $n' = n \vee (n' < n \wedge \forall n' \leq k \leq n: c \notin [t(n')]^1)$.*

Note that $\langle c \overset{n}{\vee} t \rangle$ is always well-defined and for the case in which $c \in [t(n)]^1$, it returns n itself.

2.4   From Configuration Traces to Behavior Traces

In the following, we introduce the notion of projection to extract the behavior of a certain component out of a given CT.

Definition 9 (Projection). *Given a (finite or infinite) CT* $t \in (\mathcal{K}(C))^*$ *over a healthy set of components* $C \subseteq \mathcal{C}$. *The projection to component* $c = (id, I, O) \in C$ *is denoted by* $\Pi_c(t) \in (\mathcal{B}(c))^*$ *and defined as the greatest relation satisfying the following equations:*

$$\Pi_c(t\,|_0) \quad \overset{def}{=} \quad \langle \rangle,$$

$$c \in [t(n)]^1 \implies \Pi_c(t\,|_{n+1}) \quad \overset{def}{=} \quad \Pi_c(t\,|_n) \,^\frown \left(\lambda p \in I \cup O \colon [t(n)]^3 \, (id, p) \right),$$

$$c \notin [t(n)]^1 \implies \Pi_c(t\,|_{n+1}) \quad \overset{def}{=} \quad \Pi_c(t\,|_n),$$

where $s \,^\frown e$ *denotes the sequence resulting from appending element* e *to sequence* s.

Example 3 (Projection). Applying projection of component c_3 to the CT given by Example 2 results in a BT starting as described by Example 1.

Note that for systems in which a component is activated only finitely many times, the projection to this component results in only a finite behavior trace.

3   Specifying Component Behavior

In the following, we introduce the notion of *behavior trace assertions*, a language to specify component behavior over a given interface specification. We provide its syntax as well as a formal semantics thereof in terms of *behavior traces*. Finally, we introduce a satisfaction relation for configuration traces which serves as a foundation for the calculus presented in the next section.

3.1   Behavior Trace Assertions

Component behavior can be specified by means of behavior trace assertions, i.e., temporal logic [13] formulæ over behavior assertions. Behavior assertions, on the other hand, are used to specify a component's state at a certain point in time. They are specified over a given interface specification.

Interface Specifications. Interfaces declare a set of port identifiers and associate a sort with each port. Thus, in the following, we postulate the existence of the set of all port identifiers P_{id}. Moreover, interfaces are specified over a given signature $\Sigma = (S, F, B)$ consisting of a set of sorts S, function symbols F, and predicate symbols B.

Definition 10 (Interface Specification). *An interface specification (IS) over a signature* $\Sigma = (S, F, B)$ *is a triple* (P_{in}, P_{out}, t^p), *consisting of:*

- *two disjoint sets of input and output port identifiers* $P_{in}, P_{out} \subseteq \mathsf{P}_{id}$,
- *a mapping* $t^p \colon P_{in} \cup P_{out} \to S$ *assigning a sort to each port identifier.*

The set of all interface specifications over signature Σ *is denoted by* $\mathcal{S}_I(\Sigma)$.

Behavior Assertions. Behavior assertions specify a component's state (i.e.: valuations of its ports with messages) at a certain point in time. In the following, we do not go into the details of how to specify such assertions, rather, we assume the existence of a set containing all type-compatible behavior assertions over a given interface specification.

Definition 11 (Behavior Assertions). *Given IS $S_i = (P_{in}, P_{out}, t^p)$ over signature $\Sigma = (S, F, B)$ and family of variables $V = (V_s)_{s \in S}$ with variables V_s for each sort $s \in S$. With $\varphi_\Sigma^V(S_i)$, we denote the set of all* type-compatible *(with regard to t^p) behavior assertions (BAs) for S_i, Σ, and V.*

Algebras and Variable Assignments. A BA is always interpreted over a given algebra for the signature used in the corresponding IS. Thus, in the following, we denote by $\mathcal{A}(\Sigma)$ the set of all algebras $(S', F', B', \alpha, \beta, \gamma)$ for signature $\Sigma = (S, F, B)$, consisting of sets S', functions F', predicates B', and corresponding interpretations $\alpha \colon S \to S'$, $\beta \colon F \to F'$, and $\gamma \colon B \to B'$. Moreover, with $\mathcal{I}_A^V$, we denote the set of all *variable assignments (VAs)* $\iota = (\iota_s)_{s \in S}$ (with $\iota_s \colon V_s \to \alpha(s)$ for each $s \in S$) for a family of variables $V = (V_s)_{s \in S}$ in an algebra A.

Semantics of Behavior Assertions. The semantics of behavior assertions is described in terms of component port valuations satisfying a certain behavior assertion. In the following, we denote with $A \leftrightarrow B$ a bijective function from set A to set B.

Definition 12 (Behavior Assertions: Semantics). *Given interface specification $S_i = (P_{in}, P_{out}, t^p) \in \mathcal{S}_I(\Sigma)$, a healthy set of components $C \subseteq \mathcal{C}$, component $c = (id, I, O) \in C$, algebra $A \in \mathcal{A}(\Sigma)$, and $V A \iota = (\iota_s)_{s \in S} \in \mathcal{I}_A^V$. We denote with $\mu_b \models_{(A,\iota)}^{(\delta^i,\delta^o)} \gamma$ that $\mu \in \overline{I \cup O}$ satisfies BA $\gamma \in \varphi_\Sigma^V(S_i)$ for port interpretations (PIs) $\delta^i \colon I \leftrightarrow P_{in}$ and $\delta^o \colon O \leftrightarrow P_{out}$.*

Behavior Trace Assertions. Behavior trace assertions are a means to specify a component's behavior in terms of temporal specifications over behavior assertions.

Definition 13 (Behavior Trace Assertions). *For a family of variables $V = (V_s)_{s \in S}$, rigid (fixed for the whole execution) variables $V' = (V'_s)_{s \in S}$, the set of all behavior trace assertions (BTAs) for $ISS_i \in \mathcal{S}_I(\Sigma)$ is given by $\Gamma_\Sigma^{(V,V')}(S_i)$ and defined inductively by the equations provided in Fig. 2.*

$$\phi \in \varphi_\Sigma^{V \cup V'}(S_i) \implies \phi \in \Gamma_\Sigma^{(V,V')}(S_i) \,,$$

$$\text{``}\gamma\text{''} \in \Gamma_\Sigma^{(V,V')}(S_i) \implies \text{``}\bigcirc\gamma\text{''}, \text{``}\Diamond\gamma\text{''}, \text{``}\Box\gamma\text{''} \in \Gamma_\Sigma^{(V,V')}(S_i) \,,$$

$$\text{``}\gamma\text{''}, \text{``}\gamma'\text{''} \in \Gamma_\Sigma^{(V,V')}(S_i) \implies \text{``}(\gamma \, \mathcal{U} \, \gamma')\text{''} \in \Gamma_\Sigma^{(V,V')}(S_i) \,.$$

Fig. 2. Inductive definition of behavior trace assertions.

3.2 Semantics: Behavior Traces

In the following, we define what it means for a behavior trace to satisfy a corresponding behavior trace assertion.

Definition 14 (Semantics BTs). *Given algebra A and corresponding VAs $\iota' = (\iota'_s)_{s \in S} \in \mathcal{I}_A^{V'}$ for variables V'. With $(t,n) \, {}_b^t\!\models_{(A,\iota')}^{(\delta^i,\delta^o)} \gamma$, defined recursively by the equations listed in Fig. 3, we denote that BT $t \in \mathcal{B}(c)$ satisfies BA $\gamma \in \Gamma_\Sigma^{(V,V')}(S_i)$ at time $n \in \mathbb{N}$. A BT $t \in \mathcal{B}(c)$ satisfies BA $\gamma \in \Gamma_\Sigma^{(V,V')}(S_i)$, denoted $t \, {}_b^t\!\models_{(A,\iota')}^{(\delta^i,\delta^o)} \gamma$ iff $(t,0) \, {}_b^t\!\models_{(A,\iota')}^{(\delta^i,\delta^o)} \gamma$.*

$$
\begin{aligned}
(t,n) \, {}_b^t\!\models_{(A,\iota')}^{(\delta^i,\delta^o)} \text{``}\phi\text{''} &\iff \forall \iota \in \mathcal{I}_A^V : t(n) \, {}_b^t\!\models_{(A,\iota \cup \iota')}^{(\delta^i,\delta^o)} \text{``}\phi\text{''} \; [\text{for } \phi \in \varphi_\Sigma^V(S_i)] \;, \\[4pt]
(t,n) \, {}_b^t\!\models_{(A,\iota')}^{(\delta^i,\delta^o)} \text{``}\bigcirc\gamma\text{''} &\iff (t,n+1) \, {}_b^t\!\models_{(A,\iota')}^{(\delta^i,\delta^o)} \text{``}\gamma\text{''} \;, \\[4pt]
(t,n) \, {}_b^t\!\models_{(A,\iota')}^{(\delta^i,\delta^o)} \text{``}\Diamond\gamma\text{''} &\iff \exists n' \geq n : (t,n') \, {}_b^t\!\models_{(A,\iota')}^{(\delta^i,\delta^o)} \text{``}\gamma\text{''} \;, \\[4pt]
(t,n) \, {}_b^t\!\models_{(A,\iota')}^{(\delta^i,\delta^o)} \text{``}\Box\gamma\text{''} &\iff \forall n' \geq n : (t,n') \, {}_b^t\!\models_{(A,\iota')}^{(\delta^i,\delta^o)} \text{``}\gamma\text{''} \;, \\[4pt]
(t,n) \, {}_b^t\!\models_{(A,\iota')}^{(\delta^i,\delta^o)} \text{``}(\gamma' \, \mathcal{U} \, \gamma)\text{''} &\iff \exists n' \geq n : (t,n') \, {}_b^t\!\models_{(A,\iota')}^{(\delta^i,\delta^o)} \text{``}\gamma\text{''} \; \wedge \\[4pt]
&\quad\; \forall n \leq m < n' : (t,m) \, {}_b^t\!\models_{(A,\iota')}^{(\delta^i,\delta^o)} \text{``}\gamma'\text{''} \;.
\end{aligned}
$$

Fig. 3. Recursive definition of satisfaction relation for behavior traces.

3.3 Semantics: Configuration Traces

In the following, we define what it means for a configuration trace to satisfy a behavior assertion.

Definition 15 (Semantics CTs). *Given algebra A, corresponding VAs $\iota' = (\iota'_s)_{s \in S} \in \mathcal{I}_A^{V'}$ for variables V', and behavior trace $t' \in \mathcal{B}(c)$. With*

$$(t,t',n) \, {}_k^t\!\models_{(A,\iota')}^{(c,\delta^i,\delta^o)} \gamma \overset{def}{\iff}$$

$$\left(\exists i \geq n : c \in [t(i)]^1 \wedge \left(\Pi_c(t) \circ t', \langle c \overset{n}{\#} t \rangle \right) \, {}_b^t\!\models_{(A,\iota')}^{(\delta^i,\delta^o)} \gamma \right) \; \vee \tag{3}$$

$$\left(\exists i : c \in [t(i)]^1 \wedge \not\exists i \geq n : c \in [t(i)]^1 \wedge \right.$$

$$\left. \left(\Pi_c(t) \circ t', \#(\Pi_c(t)) - 1 + (n - last(t,c)) \right) \, {}_b^t\!\models_{(A,\iota')}^{(\delta^i,\delta^o)} \gamma \right) \; \vee \tag{4}$$

$$\left(\not\exists i : c \in [t(i)]^1 \wedge (t',n) \, {}_b^t\!\models_{(A,\iota')}^{(\delta^i,\delta^o)} \gamma \right), \tag{5}$$

we denote that CT $t \in \mathcal{R}(C)$ satisfies BA $\gamma \in \Gamma_\Sigma^{(V,V')}(S_i)$ at time $n \in \mathbb{N}$ for a given continuation t'. Again, a CT $t \in \mathcal{B}(c)$ satisfies BA $\gamma \in \Gamma_\Sigma^{(V,V')}(S_i)$, denoted $t \, {}_k^t\!\models_{(A,\iota')}^{(c,\delta^i,\delta^o)} \gamma$ iff $(t,0) \, {}_k^t\!\models_{(A,\iota')}^{(c,\delta^i,\delta^o)} \gamma$.

To satisfy a given behavior assertion γ for a component c at a certain point in time n under a given continuation t', a configuration trace t is required to fulfill one of the following conditions:

- By Eq. (3): Component c is again activated (after time point n) and the projection to c for t fulfills γ at the point in time given by the current number of activations of c.
- By Eq. (4): Component c is activated at least once but not again in the future and the continuation fulfills γ at the point in time resulting from the difference of the current point in time and the last activation of c.
- By Eq. (5): Component c is never activated and the continuation fulfills γ at point in time n.

For the sake of readability, from now on, we omit symbols for algebras and port/variable interpretations for satisfaction relations. An algebra and corresponding interpretations are, however, assumed to be fixed for each property.

The following property ensures correctness of Definition 15:

Proposition 1 (Soundness of Definition 15). *A CT $t \in \mathcal{R}(c)$ satisfies BA $\gamma \in \Gamma_{\Sigma}^{(V,V')}(S_i)$ for a given continuation $t' \in \mathcal{B}(c)$ iff the corresponding projection satisfies γ:*

$$(t,t') \; _k^t \!\!\models_{(c)} \gamma \iff \Pi_c(t) \circ t' \; _b^t \!\!\models \gamma,$$

where $s \circ s'$ denotes the sequence resulting from concatenating sequences s and s'.

Remember that for architectures in which a component is activated only finitely many times, the projection to this component results in only a finite behavior trace. This is why we actually check for a valid continuation $t' \in \mathcal{B}(c)$.

4   A Calculus for Dynamic Architectures

Until now, $_k^t \!\!\models$ is only implicitly defined in terms of $_b^t \!\!\models$. While this mirrors our intuition about $_k^t \!\!\models$, it is not very useful to reason about it. Thus, in the following section, we provide an explicit characterization of $_k^t \!\!\models$ in terms of a calculus for dynamic architectures. Then, we show *soundness* and relative *completeness* of the calculus with regard to Definition 15. Using a natural deduction style, we provide introduction and elimination rules for each temporal operator.

4.1   Introduction Rules

We provide 8 rules which can be used to introduce temporal operators in a dynamic context.

Behavior Assertions. The first rules characterize introduction for *basic* behavior assertions. Therefore, we distinguish between three cases: First, the following case in which a component is guaranteed to be eventually activated in the future:

$$
\text{AssI}_a \quad
\frac{
\begin{array}{c}
\left[\, n \leq i \quad c \in [t(i)]^1 \quad \nexists n \leq k < i : c \in [t(k)]^1 \,\right] \\
\vdots \\
\lambda p \in I \cup O : [t(i)]^3 \, (c, p) \,_b\!\models \text{``}\phi\text{''}
\end{array}
}{
(t, t', n) \,{}^{t}_{k}\!\models_{(c)} \text{``}\phi\text{''}
} \quad \exists i \geq n : c \in [t(i)]^1
$$

For this case, in order to show that a BA ϕ holds at time point n, we have to show that ϕ holds at the very next point in time at which component c is active.

For the case in which a component was sometimes active, but is not activated again in the future, we get the following rule:

$$
\text{AssI}_{n1} \quad
\frac{
t'\big(n - \mathit{last}(c, t)\big) \,_b\!\models \text{``}\phi\text{''}
}{
(t, t', n) \,{}^{t}_{k}\!\models_{(c)} \text{``}\phi\text{''}
} \quad \exists i : c \in [t(i)]^1 \wedge \nexists i \geq n : c \in [t(i)]^1
$$

In order to show that BA ϕ holds at a certain point in time n, we have to show that ϕ holds for the continuation t'. Note that the corresponding time point is calculated as the difference from n to the last point in time at which component. c was active in t.

Finally, we have another rule for the case in which component is never activated:

$$
\text{AssI}_{n2} \quad
\frac{
t'(n) \,_b\!\models \text{``}\phi\text{''}
}{
(t, t', n) \,{}^{t}_{k}\!\models_{(c)} \text{``}\phi\text{''}
} \quad \nexists i : c \in [t(i)]^1
$$

For such cases, BA ϕ holds at a certain point in time n when ϕ holds for t' at time point n.

Next. The next rule characterizes introduction for the *next* operator. For this operator as well, we distinguish two cases: The first case is again the one in which a component is guaranteed to be eventually activated in the future:

$$
\text{NxtI}_a \quad
\frac{
\begin{array}{c}
\left[\, n \leq i \quad c \in [t(i)]^1 \quad \nexists n \leq k < i : c \in [t(k)]^1 \,\right] \\
\vdots \\
(t, t', i+1) \,{}^{t}_{k}\!\models_{(c)} \text{``}\gamma\text{''}
\end{array}
}{
(t, t', n) \,{}^{t}_{k}\!\models_{(c)} \text{``}\bigcirc \gamma\text{''}
} \quad \exists i \geq n : c \in [t(i)]^1
$$

For this case, in order to show that a BTA $\bigcirc \gamma$ holds at a certain point in time n, we have to show that it holds *after* the very next activation of c in t.

For the case in which a component is not activated again in the future, we get the following rule for the *next* operator:

$$
\text{NxtI}_n \quad \dfrac{(t,t',n+1) \; {}^{t}_{k}\!\models_{(c)} \text{``}\gamma\text{''}}{(t,t',n) \; {}^{t}_{k}\!\models_{(c)} \text{``}\bigcirc\gamma\text{''}} \quad \nexists i \geq n : c \in [t(i)]^1
$$

In this case, the dynamic interpretation of the operator resembles its traditional one. Thus, it suffices to show that BTA γ holds for the *next* point in time $n+1$, in order to conclude that $\bigcirc\gamma$ holds at n.

Eventually. Introduction for the *eventually* operator can be described with a single rule:

$$
\text{EvtI} \quad \dfrac{\langle c \stackrel{n}{\vee} t \rangle \leq n' \quad (t,t',n') \; {}^{t}_{k}\!\models_{(c)} \text{``}\gamma\text{''}}{(t,t',n) \; {}^{t}_{k}\!\models_{(c)} \text{``}\Diamond\gamma\text{''}}
$$

It states that in order to show that $\Diamond\gamma$ holds for a component c at some point in time n, we only have to show that γ holds at *some* time point later than the last activation (before n) of c.

Globally. Similarly, we provide a single introduction rule for the *globally* operator:

$$
\text{GlobI} \quad \dfrac{\begin{array}{c} [n \leq n'] \\ \vdots \\ (t,t',n') \; {}^{t}_{k}\!\models_{(c)} \text{``}\gamma\text{''} \end{array}}{(t,t',n) \; {}^{t}_{k}\!\models_{(c)} \text{``}\Box\gamma\text{''}}
$$

It allows us to conclude $\Box\gamma$ for time point n whenever we can show that γ holds for an *arbitrary* $n' \geq n$.

Until. Finally, we provide a single rule for introducing the *until* operator:

$$
\text{UntilI} \quad \dfrac{\begin{bmatrix} n \leq n'' & n'' \leq i'' \\ c \in [t(i'')]^1 & i'' < n' \end{bmatrix} \begin{bmatrix} n \leq n'' & n'' < n' \\ \nexists i'' \geq n'' : c \in [t(i'')]^1 \end{bmatrix}}{} \\[2pt]
\dfrac{\langle c \stackrel{n}{\vee} t \rangle \leq n' \quad (t,t',n') \; {}^{t}_{k}\!\models_{(c)} \text{``}\gamma\text{''} \quad (t,t',n'') \; {}^{t}_{k}\!\models^{(c,\delta^i,\delta^o)}_{(A,\iota)} \text{``}\gamma'\text{''} \; (t,t',n'') \; {}^{t}_{k}\!\models^{(c,\delta^i,\delta^o)}_{(A,\iota)} \text{``}\gamma'\text{''}}{(t,t',n) \; {}^{t}_{k}\!\models_{(c)} \text{``}\gamma' \; \mathcal{U} \; \gamma\text{''}}
$$

In order to show that $\gamma'\ \mathcal{U}\ \gamma$ holds for a component c at some point in time n, the rule requires to show that γ holds at some point n' later than the last activation (before n) of c and that for every time point *up to* the last activation of component c *before* n' (or the last time point $n'' < n'$ for the case component c is not activated anymore), γ' holds.

4.2   Elimination Rules

In contrast to introduction, we provide 10 rules for the elimination of the different temporal operators.

Behavior Assertions. Again, we first provide rules characterizing elimination for *basic* behavior assertions. Similar to introduction, we distinguish between three cases: The first case describes elimination for situations in which a component is guaranteed to be activated sometimes in the future:

$$
\mathrm{AssE_a} \quad \frac{(t,t',n)\ _k{\models}_{(c)}^{t}\ \text{``}\phi\text{''} \quad n\le i \quad c\in[t(i)]^1 \quad \nexists n\le k<i\colon c\in[t(k)]^1}{\lambda p\in I\cup O\colon [t(i)]^3\,(c,p)\,_b{\models}\text{``}\phi\text{''}} \quad \exists i\ge n\colon c\in[t(i)]^1
$$

The rule for such cases allows us to eliminate a basic BA ϕ and conclude that ϕ holds at the very *next* point in time where component c is active.

The next rule deals with the case in which a component was sometimes active, but is not activated again in the future.

$$
\mathrm{AssE_{n1}} \quad \frac{(t,t',n)\ _k{\models}_{(c)}^{t}\ \text{``}\phi\text{''}}{t'\bigl(n-last(c,t)\bigr)\,_b{\models}\text{``}\phi\text{''}} \quad \exists i\colon c\in[t(i)]^1\wedge\nexists i\ge n\colon c\in[t(i)]^1
$$

The rule for this case allows us to conclude that a BA ϕ holds at a certain point in time for continuation t'. Again, the corresponding time point is calculated as the difference of n and the last time component c was activated.

Finally, we have another rule for the case in which component is never activated:

$$
\mathrm{AssE_{n2}} \quad \frac{(t,t',n)\ _k{\models}_{(c)}^{t}\ \text{``}\phi\text{''}}{t'(n)\,_b{\models}\text{``}\phi\text{''}} \quad \nexists i\colon c\in[t(i)]^1
$$

For such cases, we may eliminate ϕ and conclude that ϕ holds at n for continuation t'.

Next. Similar to introduction, we provide two rules to eliminate a *next* operator: The first rule deals again with the case in which a component is guaranteed to be activated sometimes in the future:

$$\text{NxtE}_a \quad \frac{(t,t',n) \; {}^{t}_{k}\!\models_{(c)} \text{``}\bigcirc\gamma\text{''} \quad n{\leq}i \quad c{\in}[t(i)]^1 \quad \nexists n{\leq}k{<}i\colon c{\in}[t(k)]^1}{(t,t',i{+}1) \; {}^{t}_{k}\!\models_{(c)} \text{``}\gamma\text{''}} \quad \exists i{\geq}n\colon c{\in}[t(i)]^1$$

Similar to the corresponding introduction rule, this rule allows us to conclude BTA γ for a certain point in time $i+1$, whenever $\bigcirc\gamma$ holds at an earlier point in time n and i is the very next activation of component c.

If a component is not activated again, we get the following rule for eliminating a *next* operator:

$$\text{NxtE}_n \quad \frac{(t,t',n) \; {}^{t}_{k}\!\models_{(c)} \text{``}\bigcirc\gamma\text{''}}{(t,t',n{+}1) \; {}^{t}_{k}\!\models_{(c)} \text{``}\gamma\text{''}} \quad \nexists i \geq n\colon c \in [t(i)]^1$$

Again, the rule resembles the traditional interpretation of *next*, which allows us to conclude that BTA γ holds for a certain point in time $n+1$, whenever $\bigcirc\gamma$ holds at n.

Eventually. We provide two rules to eliminate an *eventually* operator:

$$\text{EvtE}_a \quad \frac{(t,t',n) \; {}^{t}_{k}\!\models_{(c)} \text{``}\Diamond\gamma\text{''}}{\exists n' \geq \langle c \overset{n}{\vee} t\rangle\colon (t,t',n') \; {}^{t}_{k}\!\models_{(c)} \text{``}\gamma\text{''}} \quad \exists i \geq n\colon c \in [t(i)]^1$$

When eliminating a $\Diamond\gamma$ for a component c at time point n, the rule allows us to conclude that BTA γ holds sometimes after the last activation (before n) of component c.

A similar rule applies for the case in which c is not activated again ($\exists n' \geq n\colon (t,t',n') \; {}^{t}_{k}\!\models_{(c)} \text{``}\gamma\text{''}$). For this case (denoted EvtE_n), however, we can conclude that the corresponding point in time n' is actually greater than n instead of $\langle c \overset{n}{\vee} t\rangle$.

Globally. Similar to introduction, we have a single rule for the elimination of a *globally* operator:

$$\text{GlobE} \quad \frac{(t,t',n) \; {}^{t}_{k}\!\models_{(c)} \text{``}\Box\gamma\text{''} \quad n' \geq \langle c \overset{n}{\vee} t\rangle}{(t,t',n') \; {}^{t}_{k}\!\models_{(c)} \text{``}\gamma\text{''}}$$

The rule allows us to eliminate $\Box\gamma$ for component c at time point n and conclude that γ holds at an arbitrary point later than the last activation of c before n.

Until. Finally, we provide two rules to eliminate *until* operators:

$$
\text{UntilE}_a \quad \frac{(t,t',n) \overset{t}{\underset{k}{\models}}_{(c)} \text{``}\gamma' \, \mathcal{U} \, \gamma\text{''}}{\begin{array}{l} \exists n' \overset{n}{\geq} \langle c \, \# \, t\rangle : (t,t',n') \overset{t}{\underset{k}{\models}}_{(c)} \text{``}\gamma\text{''} \, \wedge \\ \left(\forall n'' \overset{n}{\geq} \langle c \, \overset{n}{\vee} \, t\rangle : \left(\exists n'' \leq i' < n' : c \in [t(i')]^1 \right) \right. \\ \qquad \vee \left. (\nexists i \geq n'' : c \in [t(i)]^1 \wedge n'' < n') \right. \\ \qquad \left. \implies (t,t',n'') \overset{t}{\underset{k}{\models}}_{(c)} \text{``}\gamma'\text{''} \right) \end{array}} \quad \exists i \geq n : c \in [t(i)]^1
$$

Assuming that $\gamma' \, \mathcal{U} \, \gamma$ holds at some time point n, the rule allows us to conclude that there exists a time point in the future n', such that BTA γ holds and that up to the last activation of component c earlier to n' (or the last time point $n'' < n'$ for the case component c is not activated anymore), BTA γ' holds.

Again, a similar rule applies for the case in which c is not activated again $(\exists n' \geq n : (t,t',n') \overset{t}{\underset{k}{\models}}_{(c)} \text{``}\gamma''\text{''})$. For this case (denoted UntilE$_n$), however, we can conclude that the corresponding point in time n' is actually greater than n instead of $\langle c \overset{n}{\vee} t\rangle$.

4.3 Soundness and Completeness

In the following, we show *soundness* and relative *completeness* of the calculus. Thereby, we denote with $\vdash_{DA} \left((t,n) \overset{t}{\underset{k}{\models}}_{(c)} \gamma\right)$ that it is possible to derive $(t,n) \overset{t}{\underset{k}{\models}}_{(c)} \gamma$ with the rules introduced in Sect. 4. With $\models_{DA} \left((t,n) \overset{t}{\underset{k}{\models}}_{(c)} \gamma\right)$, on the other hand, we denote that configuration trace t indeed satisfies BTA γ at time point n.

Theorem 1 (Soundness). *The calculus presented in Sects. 4.1 and 4.2 is sound:*

Proof (Sketch). For each rule, we assume its premises and prove its conclusions from Definitions 14 and 15.

Theorem 2 (Completeness). *The calculus presented in Sects. 4.1 and 4.2 is complete (relative to the completeness of $_b\models$):*

$$
\vdash_{DA} \left((t,n) \overset{t}{\underset{k}{\models}}_{(c)} \text{``}\gamma\text{''}\right) \qquad \Longleftarrow \qquad \models_{DA} \left((t,n) \overset{t}{\underset{k}{\models}}_{(c)} \text{``}\gamma\text{''}\right).
$$

Proof (Sketch). The validity of each BTA can be derived by applying the corresponding introduction rules.

5   Verifying Properties of Dynamic Architectures

In the following, we demonstrate the practical usability of the calculus presented in Sect. 4. Therefore, we specify a dynamic version of the blackboard architecture pattern and apply our calculus to verify a simple property of such architectures.

5.1   Dynamic Blackboard Architectures: Specification

In the following, we introduce a simplified version of the blackboard pattern as described, for example, by Shaw and Garlan [18], Buschmann et al. [5], and Taylor et al. [19]. Therefore, we first specify the involved datatypes, the components interfaces, and constraints regarding the activation/deactivation of components as well as connections between their ports. Then we provide a specification of component behavior in terms of BTAs.

Datatypes. Blackboard architectures work with *problems* and *solutions* for them. Figure 4a provides the corresponding datatype specification (DTS) in terms of an algebraic specification [21]. We denote by PROB the set of all problems and by SOL the set of all solutions. To relate a problem with a corresponding solution, we assume the existence of a function $s\colon \text{PROB} \to \text{SOL}$ which assigns the *correct* solution to each problem.

Interfaces. In our example, a blackboard architecture consists of a blackboard (BB) component and a knowledgesource (KS) component. The configuration diagram (CD) [14] in Fig. 4c shows the specification of the corresponding interfaces. In our simple example, the BB component merely forwards messages to and from the KS component. Thus, it has an input port i_p which receives a problem and an output port o_s which returns the corresponding solution. Moreover, it has an output port p_p to forward a problem to a KS and a corresponding input port p_s to receive its solution. A KS, in our example, gets a problem on its input port p_p and provides a corresponding solution on its output port p_s.

DTSpec ProbSol	
sort PROB, SOL	
$s:$	PROB $\to$ SOL

(a) Datatype Specification.

PSpec BPort	**uses** ProbSol
$i_p, p_p:$	PROB
$o_s, p_s:$	SOL

(b) Port Specification.

Diagram Blackboard
based on BPort **uses** ProbSol

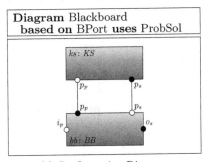

(c) Configuration Diagram.

Fig. 4. Specification of the blackboard pattern.

Spec Blackboard_Activation	**uses** *Blackboard*

$$\square\Big(bb.p_p \neq \emptyset \implies \|ks\|\Big) \tag{6}$$

$$\square\Big(\|ks\| \implies \square\big(\lozenge\|ks\|\big)\Big) \tag{7}$$

$$\square\big(\|bb\|\big) \tag{8}$$

Fig. 5. Specification of activation constraints for blackboard architectures.

Activation Constraints. Activation constraints restrict the activation or deactivation of components. They are introduced by CDs and refined by activation assertions (AAs).

In our example, the "*bb: BB*" and "*ks: KS*" annotations for a BB and KS interface, respectively, denote the condition that there are *unique* BB and KS components denoted *bb* and *ks*, respectively. Moreover, we require three more activation constraints formulated as AAs in Fig. 5:

- By Eq. (6) we require *ks* to be active whenever *bb* posts a problem.
- By Eq. (7) we require a fairness condition for the activation of an already activated *ks*.
- By Eq. (8) we require that *bb* is always active.

Connection Constraints. Connection constraints restrict the connection between components. They are introduced by CDs and refined by connection assertions CAs.

In our example, connection constraints are also specified graphically by the CD in Fig. 4c. The *solid* connections between the ports denote a constraint requiring that the ports of a KS component are connected with the corresponding ports of a BB component as depicted, whenever both components are active.

Behavior Specifications. Behavior is specified in terms of BTAs as introduced in Sect. 3. Note that we do not consider activation and deactivation of a component when specifying its behavior. Rather, this is done in a separate specification and our calculus can then be used to reason about such behavior, in a dynamic environment as well.

In Fig. 6, we specify two simple properties for BB components. They merely require messages from their input ports to be forwarded to the corresponding output ports. Figure 7 provides a specification of the KS's behavior. The property requires that whenever a problem is received it is guaranteed to be eventually solved.

Spec BB_Bhv	**uses** *Blackboard*
var p, p' :	PROB
s :	SOL
P :	PROB SET

$$\Box\left(p \in i_p \implies p \in p_p\right) \quad (9)$$
$$\Box\left(p \in p_s \implies p \in o_s\right) \quad (10)$$

Fig. 6. Specification of behavior for blackboard components.

Spec KS_Bhv	**uses** *Blackboard*
var p, q :	PROB
P :	PROB SET

$$\Box\left(p \in p_p \implies \Diamond(s(p) \in p_s)\right) \quad (11)$$

Fig. 7. Specification of behavior for knowledgesource components.

5.2 Dynamic Blackboard Architectures: Verification

In the following, we demonstrate how the calculus proposed in Sect. 4 can be used to verify a simple property of blackboard architectures as specified above.

A simple property of a blackboard architecture as specified above is that a problem is always solved. Expressed in terms of a behavior assertion over a blackboard interface, it looks as follows:

$$\Box\left(p \in i_p \implies \Diamond(s(p) \in o_s)\right). \quad (12)$$

It actually resembles the behavior property of KS components. Its proof is split into 4 parts.

First, we apply introduction for the globally and eventually operators to our goal. Thereby we use Hilbert's ε-operator to denote an arbitrary but fixed element satisfying a certain property. Moreover, we use Ass to abbreviate the assumption $(t, t', n) \underset{k}{\overset{t}{\models}}_{(bb)} p \in i_p$ for later reference.

$$
\begin{array}{c}
\vdots \\
\dfrac{(t, t', \varepsilon n'.\, n' \geq \langle bb \overset{n}{\vee} t\rangle) \underset{k}{\overset{t}{\models}}_{(bb)} (s(p) \in o_s) \quad \langle bb \overset{n}{\vee} t\rangle \leq (\varepsilon n'.\, n' \geq \langle bb \overset{n}{\vee} t\rangle)}{} \ \text{EvtI} \\
[Ass]\ \dfrac{(t, t', n) \underset{k}{\overset{t}{\models}}_{(bb)} \Diamond(s(p) \in o_s)}{\dfrac{(t, t', n) \underset{k}{\overset{t}{\models}}_{(bb)} \left(p \in i_p \implies \Diamond(s(p) \in o_s)\right)}{}}\ \text{ImpI} \\
[n \geq 0]\ \dfrac{}{(t, t', 0) \underset{k}{\overset{t}{\models}}_{(bb)} \Box\left(p \in i_p \implies \Diamond(s(p) \in o_s)\right)}\ \text{GlobI}
\end{array}
$$

We are now left with the goal of showing that the solution to the original problem p is provided by the blackboard at port o_s at some point in time later than the last activation of the blackboard. To discharge the proof obligation, we apply elimination for the globally operator and the behavior specification of blackboards. In the following, we abbreviate $\varepsilon n'.\, n' \geq \langle bb \overset{n}{\vee} t\rangle$ with n^*.

$$\frac{\overline{n^* \geq \langle c \overset{0}{\vee} t \rangle} \quad (t,t',0) \; {}_{k}{\underset{(bb)}{\overset{t}{\models}}} \Box(s(p) \in p_s \implies s(p) \in o_s)}{(t,t',n^*) \; {}_{k}{\underset{(bb)}{\overset{t}{\models}}} s(p) \in p_s \implies s(p) \in o_s} \text{ Eq. (10)}$$

$$\frac{\qquad\qquad\qquad\qquad\qquad\qquad\qquad\qquad\qquad\qquad\quad \text{GlobE} \qquad \vdots}{(t,t',n^*) \; {}_{k}{\underset{(bb)}{\overset{t}{\models}}} (s(p) \in o_s)}$$

$$(t,t',n^*) \; {}_{k}{\underset{(bb)}{\overset{t}{\models}}} (s(p) \in p_s) \qquad \text{ImpE}$$

We are left with the goal of showing that the solution for p is indeed received by the blackboard. To this end, we apply connection constraints from the CD as well as elimination rules for eventually and globally.

$$\frac{(t,t',0) \; {}_{k}{\underset{(ks)}{\overset{t}{\models}}} \Box\big(p \in p_p \implies \Diamond(s(p) \in p_s)\big) \qquad \overline{n \geq \langle c \overset{0}{\vee} t \rangle}}{(t,t',n) \; {}_{k}{\underset{(ks)}{\overset{t}{\models}}} \big(p \in p_p \implies \Diamond(s(p) \in p_s)\big)} \text{GlobE}$$

$$\frac{\vdots \qquad \qquad}{(t,t',n) \; {}_{k}{\underset{(ks)}{\overset{t}{\models}}} p \in p_p} \qquad \frac{(t,t',n) \; {}_{k}{\underset{(ks)}{\overset{t}{\models}}} \Diamond(s(p) \in p_s)}{} \text{ImpE}$$

$$\frac{(t,t',\varepsilon n'.\, n' \geq \langle bb \overset{n}{\vee} t \rangle) \; {}_{k}{\underset{(ks)}{\overset{t}{\models}}} (s(p) \in p_s)}{(t,t',\varepsilon n'.\, n' \geq \langle bb \overset{n}{\vee} t \rangle) \; {}_{k}{\underset{(bb)}{\overset{t}{\models}}} (s(p) \in p_s)} \text{Fig. 4c, Eq. (6)} \quad \text{EvtE}_a, \text{Eq. (7)}$$

Finally it remains to show that the knowledgesource indeed receives the original problem. To discharge this obligation, we simply again apply the constraints induced by the CD as well as the behavioral specification of the blackboard component.

$$\frac{(t,t',0) \; {}_{k}{\underset{(bb)}{\overset{t}{\models}}} \Box\big(p \in i_p \implies (p \in p_p)\big) \qquad \overline{n \geq \langle c \overset{0}{\vee} t \rangle}}{(t,t',n) \; {}_{k}{\underset{(bb)}{\overset{t}{\models}}} p \in i_p \implies p \in p_p} \text{GlobE}$$

$$\frac{\overline{(t,t',n) \; {}_{k}{\underset{(bb)}{\overset{t}{\models}}} p \in i_p} \text{ Ass} \qquad}{(t,t',n) \; {}_{k}{\underset{(bb)}{\overset{t}{\models}}} p \in p_p}} \qquad \text{ImpE}$$

$$\frac{(t,t',n) \; {}_{k}{\underset{(bb)}{\overset{t}{\models}}} p \in p_p}{(t,t',n) \; {}_{k}{\underset{(ks)}{\overset{t}{\models}}} p \in p_p} \text{Fig. 4c, Eq. (8)}$$

Note that one of the premises is closed by reference to the assumption *Ass* obtained at the beginning of the proof.

6 Related Work

Related work can be found in two different areas: work on the *specification* of *dynamic architectures* in general and *calculi* about *dynamic systems* specifically.

Over the last years, some approaches to the specification of dynamic architectures in general have emerged. One related approach comes from Le Métayer [12], who applies graph theory to specify architectural evolution. Similar to our work, the author proposed to model dynamic architectures as a sequence of graphs and to employ graph grammars as a technique to specify architectural evolution. A similar approach comes from Hirsch and Montanari [11], who employ hypergraphs as a formal model to represent styles and their reconfigurations. Another, closely related approach is the one used by Wermlinger et al. [20]. The authors combine behavior and structure to model dynamic reconfigurations. Recently, categorical approaches to dynamic architecture reconfiguration have appeared, such as the work of Castro et al. [7] and Fiadeiro and Lopes [9]. While they all introduce models for dynamic architectures similar to ours, they do not provide a calculus to reason about such architectures. Thus, we complement their work by providing rules to reason about such architectures.

A second area of work concerns approaches to reason about dynamic systems in general: Pioneering work in this area goes back to Milner in his well-known work on the π-calculus [17]. Here, the author provides a set of rules to reason about reconfigurable systems in general. The main idea behind the underlying model is that channels can be passed as messages between processes, which can then exchange messages over these channels. Another foundational model of dynamic systems which provides rules to reason about such systems is the Chemical Abstract Machine (CHAM) [1]. It is built upon the chemical metaphor and models a system as multi-set transformers. Thereby it also provides a set of general laws to reason about such systems. Finally, the ambient calculus [6] can be seen as an advancement of the CHAM. In contrast to membranes in CHAM, ambients provide stronger protection and provide mobility for sub-solutions as well. While all these approaches provide rules to reason about dynamic systems in general, their underlying model of dynamic systems is different from our model of dynamic architectures. Thus, we actually complement their work by providing rules to reason about different types of systems.

7   Conclusion

In this paper, we introduce a framework to reason about the behavior of components deployed to a dynamic environment. The major contributions of the paper can be summarized as follows: (i) We extend our model of dynamic architectures introduced in [15] with the notion of behavior traces to model behavior of single components. Thereby we also characterize an operator to extract the behavior of single components out of a given configuration trace. (ii) We introduce the notion of behavior trace assertions to specify behavior of single components and provide its formal semantics in terms of behavior traces. (iii) We provide a calculus to reason about the behavior of components in dynamic architectures. It is in a natural deduction style and provides introduction and elimination rules for each operator of behavior trace assertions. (iv) We show soundness and relative completeness of the calculus.

Our results can be used to support the verification of dynamic architectures. This was demonstrated by applying our calculus to verify a property for a dynamic version of the blackboard architecture pattern. Our overall research is directed towards a unified framework for the specification and verification of patterns for dynamic architectures. By introducing the calculus, we provide an important step towards this overall goal. However, future work is still required in three major directions: (i) To better support verification, we are aiming at integrating the calculus in Isabelle/HOL. Very much in the spirit of LCF [10], we are currently working on a mechanized proof of the rules of the calculus from first principles. (ii) Moreover, the calculus should be extended to better integrate port connections. (iii) We are currently looking for ways to leverage the hierarchical nature of patterns for their verification. Thus, we are interested in theoretical results of how results for one pattern can be reused for the verification of other, related patterns.

Acknowledgments. We would like to thank Manfred Broy, Mario Gleirscher, Vasileios Koutsoumpas, and the anonymous reviewers of ICTAC 2017 for their comments and helpful suggestions. The work was partially funded by the German Federal Ministry of Education and Research (BMBF) under grant "01Is16043A".

References

1. Berry, G., Boudol, G.: The chemical abstract machine. Theor. Comput. Sci. **96**(1), 217–248 (1992)
2. Bradbury, J.S., et al.: A survey of self-management in dynamic software architecture specifications. In: Proceedings of the 1st ACM SIGSOFT Workshop on Self-Managed Systems, pp. 28–33 (2004)
3. Broy, M.: A logical basis for component-oriented software and systems engineering. Comput. J. **53**(10), 1758–1782 (2010)
4. Broy, M.: A model of dynamic systems. In: Bensalem, S., Lakhneck, Y., Legay, A. (eds.) ETAPS 2014. LNCS, vol. 8415, pp. 39–53. Springer, Heidelberg (2014). doi:10.1007/978-3-642-54848-2_3
5. Buschmann, F., et al.: Pattern-Oriented Software Architecture: A System of Patterns (1996)
6. Cardelli, L., Gordon, A.D.: Mobile ambients. Theor. Comput. Sci. **240**(1), 177–213 (2000)
7. Castro, P.F., Aguirre, N.M., López Pombo, C.G., Maibaum, T.S.E.: Towards managing dynamic reconfiguration of software systems in a categorical setting. In: Cavalcanti, A., Deharbe, D., Gaudel, M.-C., Woodcock, J. (eds.) ICTAC 2010. LNCS, vol. 6255, pp. 306–321. Springer, Heidelberg (2010). doi:10.1007/978-3-642-14808-8_21
8. Clements, P.C.: A survey of architecture description languages. In: Proceedings of the 8th International Workshop on Software Specification and Design, p. 16 (1996)
9. Fiadeiro, J.L., Lopes, A.: A model for dynamic reconfiguration in serviceoriented architectures. Softw. Syst. Model. **12**(2), 349–367 (2013)
10. Gordon, M.J., Milner, A.J., Wadsworth, C.P.: Edinburgh LCF. LNCS, vol. 78. Springer, Heidelberg (1979). (Ed. by G. Goos and J. Hartmanis. 1st ed.)
11. Hirsch, D., Montanari, U.: Two graph-based techniques for software architecture reconfiguration. Electron. Notes Theor. Comput. Sci. **51**, 177–190 (2002)
12. Le Mtayer, D.: Describing software architecture styles using graph grammars. IEEE Trans. Softw. Eng. **24**(7), 521–533 (1998)
13. Manna, Z., Pnueli, A.: The Temporal Logic of Reactive and Concurrent Systems. Springer, New York (1992). doi:10.1007/978-1-4612-0931-7

14. Marmsoler, D.: On the specification of constraints for dynamic architectures. ArXiv e-prints, March 2017. arXiv: 1703.06823
15. Marmsoler, D., Gleirscher, M.: Specifying properties of dynamic architectures using configuration traces. In: Sampaio, A., Wang, F. (eds.) ICTAC 2016. LNCS, vol. 9965, pp. 235–254. Springer, Cham (2016). doi:10.1007/978-3-319-46750-4_14
16. Medvidovic, N.: ADLs and dynamic architecture changes. In: Joint Proceedings of the Second International Software Architecture Workshop and International Workshop on Multiple Perspectives in Software Development on SIGSOFT 1996 Workshops, pp. 24–27 (1996)
17. Milner, R.: Communicating and Mobile Systems: The π-calculus (1999)
18. Shaw, M., Garlan, D.: Software Architecture: Perspectives on an Emerging Discipline, vol. 1 (1996)
19. Taylor, R.N., Medvidovic, N., Dashofy, E.M.: Software Architecture: Foundations, Theory, and Practice. Wiley, Hoboken (2009)
20. Wermelinger, M., Lopes, A., Fiadeiro, J.L.: A graph based architectural (re)configuration language. Softw. Eng. Notes **26**(5), 21–32 (2001)
21. Wirsing, M.: Algebraic specification. In: van Leeuwen, J. (ed.) Handbook of Theoretical Computer Science, vol. B, Cambridge, pp. 675–788 (1990)

Class-Diagrams for Abstract Data Types

Thai Son Hoang$^{(\boxtimes)}$, Colin Snook, Dana Dghaym, and Michael Butler

ECS, University of Southampton, Southampton, UK
{t.s.hoang,cfs,dd4g12,mjb}@ecs.soton.ac.uk

Abstract. We propose to extend iUML-B class-diagrams to elaborate Abstract Data Types (ADTs) specified using Event-B theories. Classes are linked to data types, while attributes and associations correspond to operators of the data types. Axioms about the data types and operators are specified as constraints on the class. We illustrate our approach on a development of a control system in the railway domain.

Keywords: Event-B · iUML-B · Class-diagrams · Theory · Abstract Data Types (ADTs)

1 Introduction

Event-B [1] is a well-established formalism for developing systems whose components can be modelled as discrete transition systems. An Event-B model contains two parts: a dynamic part (called *machine*) modelled by a transition system and a static part (called *context*) capturing the model's parameters and assumptions about them. The main technique in Event-B to cope with system complexity is stepwise *refinement*, where design details are gradually introduced into the formal models. Refinement enables the abstraction of machines, and since abstract machines contain fewer details than concrete ones, they are usually easier to validate and verify.

To enhance the user experience with developing models, Event-B and its supporting *Rodin platform* (Rodin) is extensible. One of the extensions is iUML-B which includes state-machines and class-diagrams [9–11]. While state-machines give a visualisation of the system's dynamic state and the transitions between them, class-diagrams provide a visualisation of the model data and relationships. Another extension is the Theory plug-in [3] for extending the mathematical language of Event-B and supporting reasoning about these additional concepts. In particular, we can use Event-B theories to formalise *Abstract Data Types* (ADTs) [7] and subsequently utilise the ADTs to model the system's dynamic behaviour in the machines.

Our motivation is to provide a diagrammatic visualisation for the ADTs specified using Event-B theories. In particular, we propose to extend iUML-B class-diagrams with new and adapted diagrammatic elements, linking them to the data types and operators in the theories. The extension helps the design of the ADTs and provides a better understanding of the data types and the relationships between them.

© Springer International Publishing AG 2017
D.V. Hung and D. Kapur (Eds.): ICTAC 2017, LNCS 10580, pp. 100–117, 2017.
DOI: 10.1007/978-3-319-67729-3_7

Our contribution therefore is a proposal for extending iUML-B class-diagrams. Classes are linked to data types specified using theories. Attributes and associations elaborate operators of the data types. Axioms about the data types and operators are specified as class constraints. We illustrate our approach on a development of the RailGround case study [8] provided by Thales Austria GmbH.

The rest of the paper is structured as follows. Section 2 gives some background information about the Event-B method and the extensions such as iUML-B and the Theory plug-in. We present our proposal for extending iUML-B class-diagrams for Event-B theories in Sect. 3. We illustrate our approach using the Rail Ground case study in Sect. 4. We give a summary of our development in Sect. 5 and some conclusion of our work in Sect. 6.

2 Background

2.1 Event-B

Event-B [1] is a formal method for system development. Main features of Event-B include the use of *refinement* to introduce system details gradually into the formal model. An Event-B model contains two parts: *contexts* and *machines*. Contexts contain *carrier sets*, *constants*, and *axioms* that constrain the carrier sets and constants. Machines contain *variables* v, *invariants* $I(v)$ that constrain the variables, and *events*. An event comprises a guard denoting its enabling-condition and an action describing how the variables are modified when the event is executed. In general, an event e has the following form, where t are the event parameters, $G(t, v)$ is the guard of the event, and $v := E(t, v)$ is the action of the event[1].

e == any t where G(t,v) then v := E(t,v) end

A machine in Event-B corresponds to a transition system where *variables* represent the states and *events* specify the transitions. Contexts can be *extended* by adding new carrier sets, constants, axioms, and theorems. Machine **M** can be *refined* by machine **N** (we call **M** the abstract machine and **N** the concrete machine). The state of **M** and **N** are related by a gluing invariant $J(v, w)$ where v, w are variables of **M** and **N**, respectively. Intuitively, any "behaviour" exhibited by **N** can be simulated by **M**, with respect to the gluing invariant J. Refinement in Event-B is reasoned event-wise. Consider an abstract event e and the corresponding concrete event f. Somewhat simplifying, we say that e is refined by f iff f's guard is stronger than that of e and f's action can be simulated by e's action, taking into account the gluing invariant J. More information about Event-B can be found in [6]. Event-B is supported by Rodin [2], an extensible toolkit which includes facilities for modelling, verifying the consistency of models using theorem proving and model checking techniques, and validating models with simulation-based approaches.

---

[1] Actions in Event-B are, in the most general cases, non-deterministic [6].

2.2 iUML-B

iUML-B [9–11] provides a diagrammatic modelling notation for Event-B in the form of state-machines and class-diagrams. The diagrammatic elements are contained within an Event-B model and generate or contribute to parts of it. For example a state-machine will automatically generate the Event-B data elements (sets, constants, axioms, variables, and invariants) to implement the states, and contribute additional guards and actions to existing events. Class diagrams provide a way to visually model data relationships. Classes, attributes and associations are linked to Event-B data elements (carrier sets, constants, or variables) and generate constraints on those elements. In this paper, we focus on extending class-diagrams for visualising abstract data types specified using theories.

2.3 Theory Plug-In

The Theory plug-in [3] enables developers to define new (polymorphic) data types and operators upon those data types. These additional modelling concepts might be defined directly (including inductive definitions) or axiomatically.

An (inductive) datatype can be directly defined using several constructors. Each constructor can have zero or more destructors. A datatype without any definition is axiomatically defined. We focus on axiomatic data types in this paper. By convention, an axiomatic datatype satisfies the *non-emptiness* and *maximality* properties, i.e., for an axiomatic type S, we have $S \neq \varnothing$ and $\forall e \cdot e \in S$. As an example, an axiomatic type for *stacks* is declared as follows.

```
1 theory Stack(T)
2 types STACK(T)
3 end
```

Operators can be defined *directly*, *inductively* (on inductive data types) or *axiomatically*. An operator defined without any definition will be defined axiomatically. Operator notation is prefix by default. Operators with two arguments can be infix. Further properties can be declared for operators including *associativity* and *commutativity*.

In the following, we show the declaration for some stack operators: emptyStack, top, pop, and push.

```
1 operators
2    emptyStack: "STACK(T)"
3    top(st : "STACK(T)"): "T"
4    pop(st : "STACK(T)"): "STACK"
5       for "st ≠ emptyStack"
6    push(st : "STACK(T)", e : "T"): "STACK"
7    ≺ (e : "T", st : "STACK(T)") infix
8 axioms
9    @axm1 "∀ st, e · e ∈ T ⇒ push(st, e) ≠ emptyStack"
10   @axm2 "∀ st, e · e ∈ T ⇒ pop(push(st, e)) = st"
11   @axm3 "∀ st, e · e ∈ T ⇒ top(push(st, e)) = e"
12   @axm4 "∀ st · st ∈ STACK(T) ∧ st ≠ emptyStack ⇒ top(st) ≺ st"
13   @thm1 "∀ st, e· e ∈ T ⇒ e ≺ push(st, e)" theorem
```

An additional `infix` operator ≺ defines a predicate (without any returning type) specifying whether an element `e` is in the stack `st` or not. The axioms are the assumptions about these operators that can be used to define proof rules. Note that `@thm1` is a theorem which is derivable from the axioms defined previously. We omit the presentation of proof rules in this paper.

Finally, theories can be constructed in hierarchical manner: a theory can *extend* other theories by adding more data types, operators, and axioms.

3   Class-Diagrams for Abstract Data Types

An ADT is a mathematical model of a class of data structures. It is typically defined by a set of operations that can be performed on the ADT, along with a specification of their effect. By using Event-B theories to formalise ADTs, we can subsequently utilise the ADTs to model the system's dynamic behaviour in the machines. An ADT can be specified straightforwardly using Event-B theories with axiomatic data type and operators, e.g., the STACK data type in Sect. 2.3.

In order to aid the design of ADTs, we propose to extend class diagrams to ADTs that are specified using theories. In particular, data types are represented using classes and operators are modelled using attributes or associations. We illustrate our idea using the STACK data type example. The class-diagram for the STACK data type is shown in Fig. 1. In the diagram, there are two classes, namely STACK and T. The dashed arrow from STACK to T indicates that STACK is polymorphic and T is the type parameter of STACK. This is also denoted by the label, i.e., STACK<T>, of the STACK class. Since class T represents a formal type parameter it cannot own any child features such as associations or constraints.

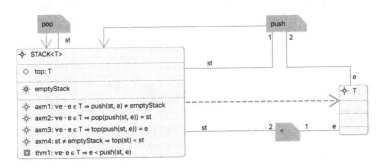

Fig. 1. A class-diagram for stack ADT

For now, we use the existing class diagram features to illustrate the proposed approach. Our intention is to add features to iUML-B to represent the ADT features with new diagram elements including a new class container for adding class constant instances, a new arrow/label feature for expressing class type parameters, a new diagram node for multi-source associations, and a new diagram node for representing abstract formal type parameters such as T.

Operators are represented by the special associations between classes. Each association operator can have one or more inputs and zero or one outputs. An operator without any output, e.g., ≺, indicates a *predicate*. The inputs to operators are labelled to indicate their formal parameters. If an operator has two or more inputs, e.g., push or ≺, each input is numbered (e.g., $1, 2, \ldots$) specifying their order.

A "query" operator, i.e., those with one input which is an instance of the data type and one output (e.g., top), can be specified as attributes of the class. An operator without any input and return an instance of the data type, i.e., a constant of the data type (e.g., emptyStack), is specified using a "constant" of the class. Finally, the axioms and theorems about the data type and its operators are specified as constraints on the class. The constraints are lifted automatically to all instances of the data type. Let st be the instance name for the STACK data type, @axm1 becomes

$$\forall \ st \ \cdot \ st \in STACK \Rightarrow (\forall \ e \ \cdot \ e \in T \Rightarrow push(st, \ e) \neq emptyStack) \ .$$

Note that in general, the class-diagrams and their corresponding theories for ADTs are developed gradually through several steps. In each step, additional data types, operators, and constraints can be added.

4   Example. An Interlocking System

The example used in this paper is based on a formal model of a railway interlocking system, which was developed by Thales Austria GmbH. This is a simplified version of interlocking systems, built specifically for research on formal validation and verification of railway systems [8]. This example is used as part of the rail use case of the European project *Enable-S3* [4].

4.1   Requirements

Railway systems, in general, aim at providing a timely, efficient and most importantly a safe train service. This requires a reliable command and control system that ensures a train can safely enter its specified route. In the system under consideration, the railway topology consists of a set of connected elements, which are controlled by signals passing information to the trains. The safety of a train is ensured by allowing its route to be set, only if it does not conflict with the current available routes. The following requirements are extracted and simplified from [8]. For illustration, we will consider the network topology with one track and two points as in Fig. 2.

Rail Elements. The railway topology is formed by a set of rail elements. A *Rail Element* is a unit which provides a physical running path for the trains, i.e. rails (e.g. track, points, crossing). Typically, a rail element is made up of one or more *segments*. The sets of segments belong to each rail element are disjoint.

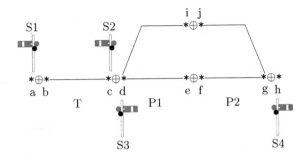

Fig. 2. An example railway topology [8]

REQ 1 The network topology is a set of rail elements.
REQ 2 A rail element contains one or more segments.

In Fig. 2, the segments are {bc,cb,di,id,de,ed,jg,gj,fg,gf}. There are three rail elements, namely T (a track), P1, P2 (points). The relationship between the rail elements and the segments are as follows:

T ↦ {bc,cb}, P1 ↦ {di,id,de,ed}, P2 ↦ {jg,gj,fg,gf}.

Element Positions. For each rail element, a *Rail Element Position* is a distinct situation of that rail element. Furthermore, each element position defines the set of possible element connections (defined by segments) for that particular rail element.

REQ 3 For each rail element, there is a set of possible element positions.
REQ 4 Each rail element and position correspond to a set of rail segments.

For example, a points has three possible position POS_X (in transition), POS_L (left), POS_R (right). Consider points P1, position POS_X corresponds to an emptyset of segments, POS_L corresponds to segments {di, id}, and POS_R corresponds to segments {de, ed}.

Paths. A path is a sequence of rail segments, with the constraint that two rail segments of the same rail element are not allowed within one path. A path can be activated so that trains are allowed to be on that path.

REQ 5 A path is a sequence of rail segments.
REQ 6 Two rail segments belonging to the same element are not allowed within one path.

Consider the example in Fig. 2, a path could be the following sequence of segments [bc,di,jg], or [gf,ed,cb]. Note that any sub-sequence of a path is also a path, e.g., [di,jg] is also a path.

Route Life-Cycle. A set of routes are defined. Each route correspond to a pre-defined path in the network. Before becoming active, a route must be requested. As soon as all conditions for the route (e.g., rail elements must be in the required position to establish its path), a requested route can be activated. A path corresponds to an active route is called active path. As a train moves along a route, rail elements that are no longer in use can be released. An active route can be removed only after all its rail elements are released. A rail element position can only be changed if the rail element is not part of an active path.

> **REQ 7** A requested route can become an active route when all conditions for that route are met.
>
> **REQ 8** An active route can be removed only after all its rail elements are released.
>
> **REQ 9** A rail element position can only be changed if it is not part of an active path.

In the example network topology, we can have the following routes R1–R4, with the following associations: R1 ↦ [bc, de, fg], R2 ↦ [bc, di, jg], R3 ↦ [gf, ed, cb], R4 ↦ [gj, id, cb].

Vacancy Detection. To simplify, we assume that each rail element corresponds to exactly one *Track Vacancy Detection* (TVD) section. The state of the TVD section is either vacant or occupied. A TVD section is occupied if there is some train on some segment belonging to the rail element.

> **REQ 10** Each rail element corresponds to exactly one TVD section.
>
> **REQ 11** A TVD section can be either in vacant or occupied state.

Signals. A signal is an entity capable of passing information to trains. A signal is associated with a rail element for a particular traversal direction. A signal aspect is an (abstract) information conveyed by a signal. Signal Default is a predefined aspect of signals. Trains are assumed to obey the signals, in particular, stop at a signal containing default aspect.

> **REQ 12** A signal is associated with a rail element.
>
> **REQ 13** A signal may be set to an aspect other than default, only if there is an active element after this signal.

In Fig. 2, we have 4 signals, S1– S4. Note that both S1 and S3 associated with T, but they protect the rail element in different traversal directions.

Safety Properties. Safety in this model is ensured by the paths which are active. The paths can only be set if all its elements are in the right positions. Safety is ensured by preventing paths to be requested if there are other paths requiring the same elements.

> **REQ 14** Two active paths cannot overlap.
>
> **REQ 15** An active path must have all its elements in the right positions.
>
> **REQ 16** A route can be requested if it is disjoint from other active or requested routes.

4.2   Development

For this paper, we omit the presentation of the proof rules associated with the theories. Most of them are directly inferred from the axioms constraining the data types. For the example, we abstract from rail segments. Details about rail segments (e.g., REQ 2, REQ 4, REQ 5, REQ 6) can be introduced later via refinement. The development is available online at http://doi.org/10.5258/ SOTON/D0162 including instructions on Rodin configuration.

Refinement Strategy. We adopt the following refinement strategy for developing a model of the system. The requirements taken into account at each refinement level is also listed.

- **M0:** To abstractly specify active routes in the system, focusing on collision-free properties (REQ 14).
- **M1:** To introduce the life-cycle of routes by specifying requested routes (REQ 7, REQ 16).
- **M2:** To formalise the rail elements and the link between rail elements and paths (REQ 1, REQ 8).
- **M3:** To specify the element positions and their association with the rail elements (REQ 3, REQ 15, REQ 9).
- **M4:** To introduce the track vacancy detection mechanism (REQ 10, REQ 11).
- **M5:** To introduce the signals controlling the trains' movement (REQ 12, REQ 13).

M0. Paths. In the initial model, we focus on the notion of paths and the relationships between them (abstractly). In particular, our model of the dynamic of the system centres around the main safety property of the system, i.e., collision-free (REQ 14). For this, we want to specify that there are no overlaps between currently active paths. The diagram for the initial theory of the PATH data type can be seen in Fig. 3. Two operators, namely $\oplus$ and $\sqsubseteq$, are introduced to specify *disjointness* and *sub-path* relationships between two paths p1 and p2. Properties of the operators are specified by constraints @axm1 and @axm2. Constraint @axm1 states that $\oplus$ is symmetric and @axm2 states that disjointness is preserved by the sub-path relationship. The corresponding theory can be seen as follows. Note that the constraints are lifted to be universally quantified over all instance p of the PATH data type.

```
1 theory Paths_01
2 types
3    PATH
4 operators
5    ⊕ (p1: "PATH", p2 : "PATH") infix
6    ⊑ (p1: "PATH", p2 : "PATH") infix
7 axioms
8    @axm1 "∀ p· p ∈ PATH ⇒ (∀ q · p ⊕ q ⇒ q ⊕ p)"
9    @axm2 "∀ p· p ∈ PATH ⇒ (∀ p1,p2 · p1 ⊑ p2 ∧ p2 ⊕ p ⇒ p ⊕ p1)"
10 end
```

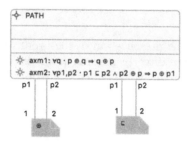

Fig. 3. Class-diagrams in M0

We can use the PATH data type to specify our dynamic system as follows. Context CO_RG_Paths declares a carrier set ROUTE denoting a set of pre-defined routes. Constant path links the routes with its initial paths (specified by the PATH data type).

```
1 context CO_RG_Paths
2 sets ROUTE
3 constants path
4 axioms
5     @axm1: "path ∈ ROUTE → PATH"
6 end
```

In machine M0_RG_Paths, variable path_curr is introduced to capture the active routes. Invariant @inv1 associates each active route with some path. Invariant @inv2 specifies the collision-free property: two different active routes must be disjoint.

```
1 machine M0_RG_Paths
2 sees CO_RG_Paths
3 variables path_curr
4 invariants
5     @inv1: "path_curr ∈ ROUTE ⇸ PATH"
6     @inv2: "∀ pth1, pth2 ·
7         pth1 ∈ dom(path_curr) ∧ pth2 ∈ dom(path_curr) ∧ pth1 ≠ pth2 ⇒
8             path_curr(pth1) ⊕ path_curr(pth2)"
9 INITIALISATION == begin @act1: "path_curr := ∅ " end
```

Three events are modelled at this specification level for adding, modifying, and removing routes. In addRoute, a new route pe, where the corresponding path (i.e., path(pe)) does not conflict with any existing routes (addRoute's @grd2), is activated. The initial path associated with pe is path(pe). Event modifyRoute updates the path corresponding to the route pe with the new path pth. Guard @grd2 of modifyRoute specifies that the new path pth must be a sub-path of the current path associated with pe (a route can only be updated by releasing rail elements which no longer in use). Finally, event removeRoute removes an active route specified by route pe from the set of active routes.

```
1 events
2     addRoute ==
3     any pe where
4         @grd1: "pe ∈ ROUTE \ dom(path_curr)"
5         @grd2: "∀ p · p ∈ dom(path_curr) ⇒ path(pe) ⊕ path_curr(p)"
6     then
7         @act1: "path_curr(pe) := path(pe)"
8     end
9
10    modifyRoute ==
11    any pe pth where
12        @grd1: "pe ∈ dom(path_curr)"
13        @grd2: "pth ⊑ path_curr(pe)"
14    then
15        @act1: "path_curr(pe) := pth"
16    end
17
18    removeRoute ==
19    any pe where
20        @grd1: "pe ∈ dom(path_curr)"
21    then
22        @act2: "path_curr := {pe} ⩤ path_curr"
23    end
24 end
```

M1. Route Life-Cycle. In the first refinement, we model the life-cycle of routes by introducing the notion of requested routes. In this refinement, there are no changes for the PATH data type. Variable path_req captures the set of requested routes (i.e., a subset of ROUTE) which must be disjoint from the set of current routes (@inv2).

```
1 invariants
2     @inv1: "path_req ⊆ ROUTE"
3     @inv2: "path_req ∩ dom(path_curr) = ∅ "
```

We refine event addRoute as follows, i.e., a requested route pe becomes an active route.

```
1 addRoute
2 refines addRoute
3 any pe where
4     @grd1: "pe ∈ path_req"
5 then
6     @act1: "path_curr(pe) := path(pe)"
7     @act2: "path_req := path_req \ {pe}"
8 end
```

In order to prove the refinement of event addRoute, we need additional invariants linking path_req and path_curr.

```
1 @inv3: "∀ pth1, pth2 · pth1 ∈ path_req ∧ pth2 ∈ dom(path_curr) ⇒ path(pth1) ⊕ path_curr
        (pth2)"
2 @inv4: "∀ pth1, pth2 · pth1 ∈ path_req ∧ pth2 ∈ path_req ∧ pth1 ≠ pth2 ⇒ path(pth1) ⊕
        path(pth2)"
```

Two new events `requestRoute` and `removeRequest` are introduced to create a new request for a path and remove an existing request. Notice the guards of `requestRoute` ensure the maintenance of invariants @inv3 and @inv4.

```
1  requestRoute ==
2  any pe where
3      @grd1: "pe ∈ ROUTE \ path_req"
4      @grd2: "pe ∉ dom(path_curr)"
5      @grd3: "∀ p · p ∈ dom(path_curr) ⇒ path(pe) ⊕ path_curr(p)"
6      @grd4: "∀ p · p ∈ path_req ⇒ path(pe) ⊕ path(p)"
7  then
8      @act1: "path_req := path_req ∪ {pe}"
9  end
10
11 removeRequest ==
12 any pth where
13     @grd1: "pth ∈ path_req"
14 then
15     @act1: "path_req := path_req \ {pth}"
16 end
```

M2. Rail Elements. In this refinement, we introduce the rail elements into the formal models. A new data type `RAIL_ELEMENT` is introduced. We extend the `PATH` data type with a new operator `rail_elements` returning the set of rail elements associated with each path (see Fig. 4). Another operator ≪ specifying whether a rail element `re` belongs to some path `p` or not is defined using the direct definition, i.e. `re ≪ p == re ∈ rail_elements(p)`. Finally, we introduce an operator `shrink` for removing a rail element `re` from the path `p`. The `shrink` operator is only defined for the rail element `re` belonging to the path `p`. Axiom @axm1 defines the disjointness between paths `p` and `q` as the disjointness of their rail elements. Axioms @axm2 and @axm3 specify the properties of

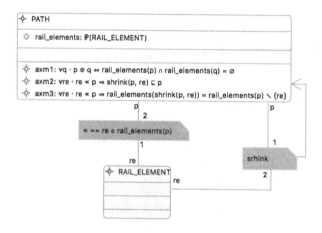

Fig. 4. Class-diagrams in M2

`shrink` operator: it makes the path `p` smaller and removes the element `re` from the path's rail elements. The corresponding theory is as follows.

```
1  theory Paths_02
2  imports Paths_01 RailElement_01
3  operators
4     rail_elements(p: "PATH"): "P(RAIL_ELEMENT)"
5     ≪ (re: "RAIL_ELEMENT", p : "PATH") infix =
6        "re ∈ rail_elements(p)"
7     shrink(p : "PATH", re : "RAIL_ELEMENT"): "PATH"
8        for "re ≪ p"
9  axioms
10    @axm1 "∀ p · p ∈ PATH ⇒ (∀ q · p ⊕ q ⇔ rail_elements(p) ∩ rail_elements(q) = ∅ )"
11    @axm2 "∀ p · p ∈ PATH ⇒ (∀ re · re ≪ p ⇒ shrink(p, re) ⊑ p)"
12    @axm3 "∀ p · p ∈ PATH ⇒ (∀ re · re ≪ p ⇒ rail_elements(shrink(p, re)) =
            rail_elements(p) \ {re})"
13 end
```

For the dynamic system, a variable `rail_element_path` is introduced to keep the relationship between the rail elements and the current active route. Each rail element is associated with at most one active route (@inv1). Invariant @inv2 states the consistency between `rail_element_path` and the set of rail elements associated with some active route `p`.

```
1  @inv1: "rail_element_path ∈ RAIL_ELEMENT ⇸ dom(path_curr)"
2  @inv2: "∀ p· p ∈ dom(path_curr) ⇒ rail_elements(path_curr(p)) = rail_element_path∼[{p}]"
```

We focus on the refinement of `modifyRoute` in this level. The changes to the other events are trivial. With the introduction of the `shrink` operator, we can now be more precise about how an active route is modified, i.e., it can be done by releasing some no longer used rail element `re`.

```
1  modifyRoute
2  refines modifyRoute
3  any pe re where
4     @grd1: "pe ∈ dom(path_curr)"
5     @grd2: "re ≪ path_curr(pe)"
6  with
7     @pth: "pth = shrink(path_curr(pe), re)"
8  then
9     @act1: "path_curr(pe) := shrink(path_curr(pe), re)"
10    @act2: "rail_element_path := {re} ⩤ rail_element_path"
11 end
```

The witness for `pth` (using the `with` clause) specifies the value of the removed abstract parameter `pth`. The rail element `re` is removed from the domain of `rail_element_path`: it is no longer associated with any active path.

M3. Element Positions. In this refinement, we introduce the positions for rail elements. We introduce a new ADT, namely `RAIL_POSITION` (see Fig. 5). A new operator ⊑ is added to the `RAIL_ELEMENT` ADT. For an element position `rp` and a rail element `re`, `ep ⊑ re` states that `rp` is a valid position for `re`. An additional operator `Default` for `RAIL_ELEMENT` which returns the default position for each rail element. Axiom @axm1 states that the default position for a rail element `re` is

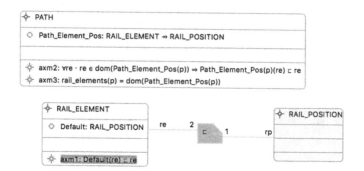

Fig. 5. Class-diagrams in M3

always a valid one for that rail element. Finally, an operator `Path_Element_Pos` is added to the `PATH` ADT which returns a (partial) function relating the rail elements (belonging to the path) with the element position. Axiom @axm2 states that the position defined for a rail element `re` of a path `p` must be a valid position for `re`. Axiom @axm3 gives the relationship between `rail_elements` and `Path_Element_Pos` as expected.

We introduce a variable `rail_positions` to capture the current position of every rail element (@inv1 below). Invariant @inv2 states that the position of every rail element `re` must be a valid one for `re`. Invariant @inv3 specifies the important safety property for each current active route: the position of the rail elements that belong to the active route must be the correct position.

```
1  invariants
2    @inv1: "rail_positions ∈ RAIL_ELEMENT ⟶ RAIL_POSITION"
3    @inv2: "∀ re · rail_positions(re) ⊑ re"
4    @inv3: "∀ p, re · p ∈ dom(path_curr) ∧ re ≪ path_curr(p) ⇒ rail_positions(re) =
             Path_Element_Pos(path_curr(p))(re)"
```

An additional guard @grd2 is added to `addRoute` event as follows.

```
1  @grd2: "∀ re · re ⊑ path(pe) ⇒ rail_positions(re) = Path_Element_Pos(path(pe))(re)"
```

The guard ensures that only when every rail element `re` that belongs to a requested route `pe` is in the correct position, can this route `pe` can be turned into a current route. Two new events are added for setting the position of a rail element: `setRailElementPos` and `setRailElementPath`.

```
1  setRailElementPos
2  any re pos where
3    @grd1: "re ∉ dom(rail_element_path)"
4    @grd2: "∀ p · p ∈ path_req ⇒ re ≪ path(p)"
5    @grd3: "pos ⊑ re" // @pos is valid
6    @grd4: "pos ≠ rail_positions(re)" // @pos is new
7  then
8    @act: "rail_positions(re) := pos"
9  end
10
```

```
11 setRailElementPath
12 any p re where
13     @grd1: "p ∈ path_req" // @p is a requested path.
14     @grd2: "re ≪ path(p)" // @re is a rail element of @p
15     @grd3: "Path_Element_Pos(path(p))(re) ≠ rail_positions(re)"
16 then
17     @act: "rail_positions(re) := Path_Element_Pos(path(p))(re)"
18 end
```

Event `setRailElementPos` sets the new position `pos` for a rail element `re` which does not belong to any active path (`@grd1`) and does not belong to any requested route (`@grd2`). Event `setRailElementPath` sets the position for a rail element `re` belonging to a requested route `p`. The new position of the element `re` is the position required for path `p` as specified by the operator `Path_Element_Pos`.

M4. Vacancy Detection. In this refinement, we introduce the track vacancy detection. Each TVD section corresponds to a rail element. As a result, we introduce a new data type `TVD_SECTION` with an operator `TVD_Element` as in Fig. 6. Axioms `@axm1` and `@axm2` ensure the one-to-one relationship between `TVD_SECTION` and `RAIL_ELEMENT`.

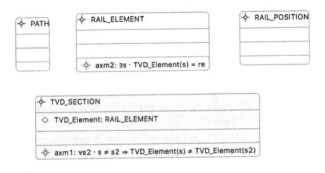

Fig. 6. Class-diagrams in M4

We introduce a new variable `TVD_status` to capture the current vacancy status of the TVD sections. The invariants for this refinement level are as follows,

```
1 @inv1: "TVD_status ∈ TVD_SECTION → TVD_STATE_ENUM"
2 @inv2: "∀ s · TVD_status(s) = TVD_STATE_OCCUPIED ⇒ TVD_Element(s) ∈ dom(
        rail_element_path)"
```

where `TVD_STATE_ENUM` is a data type with two elements: `TVD_STATE_OCCUPIED` and `TVD_STATE_VACANT`.

Invariant `@inv2` states that if a TVD section `s` is occupied then the corresponding rail element must be a part of an active path. This corresponds to the assumption that trains cannot go out of the current active paths.

Event `modifyRoute` is extended as follows.

```
1  modifyRoute extended
2  refines modifyRoute
3  any s where
4      @grd2: "TVD_status(s) = TVD_STATE_OCCUPIED"
5      @grd3: "re = TVD_Element(s)"
6  then
7      @act3: "TVD_status(s) := TVD_STATE_VACANT"
8  end
```

The additional parameter s denotes the TVD section corresponding to the rail element re (@grd3). The status of s is changed from occupied to vacant in this `modifyRoute` event. Essentially, this event models the situation where a train departs from the rail element re (hence the TVD status changed from occupied to vacant) and the rail element re is released.

A new event `setTVDStatus` is introduced for changing the status of a TVD section from vacant to occupied.

```
1  setTVDStatus
2  any s where
3      @grd1: "TVD_status(s) = TVD_STATE_VACANT"
4      @grd2: "TVD_Element(s) ∈ dom(rail_element_path)"
5  then
6      @act1: "TVD_status(s) := TVD_STATE_OCCUPIED"
7  end
```

Guard @grd2 ensures that the rail element is currently within some active path.

M5. Signal. In this refinement, we introduce the signals and signal aspects. Two new ADTs are introduced: SIGNAL and SIGNAL_ASPECT_ENUM (Fig. 7). The SIGNAL data type has one operator, namely Signal_Element, returning the rail element that the signal protects. The SIGNAL_ASPECT_ENUM has a constant, namely SIGNAL_ASPECT_DEFAULT, representing the default aspect of the signals. No additional assumptions are made about SIGNAL and SIGNAL_ASPECT_ENUM.

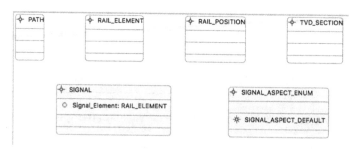

Fig. 7. Class-diagrams in M5

We introduce a variable signal_status to model the status of all the signals.

```
1  @inv1: "signal_status ∈ SIGNAL → SIGNAL_ASPECT_ENUM"
```

Event `setTVDStatus` is refined by two events according to whether or not the rail element is protected by a signal. Event `setTVDStatusPath` captures the case where the rail element corresponding to the TVD section s is not protected by a signal. This reflects the situation where a train is moving along an existing path. Event `setTVDStatusSignal` corresponds to the case where the rail element is protected by a signal. Note that the signal is turned automatically to `SIGNAL_ASPECT_DEFAULT` when the train occupied the element.

```
1 setTVDStatusPath refines setTVDStatus
2 any s where
3     @grd1: "TVD_status(s) = TVD_STATE_VACANT"
4     @grd2: "TVD_Element(s) ∈ dom(rail_element_path)"
5     @grd3: "∀ sg · TVD_Element(s) ≠ Signal_Element(sg)"
6 then
7     @act1: "TVD_status(s) := TVD_STATE_OCCUPIED"
8 end
9
10 setTVDStatusSignal refines setTVDStatus
11 any s sg where
12     @grd1: "TVD_status(s) = TVD_STATE_VACANT"
13     @grd2: "signal_status(sg) ≠ SIGNAL_ASPECT_DEFAULT"
14     @grd3: "TVD_Element(s) = Signal_Element(sg)"
15 then
16     @act1: "TVD_status(s) := TVD_STATE_OCCUPIED"
17     @act2: "signal_status(sg) := SIGNAL_ASPECT_DEFAULT"
18 end
```

In order to prove the correctness of the refinement of `setTVDStatus` by `setTVDStatusSignal`, we need the following invariants. Invariants @inv2 and @inv3 state that if the signal status for sg is not `SIGNAL_ASPECT_DEFAULT` then (1) the rail element corresponding to the signal must belong to some active path and (2) the rail element must be vacant as detected by the TVD section. Invariant @inv4 states that if two signals sg1 and sg2 protecting the same rail element and sg1 is not `SIGNAL_ASPECT_DEFAULT` then sg2 must have the default aspect.

```
1 @inv2: "∀ sg · signal_status(sg) ≠ SIGNAL_ASPECT_DEFAULT ⇒ Signal_Element(sg) ∈ dom(
        rail_element_path)"
2 @inv3: "∀ sg, s · signal_status(sg) ≠ SIGNAL_ASPECT_DEFAULT ∧ TVD_Element(s) =
        Signal_Element(sg) ⇒ TVD_status(s) = TVD_STATE_VACANT"
3 @inv4: "∀ sg1, sg2 · signal_status(sg1) ≠ SIGNAL_ASPECT_DEFAULT ∧ Signal_Element(sg1) =
        Signal_Element(sg2) ∧ sg1 ≠ sg2 ⇒ signal_status(sg2) = SIGNAL_ASPECT_DEFAULT"
```

A new event to set the signal aspect to proceed (i.e., not the default aspect) as follows, taking into account the above invariants.

```
1 setSignalAspectProceed
2 any sg asp s where
3     @grd1: "signal_status(sg) = SIGNAL_ASPECT_DEFAULT"
4     @grd2: "asp ≠ SIGNAL_ASPECT_DEFAULT"
5     @grd3: "Signal_Element(sg) ∈ dom(rail_element_path)"
6     @grd4: "TVD_Element(s) = Signal_Element(sg)"
7     @grd5: "TVD_status(s) = TVD_STATE_VACANT"
8     @grd6: "∀ sg1 · Signal_Element(sg) = Signal_Element(sg1) ∧ sg ≠ sg1 ⇒ signal_status(
            sg1) = SIGNAL_ASPECT_DEFAULT"
9 then
10     @act1: "signal_status(sg) := asp"
11 end
```

5 Summary

Our RailGround development using theories contains 6 machines, i.e., MO–M5 forming a refinement-chain. Out of the total 147 proof obligations, 95% (139) are discharged automatically. This high perchantage of automatic proofs is due to the carefully constructed ADTs with appropriate axioms and proof rules supporting the reasoning.

Typically we develop Event-B models to express important (safety) properties at a very abstract level and then make a series of refinements to gradually introduce the details of a design mechanism that maintains this property. The RailGround model is atypical in that it begins by modelling the established principals of interlocking systems without modelling the safety properties that those systems are designed to achieve. The reason for this is that the principles of interlocking are a proven design mechanism for controlling trains in a safe way. The model focusses instead on providing a precise and accurate specification of the interlocking product-line. Nevertheless, the model provides a good case study to illustrate the use of our diagrammatic representation of ADTs linked to Event-B theories including sufficient properties concerning the lack of conflicts in paths.

6 Conclusion

In this paper, we propose an extension to class-diagrams elaborating ADTs specified using Event-B theories. Classes are linked to data types, while attributes and associations correspond to operators of the data types. Axioms about the data types and operators are specified as constraints on the class. We illustrate our approach on a development of RailGround case study provided by Thales Austria GmbH. The diagrammatic visualisation helps us to design appropriate theories supporting the system development. Moreover, the diagrams and their corresponding theories can be developed gradually and integrated seamlessly with the refinement development process of Event-B.

In the future, we plan to implement our proposal by extending iUML-B. Furthermore, we plan to incorporate other techniques such as instantiation [5] to support the development of theories. Currently, during the development, we extending our class-diagrams with new data types, operators and axioms. This result in data type with several operators and constraints. A possibility for ADT is that they contain contradict axioms. An alternative to data type extension is instantation where one or more operators is "replaced" by new ones. For example, when we introduce the `rail_elements` operator for paths, we can instantiate $\oplus$ (i.e., define it) using `rail_elements` and prove the axioms about $\oplus$ can be derived from the properties of `rail_elements`. Compare to extension, instatiation will result in more concrete and smaller data types.

Acknowledgement. This work has been conducted within the ENABLE-S3 project that has received funding from the ECSEL Joint Undertaking under Grant Agreement no. 692455. This Joint Undertaking receives support from the European Union's HORIZON 2020 research and innovation programme and Austria, Denmark, Germany, Finland, Czech Republic, Italy, Spain, Portugal, Poland, Ireland, Belgium, France, Netherlands, United Kingdom, Slovakia, Norway.

References

1. Abrial, J.-R.: Modeling in Event-B: System and Software Engineering. Cambridge University Press, Cambridge (2010)
2. Abrial, J.-R., Butler, M., Hallerstede, S., Hoang, T.S., Mehta, F., Voisin, L.: Rodin: an open toolset for modelling and reasoning in Event-B. Softw. Tools Technol. Transf. **12**(6), 447–466 (2010)
3. Butler, M., Maamria, I.: Practical theory extension in Event-B. In: Liu, Z., Woodcock, J., Zhu, H. (eds.) Theories of Programming and Formal Methods. LNCS, vol. 8051, pp. 67–81. Springer, Heidelberg (2013). doi:10.1007/978-3-642-39698-4_5
4. The Enable-S3 Consortium. Enable-S3 European project (2016). www.enable-s3.eu/
5. Fürst, A., Hoang, T.S., Basin, D.A., Sato, N., Miyazaki, K.: Large-scale system development using abstract data types and refinement. Sci. Comput. Program. **131**, 59–75 (2016)
6. Hoang, T.S.: An introduction to the Event-B modelling method. In: Romanovsky, A., Thomas, M. (eds.) Industrial Deployment of System Engineering Methods, pp. 211–236. Springer, Heidelberg (2013)
7. Liskov, B., Zilles, S.: Programming with abstract data types. In: Proceedings of the ACM SIGPLAN Symposium on Very High Level Languages, pp. 50–59. ACM, New York (1974). http://doi.acm.org/10.1145/800233.807045
8. Reichl, K.: Railground Model on GitHub (2016). https://github.com/klar42/railground/. Accessed 20 Apr 2017
9. Said, M.Y., Butler, M., Snook, C.: A method of refinement in UML-B. Softw. Syst. Model. **14**(4), 1557–1580 (2015)
10. Snook, C.: iUML-B statemachines. In: Proceedings of the Rodin Workshop 2014, Toulouse, France, pp. 29–30 (2014). http://eprints.soton.ac.uk/365301/
11. Snook, C., Butler, M.: UML-B: formal modeling and design aided by UML. ACM Trans. Softw. Eng. Methodol. **15**(1), 92–122 (2006)

Value-Based or Conflict-Based? Opacity Definitions for STMs

Jürgen König$^{(\boxtimes)}$ and Heike Wehrheim

Department of Computer Science, Paderborn University, Paderborn, Germany
jkoenig@mail.upb.de

Abstract. Software Transactional Memory (STM) algorithms provide programmers with a high-level synchronization technique for concurrent access to shared state. STMs typically guarantee some sort of serializability: the concurrent execution of transactions appears to occur in a sequential order. With Guerraoui and Kapalka's 2008 paper, serializability of software transactions has been phrased as *opacity*. While opacity has been accepted as the standard correctness criterion for STMs, later verification approaches nevertheless adopt different formulations – claiming them to be opacity.

In this paper, we study the relationships between different versions of opacity, Guerraoui and Kapalka's *value-based* version and the verification-friendly, value-less *conflict-based* version. We show that even under some reasonable restrictions on executions, conflict-based remains stronger than value-based opacity, rejecting some serializable executions. We provide an alternative definition of conflict-based opacity, still not tracking values and thus keeping its verification-friendly style. This version, which we call *constraint-based*, is proven to coincide with value-based opacity. Finally, we propose a technique for checking constraint-based opacity on executions, employing the SMT-solver Z3.

1 Introduction

In modern computing, one of the greater changes was the switch from singlecore to multicore processors inducing a rising amount of concurrency in programs. (Software) Transactional Memory ((S)TM) [14,25] is a method for synchronizing multiple threads accessing shared memory. It frees the programmer from the responsibility of ensuring the atomicity of his/her code. He/she can simply mark blocks as *transactions*, and the STM then ensures that transactions will be executed seemingly atomic.

As the last sentence implies, an STM does not necessarily internally execute these blocks atomically, but externally it has to seem like it does. Formally defining this concept of "seeming atomicity" – thus also defining correctness criteria for STMs – has been the subject of past and current research. Currently, value-based opacity (value opacity in the following) [13] represents a consensus about the correct behavior of an STM. Value opacity inspects the histories generated by STM executions and checks whether transactions never read inconsistent values.

© Springer International Publishing AG 2017
D.V. Hung and D. Kapur (Eds.): ICTAC 2017, LNCS 10580, pp. 118–135, 2017.
DOI: 10.1007/978-3-319-67729-3_8

Given that there are many STM algorithms (e.g. [4,5,24,28]), an essential question is how to ensure that they are opaque. There are two main approaches for this: deductive (interactive) verification and model checking. Interactive verification approaches typically use refinement proofs to show opacity (e.g. [7,17]). To this end, they employ an intermediate specification called TMS2 [8] which is known to be opaque and prove the STM algorithm to be a refinement of TMS2 using forward or backward simulation. Lesani and Palsberg [19] on the other hand introduced a notion called *markability*, proved it to be equivalent to opacity and used interactive verification to show actual STM algorithms to be markable.

Model checking as a means for proving opacity of STM algorithms has been investigated by Guerraoui et al. [12]. Their key result is the proof of a kind of small-model-theorem: model checking for opacity of arbitrary numbers of threads operating on arbitrarily many variables can be reduced to model checking for two threads and two variables (under certain assumptions on the STM algorithm). For this, they employ a definition of opacity which is based on a notion of *conflict* between transactions, not on the idea of checking for inconsistent values of reads. Still, they refer to this as the definition of opacity of [13], which however uses a value-based formalization. Similarly, STM validation techniques based on testing frequently employ conflict-based versions. The advantage for testing as well as model checking is the possibility of completely neglecting the values written to or read from shared variables, and thus a significant gain in state space saving.

In this paper we study the question of equality of value-based and conflict-based versions of opacity. Our first result is that value and conflict opacity are basically incomparable. Under some reasonable assumptions on executions of STMs, we can show that conflict opacity implies value opacity. Taking the wish for a definition of opacity without values into account, we then propose a new definition called *constraint opacity*. Constraint opacity is fully equivalent to value opacity given two reasonable assumptions on STM executions. Interestingly, it turns out that our new definition is conceptually similar to markability [19], however ignoring variables values. Finally, we show how histories (execution sequences) of STMs can be easily checked for constraint opacity (and thus for value opacity) by encoding the constraints into first order logic and using a standard SMT solver (Z3 [21]) for satisfiability checking.

2   Notation

We start with introducing some background notation. In software transactional memory systems, programmers write *transactions* to access shared memory. We let L be the set of memory locations, V the set of possible values of these locations and T the set of transaction identifiers. The variables v, t and any variation of them are elements of their respective sets V, T. We denote locations with x, y. In executions of STMs, we observe certain *events* happening: a transaction can be started, it can read from or write to locations and it might finally end. The set of events is

$$E = \{\mathrm{write}_t(x, v), \mathrm{read}_t(x, v), \mathrm{commit}_t, \mathrm{abort}_t, \mathrm{begin}_t \mid x \in L, v \in V, t \in T\}$$

Events form *histories*, i.e., sequences $e_0 \ldots e_n$ of events where $e_i \in E$. We write $e < e'$ if there exists some i, j with $i < j$ and $e = e_i, e' = e_j$, and $e \in h$ if $e = e_i$ for some i, $0 \leq i \leq n$. We write $trans(e) = t$ iff $e_i \in \{write_t(x, v), read_t(x, v),$ $commit_t, abort_t, begin_t \mid x \in L, v \in V\}$.

We let $h|_t$ be the projection of the history h onto the events of transaction t only. A transaction t *occurs* in h, $t \in h$, if $h|_t$ is non-empty. The *write set* of a transaction t is $WS_t = \{x \mid write_t(x, v) \in h, v \in V, x \in L\}$. The *read set* RS_t is defined analogeously. Next, we define key properties of histories and introduce some conventions to simplify proofs.

We only want to consider executions where programmers use the STM according to a fixed scheme. Every transaction has to start with a begin and – if it ends – has to end with a commit or abort. Furthermore, transactions may not contain more than one begin event and not more than one commit or abort event. These requirements give rise to the notion of well formed histories.

Definition 1 (Well Formedness). *Let h be a history. A transaction t is well formed in h iff the following holds for $h|_t = e_i \ldots e_j$:*

1. $e_i = begin_t \wedge \forall k \neq i : e_k \neq begin_t$ and
2. $\forall k < j : e_k \notin \{commit_t, abort_t\}$.

A history is well formed if all transactions occurring in it are well formed.

From now on we assume all histories to be well formed. A history imposes a partial ordering on the transactions occuring in it: one transaction precedes another if the first one ends before the second one starts.

Definition 2 (Real Time Order). *Let h be a history. Two transactions t_1, t_2 in h with $h|_{t_1} = e_i, ..., e_j, h|_{t_2} = e_{i'} \ldots e_{j'}$ are called* real time ordered *in h, $t_1 <_{rt}^h t_2$, if $j < i'$ and $e_j \in \{commit_t, abort_t\}$.*

A history h is *sequential* if it is well-formed and all of its transactions are real time ordered (not concurrent), i.e., $\forall t_1 \in h, t_2 \in h : t_1 <_{rt}^h t_2 \vee t_2 <_{rt}^h t_1$. Later, we also need the completion of histories: In the completion of a history, any non committed and non-aborted transaction is aborted at the end of the history. The order of these abortions does not matter in our context. We write this completion of a history h as $complete(h)$.

For defining the correctness of an STM algorithm, we inspect the histories it generates. Basically, all opacity definitions define correctness of a history h via the ability of finding an equivalent sequential history h_s, i.e., the ability of showing that a concurrent history can be serialized in some way. They differ in the requirements they impose on h_s.

One such requirement is legality. Basically, a sequential history is *legal* if every read of a variable returns the latest written value to that variable. This in particular also has to hold for reads of aborting transactions. STM algorithms basically employ one of two ways of updating shared state: *direct* and *deferred update* semantics. In this paper, we will consider the deferred update semantics as it is the more frequently employed technique. In a deferred update STM, an

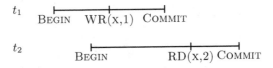

Fig. 1. Conflict-based opaque but not value-based opaque

update of memory locations occurs at commit time only. This implies that all writes of a transaction can be seen by itself after the write and be seen by other transactions only if the writing transaction has committed. For the following definition, we assume that every history starts with a committing transaction T_0 writing 0 to every location. Thereby, we need not differentiate between read events reading from other writes and reading initial values of locations. We furthermore assume that every transaction writes at most once to every location, which does not come with any cost regarding expressiveness. This lets us define what the latest write is which a read event can access.

Definition 3 (Deferred Update Latest Write). *Let* $h = e_0 \ldots e_m \ldots e_n$ *be a history. We define the* latest write *to a location* x *for an event* e_m *with* $trans(e_m) = t$ *as*

$$LW_h(x, e_m) = \begin{cases} write_t(x, v) = e_{m'}, & e_{m'} \in h, m' < m \\ commit_{t'} = e_{m'}, m' \leq m, m' \ max., x \in WS_{t'} & else \end{cases}$$

Similarly, we can define the latest written value.

Definition 4 (Deferred Update Latest Written Value). *The* latest written value *to a location* x *for an event* $trans(e_m) = t$ *in a history* $h = e_0 \ldots e_m \ldots e_n$ *is*

$$LWV_h(x, e_m) = \begin{cases} v, & \text{if } \exists write_{t'}(x, v) : commit_{t'} = LW_h(x, e_m) \\ v, & \text{if } LW_h(x, e_m) = write_t(x, v) \end{cases}$$

A sequential history is then *legal* when it always reads the latest written values: $\forall e_m = read_{t'}(x, v) : v = LWV_h(x, e_m)$. Finally, two histories h, h' are *equivalent*, $h \equiv h'$, if $\forall t : h|_t = h'|_t$. It is trivial to see that $\equiv$ is an equivalence relation.

Example 1. Figure 1 graphically depicts a history with two transactions t_1 and t_2, namely $h = begin_{t_1} begin_{t_2} write_{t_1}(x, 1) \ commit_{t_1} read_{t_2}(x, 2) \ commit_{t_2}$. The history is well formed and not sequential (the begin of t_2 happens before the commit of t_1). The latest write for $read_{t_2}(x, 2)$ is $commit_{t_1}$. Trying to find a sequential history justifying the correctness of this concurrent history fails: There are two possible sequential reorderings, $t_1 t_2$ and $t_2 t_1$, which both are not legal since the latest value written to x can never be 2.

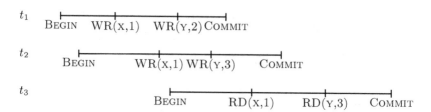

Fig. 2. Value opaque but not conflict opaque

3   Value and Conflict Opacity

The last section has introduced all neccessary notations which now let us define opacity. Basically, it remains to be defined when a sequential history can be used as a justification for a concurrent history. We give the following two definitions of value and conflict opacity according to Guerraoui et al. [13] and [12]. For value opacity, we in addition require prefix closedness which is now standardly added to opacity definitions.

Value opacity uses legality as its main correctness requirement, i.e., in a sequential history all values read have to be written by the latest write.

Definition 5 (Value Opacity). *A history h is* value final-state opaque *iff*

- *there exists a sequential legal history h_s which is equivalent to complete(h) and*
- $<^h_{rt} \subseteq <^{hs}_{rt}$.

A history h is value opaque *iff all prefixes of h are value final-state opaque.*

Conflict opacity on the other hand is characterized by a *conflict order* and the sequential history is not allowed to "reorder" conflicting transactions.

Definition 6 (Conflict Order). *The* conflict order *of h, written as $<^h_c$, is the union of the following three relations:*

1. *read-write conflicts:*
   $\{(t_1, t_2) \mid t_1, t_2 \in h, \exists e' = read_{t_1}(x, v), e = commit_{t_2} \in h, e < e', (x \in WS_{t_2})\}$,
2. *write-read conflicts:*
   $\{(t_1, t_2) \mid t_1, t_2 \in h, \exists e' = commit_{t_1}, e = read_{t_2}(x, v) \in h, e' < e, (x \in WS_{t_2})\}$,
3. *write-write conflicts:*
   $\{(t_1, t_2) \mid t_1, t_2 \in h, \exists e = commit_{t_1}, e' = commit_{t_2} \in h, e < e', WS_{t_1} \cap WS_{t_2}) \neq \emptyset\}$, *and*
4. *real-time order:* $<^h_{rt}$.

Note that we have write conflicts between commit events because we consider a deferred-update semantics. From this conflict order the definition of conflict opacity is derived.

Definition 7 (Conflict Opacity). *A history h is* conflict opaque *iff for the history $h' = complete(h)$ the conflict order $<_c^{h'}$ is a strict partial order.*

At a first glance the histories accepted by these two definitions may seem to be equal, but it can be shown that both properties do not imply each other.

Observation 1. *Conflict opacity does not imply value opacity.*

This observation can easily be confirmed by looking at Fig. 1. The conflict order only contains $t_1 <_c^h t_2$, so it is a strict partial order. But there exists no sequential equivalent history which is legal.

Observation 2. *Value opacity does not imply conflict opacity.*

This observation can easily be confirmed by looking at Fig. 2. The conflict order contains (beside other elements) $t_2 <_c^h t_3$ and $t_3 <_c^h t_2$, thus it cannot be a strict partial order. The sequential order $t_2 t_3 t_1$ is legal and equivalent to the original history, thus it is value opaque.

These two counterexamples illustrate differences between the opacity definitions which only occur in very specific situations. The differences are the following.

1. Conflict-Based Opacity is oblivious to values:
   For conflict opacity it only matters whether two events access the same location and whether one of them is a commit. Values are not part of the evaluation, which implies that non-realistic histories as the one in Fig. 1 are actually conflict opaque. One could argue that these histories are not very likely to appear in practice. However, consider the history in Fig. 3. This history could actually be produced by an STM using snapshots (e.g. the STM fulfilling snapshot isolation presented by Riegel et al. [24]). In the history, the value of x is important since the second read of t_2 on x could return either 0 or 1, because of the concurrent transaction t_1. The value of x determines whether the history is value opaque but its conflict order is always $t_1 <_c^h t_2 <_c^h t_1$, thus it is not conflict opaque in any case.

2. Value-Based Opacity does not factor in where values originated from:
   In Fig. 2, x is set to 1 by t_1 and t_2. Conflict opacity does not accept this history because its conflict order is $t_2 <_c^h t_3 <_c^h t_2$. This conflict represents the fact that t_3 reads inconsistent values of x and y, since t_2 writes to x and y but t_3 sees an older value of x namely the one of t_1. In this specific case, though, these values are equal, so the serialization $t_1 t_3 t_2$ is legal. If the value were not equal this serialization (and any other) would not be legal, and thus the history would not be value opaque.

To allow a meaningful comparison between conflict and value opacity, we exclude such specific cases in the following and check again whether value and conflict opacity coincide then.

Excluding the first case means requiring an STM to return only those values in a read which are in memory at the moment of the call to the read (or in its own

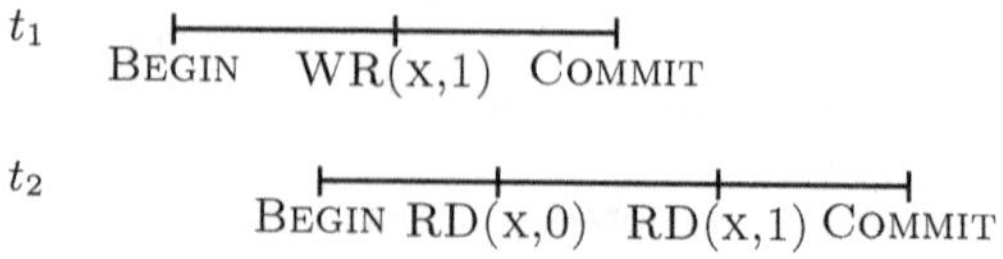

t_1

BEGIN   WR(x,1)   COMMIT

t_2

BEGIN RD(x,0)   RD(x,1) COMMIT

Fig. 3. A realistic history where the read value determines opacity

write set). Most but not all STMs do so (e.g. [7,8]). We call such STMs to have "no-out-of-thin-air-reads", using a term which is employed for a similar property in weak memory models. This property can easily be checked syntactically on the STM algorithm, looking at the read operation.

A history does not contain out-of-thin-air-reads if for every read to a location x the latest written value to that location is read. Basically, it is a form of legality for non-sequential histories.

Definition 8 (No Out-Of-Thin-Air Reads). *A history* $h = e_0...e_n$ *does not contain* out-of-thin-air reads *iff the following holds:*

$$\forall e_m = read_{t'}(x,v) : v = LWV_h(x,m).$$

Although definitely possible in real life scenarios, the second case is rather specific and not present as soon as any type of timestamp is included in the STM. Thus excluding it does not cause a significant change in the semantics of an STM. We call this second property the "unique writer" property.

Intuitively, a history has unique writers if each write to a location uses a different value.

Definition 9 (Unique Writers). *A history* $h = e_0 \dots e_n$ *has* unique writers *iff the following holds:*

$$\forall e_i = write_t(x,v) \in h, \forall e_{i'}, i \neq i', \forall t', t \neq t' : (write_{t'}(x,v) \notin h).$$

Both assumptions combined imply prefix closedness for most reasonable opacity definitions. Under these assumptions it is now possible to prove that conflict opacity does imply value opacity but not the other way round.

Lemma 1. *Conflict opacity implies value opacity for any history* h *having unique writers and no-out-of-thin-air-reads.*

Proof. W.l.o.g. assume h to be a completed history. The order $<_c^h$ is a strict partial order by definition. It also respects the real time order of h by definition. Let h' be a sequential history equivalent to h with its transaction order being an arbitrary strict total order fulfilling $<_{ct}^{h'} \supseteq <_c^h$.

We now prove that the history h' is value opaque. Thus it has to be sequential, legal, equivalent to h and respect the real time order of h. The history h' fulfills any condition but legality by definition. Thus it is left to prove that it is legal.

If h' was not legal it would intuitively not respect the conflict order of h since this order totally orders all writes and reads to a location. Thus if h' is not legal this order would have changed between h and h'. Now we assume h' is not legal thus: $\exists e^{h'}_{m'} = \text{read}_{t_1}(x, v) : v \neq LWV_{h'}(x, e_{m'})$ which implies $LW_h(x, e_m) = \text{commit}_{t_2} \neq LW_{h'}(x, e_{m'}) = \text{commit}_{t_3}$ where $e_m = e_{m'}$. In h' this implies $t_3 <^h t_1$ and $\neg(t_3 < t_2 \wedge t_2 < t_1)$ by the definition of a latest write. But in h, and by construction consecutively also in h', it holds $t_2 < t_1$ and $\neg(t_2 < t_3 \wedge t_3 < t_1)$ by definition of a latest write.

The combined statement $\neg(t_3 < t_2 \wedge t_2 < t_1) \wedge \neg(t_2 < t_3 \wedge t_3 < t_1) \wedge t_2 < t_1 \wedge t_3 < t_1$ resolves to false and is a contradiction to the assumptions, thus h' is legal, sequential and equivalent to h.   □

Observation 3. *Value opacity does not imply conflict opacity even under the assumption of unique writers and no-out-of-thin-air-reads.*

Proof. Figure 4 shows a counterexample. The sequence $t_3 t_2 t_1$ is a proof of its value opacity. But as conflicts we have $t_3 <_c t_1$ and $t_1 <_c t_3$, thus it is not conflict opaque.

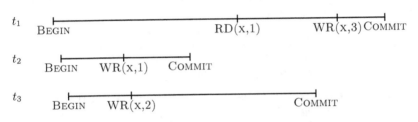

Fig. 4. Example for the semantic difference between conflict and value opacity

The counterexample in Fig. 4 demonstrates that there exists an actual semantical difference between conflict and value opacity. While value opacity in principle allows concurrent transactions to appear in any order, as long as the result is legal, conflict opacity does fix the order beforehand. It is however possible to use aspects of conflict opacity for a different defintion, which is equivalent to value opacity under these assumptions. Alike conflict opacity, this definition – given next – allows to define opacity without considering the values of read and write operations.

4   Constraint Opacity

The advantage of a conflict-based definition of opacity is its ease in opacity of a given history. Instead of having to find an equivalent sequential legal history, we only need to generate the conflict order and check for cycles in it. For testing and verification, we would like to have a similarly simple definition, which is however equivalent to value opacity. We present such a definition below, called *constraint-based opacity* (constraint opacity). Like conflict opacity it ignores the value aspect of a history. As in value opacity it still has some reordering aspects, but it mostly relies on conflicts. These conflicts can be used to reduce the search space for a possible legal equivalent sequential history. Constraint opacity is conceptually close to markability [19], the differences and similarities of both definitions are discussed in Sect. 6.

Constraint opacity requires the preservation of two orderings plus imposes a set of additional constraints on transaction ordering, called *not-in-between* (NIB) constraints. The first ordering is again real time order, as value opacity respects it and the constraint based variant needs to match it. The second ordering, called *write order*, resembles that in histories transactions are always ordered if one writes a value which the other reads. The NIB constraints state that no write may be overwritten in between where it has taken effect through a commit and where it is read by another transaction. This is another way of stating that the reordered history must be legal. The advantage is that it can be expressed via constraints of a single type.

Definition 10 (Write Order). *The* write order *of h is defined as the strict partial order between transactions for each location x written as $<_x^h$, where $t_1 <_x^h t_2$ holds iff the following is true:*

$$\exists read_{t_2}(x, v) : LW(read_{t_2}(x, v)) = commit_{t_1}$$

With this at hand, we can define constraint opacity.

Definition 11 (Constraint Opacity). *A history h is* constraint opaque *iff there exists a strict total order $<^h$ s.t.*

- *it respects the write order of h:* $\forall x \in L : <_x^h \subseteq <^h$,
- *it respects the real time order of h :* $<_{rt}^h \subseteq <^h$,
- *and it fulfills the NIB constraints:*
  $\forall t_1, t_2, t_3 \ s.t. \ t_1 <_x^h t_3 : \neg(t_1 <^h t_2 \wedge t_2 <^h t_3 \wedge x \in WS_{t_2})$.

Due to its constraint-based nature, this version of opacity is prefix-closed by definition.

Proposition 1. *Let h be a constraint opaque history which satisfies the properties of unique writers and no out-of-thin-air-reads, and let h′ be a prefix of h. Then h′ is constraint opaque.*

Constraint opacity is indeed equivalent to value-based opacity as we will prove in the following.

Lemma 2. *For any history having unique writers and no out-of-thin-air-reads constraint opacity implies value opacity.*

Proof. We show that any constraint opaque history h can be reordered to a value opaque history h′ that has the same orderings and fulfills the same constraints. We assume the strict total order of the transactions of h′ to be $<_{to}^{h'}$, where

$<_{to}^{h'} \supseteq (\bigcup_{x\in L} <_x^h) \cup <_{rt}^h$ and it respects the NIB constraints. We show that h' is legal. It is sequential and equivalent to h' by definition.

We show that the latest write for a read $read_t(x, v) = e_m^h = e_m^{h'}$ is the same for h and h', then that this implies the legality of the history.

Assume that $t_i = trans(LW_h(x, e_{m'}))$ and $t_j = trans(LW_{h'}(x, e_m))$. Intuitively, $i = j$ must hold because otherwise h' would violate the NIB constraints of h which by definition it does not. In h, $t_i <^h t$ and $\neg(t_i <^h t_j \wedge t_j <^h t)$ holds by the NIB constraints. These hold also for h' by construction. For t_j in h' it holds that $t_j <^h t$ and $\neg(t_j <^h t_i \wedge t_i <^h t)$ by the definition of a latest write. Thus in h', t_i and t_j happen before t but both cannot be in between the other in t, this statement is false except when $i = j$. Thus h' cannot exist.

In h, every read reads the value of the latest write by the no-out-of-thin-air-reads assumption since in h' the latest writer for every read is identical this still holds. Thus h' is legal. □

Lemma 3. *For any history having unique writers and no out-of-thin-air-reads value opacity implies constraint opacity.*

Proof. Let h be an arbitrary value opaque history, let $<_t^h$ be the strict total order of a sequential legal equivalent history h', which exists since h is value opaque. It holds that there is some ordering $<_t^{h'}$ such that $<_t^{h'} = <^h$. We show this for each subpart:

- $\forall x : <_x^h \subseteq <^h$: where $t_1 <_x^h t_2$ holds if $\exists read_{t_2}(x, v) : LW(read_{t_2}(x, v)) = commit_{t_1}$. By the condition of legality any latest write for a read must happen before that read. Thus $t_1 <^{h'} t_2$ which also implies $t_1 <^h t_2$.
- $<_{rt}^h \subseteq <^h$: Holds by definition of value opacity.
- $\forall t_1, t_2, t_3, t_1 <_x^h t_3 : \neg(t_1 <^h t_2 \wedge t_2 <^h t_3 \wedge x \in WS_{t_2})$: $t_1 <_x^h t_3$ holds if $\exists e_m = read_{t_3}(x, v) : trans(LW(read_{t_3}(x, v))) = t_1$. Assume that $(t_1 <^h t_2 \wedge t_2 <^h t_3 \wedge x \in WS_{t_2})$ by the no-out-of-thin-air assumption v would be the value written by t_2. Thus it would hold that $t_2 <_x^h t_3$ and $t_1 <_x^h t_3$ which by definition cannot. Thus the NIB constraints are adhered to. □

As a consequence, we obtain the following corollary stating the equivalence of constraint and value opacity.

Corollary 1. *A history h satisfying the properties of unique writer and no out-of-thin-air reads is constraint opaque if and only if it is value opaque.*

5   Checking for Constraint Opacity with Z3

Given a version of opacity without values, we next develop a way of checking histories for constraint opacity. We envisage such a checking procedure to be used in approaches for testing STMs, first of all logging the generated histories during a run of the STM and afterwards checking the logged history for opacity.

For checking opacity, we use an encoding of the constraints and required orderings in first order logic and use the SMT-solver Z3 [21] for satisfiability solving. To check a given history h with Z3, two main steps are required. First, the orders $<_{rt}, <_x$ and the NIB constraints need to be constructed and brought into suitable format. This is basic implementation work and not further specified here. Then these constraints are converted into a logical formula written in SMT code that is accepted by Z3. This conversion is shown in Fig. 5. To avoid unnecessary specifications, we use the already present semantics in Z3 of the ordering $<$ on integers. We do so by reducing the search for a sequential history to assigning to every transaction a unique positive integer so that all restrictions are fulfilled. The resulting injective function $T \to \mathbb{N}$ specifies the order of the transactions; the transaction assigned the smallest number happens first and so on.

1: **procedure** SMT TRANSFORMATION
2: **Input:** $h, \{<_x | x \in L\}, <_{rt}, Cons = \{cons \mid cons$ is a NIB constraint$\}$
3: **Output:** An SMT Command Sequence: smt
4:     **for all** $t_i \in T$ **do**
5:         Add (declare-const ti Int) to smt
6:     **for** $i = 1 \dots |T| - 1$ **do**
7:         Add (assert (not (= ti t(i+1))))
8:     **for all** $(t_1, t_2) \in <_{rt}$ **do**
9:         Add (assert($<$ t1 t2)) to smt
10:     **for all** $x \in L$ **do**
11:         **for all** $(t_1, t_2) \in <_x$ **do**
12:             **if** (assert($<$ t1 t2)) is not in smt **then**
13:                 Add (assert($<$ t1 t2)) to smt
14:     **for all** $(\neg(t_1 < t_2) \land \neg(t_2 < t_3) \in Cons$ **do**
15:         Add (assert(not(and (< t1 t2) (< t2 t3)))) to smt
16:     Add (check-sat) to smt
17:     Add (get-model) to smt

Fig. 5. SMT code transformation

Evaluation. We evaluated a prototype version of the checker on a 64 bit Windows machine with a 2.70 GHz i7-6820HQ Intel processor and 16 GB RAM. The prototype was implemented in Java using the Java API of Z3. For the evaluation, data sets from two sources were used. One source generated histories by randomly interleaving a set of read and read-write transactions. The transactions were chosen to yield balanced results, with regards to being opaque or not, and also to have a relevant number of constraints. Also a maximum amount of concurrent transactions and an upper bound of the variables used were set for each data set. Each read and write was assigned a location uniformly at random.

The other source was the benchmark test of the RingSTM implementation presented in [28]. In our evaluation the results for the RingSTM were comparable to similar configurations of randomly generated histories. Thus we focus on the latter histories, as they allow us to look at a broader spectrum of histories.

We aimed to evaluate the influence of three factors on the runtime of the checker: history size, degree of concurrency, and number of constraints. For evaluating the influence of the history size, histories with 20 transactions and 100 transactions were generated. The influence of concurrency was evaluated by changing the maximum number of transactions active at a time. This also can be viewed as the number of threads active in an STM. To measure the influence of the amount of constraints, the maximum amount of variables was changed.

We systematically evaluated combinations of both factors for a given history size. For 20 transactions the number of threads for each configuration was chosen out of the interval of 2 to 20, in steps of size 2. The interval was chosen this way, because having 1 thread would be a sequential history and having more than 20 threads has no semantical difference to having exactly 20 threads. This is because the number of active transactions cannot be higher than the number of all transactions. The maximum amount of variables for each test case was also chosen from the interval of 2 to 20 with the same step size. The amount was capped at 20. Additional testing showed that increasing the value even further did not have a significant effect. So altogether 100 different configurations were tested. For both configuration's parameters the interval of 2 was chosen to keep evaluation feasible. It also showed that choosing the intervals smaller did not result in relevant changes to the results. For 100 transactions values between 5 and 100 were chosen, with the interval being 5, for the reasons stated above. For each configuration a data set of 100 histories was given as input to the checker.

The results of the evaluation can be seen in Figs. 6 and 7. Except for a few spikes the average runtime to check one history is about 0.018 s for 20 transactions and 0.205 s for 100 transactions. This is completely sufficient for most practical testing purposes. The configurations do not yield largely different runtimes, except for the tendency that most larger spikes are found in configurations with a low thread count. Also in configurations with a low maximum amount of variables low average runtimes are more frequent.

Additionally a separate evaluation with 1000 histories was done for chosen specific configurations. The results can be found in Table 1. In these tests we only considered low variable and thread counts for better comparison and as seen in the above results, higher values did not seem to influence the run time too much.

The new measurements in these tests encompass the average runtime for opaque and not opaque histories, the number of opaque histories and not opaque histories and the average number of constraints of a history in each configuration given by constraint type.

The results show that testing an opaque history takes longer than testing a not opaque history. Also they show that history size has an exponential effect on the run time of the tool, which is not surprising given the computational complexity of the problem. For 100 transactions there could be a correlation between the number of constraints and the runtime of the checker. This effect can not be found in the configurations for 20 transactions. The assumption that the runtime for histories with 20 transactions mostly consists of the internal overhead of the Java tool excluding the Z3 libraries, could not be confirmed in further tests. Looking into Z3 was beyond the scope of this paper.

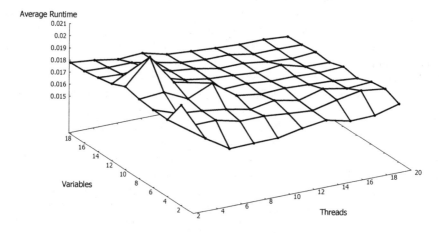

Fig. 6. Average runtimes for configurations of histories with 20 transactions

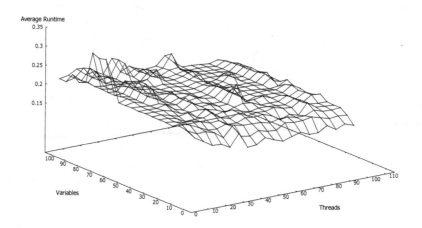

Fig. 7. Average runtimes for configurations of histories with 100 transactions

6   Related Work and Conclusion

We will give a general overview over the related work and then present options for future work.

Table 1. Specific configurations

Configuration			Runtime in seconds			# Histories		Ø # of constraints		
#Tr.	#Thr.	#V.	Total	Ø ✓	Ø ✗	✓	✗	RT	LW	NIB
20	2	2	12.879	0.0136	0.0116	620	380	174.603	30.492	15.226
20	2	5	13.657	0.0137	0.0128	930	70	174.753	26.507	8.563
20	2	20	12.211	0.0122	0.012	995	5	174.695	13.898	1.322
20	5	2	9.856	0.0116	0.0096	144	856	132.847	27.407	47.299
20	5	5	10.912	0.0114	0.0103	545	455	133.063	23.498	21.689
20	5	20	11.707	0.0117	0.0105	972	28	132.723	11.874	3.026
20	20	2	13.381	0.0143	0.0133	22	978	15.026	18.168	131.419
20	20	5	14.027	0.0144	0.0138	393	607	14.717	12.864	40.078
20	20	20	14.467	0.0145	0.0139	982	18	15.355	5.421	4.215
20	2	2	10.525	0.0111	0.0095	620	380	174.603	30.492	15.226
20	2	5	10.512	0.0107	0.0078	930	70	174.753	26.507	8.563
20	2	20	10.156	0.0102	0.0032	995	5	174.695	13.898	1.322
20	5	2	9.322	0.0114	0.009	144	856	132.847	27.407	47.299
20	5	5	10.217	0.0107	0.0096	545	455	133.063	23.498	21.689
20	5	20	10.392	0.0104	0.0098	972	28	132.723	11.874	3.026
20	20	2	9.958	0.0128	0.0099	22	978	15.026	18.168	131.419
20	20	5	10.358	0.0108	0.01	393	607	14.717	12.864	40.078
20	20	20	10.422	0.0104	0.0105	982	18	15.355	5.421	4.215
100	2	2	145.565	0.1611	0.1159	655	345	4870.689	170.37	83.059
100	2	5	174.026	0.1771	0.1353	926	74	4870.628	166.377	56.485
100	2	20	176.995	0.1774	0.0924	995	5	4870.608	145.611	15.652
100	5	2	126.599	0.1788	0.1169	157	843	4636.681	167.477	215.245
100	5	5	161.748	0.1862	0.1375	497	503	4636.243	163.048	133.474
100	5	20	192.099	0.1958	0.1178	952	48	4636.823	142.727	38.576
100	20	2	101.533	0.219	0.1012	3	997	3557.147	157.415	1026.333
100	20	5	144.64	0.2224	0.1428	23	977	3556.569	150.495	534.84
100	20	20	205.69	0.2299	0.1889	410	590	3557.211	127.93	131.426

Related Work. Several correctness criteria have been suggested for STMs. Early suggestions were serializability and linearizability [15,23]. Value opacity was proposed in [13], conflict opacity in [12]. Beside this several variants of opacity have been proposed. Elastic opacity is an extension of opacity where transactions can be elastic, such transactions can be split up into multiple subtransactions [10]. Virtual World Consistency relaxes opacity with regards to aborted transactions. Committed transactions still need to be totally ordered but aborted transactions must only be consistent with their causal past [16]. Attiya et al. defined a deferred update version of opacity which included the deferred update semantics in its legality definition [2]. Dziuma et al. introduced live opacity, a variant of opacity where values may be read from live transactions, assuming they commit

[9]. A similar approach is Last use opacity, which relaxes opacity such that under certain circumstances values from non committed transactions may be released early [26]. The property is still stronger than serializability.

There have been several approaches to validate STMs with regards to consistency criteria. Those approaches can mainly either be classified as deductive verification or as model checking. For testing, there is a fairly limited amount of research for opacity but applicable results for different consistency criteria. A main approach for deductive verification is to show an STM algorithm to be a refinement of an abstract automaton fulfilling opacity like TMS2 [8]. There have been multiple results using this approach. In [7] Doherty et al. proved the opacity of a pessimistic STM. Armstrong et al. proposed a method where proofs for the opacity of STMs can be reduced to a proof of linearizability, which yields a simpler proof [1]. Derrick et al. used KIV to verify TML using an intermediate specification between the actual implementation and the abstract automaton [6]. Another approach which uses a similar description of value opacity as constraint opacity is discussed and compared in the following.

In [19] final state opacity, which is value opacity without prefix closedness, was decomposed into several invariants together called markability. It then was shown that a history is markable if and only if it is final state opaque. So if one can prove that an STM only produces markable histories, it is final state opaque. This verification approach is then used to show that TL2 is opaque. Our definition of constraint based opacity on the other hand has been made with efficient validation techniques for generated histories in mind. Conceptually, constraint opacity and markability share similiar ideas, and coincide under the unique writers and no-out-of-thin-air-reads assumptions. We briefly describe the structure of markability and compare it to the structure of constraint opacity. For a history to be markable, there has to exist an order on transactions. As well there has to exist a order for every location where every read on that location is ordered with every transaction writing to that location. This marking has to be a superset of the real time order, which is the case for any definition equivalent to value opacity, and it has to fulfill two additional properties: write observation and read-preservation. Write observation states that for any read there has to exist a committed write which writes the value read on the location read and in the marking there is no other committed writer to that location in between. If the no-out-thin-air-reads assumption holds, the commited write exists and is known, so only the not-in-between part of the property is still relevant. Read-preservation states that no transaction may be ordered between where a transaction takes place and where a read of the same transaction takes place, this ensures atomicity. In contrast to this constraint opacity only defines a order on transactions. Thus any order generated by it is atomic and it does not require a condition similar to read-preservation. Write-Observation is matched by the combination of $<_x$ and the NIB constraints where $<_x$ defines the relation to the known writer for a read and the constraints state the second part of write observation.

For model checking there are fewer results. A main result is that, assuming certain properties, an STM that is conflict opaque or strictly serializable for two threads and two locations is also opaque for an arbitrary number of threads and locations [12]. This paper also introduced the notion of conflict opacity which we discussed in Sect. 3. As we showed in our paper, this definition is not equivalent to value opacity. Related to this, a fully automatic STM verification tool was presented in [11], which accounts for arbitrary contention managers. Their tool uses model checking to check whether the language of an STM is contained in the language of an opaque specification. In [22] this result was used to check for strict serializability. With regards to testing one of the first approaches was [20]. In this approach, the legal operation of a TM is specified, a test program is generated, run and logged on the actual implementation of the TM. Afterwards, an analysis tool checks whether the log corresponds to a sequential legal run of the TM or not. Two analysis tools are presented, one is fast but not complete while the other is complete but has an worst case runtime that is exponential in the input size. The authors claim it to be fast for practical purposes. Constraint opacity could also be used in such an approach and would replace the specific specification of legality for an STM with a more general specification. Burckhardt et al. presented Line-Up, which is a complete and automated testing tool for linearizability of concurrent programs [3]. It iterates through test cases and checks them for linearizbility. Its goal is to prove incorrectness and thus it does not terminate on correct input. Via a theoretical result it is known that any incorrect program in this context has a finite execution which is not linearizable. Thus for any incorrect program the algorithm will terminate and yield a correct result. In [27] the authors presented a method for runtime checking of serializability for STMs. Constraint opacity could be an option to do similar checking for value opacity. In general runtime checking the logged histories is a interesting direction, since for the checking of histories they will have to be generated from the STM somehow anyway. With regards to opacity, Lesani and Palsberg presented a tool that can automatically detect certain bug patterns in STMs and thus prove that they are not value opaque [18].

Conclusion and Future Work. In our paper we analyzed the relationship between existing value-based and conflict-based definitions of opacity. As general result, we showed the incomparability of these two versions of opacity. Under some mild assumptions on histories, we proved value opacity to be less strict than conflict opacity. We then proposed a new constraint based definition of opacity being equivalent to value opacity (under the same assumptions), although not tracking variable values. As such, it is a promising candidate as correctness criterion for efficient testing and model checking techniques. We furthermore showed how to check existing histories for constraint opacity with the SMT-solver Z3. The evaluation of a prototype showed that it is feasible to check large numbers of histories of medium size using this technique.

Future work could involve implementing an optimized version of this checking tool and evaluating its effectiveness. Also using this tool in combination with a model checker could be an option, if it operates fast enough, or it could be used for runtime verfication. On the theoretical side, modifiying constraint opacity to be even more accommodating to constraint solvers would be an interesting approach, as reducing the number of constraints under a modified version of the definition would improve testing performance.

Acknowledgements. Thanks to Jan Haltermann for help with Z3.

References

1. Armstrong, A., Dongol, B., Doherty, S.: Reducing opacity to linearizability: a sound and complete method. arXiv preprint arXiv:1610.01004 (2016)
2. Attiya, H., Hans, S., Kuznetsov, P., Ravi, S.: Safety of deferred update in transactional memory. In: 2013 IEEE 33rd International Conference on Distributed Computing Systems (ICDCS), pp. 601–610. IEEE (2013)
3. Burckhardt, S., Dern, C., Musuvathi, M., Tan, R.: Line-up: a complete and automatic linearizability checker. In: ACM SIGPLAN Notices, vol. 45, pp. 330–340. ACM (2010)
4. Dalessandro, L., Dice, D., Scott, M., Shavit, N., Spear, M.: Transactional mutex locks. In: D'Ambra, P., Guarracino, M., Talia, D. (eds.) Euro-Par 2010. LNCS, vol. 6272, pp. 2–13. Springer, Heidelberg (2010). doi:10.1007/978-3-642-15291-7_2
5. Dalessandro, L., Spear, M.F., Scott, M.L.: NOrec: streamlining STM by abolishing ownership records. In: ACM Sigplan Notices, vol. 45, pp. 67–78. ACM (2010)
6. Derrick, J., Dongol, B., Schellhorn, G., Travkin, O., Wehrheim, H.: Verifying opacity of a transactional mutex lock. In: Bjørner, N., de Boer, F. (eds.) FM 2015. LNCS, vol. 9109, pp. 161–177. Springer, Cham (2015). doi:10.1007/978-3-319-19249-9_11
7. Doherty, S., Dongol, B., Derrick, J., Schellhorn, G., Wehrheim, H.: Proving opacity of a pessimistic STM. In: Fatourou, P., Jiménez, E., Pedone, F. (eds.) 20th International Conference on Principles of Distributed Systems (OPODIS 2016). Leibniz International Proceedings in Informatics (LIPIcs), vol. 70, pp. 35:1–35:17. Schloss Dagstuhl-Leibniz-Zentrum fuer Informatik, Dagstuhl (2017). http://drops.dagstuhl.de/opus/volltexte/2017/7104
8. Doherty, S., Groves, L., Luchangco, V., Moir, M.: Towards formally specifying and verifying transactional memory. Formal Aspects Comput. **25**(5), 769–799 (2013). http://dx.doi.org/10.1007/s00165-012-0225-8
9. Dziuma, D., Fatourou, P., Kanellou, E.: Consistency for transactional memory computing. In: Guerraoui, R., Romano, P. (eds.) Transactional Memory. Foundations, Algorithms, Tools, and Applications. LNCS, vol. 8913, pp. 3–31. Springer, Cham (2015). doi:10.1007/978-3-319-14720-8_1
10. Felber, P., Gramoli, V., Guerraoui, R.: Elastic transactions. In: Keidar, I. (ed.) DISC 2009. LNCS, vol. 5805, pp. 93–107. Springer, Heidelberg (2009). doi:10.1007/978-3-642-04355-0_12
11. Guerraoui, R., Henzinger, T.A., Singh, V.: Completeness and nondeterminism in model checking transactional memories. In: van Breugel, F., Chechik, M. (eds.) CONCUR 2008. LNCS, vol. 5201, pp. 21–35. Springer, Heidelberg (2008). doi:10.1007/978-3-540-85361-9_6
12. Guerraoui, R., Henzinger, T.A., Singh, V.: Model checking transactional memories. Distrib. Comput. **22**(3), 129–145 (2010). http://dx.doi.org/10.1007/s00446-009-0092-6

13. Guerraoui, R., Kapalka, M.: On the correctness of transactional memory. In: Proceedings of the 13th ACM SIGPLAN Symposium on Principles and Practice of Parallel Programming (PPoPP 2008), pp. 175–184. ACM, New York (2008). http://doi.acm.org/10.1145/1345206.1345233

14. Herlihy, M., Moss, J.E.B.: Transactional memory: architectural support for lock-free data structures. In: Proceedings of the 20th Annual International Symposium on Computer Architecture, San Diego, CA, May 1993, pp. 289–300 (1993). http://doi.acm.org/10.1145/165123.165164

15. Herlihy, M.P., Wing, J.M.: Linearizability: a correctness condition for concurrent objects. ACM Trans. Program. Lang. Syst. (TOPLAS) 12(3), 463–492 (1990)

16. Imbs, D., Raynal, M.: Virtual world consistency: a condition for STM systems (with a versatile protocol with invisible read operations). Theoret. Comput. Sci. 444, 113–127 (2012)

17. Lesani, M., Luchangco, V., Moir, M.: A framework for formally verifying software transactional memory algorithms. In: Koutny, M., Ulidowski, I. (eds.) CONCUR 2012. LNCS, vol. 7454, pp. 516–530. Springer, Heidelberg (2012). doi:10.1007/978-3-642-32940-1_36

18. Lesani, M., Palsberg, J.: Proving non-opacity. In: Afek, Y. (ed.) DISC 2013. LNCS, vol. 8205, pp. 106–120. Springer, Heidelberg (2013). doi:10.1007/978-3-642-41527-2_8

19. Lesani, M., Palsberg, J.: Decomposing opacity. In: Kuhn, F. (ed.) DISC 2014. LNCS, vol. 8784, pp. 391–405. Springer, Heidelberg (2014). doi:10.1007/978-3-662-45174-8_27

20. Manovit, C., Hangal, S., Chafi, H., McDonald, A., Kozyrakis, C., Olukotun, K.: Testing implementations of transactional memory. In: Proceedings of the 15th International Conference on Parallel Architectures and Compilation Techniques, pp. 134–143. ACM (2006)

21. de Moura, L.M., Bjørner, N.: Z3: an efficient SMT solver. In: Ramakrishnan, C.R., Rehof, J. (eds.) TACAS 2008. LNCS, vol. 4963, pp. 337–340. Springer, Heidelberg (2008). doi:10.1007/978-3-540-78800-3_24

22. O'Leary, J., Saha, B., Tuttle, M.R.: Model checking transactional memory with spin. In: 2009 29th IEEE International Conference on Distributed Computing Systems (ICDCS 2009), pp. 335–342. IEEE (2009)

23. Papadimitriou, C.H.: The serializability of concurrent database updates. J. ACM (JACM) 26(4), 631–653 (1979)

24. Riegel, T., Fetzer, C., Felber, P.: Snapshot isolation for software transactional memory. In: First ACM SIGPLAN Workshop on Languages, Compilers, and Hardware Support for Transactional Computing (TRANSACT 2006), pp. 1–10. Association for Computing Machinery (ACM) (2006)

25. Shavit, N., Touitou, D.: Software transactional memory. Distrib. Comput. 10(2), 99–116 (1997)

26. Siek, K., Wojciechowski, P.T.: Last-use opacity: a strong safety property for transactional memory with early release support. CoRR abs/1506.06275 (2015). http://arxiv.org/abs/1506.06275

27. Sinha, A., Malik, S.: Runtime checking of serializability in software transactional memory. In: 2010 IEEE International Symposium on Parallel and Distributed Processing (IPDPS), pp. 1–12. IEEE (2010)

28. Spear, M.F., Michael, M.M., von Praun, C.: RingSTM: Scalable transactions with a single atomic instruction. In: Proceedings of the Twentieth Annual Symposium on Parallelism in Algorithms and Architectures, pp. 275–284. ACM (2008)

Smaller-State Implementations of 2D FSSP Algorithms

Recent Developments

Hiroshi Umeo$^{(\boxtimes)}$, Keisuke Kubo, and Akira Nomura

University of Osaka Electro-Communication,
Neyagawa-shi, Hastu-cho, 18-8, Osaka 572-8530, Japan
umeo@osakac.ac.jp

Abstract. The synchronization in ultra-fine-grained parallel computational model of cellular automata is known as the firing squad synchronization problem (FSSP) since its development, in which it was originally proposed by Myhill in the book edited by Moore [3] to synchronize all/some parts of self-reproducing cellular automata. The FSSP has been studied extensively for more than fifty years, and a rich variety of synchronization algorithms has been proposed. In this paper, we give several smaller-state implementations of the FSSP algorithms for 2D arrays based on an L-shaped zebra mapping, where synchronized configurations on 1D arrays are mapped onto 2D arrays in an L-shaped zebra form efficiently, yielding smaller-state minimum-time implementations.

1 Introduction

The synchronization in ultra-fine-grained parallel computational model of cellular automata is known as the firing squad synchronization problem (FSSP) since its development, in which it was originally proposed by Myhill in the book edited by Moore [3] to synchronize all/some parts of self-reproducing cellular automata. The FSSP has been studied extensively for more than fifty years, and a rich variety of synchronization algorithms has been proposed [1–16].

In the present article, we focus our attention to a class of 2D minimum-time FSSP algorithms that is based on an L-shaped mapping, where synchronized configurations on 1D arrays are mapped onto 2D arrays in an L-shaped form efficiently, yielding minimum-time FSSP algorithms and smaller-state implementations. In Sect. 2, we give a description of the 2D FSSP and review some basic results on the 2D FSSP algorithms. The first 2D FSSP algorithm developed by Beyer [1] and Shinahr [5] is reviewed in Sect. 3. In Sect. 4, we introduce a new class of FSSP algorithms based on the L-shaped mapping for 2D arrays and present several smaller-state implementations of the algorithms. In the last section, we give a summary of the paper.

© Springer International Publishing AG 2017
D.V. Hung and D. Kapur (Eds.): ICTAC 2017, LNCS 10580, pp. 136–152, 2017.
DOI: 10.1007/978-3-319-67729-3_9

2   Firing Squad Synchronization Problem

2.1   FSSP on 2D Cellular Arrays

Figure 1 shows a finite two-dimensional (2D) cellular array consisting of $m \times n$ cells. Each cell is an identical (except the border cells) finite-state automaton. The array operates in lock-step mode in such a way that the next state of each cell (except border cells) is determined by both its own present state and the present states of its north, south, east, and west neighbors. All cells (*soldiers*), except the north-west corner cell (*general*), are initially in the quiescent state at time $t = 0$ with the property that the next state of a quiescent cell with quiescent neighbors is the quiescent state again. At time $t = 0$, the north-west upper corner cell $C_{1,1}$ is in the *fire-when-ready* state, which is the initiation signal for the array to start the synchronization operations. The FSSP is to determine a description (state set and next-state function) for cells that ensures all cells enter the *fire* state at exactly the same time and for the first time. The tricky part of the problem is that the same kind of soldier having a fixed number of states must be synchronized, regardless of the size $m \times n$ of the array. The set of states and transition rules must be independent of m and n.

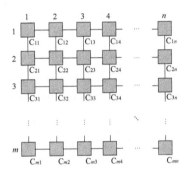

Fig. 1. A two-dimensional (2D) rectangular cellular automaton of size $m \times n$ arranged in m rows and n columns.

A formal definition of the 2D FSSP is as follows: A cellular automaton $\mathcal{M}$ is a pair $\mathcal{M} = (\mathcal{Q}, \delta)$, where

1. $\mathcal{Q}$ is a finite set of states with three distinguished states G, Q, and F, each in $\mathcal{Q}$. G is an initial general state, Q is a quiescent state, and F is a firing state, respectively.
2. δ is a next state function such that $\delta : \mathcal{Q} \times (\mathcal{Q} \cup \{*\})^4 \to \mathcal{Q}$. The state $*$ $\notin \mathcal{Q}$ is a pseudo state of the border of the array. Each tuple in the next state function δ means that:

$$S_{\text{itself}}^{t+1} = \delta(S_{\text{itself}}^t, S_{\text{north}}^t, S_{\text{south}}^t, S_{\text{east}}^t, S_{\text{west}}^t).$$

Here, we denote the state of $C_{i,j}$ at time (step) t by $S_{i,j}^t$, where $t \geq 0, 1 \leq i \leq m, 1 \leq j \leq n$.

3. The quiescent state Q must satisfy the following conditions:
$\delta(Q, Q, Q, Q, Q) = \delta(Q, *, Q, Q, *) = \delta(Q, *, Q, Q, Q) = \delta(Q, *, Q, *, Q) = \delta(Q, Q, Q, *, Q) = \delta(Q, Q, *, *, Q) = \delta(Q, Q, *, Q, Q) = \delta(Q, Q, *, Q, *) = \delta(Q, Q, Q, Q, *) = Q.$

A 2D cellular automaton of size $m \times n$, $\mathcal{M}_{m \times n}$ consisting of $m \times n$ copies of $\mathcal{M}$, is a 2D array of $\mathcal{M}$. Each $\mathcal{M}$ is referred to as a cell and denoted by $C_{i,j}$, where $1 \le i \le m$ and $1 \le j \le n$.

A *configuration* of $\mathcal{M}_{m \times n}$ at time t is a function $\mathcal{C}^t : [1, m] \times [1, n] \to Q$ and denoted as:

$$S_{1,1}^t S_{1,2}^t \dots S_{1,n}^t$$
$$S_{2,1}^t S_{2,2}^t \dots S_{2,n}^t$$
$$S_{3,1}^t S_{3,2}^t \dots S_{3,n}^t$$
$$\vdots$$
$$S_{m,1}^t S_{m,2}^t \dots S_{m,n}^t.$$

A *computation* of $\mathcal{M}_{m \times n}$ is a sequence of configurations of $\mathcal{M}_{m \times n}$, $\mathcal{C}^0$, $\mathcal{C}^1$, $\mathcal{C}^2$, ..., $\mathcal{C}^t$, ..., where $\mathcal{C}^0$ is a given initial configuration such that:

$$S_{i,j}^0 = \begin{cases} G & i = j = 1 \\ Q & \text{otherwise.} \end{cases} \tag{1}$$

A configuration at time $t + 1$, $\mathcal{C}^{t+1}$ is computed by synchronous applications of the next state function δ to each cell of $\mathcal{M}_{m \times n}$ in $\mathcal{C}^t$ such that:

$$S_{i,j}^{t+1} = \delta(S_{i,j}^t, S_{i-1,j}^t, S_{i+1,j}^t, S_{i,j+1}^t, S_{i,j-1}^t).$$

A *synchronized configuration* of $\mathcal{M}_{m \times n}$ at time t is a configuration $\mathcal{C}^t$, $S_{i,j}^t = F$, for any $1 \le i \le m$ and $1 \le j \le n$. The FSSP is to obtain an $\mathcal{M}$ such that, for any $m, n \ge 2$,

1. A synchronized configuration at time $t = T(m, n)$, $\mathcal{C}^{T(m,n)} : S_{i,j}^{T(m,n)} = F$, for any $1 \le i \le m$ and $1 \le j \le n$, can be computed from an initial configuration $\mathcal{C}^0$ in Eq. 1.
2. For any t, i, j such that $1 \le t \le T(m, n) - 1$, $1 \le i \le m, 1 \le j \le n, S_{i,j}^t \ne F$.

No cells fire before time $t = T(m, n)$. We say that the array $\mathcal{M}_{m \times n}$ is synchronized at time $t = T(m, n)$ and the function $T(m, n)$ is the time complexity for the synchronization.

2.2   Lower-Bound and Optimality in 2D FSSP Algorithms

Concerning the time optimality of the 2D FSSP algorithms, Beyer [1] and Shinahr [5] gave a lower bound of the algorithms and proposed a minimum-time FSSP algorithm. Note that there is a difference between rectangles and squares in lower bound and optimality. An a priori knowledge on the shape of a given 2D array is assumed.

Theorem 1. *There exists no cellular automaton that can synchronize any 2D array of size $m \times n$ in less than $m + n + \max(m, n) - 3$ steps, where the general is located at one corner of the array.*

Theorem 2. *There exists a cellular automaton that can synchronize any 2D array of size $m \times n$ at exactly $m + n + \max(m, n) - 3$ steps, where the general is located at one corner of the array.*

Theorem 3. *There exists no cellular automaton that can synchronize any 2D square array of size $n \times n$ in less than $2n - 2$ steps, where the general is located at one corner of the array.*

Theorem 4. *There exists a cellular automaton that can synchronize any 2D square array of size $n \times n$ at exactly $2n - 2$ optimum steps.*

3   Beyer-Shinahr Algorithm

The first 2D minimum-time FSSP algorithm $\mathcal{A}_1$, developed independently by Beyer [1] and Shinar [5], is based on a rotated L-shaped mapping which maps configurations of 1D generalized FSSP (GFSSP, for short) solution on 1D arrays onto 2D arrays in an L-shaped fashion. A rectangular array of size $m \times n$ is regarded as $\min(m, n)$ rotated L-shaped 1D arrays, where each rotated L-shaped 1D array is synchronized independently by using the GFSSP algorithm.

Figure 2 (top, left) is a space-time diagram for the original FSSP with a general at left end on which most of the minimum-time FSSP algorithms have been developed. The general at time $t = 0$ emits an infinite number of signals which propagates at $1/(2^{\ell+1} - 1)$ speed, where ℓ is positive integer. These signals meet with a reflected signal at half point, quarter points, ..., etc., denoted by $\bullet$ in Fig. 2 (top, left). It is noted that these cells indicated by $\bullet$ are synchronized. By increasing the number of *pre-synchronized* cells (not in firing state) exponentially, eventually all of the cells are synchronized at the last stage for the first time.

A key idea behind the GFSSP algorithm proposed by Moore and Langdon [4] is to reconstruct the original FSSP algorithm as if an initial general had been at the left or right end with being in the general state at time $t = -(k - 1)$, where k is the number of cells between the general and the nearest end. Figure 2 (top, right) illustrates a space-time diagram for the GFSSP. The initial general emits a left- and right-going signal with $1/1$ speed and keeps its position by marking a special symbol. The propagated signals generate a new general at each end. On reaching the end, they generate the necessary signals assuming that the end is the far end. The special marking symbol tells the first $1/1$ signal generated by the left and right end generals that that side was the just nearest end. At that point the slope $1/1$ signal is generated and it changes the slope of all the preceding signals to the next higher one, that is, $1/(2^{\ell} - 1)$ becomes $1/(2^{\ell+1} - 1)$.

Note that the original minimum-time solution is working below the dotted line in the Fig. 2 (top, right). Therefore the minimum-time complexity for the GFSSP is $\min(k - 1, n - k)$ steps smaller than the original FSSP

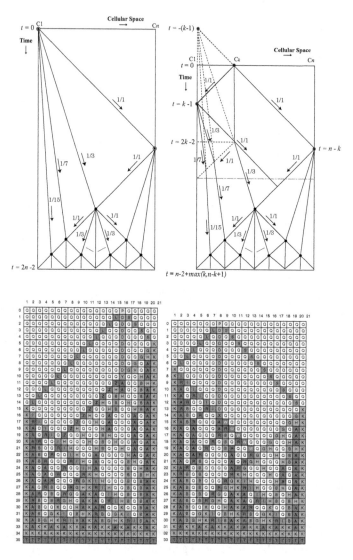

Fig. 2. Space-time diagram of the synchronization algorithms for the original FSSP with a general at one end (top, left) and the GFSSP with a general at an arbitrary position (top, right) in a 1D array of length n and snapshots (bottom) of the Moore and Langdon's [4] 17-state GFSSP algorithm implemented on 21 cells with a general on 16th and 8th cells, respectively.

with a general at one end. Thus, the time complexity is $2n - 2 - \min(k - 1, n - k) = n - 1 + \max(k - 1, n - k) = n - 2 + \max(k, n - k + 1)$. Most of the GFSSP algorithms presented in the past are based on the space-time diagram shown in Fig. 2 (top, right). Figure 2 (bottom) presents some snapshots for the Moore and Langdon's [4] 17-state implementation on 21 cells with a general on 8th and 16th cells, implemented in Umeo et al. [10]. A comprehensive survey on the GFSSP algorithms and their implementations can be seen in Umeo et al. [10]. The minimum-time GFSSP algorithm [4, 10] is stated as follows:

Theorem 5. *There exists a cellular automaton that can synchronize any 1D array of length n in minimum $n + \max(k, n - k + 1) - 2$ steps, where the general is located on the kth cell from left end.*

We overview the 2D FSSP algorithm $\mathcal{A}_1$ operating on an array of size $m \times n$. Configurations of the generalized synchronization processes on 1D array can be mapped on the rotated L-shaped array. We refer the array as L-array. See Fig. 3 (top). At time $t = 0$, the north-west cell $C_{1,1}$ is in general state and all other cells are in quiescent state. For any i such that $1 \leq i \leq \min(m, n)$, the cell $C_{i,i}$ will be in the general state at time $t = 3i - 3$. A special signal which travels towards a diagonal direction is used to generate generals on the cells $\{C_{i,i} | 1 \leq i \leq \min(m, n) \}$. For each i such that $1 \leq i \leq \min(m, n)$, the cells $\{C_{i,j} | i \leq j \leq n \}$ and $\{C_{k,i} | i \leq k \leq m\}$ constitute the ith L-shaped array. Note that the ith general generated at time $t = 3i - 3$ is on the $(m - i + 1)$th cell from the left end of the ith L-array. The length of the ith L-array is $m + n - 2i + 1$. Thus, using Theorem 5, the ith L-array can be synchronized at exactly $t_i = 3i - 3 + m + n - 2i + 1 - 2 + \max(m - i + 1, n - i + 1) = m + n + \max(m, n) - 3$, which is independent of i. In this way, all of the L-arrays can be synchronized simultaneously.

Thus, an $m \times n$ array synchronization problem is reduced to independent $\min(m, n)$ 1D GFSSP problems such that:

$$\begin{cases} \mathcal{P}(m, m + n - 1), \mathcal{P}(m - 1, m + n - 3), ..., \mathcal{P}(1, n - m + 1) & m \leq n, \\ \mathcal{P}(m, m + n - 1), \mathcal{P}(m - 1, m + n - 3), ..., \mathcal{P}(m - n + 1, m - n + 1) & m > n. \end{cases}$$

Here, $\mathcal{P}(k, \ell)$ means the 1D GFSSP problem for ℓ cells with a general on the kth cell from left end.

Shinahr [5] presented a 28-state implementation of the algorithm, where most of the transition rules (97%) had *wild cards* which can match any state. Umeo, Ishida, Tachibana, and Kamikawa [9] showed that the rule set for the implementation consists of 12849 transition rules and it is valid for the synchronization for any rectangle arrays of size $m \times n$ such that $2 \leq m, n \leq 500$. Figure 3 (bottom) illustrates snapshots of the configurations on an array of size 9×14 based on the new 28-state, 12849-rule implementation given in Umeo et al. [9]. Thus, we have:

Theorem 6. *The algorithm $\mathcal{A}_1$, implemented on a cellular automaton with 28 states and 12849 rules, can synchronize any $m \times n$ rectangular array in minimum $m + n + \max(m, n) - 3$ steps.*

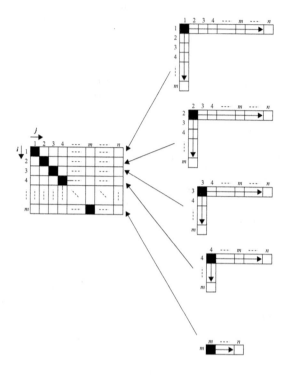

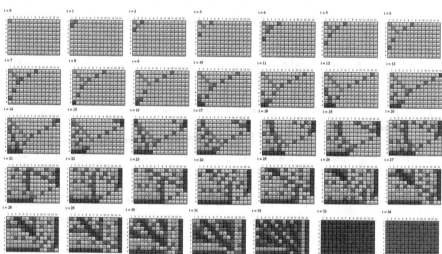

Fig. 3. A 2D synchronization scheme (top) based on an L-shaped mapping developed in Beyer [1] and Shinahr [5]. Snapshots (bottom) of the configurations of the Shinahr's 28-state synchronization algorithm on a rectangle array of size 9 × 14, implemented in Umeo et al. [9]

4   Smaller-State Zebra Implementations

4.1   Zebra Mapping on Square Arrays

The implementation is based on a zebra mapping which was originally developed for realizing a 7-state square synchronizer in Umeo and Kubo [11]. We overview an implementation technique of the zebra mapping for square arrays.

The zebra mapping is basically similar to the rotated L-shaped mapping scheme presented in the previous section, however, the mapped configuration on square arrays consists of two types of configurations: one is a one-cell smaller synchronized configuration and the other is a filled-in configuration with a stationary state. The stationary state remains unchanged once filled-in by the time before the final synchronization. Each configuration is mapped alternatively in space onto an L-shaped array *in a zebra fashion*. The mapping is referred to as *zebra mapping*. Figure 4 illustrates the zebra mapping which consists of the embedded synchronization layer and the filled-in layer.

A key idea of the zebra implementation is:

- Alternative embedding of two types of configurations. A stationary layer separates synchronization layers and it allows us to use an equal state set for the vertical and horizontal synchronization on each layer, helping us to construct a smaller-state transition rule set for the synchronization layers.
- A one-cell smaller synchronization configuration than the L-shaped mapping is embedded, where we can save synchronization time by two steps.

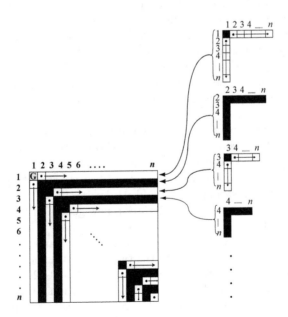

Fig. 4. A zebra mapping schema for an $n \times n$ square array.

– A single state X is used in common as an initial general state of the square synchronizer, the stationary state in stationary layers, and a firing state of the embedded one-cell-smaller synchronization algorithm. The state X itself acts as a pre-firing state.

– Any cell in state X, except $C_{n,n}$, enters the final synchronization state at the next step if all its neighbors are in state X or the boundary state of the square. The cell $C_{n,n}$ enters the synchronization state if and only if its north and west cells are in state X and its east and south cells are in the boundary state. A cell in state X that is adjacent to the cell $C_{n,n}$ is also an exception. This is an only condition that makes cells fire.

In our construction we take Mazoyer's [2] 6-state 1D synchronization rule as an embedded synchronization algorithm. The set of the 6-states is {G, Q, A, B, C, X}, where G is a general, Q is a quiescent, and X is a firing state, respectively. The other three states A, B and C are auxiliary states, respectively.

The seven-state square synchronizer that we construct has the following state set: {G, Q, A, B, C, X, F}, where F is a newly introduced firing state, X is a general, and Q is a quiescent state, respectively. The state G is the general state of the embedded synchronization. Those states A, B and C are also auxiliary states, respectively. The transition rule set is constructed in such a way that: The initial general on $C_{1,1}$ in state X generates a new general in state G on the cell $C_{1,2}$ and $C_{2,1}$ at time $t = 1$. The general in state G initiates a synchronization for the following cells {$C_{1,2}$, $C_{1,3}$, ..., $C_{1,n}$} and {$C_{2,1}$, $C_{3,1}$, ..., $C_{n,1}$}, each of length $n - 1$. Note that the length of the array where optimum-time synchronization operations are embedded is shorter by one than the usual embedding in Sect. 2. The cells on the segments are constructed to operate so that they simulate the Mazoyer's optimum-time synchronization operations. All cells on the two horizontal and vertical segments of length $n - 1$ enter the pre-firing state X at time $t = 1+2(n-1)-2 = 2n-3$. In this way, the first L_1 acts as a synchronization layer. At time $t = 2$, the cell $C_{2,2}$ takes the state X and it extends an X-arm (a cell segment in state X) in the right and lower direction, respectively, towards the cells {$C_{2,3}$, $C_{2,4}$, ..., $C_{2,n}$} and {$C_{3,2}$, $C_{4,2}$, ..., $C_{n,2}$}, respectively, each of length $n - 2$. Every cell once entered in state X remains unchanged by the time before it meets a local condition for the synchronization given later. At time $t = 2 + n - 2 = n$, the filled-in operation with the stationary state X on the second layer is finished. In this way, the second L_2 acts as a stationary layer.

Concerning the embedding on the odd ith layer, the cell $C_{i,i}$ takes the stationary state X time $t = 2i - 2$ and generates a new general in state G on the cell $C_{i,i+1}$ and $C_{i+1,i}$ at time $t = 2i - 1$. The general in state G initiates a synchronization for the following cells {$C_{i,i+1}$, $C_{i,i+2}$, ..., $C_{i,n}$} and {$C_{i+1,i}$, $C_{i+2,i}$, ..., $C_{n,i}$}, each of length $n - i$. All cells on the two horizontal and vertical segments of length $n-i$ enter the pre-firing state X at time $t = 2i-1+2(n-i)-2 = 2n-3$. In this way, for odd i, the ith L_i acts as a synchronization layer. As for the even ith layer, at time $t = 2i - 2$, the cell $C_{i,i}$ takes the state X and it extends the X-arm in the right and lower direction, respectively, towards the cells {$C_{i,i+1}$, $C_{i,i+2}$, ..., $C_{i,n}$} and {$C_{i+1,i}$, $C_{i+2,i}$, ..., $C_{n,i}$}, each of length $n - i$. Every cell

Table 1. Transition rule set used at the last synchronization step.

Q ∗ X X ∗ → F;	X Q X X ∗ → F;	X X X X X → F;	X X X X ∗ → F;
X X X ∗ X → F;	X X X ∗ ∗ → F;	X X ∗ X X → F;	X X ∗ ∗ X → F;
X ∗ X X Q → F;	X ∗ X X X → F;	X ∗ ∗ X Q → F;	X ∗ ∗ X X → F.

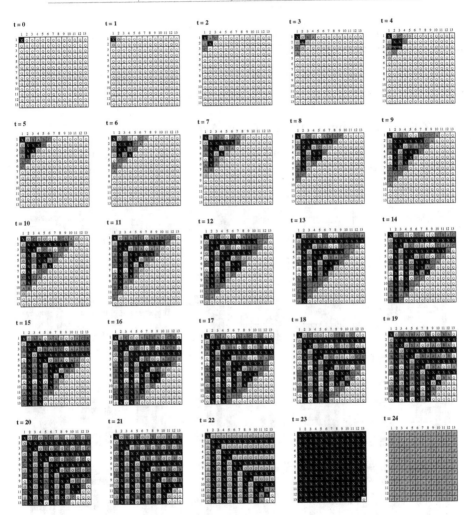

Fig. 5. Snapshots of the synchronization process on 13×13 array.

once entered in state X remains unchanged by the time before synchronization. At time $t = 2i - 2 + n - i = n + i - 2$, the filled-in operation on the ith layer for even i is finished.

At time $t = 2n - 3$, all of the cells, except $C_{n,n}$, on the square of size $n \times n$ enter the state X, which is a pre-firing state. The following twelve transition rules, shown in Table 1, are the only ones that falls into the synchronization state F in the last stage. In each 6-tuple rule such that Y1 Y2 Y3 Y4 Y5 → Y6, the symbol Y1 denotes the present state of a cell, Y2 the east state, Y3 the north state, Y4 the west state, Y5 the south state, and Y6 the next state of the cell, respectively. A symbol "*" denotes a boundary state of square arrays. The final constructed seven-state cellular automaton has 787 transition rules shown in Appendix I.

Thus we have:

Theorem 7. *The seven-state synchronization algorithm can synchronize any* $n \times n$ *square array in optimum* $2n - 2$ *steps.*

Figure 5 shows some snapshots of the synchronization process operating in optimum-steps on a 13×13 square arrays.

4.2   Zebra Mapping on Rectangular Arrays

The zebra implementation for squares can be applied to rectangles with small modifications. As is shown in Fig. 3, a 1D GFSSP configuration is mapped on an

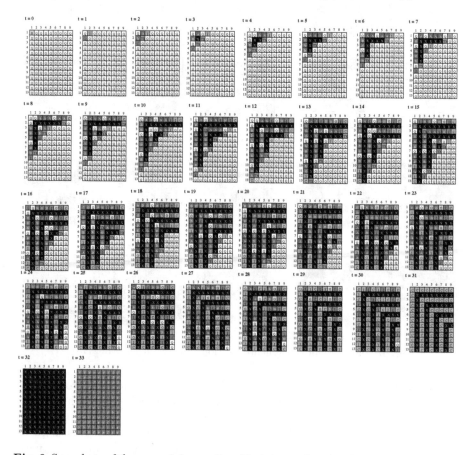

Fig. 6. Snapshots of the non-minimum-time 10-state synchronization process on a 13×9 rectangular array.

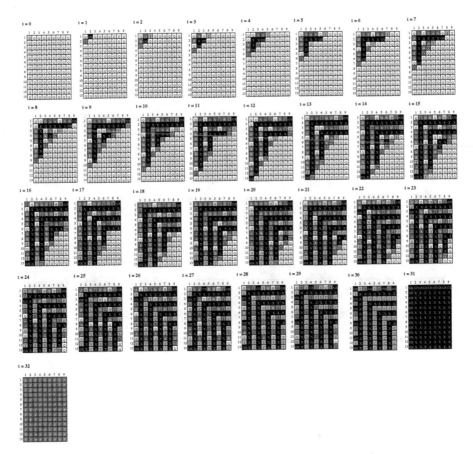

Fig. 7. Snapshots of the minimum-time 11-state synchronization process on a 13×9 array.

L-shaped array, where the cells on the horizontal and vertical segments have to cooperate with each other. Thus, in contrast to the square implementation, two independent, small-size synchronization configurations cannot be implemented on the horizontal and vertical segment on a single synchronization layer in the rectangle case. Here we do not go to the details of the implementation. All the implementations given below are variants of the zebra-mapping.

The first 10-state implementation is a straightforward implementation of the zebra-mapping, which yields a non-minimum-time algorithm. The second 11-state implementation is a variant of the zebra-mapping where the first synchronization layer L_1 and the thereafter layers $L_i, i \geq 3$ take a different set of synchronization rule set. The third one is a nine-state implementation which regards the marking symbol used in the recursive division as the pre-firing state, making the algorithm operate in minimum-steps. Those three implementations are stated in Theorems 8, 9 and 10. Some snapshots of the synchronization processes in those three implementations are given in Figs. 6, 7, and 8.

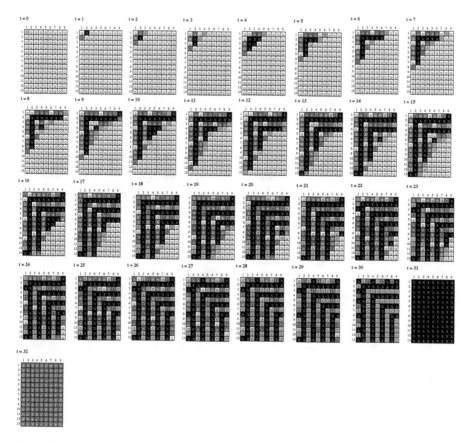

Fig. 8. Snapshots of the minimum-time nine-state synchronization process on a 13×9 array.

Theorem 8. *There exists a 10-state 2D CA that can synchronize any $m \times n$ rectangle arrays in $m + n + \max(m, n) - 2$ non-minimum steps.*

Theorem 9. *There exists an 11-state 2D CA that can synchronize any $m \times n$ rectangle arrays in $m + n + \max(m, n) - 3$ minimum steps.*

Theorem 10. *There exists a 9-state 2D CA that can synchronize any $m \times n$ rectangle arrays in $m + n + \max(m, n) - 3$ minimum steps.*

5 Summary

In the present paper, we have given several smallest-state, known at present, implementations of the FSSP algorithms for 2D square and rectangular arrays based on the L-shaped mapping. It can be seen that the L-shaped mapping presents a rich variety of 2D minimum-time FSSP algorithms. Most of the 2D algorithm proposed are *isotropic* with respect to shape of a given rectangle array, i.e. no need to control the FSSP algorithm for longer-than-wide and wider-than-long input rectangles, however, the underlying algorithm used in $\mathcal{A}_4$ presented in Umeo et al. [15] is not isotropic. The non-isotropic property led to the increase of the number of states required in its implementation. The isotropic property plays an important role in the design of higher dimensional minimum-time FSSP algorithms. A class of isotropic multi-dimensional minimum-time FSSP algorithms is given in Umeo, Kubo, and Nishide [12]. Here, we present a Table 2 based on a quantitative comparison of 2D FSSP algorithms and their transition tables discussed in this paper.

Table 2. A quantitative comparison of 2D FSSP algorithms based on L-shaped mapping.

Algorithm	Time complexity	# of states	# of transition rules	Reference
$\mathcal{A}_1$	$m + n + \max(m, n) - 3$	–	–	Beyer [1]
$\mathcal{A}_1$	$m + n + \max(m, n) - 3$	28	–	Shinahr [5]
$\mathcal{A}_1$	$m + n + \max(m, n) - 3$	28	12849	Umeo et al. [9]
$\mathcal{A}_{2-1}$	$m + n + \max(m, n) - 2$	10	1629	This paper
$\mathcal{A}_{2-2}$	$m + n + \max(m, n) - 3$	11	4044	This paper
$\mathcal{A}_{2-3}$	$m + n + \max(m, n) - 3$	9	2561	This paper
$\mathcal{A}_3$	$m + n + \max(m, n) - 3$	84	8979	Umeo et al. [16]
$\mathcal{A}_4$	$m + n + \max(m, n) - 3$	124	45128	Umeo et al. [15]

Appendix I

Transition rule set for the 7-state square synchronizer. In each 6-tuple rule such that Y1 Y2 Y3 Y4 Y5 → Y6, the symbol Y1 denotes the present state, Y2 the east state, Y3 the north state, Y4 the west state, Y5 the south state, and Y6 the next state, respectively. A symbol "*" denotes a boundary state of square arrays (to be continued).

150   H. Umeo et al.

———— Q State ————→

```
  1: Q  Q Q Q *  →  Q
  2: Q  Q Q * Q  →  Q
  3: Q  Q Q * *  →  Q
  4: Q  Q Q * *  →  Q
  5: Q  Q A A Q  →  B
  6: Q  Q A B Q  →  G
  7: Q  Q A C Q  →  A
  8: Q  Q A G Q  →  X
  9: Q  Q A G Q  →  C
 10: Q  Q A X *  →  C
 11: Q  Q A * Q  →  G
 12: Q  Q A * *  →  C
 13: Q  Q B A Q  →  G
 14: Q  Q B C *  →  X
 15: Q  Q B G Q  →  G
 16: Q  Q C Q *  →  G
 17: Q  Q C A *  →  Q
 18: Q  Q C A Q  →  A
 19: Q  Q C C Q  →  A
 20: Q  Q C C *  →  X
 21: Q  Q C G Q  →  G
 22: Q  Q C X Q  →  G
 23: Q  Q C * Q  →  A
 24: Q  Q C * *  →  G
 25: Q  Q G A Q  →  C
 26: Q  Q G B Q  →  C
 27: Q  Q G C Q  →  C
 28: Q  Q G G *  →  A
 29: Q  Q G G Q  →  X
 30: Q  Q G X *  →  A
 31: Q  Q G * Q  →  A
 32: Q  Q G * *  →  A
 33: Q  X A X *  →  Q
 34: Q  X A A *  →  G
 35: Q  X A * *  →  X
 36: Q  X B X Q  →  Q
 37: Q  X C X *  →  A
 38: Q  X C C Q  →  Q
 39: Q  X G X *  →  C
 40: Q  X X * *  →  X
 41: Q  X * Q *  →  X
 42: Q  X * * *  →  X
 43: Q  * Q Q *  →  Q
 44: Q  * Q X Q  →  G
 45: Q  * A X *  →  G
 46: Q  * A Q *  →  G
 47: Q  * B X Q  →  G
 48: Q  * C Q *  →  A
 49: Q  * C X *  →  A
 50: Q  * G X *  →  C
 51: Q  * G X *  →  C
 52: Q  * X Q *  →  G
 53: Q  A X A *  →  Q
 54: Q  A X B *  →  Q
 55: Q  A X C *  →  Q
 56: Q  A X G *  →  Q
 57: Q  A * A *  →  Q
 58: Q  A * B *  →  Q
 59: Q  A * C *  →  Q
 60: Q  A * G *  →  Q
 61: Q  B X Q *  →  Q
 62: Q  B X A *  →  Q
 63: Q  B X B *  →  Q
 64: Q  B X C *  →  Q
 65: Q  B X G *  →  Q
 66: Q  B * Q *  →  Q
 67: Q  B * A *  →  Q
 68: Q  B * B *  →  Q
 69: Q  B * C *  →  Q
 70: Q  B * G *  →  Q
 71: Q  C G X *  →  Q
 72: Q  C G * *  →  Q
 73: Q  C X Q *  →  Q
 74: Q  C X A *  →  Q
 75: Q  C X B *  →  Q
 76: Q  C X C *  →  Q
 77: Q  C X G *  →  Q
 78: Q  C X * *  →  Q
 79: Q  C * Q *  →  Q
 80: Q  C * A *  →  Q
 81: Q  C * B *  →  Q
 82: Q  C * C *  →  Q
 83: Q  C * G *  →  Q
 84: Q  C * * *  →  Q
 85: Q  G X X *  →  C
 86: Q  G X A *  →  C
 87: Q  G X B *  →  C
 88: Q  G X C *  →  G
 89: Q  G X G *  →  A
 90: Q  G * A *  →  Q
 91: Q  G * A *  →  G
 92: Q  G * B *  →  G
 93: Q  G * C *  →  G
 94: Q  G * G *  →  A
 95: Q  X X X *  →  Q
 96: Q  X Q X B  →  Q
 97: Q  X Q X C  →  Q
 98: Q  X Q X G  →  Q
 99: Q  X Q X *  →  Q
100: Q  X Q * *  →  Q
101: Q  X Q * B  →  Q
102: Q  X Q * C  →  Q
103: Q  X Q * G  →  Q
104: Q  X Q * *  →  Q
105: Q  X A X Q  →  Q
106: Q  X A X A  →  Q
107: Q  X A A B  →  Q
108: Q  X A A C  →  Q
109: Q  X A X G  →  C
110: Q  X A X *  →  C
111: Q  X A * Q  →  G
112: Q  X A * A  →  A
113: Q  X A * B  →  Q
114: Q  X A * C  →  Q
115: Q  X A * *  →  C
116: Q  X A * *  →  C
117: Q  X B X Q  →  Q
118: Q  X B X A  →  Q
119: Q  X B X B  →  Q
120: Q  X B X C  →  Q
121: Q  X B X G  →  Q
122: Q  X B X *  →  Q
123: Q  X B * Q  →  Q
124: Q  X B * A  →  Q
125: Q  X B * B  →  Q
126: Q  X B * C  →  Q
127: Q  X B * G  →  Q
128: Q  X B * *  →  Q
129: Q  X C X Q  →  A
130: Q  X C X A  →  Q
131: Q  X C X B  →  Q
132: Q  X C X C  →  Q
133: Q  X C X G  →  G
134: Q  X C X *  →  G
135: Q  X C * Q  →  A
136: Q  X C * A  →  Q
137: Q  X C * B  →  Q
138: Q  X C * C  →  Q
139: Q  X C * G  →  Q
140: Q  X C * *  →  Q
141: Q  X G X Q  →  C
142: Q  X G X A  →  Q
143: Q  X G X B  →  Q
144: Q  X G X C  →  Q
145: Q  X G X G  →  A
146: Q  X G X *  →  A
147: Q  X G * Q  →  C
148: Q  X G * A  →  Q
149: Q  X G * B  →  Q
150: Q  X G * C  →  Q
151: Q  X G * G  →  A
152: Q  X G * *  →  A
153: Q  * Q Q G  →  G
154: Q  * Q * G  →  G
155: Q  * A C Q  →  G
156: Q  * A C Q  →  X
157: Q  * A X *  →  X
158: Q  * C B Q  →  X
159: Q  * C C Q  →  X
160: Q  * C A Q  →  X
161: Q  G G G Q  →  X
162: Q  X Q X *  →  Q
163: Q  X A X *  →  C
164: Q  X A A Q  →  C
165: Q  X B X Q  →  G
166: Q  X C X Q  →  G
167: Q  X G X Q  →  G
168: Q  X G X *  →  A
169: Q  X X X *  →  X
170: Q  X X X *  →  F
171: Q  * Q Q *  →  Q
172: Q  * Q X Q  →  Q
173: Q  * A Q *  →  C
174: Q  * A X *  →  Q
175: Q  * B X *  →  G
176: Q  * C Q *  →  G
177: Q  * C X *  →  G
178: Q  * G Q *  →  A
179: Q  * G X *  →  A
180: Q  * * X Q  →  X
```

———— A State ————

```
181: A  Q A X *  →  X
182: A  Q A * *  →  X
183: A  Q B X Q  →  C
184: A  Q B X *  →  C
185: A  Q B * Q  →  G
186: A  Q B * *  →  G
187: A  Q C X Q  →  X
188: A  Q C X Q  →  A
189: A  Q C * *  →  A
190: A  Q X A X  →  A
191: A  Q X B Q  →  G
192: A  Q X X Q  →  A
193: A  Q X X C Q →  A
194: A  Q X C Q  →  A
195: A  Q * A X  →  G
196: A  Q * * A  →  G
197: A  Q * B X  →  G
198: A  Q * C Q  →  A
199: A  Q * C X  →  A
200: A  A X Q X  →  A
201: A  A X A X  →  A
202: A  A X C X  →  A
203: A  A X Q X  →  X
204: A  A * Q X  →  A
205: A  A * A X  →  A
206: A  A * C X  →  A
207: A  A X X X  →  X
208: A  B A X C  →  C
209: A  B A X G  →  B
210: A  B A * C  →  C
211: A  B A * G  →  B
212: A  B X Q X  →  G
213: A  B X A X  →  B
214: A  B B X X  →  G
215: A  B * Q X  →  Q
216: A  B * A X  →  B
217: A  B * B X  →  G
218: A  C B X C  →  C
219: A  C B * C  →  C
220: A  C X Q X  →  G
221: A  C X A X  →  C
222: A  C X A B  →  C
223: A  C X B X  →  C
224: A  C X B C  →  C
225: A  C X G X  →  C
226: A  C X X X  →  C
227: A  C * Q X  →  G
228: A  C * A B  →  C
229: A  C * A X  →  C
230: A  C * B X  →  C
231: A  C * B C  →  C
232: A  C * G X  →  C
233: A  C * X X  →  C
234: A  G X A B  →  B
235: A  G X A X  →  B
236: A  G X B X  →  C
237: A  G X G X  →  C
238: A  G * A B  →  B
239: A  G * A X  →  B
240: A  G * B X  →  C
241: A  G * G X  →  C
242: A  X Q X A  →  A
243: A  X Q X B  →  Q
244: A  X Q X C  →  C
245: A  X Q * A  →  A
246: A  X Q * B  →  Q
247: A  X Q * C  →  C
248: A  X A X A  →  A
249: A  X A X A  →  A
250: A  X A X B  →  B
251: A  X A X C  →  C
252: A  X A * A  →  B
253: A  X A * A  →  A
254: A  X A * B  →  B
255: A  X A * C  →  C
256: A  X A * *  →  C
257: A  X B X G  →  B
258: A  X B X B  →  B
259: A  X B X B  →  B
260: A  X B X B  →  C
261: A  X B X G  →  C
262: A  X B X X  →  C
263: A  X B * Q  →  B
264: A  X B * C  →  C
265: A  X B * *  →  C
266: A  X B * *  →  C
267: A  X B * *  →  C
268: A  X C X A  →  A
269: A  X C X Q  →  A
270: A  X C X *  →  A
271: A  X C * A  →  A
272: A  X G X G  →  C
273: A  X G X G  →  C
274: A  X G X G  →  C
275: A  X G * C  →  C
276: A  X G * G  →  C
277: A  X X * *  →  C
278: A  X X X A  →  X
279: A  X X X C  →  X
280: A  X X * A  →  A
281: A  X X * C  →  G
282: A  * X A Q  →  A
283: A  * X B Q  →  C
284: A  * X B Q  →  C
285: A  * X G X  →  X
286: A  * * A Q  →  X
287: A  * * B X  →  C
288: A  * * B Q  →  C
289: A  * * G X  →  C
```

———— B State ————

```
290: B  Q A X Q  →  X
291: B  Q A A Q  →  G
292: B  Q A A X  →  G
293: B  Q X B X  →  C
294: B  Q X C X  →  C
295: B  Q X G X  →  C
296: B  Q * A X  →  G
297: B  Q * B X  →  G
298: B  Q * C X  →  C
299: B  Q * G X  →  C
300: B  A X X A  →  A
301: B  A X A C  →  B
302: B  A X A X  →  B
303: B  A X B C  →  A
304: B  A X B X  →  A
305: B  A X C X  →  A
306: B  A X G X  →  C
307: B  A X G G  →  C
308: B  A * Q X  →  G
309: B  A * A C  →  B
310: B  A * A X  →  B
311: B  A * B C  →  A
312: B  A * B X  →  A
313: B  A * C X  →  A
314: B  A * G G  →  C
315: B  A * G X  →  C
316: B  B X Q X  →  B
317: B  B X A X  →  B
318: B  B X B X  →  B
319: B  B * Q X  →  B
320: B  B * A X  →  B
321: B  B * B X  →  B
322: B  C A X A  →  B
323: B  C A X C  →  Q
324: B  C A * A  →  B
325: B  C A * C  →  Q
326: B  C B X A  →  A
327: B  C B X C  →  C
328: B  C B * A  →  A
329: B  C B * C  →  C
330: B  C G X C  →  B
331: B  C G * C  →  B
332: B  C X Q X  →  Q
333: B  C X X A  →  Q
334: B  C X A X  →  Q
335: B  C X B C  →  C
336: B  C X B X  →  C
337: B  C X G C  →  B
338: B  C X G X  →  B
339: B  C * Q X  →  Q
340: B  C * X A  →  Q
341: B  C * A X  →  Q
342: B  C * B C  →  C
343: B  C * B X  →  C
344: B  C * G C  →  B
345: B  C * G X  →  B
346: B  G G X A  →  C
347: B  G G X A  →  G
348: B  G G * A  →  C
349: B  G G * *  →  G
350: B  X Q X X  →  B
351: B  X Q B X  →  B
352: B  X Q C X  →  G
353: B  X Q X X  →  G
354: B  X Q G X  →  G
355: B  X Q * *  →  G
356: B  X Q * *  →  B
357: B  X Q * *  →  B
358: B  X Q * G  →  G
359: B  X Q * G  →  G
360: B  X Q X A  →  B
361: B  X Q X B  →  B
362: B  X Q X G  →  Q
363: B  X Q X G  →  B
364: B  X Q X *  →  G
365: B  X Q * *  →  B
366: B  X Q * *  →  Q
367: B  X Q * G  →  B
368: B  X A X A  →  B
369: B  X A X A  →  B
370: B  X A X B  →  B
371: B  X A X C  →  Q
372: B  X A * Q  →  G
373: B  X A * A  →  B
374: B  X A * B  →  B
375: B  X A * C  →  Q
376: B  X B X A  →  B
377: B  X B X A  →  B
378: B  X B X B  →  B
379: B  X B X C  →  C
380: B  X B X G  →  B
381: B  X B * Q  →  B
382: B  X B * B  →  B
383: B  X B * *  →  B
384: B  X B * *  →  C
385: B  X B * G  →  B
386: B  X C X Q  →  B
387: B  X C X A  →  A
388: B  X C X G  →  A
389: B  X C X *  →  Q
390: B  X C * Q  →  B
391: B  X C * *  →  A
392: B  X C * *  →  A
393: B  X C * *  →  Q
394: B  X G X X  →  C
395: B  X G X A  →  C
396: B  X G X G  →  B
397: B  X G X *  →  Q
398: B  X G X *  →  C
399: B  X G * *  →  C
400: B  X G * A  →  C
401: B  X G * G  →  B
402: B  X G * *  →  Q
403: B  X G * *  →  G
404: B  *  X C X  →  Q
```

Appendix I. Transition rule set for the 7-state square synchronizer (continued).

```
405: B  *  X  G  X  →  G        505: C  X  A  *  *  →  B        605: G  G  X  X  X  →  X        705: X  B  X  G  *  →  X
406: B  *  *  C  X  →  Q        506: C  X  B  X  Q  →  C        606: G  G  *  B  X  →  F        706: X  C  A  X  G  →  X
407: B  *  *  G  X  →  G        507: C  X  B  X  C  →  C        607: G  G  *  C  *  →  A        707: X  C  B  X  B  →  X
                               508: C  X  B  X  G  →  G        608: G  G  *  C  X  →  A        708: X  C  B  X  G  →  X
       —— C State ——           509: C  X  B  *  *  →  G        609: G  G  *  X  X  →  X        709: X  C  C  X  X  →  X
                               510: C  X  B  *  Q  →  C        610: G  G  *  X  X  →  X        710: X  C  G  X  A  →  X
408: C  Q  A  C  Q  →  B        511: C  X  B  *  C  →  C        611: G  X  Q  X  A  →  G        711: X  C  X  Q  X  →  X
409: C  Q  A  X  C  →  X        512: C  X  B  *  G  →  G        612: G  X  Q  X  B  →  G        712: X  C  X  Q  *  →  X
410: C  Q  A  X  *  →  B        513: C  X  B  *  *  →  G        613: G  X  Q  X  C  →  G        713: X  C  X  A  X  →  X
411: C  Q  A  *  Q  →  B        514: C  X  C  X  Q  →  C        614: G  X  Q  X  A  →  G        714: X  C  X  B  X  →  X
412: C  Q  A  *  *  →  B        515: C  X  C  X  A  →  A        615: G  X  Q  *  B  →  G        715: X  C  X  C  X  →  X
413: C  Q  B  C  Q  →  C        516: C  X  C  X  B  →  B        616: G  X  Q  *  C  →  G        716: X  C  X  C  *  →  X
414: C  Q  B  X  Q  →  C        517: C  X  C  X  C  →  C        617: G  X  A  X  Q  →  B        717: X  C  X  G  X  →  X
415: C  Q  B  X  C  →  X        518: C  X  C  X  G  →  B        618: G  X  A  X  B  →  G        718: X  G  G  G  G  →  X
416: C  Q  B  X  *  →  G        519: C  X  C  *  Q  →  C        619: G  X  A  X  C  →  G        719: X  G  X  Q  X  →  X
417: C  Q  B  *  Q  →  C        520: C  X  C  *  A  →  A        620: G  X  A  *  Q  →  B        720: X  G  X  A  C  →  X
418: C  Q  B  *  *  →  G        521: C  X  C  *  B  →  B        621: G  X  A  *  B  →  G        721: X  G  X  A  X  →  X
419: C  Q  C  A  Q  →  B        522: C  X  C  *  C  →  B        622: G  X  A  *  C  →  G        722: X  G  X  B  C  →  X
420: C  Q  C  B  Q  →  C        523: C  X  C  *  G  →  B        623: G  X  B  X  Q  →  B        723: X  G  X  B  X  →  X
421: C  Q  G  X  *  →  B        524: C  X  G  X  Q  →  B        624: G  X  B  X  B  →  G        724: X  G  X  B  *  →  X
422: C  Q  G  X  Q  →  X        525: C  X  G  X  B  →  B        625: G  X  B  X  C  →  G        725: X  G  X  C  X  →  X
423: C  Q  G  *  *  →  B        526: C  X  G  X  G  →  B        626: G  X  B  X  G  →  G        726: X  G  X  G  X  →  X
424: C  Q  X  Q  X  →  C        527: C  X  G  X  *  →  B        627: G  X  B  X  *  →  G        727: X  G  X  G  *  →  X
425: C  Q  X  B  Q  →  C        528: C  X  G  *  Q  →  B        628: G  X  B  *  Q  →  B        728: X  G  X  X  X  →  X
426: C  Q  X  B  X  →  C        529: C  X  G  *  B  →  B        629: G  X  B  *  B  →  G        729: X  G  *  *  Q  →  X
427: C  Q  X  C  X  →  C        530: C  X  G  *  *  →  B        630: G  X  B  *  C  →  G        730: X  X  Q  X  Q  →  X
428: C  Q  X  G  X  →  B        531: C  X  G  *  *  →  B        631: G  X  B  *  G  →  G        731: X  X  Q  X  A  →  X
429: C  Q  X  G  Q  →  X        532: C  *  X  A  Q  →  B        632: G  X  B  *  *  →  G        732: X  X  Q  X  B  →  X
430: C  Q  *  A  Q  →  B        533: C  *  X  A  X  →  B        633: G  X  C  X  B  →  A        733: X  X  Q  X  C  →  X
431: C  Q  *  A  Q  →  B        534: C  *  X  B  Q  →  G        634: G  X  C  X  B  →  G        734: X  X  Q  X  G  →  X
432: C  Q  *  B  Q  →  C        535: C  *  X  B  X  →  G        635: G  X  C  X  C  →  G        735: X  X  A  X  Q  →  X
433: C  Q  *  B  X  →  C        536: C  *  X  G  X  →  B        636: G  X  C  X  G  →  A        736: X  X  A  X  A  →  X
434: C  Q  *  C  X  →  C        537: C  *  X  G  X  →  B        637: G  X  C  X  *  →  A        737: X  X  A  X  B  →  X
435: C  Q  *  G  X  →  B        538: C  *  *  A  Q  →  B        638: G  X  C  *  B  →  G        738: X  X  A  X  C  →  X
436: C  A  Q  X  A  →  A        539: C  *  *  A  X  →  B        639: G  X  C  *  B  →  G        739: X  X  A  X  G  →  X
437: C  A  Q  X  C  →  X        540: C  *  *  B  Q  →  G        640: G  X  C  *  C  →  G        740: X  X  B  X  Q  →  X
438: C  A  Q  X  G  →  G        541: C  *  *  B  X  →  G        641: G  X  C  *  G  →  A        741: X  X  B  X  A  →  X
439: C  A  Q  *  A  →  A        542: C  *  *  G  Q  →  B        642: G  X  C  *  *  →  A        742: X  X  B  X  B  →  X
440: C  A  Q  *  G  →  G        543: C  *  *  G  X  →  B        643: G  X  G  X  Q  →  B        743: X  X  B  X  C  →  X
441: C  A  C  X  A  →  A                                        644: G  X  G  X  B  →  G        744: X  X  B  X  G  →  X
442: C  A  C  X  C  →  X               —— G State ——            645: G  X  G  X  C  →  G        745: X  X  B  X  X  →  X
443: C  A  C  X  G  →  B                                        646: G  X  G  X  G  →  G        746: X  X  C  X  Q  →  X
444: C  A  C  *  A  →  A        544: G  Q  A  X  Q  →  B        647: G  X  G  X  *  →  X        747: X  X  C  X  A  →  X
445: C  A  C  *  G  →  B        545: G  Q  A  *  Q  →  B        648: G  X  G  *  Q  →  B        748: X  X  C  X  B  →  X
446: C  A  X  Q  A  →  A        546: G  Q  B  X  *  →  G        649: G  X  G  *  B  →  G        749: X  X  C  X  C  →  X
447: C  A  X  Q  X  →  A        547: G  Q  B  X  Q  →  X        650: G  X  G  *  C  →  G        750: X  X  C  X  G  →  X
448: C  A  X  C  A  →  A        548: G  Q  B  *  *  →  G        651: G  X  G  *  G  →  X        751: X  X  C  X  X  →  X
449: C  A  X  C  A  →  A        549: G  Q  C  X  *  →  A        652: G  X  G  *  *  →  X        752: X  X  G  G  X  →  X
450: C  A  *  Q  A  →  A        550: G  Q  C  *  *  →  A        653: G  X  X  X  B  →  G        753: X  X  G  X  B  →  X
451: C  A  *  Q  X  →  A        551: G  Q  G  X  Q  →  B        654: G  X  X  X  C  →  X        754: X  X  G  X  A  →  X
452: C  A  *  C  A  →  A        552: G  Q  G  *  *  →  B        655: G  X  X  X  G  →  X        755: X  X  G  X  B  →  X
453: C  A  *  C  X  →  A        553: G  Q  X  A  Q  →  B        656: G  X  X  *  B  →  G        756: X  X  G  X  G  →  X
454: C  B  X  Q  X  →  G        554: G  Q  X  A  X  →  B        657: G  X  X  *  C  →  G        757: X  X  G  X  G  →  X
455: C  B  X  A  X  →  B        555: G  Q  X  B  X  →  B        658: G  X  X  *  G  →  X        758: X  X  G  X  X  →  X
456: C  B  X  C  X  →  B        556: G  Q  X  B  *  →  X        659: G  *  X  B  Q  →  G        759: X  X  B  X  X  →  X
457: C  B  X  G  X  →  B        557: G  Q  X  C  X  →  A        660: G  *  X  B  X  →  A        760: X  X  C  X  X  →  X
458: C  B  *  Q  X  →  G        558: G  Q  X  G  X  →  B        661: G  *  X  C  X  →  A        761: X  X  G  X  C  →  X
459: C  B  *  A  X  →  B        559: G  Q  X  G  X  →  B        662: G  *  X  C  X  →  G        762: X  X  G  X  X  →  X
460: C  B  *  C  X  →  B        560: G  Q  X  X  Q  →  A        663: G  *  X  G  X  →  G        763: X  X  X  X  X  →  F
461: C  B  *  G  X  →  B        561: G  Q  X  *  Q  →  A        664: G  *  *  B  Q  →  G        764: X  X  X  X  *  →  F
462: C  B     X  C  →  C        562: G  Q  *  A  X  →  B        665: G  *  *  B  X  →  A        765: X  X  X  *  X  →  F
463: C  B  *     C  →  C        563: G  Q  *  A  Q  →  B        666: G  *  *  C  X  →  A        766: X  X  X  *  X  →  F
464: C  X  Q     A  →  C        564: G  Q  *  B  X  →  B        667: G  *  *  C  Q  →  X        767: X  X  *  X  X  →  F
465: C  X  Q  X     →  C        565: G  Q  *  C  X  →  A        668: G  *  *  G  X  →  X        768: X  *  X  X  X  →  F
466: C  X  A  Q     →  X        566: G  Q  *  G  Q  →  B                                       769: X  *  *  Q  X  →  X
467: C  X  B  Q     →  X        567: G  Q  *  G  X  →  B              —— X State ——            770: X  *  Q  X  A  →  X
468: C  X  B  A     →  C        568: G  Q  *  X  Q  →  A                                       771: X  *  Q  X  B  →  X
469: C  X  B  X     →  C        569: G  A  X  Q  X  →  G        669: X  Q  A  A  Q  →  X        772: X  *  Q  X  C  →  X
470: C  X  C  A     →  X        570: G  A  X  *  X  →  G        670: X  Q  A  Q  *  →  X        773: X  *  A  X  A  →  X
471: C  X  C  X     →  C        571: G  B  X  A  X  →  G        671: X  Q  X  Q  *  →  X        774: X  *  A  X  A  →  X
472: C  *  Q  X     →  C        572: G  B  X  A  X  →  G        672: X  Q  X  A  A  →  X        775: X  *  B  X  Q  →  X
473: C  *  B  X     →  C        573: G  B  X  B  X  →  G        673: X  Q  X  A  *  →  X        776: X  *  B  X  B  →  X
474: C  *  B  X     →  C        574: G  B  X  C  X  →  G        674: X  Q  X  B  Q  →  X        777: X  *  B  X  X  →  X
475: C  *  *  X     →  C        575: G  B  X  G  X  →  G        675: X  Q  X  B  X  →  X        778: X  *  C  X  Q  →  X
476: C  G  X  Q     →  G        576: G  B  X  X  Q  →  G        676: X  Q  X  C  X  →  X        779: X  *  C  X  C  →  X
477: C  G  X  Q     →  G        577: G  B  *  A  X  →  G        677: X  Q  X  C  *  →  X        780: X  *  G  X  A  →  X
478: C  G  X  A     →  B        578: G  B  *  B  X  →  G        678: X  Q  X  G  X  →  X        781: X  *  G  X  A  →  X
479: C  G  X  B     →  B        579: G  B  *  B  X  →  G        679: X  Q  X  G  *  →  X        782: X  *  G  X  B  →  X
480: C  G  X  C     →  B        580: G  B  *  C  X  →  G        680: X  Q  X  X  *  →  F        783: X  *  X  X  X  →  X
481: C  G  X  C     →  B        581: G  B  *  G  X  →  G        681: X  Q  X  X  Q  →  X        784: X  *  X  X  Q  →  F
482: C  G  *  Q     →  B        582: G  B  *  X  X  →  G        682: X  Q  X  X  *  →  X        785: X  *  X  X  *  →  F
483: C  G  *  Q     →  G        583: G  C  C  X  X  →  A        683: X  Q  *  *  Q  →  X        786: X  *  *  X  Q  →  F
484: C  G  *  Q     →  B        584: G  C  C  *  X  →  A        684: X  A  X  A  Q  →  X        787: X  *  *  X  X  →  F
485: C  G  *  A     →  G        585: G  C  C  *  C  →  G        685: X  A  X  Q  X  →  X
486: C  G  *  B     →  G        586: G  C  C  *  *  →  A        686: X  A  X  A  B  →  X
487: C  G  *  C     →  B        587: G  C  X  Q  X  →  G        687: X  A  X  A  *  →  X
488: C  G  *  C     →  B        588: G  C  X  A  X  →  G        688: X  A  X  A  *  →  X
489: C  G  *  *     →  B        589: G  C  X  B  X  →  G        689: X  A  X  B  X  →  X
490: C  X  Q  X     →  C        590: G  C  X  C  X  →  A        690: X  A  X  C  X  →  X
491: C  X  Q  X     →  A        591: G  C  X  C  *  →  G        691: X  A  X  G  X  →  X
492: C  X  Q  B     →  G        592: G  C  X  G  X  →  G        692: X  A  X  G  *  →  X
493: C  X  Q  C     →  C        593: G  C  X  X  X  →  G        693: X  A  X  G  *  →  X
494: C  X  Q  X     →  C        594: G  C  *  Q  X  →  G        694: X  A  X  X  A  →  X
495: C  X  Q  *     →  C        595: G  C  *  A  X  →  G        695: X  A  *  *  A  →  X
496: C  X  Q  *     →  A        596: G  C  *  C  X  →  G        696: X  B  A  X  A  →  X
497: C  X  Q  *     →  B        597: G  C  *  C  C  →  G        697: X  B  X  B  Q  →  X
498: C  X  Q  *     →  C        598: G  C  *  C  *  →  G        698: X  B  X  B  X  →  X
499: C  X  Q  G     →  G        599: G  C  *  G  X  →  G        699: X  B  X  A  B  →  X
500: C  X  A  X     →  B        600: G  C  *  X  X  →  G        700: X  B  X  B  C  →  X
501: C  X  A  X     →  B        601: G  X  Q  X  B  →  A        701: X  B  X  B  *  →  X
502: C  X  A  *     →  B        602: G  X  Q  C  X  →  A        702: X  B  X  B  *  →  X
503: C  X  A  *     →  B        603: G  X  G  X  C  →  A        703: X  B  X  C  X  →  X
504: C  X  A  G     →  B        604: G  X  G  X  X  →  X        704: X  B  X  C  X  →  X
```

References

1. Beyer, W.T.: Recognition of topological invariants by iterative arrays. Ph.D. thesis, p. 144. MIT (1969)
2. Mazoyer, J.: A six-state minimal time solution to the firing squad synchronization problem. Theoret. Comput. Sci. **50**, 183–238 (1987)
3. Moore, E.F.: The firing squad synchronization problem. In: Moore, E.F. (ed.) Sequential Machines, Selected Papers, pp. 213–214. Addison-Wesley, Reading (1964)
4. Moore, F.R., Langdon, G.G.: A generalized firing squad problem. Inf. Control **12**, 212–220 (1968)
5. Shinahr, I.: Two-and three-dimensional firing squad synchronization problems. Inf. Control **24**, 163–180 (1974)
6. Umeo, H.: A simple design of time-efficient firing squad synchronization algorithms with fault-tolerance. IEICE Trans. Inf. Syst. **E87–D**(3), 733–739 (2004)
7. Umeo, H.: Firing squad synchronization problem in cellular automata. In: Meyers, R.A. (ed.) Encyclopedia of Complexity and System Science, vol. 4, pp. 3537–3574. Springer, Springer (2009). doi:10.1007/978-0-387-30440-3_211
8. Umeo, H.: Synchronizing square arrays in optimum-time. Int. J. Gen. Syst. **41**(6), 617–631 (2012)
9. Umeo, H., Ishida, K., Tachibana, K., Kamikawa, N.: A transition rule set for the first 2-D optimum-time synchronization algorithm. In: Peper, F., Umeo, H., Matsui, N., Isokawa, T. (eds.) Natural Computing, vol. 2, pp. 333–341. Springer, Tokyo (2010). doi:10.1007/978-4-431-53868-4_38
10. Umeo, H., Kamikawa, N., Nishioka, K., Akiguchi, S.: Generalized firing squad synchronization protocols for one-dimensional cellular automata - a survey. Acta Physica Polonica B: Proc. Suppl. **3**, 267–289 (2010)
11. Umeo, H., Kubo, K.: A seven-state time-optimum square synchronizer. In: Bandini, S., Manzoni, S., Umeo, H., Vizzari, G. (eds.) ACRI 2010. LNCS, vol. 6350, pp. 219–230. Springer, Heidelberg (2010). doi:10.1007/978-3-642-15979-4_24
12. Umeo, H., Kubo, K., Nishide, K.: A class of FSSP algorithms for multi-dimensional cellular arrays. Commun. Nonlinear Sci. Numer. Simul. **21**, 200–209 (2015)
13. Umeo, H., Kubo, K., Takahashi, Y.: An isotropic optimum-time FSSP algorithm for two-dimensional cellular automata. In: Malyshkin, V. (ed.) PaCT 2013. LNCS, vol. 7979, pp. 381–393. Springer, Heidelberg (2013). doi:10.1007/978-3-642-39958-9_35
14. Umeo, H., Uchino, H.: A new time-optimum synchronization algorithm for rectangle arrays. Fundamenta Informaticae **87**(2), 155–164 (2008)
15. Umeo, H., Yamawaki, T., Nishide, K.: An optimum-time firing squad synchronization algorithm for two-dimensional rectangle arrays –freezing-thawing technique based–. J. Cell. Automata **7**, 31–46 (2012)
16. Umeo, H., Yunès, J.-B., Yamawaki, T.: A simple-optimum-time firing squad synchronization algorithms for two-dimensional arrays. In: Proceedings of 2009 International Conference on Computational Intelligence, Modelling and Simulation, CSSim 2009, pp. 120–125. IEEE Computer Society (2009)

Automata

Derived-Term Automata of Weighted Rational Expressions with Quotient Operators

Akim Demaille$^{(\boxtimes)}$ and Thibaud Michaud

EPITA Research and Development Laboratory (LRDE),
14-16, Rue Voltaire, 94276 Le Kremlin-Bicêtre, France
{akim,tmichaud}@lrde.epita.fr

Abstract. Quotient operators have been rarely studied in the context of weighted rational expressions and automaton generation—in spite of the key role played by the quotient of words in formal language theory. To handle both left- and right-quotients we generalize an *expansion*-based construction of the *derived-term* (or *Antimirov*, or *equation*) automaton and rely on support for a *transposition* (or *reversal*) operator. The resulting automata may have spontaneous transitions, which requires different techniques from the usual derived-term constructions.

1 Introduction

There are several well-known algorithms to build an automaton from a rational expression. We are particularly interested in the construction of the *derived-term* automaton, pioneered by the *derivatives* of Brzozowski [4], improved as *partial derivatives* by Antimirov [3], and generalized to *weighted* expressions by Lombardy and Sakarovitch [13].

Thiemann [16] explores the properties of rational expression operators that enable the construction of the derived-term automaton. In particular, he shows that the left- and right- *quotients* are not "ε-testable", and that *transposition* (aka *reversal*) is neither "left nor right derivable". Our purpose is to show how *expansions* allow to overcome these issues and succeed in supporting the operators.

Our contributions include (i) a proof of the "super **S**" property, (ii) an extension of rational expressions to support transpose, left- and right-quotient operators, (iii) an algorithm to build the derived-term automaton of such an expression which requires (iv) the support of spontaneous transitions in derived-term automata.

We settle the notations and left quotient in Sect. 2. Rational expansions are introduced and computed from an expression in Sect. 3; they are used in Sect. 4 to construct the derived-term automaton. Handled in a different way, the transpose operator is introduced in Sect. 5 and used to define the right quotient. In Sect. 6 we present related work and conclude in Sect. 7.

© Springer International Publishing AG 2017
D.V. Hung and D. Kapur (Eds.): ICTAC 2017, LNCS 10580, pp. 155–173, 2017.
DOI: 10.1007/978-3-319-67729-3_10

Vcsn is a free-software platform dedicated to weighted automata and rational expressions [9]. All of constructs presented in this paper can be experimented from a simple web-browser[1].

2   Notations

Our purpose is to introduce a left-quotient operator $\backslash$ for weighted rational expressions (e.g., $\mathsf{E}_1 := (\langle 2\rangle a)\backslash(\langle 3\rangle(a+b) + \langle 5\rangle(aa^*) + \langle 7\rangle(ab^*)) + \langle 11\rangle(ab^*)$, weights are in angle brackets), and to build an equivalent automaton from it (Fig. 1). To this end we compute *the rational expansion* of an expression [7]:

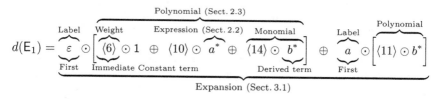

Expansions can be thought as a (non unique) normal form for expressions. Defining them requires several concepts, introduced bottom-up in this section.

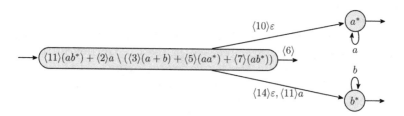

Fig. 1. The derived-term automaton of our running example, $\mathsf{E}_1 := (\langle 2\rangle a)\backslash(\langle 3\rangle(a+b) + \langle 5\rangle aa^* + \langle 7\rangle ab^*) + \langle 11\rangle ab^*$.

2.1   Rational Series

Series are to weighted automata what languages are to Boolean automata. Not all languages are rational (denoted by an expression), and similarly, not all series are rational (denoted by a weighted expression). We follow Sakarovitch [15].

Let A be a (finite) alphabet; a *word* m is a finite sequence of letters of A. The empty word is denoted ε. The set of words is written A^*, and $A^?$ denotes $A\cup\{\varepsilon\}$. A *language* is a subset of A^*. Let $\langle \mathbb{K}, +, \cdot, 0_{\mathbb{K}}, 1_{\mathbb{K}}\rangle$ be a commutative semiring whose multiplication will be denoted by implicit concatenation. A (formal power) *series* over A^* with *weights* (or *multiplicities*) in $\mathbb{K}$ is any map from A^* to $\mathbb{K}$. The weight of a word m in a series s is denoted $s(m)$. The *empty series*, $m \mapsto 0_{\mathbb{K}}$, is

---

[1] See the interactive environment, http://vcsn-sandbox.lrde.epita.fr, or the companion notebook, http://vcsn.lrde.epita.fr/dload/doc/ICTAC-2017.html.

denoted 0; for any word u (including ε), u denotes the series $m \mapsto 1_{\mathbb{K}}$ if $m = u$, $0_{\mathbb{K}}$ otherwise. Equipped with the pointwise addition $(s + t := m \mapsto s(m) + t(m))$ and the Cauchy product $(s \cdot t := m \mapsto \sum_{u,v \in A^* | u \cdot v = m} s(u) \cdot t(v))$ as multiplication, the set of these series forms a semiring denoted $\langle \mathbb{K}\langle\langle A^* \rangle\rangle, +, \cdot, 0, \varepsilon \rangle$.

The *constant term* of a series s, denoted s_ε, is $s(\varepsilon)$, the weight of the empty word. A series s is *proper* if $s_\varepsilon = 0_{\mathbb{K}}$. The *proper part* of s, denoted s_p, is the proper series which coincides with s on non empty words: $s = s_\varepsilon \varepsilon + s_p$ (or, with a slight abuse of notations $s = s_\varepsilon + s_p$).

Star. A weight $k \in \mathbb{K}$ is *starrable* if its star, $k^* := \sum_{n \in \mathbb{N}} k^n$, is defined. We suppose that $\mathbb{K}$ is a *topological semiring*, i.e., it is equipped with a topology, and both addition and multiplication are continuous. Besides, it is supposed to be *strong*, i.e., the product of two summable families is summable. This ensures that $\mathbb{K}\langle\langle A^* \rangle\rangle$, equipped with the product topology derived from the topology on $\mathbb{K}$, is also a strong topological semiring. The *star* of a series is an infinite sum: $s^* := \sum_{n \in \mathbb{N}} s^n$.

To prove the correctness of our construct (Proposition 6), we will need a property of star (Proposition 2) which follows from the following result. In various forms it is named the "denesting rule" [11, p. 57], the "property S" [15, Propositions III.2.5 and III.2.6], or the "sum-star equation" [10, p. 188]. Proofs can be found for the axiomatic approach of star (based on Conway semirings), but we followed the topology-based one, for which we did not find a published version.

Proposition 1 (Super S). *Let $\mathbb{K}$ be a strong topological semiring. For any series $s, t \in \mathbb{K}\langle\langle A^* \rangle\rangle$, if s_ε^*, $(t_\varepsilon s_\varepsilon^*)^*$, and $(s_\varepsilon + t_\varepsilon)^*$ are defined and $(s_\varepsilon + t_\varepsilon)^* = s_\varepsilon^*(t_\varepsilon s_\varepsilon^*)^*$, then $(s + t)^* = s^*(ts^*)^*$.*

Proof. This proof climbs from restricted forms (e.g., s being a weight and t being proper) to the general cases using previous steps. See Appendix A.1. □

All the usual semirings $(\mathbb{Q}, \mathbb{R}, \mathbb{R}_{\min}, \text{Log}, \text{etc.})$ are strong topological semirings, in which if s_ε^*, $(t_\varepsilon s_\varepsilon^*)^*$, and $(s_\varepsilon + t_\varepsilon)^*$ are defined then $(s_\varepsilon + t_\varepsilon)^* = s_\varepsilon^*(t_\varepsilon s_\varepsilon^*)^*$. Proposition 1 (and Proposition 2) actually do not need $\mathbb{K}$ to be commutative.

Proposition 2. *Let $\mathbb{K}$ be a strong topological semiring. Let $s \in \mathbb{K}, t \in \mathbb{K}\langle\langle A^* \rangle\rangle$, if s^*, $(t_\varepsilon s^*)^*$, and $(s + t_\varepsilon)^*$ are defined and $(s + t_\varepsilon)^* = s^*(t_\varepsilon s^*)^*$ then $(s + t)^* = s^* + s^* t(s + t)^*$.*

Proof. The result follows from Proposition 1, and from $(ts^*)^* = \varepsilon + (ts^*)(ts^*)^*$: $(s + t)^* = s^*(ts^*)^* = s^*(\varepsilon + (ts^*)(ts^*)^*) = s^* + s^* t(s^*(ts^*)^*) = s^* + s^* t(s + t)^*$. □

Left Quotient. Like Li et al. [12], we define the left quotient by series s of series t as: $s \backslash t := v \mapsto \sum_{u \in A^*} s(u) \cdot t(uv)$.

Proposition 3 (Quotient is Bilinear *[12, Proposition 6]). For weight $k \in \mathbb{K}$ and series $s, s', t, t' \in \mathbb{K}\langle\!\langle A^* \rangle\!\rangle$:*

$$s\backslash(t + t') = s\backslash t + s\backslash t' \qquad\qquad s\backslash kt = k(s\backslash t)$$
$$(s + s')\backslash t = s\backslash t + s'\backslash t \qquad\qquad (ks)\backslash t = k(s\backslash t)$$

Let u, v be two words, their *root* $r(u, v)$ is u if u is a prefix of v, v if v is a prefix of u, undefined otherwise.

Proposition 4. *For series $s, t \in \mathbb{K}\langle\!\langle A^* \rangle\!\rangle$ and words $u, v \in A^*$:*

$$us\backslash vt = \begin{cases} 0 & \text{if } r(u,v) \text{ is undefined} \\ u's\backslash v't & \text{otherwise, with } u' = r(u,v)\backslash u, v' = r(u,v)\backslash v \end{cases}$$

2.2   Extended Weighted Rational Expressions

Definition 1 (Extended Weighted Rational Expression). *A* rational expression E *is a term built from the following grammar, where $a \in A$ is a letter, and $k \in \mathbb{K}$ a weight:* $\mathsf{E} ::= 0 \mid 1 \mid a \mid \mathsf{E} + \mathsf{E} \mid \langle k \rangle \mathsf{E} \mid \mathsf{E} \cdot \mathsf{E} \mid \mathsf{E}^* \mid \mathsf{E}\backslash\mathsf{E}.$

Example 1. Let $\mathsf{E}_1 := (\langle 2 \rangle a)\backslash(\langle 3 \rangle(a + b) + \langle 5 \rangle aa^* + \langle 7 \rangle ab^*) + \langle 11 \rangle ab^*$. By "simplifying" the left quotient (distributivity and $(\langle 2 \rangle a)\backslash(\langle 3 \rangle(a + b)) \equiv \langle 6 \rangle 1$, etc.), it can be shown to be equivalent to $\langle 6 \rangle 1 + \langle 10 \rangle a^* + \langle 14 \rangle b^* + \langle 11 \rangle ab^*$.

Rational expressions are syntactic objects; they provide a finite notation for (some) series, which are semantic objects.

Definition 2 (Series Denoted by an Expression). *Let E be an expression. The series denoted by E, noted $[\![\mathsf{E}]\!]$, is defined by induction on E:*

$$[\![0]\!] := 0 \qquad [\![1]\!] := \varepsilon \qquad [\![a]\!] := a \qquad [\![\mathsf{E} + \mathsf{F}]\!] := [\![\mathsf{E}]\!] + [\![\mathsf{F}]\!] \qquad [\![\langle k \rangle \mathsf{E}]\!] := k[\![\mathsf{E}]\!]$$
$$[\![\mathsf{E} \cdot \mathsf{F}]\!] := [\![\mathsf{E}]\!] \cdot [\![\mathsf{F}]\!] \qquad [\![\mathsf{E}^*]\!] := [\![\mathsf{E}]\!]^* \qquad [\![\mathsf{E}\backslash\mathsf{F}]\!] := [\![\mathsf{E}]\!]\backslash[\![\mathsf{F}]\!]$$

An expression is *valid* if it denotes a series. More specifically, this requires that $[\![\mathsf{F}]\!]^*$ is well defined for each sub-expression of the form F^*, i.e., that the constant term of $[\![\mathsf{F}]\!]$ is *starrable* in $\mathbb{K}$ (Proposition 2). So for instance, $1_\mathbb{K}^*$ and $(a^*)^*$ are valid in $\mathbb{B}$, but invalid in $\mathbb{Q}$.

Two expressions E and F are *equivalent* iff $[\![\mathsf{E}]\!] = [\![\mathsf{F}]\!]$. Some expressions are "trivially equivalent"; any candidate expression will be rewritten via the following *trivial identities*. Any sub-expression of a form listed to the left of a '$\Rightarrow$' is rewritten as indicated on the right.

$$\mathsf{E} + 0 \Rightarrow \mathsf{E} \qquad 0 + \mathsf{E} \Rightarrow \mathsf{E}$$
$$\langle 0_\mathbb{K} \rangle \mathsf{E} \Rightarrow 0 \qquad \langle 1_\mathbb{K} \rangle \mathsf{E} \Rightarrow \mathsf{E} \qquad \langle k \rangle 0 \Rightarrow 0 \qquad \langle k \rangle\langle h \rangle \mathsf{E} \Rightarrow \langle kh \rangle \mathsf{E}$$
$$(\langle k \rangle^? 1) \cdot \mathsf{E} \Rightarrow \langle k \rangle \mathsf{E} \qquad \mathsf{E} \cdot (\langle k \rangle^? 1) \Rightarrow \langle k \rangle \mathsf{E}$$
$$\mathsf{E} \cdot 0 \Rightarrow 0 \qquad 0 \cdot \mathsf{E} \Rightarrow 0 \qquad 0^* \Rightarrow 1 \qquad 0\backslash\mathsf{E} \Rightarrow 0 \qquad \mathsf{E}\backslash 0 \Rightarrow 0 \qquad 1\backslash\mathsf{E} \Rightarrow \mathsf{E}$$

where E stands for a rational expression, $\ell \in A^?$ is a *label*, $k, h \in \mathbb{K}$ are weights, and $\langle k \rangle^? \ell$ denotes either $\langle k \rangle \ell$, or ℓ in which case $k = 1_\mathbb{K}$ in the right-hand side of $\Rightarrow$. The choice of these identities is beyond the scope of this paper [13, p. 149], they are limited to trivial properties; in particular *linearity* ("weighted ACI": associativity, commutativity, and $\langle k \rangle^? \mathsf{E} + \langle h \rangle^? \mathsf{E} \Rightarrow \langle k + h \rangle \mathsf{E}$) is not enforced — polynomials will take care of it (Sect. 2.3). In practice, additional identities help reducing the number of derived terms, hence the final automaton size.

2.3 Rational Polynomials

The "partial derivatives" [3] rely on *sets* of rational expressions, later generalized to *weighted sets* [13], i.e., functions (partial, with finite domain) from the set of expressions into $\mathbb{K} \setminus \{0_\mathbb{K}\}$. It proves useful to view such structures as *polynomials* of rational expressions. In essence, they capture the linearity of addition.

Definition 3 (Rational Polynomial). *A* polynomial *(of rational expressions) is a finite (left) linear combination of rational expressions. Syntactically it is represented by a term built from the grammar* $\mathsf{P} ::= 0 \mid \langle k_1 \rangle \odot \mathsf{E}_1 \oplus \cdots \oplus \langle k_n \rangle \odot \mathsf{E}_n$ *where* $k_i \in \mathbb{K} \setminus \{0_\mathbb{K}\}$ *denote non-zero weights, and* E_i *denote non-zero expressions. Expressions may not appear more than once in a polynomial. A* monomial *is a pair* $\langle k_i \rangle \odot \mathsf{E}_i$. *The* terms *of* P *is the set* $\mathsf{exprs}(\mathsf{P}) := \{\mathsf{E}_1, \ldots, \mathsf{E}_n\}$.

We use specific symbols ($\odot$ and $\oplus$) to clearly separate the outer polynomial layer from the inner expression layer. A polynomial P of expressions can be "projected" as a rational expression $\mathsf{expr}(\mathsf{P})$ by mapping its sum and left multiplication by a weight onto the corresponding operators on rational expressions. This operation is performed on a canonical form of the polynomial (expressions are sorted in a well defined order). Polynomials denote series: $[\![\mathsf{P}]\!] := [\![\mathsf{expr}(\mathsf{P})]\!]$.

Example 2 (Example 1 continued). Let $\mathsf{E}_1 := ((\langle 2 \rangle a) \setminus (\langle 3 \rangle (a + b) + \langle 5 \rangle a a^* + \langle 7 \rangle a b^*) + \langle 11 \rangle a b^*$. The polynomial '$\mathsf{P}_{1\varepsilon} := \langle 6 \rangle \odot 1 \oplus \langle 10 \rangle \odot a^* \oplus \langle 14 \rangle \odot b^*$' has three monomials, and $\mathsf{expr}(\mathsf{P}_{1\varepsilon}) = \langle 6 \rangle 1 + \langle 10 \rangle a^* + \langle 14 \rangle b^*$.

Let $\ell \in A^?$ be a label, $\mathsf{P} = \langle k_1 \rangle \odot \mathsf{E}_1 \oplus \cdots \oplus \langle k_n \rangle \odot \mathsf{E}_n$ a polynomial, k a weight (possibly zero) and F an expression (possibly zero), we introduce:

$$\ell \cdot \mathsf{P} := \langle k_1 \rangle \odot (\ell \cdot \mathsf{E}_1) \oplus \cdots \oplus \langle k_n \rangle \odot (\ell \cdot \mathsf{E}_n)$$
$$\mathsf{P} \cdot \mathsf{F} := \langle k_1 \rangle \odot (\mathsf{E}_1 \cdot \mathsf{F}) \oplus \cdots \oplus \langle k_n \rangle \odot (\mathsf{E}_n \cdot \mathsf{F})$$
$$\langle k \rangle \mathsf{P} := \langle k k_1 \rangle \odot \mathsf{E}_1 \oplus \cdots \oplus \langle k k_n \rangle \odot \mathsf{E}_n$$
$$\mathsf{P}_1 \setminus \mathsf{P}_2 := \bigoplus_{\substack{\langle k_1 \rangle \odot \mathsf{E}_1 \in \mathsf{P}_1 \\ \langle k_2 \rangle \odot \mathsf{E}_2 \in \mathsf{P}_2}} \langle k_1 \cdot k_2 \rangle \odot (\mathsf{E}_1 \setminus \mathsf{E}_2) \tag{1}$$

Trivial identities might simplify the result, e.g., $((\langle 1_\mathbb{K} \rangle \odot 1) \setminus (\langle 1_\mathbb{K} \rangle \odot a) = \langle 1_\mathbb{K} \rangle \odot a$. Note the asymmetry between left and right exterior products. Addition is commutative, multiplication by zero (be it an expression or a weight) evaluates to the polynomial zero, and left multiplication by a weight is distributive.

Lemma 1. $[\![\ell \cdot \mathsf{P}]\!] = \ell \cdot [\![\mathsf{P}]\!]$ $[\![\mathsf{P} \cdot \mathsf{F}]\!] = [\![\mathsf{P}]\!] \cdot [\![\mathsf{F}]\!]$
$[\![\langle k \rangle \mathsf{P}]\!] = \langle k \rangle [\![\mathsf{P}]\!]$ $[\![\mathsf{P}_1 \backslash \mathsf{P}_2]\!] = [\![\mathsf{P}_1]\!] \backslash [\![\mathsf{P}_2]\!]$.

Proof. These properties are trivial. In particular, the case of $\backslash$ follows from Proposition 3 (see Appendix A.2). $\qquad\qquad\qquad\qquad\qquad\qquad\qquad\qquad\qquad\qquad$ □

2.4   Weighted Automata

Definition 4. *A* finite *weighted automaton* $\mathcal{A}$ *is a tuple* $\langle A, \mathbb{K}, Q, E, I, T \rangle$ *where:*

- *A is an alphabet,*
- $\mathbb{K}$ *(the set of weights) is a semiring,*
- *Q is a finite set of states,*
- *I and T are the* initial *and* final *functions from Q into* $\mathbb{K}$,
- *E is a (partial) function from* $Q \times A^? \times Q$ *into* $\mathbb{K} \backslash \{0_{\mathbb{K}}\}$; *its domain represents the* transitions: *(source, label, destination).*

Our automata are "ε-NFAs": they may have spontaneous transitions ($\ell \in A^?$). A *path* π is a sequence of transitions $(q_0, \ell_1, q_1)(q_1, \ell_2, q_2) \cdots (q_{n-1}, \ell_n, q_n)$ where the source of each is the destination of the previous one; its *source* is $\iota(\pi) := q_0$, its *destination* is $\tau(\pi) := q_n$, its *label* is the word $\ell(\pi) := \ell_1 \cdots \ell_n$, its *weight* is $w(\pi) := E(q_0, \ell_1, q_1) \cdot \ldots \cdot E(q_{n-1}, \ell_n, q_n)$, and its *weighted label* [14] is the monomial $wl(\pi) := w(\pi)\ell(\pi)$. The set of paths of $\mathcal{A}$ is denoted $\mathsf{Path}(\mathcal{A})$. A *computation* c is a path π together with its initial and final functions at the ends: $c := (I(\iota(\pi)), \pi, T(\tau(\pi)))$, its weight is $w(c) := I(\iota(\pi))w(\pi)T(\tau(\pi))$.

The *evaluation* of word u by an automaton $\mathcal{A}$, $\mathcal{A}(u)$, is the sum of the weights of all the computations labeled by u, or $0_{\mathbb{K}}$ if there are none. The *behavior* of $\mathcal{A}$ is the series $[\![\mathcal{A}]\!] := u \mapsto \mathcal{A}(u)$. A state q is *initial* if $I(q) \neq 0_{\mathbb{K}}$. A state q is *accessible* if there is a path from an initial state to q. The *accessible* part of an automaton $\mathcal{A}$ is the sub-automaton whose states are the accessible states of $\mathcal{A}$.

Automata with spontaneous transitions may be *invalid*, if they have cycles of spontaneous transitions whose weight is not starrable [14].

Definition 5 (Semantics of a State). *Given a weighted automaton* $\mathcal{A} = \langle A, \mathbb{K}, Q, E, I, T \rangle$, *the semantics of state* q *(aka, its* future*) is the series:*

$$[\![q]\!] := T(q) + \sum_{\pi \in \mathsf{Path}(\mathcal{A})|q=i(\pi)} wl(\pi)T(\tau(\pi)) \qquad (2)$$

Clearly, $[\![\mathcal{A}]\!] = \sum_{q \in Q} I(q)[\![q]\!]$.

Proposition 5. *For any automaton* $\mathcal{A}$, *we have:*

$$[\![q]\!] = T(q) + \sum_{\ell \in A^?, q' \in Q} E(q, \ell, q')\ell[\![q']\!] \qquad (3)$$

The equivalence of (2) and (3) can be seen as two different strategies of evaluation: the first one is by depth first (follow each path individually, then sum their weights), the second one by breadth (starting from the set of initial states, descend "simultaneously" each transition, and repeat).

A simple proof by induction [7, Sect. 2.5] suffices in the absence of spontaneous transitions. With cycles of spontaneous transitions, we face infinite sums whose formal treatment requires arguments that go way beyond the scope of this paper. This is in fact the core of the work of Lombardy and Sakarovitch [14].

3   Rational Expansions

Expansions (Sect. 3.1) can be viewed as a normal form of rational expansions from which the construction of the derived-term automaton is straightforward. For instance, *the* (see Sect. 3.2) expansion of $\langle 2 \rangle ac + \langle 3 \rangle bc$ is $a \odot [\langle 2 \rangle \odot c] \oplus b \odot [\langle 3 \rangle \odot c]$.

3.1   Rational Expansions

An *expansion* [6,7] is a syntactic object that denotes a linear form of a series/expressions: it maps each label to a polynomial. From systems of expansions, building the "equation" automaton is straightforward (Sect. 4). Although closely related to the derivatives of an expression, expansions can cope more easily with new operators (such as quotient) than derivatives [6]. They also have a more "forward" flavor: their computation follow very simple rules such as distributivity. Let $[n]$ denote $\{1, \ldots, n\}$.

Definition 6 (Rational Expansion). *A rational expansion* X *is a term built from the grammar* $\mathsf{X} ::= 0 \mid \ell_1 \odot [\mathsf{P}_1] \oplus \cdots \oplus \ell_n \odot [\mathsf{P}_n]$ *where* $\ell_i \in A^?$ *are labels (occurring at most once), and* P_i *non-zero polynomials. The* firsts *of* X *is* $f(\mathsf{X}) := \{\ell_1, \ldots, \ell_n\}$ *(possibly empty), and its* terms *are* $\mathsf{exprs}(\mathsf{X}) := \bigcup_{i \in [n]} \mathsf{exprs}(\mathsf{P}_i)$.

Polynomials are written in square brackets to ease reading. Given an expansion X, we denote by X_ℓ (or $\mathsf{X}(\ell)$) the polynomial corresponding to ℓ in X, or the polynomial zero if $\ell \notin f(\mathsf{X})$. Expansions will thus be written: $\mathsf{X} = \bigoplus_{\ell \in f(\mathsf{X})} \ell \odot [\mathsf{X}_\ell]$.

An expansion X can be "projected" as a rational expression $\mathsf{expr}(\mathsf{X})$ by mapping labels and polynomials to their corresponding rational expressions, and $\oplus/\odot$ to the sum/concatenation of rational expressions. Again, this is performed on a canonical form of the expansion: labels and polynomials are sorted. Expansions also denote series: $[\![\mathsf{X}]\!] := [\![\mathsf{expr}(\mathsf{X})]\!]$. An expansion X is said to be *equivalent* to an expression E iff $[\![\mathsf{X}]\!] = [\![\mathsf{E}]\!]$.

The *immediate constant term* of an expansion X, $\mathsf{X}_\$$, is the weight of 1 in $\mathsf{X}(\varepsilon)$, or $0_\mathbb{K}$ if it does not exist. The *immediate proper part* of X, X_p, is the expansion which coincides with X but with a null immediate constant term; hence[2] $\mathsf{X} = \varepsilon \odot [\langle \mathsf{X}_\$ \rangle \odot 1] \oplus \mathsf{X}_p$. Beware that $[\![\mathsf{X}_p]\!]$ might not be proper; e.g., with $\mathsf{X} := \varepsilon \odot [\langle 2 \rangle \odot 1 \oplus \langle 3 \rangle \odot a \backslash a]$, we have $\mathsf{X}_p = \varepsilon \odot [\langle 3 \rangle \odot a \backslash a]$, yet $[\![\mathsf{X}_p]\!] = 3$.

---

[2] The (straightforward) definition of addition of expansions, $\oplus$, will be given below.

Example 3 (Examples 1 and 2 continued). Let $P_{1a} := \langle 11 \rangle \odot b^*$. Expansion $X_1 := \varepsilon \odot P_{1\varepsilon} \oplus a \odot P_{1a} = \varepsilon \odot [\langle 6 \rangle \odot 1 \oplus \langle 10 \rangle \odot a^* \oplus \langle 14 \rangle \odot b^*] \oplus a \odot [\langle 11 \rangle \odot b^*]$ maps the label ε (resp. a) to the polynomial $P_{1\varepsilon}$ (resp. P_{1a}). The immediate constant term of X_1 is 6. X_1 is equivalent to E_1.

Let X, Y be expansions, k a weight, and E an expression (all possibly zero):

$$X \oplus Y := \bigoplus_{\ell \in f(X) \cup f(Y)} \ell \odot [X_\ell \oplus Y_\ell] \qquad \langle k \rangle X := \bigoplus_{\ell \in f(X)} \ell \odot [\langle k \rangle X_\ell]$$

$$X \cdot E := \bigoplus_{\ell \in f(X)} \ell \odot [X_\ell \cdot E]$$

$$X \backslash Y := \bigoplus \begin{cases} \varepsilon \odot [X_\ell \backslash Y_\ell] & \forall \ell \in f(X) \cap f(Y) \\ \varepsilon \odot [X_\varepsilon \backslash (\ell' \cdot Y_{\ell'})] & \forall \ell' \in f(Y) \quad \text{if } \varepsilon \in f(X) \\ \varepsilon \odot [(\ell \cdot X_\ell) \backslash Y_\varepsilon] & \forall \ell \in f(X) \quad \text{if } \varepsilon \in f(Y) \end{cases} \qquad (4)$$

Since by definition expansions never map to null polynomials, some firsts might be smaller sets than suggested by these equations. For instance in $\mathbb{Z}$ the sum of $\varepsilon \odot [\langle 1 \rangle \odot 1] \oplus a \odot [\langle 1 \rangle \odot b]$ and $\varepsilon \odot [\langle 1 \rangle \odot 1] \oplus a \odot [\langle -1 \rangle \odot b]$ is $\varepsilon \odot [\langle 2 \rangle \odot 1]$.

With the convention that terms with undefined roots are ignored (i.e., equal to 0), the definition (4) can be stated as

$$X \backslash Y = \bigoplus_{\substack{\ell \in f(X), \ell' \in f(Y) \\ p = r(\ell, \ell')}} \varepsilon \odot \left[((p \backslash \ell) \cdot X_\ell) \backslash ((p \backslash \ell') \cdot Y_{\ell'}) \right] \qquad (5)$$

The following lemma is simple to establish: lift semantic equivalences, such as those of Propositions 3 and 4, to syntax, using Lemma 1 (Appendix A.3).

Lemma 2. $[\![X \oplus Y]\!] = [\![X]\!] + [\![Y]\!] \qquad [\![\langle k \rangle X]\!] = \langle k \rangle [\![X]\!]$
$[\![X \cdot E]\!] = [\![X]\!] \cdot [\![E]\!] \qquad [\![X \backslash Y]\!] = [\![X]\!] \backslash [\![Y]\!]$.

3.2   Expansion of a Rational Expression

Definition 7 (Expansion of a Rational Expression). *The expansion of a rational expression E, written $d(E)$, is defined inductively as follows:*

$$d(0) := 0 \qquad d(1) := \varepsilon \odot [\langle 1_{\mathbb{K}} \rangle \odot 1] \qquad d(a) := a \odot [\langle 1_{\mathbb{K}} \rangle \odot 1]$$
$$d(E + F) := d(E) \oplus d(F) \qquad d(\langle k \rangle E) := \langle k \rangle d(E)$$
$$d(E \cdot F) := d_p(E) \cdot F \oplus \langle d_{\$}(E) \rangle d(F)$$
$$d(E^*) := \varepsilon \odot [\langle d_{\$}(E)^* \rangle \odot 1] \oplus \langle d_{\$}(E)^* \rangle d_p(E) \cdot E^* \qquad (6)$$
$$d(E \backslash F) := d(E) \backslash d(F) \qquad (7)$$

where $d_{\$}(E)$ and $d_p(E)$ are the immediate constant term/immediate proper part of $d(E)$.

The right-hand sides are indeed expansions. The computation trivially terminates: induction is performed on strictly smaller sub-expressions.

Proposition 6. *An expression is equivalent to its expansion.*

Proof. Follows from a straightforward induction on E [7]. For instance, the case of left quotient follows from $[\![d(E\backslash F)]\!] = [\![d(E)\backslash d(F)]\!]$(by Definition (7)) = $[\![d(E)]\!]\backslash[\![d(F)]\!]$(by Lemma 2). The case of star is more delicate than in our previous work [7] as $d_p(E)$ might not denote a proper series. This is handled by Proposition 2, much more powerful than its predecessor [7, Proposition 2]. □

4   Expansion-Based Derived-Term Automaton

Definition 8 (Expansion-Based Derived-Term Automaton).   *The derived-term automaton of an expression E over G is the accessible part of the automaton $\mathcal{A}_E := \langle M, G, \mathbb{K}, Q, E, I, T \rangle$ defined as follows:*

- *Q is the set of rational expressions on alphabet A with weights in $\mathbb{K}$,*
- *$I = E \mapsto 1_{\mathbb{K}}$,*
- *$E(F, \ell, F') = k$ iff $\ell \in f(d(F))$ and $\langle k \rangle \odot F' \in d_p(F)(\ell)$,*
- *$T(F) = d_\$(F)$.*

It is straightforward to extract an algorithm from Definition 8, using a worklist of states whose outgoing transitions need to be computed [7, Algorithm 1]. However, we must justify Definition 8 by proving that this automaton is finite.

Example 4 (Examples 1 to 3 continued). With $E_1 := (\langle 2 \rangle a)\backslash(\langle 3 \rangle(a + b) + \langle 5 \rangle aa^* + \langle 7 \rangle ab^*) + \langle 11 \rangle ab^*$, one has:
$$d(E_1) = \varepsilon \odot [\langle 6 \rangle \odot 1 \oplus \langle 10 \rangle \odot a^* \oplus \langle 14 \rangle \odot b^*] \oplus a \odot [\langle 11 \rangle \odot b^*] \quad \text{(Example 3)}$$
$$d(a^*) = \varepsilon \odot [\langle 1 \rangle \odot 1] \oplus a \odot [\langle 1 \rangle \odot a^*] \qquad d(b^*) = \varepsilon \odot [\langle 1 \rangle \odot 1] \oplus b \odot [\langle 1 \rangle \odot b^*]$$

Therefore $d_\varepsilon(E_1)$ is 6, and $d_\varepsilon(a^*) = d_\varepsilon(b^*) = 1$, from which $\mathcal{A}_{E_1}$ follows: Fig. 1.

Example 5. The derived-term automaton of $(((\langle \frac{1}{2} \rangle ab)\backslash(ab^*))^*$ is as follows. It has a non coaccessible state with a spontaneous loop whose weight, 1, is not starrable. This automaton must be trimmed to be valid.

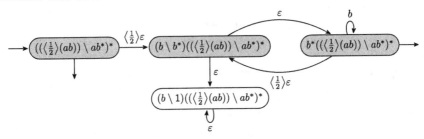

Theorem 1. *For any expression E, $\mathcal{A}_E$ is finite.*

Proof. The proof goes in several steps (see Appendix A.5). First introduce the *proper derived terms* of E, a set of expressions noted PD(E), and the *derived terms* of E, D(E) := PD(E) ∪ {E}. PD(E) admits a simple inductive definition similar to [2, Definition 3], to which we add PD(E\F) := {E'\F' | E' ∈ PD(E), F' ∈ PD(F)}. Second, verify that PD(E) is finite. Third, prove that D(E) is "stable by expansion", i.e., ∀F ∈ D(E), exprs(d(F)) ⊆ D(E). Finally, observe that the states of $\mathcal{A}_E$ are therefore members of D(E).   □

Theorem 2. *If valid, any expression* E *and its expansion-based derived-term automaton* $\mathcal{A}_E$ *denote the same series, i.e.,* $[\![\mathcal{A}_E]\!] = [\![E]\!]$.

Proof. We show that the semantics of the states of $\mathcal{A}_E$ (3) and of the expressions in D(E) define the same system of linear equations (Appendix A.6).   □

The constant term of expressions without quotient can be computed syntactically [7, Definition 8], thus invalid expressions can be rejected during the construction of the derived-term automaton (when computing $d_\$(E)^*$ in (6)). This is no longer true with the quotient operator: the procedure may succeed on invalid expressions, the validity of the automaton [14] must be verified at end. The elimination of the spontaneous transitions is a means to check the validity of the automaton, but the computations highly depend on the semiring.

Example 6. In $\mathbb{Q}$, E := $(ab\backslash ab)^*$ is invalid as $[\![ab\backslash ab]\!]$ = $[\![\varepsilon]\!]$ whose constant-term, 1, is not starrable in $\mathbb{Q}$. Therefore its derived-term automaton is invalid in $\mathbb{Q}$. However they are valid in $\mathbb{B}$.

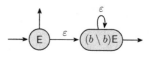

The procedure may also build invalid automata from valid expressions. Consider for instance F := $ab\backslash ab + \langle -1\rangle 1$: clearly $[\![F]\!] = 0$, so $[\![F^*]\!] = 1$. However the derived-term automaton of F^* is invalid: it has spontaneous loops whose weights are not starrable. This cannot happen in positive semirings.

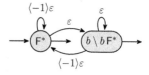

5   Transposition and Right Quotient

This section introduces the support for the right quotient. We build it on top of a transpose operator, which might be used eventually with other operators.

Transpose. The *transpose* (aka *reversal* or *mirror image*) of a word $m = a_1 a_2 \ldots a_n$ is $m^t := a_n a_{n-1} \ldots a_1$. The transpose of a series s is $s^t := m \mapsto s(m^t)$.

Proposition 7. *For series* $s, t \in \mathbb{K}\langle\!\langle A^*\rangle\!\rangle$:

$$(s+t)^t = s^t + t^t \quad (ks)^t = k(s^t) \quad (sk)^t = (s^t)k \quad (st)^t = t^t s^t \quad s^{tt} = s$$

Right quotient. We define the *right quotient* of two series s by t as $s/t := v \mapsto \sum_{u \in A^*} s(vu) \cdot t(u)$. Since $\mathbb{K}$ is commutative, quotients are dual (see Appendix A.7).

Proposition 8. *If $\mathbb{K}$ is commutative, then* $s/t = (t^t \backslash s^t)^t$ $s \backslash t = (t^t / s^t)^t$.

We extend Definition 1 with: $\mathsf{E} ::= 0 \mid 1 \mid a \mid \mathsf{E} + \mathsf{E} \mid \langle k \rangle \mathsf{E} \mid \mathsf{E} \cdot \mathsf{E} \mid \mathsf{E}^* \mid \mathsf{E} \backslash \mathsf{E} \mid \mathsf{E}^t$, with additional identities $0^t \Rightarrow 0, \ell^t \Rightarrow \ell$ and we add $\llbracket \mathsf{E}^t \rrbracket := \llbracket \mathsf{E} \rrbracket^t$ to Definition 2. Thanks to Proposition 8, we may add support for the right quotient as syntactic sugar on top of transposition and left quotient: $\mathsf{E}/\mathsf{F} := (\mathsf{F}^t \backslash \mathsf{E}^t)^t$.

Definition 9. *The transposed expansion of an expression E, written $d^t(\mathsf{E})$, is defined inductively as follows:*

$$d^t(0) := d(0) \qquad d^t(1) := d(1) \qquad d^t(a) := d(a)$$

$$d^t(\mathsf{E} + \mathsf{F}) := d^t(\mathsf{E}) \oplus d^t(\mathsf{F}) \qquad d^t(\langle k \rangle \mathsf{E}) := \langle k \rangle d^t(\mathsf{E})$$

$$d^t(\mathsf{E} \cdot \mathsf{F}) := d^t_p(\mathsf{F}) \cdot \mathsf{E}^t \oplus \langle d^t_\$(\mathsf{F}) \rangle d^t(\mathsf{E}) \quad d^t(\mathsf{E}^*) := \langle d^t_\$(\mathsf{E})^* \rangle \oplus \langle d^t_\$(\mathsf{E})^* \rangle d^t_p(\mathsf{E}) \cdot \mathsf{E}^{*t}$$

$$d^t(\mathsf{E} \backslash \mathsf{F}) := d^t(\mathsf{E}) \backslash d^t(\mathsf{F}) \qquad d^t(\mathsf{E}^t) := d(\mathsf{E})$$

where $d^t_\$(\mathsf{E})$ and $d^t_p(\mathsf{E})$ are the immediate constant term/immediate proper part of $d^t(\mathsf{E})$. Then Definition 7 is extended with $d(\mathsf{E}^t) := d^t(\mathsf{E})$.

Proposition 6 is generalized by proving $\llbracket d^t(\mathsf{E}) \rrbracket = \llbracket \mathsf{E} \rrbracket^t$ (Appendix A.4).

Example 7. It is well known that the prefix of a language can be defined with $\text{Pref}(\mathsf{E}) := \mathsf{E}/A^*$. Let $\mathsf{E}_5 := (ab)/(a + b)^* = ((a + b)^{*t} \backslash (ab)^t)^t$. We have $d(\mathsf{E}_5) = \varepsilon \odot [(ba)^t \oplus ((a + b)^{*t} \backslash a)^t]$. Its derived-term automaton is:

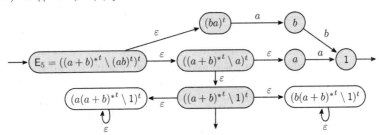

6   Related Work

The quotient between rational series is surprisingly little treated in the literature. Even Sakarovitch [15] defines the quotient by a word only: Sect. 1.2.3 p. 62 for the quotient of a word and of a language, and Sect. 4.1.1 p. 438 for the quotient of a series. It is quite rare to find the definition of the quotient of languages, and to define the quotient of *series* seems a unique feature of Li et al. [12][3].

---

[3] When lifting the quotient of a language (or series) by a word to a quotient of languages, there are two options: *union* vs. *intersection* of the quotients by words. Li et al. [12] name *quotient* the union-based versions and write $s^{-1}t$ and st^{-1}, and name *residual* the intersection-based ones, written $s \backslash t$ and s/t. In this paper, we focus only on left and right quotients, but denoted $s \backslash t$ and s/t.

Expansions were previously introduced [7] to optimize the construction of the derived-term automaton [13], and to add additional operators (the Hadamard product and complement). It was shown that they can also support multi-tape expressions [6]. Expansions previously appeared as an orphan concept from Brzozowski [4, last line of p. 484], and as "linear forms" by Antimirov [3, Definition 2.3].

For basic (weighted) expressions, there are more efficient algorithms to build the derived-term automaton [1,5], but it is unclear how they could be extended to support operators such quotients. Actually, it is also doubtful whether the derivative-based approach [13] could be generalized to quotient, as the possible presence of ε in the firsts would correspond to derivatives with respect to ε.

Being able to feature ε in the firsts of expansions is a key feature. Indeed, Thiemann [16] shows that quotients have bad properties, in particular, they are not ε-testable. We avoided these issues by constructing an automaton with spontaneous transitions, which allows us to "delay" the computation of the constant-term of $a\backslash ab^*$ to the one of b^*. Besides, although transpose is neither left nor right derivable Thiemann [16], our procedure succeeds thanks to the introduction of the transposed computation of the expansion: d^t.

7   Conclusion

Thiemann [16] reported that the quotient and transpose operators pose real problems to the derivative-based construction of the derived-term automaton. We have addressed these issues in different ways. First, we rely on expansions rather than on derivatives, which allows us to cope naturally with spontaneous transitions, something that would correspond to nonsensical derivatives wrt the empty word. Second, since we can no longer determine the validity of an expression by a simple inductive computation, it is actually the validity of the derived-term automaton that ensures it. Finally, we introduce the transposed computation of expansions to handle the transpose operator.

In the future we will study the *residuals*, which, in the case of languages, rely on the intersection of quotients of words, rather than their union. We also want to explore other definitions of quotients, so that $\langle 2 \rangle a \backslash \langle 2 \rangle ab = a$, not $\langle 4 \rangle a$.

Acknowledgments. We thank the anonymous reviewers for their very helpful comments.

A   Proofs

A.1   Proof of Proposition 1

This proof goes in several steps, with different constraints over s and t. From a formal point of view, it is actually "trivial": a simple look at the proof of Sakarovitch [15, Proposition III.2.6] shows that both expressions are *formally* equivalent. The real technical difficulty is semantic: ensuring that all the (infinite) sums are properly defined.

We actually only need Item 4 to establish Proposition 2.

1. *When s and t are proper.* This is a well-known consequence of Arden's lemma [15, Proposition III.2.5].
2. *When $s \in \mathbb{K}$, and t is proper.* This property holds when $\mathbb{K}$ is a strong topological semiring, and when s^* is defined [15, Proposition III.2.6].
3. *When $s, t \in \mathbb{K}$.* This result follows directly from the hypothesis of this property. Note however that $s^*(ts^*)^* = (s+t)^*$ is verified in all the "usual" semirings.
   - If $\mathbb{K}$ is a "usual numerical semiring" (i.e., $\mathbb{Q}, \mathbb{R}$, or more generally, a subring of $\mathbb{C}^n$), then s^* is the inverse of $1 - s$, i.e., $(1 - s)s^* = s^*(1 - s) = 1$. To establish the result, we show that $s^*(ts^*)^*$ is the inverse of $1 - (s + t)$. By hypothesis, s^* and $(ts^*)^*$ are defined. $(1 - (s + t))s^*(ts^*)^* = (1 - s)s^*(ts^*)^* - ts^*(ts^*)^* = (ts^*)^* - ts^*(ts^*)^* = (1 - ts^*)(ts^*)^* = 1$, which shows that $(s + t)^*$ is defined.
   - If $\mathbb{K}$ is a tropical semiring, say, $\langle \mathbb{Z} \cup \{\infty\}, \min, +, \infty, 0 \rangle$, then s^* is defined iff $s \geq 0$, and then $s^* = 0$, hence the result trivially follows.
   - If $\mathbb{K}$ is the Log semiring, $\langle \mathbb{R}^+ \cup \{\infty\}, +_{\text{Log}}, +, \infty, 0 \rangle$ where $+_{\text{Log}} := x, y \mapsto -\log(\exp(-x) + \exp(-y))$. Then we get $x^* = \log(1 - \exp(-x))$. Again, one can verify the identity.
4. *When $s \in \mathbb{K}$ and t is any series.* By hypothesis, $(ts^*)^*$ is defined, i.e., $(t_\varepsilon s^*)^*$ is defined, so by Item 3, $(s + t_\varepsilon)^*$ is defined.

$$(s + t)^* = (s + t_\varepsilon + t_p)^*$$
$$= (s + t_\varepsilon)^*(t_p(s + t_\varepsilon)^*)^* \qquad \text{by Item 2, } t_p \text{ proper, } (s + t_\varepsilon)^* \text{ defined}$$
$$= s^*(t_\varepsilon s^*)^*(t_p s^*(t_\varepsilon s^*)^*)^* \qquad \qquad \text{by Item 3}$$
$$= s^*(t_\varepsilon s^* + t_p s^*)^* \qquad \text{by Item 2, } t_p s^* \text{ proper, } (t_\varepsilon s^*)^* \text{ defined}$$
$$= s^*((t_\varepsilon + t_p)s^*)^*$$
$$= s^*(ts^*)^*$$

5. *When s is any series and t is proper.* By hypothesis, s^* is defined, so s_ε^* is defined.

$$(s + t)^* = (s_\varepsilon + (s_p + t))*$$
$$= s_\varepsilon^*((s_p + t)s_\varepsilon^*)^* \qquad \qquad \text{by Item 2, } s_p + t \text{ proper}$$
$$= s_\varepsilon^*(s_p s_\varepsilon^* + t s_\varepsilon^*)^*$$
$$= s_\varepsilon^*(s_p s_\varepsilon^*)^*(t s_\varepsilon^*(s_p s_\varepsilon^*)^*)^* \qquad \text{by Item 1, } s_p s_\varepsilon^* \text{ and } t s_\varepsilon^* \text{ are proper}$$
$$= (s_\varepsilon + s_p)^*(t(s_\varepsilon + s_p)^*)^* \qquad \text{by Item 2 } s_\varepsilon^* \text{ is defined, } s_p \text{ is proper}$$
$$= s^*(ts^*)^*$$

6. *When s and t are any series.* By hypothesis, s^* is defined.

$$
\begin{aligned}
(s+t)^* &= (s+t_\varepsilon+t_p)^* \\
&= (s+t_\varepsilon)^*(t_p(s+t_\varepsilon)^*)^* && \text{by Item 5, } t_p \text{ proper} \\
&= s^*(t_\varepsilon s^*)(t_p s^*(t_\varepsilon s^*)^*)^* && \text{by Item 4, } t_\varepsilon \in \mathbb{K} \\
&= s^*(t_\varepsilon s^* + t_p s^*)^* && \text{by by Item 5, } t_p s^* \text{ proper} \\
&= s^*(ts^*)^*
\end{aligned}
$$

A.2 Proof of Lemma 1

These are trivial consequences of the properties of the corresponding operations on series. For instance, let $\mathsf{P} = \bigoplus_{i\in[m]}\langle k_i\rangle \odot \mathsf{E}_i,\ \mathsf{Q} = \bigoplus_{j\in[n]}\langle h_j\rangle \odot \mathsf{F}_j$, we have:

$$
\begin{aligned}
[\![\mathsf{P}\backslash\mathsf{Q}]\!] &= \left[\!\!\left[\bigoplus_{i\in[m],j\in[n]} \langle k_i \cdot h_j\rangle \odot (\mathsf{E}_i\backslash\mathsf{F}_j) \right]\!\!\right] && \text{by definition} \\
&= \sum_{i\in[m],j\in[n]} [\![\langle k_i \cdot h_j\rangle \odot (\mathsf{E}_i\backslash\mathsf{F}_j)]\!] \\
&= \sum_{i\in[m],j\in[n]} (k_i \cdot h_j) \cdot [\![\mathsf{E}_i\backslash\mathsf{F}_j]\!] \\
&= \sum_{i\in[m],j\in[n]} (k_i \cdot h_j) \cdot [\![\mathsf{E}_i]\!]\backslash[\![\mathsf{F}_j]\!] \\
&= \sum_{i\in[m],j\in[n]} (k_i \cdot [\![\mathsf{E}_i]\!])\backslash(h_j \cdot [\![\mathsf{F}_j]\!]) && \text{by Proposition 3} \\
&= \sum_{i\in[m],j\in[n]} [\![\langle k_i\rangle \odot \mathsf{E}_i]\!]\backslash[\![\langle h_j\rangle \odot \mathsf{F}_j]\!] \\
&= \left(\sum_{i\in[m]} [\![\langle k_i\rangle \odot \mathsf{E}_i]\!]\right)\backslash\left(\sum_{j\in[n]} [\![\langle h_j\rangle \odot \mathsf{F}_j]\!]\right) && \text{by Proposition 3} \\
&= \left[\!\!\left[\bigoplus_{i\in[m]} \langle k_i\rangle \odot \mathsf{E}_i\right]\!\!\right]\backslash\left[\!\!\left[\bigoplus_{j\in[n]} \langle h_j\rangle \odot \mathsf{F}_j\right]\!\!\right] \\
&= [\![\mathsf{P}]\!]\backslash[\![\mathsf{Q}]\!]
\end{aligned}
$$

A.3 Proof of Lemma 2

The proofs are straightforward: lift semantic equivalences, such as those of Propositions 3 and 4, to syntax.

We prove for instance the case of the left quotient. However, we will use (5) rather than (4) for two reasons: not only is the proof more compact, it is also more general as it provides support for expressions and automata whose labels are words (e.g., "*abcd*"), not just letters or ε. In that case, one can verify that $d(\text{"}ab\text{"}\backslash\text{"}abcd\text{"}) = \varepsilon \odot [\langle 1_\mathbb{K}\rangle \odot \text{"}cd\text{"}]$.

The proof is as follows.

$$[\![X\backslash Y]\!] = \Bigg[\!\!\Bigg[\bigoplus_{\substack{\ell \in f(X), \ell' \in f(Y) \\ p = r(\ell,\ell')}} \varepsilon \odot \Big[((p\backslash\ell) \cdot X_\ell)\backslash((p\backslash\ell') \cdot Y_\ell) \Big] \Bigg]\!\!\Bigg] \qquad \text{by (5)}$$

$$= \sum_{\substack{\ell \in f(X), \ell' \in f(Y) \\ p = r(\ell,\ell')}} [\![((p\backslash\ell) \cdot X_\ell)\backslash((p\backslash\ell') \cdot Y_\ell)]\!] \qquad \text{by Lemma 2 on } \oplus$$

$$= \sum_{\substack{\ell \in f(X), \ell' \in f(Y) \\ p = r(\ell,\ell')}} \Big((p\backslash\ell) \cdot [\![X_\ell]\!] \Big) \backslash \Big((p\backslash\ell') \cdot [\![Y_{\ell'}]\!] \Big) \qquad \text{by Lemma 1}$$

$$= \sum_{\ell \in f(X), \ell' \in f(Y)} \ell \cdot [\![X_\ell]\!] \backslash \ell' \cdot [\![Y_{\ell'}]\!] \qquad \text{by Proposition 4}$$

$$= \sum_{\ell \in f(X), \ell' \in f(Y)} [\![\ell \cdot X_\ell]\!] \backslash [\![\ell' \cdot Y_{\ell'}]\!] \qquad \text{by Lemma 1}$$

$$= \Big(\sum_{\ell \in f(X)} [\![\ell \cdot X_\ell]\!] \Big) \backslash \Big(\sum_{\ell' \in f(Y)} [\![\ell' \cdot Y_{\ell'}]\!] \Big) \qquad \text{by Proposition 3}$$

$$= \Bigg[\!\!\Bigg[\bigoplus_{\ell \in f(X)} \ell \odot X_\ell \Bigg]\!\!\Bigg] \backslash \Bigg[\!\!\Bigg[\bigoplus_{\ell' \in f(Y)} \ell' \odot Y_{\ell'} \Bigg]\!\!\Bigg] \qquad \text{by Lemma 2}$$

$$= [\![X]\!]\backslash[\![Y]\!]$$

A.4   Proof of Proposition 6

A simple induction on E proves $[\![d(E)]\!] = [\![E]\!]$, see the details in Demaille [7]. To handle transpose, we add the following case:

$$[\![d^t(EF)]\!] = [\![d^t_p(F) \cdot E^t \oplus \langle d^t_\$(F) \rangle d^t(E)]\!] \qquad \text{by Definition 9}$$

$$= [\![d^t_p(F)]\!][\![E]\!]^t + d^t_\$(F)[\![d(E)]\!]^t \qquad \text{by Definition 2 and } [\![E^t]\!]$$

$$= [\![d^t_p(F)]\!][\![E]\!]^t + d^t_\$(F)[\![E]\!]^t \qquad \text{by induction hypothesis}$$

$$= [\![d^t_p(F) + d^t_\$(F)]\!][\![E]\!]^t$$

$$= [\![d^t(F)]\!][\![E]\!]^t$$

$$= [\![F]\!]^t[\![E]\!]^t = ([\![E]\!][\![F]\!])^t = [\![EF]\!]^t \qquad \text{by Proposition 7}$$

A.5   Proof of Theorem 1

This proof shares large parts with the corresponding proof in Demaille [8, Appendix C], itself being based on the work from Lombardy and Sakarovitch [13]. As in the former we introduce $PD(E)$, the *proper derived terms* of E, rather than $TD(E)$, the *true derived terms* of E, as in the latter.

We will manipulate sets of expressions. To simplify notations, operations on expressions are lifted additively on sets of expressions. For instance:

$$\{E_i \mid i \in [n]\}\backslash\{F_j \mid j \in [m]\} := \{E_i\backslash F_j \mid i \in [n], j \in [m]\}$$

Definition 10 (Derived Terms). *Given an expression* E, *its* proper derived terms *is the set* PD(E) *defined as follows:*

$$PD(0) := \emptyset \qquad PD(1) := \{1\} \qquad PD(a) := \{1\} \quad \forall a \in A$$
$$PD(E + F) := PD(E) \cup PD(F) \qquad PD(\langle k \rangle E) := PD(E) \quad \forall k \in \mathbb{K}$$
$$PD(E \cdot F) := PD(E) \cdot F \cup PD(F) \qquad PD(E^*) := PD(E) \cdot E^*$$
$$PD(E \backslash F) := PD(E) \backslash PD(F)$$

The derived terms *of an expression* E *is* D(E) := PD(E) $\cup$ {E}.

Lemma 3. *For any expression* E, D(E) *is finite.*

Proof. Follows from the finiteness of PD(E), which is a direct consequence from Definition 10: finiteness propagates during the induction.   □

Lemma 4 (Proper Derived Terms and Single Expansion). *For any expression* E, exprs(d(E)) $\subseteq$ PD(E).

Proof. Established by a simple verification of Definition 7.   □

The derived terms of derived terms of E are derived terms of E. In other words, repeated expansions never "escape" the set of derived terms.

Lemma 5 (Proper Derived Terms and Repeated Expansions). *Let* E *be an expression. For all* F $\in$ PD(E), exprs(d(F)) $\subseteq$ PD(E).

Proof. This will be proved by induction over E.

Case E = 0 or E = 1. Trivially true, since there is no such F, as PD(E) = $\emptyset$.

Case E = a. Then PD(E) = {1}, hence F = 1 and therefore d(F) = d(1) = $\langle 0_{\mathbb{K}} \rangle$, so exprs($d$(F)) = $\emptyset \subseteq$ PD(E).

Case E = G + H. Then PD(E) = PD(G) $\cup$ PD(H). Suppose, without loss of generality, that F $\in$ PD(G). Then, by induction hypothesis, exprs(d(F)) $\subseteq$ PD(G) $\subseteq$ PD(E).

Case E = $\langle k \rangle$G. Then if F $\in$ PD($\langle k \rangle$G) = PD(G), so by induction hypothesis exprs(d(F)) $\subseteq$ PD(G) = PD($\langle k \rangle$G) = PD(E).

Case E = G $\cdot$ H. Then PD(E) = {G$_i$ $\cdot$ H | G$_i$ $\in$ PD(G)} $\cup$ PD(H).
- If F = G$_i$ $\cdot$ H with G$_i$ $\in$ PD(G), then d(F) = d(G$_i$ $\cdot$ H) = d_p(G$_i$) $\cdot$ H $\oplus$ $\langle d_\$(G_i) \rangle d$(H).
  Since G$_i$ $\in$ PD(G) by induction hypothesis exprs(d_p(G$_i$)) = exprs(d(G$_i$)) $\subseteq$ PD(G). By definition of the product of an expansion by an expression, exprs(d_p(G$_i$) $\cdot$ H) $\subseteq$ {G$_j$ $\cdot$ H | G$_j$ $\in$ PD(G)} $\subseteq$ PD(G $\cdot$ H) = PD(E).
- If F $\in$ PD(H), then by induction hypothesis exprs(d(F)) $\subseteq$ PD(H) $\subseteq$ PD(E).

Case E = G*. If F $\in$ PD(E) = {G$_i$ $\cdot$ G* | G$_i$ $\in$ PD(G)}, i.e., if F = G$_i$ $\cdot$ G* with G$_i$ $\in$ PD(G), then d(F) = d(G$_i$ $\cdot$ G*) = d_p(G$_i$) $\cdot$ G* $\oplus$ $\langle d_\$(G_i) \rangle d$(G*), so

$\mathsf{exprs}(d(\mathsf{F})) \subseteq \mathsf{exprs}(d_p(\mathsf{G}_i) \cdot \mathsf{G}^*) \cup \mathsf{exprs}(d(\mathsf{G}^*)).^4$ We will show that both are subsets of $\mathrm{PD}(\mathsf{E})$, which will prove the result.

Since $\mathsf{G}_i \in \mathrm{PD}(\mathsf{G})$, by induction hypothesis, $\mathsf{exprs}(d_p(\mathsf{G}_i)) = \mathsf{exprs}(d(\mathsf{G}_i)) \subseteq \mathrm{PD}(\mathsf{G})$, so by definition of a product of an expansion by an expression, $\mathsf{exprs}(d_p(\mathsf{G}_i) \cdot \mathsf{G}^*) \subseteq \{\mathsf{G}_j \cdot \mathsf{G}_j^* \mid \mathsf{G}_j \in \mathrm{PD}(\mathsf{G})\} = \mathrm{PD}(\mathsf{E})$.

By Lemma 4 $\mathsf{exprs}(d(\mathsf{G}^*)) \subseteq \mathrm{PD}(\mathsf{G}^*) = \mathrm{PD}(\mathsf{E})$.

Case $\mathsf{E} = \mathsf{G} \backslash \mathsf{H}$. (1) and (4) show that for all expansions X, Y,

$$\mathsf{exprs}(\mathsf{X} \backslash \mathsf{Y}) \subseteq \mathsf{exprs}(\mathsf{X}) \backslash \mathsf{exprs}(\mathsf{Y}) \tag{8}$$

Let $\mathsf{F} \in \mathrm{PD}(\mathsf{E}) = \mathrm{PD}(\mathsf{G}) \backslash \mathrm{PD}(\mathsf{H})$, i.e., let $\mathsf{F} = \mathsf{G}_i \backslash \mathsf{H}_j$ with $\mathsf{G}_i \in \mathrm{PD}(\mathsf{G}), \mathsf{H}_j \in \mathrm{PD}(\mathsf{H})$, then

$$\begin{aligned}
\mathsf{exprs}(d(\mathsf{F})) &= \mathsf{exprs}(d(\mathsf{G}_i \backslash \mathsf{H}_j)) & \\
&= \mathsf{exprs}(d(\mathsf{G}_i) \backslash d(\mathsf{H}_j)) & \text{by (7)} \\
&\subseteq \mathsf{exprs}(d(\mathsf{G}_i)) \backslash \mathsf{exprs}(d(\mathsf{H}_j)) & \text{by (8)} \\
&\subseteq \mathrm{PD}(\mathsf{G}) \backslash \mathrm{PD}(\mathsf{H}) & \text{by induction hypothesis} \\
&= \mathrm{PD}(\mathsf{G} \backslash \mathsf{H}) & \text{by Definition 10} \\
&= \mathrm{PD}(\mathsf{E}) &
\end{aligned}$$

$\square$

Lemma 6 (Derived Terms and Repeated Expansions). *Let E be an expression. For all $\mathsf{F} \in D(\mathsf{E})$, $\mathsf{exprs}(d(\mathsf{F})) \subseteq \mathrm{PD}(\mathsf{E})$.*

Proof Immediate consequence of Lemmas 4 and 5, since $D(\mathsf{E}) = \mathrm{PD}(\mathsf{E}) \cup \{\mathsf{E}\}$. $\square$

We may now prove Theorem 1.

Theorem 1. *1 For any expression E, $\mathcal{A}_\mathsf{E}$ is finite.*

Proof. The states of $\mathcal{A}_\mathsf{E}$ are members of $D(\mathsf{E})$ (Lemma 6), which is finite (Lemma 3). $\square$

A.6 Proof of Theorem 2

The Definition 8 shows that each state q_F of the $\mathcal{A}_\mathsf{E}$ has the following semantics:

$$\llbracket q_\mathsf{F} \rrbracket = \sum_{\substack{\ell \in f(d(\mathsf{F})) \\ \langle k \rangle \odot \mathsf{F}' \in d(\mathsf{F})(\ell)}} k_{\ell, \mathsf{F}'} \, \ell \, \llbracket q_{\mathsf{F}'} \rrbracket \tag{9}$$

---

[4] Given two expansions X, Y, $\mathsf{exprs}(\mathsf{X} \oplus \mathsf{Y}) \subseteq \mathsf{exprs}(\mathsf{X}) \cup \mathsf{exprs}(\mathsf{Y})$, but they may be different; consider for instance $\mathsf{X} = a \odot [\langle 1 \rangle \odot 1]$ and $\mathsf{Y} = a \odot [\langle -1 \rangle \odot 1]$ in $\mathbb{Z}$.

Besides:

$$[\![\mathsf{F}]\!] = [\![d(\mathsf{F})]\!] \qquad \text{(by Proposition 6)}$$

$$= \Bigl[\!\!\Bigl[\bigoplus_{\ell \in f(d(\mathsf{F}))} \ell \odot d(\mathsf{F})(\ell) \Bigr]\!\!\Bigr] \quad = \sum_{\ell \in f(d(\mathsf{F}))} \ell [\![d(\mathsf{F})(\ell)]\!]$$

$$= \sum_{\ell \in f(d(\mathsf{F}))} \ell \Bigl[\!\!\Bigl[\bigoplus_{\langle k_{\ell,i}\rangle \odot \mathsf{F}_{\ell,i} \in d(\mathsf{F})(\ell)} \langle k_{\ell,i}\rangle \odot \mathsf{F}_{\ell,i} \Bigr]\!\!\Bigr]$$

$$= \sum_{\ell \in f(d(\mathsf{F}))} \ell \sum_{\langle k_{\ell,i}\rangle \odot \mathsf{F}_{\ell,i} \in d(\mathsf{F})(\ell)} k_{\ell,i} [\![\mathsf{F}_{\ell,i}]\!]$$

$$= \sum_{\substack{\ell \in f(d(\mathsf{F})) \\ \langle k_{\ell,i}\rangle \odot \mathsf{F}_{\ell,i} \in d(\mathsf{F})(\ell)}} k_{\ell,i}\, \ell\, [\![\mathsf{F}_{\ell,i}]\!] \qquad (10)$$

(9) and (10) define the same system of linear equations, hence $[\![\mathcal{A}_\mathsf{E}]\!] = [\![\mathsf{E}]\!]$. □

A.7　Proof of Proposition 8

$$(t^t \backslash s^t)^t(v) = (t^t \backslash s^t)(v^t)$$

$$= \sum_{u \in A^*} t^t(v^t u) \cdot s^t(u)$$

$$= \sum_{u \in A^*} t(u^t v) \cdot s(u^t) \qquad \text{by definition of transpose}$$

$$= \sum_{u \in A^*} t(uv) \cdot s(u) \qquad \text{by change of variable: } u \to u^t$$

$$= \sum_{u \in A^*} s(u) \cdot t(uv) \qquad \text{by commutativity of } \mathbb{K}$$

$$= (s/t)(v)$$

Commutativity may be replaced by a weaker condition: $\forall u, v \in A^*, t(uv) \cdot s(u) = s(u) \cdot t(uv)$.

The right-quotient is treated similarly.

References

1. Allauzen, C., Mohri, M.: A unified construction of the Glushkov, follow, and Antimirov automata. In: Královič, R., Urzyczyn, P. (eds.) MFCS 2006. LNCS, vol. 4162, pp. 110–121. Springer, Heidelberg (2006). doi:10.1007/11821069_10
2. Angrand, P.-Y., Lombardy, S., Sakarovitch, J.: On the number of broken derived terms of a rational expression. J. Autom. Lang. Comb. **15**(1/2), 27–51 (2010)
3. Antimirov, V.: Partial derivatives of regular expressions and finite automaton constructions. TCS **155**(2), 291–319 (1996)
4. Brzozowski, J.A.: Derivatives of regular expressions. J. ACM **11**(4), 481–494 (1964)

5. Champarnaud, J.-M., Ouardi, F., Ziadi, D.: An efficient computation of the equation $\mathbb{K}$-automaton of a regular $\mathbb{K}$-expression. In: Harju, T., Karhumäki, J., Lepistö, A. (eds.) DLT 2007. LNCS, vol. 4588, pp. 145–156. Springer, Heidelberg (2007). doi:10.1007/978-3-540-73208-2_16

6. Demaille, A.: Derived-term automata of multitape rational expressions. In: Han, Y.-S., Salomaa, K. (eds.) CIAA 2016. LNCS, vol. 9705, pp. 51–63. Springer, Cham (2016). doi:10.1007/978-3-319-40946-7_5

7. Demaille, A.: Derived-term automata for extended weighted rational expressions. In: Sampaio, A., Wang, F. (eds.) ICTAC 2016. LNCS, vol. 9965, pp. 351–369. Springer, Cham (2016). doi:10.1007/978-3-319-46750-4_20

8. Demaille, A.: Derived-term automata for extended weighted rational expressions. Technical report 1605.01530, arXiv, May 2016. http://arxiv.org/abs/1605.01530

9. Demaille, A., Duret-Lutz, A., Lombardy, S., Sakarovitch, J.: Implementation concepts in Vaucanson 2. In: Konstantinidis, S. (ed.) CIAA 2013. LNCS, vol. 7982, pp. 122–133. Springer, Heidelberg (2013). doi:10.1007/978-3-642-39274-0_12

10. Ésik, Z., Kuich, W.: Equational Axioms for a Theory of Automata. Springer, Heidelberg (2004)

11. Kozen, D.C.: Automata and Computability, 1st edn. Springer, Secaucus (1997)

12. Li, Y., Wang, Q., Li, S.: On quotients of formal power series. Comput. Res. Repos. abs/1203.2236 (2012)

13. Lombardy, S., Sakarovitch, J.: Derivatives of rational expressions with multiplicity. TCS **332**(1–3), 141–177 (2005)

14. Lombardy, S., Sakarovitch, J.: The validity of weighted automata. Int. J. Algebra Comput. **23**(4), 863–914 (2013)

15. Sakarovitch, J.: Elements of Automata Theory. Cambridge University Press, Cambridge (2009). (Corrected English translation of Éléments de théorie des automates, Vuibert, 2003)

16. Thiemann, P.: Derivatives for Enhanced Regular Expressions. Springer, Cham (2016)

Polynomial Time Learner for Inferring Subclasses of Internal Contextual Grammars with Local Maximum Selectors

Abhisek Midya[1]([✉]), D.G. Thomas[2], Saleem Malik[3], and Alok Kumar Pani[4]

[1] Computer Science and Engineering, Icfai Tech School, Hyderabad 501203, India
abhisekmidyacse@gmail.com
[2] Department of Mathematics, Madras Christian College, Chennai 600059, India
dgthomasmcc@yahoo.com
[3] Computer Science and Engineering, Alliance University, Bangalore 562106, India
baronsaleem@gmail.com
[4] Computer Science and Engineering, Faculty of Engineering, Christ University,
Bangalore 560074, India
alok.kumar@christuniversity.in

Abstract. Natural languages contain regular, context-free, and context-sensitive syntactic constructions, yet none of these classes of formal languages can be identified in the limit from positive examples. Mildly context-sensitive languages are capable to represent some context-sensitive constructions such as multiple agreement, crossed agreement, and duplication. These languages are important for natural language applications due to their expressiveness, and the fact that they are not fully context-sensitive. In this paper, we present a polynomial-time algorithm for inferring subclasses of internal contextual languages using positive examples only, namely strictly and k-uniform internal contextual languages with local maximum selectors which can contain mildly context-sensitive languages.

Keywords: Internal contextual grammar with local maximum selectors · Identification in the limit from positive data

1 Introduction

In theoretical computer science, formal language theory is one of the fundamental areas. This study has its origin in Chomskian grammars. Contextual grammars which are different from Chomskian grammars, have been studied in [9,13,14,17] by formal language theorists, as they provide novel insight into a number of issues central to formal language theory. In a total contextual grammar, a context is adjoined depending on the whole current string. Two special cases of total contextual grammars, namely internal and external are very natural and have been extensively investigated. (External) Contextual grammars are introduced by Marcus in 1969 [9] with a linguistic motivation in mind. An internal contextual

D.V. Hung and D. Kapur (Eds.): ICTAC 2017, LNCS 10580, pp. 174–191, 2017.
DOI: 10.1007/978-3-319-67729-3_11

grammar generates a language starting from a finite set of strings (the base) and iteratively adjoining to its contexts outside the current string. In other families of contextual grammars, such as internal contextual grammars [9], the contexts are adjoined inside the current string.

According to [12], it is known that many classes of formal languages, such as regular and context-free, cannot be learned from positive data only. Now it natural to look for subclasses of these languages which can be identified in the limit from positive data only.

In this paper, we present a polynomial-time algorithm for learning Strictly and k-uniform internal contextual languages with local maximum selector ($SLICG_M, k-UICG_{LM}$) from positive data. Using these two languages, mildly context sensitive languages can be generated. That is, they can express the context-sensitive syntactic constructions that are most prevalent in natural languages, such as multiple agreement, crossed agreement, and duplication [3].

Currently, there is an algorithm known for inferring the subclasses of the class of internal contextual grammars with finite selector set [10]. Also, polynomial time inferring algorithm is available for very attractive subclasses of the class of external contextual grammars [8].

The paper is organized as follows. Section 2 describes the basic classes of contextual grammars in more detail. Section 3 describes the newly defined subclasses. In Sect. 4, we discuss the generative power of the subclasses. Sections 5, 6 and 7 present the pseudocode and discuss the complete algorithm in detail along with the correctness. Section 8 discusses the characteristic sample of the algorithm. Running time complexity of the algorithm has been described in Sect. 9. In Sect. 10, we present a complex example for better understanding of the algorithm.

2   Basic Classes of Contextual Languages

This section recalls the definition of the basic classes of contextual languages. [11] For an alphabet Σ, we denote by Σ^* the free monoid generated by Σ, by λ its identity, and $\Sigma^+ = \Sigma^* - \{\lambda\}$.

Definition 1. *A Contextual grammar is a construct* $G = (\Sigma, A, (sel_1, C_1), (sel_2, C_2), \ldots, (sel_k, C_k))$, *for some* $k \geq 1$, *where* Σ *is an alphabet,* $A \subset \Sigma^*$ *is a finite set, called the axiom set,* $sel_i \subseteq \Sigma^*, 1 \leq i \leq k$, *are the sets of selectors, and* $C_i \subset \Sigma^* \times \Sigma^*$ *where* $1 \leq i \leq k$, *and* C_i *is a finite set of contexts. There are two basic modes of derivation as follows. For two words* $x, y \in \Sigma^*$, *we have the internal mode of derivation:*

$x \Longrightarrow_{in} y$ *iff* $x = x_1 x_2 x_3, y = x_1 u x_2 v x_3, x_2 \in sel_i, (u, v) \in C_i$, *for some* $1 \leq i \leq k$. *The external mode of derivation:*

$x \Longrightarrow_{ex} y$ *iff* $y = uxv, x \in sel_i, (u, v) \in C_i$, *for some* $1 \leq i \leq k$. *The language generated by* G *with respect to each of the two modes of derivation is:* $L_\alpha(G) = \{w \in \Sigma^* \mid x \in A, x \Longrightarrow_\alpha^* w\}$, *for* $\alpha \in \{in, ex\}$, *where* $\Longrightarrow_\alpha^*$ *denotes the reflexive - transitive closure of* $\Longrightarrow_\alpha$.

A *contextual grammar with internal (external) mode of derivation is called an internal (external) contextual grammar. The corresponding languages are called an internal contextual languages and external contextual languages.*

If $sel_1, sel_2, \ldots, sel_k$ are languages in the family of regular languages REG, then G is said to be with REG choice. The family of languages generated by contextual grammars with REG choice in the mode α of derivation is denoted by $L\alpha(REG)$.

Now consider the local maximum selector in internal local mode of derivation. One natural restriction has been imposed on the use of selectors as seen in [15]. In fact, there is a need for some length conditions on the selector to be used, such as minimality or maximality. It implies that we can put the restriction that any time when a context is adjoined around a selector, no factor of the selector (minimal case) can be used as a selector, or no word containing the current selector as a factor can be used as a selector (maximal case). This restriction can be imposed with respect to the specified pair of selectors or to the whole grammar. Now we discuss some details about the maximal case only because using maximal use of selectors, we will be able to generate mildly context-sensitive family of languages which is one the most important component to characterize natural languages.

Definition 2. *Given a contextual grammar* $G = (\Sigma, A, (sel_1, C_1), (sel_2, C_2), \ldots, (sel_k, C_k))$, *we define, for two words* $x, y \in \Sigma^*$, *the local maximal mode of derivation in* G *is defined as follows:* $x \Longrightarrow_{lm} y$ *iff* $x = x_1 x_2 x_3, y = x_1 u x_2 v x_3,$ *for* $x_2 \in sel_i, (u, v) \in C_i, i \leq i \leq k$ *and for no* $x_1', x_2', x_3' \in sel_i, x = x_1' x_2' x_3', x_2' \in sel_i, x_2$ *a factor of* x_2'. *Here lm denotes the local maximal mode.*

Example: Consider the following contextual grammar

- $G = (\{a, b, c\}, \{abc\}, (b^+, \{(a, bc)\}))$

Now we show one sample derivation - here [] denotes the contexts and underlined string is the selector.

- $a\underline{b}c \Longrightarrow_G a[a]\underline{b}[bc]c$
- $aa\underline{bb}cc \Longrightarrow_G aa[a]\underline{bb}[bc]cc$
- $aaa\underline{bbb}ccc \Longrightarrow_G aaa[a]\underline{bbb}[bc]ccc$
- The language generated by G is $L_{lm}(G) = \{a^n b^n c^n \mid n \geq 1\}$.

3   Subclasses of the Class of Internal Contextual Grammars with Local Maximum Selectors

In this paper our learning paradigm is identification in the limit which is defined as follows:

Definition 3 [12]. *Method M identifies language L in the limit if, after a finite number of examples, M makes a correct guess and does not alter its guess thereafter. A class of languages is identifiable in the limit if there is a method M such that given any language of the class and given any admissible example sequence for this language, M identifies the language in the limit.*

Here our main focus is on designing an identification algorithm to infer internal contextual languages, but according to Gold model [12], no superfinite class of languages is inferable from positive data only. A class of languages which consists of all finite languages but atleast one infinite language, is called super finite class of languages. From [10], we have the following result.

Theorem 1 [10]. *The class of internal contextual languages (ICL), is not inferable from positive data only.*

As we know that the class ICL is not inferable from positive data only, it is natural to look for subclasses of these languages which can be identified in the limit from positive data only. We now define strictly internal contextual grammar with local maximum selectors $(SICG_{LM})$ and k-uniform internal contextual grammar with local maximum selectors $(k - UICG_{LM})$.

Definition 4. *A strictly internal contextual grammar with local maximum selectors $(SICG_{LM})$ is an internal contextual grammar $G = (\Sigma, A, (sel_1, C_1), (sel_2, C_2), \ldots, (sel_k, C_k))$, for some $k \geq 1$, where*

- *Σ is the alphabet.*
- *$A \subset \Sigma^*$ is a finite set, called axiom set.*
- *$sel_i \subseteq \Sigma^*, 1 \leq i \leq k$, are the sets of selectors.*
- *$C_i \subset \Sigma^* \times \Sigma^*$, are sets of contexts.*

with the following restrictions,

- *If the rule is (sel_i, C_i) where $C_i = \{(u_i, v_i)\}$ then $first(u_i) \neq first(v_i)$ where $first(u)$ denotes the first alphabet of u.*
- *for each selector, there exists exactly one context (u, v).*

The language generated by $SICG_{LM} G$ is given by $L_{slm}(G) = \{w \in \Sigma^* \mid x \Longrightarrow^*_{slm} w, x \in A\}$ where $\Longrightarrow_{slm}$ denotes the one step derivation in strictly local maximal mode. Now, SLM denotes the family of languages generated by $SICG_{LM}$.

Now we present two examples of $SICG_{LM}, G_1, G_2$:

- $G_1 = (\{a, b, c\}, \{abc\}, (b^+, \{(a, bc)\}))$ where $first(u) = a \neq first(v) = b, L(G_1) = \{a^n b^n c^n \mid n \geq 1\}$. For better understanding, see the derivation example of Definition 2.
- $G_2 = (\{a, b, c, d\}, \{abcd\}, (ab^+c, \{(a, c)\}), (bc^+d, \{(b, d)\}))$ where $first(u) = a \neq first(v) = b$ and $first(u) = b \neq first(v) = d, L(G_2) = \{a^n b^m c^n d^m \mid n \geq 1\}$.

Definition 5. *A k - uniform internal contextual grammar with local maximum selectors $(k - UICG_{LM})$ is an internal contextual grammar $G = (\Sigma, A, (sel_1, C_1), (sel_2, C_2), \ldots, (sel_k, C_k))$, for some $k \geq 1$, where*

- *Σ is the alphabet.*
- *A is the finite subset of Σ^*, called axiom set.*

- $sel_i \subseteq \Sigma^*, 1 \leq i \leq k$, are the sets of selectors.
- $C_i \subset \Sigma^* \times \Sigma^*$, are sets of contexts.
  With the following restrictions, if the rule is (sel_i, C_i) where $C_i = \{(u_i, v_i)\}$
  then $|u| = |v| = k$.
- The language generated by a $k - UICG_{LM}$ G is given by $L_{klm}(G) = \{w \in \Sigma^* \mid x \Longrightarrow^*_{klm} w, x \in A\}$ where $\Longrightarrow_{klm}$ denotes the one step derivation in
  k-local maximal mode. Now, KLM denotes the family of languages generated
  by $k - UICG_{LM}$.

Now we present a $k - UICG_{LM}$ $G_3 = (\{a, b, c\}, \{c\}, (\{c\}\{a, b\}^*, \{(a, a), (b, b)\}))$,
$L_{klm}(G_3) = \{wcw \mid w \in \{a, b\}^*\}$.

4   Power of the Subclasses

In this section we discuss the generative power of these subclasses. We know that
several natural languages are not context-free and these languages are consisting
of non-context-free properties. Thus, in order to obtain formal grammars focusing to model natural languages, we have to look for classes of grammars that
are able to generate non-context-free languages. On the other hand they should
not be too powerful, that means they should not generate languages without
any linguistic relevance. So, the idea of keeping the generative power under control has lead to the notion of *mildly context-sensitive* family of languages. The
properties of such families are the following [11]:

1. It contains all three basic non-context-free constructions in, that is,
   - *multiple agreements:* $L_1 = \{a^n b^n c^n \mid n \geq 1\}$
   - *crossed agreements:* $L_2 = \{a^n b^m c^n d^m \mid n, m \geq 1\}$
   - *duplication:* $L_3 = \{wcw \mid w \in (a + b)^*\}$.
2. All the languages in the family, are *polynomial time* parsable.
3. It contains *semilinear* languages.

Here, our defined subclasses can generate three basic non-context-free
constructions.

Theorem 2

(i) $L_1, L_2 \in SLM$ *(See examples of Definition 4).*
(ii) $L_3 \in KLM$ *(See example of Definition 5).*

Lemma 1. $KLM - SLM \neq \phi$.

Proof. From Theorem 2 we know that $L_3 \in KLM$. The appropriate gram-
mar to generate L_3 is $G_3 = (\{a, b, c\}, \{c\}, (\{c\}\{(a + b)^*\}, \{(a, a), (b, b)\}))$ where
$k = 1$. But $L_3 \notin SLM$, as we know from Definition 3 that if the rule is (sel_i, C_i)
where $C_i = \{(u_i, v_i)\}$ then $first(u_i) \neq first(v_i)$. Here it needs to be always
$first(u_i) = a = first(v_i)$ or $first(u_i) = b = first(v_i)$.   □

Lemma 2. $SLM - KLM \neq \phi$.

Proof. From Theorem 2, we can conclude that $L_1, L_2 \in SLM$. The appropriate grammar to generate L_1 and L_2 are respectively $G_1 = (\{a, b, c\}, \{abc\}, (b^+, \{(a, bc)\}))$ where $|u| = |a| = 1$ and $|v| = |bc| = 2$ and $G_2 = (\{a, b, c, d\}, \{abcd\}, (ab^+c, \{(a, bc)\}), (bc^+d, \{(b, d)\}))$ where for selector ab^+c the required contexts are always $|u| = |a| = 1$ and $|v| = |bc| = 2$. So it can be understood easily that $L_1, L_2 \notin KLM$.   □

Lemma 3. $SLM \cap KLM \neq \phi$.

Proof. $L_5 = \{a^n cb^n \mid n \geq 0\}, L_5 \in SLM \cap KLM$. The appropriate grammar to generate L_5 is $G = (\{a, b, c\}, \{c\}, (c, \{(a, b)\}))$ and it satisfies Definitions 4 and 5.   □

Theorem 3. *SLM is incomparable with KLM and but they are not disjoint.*

Proof. We can conclude this fact from Lemmas 1, 2 and 3.   □

5   Identification of Subclasses of Internal Contextual Languages with Local Maximum Selectors and Correctness

In this section, we propose an identification algorithm IA to infer $SICG_{LM}$ from positive examples only. We recall the notion of an insertion rule. The insertion operation is first considered by Haussler in [6] and based on the operation, insertion systems are introduced by Kari in [7]. Informally, if a string α is inserted between two parts w_1 and w_2 of a string $w_1 w_2$ to get $w_1 \alpha w_2$, we call the operation as insertion.

Our identification algorithm IA takes finite sequences of positive examples i_{t_j} in the different time interval t_j where $j \geq 1$. Our goal is to find out $SICG_{LM}$, such that $IPS \subseteq L(G)$ where IPS is the input set. The algorithm works in the following way.

- After receiving the first set as an input, based on the size of each input, firstly the algorithm determines the axiom.
- Then it defines insertion rules in order to find out the contexts and selectors from input example.
- After that, insertion rules are converted into 1-sided[1] contextual rules.
- Next it updates with new contextual rules if the next input cannot be generated by the existing contextual rules, that is called the correction phase. All the guessing will be done in a flexible way in the sense that the correction can be done at every instance.
- Then it will convert 1-sided contextual rule into 2-sided contextual rule to take care of over generalization, that could be the temporary guess g_j at particular time interval t_j, about the unknown grammar.
- Finally we will take care of maximal use of selectors.

---

[1] In an 1-sided contextual rule either left context is λ or right context is λ.

Lemma 4. *Let $g_{t_1}, g_{t_2}, \ldots, g_{t_i}$ be the sequences of guesses (grammar) about the unknown grammar produced by identification algorithm IA at different time interval $t_1, t_2, \ldots, t_i$ based on different information, $i_{t_1}, i_{t_2}, \ldots, i_{t_i}$ such that $g_f = g_{f+1}$.*

Proof. The behavior of the algorithm, in particular, there is an upper bound(in terms of the size the current input set) to make the guess g_i about the unknown grammar where $L(g_{i-1}) \subset L(g_i)$. Thus, there exist a $f \geq 1$ such that $g_f = g_{f+1}$ where $L(g_{f-1}) \subset L(g_f)$. So, we conclude this lemma. $\square$

From this, we have the following result.

Theorem 4. *SLM is identifiable in the limit from positive examples only.*

6   Pseudocode of Our Algorithm

In this section we present the pseudocode of our algorithm IA and also in further subsections we explain that in detail.

1: $axiom \leftarrow FIND - SMALLEST(IPS)$
2: $inser \leftarrow GENERATE - INSR(axiom, s_i)$
3: $1 - Sided - Contextual - Rule \leftarrow \{\}$
4: $1 - Sided - Correct - Rule \leftarrow \{\}$
5: $2 - Sided - Correct - Rule \leftarrow \{\}$
6: $Table \leftarrow \sqcap$
7: $1 - Sided - Contextual - Rule.push[CONVERT - into - CONTEXTUAL - RULE(inser)]$
8: $IPS \leftarrow REMOVE(IPS, s_i)$
9: **for** $(1 - Sided - Contextual - Rule_i \in \{1 - Sided - Contextual - Rule\})$ **do**
10:    **for** $(s_i \in IPS)$ **do**
11:        $S \leftarrow CHECK - CONTEXTUAL - RULE(1 - Sided - Contextual - Rule_i, s_i)$
12:        **if** $S = 1$ **then**
13:            $1 - Sided - Correct - Rule.push[1 - Sided - Contextual - Rule_i]$
14:        **if** $S = 0$ **then**
15:            $1 - Sided - Correct - Rule.push[CORRECTION - CONTEXTUAL - RULE(1 - Sided - Contextual - Rule_i, s_i)]$
16: **for** $(1 - Sided - Correct - Rule_i \in \{1 - Sided - Correct - Rule\})$ **do**
17:    **for** $(s_i \in IPS)$ **do**
18:        $Table.insert[FIND - NOF - APP - of - EACHRULE - in - EACHMEMBER(1 - Sided - Correct - Rule_i, s_i)]$
19: **if** $TableRow_i = TableRow_j$ **then**
20:    $2 - Sided - Correct - Rule.push[MERGE(1 - Sided - Correct - Rule_i, 1 - Sided - Correct - Rule_j)]$
21: $LOC - MAX - SEL_i \leftarrow LMS(sel_i, u_i, v_i)$

6.1   Finding Axiom - Pseudocode-Step: 1

axiom ← **FIND – SMALLEST(IPS):**

- **case 1:** It finds the smallest string from the current IPS. The smallest string will be considered as an axiom.
- **case 2:** If two strings are given with same length then both of them will be there in the axiom set A.
- **case 3:** At any point of time a string can be given as an input which is smaller than some members of the existing axiom set. In such cases, if the strings existing in the axiom set can be generated from this new smaller string, then this new smaller string will replace them.
- **case 4:** If no member of the existing axiom set can be generated from the new smaller string then the new smaller string will be added to the axiom set as a new member of the axiom set.

Let IPS be the set of input strings. $IPS = \{s_1, s_2, \ldots, s_k\}$ where $s_j = s_{j_1} s_{j_2} \ldots s_{j_r}, 1 \leq j \leq k, 1 \geq r$. (i.e., s_j is of length r). Then the axiom will be $Min(IPS)$ where $Min(A)$ denotes the minimum size member of set A.

6.2   Defining Insertion Rule and Converting It into Contextual Rule - Pseudocode-Steps: 2, 7, 8

- insr ← **GENERATE – INS(axiom, s_i):** It generates the insertion rule from axiom and any member (s_i) of input set IPS. The output of the function will be stored in $insr$ as an insertion rule.
- 1 – Sided – Contextual – Rule.push[**CONVERT – into – CONTEXT –UAL – RULE(inser)**]: It converts $insr$ into $1 - Sided - Contextual - Rule$ and push that into $1 - Sided - Contextual - Rule$ set.
- IPS ← **REMOVE(IPS, IP$_i$):** It removes the current input member IP_i from IPS.

We now shortly describe about the intuitive idea of the parts 1–4. We try to identify the selectors from the axiom and contexts from examining input. If the format of the insertion rule is uxv where $u, x, v \in \Sigma^+$ are left context, inserted portion, and right context respectively.

- Let the axiom be $s_j^a = s_{j_1}^a s_{j_2}^a s_{j_3}^a \ldots s_{j_n}^a$ and the examining (scanning) string be $s_j^e = s_{j_1}^e s_{j_2}^e \ldots s_{j_r}^e$ where $r = $ length of the examining string. Now from the axiom we can have the following consideration. In the following four parts, if a string x is a substring of y, then it is denoted by $x \in sub(y)$.

- **Part 1:** let the initial rule be $(u, x, v)_{ins}$ where $u = s_{j_1}^a, v = s_{j_2}^a s_{j_3}^a \ldots s_{j_n}^a$, check whether any $|x| \leq r$ exists with $uxv \in sub(s_j^e)$ or not. If yes then fix that x (i.e., and go to part 3. Else, go to part 2.

- **Part 2:** Remove the last alphabet of the right context v and the rule becomes $(u, x, v)_{ins}$ where $u = s_{j_1}^a, v = s_{j_2}^a s_{j_3}^a \ldots s_{j_{n-1}}^a$, Check whether any $|x| \leq r$ exists with $uxv \in sub(s_j^e)$ or not, if yes, go to part 3. Else, go to (recursively) part 2 until the rule becomes of the form $(u, x, v) \mid u = s_{j_1}^a, v = s_{j_2}^a$. Then go to part 4.

- **Part 3: Conversion into Contextual Rule: 7.** After getting correct insertion rules (which necessarily satisfy $uxv \in sub(s_j^e)$), they are converted into 1-sided contextual rules as follows: $(u, x, v)_{ins} \longrightarrow (sel, (u, v))_{icg}$ where $sel_{icg} = u_{ins}, v_{icg} = x, u_{icg} = \lambda$ and the omitted right context v_{ins} will be treated as the left context u_{ins} for the next insertion rule. Now, we remove $(ux)_{ins}$ as a substring from the examining string and only u_{ins} from the axiom. Once we get a selector and associated context with it, we have the following conditions for each insertion rule.

- **Condition 1:** If $(|u| + |x| + |v|)_{ins} = |E|$ where $|E|$ denotes the length of examining string, it implies that only one rule has been applied and we have obtained that already.

- **Condition 2:** If $(|u|+|v|)^{ins} \leq |s_j^a|$ where $|s_j^a|$ denotes the length of the axiom, then we remove u_{ins} from axiom s_j^a, and obtain a new temporary axiom. Also consider $v_{ins} = u_{ins}$ for the next insertion rule. Next, it removes $(ux)_{ins}$ as a substring from s_j^e and obtain a new temporary input. Here after we continue our procedure with this temporary axiom and temporary examining input in the same way.

- **Condition 3:** If $(|u| + |x| + |v|)_{ins} \leq |E|$ but $(|u| + |v|)_{ins} = |s_j^a|$, it implies that some part is still left to scan and that is left context u_{icg} of the first selector sel_{icg}^{first} or right context v_{icg} of the last selector sel_{icg}^{last}, then we will include them as a new rule.
  $(sel_{new}, \{u_{mew}, v_{new}\})_{new}$ where $u_{new} = u_{icg}, v_{new} = \lambda, sel_{new} = sel_{icg}^{first}$, in another case, $v_{new} = v_{icg}, sel_{new} = sel_{icg}^{last}$. For these rules, we will never go for correction.

- **Part 4:** If $u_{ins} = s_{j_1}^a$ and $v_{ins} = s_{j_2}^a$, this time we consider $u_{ins} = s_{j_1}^a s_{j_2}^a$. Rest of the axiom part will be considered as right context v_{ins} of the new rule as follows, $(u, x, v)_{ins}$ where $u = s_{j_1}^a s_{j_2}^a, v = s_{j_3}^a \ldots s_{j_n}^a$ and go to part 1 until $u_{ins} = s_{j_1}^a s_{j_2}^a s_{j_3}^a \ldots s_{j_n}^a$. In that case, defining insertion rule is not possible. Here our selection of axiom is wrong, so we need to start with different axiom.

In this section, we get the selectors from axiom and contexts from examining input. Later on for new input, we may need to change our it for wrong guess (next section).

6.3   Making Correction and Updating Rules - Pseudocode-Steps: 9–15

- **S ← CHECK – CONTEXTUAL – RULE(1 – Sided – Contextual– Rule$_i$, s$_i$):** It checks the correctness of $1 - Sided - Contextual - Rule_i$ for another input.
- If S is true then the correct $1 - Sided - Contextual - Rule_i$ will be pushed onto set $\{1 - Sided - Correct - Rule_i\}$ and continue the process for the next input.

- **CORRECTION – CONTEXTUAL – RULE(1 – Sided – Contextual– Rule$_i$, s$_i$):** Otherwise it goes for correction.

Below we have discussed that if the new examining string is not derivable with the existing set of contextual rules, then we need to go for correction and updating with new rules.

Let the rule be $R_i : (sel_i, (u_i, v_i))_{icg}$ where $u_i = \lambda$. Examining string $s^e_j = s^e_{j_1} s^e_{j_2} \ldots s^e_{j_r}$. We can represent the examining as $X \; sel_i s^e_{j_y+1} s^e_{j_y+2} \ldots s^e_{j_{y'}} \; sel_{i+1} \; Z$ where $X, Z \in \Sigma^*$ and the remaining parts of the string. The examining string is presented in this form $X \; sel_i s^e_{j_y+1} s^e_{j_y+2} \ldots s^e_{j_{y'}} \; sel_{i+1} \; Z$ because we make the correction of rule R_i using rule R_{i+1}, so it is needed to introduce the sel_i and sel_{i+1} both.

Proposition 1. *In case of correction, we deal with only 1-sided contextual rules where left context is always empty. (see condition 3 of Subsect. 6.2)*

If $sel_i = s^e_{j_l} s^e_{j_{l+1}} \ldots s^e_{j_y}$. If selector sel_i, sel_{i+1} are not present in s^e_j then new insertion rule has to be defined again to find out the correct selectors and go to Sect. 6.2. If defining insertion rule is not possible even after this step, then it indicates that the chosen axiom is wrong. In that case, we will choose some other axiom, if available. If no other axiom is available then we add the examining string into the axiom set as a new member of axiom set (recall that we have positive examples only).

If $v_i \neq s^e_{j_y+1} s^e_{j_y+2} \ldots s^e_{j_{y'}}$, then correction and updating is required. Let v_i be $V_1 V_2 \ldots V_w$ and $s^e_{j_y+1} s^e_{j_y+2} \ldots s^e_{j_{y'}}$ be $Q_1 Q_2 \ldots Q_z$ for convenience sake.

To apply the rule properly the following condition is required, $V_1 V_2 \ldots V_w = Q_1 Q_2 \ldots Q_z$ where $w = z$.

Here we are making an analysis to find out the partially equal part (prefix/suffix) of $V_1 V_2 \ldots V_w$ and $Q_1 Q_2 \ldots Q_z$.

We have shown that the correction part for one rule, in the same way the correction can be done for other rules.

Theorem 5. *If the analysis starts with equality such that $Q_1 = V_1, Q_2 = V_2, \ldots, Q_f = V_s$, and $Q_{f+1} \neq V_{s+1}$ or $f = z$ or $s = w$, then we can have four different type of errors which are stated in terms of following lemmas. (Finding common prefix part).*

Lemma 5. *If $(f = z$ and $s = w)$ then it implies that matching is correct, so no need to make any correction for this rule and the rule is correct.*

Lemma 6. *If $(f = z$ and $s < w)$ then we infer two new rules.*

Proof. – $Rule_{i'} : (sel_{i'}, C_{i'})$ where $C_i = \{(u_{i'}, v_{i'})\}, v_{i'} = V_1 V_2 \ldots V_s = Q_1 Q_2 \ldots Q_z, u_{i'} = \lambda, sel_{i'} = sel_i.$
 – $Rule_{(i+1)'} : (sel_{(i+1)'}, C_{(i+1)'})$ where $C_{(i+1)'} = \{(u_{(i+1)'}, v_{(i+1)'})\}, u_{(i+1)'} = V_{s+1} V_{s+2} \ldots V_w, v_{(i+1)'} = \lambda, sel_{(i+1)'} = sel_{(i+1)}.$ □

Lemma 7. *If $(f < z$ and $s = w)$ then we infer two new rules.*

Proof.   – $Rule_{i'} : (sel_{i'}, C_{i'})$ where $C_i = \{(u_{i'}, v_{i'})\}, v_{i'} = V_1 V_2 \ldots V_w = Q_1 Q_2 \ldots$
$Q_f, u_{i'} = \lambda, sel_{i'} = sel_i$.
– $Rule_{(i+1)'} = (sel_{(i+1)'}, C_{(i+1)'})$ where $C_{(i+1)'} = \{(u'_{(i+1)}, v_{(i+1)'})\}, u_{(i+1)'} = Q_{f+1} Q_{f+2} \ldots Q_z, v_{(i+1)'} = \lambda, sel_{(i+1)'} = sel_{(i+1)}$. $\square$

Lemma 8. *If $(f < z$ and $s < w)$ then we infer three new rules.*

Proof.   – $Rule_{i'} : (sel_{i'}, C_{i'})$ where $C_i = \{(u_{i'}, v_{i'})\}, v_{i'} = V_1 V_2 \ldots V_s = Q_1 Q_2 \ldots$
$Q_f, u_{i'} = \lambda, sel_{i'} = sel_i$.
– $Rule_{(i+1)'} : (sel_{(i+1)'}, C_{(i+1)'})$ where $u_{(i+1)'} = V_{s+1} V_{s+2} \ldots V_w, u_{(i+1)'} = \lambda, sel_{(i+1)'} = sel_{i+1}$.
– $Rule_{(i+2)'} : Rule_{(i+2)'} : (sel_{(i+2)'}, C_{(i+2)'})$ where $u_{(i+2)'} = Q_{f+1} Q_{f+2} \ldots Q_z, v_{(i+2)'} = \lambda, sel_{(i+2)'} = sel_{i+1}$. $\square$

Theorem 6. *If the analysis starts with inequality such that $Q_1 \neq V_1$, but $Q_z = V_w, Q_{z-1} = V_{w-1} \ldots Q_f = V_s$, and $Q_{f-1} \neq V_{s-1}$ then we can have three different type of errors which can be seen in the following lemmas. (Finding common suffix part).*

Lemma 9. *If $(s = 1, f > 1)$ then we infer two new rules.*

Proof.   – $Rule_{i'} : (sel_{i'}, C_{i'})$ where $C_{i'} = \{(u_{i'}, v_{i'})\}, u_{i'} = V_1 V_2 \ldots V_w, v_{i'} = \lambda, sel_{i'} = sel_{i+1}$.
– $Rule_{(i+1)'} : (sel_{(i+1)'}, C_{(i+1)'})$ where $C_{(i+1)'} = (u'_{(i+1)}, v_{(i+1)'})$ where $v_{(i+1)'} = Q_1 Q_2 \ldots Q_{f-1}, u_{(i+1)'} = \lambda, sel_{(i+1)'} = sel_i$. $\square$

Lemma 10. *If $(s > 1)$ then we infer three new rules.*

Proof.   – $Rule_{i'} : (sel'_i, C'_i)$ where $C_{i'} = \{(u_{i'}, v_{i'})\}, u_{i'} = V_s V_{s+1} \ldots V_w, v_{i'} = \lambda, sel_{i'} = sel_{i+1}$.
– $Rule_{(i+1)'} : (sel_{(i+1)'}, C_{(i+1)'})$ where $C_{(i+1)'} = (u_{(i+1)'}, v_{(i+1)'}), v_{(i+1)'} = Q_1 Q_2 \ldots Q_{f-1}, u_{(i+1)'} = \lambda, sel_{(i+1)'} = sel_i$.
– $Rule_{(i+2)'} : (sel_{(i+2)'}, C_{(i+2)'})$ where $C_{(i+2)'} = (u_{(i+2)'}, v_{(i+2)'}), u_{(i+2)'} = \lambda, v_{(i+2)'} = V_1 V_2 \ldots V_{s-1}, sel_{(i+2)'} = sel_i$. $\square$

Lemma 11. *If $Q_z \neq R_w$ then we infer two new rules. (In this case Theorem 6 is not applicable here because common prefix/suffix part is absent).*

Proof.   – $Rule_{i'} : (sel'_i, C'_i)$ where $C_i = \{(u_{i'}, v_{i'})\}, v_{i'} = V_1 V_2 \ldots V_w, u_{i'} = \lambda, sel_{i'} = sel_i$.
– $Rule_{(i+1)'} : (sel_{(i+1)'}, C_{(i+1)'})$ where $C_{(i+1)'} = (u'_{(i+1)}, v_{(i+1)'} = Q_1 Q_2 \ldots Q_z, u_{(i+1)'} = \lambda, sel_{(i+1)'} = sel_i$. $\square$

In this section, we must notice that we have different rules with same selectors. According to Definition 4, for each selector there must be one rule. As we are inferring 1-sided contextual rule, it does not satisfy our Definition 4. In the next section we will convert 1-sided contextual rule into 2-sided contextual rule in order to take care of over generalization.

7 Controlling over Generalization - Pseudocode-Steps: 16–20

In this section we determine the number of applications of each rule to generate the given input set. It is presented in table. We put priority in applying rules where left context is empty and context is smaller in size. If it is found that without using any rule we can generate full input set then we can ignore that rule.

- Using steps 16, 17 - we scan all the correct contextual rule for all the member of input set.
- **Table.insert[FIND – NOF – APP – of – EACHRULE – in – EACH MEMBER($1 - Sided - Correct - Rule_i, IP_i$)]:** It finds out the application of each rule on each member of the input and insert that record into the table.
- $2 - Sided - Correct - Rule$.push[**MERGE($1 - Sided - Correct - Rule_i$, $1 - Sided - Correct - Rule_j$)**]: In this case if we find that ith row ($TableRow_i$) and jth row ($TableRow_j$) of the table are same then we merge these two rules and store as a $2 - Sided - Correct - Rule$.

Actually all the rules are 1-sided where left contexts or right contexts are empty that generates more elements. Thus, to control this over generalization, we check that how many times each rule is applied in each member of the input set. Rules which are applied equal number of times in each member, those can be merged into one rule based on condition.(discussed in Lemmas 12 and 13)

Lemma 12. *If consecutive selectors are sel_i, sel_j with $(j - i) = 1$ and left contexts(right contexts) are null in both of the rule then we can get 2-sided internal contextual rule after merging them.*

Proof. Here sel_i, sel_j denote ith and jth selector, v_i, v_j are right contexts of them respectively, and u_i, u_j are ith and jth left context of them respectively.

- $R_i : (sel_i, (u_i, v_i))_{icg}, R_j : (sel_j, (u_j, v_j))_{icg}.$
- **case 1:** If sel_i, sel_j where $(j - i) = 1$, if $v_i = v_j = \lambda$ then rule becomes $R_{new} : (sel_{new}, (u_{new}, v_{new}))_{icg}$ where $sel_{new} = sel_i, v_{new} = u_j.$
- **case 2:** If sel_i, sel_j where $(j - i) = 1$, if $u_i = u_j = \lambda$ then rule becomes $R_{new} : (sel_{new}, (u_{new}, v_{new}))_{icg}$ where $u_{new} = v_i, sel_{new} = sel_j.$

Lemma 13. *If consecutive selectors are sel_i, sel_j with $(j - i) = 1$ and left contexts of ith rule and right context of jth rule is null then we can get 1-sided internal contextual rule after merging them.*

Proof. Here sel_i, sel_j denote ith and jth selector, u_i, v_j are left contexts of ith rule and right context of jth rule respectively.

- $R_i : (sel_i, (u_i, v_i))_{icg}, R_j : (sel_j, (u_j, v_j))_{icg}.$
- If sel_i, sel_j where $(j - i) = 1$, if $u_i = v_j = \lambda$ then rule becomes $R_{new} : (sel_{new}, (u_{new}, v_{new}))_{icg}$ where $sel_{new} = sel_i, v_{new} = v_i u_j.$

7.1 Finding Maximal Use of Selectors - Step 21

In this subsection we show how to identify regular selector set and use the maximal idea. In this section we denote our already obtained individual selectors as SEL.

$COM(A, B)$ computes the common subword between A, B. On the other hand, $PREF(A), SUFF(B)$ denote the prefix and suffix part of A, B respectively, sel stands for selector.

Lemma 14. *For any selector and associated context with it, if $COM(PREF$ $(SEL), SUFF(u)) \neq \lambda$ or $COM(PREF(v), SUFF(SEL)) \neq \lambda$ then we get regular selector set and we focus on the maximal use of selectors.*

Proof. – $COM(PREF(sel)), SUFF(u))$: If a rule is $(SEL, (u, v))_{icg}$ where $SEL = X_1 X_2 .. X_k, u = u_1 u_2 \ldots u_m$ where $X_1 = u_j, X_2 = u_{j+1}, \ldots, X_n = u_m, j \geq 1$ then the regular selector set becomes $SEL = (X_1 X_2 \ldots X_n)^* X_{n+1} X_{n+2} \ldots X_k$.
- $COM(PREF(v), SUF(SEL))$: If a rule is $(SEL, (u, v))_{icg}$ where $SEL = X_1 X_2 \ldots X_k, v = v_1 v_2 \ldots v_m$ where $X_j = v_1, X_{j+1} = v_2, \ldots, X_k = v_n, j \geq 1$ then the selector set becomes $SEL = X_1 X_2 \ldots (X_j X_{j+2} \ldots X_k)^*$. (see example)

Remark 1. The above algorithm can also be used to identify a k-uniform internal contextual grammar with local maximum selectors. A required modification is that k is also given along with the input set.

In this case, at the time of defining insertion rule (Sect. 6.2), we need to focus on the size of selectors and contexts in terms of column as k is given as an input. Defining insertion rule should be done in the following way, $uxv \in sub(s_j^e)$ where $|u| = |v| = k$.

8 Characteristic Sample

The most widely used definition of data efficiency relies on the notion of characteristic sample. The characteristic sample is a finite set of data from a language L that ensures the correct convergence of the algorithm on any presentation of L as soon as it is included in the data seen so far.

Definition 6 (Characteristic Sample - CS). *If Let L be a $SICL_{LM}$ then a finite set CS is called a characteristic sample of L if and only if L is the smallest $SICL_{LM}$ containing CS.*

Consider $G_1 = (\{a, b, c\}, \{abc\}, (b^+, \{(a, bc)\}))$ where $first(u) = a \neq first(v) = b, L(G_1) = \{a^n b^n c^n \mid n \geq 1\}$. Here, $CS = \{abc, aaabbbccc, aabbcc, aaaabbbbcccc\}$.

When the input set IPS of the identification algorithm IA contains all the elements of CS, the algorithm converges to a correct final guess for the target $SICL_{LM}$. Hence, it is clear from the manner in which the characteristic sample CS is formed that, the class SLM is identifiable in the limit from positive data.

9   Time Complexity of Our Algorithm

We analyze the time complexity of our algorithm in two aspects, *time for updating a conjecture* and a bound on the *number of implicit errors* of guesses. We adapt this idea of time complexity analysis from [16]. Here we make an analysis of our pseudocode step by step.

- Step 1: If k number of strings are given in the input set, then we need to find out the size of each member of the set, so here the time complexity depends on the number of input member k and size of each member of input set. So, the time taken by step 1 is $SumofSize(IPS)$.
- Step 2: In order to generate all the possible subarrays, it takes polynomial time in the size of the axiom that is $Size(axiom)$. Also when we search the substring (uxv) in the examining input then it takes even linear time of the size of the examining input that is $Size(ExaminingInput)$.
- Step 3–6: It is only declaration.
- Step 7, 8: It can be seen easily that these two steps take constant time. Also removing one element from the input set, takes constant time. 5
- Step 9–15: Let k be the number of input arrays in the input set. If all the rules are correct then we do not need to go for any correction, so time complexity depends on k and $SumofSize(IPS)$. Also for any incorrect rule we need go for correction and the correction part takes polynomial time in the size of the input set that is $SumofSize(IPS')$, finally these step 9–15 can be executed in polynomial time in the size of the set.
- Step 16–18: These three steps depend on the number of 1-sided-contextual-rule, let it be l and again the size of the input set.
- Step 19–20: In these two steps, firstly we search the table we if we find any two rows are same then merge these two 1-sided-contextual-rule. So, it depends on the size of the table.
- Step 21: It finds the regular selector. In this case, running time depends on the size of the correct contextual rule.

Lemma 15 (Time for updating a conjecture). *The identification algorithm IA identifies a target grammar g_f, in the limit, from positive data, satisfying the property that the time for updating the conjecture is bounded by polynomial in the size of the, $SumofSize(IPS)$.*

Proof. From the above discussion we can conclude that.   □

Lemma 16 (Number of implicit errors of guesses). *The number of implicit errors of guesses of IA, is bounded by polynomial in the cardinality of set IPS.*

Proof. From the previous step by step running time discussion we can conclude that.   □

Summing up the previous discussion about the definition of running time complexity [16] and last two lemmas, we have the following theorem.

Theorem 7. *The identification algorithm IA can be implemented to run in time polynomial in the size of IPS for updating conjecture, and the number of implicit errors of guesses is bounded by polynomial in the cardinality of set IPS.*

10   Example Run

Given input at time-unit t_1 is $i_{t1} = IPS = \{s_1 = abbcdd, s_2 = aabbbccddd\}$. Examining string $s_2^e = s_{21}^e s_{22}^e \ldots s_{210}^e = aabbbccddd$, Axiom $s_1^a = s_{11}^a s_{12}^a \ldots s_{16}^a = abbcdd$.

Defining Insertion Rule:

- $(u, x, v)_{ins}$ where $u = a, v = bbcdd$, Check whether any $|x| \leq r$ exists with $uxv \in sub(s_2^e)$? No-go to part 2.
- $(u, x, v)_{ins}$ where $u = a, v = bbcd$, Check whether any $|x| \leq r$ exists with $uxv \in sub(s_2^e)$? No-go to part 2.
- $(u, x, v)_{ins}$ where $u = a, v = bbc$, Check whether any $|x| \leq r$ exists with $uxv \in sub(s_2^e)$? Yes- $x = ab$, go to part 3.

According to condition 2 of Subsect. 6.2, $(|u| + |v|)^{ins} \leq |s_j^a|$, so for the next insertion rule - $u = a, x = ab$ are removed from the examining string and u is removed from axiom. Therefore string becomes $bbccddd$ and temporary axiom will be $bbcdd$. Existing $v = bbc$ will be considered as u (left context) for the next insertion rule. $(u, x, v)_{ins}$ where $u = bbc, v = dd, x = c$.

Now according to condition 3 of Subsect. 6.2, $(|u| + |x| + |v|)_{ins} \leq |E|$ but $(|u|+|v|)_{ins} = |s_j^a|$, so in this new insertion rule existing $v = dd$ will be considered as a u (for last selector) of the new rule. Now the axiom is covered completely and the rest part of the string will be considered as x of the next insertion rule. $(u, x, v)_{ins}$ where $u = dd, v = \lambda, x = d$. Finally the insertion rules are

- $(u, x, v)_{ins}$ where $u = a, v = bbc, x = ab$
- $(u, x, v)_{ins}$ where $u = bbc, v = dd, x = c$
- $(u, x, v)_{ins}$ where $u = dd, v = \lambda, x = d$

Converting into Contextual Rule: For A_1

- $R_1 : (sel_1, (u_1, v_1))_{icg}$ where $sel_1 = a, v_1 = ab, u_1 = \lambda, R_2 : (sel_2, (u_2, v_2))_{icg}$ where $sel_2 = bbc, v_2 = c, u_2 = \lambda, R_3 : (sel_3, (u_3, v_3))_{icg}$ where $sel_3 = dd, v_3 = d, u_3 = \lambda$.

Next input set at time-unit t_2 is $i_{t2} = IPS = \{s_3 = aaabcccd, s_4 = aabccd\}$. s_4 will be the new member of axiom set because s_1, s_4 both are of same lengths. $abbcdd, aabccd$ are considered as A_1, A_2 respectively.

Try to apply R_1, R_2, R_3 on s_3 but here we are not getting proper selectors also, so we need to define the insertion rule again. But here defining insertion is not possible from axiom A_1, so we define he insertion rule from A_2.

- $(u, x, v)_{ins}$ where $u = a, v = abcc, x = a$.
- $(u, x, v)_{ins}$ where $u = abcc, v = d, x = c$.

After converting into contextual rules: for A_2-

- $R_1 : (sel_1, (u_1, v_1))_{icg}$ where $sel_1 = a, v_1 = a, u_1 = \lambda, R_2 : (sel_2, (u_2, v_2))_{icg}$ where $sel_2 = abcc, v_2 = c, u_2 = \lambda$.

Now we will check that from A_2, generating S_1 is possible or not. Here A_2 is correct axiom for s_1. So the rules will be after converting into contextual rule-

- $R_3 : \{(sel_3, (u_3, v_3))_{icg}$ where $sel_3 = aa, v_3 = bb, u_6 = \lambda \mid (i \geq 1)\}, R_4 : \{(sel_4, (u_4, v_4))_{icg}$ where $sel_4 = bccd, v_4 = d, u_4 = \lambda \mid (i \geq 1)\}$.

Input at time-unit t_3 is $i_{t3} = IPS = \{s_5 = aabbccdd\}$.

- From A_1, deriving s_5 is possible because selectors are matching but needs to make the correction.
- In the same way we can verify that from A_2 it is possible to generate s_5 or not, using second set of rule. Selectors are not matching, so need to define insertion rule. Here defining insertion rule is possible, it suggests that axiom is correct for S_5.
- In the same way we can define insertion rules and convert insertion rules into contextual rule to reach S_5 from A_2.
- $R_5 : (sel_4, (u_4, v_4))_{icg}$ where $sel_4 = aa, v_1 = b, u_1 = \lambda, R_6 : (sel_5, (u_5, v_5))_{icg}$ where $sel_5 = bccd, v_5 = d, u_5 = \lambda$.
- Now with this new existing set of rule for A_2, generating S_2 is possible.

Making Correction and Updating Rules

- Here we are making the correction of R_1 (for A_1) to generate S_5. Now let v_1 be $V_1 V_2 = ab$ where $w = 2$. $X sel_1 Q_1 sel_2 Z = aabbccdd$ where $sel_1 = a, Q_1 = a, sel_2 = bbc, X = \lambda, Z = cdd$.
- $Q_1 = a = V_1$, Here $(f = z = 1$ and $s < w = 2)$. (According to Lemma 6)
- R_1 is changed and it becomes $R_1 : (sel_1, (u_1, v_1))_{icg}$ where $sel_1 = a, v_1 = a, u_1 = \lambda$.

New the set of rule will be after making the correction-for A_1 to generate S_2, S_5.

- $R_1 : (sel_1, (u_1, v_1))_{icg}$ where $sel_1 = a, v_1 = a, u_1 = \lambda$
- $R_2 : (sel_2, (u_2, v_2))_{icg}$ where $sel_2 = bbc, v_2 = c, u_2 = \lambda$
- $R_3 : (sel_3, (u_3, v_3))_{icg}$ where $sel_3 = dd, v_3 = d, u_3 = \lambda$
- $R_4 : (sel_4, (u_4, v_4))_{icg}$ where $sel_4 = bbc, v_4 = \lambda, u_4 = b$

From A_2-possible to generate s_2, s_3, s_5

- $R_1 : (sel_1, (u_1, v_1))_{icg}$ where $sel_1 = a, v_1 = a, u_1 = \lambda$
- $R_2 : (sel_2, (u_2, v_2))_{icg}$ where $sel_2 = abcc, v_2 = c, u_2 = \lambda$
- $R_3 : (sel_3, (u_3, v_3))_{icg}$ where $sel_4 = aa, v_4 = b, u_4 = \lambda$
- $R_4 : (sel_4, (u_4, v_4))_{icg}$ where $sel_5 = bccd, v_5 = d, u_5 = \lambda$

Controlling over Generalization and Finding Maximum Selectors. So

two sets of rules are here, one is for axiom A_1 and another one is for axiom A_2. Now we will check that how many times each rule has been used in each string and that controls the over generalization. Table 1 contains application of each rule for $A_1, s_2 = aabbbccddd, s_5 = aabbccdd$. Also Table 2 contains application of each rule for $A_2, s_2 = aabbbccdddd, s_3 = aaabcccd, s_5 = aabbccdd$.

Table 1. Finding application of each rule for A_1

Rules	s_2	s_5
$R_1 = (a, (\lambda, a))$	1	1
$R_2 = (bbc, (\lambda, c))$	1	1
$R_3 = (dd, (\lambda, d))$	1	0
$R_4 = (bbc, (b, \lambda))$	1	0

For A_1, we can merge $(R_1, R_2), (R_3, R_4)$, So according to Lemmas 12, 13 and 14. $R_{12} = (bbc^+, (a, c)), R_{34} = (b^+bc, (b, d))$, we can write $R_{12} = (b^+c^+, (a, c))$, $R_{34} = (b^+c^+, (b, d))$.

Table 2. Finding application of each rule for A_2

RULE	s_2	s_3	s_5
$R_1 = (a, (\lambda, a))$	0	1	0
$R_2 = (abcc, (\lambda, c))$	0	1	0
$R_3 = (aa, (\lambda, b))$	2	0	1
$R_4 = (bccd, (\lambda, d))$	2	0	1

For A_2, we can merge $(R_1, R_2), (R_3, R_4)$, So according to Lemmas 12, 13 and 14 - $R_{12} = (a^+b^+c^+, (a, c)), R_{34} = (b^+c^+d^+, (b, d))$.

References

1. Marcus, G.F.: Negative evidence in language acquisition. Cognition **46**, 53–85 (1993)
2. Oates, T., Desai, D., Bhat, V.: Learning k-reversible context-free grammars from positive structural examples. In: Proceedings of the Nineteenth International Conference on Machine Learning (2002)
3. Oates, T., Armstrong, T., Harris, J., Nejman, M.: On the relationship between lexical semantics and syntax for the inference of context-free grammars. In: Proceedings of AAAI, pp. 431–436 (2004)
4. Giammarresi, D., Restivo, A.: Two dimensional languages. In: Rozenberg, G., Salomaa, A. (eds.) Handbook of Formal Languages, pp. 215–267. Springer, Heidelberg (1997). doi:10.1007/978-3-642-59126-6_4
5. Rosenfeld, A., Sironmoney, R.: Picture languages - a survey. Lang. Des. **1**, 229–245 (1993)
6. Haussler, D.: Insertion and iterated insertion as operations on formal languages. Ph.D. Thesis, University of Colorado, Boulder (1982)
7. Kari, L.: Contextual insertions/deletions and computability. Inf. Comput. **1**, 47–61 (1996)

8. Oates, T., Armstrong, T., Bonache, L.B., Atamas, M.: Inferring grammars for mildly context sensitive languages in polynomial-time. In: Sakakibara, Y., Kobayashi, S., Sato, K., Nishino, T., Tomita, E. (eds.) ICGI 2006. LNCS, vol. 4201, pp. 137–147. Springer, Heidelberg (2006). doi:10.1007/11872436_12

9. Marcus, S.: Contextual grammars. Revue Roumane de Mathematiques Pures et appliques **14**(10), 1525–1534 (1969)

10. Emerald, J.D., Subramanian, K.G., Thomas, D.G.: Inferring subclasses of contextual languages. In: Oliveira, A.L. (ed.) ICGI 2000. LNCS, vol. 1891, pp. 65–74. Springer, Heidelberg (2000). doi:10.1007/978-3-540-45257-7_6

11. Ilie, L.: Some recents results on contextual languages. TUCS Technical report No 96 (1997)

12. Gold, E.M.: Language identification in the limit. Inf. Control **10**, 447–474 (1967)

13. Ehrenfeucht, A., Paun, G., Rozenberg, G.: Contextual grammars and formal languages. In: Rozenberg, G., Salomaa, A. (eds.) Handbook of Formal Language, vol. 2, pp. 237–293. Springer, Heidelberg (1997). doi:10.1007/978-3-662-07675-0_6

14. Fernau, H., Freund, R., Holzer, M.: Representations of recursively enumerable array languages by contextual array grammars. Fundamenta Informatica **64**, 159–170 (2005)

15. Martin-Vide, C., Mateescu, A., Miguel-Verges, J., Paun, G.: Internal contextual grammars: minimal, maximal, and scattered use of selectors. In: Kappel, M., Sgamir, E. (eds.) Bisfai 95 Conference on Natural Languages and AI, Jerusalem, pp. 132–142 (1995)

16. Yokomori, T.: Polynomial-time identification algorithm of very simple grammars from positive data. Theor. Comput. Sci. **1**(298), 179–206 (2003)

17. Rama, R., Smitha, T.A.: Some results on array contextual grammars. Int. J. Pattern Recogn. Artif. Intell. **14**, 537–550 (2000)

Trace Relations and Logical Preservation for Continuous-Time Markov Decision Processes

Arpit Sharma$^{(\boxtimes)}$

Department of Electrical Engineering and Computer Science,
Indian Institute of Science Education and Research Bhopal, Bhopal, India
arpit@iiserb.ac.in

Abstract. Equivalence relations are widely used for comparing the behavior of stochastic systems. This paper introduces several variants of trace equivalence for continuous-time Markov decision processes (CTMDPs). These trace equivalences are obtained as a result of button pushing experiments with a black box model of CTMDP. For every class of CTMDP scheduler, a corresponding variant of trace equivalence has been introduced. We investigate the relationship among these trace equivalences and also compare them with bisimulation for CTMDPs. Finally, we prove that the properties specified using deterministic timed automaton (DTA) specifications and metric temporal logic (MTL) formulas are preserved under some of these trace equivalences.

Keywords: Scheduler · Trace equivalence · Bisimulation · Timed automaton · Temporal logic

1 Introduction

Continuous-time Markov decision processes (CTMDPs) provide a mathematical framework for modeling systems that exhibit both non-deterministic and stochastic behavior. CTMDPs have applications in queueing systems, economics, dynamic power management, epidemic and population processes. They have been used as a semantic model for amongst others generalized stochastic Petri nets [20] and interactive Markov chains [15]. Equivalence relations can be used to compare the behavior of CTMDPs. For instance, bisimulation is a well-known equivalence that preserves the validity of continuous stochastic logic (CSL) [21], a timed probabilistic version of the branching-time temporal logic CTL [5].

This paper focuses on linear-time equivalences for CTMDPs and investigates which kind of logical properties do they preserve. We use button pushing experiments on a black box model of CTMDP (i.e., trace machine) to define several variants of trace equivalence. Our machine is equipped with an action display, a state label display, a timer and a reset button. Action and state label displays enable the external observer to observe the trace of the current run of machine $\mathcal{M}$ and timer provides the absolute time. An alternating sequence of actions and state labels, denoted σ, and a sequence of time checks, denoted θ, form an

D.V. Hung and D. Kapur (Eds.): ICTAC 2017, LNCS 10580, pp. 192–209, 2017.
DOI: 10.1007/978-3-319-67729-3_12

outcome (or timed trace), i.e., (σ, θ), of the trace machine. Since schedulers are used to resolve non-deterministic choices in CTMDPs, we always fix a class of scheduler $\mathcal{C}$ and allow the machine to execute infinitely many runs for all possible schedulers of that class. This process is repeated for every scheduler class $\mathcal{C}$ of the trace machine $\mathcal{M}$. Roughly speaking, two CTMDPs $\mathcal{M}_1, \mathcal{M}_2$ are trace equivalent (w.r.t. class of scheduler $\mathcal{C}$), denoted $\equiv_{\mathcal{C}}$, if for every scheduler $\mathcal{D} \in \mathcal{C}$ of $\mathcal{M}_1$ there exists a scheduler $\mathcal{D}' \in \mathcal{C}$ of $\mathcal{M}_2$ such that for all outcomes/timed traces (σ, θ) we have $P^{trace}_{\mathcal{M}_1, \mathcal{D}}(\sigma, \theta) = P^{trace}_{\mathcal{M}_2, \mathcal{D}'}(\sigma, \theta)$ and vice versa. Here, $P^{trace}_{\mathcal{M}_1, \mathcal{D}}(\sigma, \theta)$ denote the probability of all timed paths that are compatible with the outcome/timed trace (σ, θ) in $\mathcal{M}_1$ under scheduler $\mathcal{D}$. We define six variants of trace equivalence on the basis of increasing power of schedulers, namely stationary deterministic (SD), stationary randomized (SR), history-dependent deterministic (HD), history-dependent randomized (HR), timed history-dependent deterministic (THD) and timed history-dependent randomized (THR) trace equivalence. We compare these trace equivalences with bisimulation for CTMDPs [21]. We also study the connections among these equivalences.

Our main focus and motivation, however, is to investigate the preservation of linear real-time objectives under the above mentioned trace equivalences. We prove that if two CTMDPS are trace equivalent under (THD) class of schedulers then they have the same probability of satisfying a DTA specification. A model-checking algorithm that verifies a CTMDP against a DTA specification has recently been developed [11]. In addition, we study MTL [10, 23], a real-time variant of LTL that is typically used for timed automata (and not for CTMDPs). We define the semantics of MTL formulas over CTMDP paths and prove that under (THR) trace equivalence probability of satisfying MTL formulas is preserved. Note that DTA and MTL have incomparable expressiveness [5, 10, 30]. Put in a nutshell, the major contributions of this paper are as follows:

- We define six variants of trace equivalence by experimenting with the trace machines, investigate the relationship between them and compare these equivalences with bisimulation for CTMDPs.
- We prove that THD and THR trace equivalences preserve DTA and MTL specifications, respectively.

1.1 Related Work

In the discrete-time setting, various branching-time relations (e.g., weak and strong variants of bisimulation equivalence and simulation pre-orders) [4–6, 13, 17–19, 25, 26, 28], trace relations [9, 16, 18, 24, 26, 29] and testing relations [9, 27, 31] have been defined.

For continuous-time Markov chains (CTMCs), several variants of weak and strong bisimulation equivalence and simulation pre-orders have been defined in [6]. Their compatibility to (fragments of) stochastic variants of CTL has been thoroughly investigated, cf. [6]. In [7], Bernardo considered Markovian testing equivalence over sequential Markovian process calculus (SMPC), and coined the term T-lumpability [8] for the induced state-level aggregation, where T stands for testing. His testing equivalence is a congruence w.r.t. parallel composition, and preserves transient as well as steady-state probabilities. Bernardo's T-lumpability has been reconsidered in [30] where weighted lumpability (WL) is defined as a structural notion on CTMCs. Note that DTA and MTL specifications are preserved under WL [30]. In [32], several linear-time equivalences (Markovian trace equivalence, failure and ready trace equivalence) for CTMCs have been investigated. Testing scenarios based on push-button experiments have been used for defining these equivalences. In [21], authors have defined strong bisimulation relation for CTMDPs. This paper also proves that CSL properties are preserved under bisimulation for CTMDPs. Trace semantics for interactive Markov chains (IMCs) have been defined in [33]. In this paper, testing scenarios using button pushing experiments have been used to define several variants of trace equivalence that arise by varying the type of schedulers. Our definitions of trace equivalence for CTMDPs here build on that investigated in [33] for IMCs. We take a similar approach and use the button pushing experiments [33] with trace machines to define trace equivalences.

Organisation of the Paper. Section 2 briefly recalls the main concepts of CTMDPs. Section 3 defines trace equivalence relation. Sections 4 and 5 discuss the preservation of DTA properties and MTL-formulas, respectively. Finally, Sect. 6 concludes the paper.

2   Preliminaries

This section presents the necessary definitions and basic concepts related to continuous-time Markov decision processes (CTMDPs) that are needed for an understanding of the rest of this paper. Let AP is a finite set of atomic propositions.

Definition 1 (CTMDP). *A continuous-time Markov decision process is a tuple* $\mathcal{M} = (S, s_0, Act, P, E, L)$*, where*

- *S is a finite set of states,*
- *s_0 is the initial state,*
- *Act is a finite set of actions,*
- *$P : S \times Act \times S \to [0,1]$ is a transition probability matrix, such that for any state $s \in S$ and action $\alpha \in Act$, $\Sigma_{s' \in S} P(s, \alpha, s') \in \{0,1\}$,*
- *$E : S \times Act \to \mathbb{R}_{\geq 0}$ is an exit rate function, and*
- *$L : S \to 2^{AP}$ is a labeling function.*

A state s is called *deadlock* iff $E(s, \alpha) = 0$ for all $\alpha \in Act$. Let $Act(s)$ denote the set of enabled actions from state s, i.e., $Act(s) = \{\alpha \in Act | E(s, \alpha) > 0\}$. Throughout this paper, we only consider CTMDPs that do not have any deadlock states. A possible behavior of a CTMDP is obtained from the resolution of non-deterministic and probabilistic choices. On entering a state s, an action α, say, in $Act(s)$ is non-deterministically selected. The probability to exit the state s via action α within t time units is given by $1 - e^{-E(s,\alpha) \cdot t}$. The probability to move

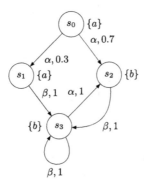

Fig. 1. An example CTMDP $\mathcal{M}$

from state s to s' via action α within t time units equals $P(s,\alpha,s')\cdot(1-e^{-E(s,\alpha)\cdot t})$. Let the rate of moving from s to s' via action α be defined as $R(s,\alpha,s') = P(s,\alpha,s')\cdot E(s,\alpha)$. Similarly, for $C \subseteq S$, $R(s,\alpha,C) = \Sigma_{s'\in C}P(s,\alpha,s')\cdot E(s,\alpha)$. Note that every CTMDP is in fact a CTMC when $\forall s \in S, |Act(s)| = 1$.

Example 1. Consider the CTMDP $\mathcal{M}$ shown in Fig. 1, where $S = \{s_0, s_1, s_2, s_3\}$, $AP = \{a, b\}$, $Act = \{\alpha, \beta\}$ and s_0 is the initial state. The transition probabilities are associated with the transitions. The exit rates are defined as follows: $E(s_0,\alpha) = 4$, $E(s_1,\beta) = 3$, $E(s_2,\beta) = 5$, $E(s_3,\alpha) = 7$, $E(s_3,\beta) = 7$. In s_0, there is a probabilistic choice on action α. In s_3, there is a non-deterministic choice between actions α and β.

Definition 2 (CTMDP timed paths). *Let* $\mathcal{M} = (S, s_0, Act, P, E, L)$ *be a CTMDP. An infinite* path π *in* $\mathcal{M}$ *is a sequence* $s_0 \xrightarrow{\alpha_0, t_0} s_1 \xrightarrow{\alpha_1, t_1} s_2 \ldots s_{n-1} \xrightarrow{\alpha_{n-1}, t_{n-1}} s_n \ldots$ *where for each* $i \geq 0$, $s_i \in S$ *is a state,* $\alpha_i \in Act$ *is an action, and* $t_i \in \mathbb{R}_{>0}$ *is the sojourn time in state* s_i. *A finite path* π *is a finite prefix of an infinite path. The length of an infinite path* π, *denoted* $|\pi|$ *is* ∞; *the length of a finite path* π *with* $n + 1$ *states is* n.

Let $Paths^{\mathcal{M}} = Paths^{\mathcal{M}}_{fin} \cup Paths^{\mathcal{M}}_{\omega}$ denote the set of all paths in $\mathcal{M}$ that start in s_0, where $Paths^{\mathcal{M}}_{fin} = \bigcup_{n\in\mathbb{N}} Paths^{\mathcal{M}}_n$ is the set of all finite paths in $\mathcal{M}$ and $Paths^{\mathcal{M}}_n$ denote the set of all finite paths of length n that start in s_0. Let $Paths^{\mathcal{M}}_{\omega}$ is the set of all infinite paths in $\mathcal{M}$ that start in s_0. For infinite path $\pi = s_0 \xrightarrow{\alpha_0, t_0} s_1 \xrightarrow{\alpha_1, t_1} s_2 \ldots$ and any $i \in \mathbb{N}$, let $\pi[i] = s_i$, the $(i+1)$st state of π. Let $\delta(\pi, i) = t_i$ be the time spent in state s_i. For any $t \in \mathbb{R}_{\geq 0}$ and i, the smallest index s.t. $t \leq \sum_{j=0}^{i} t_j$, let $\pi@t = \pi[i]$, the state occupied at time t. For finite path $s_0 \xrightarrow{\alpha_0, t_0} s_1 \xrightarrow{\alpha_1, t_1} s_2 \ldots s_{n-1} \xrightarrow{\alpha_{n-1}, t_{n-1}} s_n$, which is a finite prefix of an infinite path, $\pi[i]$, $\delta(\pi, i)$ are only defined for $i \leq n$, and for $i < n$ defined as in the case of infinite paths. For all $t > \sum_{j=0}^{n-1} t_j$, let $\pi@t = s_n$; otherwise $\pi@t$ is defined as in the case of infinite paths. Let $\delta(\pi, n) = \infty$. Let π

be a finite path of length n then $time(\pi) = \sum_{i=0}^{n-1} t_i$. Trace of an infinite path $\pi = s_0 \xrightarrow{\alpha_0, t_0} s_1 \xrightarrow{\alpha_1, t_1} s_2 \ldots s_{n-1} \xrightarrow{\alpha_{n-1}, t_{n-1}} s_n \ldots$ denoted $Trace(\pi)$ is given as $L(s_0)\alpha_0 L(s_1)\alpha_1 \ldots L(s_{n-1})\alpha_{n-1} L(s_n) \ldots$. Trace of a finite path π can be defined in an analogous manner.

Example 2. Consider the CTMDP $\mathcal{M}$ shown in Fig. 1. An example timed path in $\mathcal{M}$ is $\pi = s_0 \xrightarrow{\alpha, 3.7} s_1 \xrightarrow{\beta, 1.5} s_3 \xrightarrow{\alpha, 1.4} s_2 \ldots$. Here we have $\pi[2] = s_3$ and $\pi@4 = s_1$. $Trace(\pi) = \{a\}\alpha\{a\}\beta\{b\}\alpha\{b\} \ldots$

In order to construct a measurable space over $Paths_\omega^{\mathcal{M}}$, we define the following sets: $\Omega = Act \times \mathbb{R}_{\geq 0} \times S$ and the σ-field $\mathcal{J} = (2^{Act} \times \mathcal{J}_R \times 2^S)$, where $\mathcal{J}_R$ is the Borel σ-field over $\mathbb{R}_{\geq 0}$ [2,3]. The σ-field over $Paths_n^{\mathcal{M}}$ is defined as $\mathcal{J}_{Paths_n^{\mathcal{M}}} = \sigma(\{S_0 \times M_0 \times \ldots \times M_{n-1} | S_0 \in 2^S, M_i \in \mathcal{J}, 0 \leq i \leq n-1\})$. A set $B \in \mathcal{J}_{Paths_n^{\mathcal{M}}}$ is a base of a cylinder set C if $C = Cyl(B) = \{\pi \in Paths_\omega^{\mathcal{M}} | \pi[0 \ldots n] \in B\}$, where $\pi[0 \ldots n]$ is the prefix of length n of the path π. The σ-field $\mathcal{J}_{Paths_\omega^{\mathcal{M}}}$ of measurable subsets of $Paths_\omega^{\mathcal{M}}$ is defined as $\mathcal{J}_{Paths_\omega^{\mathcal{M}}} = \sigma(\cup_{n=0}^{\infty}\{Cyl(B) | B \in \mathcal{J}_{Paths_n^{\mathcal{M}}}\})$. In simple words, σ-fields are made up of events, such that a probability measure can be assigned.

2.1   Schedulers

Non-determinism in a CTMDP is resolved by a scheduler. Schedulers are also known as adversaries or policies[1]. More formally, schedulers are defined as follows:

Definition 3 (Scheduler). *A scheduler for CTMDP $\mathcal{M} = (S, s_0, Act, P, E, L)$ is a measurable function $\mathcal{D} : Paths_{fin}^{\mathcal{M}} \to Distr(Act)$, such that for $n \in \mathbb{N}$,*

$$\mathcal{D}(s_0 \xrightarrow{\alpha_0, t_0} s_1 \xrightarrow{\alpha_1, t_1} \ldots \xrightarrow{\alpha_{n-1}, t_{n-1}} s_n)(\alpha) > 0 \text{ implies } \alpha \in Act(s_n)$$

where $Distr(Act)$ denotes the set of all distributions on Act.

Schedulers can be classified according to the way they resolve non-determinism and the information that is available when making a decision. For example, the next action can be chosen with probability one (deterministic schedulers) or at random according to a specific probability distribution (randomized schedulers). Similarly, non-determinism can be resolved by only considering the current state (stationary schedulers) or complete (time-abstract/timed) history. More formally, schedulers can be classified as follows:

Definition 4 (Classes of schedulers). *A scheduler $\mathcal{D}$ for CTMDP $\mathcal{M}$ is*

- *stationary deterministic (SD) if $\mathcal{D} : S \to Act$ such that $\mathcal{D}(s) \in Act(s)$*
- *stationary randomized (SR) if $\mathcal{D} : S \to Distr(Act)$ such that $\mathcal{D}(s)(\alpha) > 0$ implies $\alpha \in Act(s)$*

---

[1] We only consider schedulers that make a decision as soon as a state is entered. Such schedulers are called early schedulers.

- *history-dependent deterministic (HD) if* $\mathcal{D} : (S \times Act)^* \times S \to Act$ *such that we have* $\mathcal{D}(\underbrace{s_0 \xrightarrow{\alpha_0} s_1 \xrightarrow{\alpha_1} \ldots \xrightarrow{\alpha_{n-1}} s_n}_{time-abstract\ history}) \in Act(s_n)$

- *history-dependent randomized (HR) if* $\mathcal{D} : (S \times Act)^* \times S \to Distr(Act)$ *such that* $\mathcal{D}(\underbrace{s_0 \xrightarrow{\alpha_0} s_1 \xrightarrow{\alpha_1} \ldots \xrightarrow{\alpha_{n-1}} s_n}_{time-abstract\ history})(\alpha) > 0$ *implies* $\alpha \in Act(s_n)$

- *timed history-dependent deterministic (THD) if* $\mathcal{D} : (S \times Act \times \mathbb{R}_{>0})^* \times S \to Act$ *such that* $\mathcal{D}(\underbrace{s_0 \xrightarrow{\alpha_0,t_0} s_1 \xrightarrow{\alpha_1,t_1} \ldots \xrightarrow{\alpha_{n-1},t_{n-1}} s_n}_{timed\ history}) \in Act(s_n)$

- *timed history-dependent randomized (THR) schedulers have been already defined in Definition 3*

Let $Adv(\mathcal{M})$ denote the set of all schedulers of $\mathcal{M}$. Let $Adv_{\mathcal{C}}(\mathcal{M})$ denote the set of all schedulers of class $\mathcal{C}$, e.g., $Adv_{\mathrm{THD}}(\mathcal{M})$ denote the set of all THD schedulers of CTMDP $\mathcal{M}$. Let $Paths_{\mathcal{D}}^{\mathcal{M}}$ denote the set of all infinite paths of $\mathcal{M}$ under $\mathcal{D} \in Adv(\mathcal{M})$ that start in s_0.

Definition 5 (Probability measure). *Let* $\mathcal{M} = (S, s_0, Act, P, E, L)$ *be a CTMDP and* $\mathcal{D} \in Adv(\mathcal{M})$. *The probability measure* $Pr_{\mathcal{D}}$ *on* $\mathcal{J}_{Paths_n^{\mathcal{M}}}$ *is the unique measure defined by induction on* k *in the following way. Let* $Pr_{\mathcal{D}}(Cyl(s_0)) = 1$ *and for* $k > 0$:

$$Pr_{\mathcal{D}}(Cyl(s_0, \alpha_0, I_0, \ldots, s_k, \alpha', I', s')) = \mathcal{P}_{(s_0, s_k)} \cdot \mathcal{D}(\pi[0 \ldots k])(\alpha') \cdot P(s_k, \alpha', s', I')$$

where $\mathcal{P}_{(s_0, s_k)} = Pr_{\mathcal{D}}(Cyl(s_0, \alpha_0, I_0, \ldots, s_k))$, $\pi[0 \ldots k]$ *is the prefix of any infinite path* $\pi \in Cyl(s_0, \alpha_0, I_0, \ldots, s_k)$ *and* $\mathcal{D}(\pi[0 \ldots k])(\alpha')$ *is the probability by which* α' *is selected by scheduler* $\mathcal{D}$. *Here,* $P(s_k, \alpha', s', I') = P(s_k, \alpha', s') \cdot \left(e^{E(s_k, \alpha') \cdot a} - e^{E(s_k, \alpha') \cdot b}\right)$ *for* $I' = [a, b]$.

Intuitively, the probability of the set of paths of length $(n + 1)$ *is defined as a product between the probability of the set of paths of length* n *and the one-step transition probability to go from* $(n + 1)$-*th state to* $(n + 2)$-*th state by executing action* α' *selected by the scheduler* $\mathcal{D}$.

Assumptions. Note that to avoid the issues related to probability measure of randomized schedulers, we assume that every state in CTMDP $\mathcal{M}$ with multiple outgoing actions need to have the same exit rate for all its enabled actions. More formally, $\forall s \in S : |Act(s)| > 1 \implies \forall \alpha, \alpha' \in Act(s) : E(s, \alpha) = E(s, \alpha')$. This assumption is less limiting than may appear at first sight, since a more restrictive class of MDP models, i.e., uniform[2] CTMDPs are widely used for performance and dependability evaluation.

---

[2] A CTMDP in which the delay time distribution per state visit is the same for all states.

Example 3. Consider the CTMDP $\mathcal{M}$ shown in Fig. 1. Let E be the exit rate function[3] defined as follows: $E(s_0, \alpha) = 4$, $E(s_1, \beta) = 3$, $E(s_2, \beta) = 5$, $E(s_3, \alpha) = 7$, $E(s_3, \beta) = 7$. Let $\mathcal{D}$ be a SR scheduler for $\mathcal{M}$ such that $\mathcal{D}(s_3)(\alpha) = \frac{3}{4}$ and $\mathcal{D}(s_3)(\beta) = \frac{1}{4}$. Then we can compute the probability of set of paths $\mathcal{B} = Cyl(s_0, \alpha, [0, 2], s_1, \beta, [0, 4], s_3, \alpha, [1, 3], s_2)$ of $\mathcal{M}$ under $\mathcal{D}$ as follows:

$$Pr_{\mathcal{D}}(\mathcal{B}) = (1 - e^{-(4 \cdot 2)}) \cdot (1 - e^{-(3 \cdot 4)}) \cdot \frac{3}{4} \cdot (e^{-(7 \cdot 1)} - e^{-(7 \cdot 3)}) \approx .0006836$$

3   Trace Equivalence Relations

This section proposes several variants of trace equivalence for CTMDPs. These equivalences are obtained by performing push-button experiments with a trace machine $\mathcal{M}$. Consider the stochastic trace machine $\mathcal{M}$ shown in Fig. 2. The machine is equipped with an action display, a state label display, a timer and a reset button. Action display shows the last action that has been executed by the trace machine. Note that this display is empty at the beginning of the experiment. The state label display shows the set of atomic propositions that are true in the current state of the machine $\mathcal{M}$. The timer display shows the absolute time. The reset button is used to restart the machine for another run starting from the initial state. Consider a run of the machine (under scheduler $\mathcal{D}$ of class $\mathcal{C}$) which always starts from the initial state. The state label shows the label of the current state and action display shows the last action that has been executed. Note that the action display remains unchanged until the next action is executed by the machine. The observer records the sequence of state labels, actions and time checks where each time check is recorded at an arbitrary time instant between the occurrence of two successive actions. The observer can press the reset button to stop the current run. Once the reset button is pressed, the action display will be empty and the state label display shows the set of atomic propositions that are true in the initial state. The machine then starts for another run and the observer again records the sequence of actions, state labels and time checks. Note that the machine needs to be executed for infinitely many runs to complete

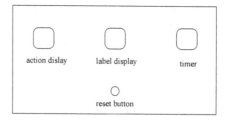

Fig. 2. Trace machine $\mathcal{M}$

---

[3] Note that the exit rate of s_3 for both α and β is the same. This is in accordance with the assumption that the exit rates need to be the same for any state s with $|Act(s)| > 1$.

the whole experiment. It is assumed that the observer can distinguish between the consecutive execution of the same action. An outcome of this machine say $(\sigma, \theta) = (< L(s_0)\alpha_0 L(s_1)\alpha_1 \ldots L(s_{n-1})\alpha_{n-1} L(s_n) >, < t'_0 t'_1 \ldots t'_n >)$ can be interpreted as follows: for $0 \leq m < n$, action α_m of machine is performed in the time interval $(y_m, y_{m+1}]$ where $y_m = \Sigma_{i=0}^m t'_i$.

Definition 6 (Compatible paths). *Let* $(\sigma, \theta) = (< L(s_0)\alpha_0 L(s_1)\alpha_1 \ldots L(s_{n-1})\alpha_{n-1} L(s_n) >, < t'_0 t'_1 \ldots t'_n >)$ *be an outcome of* $\mathcal{M}$ *under* $\mathcal{D} \in Adv(\mathcal{M})$, *then a path* $\pi = s_0 \xrightarrow{\alpha_0, t_0} s_1 \xrightarrow{\alpha_1, t_1} s_2 \ldots s_{n-1} \xrightarrow{\alpha_{n-1}, t_{n-1}} s_n \ldots \in Paths_{\mathcal{D}}^{\mathcal{M}}$ *is said to be compatible with* (σ, θ), *denoted* $\pi \triangleright (\sigma, \theta)$, *if the following holds:*

$$Trace(\pi[0 \ldots n]) = \sigma \text{ and } \Sigma_{j=0}^i t_j \in (y_i, y_{i+1}] \text{ for } 0 \leq i < n$$

where $y_i = \Sigma_{j=0}^i t'_j$.

The probability of all the paths compatible with an outcome is defined as follows:

Definition 7 (Probability of compatible paths). *Let* (σ, θ) *be an outcome of trace machine* $\mathcal{M}$ *under* $\mathcal{D} \in Adv(\mathcal{M})$. *Then the probability of all the paths compatible with* (σ, θ) *is defined as follows:*

$$P_{\mathcal{M}, \mathcal{D}}^{trace}(\sigma, \theta) = Pr_{\mathcal{D}}(\{\pi \in Paths_{\mathcal{D}}^{\mathcal{M}} | \pi \triangleright (\sigma, \theta)\})$$

Informally, $P_{\mathcal{M}, \mathcal{D}}^{trace}$ is a function that gives the probability to observe (σ, θ) in machine $\mathcal{M}$ under scheduler $\mathcal{D}$.

Definition 8 (Set of observations). *Let* $P_{\mathcal{M}, \mathcal{D}}^{trace}$ *be an observation of machine* $\mathcal{M}$ *under* $\mathcal{D} \in Adv(\mathcal{M})$. *Then the set of observations for scheduler class* $\mathcal{C}$, *denoted* $O_{\mathcal{C}}(\mathcal{M})$, *is defined as follows:*

$$O_{\mathcal{C}}(\mathcal{M}) = \{P_{\mathcal{M}, \mathcal{D}}^{trace} | \mathcal{D} \in Adv_{\mathcal{C}}(\mathcal{M})\}$$

Informally, $O_{\mathcal{C}}(\mathcal{M})$ denote a set of functions where each function assigns a probability value to every possible outcome of the trace machine, i.e., (σ, θ).

Definition 9 (Trace equivalence). *Two CTMDPs* $\mathcal{M}_1$, $\mathcal{M}_2$ *are trace equivalent w.r.t. scheduler class* $\mathcal{C}$ *denoted* $\mathcal{M}_1 \equiv_{\mathcal{C}} \mathcal{M}_2$ *iff* $O_{\mathcal{C}}(\mathcal{M}_1) = O_{\mathcal{C}}(\mathcal{M}_2)$.

This definition says that for every $\mathcal{D} \in Adv_{\mathcal{C}}(\mathcal{M}_1)$ there exists a scheduler $\mathcal{D}' \in Adv_{\mathcal{C}}(\mathcal{M}_2)$ such that for all outcomes (σ, θ) we have $P_{\mathcal{M}_1, \mathcal{D}}^{trace}(\sigma, \theta) = P_{\mathcal{M}_2, \mathcal{D}'}^{trace}(\sigma, \theta)$ and vice versa.

Example 4. Consider the two CTMDPs shown in Fig. 3. Let all the states of $\mathcal{M}$ and $\mathcal{M}'$ have the same exit rate for every enabled action. It is easy to check that these two CTMDPs are $\equiv_{SD}$. Note that they are not $\equiv_{SR}$. This is because there exists a SR-scheduler $\mathcal{D}$ for $\mathcal{M}$ such that the trace $(a\alpha a\beta)^*$ has a probability greater than 0, but this is not possible in $\mathcal{M}'$ for any SR-scheduler $\mathcal{D}'$. For similar reason, $\mathcal{M}$, $\mathcal{M}'$ are not $\equiv_{HD}$, $\equiv_{HR}$, $\equiv_{THD}$ and $\equiv_{THR}$.

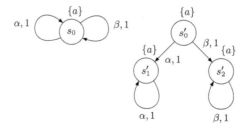

Fig. 3. *SD* trace equivalent CTMDPs $\mathcal{M}$ (left) and $\mathcal{M}'$ (right)

3.1   Relationship Between Trace Equivalence and Bisimulation

This section investigates the relationship of bisimulation to several variants of trace equivalence defined in this paper. Informally, two states are bisimilar if they are able to mimic each other's behavior step-wise. Note that bisimulation for CTMDPs preserves continuous stochastic logic (CSL) [21]. We first recall the definition of bisimulation.

Definition 10 (Bisimulation [21]**).** *Let* $\mathcal{M}$ = (S, s_0, Act, P, E, L) *be a CTMDP. An equivalence* $\mathcal{R} \subseteq S \times S$ *is a strong bisimulation relation if* $L(s) = L(s')$ *for all* $(s, s') \in \mathcal{R}$ *and* $R(s, \alpha, C) = R(s', \alpha, C)$ *for all* $\alpha \in Act$ *and all* $C \in S/\mathcal{R}$.

Two states s *and* s' *are strongly bisimilar* ($s \sim s'$) *if there exists a strong bisimulation relation* $\mathcal{R}$ *such that* $(s, s') \in \mathcal{R}$. *Strong bisimilarity is the union of all strong bisimulation relations.*

These conditions require that any two bisimilar states are equally labeled and have identical cumulative rates to move to any equivalence class C via some action α. This definition of bisimulation can be easily extended to compare the behavior of two CTMDPs $\mathcal{M}_1$ (with state space S_1) and $\mathcal{M}_2$ (with state space S_2). This is achieved by taking the disjoint union of state spaces ($S = S_1 \uplus S_2$) and requiring that initial states of two systems are bisimilar with respect to S.

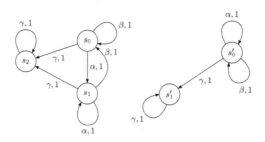

Fig. 4. CTMDPs $\mathcal{M}_1$ (left) and $\mathcal{M}_2$ (right)

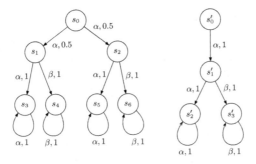

Fig. 5. SR trace equivalent and bisimilar CTMDPs $\mathcal{M}$ (left) and $\mathcal{M}'$ (right)

Example 5. Consider the CTMDPs $\mathcal{M}_1$ and $\mathcal{M}_2$ shown in Fig. 4. Let all the states of $\mathcal{M}_1$ and $\mathcal{M}_2$ have the same labeling and the same exit rate for every enabled action. It is easy to check that these two systems are bisimilar.

Theorem 1. *The following holds:*

- $\sim \not\Rightarrow \equiv_{SD}$ *and* $\equiv_{SD} \not\Rightarrow \sim$
- $\sim \not\Rightarrow \equiv_{SR}$ *and* $\equiv_{SR} \Rightarrow \sim$
- $\sim \not\Rightarrow \equiv_{HD}$ *and* $\equiv_{HD} \Rightarrow \sim$

- $\sim \Rightarrow \equiv_{HR}$ *and* $\equiv_{HR} \Rightarrow \sim$
- $\sim \not\Rightarrow \equiv_{THD}$ *and* $\equiv_{THD} \Rightarrow \sim$
- $\sim \Rightarrow \equiv_{THR}$ *and* $\equiv_{THR} \Rightarrow \sim$

Example 6. Consider the two CTMDPs shown in Fig. 4. Let all the states of $\mathcal{M}_1$ and $\mathcal{M}_2$ have the same labeling and the same exit rate for every enabled action. These two CTMDPs are bisimilar but they are neither SD nor SR trace equivalent. Similarly, the two CTMDPs shown in Fig. 3 are SD trace equivalent but they are not bisimilar.

Example 7. Consider the two CTMDPs shown in Fig. 5. Let all the states of these CTMDPs have the same labeling and the same exit rate for every enabled action. These two CTMDPs are bisimilar but they are neither HD nor THD trace equivalent.

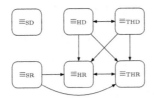

Fig. 6. Connections among six trace equivalences

3.2   Relationship Between Trace Equivalences

Next, we study the relationship between several variants of trace equivalence defined in Sect. 3. Connections among these equivalences can be understood from Fig. 6. Here a directed edge from node labeled with $\equiv_{C_1}$ to node labeled with $\equiv_{C_2}$ denotes implication, i.e., $\equiv_{C_1} \Rightarrow \equiv_{C_2}$. Similarly, an edge that connects two nodes in both the directions denotes bi-implication, i.e., coincidence.

Theorem 2. *The following holds:*

- $\equiv_{SD} \not\Rightarrow \equiv_{SR}, \equiv_{SD} \not\Rightarrow \equiv_{HD}, \equiv_{SD} \not\Rightarrow \equiv_{HR}, \equiv_{SD} \not\Rightarrow \equiv_{THD}, \equiv_{SD} \not\Rightarrow \equiv_{THR}$
- $\equiv_{SR} \not\Rightarrow \equiv_{SD}, \equiv_{SR} \not\Rightarrow \equiv_{HD}, \equiv_{SR} \not\Rightarrow \equiv_{THD}, \equiv_{SR} \Rightarrow \equiv_{HR}, \equiv_{SR} \Rightarrow \equiv_{THR}$
- $\equiv_{HD} \not\Rightarrow \equiv_{SD}, \equiv_{HD} \not\Rightarrow \equiv_{SR}, \equiv_{HD} \Rightarrow \equiv_{THD}, \equiv_{HD} \not\Rightarrow \equiv_{HR}, \equiv_{HD} \Rightarrow \equiv_{THR}$
- $\equiv_{HR} \not\Rightarrow \equiv_{SD}, \equiv_{HR} \not\Rightarrow \equiv_{SR}, \equiv_{HR} \not\Rightarrow \equiv_{HD}, \equiv_{HR} \not\Rightarrow \equiv_{THD}, \equiv_{HR} \Rightarrow \equiv_{THR}$
- $\equiv_{THD} \not\Rightarrow \equiv_{SD}, \equiv_{THD} \not\Rightarrow \equiv_{SR}, \equiv_{THD} \Rightarrow \equiv_{HD}, \equiv_{THD} \Rightarrow \equiv_{HR}, \equiv_{THD} \Rightarrow \equiv_{THR}$
- $\equiv_{THR} \not\Rightarrow \equiv_{SD}, \equiv_{THR} \not\Rightarrow \equiv_{SR}, \equiv_{THR} \not\Rightarrow \equiv_{HD}, \equiv_{THR} \Rightarrow \equiv_{HR}, \equiv_{THR} \not\Rightarrow \equiv_{THD}$

Example 8. Consider the two CTMDPs shown in Fig. 5. Let all the states have the same labeling in both the systems and the same exit rate for every enabled action. These CTMDPs are SR trace equivalent but they are not SD trace equivalent. Similarly, these two CTMDPs are neither HD nor THD trace equivalent.

Example 9. Consider the two CTMDPs shown in Fig. 4. These two CTMDPS are HD trace equivalent but they are neither SD nor SR trace equivalent.

4   Deterministic Timed Automaton

In this section we show that THD trace equivalent CTMDPs preserve the probability of satisfying DTA specifications. Note that model-checking algorithms that verify a CTMDP against a DTA specification have recently been developed [11]. We first recall the definition of DTA [1].

Definition 11 (DTA). *A deterministic timed automaton (DTA) is a tuple* $\mathcal{A} = (\Sigma, \mathcal{X}, Q, q_0, F, \rightarrow)$ *where:*

- *Σ is a finite alphabet,*
- *$\mathcal{X}$ is a finite set of clocks,*
- *Q is a nonempty finite set of locations with the initial location $q_0 \in Q$,*
- *$F \subseteq Q$ is a set of accepting (or final) locations,*
- *$\rightarrow \subseteq Q \times \Sigma \times \mathcal{CC}(\mathcal{X}) \times 2^{\mathcal{X}} \times Q$ is the edge relation satisfying:*

$$\left(q \xrightarrow{a,g,X} q' \text{ and } q \xrightarrow{a,g',X'} q'' \text{ with } g \neq g'\right) \quad implies \quad g \cap g' = \varnothing.$$

Intuitively, the edge $q \xrightarrow{a,g,X} q'$ asserts that the DTA $\mathcal{A}$ can move from location q to q' when the input symbol is a and the guard g holds, while the clocks in X should be reset when entering q' (all other clocks keep their value). DTA are deterministic as they have a single initial location, and outgoing edges of a

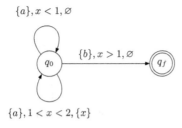

{a}, x < 1, ∅

{b}, x > 1, ∅

q_0

q_f

{a}, 1 < x < 2, {x}

Fig. 7. An example DTA $\mathcal{A}$

location labeled with the same input symbol are required to have disjoint guards. In this way, the next location is uniquely determined for a given location and a given set of clock values. In case no guard is satisfied in a location for a given clock valuation, time can progress. If the advance of time will never reach a situation in which a guard holds, the DTA will stay in that location *ad infinitum*. Note that DTA do not have location invariants. The semantics of a DTA is given by an infinite-state transition system [1]. Next, we define the notion of paths, i.e., runs or executions of a DTA. This is done using some auxiliary notions. A *clock valuation* η for a set $\mathcal{X}$ of clocks is a function $\eta : \mathcal{X} \to \mathbb{R}_{\geq 0}$, assigning to each clock $x \in \mathcal{X}$ its current value $\eta(x)$. The clock valuation η over $\mathcal{X}$ satisfies the clock constraint g, denoted $\eta \models g$, iff the values of the clocks under η fulfill g. For instance, $\eta \models x - y > c$ iff $\eta(x) - \eta(y) > c$. Other cases are defined analogously. For $d \in \mathbb{R}_{\geq 0}$, $\eta + d$ denotes the clock valuation where all clocks of η are increased by d. That is, $(\eta + d)(x) = \eta(x) + d$ for all clocks $x \in \mathcal{X}$. Clock *reset* for a subset $X \subseteq \mathcal{X}$, denoted by $\eta[X := 0]$, is the valuation η' defined by: $\forall x \in X.\eta'(x) := 0$ and $\forall x \notin X.\eta'(x) := \eta(x)$. The valuation that assigns 0 to all the clocks is denoted by $\mathbf{0}$. An (infinite) path of DTA $\mathcal{A}$ has the form $\rho = q \xrightarrow{a_0, t_0} q_1 \xrightarrow{a_1, t_1} \dots$ such that $\eta_0 = \mathbf{0}$, and for all $j \geq 0$, it holds $t_j > 0$, $\eta_j + t_j \models g_j$, $\eta_{j+1} = (\eta_j + t_j)[X_j := 0]$, where η_j is the clock evaluation on entering q_j. Here, g_j is the guard of the j-th edge taken in the DTA and X_j the set of clock to be reset on that edge. A path ρ is accepted by $\mathcal{A}$ if $q_i \in F$ for some $i \geq 0$. Since the DTA is deterministic, the successor location is uniquely determined; for convenience we write $q' = succ(q, a, g)$.

Example 10. Consider the DTA $\mathcal{A}$ shown in Fig. 7, where $\Sigma = \{a, b\}$, $Q = \{q_0, q_f\}$, $\mathcal{X} = \{x\}$, $F = \{q_f\}$ and q_0 is the initial location. An example timed path is $q_0 \xrightarrow{a, 1.4} q_0 \xrightarrow{b, 2.1} q_f$.

A path in a CTMDP $\mathcal{M}$ can be "matched" by a path through DTA $\mathcal{A}$ by regarding sets of atomic propositions in $\mathcal{M}$ as input symbols of $\mathcal{A}$. Such a path is accepted, if at some point an accepting location in the DTA is reached:

Definition 12 (Path acceptance). *Let CTMDP* $\mathcal{M} = (S, s_0, Act, P, E, L)$ *and DTA* $\mathcal{A} = (2^{AP}, \mathcal{X}, Q, q_0, F, \to)$. *The CTMDP path* $\pi = s_0 \xrightarrow{\alpha_0, t_0} s_1 \xrightarrow{\alpha_1, t_1}$

$s_2 \ldots$ *is accepted by* $\mathcal{A}$ *if there exists a corresponding DTA path*

$$q_0 \xrightarrow{L(s_0),t_0} \underbrace{succ\big(q_0, L(s_0), g_0\big)}_{=q_1} \xrightarrow{L(s_1),t_1} \underbrace{succ\big(q_1, L(s_1), g_1\big)}_{=q_2} \ldots$$

such that $q_j \in F$ *for some* $j \geq 0$. *Here,* $\eta_0 = \mathbf{0}$, g_i *is the (unique) guard in* q_i *(if it exists) such that* $\eta_i + t_i \models g_i$ *and* $\eta_{i+1} = (\eta_i + t_i)[X_i := 0]$, *and* η_i *is the clock evaluation on entering* q_i, *for* $i \geq 0$. *Let* $Paths^{\mathcal{M}}(\mathcal{A}) = \{\pi \in Paths^{\mathcal{M}} \mid \pi$ *is accepted by DTA* $\mathcal{A}\}$.

Theorem 3. *For any CTMDP* $\mathcal{M}$ *and DTA* $\mathcal{A}$, *the set* $Paths^{\mathcal{M}}(\mathcal{A})$ *is measurable* [12,14].

The main result of this theorem is that $Paths^{\mathcal{M}}(\mathcal{A})$ can be rewritten as the combination of cylinder sets of the form $Cyl = (s_0, \alpha_0, I_0, \ldots, \alpha_{n-1}, I_{n-1}, s_n)$ (*Cyl* for short) which are all accepted by DTA $\mathcal{A}$. A cylinder set (*Cyl*) is accepted by DTA $\mathcal{A}$ if all its paths are accepted by $\mathcal{A}$.

Definition 13 (Probability of accepted paths). *For CTMDP* $\mathcal{M}$, $\mathcal{D} \in Adv(\mathcal{M})$ *and DTA* $\mathcal{A}$, *let* $Pr_{\mathcal{D}}(\mathcal{M} \models \mathcal{A}) = Pr_{\mathcal{D}}(Paths^{\mathcal{M}}(\mathcal{A}))$

Definition 14 (Maximum probability of DTA). *For CTMDP* $\mathcal{M}$ *and DTA* $\mathcal{A}$, *let* $Pr^{max}(\mathcal{M} \models \mathcal{A}) = \sup_{\mathcal{D} \in Adv(\mathcal{M})} Pr_{\mathcal{D}}(\mathcal{M} \models \mathcal{A})$

In simple words, $Pr^{max}(\mathcal{M} \models \mathcal{A})$ is the maximum probability of CTMDP $\mathcal{M}$ satisfying a DTA $\mathcal{A}$ computed over all possible schedulers of $\mathcal{M}$, i.e., $Adv(\mathcal{M})$. $Pr^{min}(\mathcal{M} \models \mathcal{A})$ can be defined in an analogous manner. For CTMDPs, THD schedulers suffice for computing $Pr^{max}(\mathcal{M} \models \mathcal{A})$ and $Pr^{min}(\mathcal{M} \models \mathcal{A})$ [11,22].

Theorem 4 (Preservation of DTA). *Let* $\mathcal{M}_1$, $\mathcal{M}_2$ *be two CTMDPs such that* $\mathcal{M}_1 \equiv_{THD} \mathcal{M}_2$. *Then for any DTA* $\mathcal{A}$ *we have:*

$$Pr^{max}(\mathcal{M}_1 \models \mathcal{A}) = Pr^{max}(\mathcal{M}_2 \models \mathcal{A})$$

$$Pr^{min}(\mathcal{M}_1 \models \mathcal{A}) = Pr^{min}(\mathcal{M}_2 \models \mathcal{A})$$

In simple words, this theorem states that if two CTMDPs are THD trace equivalent, then their maximum (resp. minimum) probability to satisfy any DTA specification coincides.

Proof (Proof of Theorem 4). Let $\mathcal{D}_1$ be a THD scheduler for $\mathcal{M}_1$ such that $Pr^{max}(\mathcal{M}_1 \models \mathcal{A}) = Pr_{\mathcal{D}_1}(\mathcal{M}_1 \models \mathcal{A})$. In simple words, this means that the maximum probability of CTMDP $\mathcal{M}_1$ satisfying DTA $\mathcal{A}$ is obtained under THD scheduler $\mathcal{D}_1$. Let Π be the set of all cylinder sets of $\mathcal{M}_1$ under scheduler $\mathcal{D}_1$ that are accepted by DTA $\mathcal{A}$. This means, $Pr_{\mathcal{D}_1}(\mathcal{M}_1 \models \mathcal{A}) = Pr_{\mathcal{D}_1}(\Pi)$. Let $\bar{\Lambda}_i \subseteq \Pi$ $(1 \leq i \leq n)$ such that $\bigcup_{1 \leq i \leq n} \bar{\Lambda}_i = \Pi$ and $\bigcap_{1 \leq i \leq n} \bar{\Lambda}_i = \varnothing$. In simple words, Π is a disjoint union of the subsets $\bar{\Lambda}_i$ $(1 \leq i \leq n)$. Note that each $\bar{\Lambda}_i$ is a set of cylinder sets. Let each $\bar{\Lambda}_i$ consists of exactly those cylinder sets whose paths are compatible with some outcome $(\sigma, \theta) = (< L(s_0)\alpha_0 L(s_1)\alpha_1 \ldots L(s_{n-1})\alpha_{n-1}L(s_n) >, < t'_0 t'_1 \ldots t'_n >)$ of machine $\mathcal{M}_1$ under $\mathcal{D}_1$ (for some $n \in \mathbb{N}$). More formally, for any $\bar{\wedge}_i \in \Pi$, $\forall Cyl_1, Cyl_2 \in \bar{\wedge}_i$ and some $(\sigma, \theta) = (< L(s_0)\alpha_0 L(s_1)\alpha_1 \ldots L(s_{n-1})\alpha_{n-1}L(s_n) >, < t''_0 t''_1 \ldots t''_n >)$, the following should hold:

$$\forall \pi \in Cyl_1, \forall \pi' \in Cyl_2 \implies \pi \triangleright (\sigma, \theta) \land \pi' \triangleright (\sigma, \theta)$$

From the definition of THD trace equivalence (Definition 9) we know that for every THD scheduler $\mathcal{D}_1$ of $\mathcal{M}_1$ there exists a scheduler $\mathcal{D}_2$ of $\mathcal{M}_2$ such that the total probability of all the paths under $\mathcal{D}_1$ that are compatible with any outcome (σ, θ) is same as the total probability of all the paths under $\mathcal{D}_2$ that are compatible with (σ, θ). The same holds true in the other direction. This means that for every set of cylinder sets $\bar{\wedge}_i$ in $\mathcal{M}_1$ (under $\mathcal{D}_1$) there exists a corresponding set of cylinder sets $\bar{\wedge}'_i$ in $\mathcal{M}_2$ (under $\mathcal{D}_2$) such that $Pr_{\mathcal{D}_1}(\bar{\wedge}_i) = \Sigma_{i=1}^{|\bar{\wedge}_i|} Pr_{\mathcal{D}_1}(Cyl_i) = \Sigma_{j=1}^{|\bar{\wedge}'_i|} Pr_{\mathcal{D}_2}(Cyl'_j) = Pr_{\mathcal{D}_2}(\bar{\wedge}'_i)$. Note that the number of cylinder sets in $\bar{\wedge}_i$ and $\bar{\wedge}'_i$ could be different, i.e., it is possible that $|\bar{\wedge}_i| \neq |\bar{\wedge}'_i|$. From this we can conclude that $Pr^{max}(\mathcal{M}_1 \models \mathcal{A}) = Pr_{\mathcal{D}_1}(\mathcal{M}_1 \models \mathcal{A}) = \Sigma_{i=1}^{n} Pr_{\mathcal{D}_1}(\bar{\wedge}_i) = \Sigma_{i=1}^{n} Pr_{\mathcal{D}_2}(\bar{\wedge}'_i) = Pr_{\mathcal{D}_2}(\mathcal{M}_2 \models \mathcal{A}) = Pr^{max}(\mathcal{M}_2 \models \mathcal{A})$. A similar proof can be given to show that $Pr^{min}(\mathcal{M}_1 \models \mathcal{A}) = Pr^{min}(\mathcal{M}_2 \models \mathcal{A})$. $\qquad \square$

Corollary 1. *THD trace equivalence preserves maximum and minimum transient state probabilities.*

5   Metric Temporal Logic

In this section we show that THR trace equivalence for CTMDPs preserves the probability of satisfying MTL specifications. Note that expressive power of MTL is different from that of DTA. For example, the following property specified using an MTL formula $\Diamond^{[0,100]}\Box^{[0,5]}a$ cannot be expressed using deterministic timed automata. On the other hand, the following DTA property cannot be expressed using MTL: what is the probability to reach a given target state within the deadline, while avoiding forbidden states and not staying too long in any of the dangerous states on the way [30]. We now recall the syntax and semantics of Metric Temporal Logic [10,23].

Definition 15 (Syntax of MTL). *Let AP be a set of atomic propositions, then the formulas of MTL are built from AP using Boolean connectives, and time-constrained versions of the* until *operator U as follows:*

$$\varphi ::= tt \mid a \mid \neg\varphi \mid \varphi \land \varphi \mid \varphi \, U^I \, \varphi$$

where $I \subseteq \mathbb{R}_{\geq 0}$ is a non-empty interval with rational bounds, and $a \in AP$.

Next, we define the semantics of MTL formulas over CTMDP paths.

Definition 16 (Semantics of MTL formulas). *The meaning of MTL formulas is defined by means of a satisfaction relation, denoted by $\models$, between a CTMDP $\mathcal{M}$, one of its paths π, MTL formula φ, and time $t \in \mathbb{R}_{\geq 0}$. Let*
$$\pi = s_0 \xrightarrow{\alpha_0, t_0} s_1 \ldots s_{n-1} \xrightarrow{\alpha_{n-1}, t_{n-1}} s_n \ldots \text{ be a finite or infinite path of } \mathcal{M}, \text{ then}$$
$(\pi, t) \models \varphi$ is defined inductively by:

$$
\begin{aligned}
&(\pi, t) \models tt \\
&(\pi, t) \models a && \text{iff } a \in L(\pi@t) \\
&(\pi, t) \models \neg\varphi && \text{iff } not\ (\pi, t) \models \varphi \\
&(\pi, t) \models \varphi_1 \wedge \varphi_2 && \text{iff } (\pi, t) \models \varphi_1\ and\ (\pi, t) \models \varphi_2 \\
&(\pi, t) \models \varphi_1\, U^I\, \varphi_2 && \text{iff } \exists t' \in t+I.\ ((\pi, t') \models \varphi_2 \wedge \forall t \leq t'' < t'.\ (\pi, t'') \models \varphi_1).
\end{aligned}
$$

The semantics for the propositional fragment is straightforward. Recall that $\pi@t$ denotes the state occupied along path π at time t. Path π at time t satisfies $\varphi_1\, U^I\, \varphi_2$ whenever for some time point t' in the interval $I+t$, defined as $[a, b]+t = [a+t, b+t]$ (and similarly for open intervals), φ_2 holds, and at all time points between t and t', path π satisfies φ_1. Let $\pi \models \varphi$ if and only if $(\pi, 0) \models \varphi$. Timed variant of standard temporal operator $\Diamond$ ("eventually") is derived in the following way: $\Diamond^I \varphi = tt\, U^I\, \varphi$. Similarly, timed variant of $\Box$ ("globally") is derived as follows:

$$\Box^I \varphi = \neg(\Diamond^I \neg\varphi).$$

MTL can be used to specify various interesting properties, e.g., $\Box^{[0,100]}(down \rightarrow \Diamond^{[0,5]}up)$, which says that whenever the system is down in the interval $[0, 100]$, it should be up again within 5 time units. Let $Paths^{\mathcal{M}}(\varphi) = \{\pi \in Paths^{\mathcal{M}} \mid \pi \models \varphi\}$.

Theorem 5. *For any CTMDP $\mathcal{M}$ and MTL formula φ, the set $Paths^{\mathcal{M}}(\varphi)$ is measurable* [30].

In simple words, this theorem says that paths that satisfy an MTL formula φ can be written as a set of cylinder sets.

Definition 17 (Probability of MTL paths). *For CTMDP $\mathcal{M}$, $\mathcal{D} \in Adv(\mathcal{M})$ and MTL formula φ, let $Pr_{\mathcal{D}}(\mathcal{M} \models \varphi) = Pr_{\mathcal{D}}(Paths^{\mathcal{M}}(\varphi))$*

$Pr_{\mathcal{D}}(\mathcal{M} \models \varphi)$ denote the probability of all paths of $\mathcal{M}$ under scheduler $\mathcal{D}$ that satisfy an MTL formula φ.

Definition 18 (Maximum probability of MTL). *For CTMDP $\mathcal{M}$ and MTL formula φ,* $Pr^{max}(\mathcal{M} \models \varphi) = \sup_{\mathcal{D} \in Adv(\mathcal{M})} Pr_{\mathcal{D}}(\mathcal{M} \models \varphi)$

$Pr^{min}(\mathcal{M} \models \varphi)$ can be defined in an analogous manner.

Theorem 6 (Preservation of MTL). *Let $\mathcal{M}_1, \mathcal{M}_2$ be two CTMDPs such that $\mathcal{M}_1 \equiv_{THR} \mathcal{M}_2$. Then for any MTL formula φ we have:*

$$Pr^{max}(\mathcal{M}_1 \models \varphi) = Pr^{max}(\mathcal{M}_2 \models \varphi)$$

$$Pr^{min}(\mathcal{M}_1 \models \varphi) = Pr^{min}(\mathcal{M}_2 \models \varphi)$$

This theorem asserts that THR-trace equivalent CTMDPs have the same maximum (resp. minimum) probability of satisfying any MTL formula φ.

Proof (Proof of Theorem 6). Let $\mathcal{D}_1$ be a THR scheduler for $\mathcal{M}_1$ such that $Pr^{max}(\mathcal{M}_1 \models \varphi) = Pr_{\mathcal{D}_1}(\mathcal{M}_1 \models \varphi)$. In simple words, this means that the maximum probability of CTMDP $\mathcal{M}_1$ satisfying MTL formula φ is obtained under THR scheduler $\mathcal{D}_1$. Let Π be the set of all cylinder sets of $\mathcal{M}_1$ under scheduler $\mathcal{D}_1$ that satisfy MTL formula φ. The rest of the proof is similar to the proof of Theorem 4, i.e., we can show that there exists a scheduler $\mathcal{D}_2$ in $\mathcal{M}_2$ such that $Pr_{\mathcal{D}_1}(\mathcal{M}_1 \models \varphi) = Pr_{\mathcal{D}_2}(\mathcal{M}_2 \models \varphi)$. This can be done by reasoning over the set of cylinder sets.   □

6 Conclusions

This paper presented several variants of trace equivalence on the basis of increasing power of schedulers for CTMDPs. Button pushing experiments on a black box model of CTMDP have been used to define these trace equivalences. We investigated the relationship among these trace relations and also compared them with strong bisimulation for CTMDPs. Finally, we proved that trace equivalent CTMDPs have the same probability of satisfying DTA and MTL properties. In the future, we plan to study ready trace and failure trace semantics for CTMDPs.

Acknowledgments. A special thanks goes to Michele Loreti for valuable discussions and suggestions.

References

1. Alur, R., Dill, D.L.: A theory of timed automata. Theor. Comput. Sci. **126**(2), 183–235 (1994)
2. Ash, R.B., Doleans-Dade, C.A.: Probability and Measure Theory. Academic Press, Cambridge (2000)
3. Baier, C., Haverkort, B.R., Hermanns, H., Katoen, J.-P.: Model-checking algorithms for continuous-time Markov chains. IEEE Trans. Softw. Eng. **29**(6), 524–541 (2003)
4. Baier, C., Hermanns, H.: Weak bisimulation for fully probabilistic processes. In: Grumberg, O. (ed.) CAV 1997. LNCS, vol. 1254, pp. 119–130. Springer, Heidelberg (1997). doi:10.1007/3-540-63166-6_14
5. Baier, C., Katoen, J.-P.: Principles of Model Checking. MIT Press, Cambridge (2008)
6. Baier, C., Katoen, J.-P., Hermanns, H., Wolf, V.: Comparative branching-time semantics for Markov chains. Inf. Comput. **200**(2), 149–214 (2005)
7. Bernardo, M.: Non-bisimulation-based Markovian behavioral equivalences. J. Log. Algebr. Program. **72**(1), 3–49 (2007)
8. Bernardo, M.: Towards state space reduction based on t-lumpability-consistent relations. In: Thomas, N., Juiz, C. (eds.) EPEW 2008. LNCS, vol. 5261, pp. 64–78. Springer, Heidelberg (2008). doi:10.1007/978-3-540-87412-6_6

9. Bernardo, M., De Nicola, R., Loreti, M.: Revisiting trace and testing equivalences for nondeterministic and probabilistic processes. LMCS, **10**(1) (2014)
10. Bouyer, P.: From Qualitative to Quantitative Analysis of Timed Systems. Mémoire d'habilitation. Université Paris 7, Paris, France, January 2009
11. Chen, T., Han, T., Katoen, J.-P., Mereacre, A.: Observing continuous-time MDPs by 1-Clock timed automata. In: Delzanno, G., Potapov, I. (eds.) RP 2011. LNCS, vol. 6945, pp. 2–25. Springer, Heidelberg (2011). doi:10.1007/978-3-642-24288-5_2
12. Chen, T., Han, T., Katoen, J.-P., Mereacre, A.: Quantitative model checking of continuous-time Markov chains against timed automata specifications. In: LICS, pp. 309–318. IEEE Computer Society (2009)
13. Desharnais, J., Gupta, V., Jagadeesan, R., Panangaden, P.: Weak bisimulation is sound and complete for pCTL*. Inf. Comput. **208**(2), 203–219 (2010)
14. Fu, H.: Approximating acceptance probabilities of CTMC-paths on multi-clock deterministic timed automata. In: HSCC, pp. 323–332. ACM (2013)
15. Hermanns, H. (ed.): Interactive Markov Chains: And the Quest for Quantified Quality. LNCS, vol. 2428. Springer, Heidelberg (2002). doi:10.1007/3-540-45804-2
16. Huynh, D.T., Tian, L.: On some equivalence relations for probabilistic processes. Fundam. Inf. **17**(3), 211–234 (1992)
17. Jonsson, B., Larsen, K.G.: Specification and refinement of probabilistic processes. In: LICS, pp. 266–277. IEEE Computer Society (1991)
18. Jou, C.-C., Smolka, S.A.: Equivalences, congruences, and complete axiomatizations for probabilistic processes. In: Baeten, J.C.M., Klop, J.W. (eds.) CONCUR 1990. LNCS, vol. 458, pp. 367–383. Springer, Heidelberg (1990). doi:10.1007/BFb0039071
19. Larsen, K.G., Skou, A.: Bisimulation through probabilistic testing. In: POPL, pp. 344–352 (1989)
20. Marsan, M.A., Balbo, G., Conte, G., Donatelli, S., Franceschinis, G.: Modelling with Generalized Stochastic Petri Nets, 1st edn. Wiley, Hoboken (1994)
21. Neuhäußer, M.R., Katoen, J.-P.: Bisimulation and logical preservation for continuous-time Markov decision processes. In: Caires, L., Vasconcelos, V.T. (eds.) CONCUR 2007. LNCS, vol. 4703, pp. 412–427. Springer, Heidelberg (2007). doi:10.1007/978-3-540-74407-8_28
22. Neuhäußer, M.R., Stoelinga, M., Katoen, J.-P.: Delayed nondeterminism in continuous-time Markov decision processes. In: Alfaro, L. (ed.) FoSSaCS 2009. LNCS, vol. 5504, pp. 364–379. Springer, Heidelberg (2009). doi:10.1007/978-3-642-00596-1_26
23. Ouaknine, J., Worrell, J.: Some recent results in metric temporal logic. In: Cassez, F., Jard, C. (eds.) FORMATS 2008. LNCS, vol. 5215, pp. 1–13. Springer, Heidelberg (2008). doi:10.1007/978-3-540-85778-5_1
24. Parma, A., Segala, R.: Axiomatization of trace semantics for stochastic nondeterministic processes. In: QEST, pp. 294–303 (2004)
25. Philippou, A., Lee, I., Sokolsky, O.: Weak bisimulation for probabilistic systems. In: Palamidessi, C. (ed.) CONCUR 2000. LNCS, vol. 1877, pp. 334–349. Springer, Heidelberg (2000). doi:10.1007/3-540-44618-4_25
26. Segala, R.: Modelling and verification of randomized distributed real time systems. Ph.D. thesis. MIT (1995)
27. Segala, R.: Testing probabilistic automata. In: Montanari, U., Sassone, V. (eds.) CONCUR 1996. LNCS, vol. 1119, pp. 299–314. Springer, Heidelberg (1996). doi:10.1007/3-540-61604-7_62
28. Segala, R., Lynch, N.A.: Probabilistic simulations for probabilistic processes. Nord. J. Comput. **2**(2), 250–273 (1995)

29. Sharma, A.: Weighted probabilistic equivalence preserves ω-regular properties. In: Schmitt, J.B. (ed.) MMB&DFT. LNCS. Springer, Heidelberg (2012). doi:10.1007/978-3-642-28540-0_9

30. Sharma, A., Katoen, J.-P.: Weighted lumpability on Markov chains. In: Clarke, E., Virbitskaite, I., Voronkov, A. (eds.) PSI 2011. LNCS, vol. 7162, pp. 322–339. Springer, Heidelberg (2012). doi:10.1007/978-3-642-29709-0_28

31. Stoelinga, M., Vaandrager, F.: A testing scenario for probabilistic automata. In: Baeten, J.C.M., Lenstra, J.K., Parrow, J., Woeginger, G.J. (eds.) ICALP 2003. LNCS, vol. 2719, pp. 464–477. Springer, Heidelberg (2003). doi:10.1007/3-540-45061-0_38

32. Wolf, V., Baier, C., Majster-Cederbaum, M.E.: Trace machines for observing continuous-time Markov chains. ENTCS 153(2), 259–277 (2006)

33. Wolf, V., Baier, C., Majster-Cederbaum, M.E.: Trace semantics for stochastic systems with nondeterminism. Electr. Notes Theo. Comput. Sci. 164(3), 187–204 (2006)

SMT Solvers and Algorithms

Constructing Cycles in the Simplex Method for DPLL(T)

Bertram Felgenhauer[(✉)] and Aart Middeldorp

Department of Computer Science, University of Innsbruck, Innsbruck, Austria
{bertram.felgenhauer,aart.middeldorp}@uibk.ac.at

Abstract. Modern SMT solvers use a special DPLL(T) variant of the simplex algorithm to solve satisfiability problems in linear real arithmetic. Termination is guaranteed by Bland's pivot selection rule, but it is not immediately obvious that such a rule is required. For the traditional simplex method non-termination is well-understood, but the cycling examples from the literature do not immediately carry over to the DPLL(T) variant. We present two SMT encodings of the problem of finding cycles, using linear and nonlinear real arithmetic.

1 Introduction

The simplex algorithm (Dantzig 1947) is the most popular method for solving linear programs, despite its worst-case exponential complexity. Termination of the simplex algorithm is guaranteed by pivot selection strategies, like Bland's rule [6].

Dutertre and de Moura [9] proposed an adaptation of the simplex method to decide quantifier-free linear arithmetic (QF_LRA) that works well in a DPLL(T) setting and which is used in SMT solvers like Yices [8] and Z3 [5]. The correctness of the decision procedure follows from termination of the algorithm [10, Theorem 1], which relies on Bland's pivot selection rule. The algorithm is covered in the textbook [14] by Kroening and Strichman, where it is called the *general simplex algorithm*. We prefer the name *DPLL(T) simplex algorithm*, because the algorithm does not, in fact, generalize the simplex method. Teaching a course on decision procedures using this book (as well as [7]) led to the question whether Bland's pivot selection rule is essential for termination. This paper reports on our quest to answer this question.

The literature on the simplex method contains several cycling examples, e.g. [2,4,13,20], but these typically do no carry over to the DPLL(T) setting without further ado because they start from a feasible solution and the cycling behavior is triggered by the objective function, which is absent in the DPLL(T) simplex method.

We describe two new approaches to automatically find cycling examples. The first approach targets the DPLL(T) simplex method. A sequence of pivoting steps is fixed such that the induced tableau cycles. This is followed by

This research was supported by Austrian Science Fund (FWF) project P27528.

D.V. Hung and D. Kapur (Eds.): ICTAC 2017, LNCS 10580, pp. 213–228, 2017.
DOI: 10.1007/978-3-319-67729-3_13

the use of an SMT solver for linear real arithmetic to find bounds on the variables and an initial assignment for the variables such that the pivoting steps are valid. This approach works well and is able to find small cycles which are useful for didactic purposes. In the second approach the complete search is encoded into nonlinear real arithmetic, both for the DPLL(T) simplex method and the standard simplex method with Dantzig's pivoting rule. The resulting SMT problems in quantifier-free nonlinear real arithmetic are nontrivial and could serve as interesting benchmarks for SMT solvers. The code we produced while preparing this paper is available online.[1]

The remainder of the paper is organized as follows. In the next section we briefly recall the DPLL(T) simplex algorithm. In Sect. 3 we give two examples showing that the algorithm may cycle if Bland's pivot selection rule is violated. The first one is found by our program. The second one originates from [2] and relies on the fact that the constant vector in the linear program is zero and hence the objective function of the dual linear program is constant, which ensures that it cannot affect the cyclic behavior. In Sect. 4 we explain how to construct cycles using an SMT solver for linear real arithmetic to find bounds on the variables and the initial assignment, after the initial tableau and the sequence of pivoting steps is fixed. Encoding the whole search for cycles as a satisfiability problem requires solving nonlinear real arithmetic constraints. This is described in Sect. 5 for the DPLL(T) simplex method as well as the original simplex method. In Sect. 6 we comment on related work. In particular, we analyzed the examples from the survey paper by Avis et al. [1], where we observed violations of Dantzig's pivot selection rule and a few typographical errors. We conclude in Sect. 7.

2   DPLL(T) Simplex Algorithm

The DPLL(T) simplex algorithm is a constraint solving method for linear arithmetic over real (or rational) numbers $x_1, \ldots, x_n$. The unknowns $x_1, \ldots, x_n$ are divided into *basic* variables B and *nonbasic* variables N that are related as follows:

$$x_i = \sum_{j \in N} a_{ij} x_j \tag{1}$$

for all $i \in B$. Here $\{1, \ldots, n\} = B \uplus N$ and $a_{ij} \in \mathbb{R}$ for all $i \in B$ and $j \in N$. The coefficients a_{ij} form a $|B| \times |N|$ matrix which is called the *tableau* of the problem. In addition, every variable x_i with $1 \leqslant i \leqslant n$ is equipped with upper and lower bounds u_i and l_i:

$$-\infty \leqslant l_i \leqslant x_i \leqslant u_i \leqslant +\infty \tag{2}$$

The infinities signal the absence of a corresponding bound. Throughout the algorithm, an assignment for the variables is maintained such that (1) is satisfied and (2) holds for every $i \in N$. If (2) holds also for every $i \in B$ then the algorithm returns the current, satisfying, assignment. Otherwise $i \in B$ is selected such

---

[1] http://cl-informatik.uibk.ac.at/research/simplex/

that (2) is violated. Next a suitable $j \in N$ is selected such that x_i and x_j can be swapped in a pivoting operation. If there is no suitable $j \in N$ then the algorithm terminates and reports that the constraint problem is unsatisfiable. The index $j \in N$ is *suitable* if one of the following mutually exclusive conditions is satisfied:

(L_+) $x_i < l_i$, $a_{ij} > 0$, and $x_j < u_j$,
(L_-) $x_i < l_i$, $a_{ij} < 0$, and $l_j < x_j$,
(U_+) $u_i < x_i$, $a_{ij} > 0$, and $l_j < x_j$,
(U_-) $u_i < x_i$, $a_{ij} < 0$, and $x_j < u_j$.

Once $j \in N$ is selected, a pivoting step is performed: $B' = B \cup \{j\} - \{i\}$, $N' = N \cup \{i\} - \{j\}$, and the coefficients in (1) are updated such that

$$x_{i'} = \sum_{j' \in N'} a_{i'j'} x_{j'} \tag{3}$$

holds for all $i' \in B'$. This amounts to substituting

$$x_j = \frac{1}{a_{ij}} \left(x_i - \sum_{j' \in N - \{j\}} a_{ij'} x_{j'} \right)$$

into the previous tableau. Next the value of x_j is changed to l_i in cases (L_+) or (L_-) and to u_i in cases (U_+) or (U_-). This is followed by a recomputation of the values of the new basic variables such that (3) remains true.

Example 1. Consider the tableau

$$\begin{array}{c} \quad\ x_1\ x_2\ x_3 \\ \begin{array}{c} x_4 \\ x_5 \end{array} \left(\begin{array}{ccc} 2 & 2 & -1 \\ -1 & 1 & 3 \end{array} \right) \end{array}$$

with bounds

$$x_1 \geqslant 0 \qquad x_2 \geqslant 0 \qquad x_3 \geqslant 0 \qquad x_4 \geqslant 3 \qquad x_5 \leqslant -2$$

and assignment $x_1 = x_2 = x_3 = x_4 = x_5 = 0$. Both x_4 and x_5 violate their respective bounds. We can pivot x_4 with x_1 or x_2, but not with x_3; in order to increase the value of x_4 we have to decrease the value of x_3 (due to the negative coefficient -1) but x_3 is at its lower bound. So the nonbasic variable x_3 is not suitable for the basic variable x_4 because $x_4 < l_4$, $a_{43} < 0$, but condition (L_-) above is violated. Likewise, x_5 can be pivoted with x_1, but not with x_2 or x_3. So there are three different options for a pivoting step: (x_4, x_1), (x_4, x_2), and (x_5, x_2).

In the simplex method, the selection of the pair (x_i, x_j) with $i \in B$ and $j \in N$ is determined by a *pivot selection rule* and critical for ensuring termination of the method. Different pivoting rules have been proposed in the literature (e.g. [6,11,12,16]). Termination of the DPLL(T) simplex algorithm has been established in [10] for *Bland's rule* [6], which selects the smallest $i \in B$ such that x_i violates its bounds and smallest suitable $j \in N$.

Example 2. In the preceding example, the pair (x_4, x_1) is selected by Bland's rule, resulting in the new tableau

$$
\begin{array}{c}
\quad\quad x_4 \;\; x_2 \;\; x_3 \\
\begin{array}{c} x_1 \\ x_5 \end{array}
\left(
\begin{array}{ccc}
\frac{1}{2} & -1 & \frac{1}{2} \\
-\frac{1}{2} & 2 & \frac{5}{2}
\end{array}
\right)
\end{array}
$$

and the assignment $x_1 = \frac{3}{2}$, $x_2 = x_3 = 0$, $x_4 = 3$, $x_5 = -\frac{3}{2}$.

3 Two Cycles

We give two examples where the DPLL(T) simplex algorithm may loop if one does not impose any constraints on pivots beyond suitability. The first one is obtained by the method that we describe in the next section.

Example 3. We use four variables, x_1 to x_4, with the following constraints:

$$
\begin{array}{lll}
x_3 = x_1 + 2x_2 & -1 \leqslant x_1 \leqslant 0 & -5 \leqslant x_3 \leqslant -4 \\
x_4 = 2x_1 + x_2 & -4 \leqslant x_2 \leqslant 0 & -7 \leqslant x_4 \leqslant 1
\end{array}
$$

The resulting cycle is given in Fig. 1, with the pivoting element indicated in each tableau. Note that after the first four steps (which are given in the left column), the tableaux repeat, but the assignments are different. In fact, any nonbasic variable that is at its lower bound will be at its upper bound fours steps later, and vice versa. Figure 2 displays the trajectory of the (x_1, x_2) coordinates of the eight assignments, along with the lines corresponding to the lower and upper bounds of each variable. Every assignment lies at the intersection of two of these lines, because in each step of the cycle, the two nonbasic variables are at one of their bounds. Each pair of subsequent assignments lie on one of those lines, determined by the nonbasic variable that is *not* pivoted in the corresponding pivoting step. It is noteworthy that the trajectory alternates between left and right turns, a behavior already observed by Beale [4]. The second step violates Bland's pivot selection rule as the basic variable x_1, which precedes the selected basic variable x_4, also violates its bounds. The nonbasic variable x_2 is suitable for pivoting with x_1, and the resulting pivoting step produces the tableau

$$
\begin{array}{c}
\quad\quad x_2 \;\; x_4 \\
\begin{array}{c} x_3 \\ x_1 \end{array}
\left(
\begin{array}{cc}
\frac{1}{2} & -\frac{1}{2} \\
\frac{3}{2} & -\frac{1}{2}
\end{array}
\right)
\end{array}
$$

and assignment $x_1 = -1$, $x_2 = -\frac{3}{2}$, $x_3 = -4$, and $x_4 = -\frac{7}{2}$, which satisfies the constraints. A simpler satisfying assignment is $x_1 = -1$, $x_2 = -2$, $x_3 = -5$, and $x_4 = -4$.

Note that the selection of nonbasic variables follows Bland's rule when using the (natural) variable ordering $x_1 < x_2 < x_3 < x_4$. If one instead considers the variable ordering $x_4 < x_1 < x_2 < x_3$, then the selection of basic variables follows Bland's rule. However, the third pivoting step, which pivots the basic variable x_1 with the nonbasic variable x_3, should pivot x_1 with x_4 instead, because x_4 precedes x_3 in this variable ordering. Consequently, both parts of Bland's pivot selection rule are required in order to ensure termination.

$$\begin{array}{c} \\ x_3 \\ x_4 \end{array} \begin{array}{c} \begin{array}{cc} x_1 & x_2 \end{array} \\ \begin{pmatrix} \boxed{1} & 2 \\ 2 & 1 \end{pmatrix} \end{array} \quad \begin{array}{cccc} x_1 & x_2 & x_3 & x_4 \\ \hline 0 & 0 & 0 & 0 \end{array} \qquad\Bigg|\qquad \begin{array}{c} \\ x_3 \\ x_4 \end{array} \begin{array}{c} \begin{array}{cc} x_1 & x_2 \end{array} \\ \begin{pmatrix} \boxed{1} & 2 \\ 2 & 1 \end{pmatrix} \end{array} \quad \begin{array}{cccc} x_1 & x_2 & x_3 & x_4 \\ \hline -1 & -4 & -9 & -6 \end{array}$$

$$\begin{array}{c} \\ x_1 \\ x_4 \end{array} \begin{array}{c} \begin{array}{cc} x_3 & x_2 \end{array} \\ \begin{pmatrix} 1 & -2 \\ 2 & \boxed{-3} \end{pmatrix} \end{array} \quad \begin{array}{cccc} x_1 & x_2 & x_3 & x_4 \\ \hline -4 & 0 & -4 & -8 \end{array} \qquad\Bigg|\qquad \begin{array}{c} \\ x_1 \\ x_4 \end{array} \begin{array}{c} \begin{array}{cc} x_3 & x_2 \end{array} \\ \begin{pmatrix} 1 & -2 \\ 2 & \boxed{-3} \end{pmatrix} \end{array} \quad \begin{array}{cccc} x_1 & x_2 & x_3 & x_4 \\ \hline 3 & -4 & -5 & 2 \end{array}$$

$$\begin{array}{c} \\ x_1 \\ x_2 \end{array} \begin{array}{c} \begin{array}{cc} x_3 & x_4 \end{array} \\ \begin{pmatrix} \boxed{-\frac{1}{3}} & \frac{2}{3} \\ \frac{2}{3} & -\frac{1}{3} \end{pmatrix} \end{array} \quad \begin{array}{cccc} x_1 & x_2 & x_3 & x_4 \\ \hline -\frac{10}{3} & -\frac{1}{3} & -4 & -7 \end{array} \qquad\Bigg|\qquad \begin{array}{c} \\ x_1 \\ x_2 \end{array} \begin{array}{c} \begin{array}{cc} x_3 & x_4 \end{array} \\ \begin{pmatrix} \boxed{-\frac{1}{3}} & \frac{2}{3} \\ \frac{2}{3} & -\frac{1}{3} \end{pmatrix} \end{array} \quad \begin{array}{cccc} x_1 & x_2 & x_3 & x_4 \\ \hline \frac{7}{3} & -\frac{11}{3} & -5 & 1 \end{array}$$

$$\begin{array}{c} \\ x_3 \\ x_2 \end{array} \begin{array}{c} \begin{array}{cc} x_1 & x_4 \end{array} \\ \begin{pmatrix} -3 & 2 \\ -2 & \boxed{1} \end{pmatrix} \end{array} \quad \begin{array}{cccc} x_1 & x_2 & x_3 & x_4 \\ \hline -1 & -5 & -11 & -7 \end{array} \qquad\Bigg|\qquad \begin{array}{c} \\ x_3 \\ x_2 \end{array} \begin{array}{c} \begin{array}{cc} x_1 & x_4 \end{array} \\ \begin{pmatrix} -3 & 2 \\ -2 & \boxed{1} \end{pmatrix} \end{array} \quad \begin{array}{cccc} x_1 & x_2 & x_3 & x_4 \\ \hline 0 & 1 & 2 & 1 \end{array}$$

Fig. 1. The cycle of length 8 in Example 3.

The second example is an adaptation of an example attributed to Kuhn in [2].

Example 4. The linear program in [2, Example 2] (without the third row) amounts to:

$$\begin{array}{lll} x_4 = -2x_1 + \frac{1}{3}x_2 - 2 & x_6 = x_1 - \frac{1}{3}x_2 + 1 & \max u = 0x_1 + 0x_2 \\ x_5 = -9x_1 + x_2 - 3 & x_7 = 9x_1 - x_2 + 12 & x_i \geqslant 0 \end{array}$$

Using the transformation $x_3 := x_4 + 2$, $x_4 := x_5 + 3$, $x_5 := x_6 - 1$, $x_6 := x_7 - 12$ we obtain the following constraints:

$$\begin{array}{lllll} x_3 = -2x_1 + \frac{1}{3}x_2 & x_5 = x_1 - \frac{1}{3}x_2 & x_1 \geqslant 0 & x_3 \geqslant 2 & x_5 \geqslant -1 \\ x_4 = -9x_1 + x_2 & x_6 = 9x_1 - x_2 & x_2 \geqslant 0 & x_4 \geqslant 3 & x_6 \geqslant -12 \end{array}$$

With these constraints, a cycle of length 6 is obtained. However, some of the beauty of the original example is lost, where after just two pivoting steps, the tableau becomes identical to the initial tableau under a cyclic shift of the variables.

In order to restore this symmetry, we have to assign lower bounds such that all odd numbered variables have the same lower bound, and all even numbered

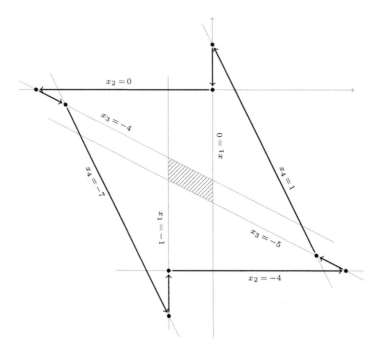

Fig. 2. Trajectory of the assignments (x_1, x_2) in Example 3.

variables as well. A suitable choice is

$$x_3 = -2x_1 + \tfrac{1}{3}x_2 \qquad x_5 = x_1 - \tfrac{1}{3}x_2 \qquad x_1, x_3, x_5 \geqslant \tfrac{1}{3}$$
$$x_4 = -9x_1 + x_2 \qquad x_6 = 9x_1 - x_2 \qquad x_2, x_4, x_6 \geqslant -3$$

The first two steps of the corresponding cycle of length 6 are given in Fig. 3, after which a cyclic shift of the variables is obtained.

4   Constructing Cycles Using Linear Real Arithmetic

Our first approach to finding cycles in the DPLL(T) simplex method works by fixing the initial tableau and a sequence of pivoting steps, and then setting up an SMT problem to find bounds on the variables and an initial assignment such that the pivoting steps cycle. If the resulting SMT problem is satisfiable then we have found a cycle; otherwise we try again with a different initial tableau. The procedure is outlined in Fig. 4.

Our goal is to obtain a cycle with simple pivoting steps, that is, we want the tableau entries corresponding to the pivoting steps to be simple.[2] In order to

---

[2] We use $\max(|p|, |q|)$ as a measure of simplicity of a rational number p/q; the smaller the measure the simpler the number.

$$
\begin{array}{c}
\begin{array}{c}
\begin{array}{cc} x_1 & x_2 \end{array} \\
\begin{array}{c} x_3 \\ x_4 \\ x_5 \\ x_6 \end{array}
\begin{pmatrix} -2 & \frac{1}{3} \\ -9 & \boxed{1} \\ 1 & -\frac{1}{3} \\ 9 & -2 \end{pmatrix}
\end{array}
\qquad
\begin{array}{c}
\begin{array}{ccc} x_1 & x_2 & x_3 \end{array} \\
\hline
\begin{array}{ccc} \frac{1}{3} & -3 & -\frac{5}{3} \end{array} \\
\begin{array}{ccc} x_4 & x_5 & x_6 \end{array} \\
\hline
\begin{array}{ccc} -6 & \frac{4}{3} & 9 \end{array}
\end{array}
\qquad\Bigg|\qquad
\begin{array}{c}
\begin{array}{cc} x_3 & x_4 \end{array} \\
\begin{array}{c} x_1 \\ x_2 \\ x_5 \\ x_6 \end{array}
\begin{pmatrix} 1 & -\frac{1}{3} \\ 9 & -2 \\ -2 & \frac{1}{3} \\ -9 & \boxed{1} \end{pmatrix}
\end{array}
\qquad
\begin{array}{c}
\begin{array}{ccc} x_1 & x_2 & x_3 \end{array} \\
\hline
\begin{array}{ccc} \frac{4}{3} & 9 & \frac{1}{3} \end{array} \\
\begin{array}{ccc} x_4 & x_5 & x_6 \end{array} \\
\hline
\begin{array}{ccc} -3 & -\frac{5}{3} & -6 \end{array}
\end{array}
$$

$$
\begin{array}{c}
\begin{array}{cc} x_1 & x_4 \end{array} \\
\begin{array}{c} x_3 \\ x_2 \\ x_5 \\ x_6 \end{array}
\begin{pmatrix} -2 & -\frac{1}{3} \\ -9 & -2 \\ \boxed{1} & \frac{1}{3} \\ 9 & 1 \end{pmatrix}
\end{array}
\qquad
\begin{array}{c}
\begin{array}{ccc} x_1 & x_2 & x_3 \end{array} \\
\hline
\begin{array}{ccc} \frac{1}{3} & -2 & \frac{1}{3} \end{array} \\
\begin{array}{ccc} x_4 & x_5 & x_6 \end{array} \\
\hline
\begin{array}{ccc} -3 & -\frac{2}{3} & 0 \end{array}
\end{array}
\qquad\Bigg|\qquad \vdots
$$

Fig. 3. One third of a cycle of length 6 in Example 4.

```
1: fix sequence of pivoting steps
2: repeat
3:     guess initial tableau
4:     generate linear real arithmetic SMT problem for bounds and initial assignment
5: until SMT problem is satisfiable with a cycle of desired simplicity
6: print cycle based on model generated by SMT solver
```

Fig. 4. Constructing cycles using linear real arithmetic

control these entries we take a detour via *full tableaux*. The full tableau corresponding to

$$
x_i = \sum_{j \in N} a_{ij} x_j
$$

for $i \in B$ is the $|B| \times n$ matrix with entries a_{ij} where a_{ij} for $j \in B$ is defined as -1 if $i = j$ and 0 otherwise. That is, the full tableau is obtained from the (shortened) tableau by adjoining a negated identity matrix in the columns corresponding to the basic variables.

Full tableaux allow an elegant description of pivoting steps: From the tableau A, where the basic variable x_i being pivoted corresponds to a column equal to a negated unit vector $-e_k$ (we use e_k to denote the unit vector of length $|N|$ whose k-th entry equals 1), we use row operations to move to the tableau RA, where R differs from the identity matrix in the i-th column. The matrix R is chosen such that the column corresponding to the variable entering the basis in RA equals $-e_k$.

Example 5. The full tableau corresponding to the initial tableau in Example 3 is

$$
\begin{array}{c}
\begin{array}{cccc} x_1 & x_2 & x_3 & x_4 \end{array} \\
\begin{array}{c} x_3 \\ x_4 \end{array}
\begin{pmatrix} 1 & 2 & -1 & 0 \\ 2 & 1 & 0 & -1 \end{pmatrix}
\end{array}
$$

The first pivoting step corresponds to subtracting 2 times the first row from the second row and multiplying the first row by -1 in the full tableau, i.e.,

$$\begin{pmatrix} -1 & 0 \\ -2 & 1 \end{pmatrix} \begin{pmatrix} 1 & 2 & -1 & 0 \\ 2 & 1 & 0 & -1 \end{pmatrix} = \begin{pmatrix} -1 & -2 & 1 & 0 \\ 0 & -3 & 2 & -1 \end{pmatrix}$$

Now if we assume that there is a cycle with initial full tableau A and pivoting steps given by R_1 to R_n, then from

$$R_n R_{n-1} \cdots R_1 A = A$$

we may conclude that $R_n R_{n-1} \cdots R_1 = I$ by focusing on the variables that are initially basic. Conversely, given $R_n R_{n-1} \cdots R_1 = I$ with R_i of the shape described above, we can construct a corresponding initial tableau under the additional assumption that the variable entering the basis in the j-th pivoting step is x_j. In that case, the j-th column $a_{\bullet j}$ of A satisfies

$$R_j R_{j-1} \cdots R_1 a_{\bullet j} = -e_k$$

where k is the index of the column of R_j that differs from the identity matrix. Consequently,

$$a_{\bullet j} = R_n R_{n-1} \cdots R_1 a_{\bullet j} = -R_n R_{n-1} \cdots R_{j+1} e_k$$

This gives us the desired control over the pivoting elements, whose inverse can be found on the diagonals of the R_i in the non-unit columns.

Example 6. The following four matrices satisfy $R_4 R_3 R_2 R_1 = I$:

$$R_1 = \begin{pmatrix} -1 & 0 \\ -2 & 1 \end{pmatrix} \qquad R_2 = \begin{pmatrix} 1 & -\frac{2}{3} \\ 0 & \frac{1}{3} \end{pmatrix} \qquad R_3 = \begin{pmatrix} 3 & 0 \\ 2 & 1 \end{pmatrix} \qquad R_4 = \begin{pmatrix} 1 & -2 \\ 0 & -1 \end{pmatrix}$$

We have

$$-R_4 R_3 R_2 e_1 = \begin{pmatrix} 1 \\ 2 \end{pmatrix} \qquad -R_4 R_3 e_2 = \begin{pmatrix} 2 \\ 1 \end{pmatrix} \qquad -R_4 e_1 = \begin{pmatrix} -1 \\ 0 \end{pmatrix} \qquad -e_2 = \begin{pmatrix} 0 \\ -1 \end{pmatrix}$$

and the resulting full tableau

$$\begin{pmatrix} 1 & 2 & -1 & 0 \\ 2 & 1 & 0 & -1 \end{pmatrix}$$

is the one underlying Example 3.

For the SMT encoding, we generate variables for the lower and upper bounds l_i and u_i and the assignments x_{ri} after each round r (using $r = 0$ for the initial assignment). For each round, we assert that the assignment satisfies the initial tableau, that the nonbasic variables that remain nonbasic do not change their value, that the pivoting step is suitable, and that the new nonbasic variable is assigned its lower bound in cases (L_+) and (L_-) of the suitability conditions or its upper bound in cases (U_+) and (U_-). Finally we assert that the final assignment equals the initial one.

We automated the above process for the case of two constraints, with pivoting steps alternating between the first and the second row. All but two of the matrices R_i are generated randomly, picking coefficients from the set of simple numbers $\{p/q \mid |p|, |q| < 4\}$. The final two matrices are computed from the constraint $R_n R_{n-1} \ldots R_1 = I$: Denoting the unknown coefficients of R_2 and R_1 by a, b, c, and d, the constraint can be written as

$$(R_n R_{n-1} \ldots R_3)^{-1} = R_2 R_1 = \begin{pmatrix} 1 & a \\ 0 & b \end{pmatrix} \begin{pmatrix} c & 0 \\ d & 1 \end{pmatrix} = \begin{pmatrix} c + ad & a \\ bd & b \end{pmatrix}$$

From this we can read off a, b, d, and c, in that order, provided that $b \neq 0$.

As a final refinement, we let the number of rounds be $2n$ instead of n. This means that we perform the sequence of pivoting steps twice. This is useful because the assignment of the nonbasic variables may alternate between lower and upper bounds. Indeed exactly this happens in Example 3. The resulting set of constraints is passed to an SMT solver (in our case, Yices [8]).

We rely on the SMT solver to produce simple numbers for the assignments, which, as evidenced by Example 3, works well enough. In order to obtain this simple cycle, the termination condition in Fig. 4 takes simplicity into account. The individual SMT problems are very simple; generating a problem and solving it with Yices takes well under 0.01 s on a Core i7-4600U (2.1 GHz) CPU, with most of the time spent in the OS rather than doing productive work. For Example 3 we filtered out unsatisfiable problems, and discarded all answers that contain numbers greater than 11; an average run succeeded after about 2000 iterations and took under 15 s to complete on the mentioned hardware.

5 Constructing Cycles Using Nonlinear Real Arithmetic

The approach outlined in Sect. 4 is slightly unsatisfactory, because it involves guessing. We also tried using support for nonlinear real arithmetic (NRA) to delegate this task to the SMT solver. We tried this for both the DPLL(T) simplex method and the standard simplex method using Dantzig's pivot selection rule.

5.1 DPLL(T) Simplex

For the DPLL(T) simplex method, we fix a sequence of pivoting steps. Here we include the information which of the bounds the basic variable being pivoted violates. Then we introduce variables for the entries of the initial tableau, the lower and upper bounds, and the assignments after each round. As in Sect. 4, we assert that each assignment satisfies the initial tableau, and that the basic variable chosen in each step violates its selected bound. In order to ensure suitability, we encode that the nonbasic variable changes in the right direction; formally, if x_j denotes the value before the pivoting step and x_j' the value after the pivoting step, we assert that

$$(x_j < u_j \wedge x_j < x_j') \vee (x_j > l_j \wedge x_j > x_j')$$

This way we avoid having to compute the entries of the intermediate tableaux. With this approach we obtain the following examples using Yices (version 2.5.2) and Z3 (version 4.5.0):[3]

Example 7. The DPLL(T) simplex method cycles with the constraints

$$
\begin{array}{lll}
x_3 = x_1 + 2x_2 & -\frac{5}{8} \leqslant x_1 \leqslant -\frac{9}{16} & -4 \leqslant x_2 \leqslant 1 \\
x_4 = -x_1 - \frac{1}{2}x_2 & -\frac{9}{2} \leqslant x_3 \leqslant -4 & 0 \leqslant x_4 \leqslant 4
\end{array}
$$

and initial assignment $x_1 = -\frac{5}{8}$, $x_2 = -4$, $x_3 = -\frac{69}{8}$, and $x_4 = \frac{21}{8}$. This example was obtained using Yices. Z3 produces the following cycling problem:

$$
\begin{array}{lll}
x_3 = x_1 + 8x_2 & \frac{1}{2} \leqslant x_1 \leqslant 2 & \frac{1}{8} \leqslant x_2 \leqslant 2 \\
x_4 = -x_1 - x_2 & 6 \leqslant x_3 \leqslant 13 & -\frac{17}{4} \leqslant x_4 \leqslant \frac{1}{8}
\end{array}
$$

with initial assignment $x_1 = \frac{1}{2}$, $x_2 = \frac{1}{8}$, $x_3 = \frac{3}{2}$, and $x_4 = -\frac{5}{8}$.

The numbers obtained this way are not nearly as nice as those obtained by the approach based on linear real arithmetic. We tried tweaking the result by fixing some of the bounds or tableau entries, but found that it's hard to steer Yices and Z3 towards nice solutions.

5.2   Standard Simplex

This section is concerned with the standard simplex method, which is used for solving linear optimization problems of the shape

$$
\begin{array}{ll}
\text{minimize} & \sum_{j \in N} c_j x_j \\
\text{subject to} & x_i + \sum_{j \in N} a_{ij} x_j = b_i \quad \text{for } i \in B \\
& x_i \geqslant 0 \qquad\qquad\quad \text{for } i \in N \cup B
\end{array}
$$

where we again distinguish between basic variables x_i ($i \in B$) and nonbasic variables x_j ($j \in N$). The simplex method maintains a tableau consisting of the coefficients a_{ij}, b_i, and c_j for $i \in B$ and $j \in N$ satisfying the condition $b_i \geqslant 0$ for $i \in B$, which ensures that the assignment $x_j = 0$ for $j \in N$ and $x_i = b_i$ for $i \in B$ satisfies the constraints. If no c_j ($j \in N$) is negative then the optimum has been

---

[3] While CVC4 [3] (snapshot version 2017-06-14) also has support for NRA, it cannot produce models, making it unfit for our purposes.

reached; otherwise, we select a nonbasic variable x_j corresponding to a negative c_j, and look for a basic variable x_i such that a_{ij} is positive. (If there is no such basic variable then the problem is unbounded.) These two constraints determine the *suitable* pivoting pairs. To pivot x_i and x_j, we use the substitution

$$x_j = \frac{1}{a_{ij}} \left(b_i - x_i - \sum_{j' \in N - \{j\}} a_{ij'} x_{j'} \right)$$

in the given tableau and the objective function. There are several pivot selection rules for the standard simplex method. One is Bland's rule, which ensures termination; it picks the smallest (nonbasic) variable index among the negative values c_j, and the smallest index among the basic variables that are suitable for pivoting with the selected nonbasic variable.

Here we focus on Dantzig's traditional pivoting rule, which tries to reduce the value of the objective function as quickly as possible. This is the oldest pivoting rule, and it is of interest to us because it fails to ensure termination. To this end, the nonbasic variable x_j is selected such that the value c_j is as small as possible (ties are broken by variable index). The basic variable x_i is selected such that $\frac{b_i}{a_{ij}}$ is minimized. Again, ties are broken in favor of smaller variable indices.

For the standard simplex method, we first tried a very naive encoding in an attempt to find cycles of length 6. However, the trick from Sect. 5.1, to express all constraints in terms of the initial tableau, does not work here, because pivot selection depends on the objective function (which has to be expressed in terms of the nonbasic variables) and the pivoting elements in the tableau. Therefore, as a first attempt, we introduced variables for all tableau entries for each rounds in the assumed cycle, which were defined in terms of the pivoting element and the preceding tableau. As a simplification, which is inspired by Avis *et al.* [1], we assume that $b_i = 0$ for $i \in B$, so the minimization of $\frac{b_i}{a_{ij}}$ has no effect.

This turned out to be too much for Yices and Z3, perhaps because of the large number of functions and variables (for 6 pivoting steps and 6 variables in the tableau, the encoding requires 98 real variables for coefficients and tableau entries) and we did not obtain any cycling tableau from this encoding.

In the end we adopted an approach by Zörnig [20], which avoids divisions and requires fewer variables (26 instead of 98 for a cycle of length 6 with 6 variables). In this approach, all constraints are expressed in terms of the initial tableau using subdeterminants. We demonstrate this by an example, where we try to find a cycling tableau with two constraints and six variables $x_1, \ldots, x_6$ where the basic variables follow the cycle

$$x_5, x_6 \rightarrow x_1, x_6 \rightarrow x_1, x_2 \rightarrow x_3, x_2 \rightarrow x_3, x_4 \rightarrow x_5, x_4 \rightarrow x_5, x_6 \rightarrow \cdots$$

We can express the initial tableau by

$$Ax = \begin{pmatrix} a_{11} & a_{12} & a_{13} & a_{14} & 1 & 0 \\ a_{21} & a_{22} & a_{23} & a_{24} & 0 & 1 \\ \hline c_1 & c_2 & c_3 & c_4 & 0 & 0 \end{pmatrix} \quad x = \begin{pmatrix} 0 \\ 0 \\ z \end{pmatrix}$$

where $\boldsymbol{x} = (x_1, x_2, x_3, x_4, x_5, x_6)^T$, z is the value of the objective function, and we have already set $b_i = 0$ for $i \in \{1, 2\}$. In order to obtain the tableau with basic variables x_i, x_j, we have to perform row operations that result in the corresponding columns to become unit vectors; this can be expressed as

$$A'\boldsymbol{x} = \begin{pmatrix} a_{1i} & a_{1j} & 0 \\ a_{2i} & a_{2j} & 0 \\ c_i & c_j & 1 \end{pmatrix}^{-1} \begin{pmatrix} a_{11} & a_{12} & a_{13} & a_{14} & 1 & 0 \\ a_{21} & a_{22} & a_{23} & a_{24} & 0 & 1 \\ c_1 & c_2 & c_3 & c_4 & 0 & 0 \end{pmatrix} \boldsymbol{x} = \begin{pmatrix} 0 \\ 0 \\ z \end{pmatrix}$$

Following Zörnig, let D_{ij} and $\overline{D}_{ijk}$ be defined as

$$D_{ij} = \begin{vmatrix} a_{1i} & a_{1j} \\ a_{2i} & a_{2j} \end{vmatrix} \qquad\qquad \overline{D}_{ijk} = \begin{vmatrix} a_{1i} & a_{1j} & a_{1k} \\ a_{2i} & a_{2j} & a_{2k} \\ c_i & c_j & c_k \end{vmatrix}$$

Using what is essentially Cramer's rule, the k-th column of the tableau A' equals

$$\begin{pmatrix} a'_{1k} \\ a'_{2k} \\ c'_k \end{pmatrix} = \frac{1}{D_{ij}} \begin{pmatrix} D_{kj} \\ D_{ik} \\ \overline{D}_{ijk} \end{pmatrix}$$

Now, for the pivoting step from x_i, x_j to x_k, x_j to be valid, the following constraints need to be satisfied:

- $a'_{1,k} > 0$: D_{ij} and D_{kj} have equal signs, and $D_{ij} \neq 0$.
- $c'_k < 0$: $\overline{D}_{ijk}$ and D_{ij} have opposite signs.
- c'_k is minimal, and ties are broken by smaller variable index: if $D_{ij} > 0$ ($D_{ij} < 0$), then $\overline{D}_{ijk'} > \overline{D}_{ijk}$ ($\overline{D}_{ijk'} < \overline{D}_{ijk}$) for $k' < k$ and $\overline{D}_{ijk'} \geqslant \overline{D}_{ijk}$ ($\overline{D}_{ijk'} \leqslant \overline{D}_{ijk}$) for $k' > k$.
- no variable with smaller index can enter the basis: if $j < k$ then $a'_{2,k} < 0$, i.e., D_{ij} and D_{ik} have opposite signs.

Analogous conditions can be derived for pivoting steps from x_i, x_j to x_i, x_k. In fact by the first constraint, we will always have $D_{ij} > 0$, because $D_{56} = 1 > 0$ in the initial tableau. Using this encoding the following example is obtained using Yices; Z3 did not produce an answer within 600 s.

Example 8. The following optimization problem cycles when using the standard simplex method with Dantzig's pivot selection rule:

$$\begin{aligned}
\text{minimize} \quad & -6x_1 + 46x_2 + 7x_3 + \tfrac{97}{32}x_4 \\
\text{subject to} \quad & -x_5 = \tfrac{1}{2}x_1 - 4x_2 - \tfrac{3}{4}x_3 - \tfrac{25}{64}x_4 \\
& -x_6 = 4x_2 + x_3 + \tfrac{1}{2}x_4 \\
& x_1, \ldots, x_6 \geqslant 0
\end{aligned}$$

With some manual tweaking (by fixing some of the values of the tableau in the SMT encoding), we obtain the following, nicer optimization problem:

$$\text{minimize} \quad -\tfrac{3}{4}x_1 + 4x_2 + x_3 + \tfrac{5}{13}x_4$$
$$\text{subject to} \quad -x_5 = \tfrac{1}{3}x_1 - 2x_2 - \tfrac{2}{3}x_3 - \tfrac{1}{3}x_4$$
$$-x_6 = 2x_2 + x_3 + \tfrac{6}{13}x_4$$
$$x_1, \dots, x_6 \geqslant 0$$

The cycle is given in Fig. 5.

$$
\begin{array}{c}
\begin{array}{cccc} x_1 & x_2 & x_3 & x_4 \end{array} \\
\begin{array}{c} -x_5 \\ -x_6 \\ \text{min:} \end{array}
\left(\begin{array}{cccc}
\boxed{\tfrac{1}{3}} & -2 & -\tfrac{2}{3} & -\tfrac{1}{3} \\
0 & 2 & 1 & \tfrac{6}{13} \\
-\tfrac{3}{4} & 4 & 1 & \tfrac{5}{13}
\end{array}\right)
\end{array}
\qquad
\begin{array}{c}
\begin{array}{cccc} x_5 & x_6 & x_1 & x_4 \end{array} \\
\begin{array}{c} -x_3 \\ -x_2 \\ {} \end{array}
\left(\begin{array}{cccc}
3 & 3 & 1 & \tfrac{5}{13} \\
-\tfrac{3}{2} & -1 & -\tfrac{1}{2} & \boxed{\tfrac{1}{26}} \\
3 & 1 & \tfrac{1}{4} & -\tfrac{2}{13}
\end{array}\right)
\end{array}
$$

$$
\begin{array}{c}
\begin{array}{cccc} x_5 & x_2 & x_3 & x_4 \end{array} \\
\begin{array}{c} -x_1 \\ -x_6 \\ {} \end{array}
\left(\begin{array}{cccc}
3 & -6 & -2 & -1 \\
0 & \boxed{2} & 1 & \tfrac{6}{13} \\
\tfrac{9}{4} & -\tfrac{1}{2} & -\tfrac{1}{2} & -\tfrac{19}{52}
\end{array}\right)
\end{array}
\qquad
\begin{array}{c}
\begin{array}{cccc} x_5 & x_6 & x_1 & x_2 \end{array} \\
\begin{array}{c} -x_3 \\ -x_4 \\ {} \end{array}
\left(\begin{array}{cccc}
\boxed{18} & 13 & 6 & -10 \\
-39 & -26 & -13 & 26 \\
-3 & -3 & -\tfrac{7}{4} & 4
\end{array}\right)
\end{array}
$$

$$
\begin{array}{c}
\begin{array}{cccc} x_5 & x_6 & x_3 & x_4 \end{array} \\
\begin{array}{c} -x_1 \\ -x_2 \\ {} \end{array}
\left(\begin{array}{cccc}
3 & 3 & \boxed{1} & \tfrac{5}{13} \\
0 & \tfrac{1}{2} & \tfrac{1}{2} & \tfrac{3}{13} \\
\tfrac{9}{4} & \tfrac{1}{4} & -\tfrac{1}{4} & -\tfrac{1}{4}
\end{array}\right)
\end{array}
\qquad
\begin{array}{c}
\begin{array}{cccc} x_3 & x_6 & x_1 & x_2 \end{array} \\
\begin{array}{c} -x_5 \\ -x_4 \\ {} \end{array}
\left(\begin{array}{cccc}
\tfrac{1}{18} & \tfrac{13}{18} & \tfrac{1}{3} & -\tfrac{5}{9} \\
\tfrac{13}{6} & \boxed{\tfrac{13}{6}} & 0 & \tfrac{13}{3} \\
\tfrac{1}{6} & -\tfrac{5}{6} & -\tfrac{3}{4} & \tfrac{7}{3}
\end{array}\right)
\end{array}
$$

Fig. 5. The cycle of length 6 in Example 8.

In contrast to the encoding in Sect. 4, the SMT encodings for this section were produced manually. This is made feasible by the fact that the SMT-LIB format supports function definitions. For example, we defined an abbreviation for the determinant of a 3×3 matrix:

```
(define-fun det3
  ((c11 Real) (c12 Real) (c13 Real)
   (c21 Real) (c22 Real) (c23 Real)
   (c31 Real) (c32 Real) (c33 Real))
  Real
  (- (+ (* c11 c22 c33) (* c12 c23 c31) (* c13 c21 c32))
     (+ (* c11 c23 c32) (* c12 c21 c33) (* c13 c22 c31)))))
```

6 Related Work

Perhaps the closest related work is Zörnig's paper [20], which explores the idea of employing a computer program for finding cycles in the standard simplex method.

Zörnig uses LINGO (a commercial program for nonlinear optimization) for this purpose. His work goes into a different direction from ours. Whereas we are mainly interested in the DPLL(T) simplex method, Zörnig explores several pivot selection rules and also synthesizes a cycle of odd length. The latter requires working with more than 2 constraints, cf. [20, Eq. (5.6)].

There is a rich body of literature about loops in the standard simplex method, starting with Hoffmann [13] and Beale [4]. A survey of cycles with visualizations of the trajectories was produced by Avis *et al.* [1]. As far as we know, all of these examples have been found manually. As part of this work, we reconstructed the cycles presented in the latter paper. Below we make a few observations.

- The example attributed to Beale does not appear in [4], where instead the following cycling tableau is given:

$$
\begin{aligned}
\text{minimize} \quad & -\tfrac{3}{4}x_1 + 20x_2 - \tfrac{1}{2}x_3 + 6x_4 \\
\text{subject to} \quad & \tfrac{1}{4}x_1 - 8x_2 - x_3 + 9x_4 + x_5 = 0 \\
& \tfrac{1}{2}x_1 - 12x_2 - \tfrac{1}{2}x_3 + 3x_4 + x_6 = 0
\end{aligned}
$$

- There are sign errors in the objective functions of Beale's example ($+150x_2$ should be $-150x_2$) and Marshall and Suurballe's example [15] (which should read $z = 0 + x_3 - 7x_4 - 1x_5 - 2x_6$).
- The examples by Sierksma [17], Yudin and Gol'shtein [19], and Solow [18] violate Dantzig's pivot selection rule; in the last case, only the tie-breaking rule for the basic variable is violated. Solow's cycle is similar to Kuhn's in that it is based on two pivoting steps that result in a cyclic shift of the variables. After four steps, the first tableau of Fig. 6 is reached. Then x_1 is pivoted with x_5. In the sixth step, x_2 is pivoted with x_6, but by Dantzig's rule we should select x_1 as the new basic variable instead of x_6.

$$
\begin{array}{c|cccc}
 & x_1 & x_2 & x_3 & x_4 \\
\hline
-x_5 & \boxed{2} & 1 & -3 & -1 \\
-x_6 & -7 & -3 & 7 & 2 \\
\hline
\text{min:} & -2 & -2 & 8 & 2
\end{array}
\qquad
\begin{array}{c|cccc}
 & x_5 & x_6 & x_3 & x_4 \\
\hline
-x_1 & -3 & -1 & \boxed{2} & 1 \\
-x_2 & 7 & 2 & -7 & -3 \\
\hline
 & 8 & 2 & -2 & -2
\end{array}
$$

$$
\begin{array}{c|cccc}
 & x_5 & x_2 & x_3 & x_4 \\
\hline
-x_1 & \tfrac{1}{2} & \tfrac{1}{2} & -\tfrac{3}{2} & -\tfrac{1}{2} \\
-x_6 & \tfrac{7}{2} & \boxed{\tfrac{1}{2}} & -\tfrac{7}{2} & -\tfrac{3}{2} \\
\hline
 & 1 & -1 & 5 & 1
\end{array}
\qquad \vdots
$$

Fig. 6. One third of Solow's cycle of length 6 [18]

7   Conclusion

In this paper we have presented a new approach for finding cycles in the simplex method, both for the traditional method and, for the first time, for the DPLL(T) variant which is used in SMT solvers to solve quantifier-free linear arithmetic constraint problems.

Any cycle in the simplex method induces a cycle in the dual simplex method by switching to the dual optimization problem. The absence of an objective function means that this observation does not immediately carry over to the DPLL(T) simplex method. However, if a cycling tableau has shape $x_B + Ax_N = 0$, which is the case for all examples collected by Avis et al. [1], then dualization produces a constant objective function, and in this case, the cycle can be reproduced in the DPLL(T) simplex method. We have seen this in Example 4. It is noteworthy that this approach cannot produce Example 3, which relies on the fact that every variable comes with two constraints. In fact, Beale [4] observed that any cycle in the standard simplex method with two constraints requires at least 6 steps, and correspondingly, 6 variables, because each bound $x_i \geqslant 0$ produces one of the potential lines the trajectory can move along. Our 4 variable example works because for each variable, we get a pair of two parallel lines that can be used on the trajectory. Beale's first observation remains valid; indeed our cycle length 8 is greater than 6.

While working on Zörnig's encoding for the standard simplex we noticed that sometimes small changes (like switching from a strict inequality to a nonstrict one) resulted in Yices taking a longer time than we were willing to wait; we did not study this phenomenon systematically, but this suggests that these encodings are interesting benchmarks for nonlinear real arithmetic.

Acknowledgements. We thank the reviewers for their constructive feedback.

References

1. Avis, D., Kaluzny, B., Titley-Péloquin, D.: Visualizing and constructing cycles in the simplex method. Oper. Res. **56**(2), 512–518 (2008). doi:10.1287/opre.1070.0474
2. Balinski, M.L., Tucker, A.W.: Duality theory of linear programs: a constructive approach with applications. SIAM Rev. **11**(3), 347–377 (1969). doi:10.1137/1011060
3. Barrett, C., Conway, C.L., Deters, M., Hadarean, L., Jovanović, D., King, T., Reynolds, A., Tinelli, C.: CVC4. In: Gopalakrishnan, G., Qadeer, S. (eds.) CAV 2011. LNCS, vol. 6806, pp. 171–177. Springer, Heidelberg (2011). doi:10.1007/978-3-642-22110-1_14
4. Beale, E.M.L.: Cycling in the dual simplex algorithm. Naval Res. Logistics Q. **2**, 269–275 (1955). doi:10.1002/nav.3800020406
5. Moura, L., Bjørner, N.: Z3: an efficient SMT solver. In: Ramakrishnan, C.R., Rehof, J. (eds.) TACAS 2008. LNCS, vol. 4963, pp. 337–340. Springer, Heidelberg (2008). doi:10.1007/978-3-540-78800-3_24
6. Bland, R.G.: New finite pivoting rules for the simplex method. Math. Oper. Res. **2**(2), 103–107 (1977). doi:10.1287/moor.2.2.103

7. Bradley, A.R., Manna, Z.: The Calculus of Computation—Decision Procedures with Applications to Verification. Springer, Heidelberg (2007). doi:10.1007/978-3-540-74113-8

8. Dutertre, B.: Yices 2.2. In: Biere, A., Bloem, R. (eds.) CAV 2014. LNCS, vol. 8559, pp. 737–744. Springer, Cham (2014). doi:10.1007/978-3-319-08867-9_49

9. Dutertre, B., Moura, L.: A fast linear-arithmetic solver for DPLL(T). In: Ball, T., Jones, R.B. (eds.) CAV 2006. LNCS, vol. 4144, pp. 81–94. Springer, Heidelberg (2006). doi:10.1007/11817963_11

10. Dutertre, B., de Moura, L.: Integrating simplex with DPLL(T). Technical report SRI-CSL-06-01, SRI International (2006)

11. Goldfarb, D., Reid, J.K.: A practicable steepest-edge simplex algorithm. Math. Program. **12**(1), 361–371 (1977). doi:10.1007/BF01593804

12. Harris, P.M.J.: Pivot selection methods of the Devex LP code. Math. Program. **5**(1), 1–28 (1973). doi:10.1007/BF01580108

13. Hoffman, A.J.: Cycling in the simplex algorithm. Technical report, 2974. National Bureau of Standards (1953)

14. Kroening, D., Strichman, O.: Decision Procedures—An Algorithmic Point of View. Springer, Heidelberg (2008). doi:10.1007/978-3-540-74105-3

15. Marshall, K., Suurballe, J.: A note on cycling in the simplex method. Naval Res. Logistics Q. **16**(1), 121–137 (1969). doi:10.1002/nav.3800160110

16. Pan, P.Q.: A largest-distance pivot rule for the simplex algorithm. Eur. J. Oper. Res. **187**(2), 393–402 (2008). doi:10.1016/j.ejor.2007.03.026

17. Sierksma, G.: Linear and Integer Programming, 2nd edn. Marcel Dekker Inc., New York City (1996)

18. Solow, D.: Linear Programming: An Introduction to Finite Improvement Algorithms. North-Holland, Amsterdam (1984)

19. Yudin, D.B., Gol'shtein, E.G.: Linear programming. In: Israel Program of Scientific Translations (1965)

20. Zörnig, P.: Systematic construction of examples for cycling in the simplex method. Comput. Oper. Res. **33**(8), 2247–2262 (2006). doi:10.1016/j.cor.2005.02.001

Tableaux with Partial Caching for Hybrid PDL with Satisfaction Statements

Agathoklis Kritsimallis$^{(\boxtimes)}$

Larissa, Greece
agiskr@gmail.com

Abstract. We give a novel deterministic tableau-based satisfiability algorithm for Hybrid Propositional Dynamic Logic (i.e. PDL with nominals) with satisfaction statements (HPDL@). It builds and-or graphs in which it detects unfulfilled eventualities and unifies nodes (due to nominals) on-the-fly. There are two kinds of nodes: *sentential* nodes that represent partial descriptions of worlds of a model and *unification* nodes that deal with nominals. The main technical achievement of this work is the determination of the necessary information that a sentential node should have so that caching is feasible. Each saturated sentential node is available for reuse until it becomes out of date, due to loop dependencies. Thus, the algorithm runs in double exponential time. However, for iteration-free formulas, loops do not occur and thus, it works in exponential time. Nevertheless, despite the iteration operator, thanks to partial caching, the algorithm has the potential to achieve acceptable performance.

1 Introduction

The satisfiability problem of Propositional Dynamic Logic (PDL) [5,12] is ExpTime-complete. Various decision procedures have been given such as best-case exponential [22], working in multiple stages [19,23], on-the-fly [6] and with analytic cut-rule for the converse [6,19], most of them based on and-or tableaux [7]. The algorithm of [10] and its extension for the converse [11] reveal the crucial role that global caching plays to the achievement of an optimal algorithm.

The origin of Hybrid Logics [2,4] goes back to Arthur Prior's work on tense logic [24]. In the literature, various extensions of the basic modal logic with nominals have been studied. They usually include satisfaction statements, the universal modality, the difference modality and the converse modality. In [3,13,25], prefixed tableau systems are given for such logics.

Nominals are also met in description logics as (named) instances of concepts. The algorithm in [8] concerns hybrid logics with coalgebraic semantics (which can be instantiated for $\mathcal{ALCO}$). Nominals are handled through @-constraints which correspond to sets of satisfaction statements that concern appropriate and-subgraphs of a tableau. In the algorithms of [17] and [18] for $\mathcal{SHIO}$ and $\mathcal{SHOQ}$, respectively, an on-demand cut rule is used. It is restricted to formulas that are imposed by the nominals and it requires the re-expansion of nodes.

© Springer International Publishing AG 2017
D.V. Hung and D. Kapur (Eds.): ICTAC 2017, LNCS 10580, pp. 229–247, 2017.
DOI: 10.1007/978-3-319-67729-3_14

We refer to the extension of PDL with nominals as hybrid PDL (HPDL) and we denote HPDL with satisfaction statements as HPDL@. Hybrid PDL with the universal modality was introduced in [20,21]. Similarly to PDL, the satisfiability problem of HPDL@ is ExpTime-complete [1,14]. A best-case exponential algorithm for HPDL with the difference modality and the converse is given in [14].

The issues that arise with HPDL@ are the same with PDL, such as fulfillment of eventualities, caching and working on-the-fly. In addition to them, we have to consider the nominals which make things even more complex. It is clear that any unifications of nodes that may take place due to nominals affect the fulfilling paths of eventualities, as well as the required cached information for a node.

In [15], a tableau-based satisfiability algorithm for HPDL is given which succeeds to handle eventualities and nominals. It is a NExpTime algorithm and it processes graphs of exponential size. In these graphs, only and-branching is permitted, whereas whenever disjunctions occur, backtracking is used. The literature [8–11,17–19] has shown that caching is very important in devising optimal algorithms. Since the approach of [15] works on graphs and not on sets of formulas, in our view, it does not seem possible to be extended to exploit caching. The authors of [15] state that devising worst-case optimal decision procedures for modal logics with nominals and eventualities is an open problem.

Here, we give a novel deterministic tableau-based satisfiability algorithm for HPDL@. It defines a tableau as a variant of an and-or graph in which there are two kinds of nodes: *sentential* nodes that represent partial descriptions of worlds of a model and *unification* nodes that deal with nominals which appear in more than one sentential node. To avoid world cycles of eventualities within a node, inspired by the approach of [15], the algorithm examines in advance the way that the eventualities are reduced by the usual static rules. Without being necessary to examine global properties of a tableau in multiple subsequent passes, the algorithm detects unfulfilled eventualities on-the-fly and unifies sentential nodes (due to some nominal), based on the local information of a unification node.

The main technical achievement of this work is the determination of the necessary information that a sentential node should have so that its reuse is possible. This allows us to partially cache the saturated sentential nodes, ensure the termination of the algorithm and restrict the expansion of a tableau in a more effective way. The nodes of the branch under expansion are cached so that we can block its possible infinite expansion due to the iteration operator. Nodes of earlier defined branches are also cached. In general, each saturated sentential node is available for possible reuse, but the moment that it becomes out of date due to loop dependencies, its reuse is not allowed anymore.

The algorithm runs in double exponential time, as loop dependencies restrict the caching of nodes. On the other hand, in the case of iteration-free formulas, loops do not occur and thus, all the nodes are free from dependencies. Therefore, all the saturated sentential nodes are cached and the algorithm works in single exponential time. Moreover, in the general case, despite the iteration operator, since all the saturated nodes which are not involved in a loop are cached, the algorithm has the potential to achieve acceptable performance.

Due to lack of space and due to the technical nature of the algorithm, detailed proofs of correctness are available in the extended version of this paper [16].

The paper is organized as follows. In Sect. 2, we give the syntax and the semantics of HPDL@ and we introduce all the necessary concepts related to the reduction sets of α/β formulas. In Sect. 3, we present our algorithm along with an example and in Sect. 4, we conclude our work.

2   Preliminaries

HPDL@ extends PDL with nominals and satisfaction statements. Nominals designate atomic properties, but with the difference that they uniquely identify states. The satisfaction statements $@_x\varphi$ express that the single state which satisfies the nominal x should also satisfy the formula φ. We consider countable disjoint sets of atomic propositions and of nominals, denoted as AtF and N, respectively, designating their union by At. We also consider a countable set AtP of atomic programs. In what follows, p, q range over atomic formulas, x, y, z over nominals and a, b, c over atomic programs. The formal syntax of HPDL@ is presented below.

$$\mathcal{L}_s \ni \varphi := p \mid x \mid \neg\varphi \mid [A]\varphi \mid @_x\varphi \qquad \mathcal{L}_a \ni A := a \mid \varphi \mid AA \mid A + A \mid A^*$$

We adopt a slightly different notation from the one usually met in the literature and we write AA for $A; A, A + A$ for $A \cup A$, and φ for φ?, when φ acts as a program. The possibility operator $\langle\rangle$ and the propositional connectives are not taken as primitive, but they can be defined as usual.

Definition 1. *A frame $\mathcal{F}$ is a structure $\langle W, (\overset{a}{\rightsquigarrow})_{a \in AtP} \rangle$ where W is a set of states and $\rightsquigarrow$ is a transition function assigning to each atomic program a a binary relation $\overset{a}{\rightsquigarrow} \subseteq W \times W$. A model $\mathcal{M}$ is a structure $\langle \mathcal{F}, \rho \rangle$ where $\mathcal{F}$ is a frame and $\rho : At \longrightarrow 2^W$ is an interpretation function of atomic formulas with the restriction that $\forall x \in N \ |\rho(x)| = 1$. The interpretation function ρ and the transition function $\rightsquigarrow$ are extended to all the formulas φ (through the function $[\![]\!]_\rho^{\mathcal{F}} : \mathcal{L}_s \longrightarrow 2^W$) and to all the programs A, respectively, as shown in Table 1.*

Table 1. The interpretation of the HPDL@ language

$[\![p]\!]_\rho^{\mathcal{F}} = \rho(p)$	$\overset{a}{\rightsquigarrow} \subseteq W \times W$
$[\![x]\!]_\rho^{\mathcal{F}} = \rho(x)$	$\overset{\varphi}{\rightsquigarrow} = \{(w, w) \mid w \in [\![\varphi]\!]_\rho^{\mathcal{F}}\}$
$[\![@_x\varphi]\!]_\rho^{\mathcal{F}} = \begin{cases} W & \text{if } \rho(x) \subseteq [\![\varphi]\!]_\rho^{\mathcal{F}} \\ \emptyset & \text{if } \rho(x) \not\subseteq [\![\varphi]\!]_\rho^{\mathcal{F}} \end{cases}$	$\overset{A+B}{\rightsquigarrow} = \overset{A}{\rightsquigarrow} \cup \overset{B}{\rightsquigarrow}$
$[\![\neg\varphi]\!]_\rho^{\mathcal{F}} = W \setminus [\![\varphi]\!]_\rho^{\mathcal{F}}$	$\overset{AB}{\rightsquigarrow} = \overset{A}{\rightsquigarrow}\overset{B}{\rightsquigarrow}$
$[\![[A]\varphi]\!]_\rho^{\mathcal{F}} = \{w \in W \mid \forall w' \in W(w \overset{A}{\rightsquigarrow} w' \Rightarrow w' \in [\![\varphi]\!]_\rho^{\mathcal{F}})\}$	$\overset{A^*}{\rightsquigarrow} = \bigcup_{n \geq 0} \left(\overset{A}{\rightsquigarrow}\right)^n$

Due to the iteration operator, we are interested in formulas of the form $\neg[A_1]\cdots[A_k][A^*]\varphi$, for some $k \geq 0$. We call them *eventualities* and their set is designated by Ev. In Table 2, we follow the Smullyan's unifying notation which classifies the conjunctive cases as α-formulas and the disjunctive as β-formulas.

Table 2. The α and β-formulas

α	$\neg\neg\varphi$	$\neg[\psi]\varphi$	$[AB]\varphi$	$\neg[AB]\varphi$	$[A{+}B]\varphi$	$[A^*]\varphi$	β	$[\psi]\varphi$	$\neg[A{+}B]\varphi$	$\neg[A^*]\varphi$
α_1	φ	$\neg\varphi$	$[A][B]\varphi$	$\neg[A][B]\varphi$	$[A]\varphi$	φ	β_1	$\neg\psi$	$\neg[A]\varphi$	$\neg\varphi$
α_2		ψ			$[B]\varphi$	$[A][A^*]\varphi$	β_2	φ	$\neg[B]\varphi$	$\neg[A][A^*]\varphi$

Definition 2. *The* decomposition set $\mathcal{D}(\varphi)$ *of an* α/β *eventuality* φ *is a set of triples* $(\mathcal{P}, \mathcal{T}, \vartheta)$ *where* $\mathcal{P}, \mathcal{T} \subseteq \mathcal{L}_s$ *are sets of formulas and* ϑ *is a formula. It contains the triple* $(\emptyset, \emptyset, \varphi)$ *and it is closed under the following decomposition rules, where a rule* $\frac{(\mathcal{P}, \mathcal{T}, \vartheta)}{(\mathcal{P}', \mathcal{T}', \vartheta')}$ *is applied iff* ϑ *is an eventuality and* $\vartheta \notin \mathcal{P}$:

$$\frac{(\mathcal{P}, \mathcal{T}, \beta)}{(\mathcal{P} \cup \{\beta\}, \mathcal{T}, \beta_1)} \qquad \frac{(\mathcal{P}, \mathcal{T}, \beta)}{(\mathcal{P} \cup \{\beta\}, \mathcal{T}, \beta_2)} \qquad \frac{(\mathcal{P}, \mathcal{T}, \alpha)}{(\mathcal{P} \cup \{\alpha\}, \mathcal{T} \cup \{\alpha_2\}, \alpha_1)}$$

The finalized decomposition set $\mathcal{FD}(\varphi)$ *is the set of all the pairs* $(\mathcal{T}, \vartheta)$ *such that there is a triple* $(\mathcal{P}, \mathcal{T}, \vartheta)$ *in* $\mathcal{D}(\varphi)$ *such that no decomposition rule can be applied to it and at the same time,* ϑ *is not in* $\mathcal{P}$.

Definition 3. *The (family of)* reduction sets $\mathcal{R}_1^\varphi, \ldots, \mathcal{R}_n^\varphi \subseteq \mathcal{L}_s$ *of an* α/β *formula* φ, *for some* $n \geq 1$ *(called the* reduction degree *of* φ), *are defined as follows:*

- *If* φ *is an* α *non-eventuality, then* $\mathcal{R}_1^\varphi = \{\alpha_1, \alpha_2\}$ *is its only reduction set.*
- *If* φ *is a* β *non-eventuality, then the family of its reduction sets consists of the singletons* $\mathcal{R}_1^\varphi = \{\beta_1\}$ *and* $\mathcal{R}_2^\varphi = \{\beta_2\}$.
- *If* φ *is an eventuality, then for each pair* $(\mathcal{T}, \vartheta) \in \mathcal{FD}(\varphi)$ *and for* $i = 1, \ldots, n$, *where* n *is equal to the cardinality of* $\mathcal{FD}(\varphi)$, *we define* $\mathcal{R}_i^\varphi = \mathcal{T} \cup \{\vartheta\}$.

Definition 4. *The binary relation* $\triangleright$ *relates formulas* φ *and* ψ *and we write* $\varphi \triangleright \psi$ *iff all the following conditions hold:*

- φ *is an* α/β *formula of the form* $\neg[A]\chi$ *and* ψ *is in one of its reduction sets.*
- *If* φ *is an* α *non-eventuality, then* $\psi = \alpha_1$.
- *If* φ *is a* β *non-eventuality, then* $\psi \in \{\beta_1, \beta_2\}$.
- *If* φ *is an eventuality, then there is a pair* $(\mathcal{T}, \vartheta) \in \mathcal{FD}(\varphi)$ *such that* $\vartheta = \psi$ *(notice that the set* $\mathcal{T} \cup \{\vartheta\}$ *is a reduction set of* φ).

3   The Tableau-Based Satisfiability Algorithm

3.1   Basic Definitions

The following technical definitions facilitate the presentation of the algorithm.

Definition 5. *A* label l *is a pair* $\langle \Phi, \mathbf{rd} \rangle$, *where* Φ *is a set of formulas and* $\mathbf{rd}$ *is a reduction function which assigns to the* α/β *eventualities of* Φ *one of the values 1 and 0 such that for each* α/β *eventuality* $\varphi \in \Phi$, *if* $\mathbf{rd}(\varphi) = 1$, *then at least one of the reduction sets of* φ *is a subset of* Φ.

The active set $\mathbf{actF}$ *of a label* $l = \langle \Phi, \mathbf{rd} \rangle$ *consists of all the formulas of* Φ *such that they are: (i) formulas of the form* $p, \neg p, x, \neg x, @_x\varphi, \neg @_x\varphi, [a]\psi, \neg[a]\psi,$ *or (ii)* α/β *non-eventualities for which none of their reduction sets is a subset of* Φ, *or (iii)* α/β *eventualities* φ *such that* $\mathbf{rd}(\varphi) = 0$.

The reduced set $\mathbf{rdF}$ *of a label* $l = \langle \Phi, \mathbf{rd} \rangle$ *consists of the* α/β *formulas* φ *of* Φ *such that: (i) if* φ *is a non-eventuality, then at least one of its reduction sets is a subset of* Φ *and (ii) if* φ *is an eventuality, then* $\mathbf{rd}(\varphi) = 1$.

A partial label is a label such that its active set contains α/β *formulas. A saturated label is a label which is not a partial one.*

Finally, if l *is a label, then* $\tilde{l}$ *is also a label such that* $\Phi_{\tilde{l}} = \Phi_l \setminus \mathbf{rdF}_l$ *and for all the* α/β *eventualities* φ *of* $\Phi_{\tilde{l}}, \mathbf{rd}_{\tilde{l}}(\varphi) = \mathbf{rd}_l(\varphi)$ *(thus,* $\mathbf{actF}_{\tilde{l}} = \mathbf{actF}_l$ *and* $\mathbf{rdF}_{\tilde{l}} = \emptyset$). *Moreover, if* L *is a set of labels, then* $\tilde{L}$ *is the set* $\{\tilde{l} \mid l \in L\}$.

Intuitively speaking, a label constitutes the main element of a sentential node and its active formulas are used as the principal formulas of the rules of the algorithm. In the case of an α/β eventuality φ of a label $l = \langle \Phi, \mathbf{rd} \rangle$, despite the possible existence of one or more of its reduction sets as subsets of Φ, we consider it as active, until we examine all the ways to fulfill it. This is indicated by the reduction function which assigns to φ the value 1.

Definition 6. *Let* l *be a label and* $\varphi \in \Phi_l$ *an eventuality. The set* $\mathbf{reach}(\varphi, l)$ *is defined as the set of formulas* $\psi \in \Phi_l$ *such that there is a sequence of formulas* $\psi_1, \ldots, \psi_k$ *of* Φ_l, *with* $k \geq 1$, *such that (i)* $\psi_1 = \varphi$ *and* $\psi_k = \psi$, *(ii) for* $i = 1, \ldots, k-1, \psi_i \in (\mathbf{rdF}_l \cap Ev)$ *and* $\psi_i \rhd \psi_{i+1}$ *and there is a reduction set* $\mathcal{R}$ *of* ψ_i *such that* $\psi_{i+1} \in \mathcal{R}$ *and* $\mathcal{R} \subseteq \Phi_l$ *and (iii)* ψ_k *is either an active eventuality of* l, *or a non-eventuality formula of* l.

Definition 7. *A history* h *for a label* l_0, *over a set* L *of saturated labels, is a triple* $\langle \Lambda, \mathbf{r}, \rightarrowtail \rangle$:

- *The set* $\Lambda \subseteq \tilde{L}$ *of nominal labels of* h *is a set of saturated labels such that for each* $l \in \Lambda$, *there is at least one nominal* $x \in N$ *such that* $x \in \mathbf{actF}_l$.
- *The reachability function* $\mathbf{r} : Ev \cap \mathbf{actF}_{l_0} \longrightarrow (\tilde{L} \times Ev) \cup \{\emptyset\} \cup \{FL\}$ *assigns to each active eventuality of* l_0 *a pair of a label and one of that label's active eventualities or the empty set or the constant* FL *(Fulfilling Label).*
- *The fulfillment relation* $\rightarrowtail \subseteq (\Lambda \times Ev) \times ((\tilde{L} \times Ev) \cup \{FL\})$ *relates pairs of labels and their active eventualities, either with pairs of the same form, or with* FL.

Intuitively, a history $h = \langle \Lambda, \mathbf{r}, \rightarrowtail \rangle$ concerns the label of a sentential node and records information for an appropriate and-subgraph of a tableau. Due to or-branching, there are many and-subgraphs for a label and as a result, we should consider the corresponding number of histories. Roughly speaking, a history can be seen as a combination and extension of the information that is maintained in [10] and [8] (i.e. the potential rescuers function and the nominal constraints, respectively). The set Λ records the nominal saturated labels of an and-subgraph, while the function $\mathbf{r}$ and the relation $\rightarrowtail$ record the fulfilling paths of eventualities. These paths concern saturated labels with nominals. We use $\mathbf{r}$ to remember the most recent label that an eventuality reaches in such a path, while $\rightarrowtail$ records the rest of it. Since labels are merged due to nominals, thanks to $\mathbf{r}$ and $\rightarrowtail$, we record the changes in the fulfilling paths and detect unfulfilled eventualities on-the-fly. If a tableau concerns a PDL formula, Λ and $\rightarrowtail$ are of no use.

Definition 8. *Let $h = \langle \Lambda, r, \rightarrowtail \rangle$ be a history, defined over a set L of saturated labels, for a label $\imath$. The history h is* normal *iff for each $x \in N$, there is at most one label $\imath \in \Lambda$ such that $x \in \mathbf{actF_\imath}$,* concise *iff for any labels $\imath_1, \imath_2 \in \Lambda, \mathbf{actF_{\imath_1}} \not\subseteq \mathbf{actF_{\imath_2}}$ and* deterministic *iff for each label $\imath \in \Lambda$, for each active eventuality φ of $\imath$, the cardinality of $\{P \mid (\imath, \varphi) \rightarrowtail P\}$ is not greater than 1.*

We say that h is cyclic *iff either there is an active eventuality φ of $\imath$ such that $r(\varphi) = \emptyset$, or there is a pair $(\imath_1, \varphi_1)$ in the domain of $\rightarrowtail$ such that $(\imath_1, \varphi_1) \rightarrowtail^+ (\imath_1, \varphi_1)$. An* acyclic *history is a history which is not cyclic.*

The criterion for unifications of labels of nodes is the information of a history. A normal history requires no unifications of labels. We work with concise histories so that there is no need for explicit unifications of unnecessary labels and with deterministic histories in order to examine deterministic fulfilling paths of eventualities. Notice that the cyclic histories indicate unfulfilled eventualities.

Definition 9. *If $h = \langle \Lambda, r, \rightarrowtail \rangle$ is a history, then $\mathbf{Det}(h)$ is the set of all the deterministic histories $\langle \Lambda, r, \rightarrowtail' \rangle$ such that $\rightarrowtail'$ is a subset of $\rightarrowtail$ and for each label $\imath \in \Lambda$, for each active eventuality φ of $\imath$, for only one value P of the set $\{P \mid (\imath, \varphi) \rightarrowtail P\}$, we have that $(\imath, \varphi) \rightarrowtail' P$.*

Definition 10. *We call a set H of histories a* hybrid set *iff its histories are normal, acyclic and deterministic.*

Definition 11. *A* sentential node *ν of a rooted directed graph G, over a set L of saturated labels, is a triple $\langle \imath_\nu, H_\nu, D_\nu \rangle$, where:*

- *$\imath_\nu$ is a label,*
- *H_ν is a hybrid set of histories, defined over L, for the label $\imath_\nu$,*
- *D_ν is a set of sentential nodes of G, called* dependency set *and its elements* dependency nodes, *such that they are ancestors of ν (i.e. closer to the root).*

We refer to the pair (H_ν, D_ν) as the status *of ν, denoted as $\mathbf{sts}_\nu$, and we may equivalently write $\langle \imath_\nu, \mathbf{sts}_\nu \rangle$. We call a sentential node* partial *iff its label is partial and saturated or* state *iff its label is saturated.*

We use the sentential nodes to unfold the properties that their formulas require. A history in a hybrid set reveals the existence of an and-subgraph which suggests the satisfiability of the corresponding label. Since loops are very likely to occur in a tableau, the fulfillment of eventualities of a node and the set of nominal labels that corresponds to it might depend on ancestor nodes. A dependency set is used to record these ancestor nodes.

Definition 12. *A* unification node *u of a rooted directed graph G, over a set L of saturated labels is a quintuple $\langle \imath_u, h_u, \widetilde{D}_u, H_u, D_u \rangle$, where:*

- l_u is a saturated label,
- h_u is a concise and a deterministic history, defined over L, for l_u,
- $\widetilde{D}_u$ is a set of sentential nodes of G called the initial dependency set of u,
- H_u is a hybrid set of histories, defined over L, for the label l_u,
- D_u is a set of sentential nodes of G, called the final dependency set of u.

We refer to the pair (H_u, D_u) as the status of u, denoted as $\mathtt{sts}_u$, and we may equivalently write $\langle l_u, h_u, \widetilde{D}_u, \mathtt{sts}_u \rangle$.

A unification node is always a descendant of a state and its label is the label of this state. States are considered as and-nodes and they can be seen as roots of and-subgraphs of a tableau. A unification node combines the information of the sentential children of a state so that its history gathers all the nominal saturated labels of an and-subgraph and records the fulfilling paths of eventualities. Labels with common nominals are merged based on the history of a unification node. New unification nodes are defined to incorporate the new nodes and this continues until we reach a unification node with a normal history.

Definition 13. *A* tableau *for a formula φ is a directed graph $G = (V, E_f, E_b, E_c)$, where V is a set of sentential and unification nodes and E_f, E_b and E_c are sets of forward, backward and cyclic edges, respectively, which may be labelled with a formula of the form $\neg[a]\chi$ or with a nominal. Its root is a sentential node whose label is the pair $\langle \{\varphi\}, \mathbf{rd} \rangle$, where $\mathbf{rd}$ is the reduction function which assigns to all the values of its domain the value 0. For simplicity of notation, we assume that E is the set of all the edges of G and we equivalently write $G = (V, E)$.*

Remark 1 (Notational Conventions). When we do not know or are not interested in the type of a node of a tableau $G = (V, E)$, we just write $v \in V$. When we refer to the attributes of a label l_ν of a node ν, we may write $\mathtt{actF}_\nu, \mathtt{rdF}_\nu$ and Φ_ν, without further disambiguation. To deal with the undefined attributes of the nodes of a tableau, we let the 'undefined value' be denoted by $\perp$. For the status value $\mathtt{sts}_v$ of some node v, we write $\mathtt{sts}_v = \perp$ when both of its attributes are undefined. Finally, for some value v of a set B, we denote as $f^v : A \to B$ the function which assigns to all the values of its domain the value v.

3.2   Tableau Construction

In this section, we present the way that the algorithm constructs a tableau and we describe all the required procedures. The algorithm expands the nodes in a depth-first, left-to-right fashion and defines their statuses in a postorder manner.

The procedure $\mathtt{isSat}$ takes as input the formula whose satisfiability we want to examine. First, we initialize an empty graph G which gradually evolves into the tableau for the input formula. Moreover, we initialize a cache set C of sentential state nodes of G which is used to restrict the tableau expansion. Then, we define the root node of G whose label contains only the input formula, while its status is left undefined. Next the procedure $\mathtt{constructTableau}$ is used which, roughly speaking, builds a tableau and defines the status of the root node. If the hybrid

---

Procedure isSat(φ_0)

Input: A formula $\varphi_0 \in \mathcal{L}_s$.
Output: Whether the formula φ_0 is satisfiable or not.

  1 Define a global variable G to hold a graph (V, E) such that $V := \emptyset$ and $E := \emptyset$
  2 Define a global variable C to hold a set of sentential state nodes of G: $C := \emptyset$
  3 Define the sentential node $\nu = \langle 1_\nu, \mathtt{sts}_\nu \rangle$: $1_\nu := \langle \{\varphi_0\}, \mathtt{rd}^0 \rangle$, $\mathtt{sts}_\nu := \bot$
  4 constructTableau($\bot, \bot, \nu$)
  5 **if** ($H_\nu \neq \emptyset$) **then return** *true* **else return** *false*

---

set of the root node is the empty set, isSat concludes that the input formula is unsatisfiable, otherwise, that it is satisfiable.

The procedure constructTableau is the backbone of our algorithm, as it handles all the cases that occur. It accepts as input two nodes, v_0 and v_1, and an edge tag t. In the case that $v_0 \neq \bot, v_0$ is already a node of the tableau, whereas v_1 is treated as a candidate child of v_0. We first examine what type of node v_1 is. Lines 2–18 concern a sentential node, whereas lines 20–25 a unification one.

First, we consider the case of a sentential node ν_1. In the case that ν_1 is a state, we initially search the cache set C for another state ν_1' with the same active set of formulas as that of ν_1. If this is the case, we ignore ν_1. According to line 3^1, if ν_1' is a forward ancestor of v_0, then a cyclic edge is defined between the nodes v_0 and ν_1'. If not, then ν_1' belongs to an earlier defined branch and a backward edge is defined. Now, in the case that we cannot reuse another state or ν_1 is not a state, ν_1 is added to the graph as a forward child of v_0 (see line 6 (see footnote 1)). Moreover, if ν_1 is a state, it is also added to the cache set C (see line 7).

After the addition of ν_1, if it has no local inconsistencies (see line 8), it is expanded and then, its status is calculated. Lines 10–11 concern a partial node and lines 13–14 a non-leaf state (note that the names of the involved procedures indicate what they do). In the case of a leaf state (lines 16–17), its status is calculated at once by distinguishing cases on whether it has nominals or not.

After the definition of the status of ν_1, if it is a state, all the nodes of C which are dependent on it are removed from C (see line 18). As the dependent states are not updated to consider $\mathtt{sts}_{\nu_1}$, the algorithm cannot reuse them.

In the case of a unification node u_1, since we do not cache this type of nodes, it is immediately added to the tableau, as a child of v_0. Recall that we use the unification nodes to detect labels that should be merged. Thus, we distinguish three cases based on $h_{u_1} = \langle \Lambda, \mathbf{r}, \rightarrowtail \rangle$. Intuitively speaking, if h_{u_1} is cyclic, then an unfulfilled eventuality has been detected and thus, the status of u_1 is defined as the pair $(\emptyset, \emptyset)$. In the case of a normal and acyclic history, all the necessary unifications have taken place. The node u_1 is a leaf and its status sts_{u_1} is defined

---

[1] The procedure calls backwEdge(G, v_0, t, v_1) and cyclEdge(G, v_0, t, v_1) define a backward and a cyclic edge (v_0, v_1) (labelled with t), respectively. The procedure call addNode(G, v_0, t, v_1) extends G with v_1 (i.e. $V := V \cup \{v_1\}$) and if $v_0 \neq \bot$, then it defines the forward edge (v_0, v_1) (i.e. $E_f := E_f \cup \{(v_0, v_1)\}$) and labels it with t.

as the pair (H_{u_1}, D_{u_1}) in which the hybrid set H_{u_1} is the singleton $\{h_{u_1}\}$ and the final dependency set D_{u_1} is the same as the initial $\widetilde{D}_{u_1}$. In the case of a non-normal history, the procedure $\texttt{unify}$ creates a sentential node as a child of u_1 by merging labels of Λ (more than one) due to a specific nominal of theirs. Then, the procedure $\texttt{calcStsUnification}$ calculates the status of u_1.

In the sequel, we present the procedures which expand a partial, a state and a unification node and those which calculate their statuses. But before that, we introduce the procedures $\texttt{hybrid}$ and $\texttt{dependency}$ which are involved in the calculation of the statuses of the previous three types of nodes.

Procedure $\mathrm{construct}\mathrm{Tableau}(v_0, t, v_1)$

Input: A node $v_0 \in V \cup \{\bot\}$, an edge tag t (i.e. some formula $\neg[a]\chi$ or a nominal), potentially undefined, and a node $v_1 \notin V$ which is either sentential (denoted as $\nu_1 = \langle \mathbf{l}_{\nu_1}, \mathbf{sts}_{\nu_1} \rangle$), or unification (denoted as $u_1 = \langle \mathbf{l}_{u_1}, h_{u_1}, \widetilde{D}_{u_1}, \mathbf{sts}_{u_1} \rangle$).

Output: -

```
 1  if (v₁ is a sentential node ν₁) then
 2      if (ν₁ is a state and ∃ν₁' ∈ C such that actF_{ν₁'} = actF_{ν₁}) then
 3          if ((ν₁',v₀)∈E_f⁺) then cyclEdge(G,v₀,t,ν₁') else backwEdge(G,v₀,t,ν₁')
 4          Extend rdF_{ν₁'} with rdF_{ν₁}:   Φ_{ν₁'} := Φ_{ν₁'}∪rdF_{ν₁} and rd_{ν₁'} := rd¹
 5      else
 6          Extend G with ν₁: addNode(G,v₀,t,ν₁)
 7          Extend C with ν₁: if (ν₁ is a state) then C := C∪{ν₁}
 8          if (∃φ ∈ Φ_{ν₁} such that ¬φ ∈ Φ_{ν₁}) then  sts_{ν₁} := (∅,∅)
 9          else if (ν₁ is a partial node, i.e. there is an α/β formula in actF_{ν₁}) then
10              applyStaticRule(ν₁)
11              sts_{ν₁} := calcStsPartial(ν₁)
12          else if (there is a formula in ν₁ of the form ¬[a]χ, @_xφ or ¬@_xφ) then
13              applyNonStaticRules(ν₁)
14              sts_{ν₁} := calcStsState(ν₁)
15          else                              /* ν₁ is a leaf state with no active eventualities */
16              sts_{ν₁} := if (∃φ∈actF_{ν₁}∩N) then ({h},∅), where h := ⟨{ĩ_{ν₁}},∅,∅⟩
17                         else  ({h},∅), where h := ⟨∅,∅,∅⟩
18          if (ν₁ is a state) then foreach (ν ∈ C s.t. ν₁ ∈ D_ν) do C := C \ {ν}
19  else /* v₁ is a unification node u₁ = ⟨l_{u₁}, h_{u₁}, D̃_{u₁}, sts_{u₁}⟩ with h_{u₁}=⟨Λ,r,↦⟩ */
20      Extend G with u₁: addNode(G,v₀,t,u₁)
21      if (h_{u₁} is a cyclic history) then  sts_{u₁} := (∅,∅)
22      else if (h_{u₁} is not normal due to some x, i.e. |{l'∈Λ | x∈actF_{l'}}|>1) then
23          unify(u₁,x)
24          sts_{u₁} := calcStsUnification(u₁)
25      else sts_{u₁} := ({h_{u₁}}, D̃_{u₁})                  /* h_{u₁} is normal and acyclic */
```

The procedures $\texttt{hybrid}$ and $\texttt{dependency}$ accept as input two tableau nodes, denoted as v and ν. The node v can be of any type, whereas ν is sentential and it is also a child of v. As their names indicate, $\texttt{hybrid}$ returns a hybrid set of histories and $\texttt{dependency}$ a set of sentential nodes. Both sets concern ν and they are used for the definition of the status of the parent v.

There are two cases depending on the edge that connects the nodes v and ν. If ν is a forward or a backward child of v, then **hybrid** returns the hybrid set of ν and **dependency** returns its dependency set. In the case of a backward edge, ν is a node of a previously defined branch. So, no matter whether the edge is forward or backward, since the algorithm defines the statuses of nodes in a postorder manner, the status of ν has already been calculated. If ν is a cyclic child of v, according to lines 2–4 of **constructTableau**, a loop has been formed and ν is also a forward ancestor state of v whose status has not been calculated yet. In this case, **hybrid** defines a single history which, intuitively speaking, clearly declares that the fulfillment of any eventualities that may be involved depends on ν which does not have the required information to help us decide on their fulfillment yet. In the same case, **dependency** returns the singleton $\{\nu\}$ to record the created loop dependency. Intuitively, since the status of ν is undefined at that moment, all the nodes of the loop are transitively dependent on ν.

Procedure hybrid(v, ν)

Input: A tableau node v and a sentential node ν which is a child of v.
Output: A hybrid set of histories.
  1 **if** (ν *is a forward or a backward child of* v) **then return** H_ν
  2 **else**   /* ν is a cyclic child of v and it is a state */
  3 $\quad$ | **Definition** The history $h = \langle \Lambda, \mathbf{r}, \rightarrowtail \rangle$ is defined as follows:
  4 $\quad$ | $\quad$ – $\Lambda :=$ **if** (ν *has some nominal*) **then** $\{\widetilde{1}_\nu\}$ **else** $\emptyset$
  5 $\quad$ | $\quad$ – The reachability function $\mathbf{r}$ for 1_ν: $\forall \varphi \in \mathbf{Ev} \cap \mathbf{actF}_\nu$, $\mathbf{r}(\varphi) := (\widetilde{1}_\nu, \varphi)$
  6 $\quad$ | $\quad$ – $\rightarrowtail := \emptyset$
  7 $\quad$ | **return** $\{h\}$

Procedure dependency(v, ν)

Input: A tableau node v and a sentential node ν which is a child of v.
Output: A dependency set of state nodes.
  1 **if** $((v, \nu) \in E_f \cup E_b)$ **then return** D_ν **else return** $\{\nu\}$

The algorithm reuses the states of a tableau by taking advantage of their statuses. On the other hand, it may stop reusing nodes due to loop dependencies. Loops are formed as usual due to the iteration operator and nodes become dependent on ancestor nodes because at the moment that a loop is formed, the latter nodes do not have the required information yet. Recall how the procedures **hybrid** and **dependency** work and that a cyclic edge indicates the existence of a loop. So, intuitively speaking, each loop has a dependency node such that every other node of the loop is dependent on it. From the moment that the status of such a dependency node is calculated, the corresponding dependent nodes are considered out of date, as they do not become aware of this status value. As a result, the algorithm removes them from the cache set. The empty dependency set of a state indicates that it is not involved in any loop and that it is not dependent on any node. Hence, it remains in the cache set the whole time.

The Procedures for a Partial Node (see lines 9–11 of `constructTableau`*).* The procedure `applyStaticRule` expands a partial node ν with as many sentential children as the reduction degree of an active α/β formula φ of ν. The set of formulas of each child is defined by adding to that of ν, one of the reduction sets of φ. The reduction function is defined (see line 5) so that the principal formula is considered as reduced and all the new α/β eventualities as active.

After the expansion of a partial node ν, the procedure `calcStsPartial` calculates its status. It uses the histories and the dependency nodes of its children as they are determined by the procedures `hybrid` and `dependency`, respectively. By using the auxiliary procedure `reachableLabels`, it defines reachability functions for the active eventualities of ν to record their fulfilling paths.

Procedure applyStaticRule(ν)

Input: A partial node ν.
Output: -
1   Let φ be an α/β formula in $\mathtt{actF}_\nu$ and $\mathcal{R}_1^\varphi, \ldots, \mathcal{R}_k^\varphi$ its reduction sets with $k \geq 1$.
2   **for** $(i := 1$ **to** $k)$ **do**
3   Define the sentential node $\nu_i = \langle\langle \Phi_i, \mathbf{rd}_i \rangle, \mathtt{sts}_i \rangle$ as follows:
4      $-\; \Phi_i := \Phi_\nu \cup \mathcal{R}_i^\varphi$

5      $-$ For each $\alpha/\beta\; \psi \in \mathbf{Ev} \cap \Phi_i$, $\mathbf{rd}_i(\psi) := \begin{cases} \mathbf{rd}_\nu(\psi) & \text{if } \psi \in \Phi_\nu \setminus \{\varphi\} \\ 1 & \text{if } \psi = \varphi \\ 0 & \text{if } \psi \in \mathcal{R}_i^\varphi \setminus \Phi_\nu \end{cases}$

6      $-\; \mathtt{sts}_i := \bot$
7   `constructTableau`$(\nu, \bot, \nu_i)$

Procedure calcStsPartial(ν)

Input: A partial node ν.
Output: The status of ν.
1   Let $\psi_1, \ldots, \psi_m$ be the active eventualities of ν, with $m \geq 0$.
2   Let H be an empty set of histories.
3   **foreach** $($*child node* ν' *of* ν *(i.e.* $(\nu, \nu') \in E))$ **do**
4   **foreach** $($*history* $\langle \Lambda, r, \rightarrowtail \rangle \in hybrid(\nu, \nu'))$ **do**
5   **for** $(j := 1$ **to** $m)$ **do** $\Gamma_j :=$ `reachableLabels`$(1_{\nu'}, r, \psi_j)$
6   **foreach** $($*tuple* $(P_1, \ldots, P_m)$ *such that, for* $j = 1, \ldots, m,\; P_j \in \Gamma_j)$ **do**
7   The reachability function $\mathbf{r}'$ for 1_ν: **for** $(j := 1$ **to** $m)$ **do** $\mathbf{r}'(\psi_j) := P_j$
8              $H := H \cup \{\langle \Lambda, \mathbf{r}', \rightarrowtail \rangle\}$

9   **return** $\left(H, \bigcup_{(\nu, \nu_0) \in E} dependency(\nu, \nu_0) \right)$

The procedure `reachableLabels` determines how the fulfillment of an eventuality φ of a label 1 evolves. This is achieved through the relation $\rhd$ and the set $\mathtt{reach}(\varphi, 1)$ (see Definition 6) and through a reachability function $\mathbf{r}$ for 1.

Procedure reachableLabels$(1, \mathbf{r}, \varphi)$

Input: A label 1, a reachability function $\mathbf{r}$ for 1 and an eventuality φ of Φ_1.
Output: Either a set of pairs of labels and eventualities, or the singleton $\{FL\}$.
1   $\Gamma := \mathtt{reach}(\varphi, 1)$
2   **if** $(\exists \psi \in \Gamma(\psi \notin Ev$ *or* $(\psi \in Ev$ *and* $r(\psi) = FL)))$ **then return** $\{FL\}$ **else**
    return $\bigcup_{\psi \in \Gamma} \{r(\psi)\}$

The Procedures for a State Node (see lines 12–14 of `constructTableau`*).* The procedure `applyNonStaticRules` expands a state ν with the appropriate sentential children. It creates a node for each formula $\neg[a]\chi$ of ν and for each nominal x such that there is a formula in ν of the form $@_x\psi$ or $\neg@_x\psi$.

Procedure applyNonStaticRules(ν)

Input: A state node ν.
Output: -
1   **foreach** $(\varphi \in \{\neg[a]\chi \mid \neg[a]\chi \in \Phi_\nu\} \cup \{x \mid \exists \psi \in \Phi_\nu(\psi = @_x\varphi$ *or* $\psi = \neg@_x\varphi)\})$ **do**
2   **if** *(there is no sentential child ν_c of ν such that* $\mathtt{hybrid}(\nu, \nu_c) = \emptyset$*)* **then**
3   Define the sentential node $\nu' = \langle\langle\Phi, \mathbf{rd}\rangle, \mathtt{sts}\rangle$ *as follows:*
4       $-\ \Phi :=$ **if** *(φ is some formula $\neg[a]\chi$)* **then** $\{\neg\chi\} \cup \{\vartheta \mid [a]\vartheta \in \mathtt{actF}_\nu\}$
5   **else if** *(φ is some x)* **then** $\{x\} \cup \{\psi \mid @_x\psi \in \Phi_\nu\} \cup \{\neg\psi \mid \neg@_x\psi \in \Phi_\nu\}$
6       $-\ \mathbf{rd} := \mathbf{rd}^0$
7       $-\ \mathtt{sts} := \perp$
8   constructTableau(ν, φ, ν')
9   **else** break the for loop

After the expansion of a state ν with the appropriate sentential children, the procedure `calcStsState` calculates its status. If the hybrid sets that correspond to these sentential children do not imply unsatisfiability, the procedure `expandStWithUnifNodes` expands ν with the appropriate unification nodes.

Procedure calcStsState(ν)

Input: A state node ν with at least one sentential child node.
Output: The status of ν.
1   Let $\nu_1, \ldots, \nu_k$ be the sentential children of ν, with $k \geq 1$.
2   **if** $(\exists i \in \{1, \ldots, k\}$ *such that* $\mathtt{hybrid}(\nu, \nu_i) = \emptyset)$ **then return** $(\emptyset, \emptyset)$ **else**
    return *expandStWithUnifNodes*(ν)

Procedure expandStWithUnifNodes(ν)

Input: A state node ν.
Output: A status value for ν.

1 Let $\nu_1, \ldots, \nu_k$ be the sentential children of ν, with $k \geq 1$, such that there is
   $0 \leq n \leq k$ such that for $i = 1, \ldots, n$, the edge (ν, ν_i) is labelled with a formula
   $\neg[a]\chi$ and for $i = n+1, \ldots, k$ the edge (ν, ν_i) is labelled with a nominal x.

2 **foreach** (*tuple* $(h_1, \ldots, h_k)$ *such that for* $i = 1, \ldots, k$, $h_i \in hybrid(\nu, \nu_i)$) **do**

3 $\quad$ $h := \mathtt{filterHist}(1_\nu, \mathtt{defConciseHist}(1_\nu, \mathtt{defCombinedHist}(\nu, (h_1, \ldots, h_k))))$

4 $\quad$ **foreach** ($h' \in Det(h)$) **do**

5 $\quad\quad$ Define the unification node $u = \langle 1_u, h_u, \widetilde{D}_u, \mathtt{sts}_u \rangle$:

6 $\quad\quad$ $1_u := 1_\nu$, $\quad h_u := h'$, $\quad \widetilde{D}_u := \left(\bigcup_{1 \leq i \leq k} \mathtt{dependency}(\nu, \nu_i) \right) \setminus \{\nu\}$, $\quad \mathtt{sts}_u := \bot$

7 $\quad\quad$ $\mathtt{constructTableau}(\nu, \bot, u)$

8 **return** $\left(\bigcup_{(\nu, u_0) \in E} H_{u_0}, \bigcup_{(\nu, u_0) \in E} D_{u_0} \right)$

The procedure **expandStWithUnifNodes** defines a status value for a state ν. Since the satisfiability of a state requires the satisfiability of all of its sentential children, for each possible combination of histories of their hybrid sets (see line 2), the procedure defines a new history for ν. According to line 3, the procedure **defCombinedHist** combines them into a single history, **defConciseHist** makes it concise and **filterHist** removes the label $\widetilde{1}_\nu$ from it under the condition that $\widetilde{1}_\nu$ has no nominals. Additionally, we consider the set of deterministic histories that correspond to the defined history. Intuitively speaking, our goal is to determine a history which gathers all the necessary information for an and-subgraph whose root is ν. Thus, we define the appropriate unification node (see line 6) so that we can examine if any labels of this and-subgraph should be merged.

The procedure **defCombinedHist** takes as input a state ν and a tuple of histories and it returns a single history $\langle \Lambda, \mathbf{r}, \rightarrowtail \rangle$ for 1_ν. It combines the input histories into a single history $\langle \Lambda, \mathbf{r}, \rightarrowtail \rangle$ so that Λ gathers all the saturated labels with some nominal and $\mathbf{r}$ and $\rightarrowtail$ record the fulfilling paths of the eventualities of ν. Depending on whether there is a nominal in 1_ν, or not, the procedure distinguishes two cases on how each attribute of $\langle \Lambda, \mathbf{r}, \rightarrowtail \rangle$ is defined.

Procedure defCombinedHist($\nu, (h_1, \ldots, h_k)$)

Input: A state ν and a tuple $(\langle \Lambda_1, \mathbf{r}_1, \rightarrowtail_1 \rangle, \ldots, \langle \Lambda_k, \mathbf{r}_k, \rightarrowtail_k \rangle)$ of histories, with $k \geq 1$.
Output: A history $h = \langle \Lambda, \mathbf{r}, \rightarrowtail \rangle$ for 1_ν.

1 Let $\nu_1, \ldots, \nu_n$ be all the children of ν with $0 \leq n \leq k$ and $\vartheta_1, \ldots, \vartheta_n$ all the active
   formulas of ν such that for $i = 1, \ldots, n$, $\vartheta_i = \neg[a_i]\chi_i$ and $(\nu, \nu_i) \in E$ is labelled
   with ϑ_i and $h_i \in \mathtt{hybrid}(\nu, \nu_i)$.

2 **Definition** The history $h = \langle \Lambda, \mathbf{r}, \rightarrowtail \rangle$ for 1_ν is defined as follows:

3 $\quad$ $\Lambda := \quad$ **if** $(\exists \varphi \in actF_\nu (\varphi \in N))$ **then** $\{\widetilde{1}_\nu\} \cup \Lambda_1 \cup \cdots \cup \Lambda_k$ **else** $\Lambda_1 \cup \cdots \cup \Lambda_k$

4 $\quad$ **if** $(\widetilde{1}_\nu \in \Lambda)$ **then** **foreach** ($\varphi \in (Ev \cap actF_\nu)$) **do** $(\mathbf{r}(\varphi) := (\widetilde{1}_\nu, \varphi))$

5 $\quad$ **else** **for** ($i := 1$ to n) **do** **if** ($\vartheta_i \in Ev$) **then** $\mathbf{r}(\neg[a_i]\chi_i) := \mathbf{r}_i(\neg\chi_i)$

6 $\quad$ $\rightarrowtail := $ **if** $(\widetilde{1}_\nu \in \Lambda)$ **then** $\{((\widetilde{1}_\nu, \vartheta_i), \mathbf{r}_i(\neg\chi_i)) \mid \vartheta_i \in Ev$ and $1 \leq i \leq n\} \cup \bigcup_{1 \leq i \leq k} \rightarrowtail_i$

   $\quad\quad$ **else** $\bigcup_{1 \leq i \leq k} \rightarrowtail_i$

7 **return** $\langle \Lambda, \mathbf{r}, \rightarrowtail \rangle$

The procedure `defConciseHist` takes as input a history $h = \langle \Lambda, \mathbf{r}, \rightarrowtail \rangle$ for some saturated label $\mathbf{l}_0$, possibly not a concise one, and it processes it so that it is definitely concise. Recall that h is not concise iff there are labels $\mathbf{l}_1, \mathbf{l}_2 \in \Lambda$ such that $\mathtt{actF}_{\mathbf{l}_1} \subset \mathtt{actF}_{\mathbf{l}_2}$. So, if there are such labels $\mathbf{l}_1, \mathbf{l}_2$ in Λ, it eliminates the unnecessary label $\mathbf{l}_1$ from h. It is immediate that there is at least one nominal which belongs to both labels and consequently, they should be merged.

Procedure defConciseHist$(\mathbf{l}_0, h)$

Input: A saturated label $\mathbf{l}_0$ and a (not necessarily concise) history $\langle \Lambda, \mathbf{r}, \rightarrowtail \rangle$ for $\mathbf{l}_0$.
Output: A redefined concise history $\langle \Lambda, \mathbf{r}, \rightarrowtail \rangle$ for $\mathbf{l}_0$.

1 **while** (*there are labels* $\mathbf{l}_1, \mathbf{l}_2 \in \Lambda$ *such that* $\mathtt{actF}_{\mathbf{l}_1} \subset \mathtt{actF}_{\mathbf{l}_2}$) **do**
2   **Definition** The history $\langle \Lambda, \mathbf{r}, \rightarrowtail \rangle$ for $\mathbf{l}_0$ is redefined as follows:
3         $\Lambda := \Lambda \setminus \{\mathbf{l}_1\}$
4   **foreach** ($\varphi \in (Ev \cap \mathtt{actF}_{\mathbf{l}_0})$ *such that* $\mathbf{r}(\varphi) = (\mathbf{l}_1, \psi)$) **do** $\mathbf{r}(\varphi) := (\mathbf{l}_2, \psi)$
5         $\rightarrowtail := \rightarrowtail \setminus \{((\mathbf{1}, \varphi), P) \in \rightarrowtail \mid \mathbf{1} = \mathbf{l}_1\}$
6   **while** (*there are related pairs* $(\mathbf{1}, \varphi) \rightarrowtail (\mathbf{1}', \varphi')$ *such that* $\mathbf{1}' = \mathbf{l}_1$) **do**
7           $\rightarrowtail := \left(\rightarrowtail \setminus \{((\mathbf{1}, \varphi), (\mathbf{1}', \varphi'))\}\right) \cup \{((\mathbf{1}, \varphi), (\mathbf{l}_2, \varphi'))\}$

8 **return** $\langle \Lambda, r, \rightarrowtail \rangle$

The procedure `filterHist` modifies the reachability function and the fulfillment relation of a history $h = \langle \Lambda, \mathbf{r}, \rightarrowtail \rangle$ which has been defined for a saturated label $\mathbf{l}_0$ with no nominals. Any pairs of labels and eventualities in which $\widetilde{\mathbf{l}}_0$ occurs within h are modified so that the specific label does not appear anymore. Roughly speaking, having in mind that h concerns the label $\mathbf{l}_0$, if $\widetilde{\mathbf{l}}_0$ occurs within h (e.g. there are φ, ψ in $\mathtt{actF}_{\mathbf{l}_0}$ such that $\mathbf{r}(\varphi) = (\widetilde{\mathbf{l}}_0, \psi)$ or $\mathbf{r}(\varphi) \rightarrowtail^+ (\widetilde{\mathbf{l}}_0, \psi)$), a loop may have been formed. Recall that our concern is to maintain paths for the eventualities in which nominal saturated labels appear so that we can record the changes that unifications of labels impose. Since $\mathbf{l}_0$ has no nominals, the pairs in which it appears should be modified appropriately. Of course, since a loop may have been formed, we might obtain a cyclic history.

Procedure filterHist$(\mathbf{l}_0, h)$

Input: A saturated label $\mathbf{l}_0$ and a history $h = \langle \Lambda, \mathbf{r}, \rightarrowtail \rangle$ for $\mathbf{l}_0$.
Output: A redefined history $h = \langle \Lambda, \mathbf{r}, \rightarrowtail \rangle$ for $\mathbf{l}_0$.

1 **if** ($\mathbf{l}_0$ *is a label with no nominals*) **then**
2   **foreach** ($\varphi \in Ev \cap \mathtt{actF}_{\mathbf{l}_0}$) **do**   /* redefinition of $\mathbf{r}$ */
3   **if** (*there is* $\varphi_1, \ldots, \varphi_k$ *with* $k \geq 1$ *s.t.* $\varphi_1 = \varphi$ *and* (*for* $i = 1, \ldots, k - 1$,
          $\mathbf{r}(\varphi_i) = (\widetilde{\mathbf{l}}_0, \varphi_{i+1})$) *and* ($\mathbf{r}(\varphi_k) = FL$ *or* $\mathbf{r}(\varphi_k) = (\mathbf{1}, \psi)$ *s.t.* $\mathbf{1} \neq \widetilde{\mathbf{l}}_0$)) **then**
4           $\mathbf{r}(\varphi) := \mathbf{r}(\varphi_k)$
5   **else** $\mathbf{r}(\varphi) := \emptyset$
6   **if** ($\forall \varphi \in Ev \cap \mathtt{actF}_{\mathbf{l}_0}(\mathbf{r}(\varphi) \neq \emptyset)$) **then**   /* redefinition of $\rightarrowtail$ */
7         $\rightarrowtail := \rightarrowtail \cup \{((\mathbf{l}_1, \psi_1), \mathbf{r}(\psi)) \mid (\mathbf{l}_1, \psi_1) \rightarrowtail (\widetilde{\mathbf{l}}_0, \psi)\}$
8         $\rightarrowtail := \rightarrowtail \setminus \{((\mathbf{l}_1, \psi_1), (\mathbf{l}_2, \psi_2)) \in \rightarrowtail \mid \mathbf{l}_2 = \widetilde{\mathbf{l}}_0\}$

9 **return** $\langle \Lambda, r, \rightarrowtail \rangle$

The Procedures for a Unification Node (see lines 22–24 of `constructTableau`*).* The procedure `unify` takes as input a unification node u such that its concise history $h_u = \langle \Lambda_u, \mathbf{r}_u, \rightarrowtail_u \rangle$ is not normal and a nominal which proves that. This nominal belongs to more than one label of Λ_u and we denote their set as L. Intuitively speaking, the labels of L, as well as the labels of $\Lambda_u \setminus L$ which have a common nominal with those of L, should all be satisfied by the same state of a model. Thus, `unify` expands the set L with the appropriate labels (see lines 2–3) and then, it merges all of them into a new node (see line 4).

Procedure unify(u, x)

Input: A node $u = \langle \mathbf{1}_u, h_u, \widetilde{D}_u, \mathtt{sts}_u \rangle$, where $h_u = \langle \Lambda_u, \mathbf{r}_u, \rightarrowtail_u \rangle$, and a nominal x.
Output: -

1 $L := \{ \mathbf{1} \in \Lambda_u \mid x \in \mathtt{actF_1} \}$ /* L is a set of saturated labels such that $|L| > 1$ */
2 **while** $(\exists l \in (\Lambda_u \setminus L)$ *such that* $\exists y \in \mathtt{actF_1}$ *such that* $y \in \bigcup\limits_{l' \in L} \mathtt{actF_{l'}})$ **do**
3 $\quad \Big\lfloor \quad L := L \cup \{ \mathbf{1} \in (\Lambda_u \setminus L) \mid \exists y \in \mathtt{actF_1}$ such that $y \in \bigcup\limits_{1' \in L} \mathtt{actF_{1'}} \}$

4 Define the node $\nu = \langle \langle \Phi_\nu, \mathbf{rd}_\nu \rangle, \mathtt{sts}_\nu \rangle$: $\Phi_\nu := \bigcup\limits_{1 \in L} \Phi_1, \quad \mathbf{rd}_\nu := \emptyset, \quad \mathtt{sts}_\nu := \bot$
5 `constructTableau`(u, x, ν)

The procedure `calcStsUnification` takes as input a unification node u and it returns its status. A unification node with an acyclic and a non-normal history has a single sentential child which is the result of `unify`. If the hybrid set that corresponds to this child of u does not imply unsatisfiability, the procedure `expandUnWithUnifNodes` expands u with the appropriate unification nodes.

Procedure calcStsUnification(u)

Input: A unification node u.
Output: The status of u.
1 Let ν be the sentential child of u.
2 **if** $(hybrid(u,\nu) = \emptyset)$ **then return** $(\emptyset, \emptyset)$ **else return** *expandUnWithUnifNodes*(u)

The procedure `expandUnWithUnifNodes` expands a unification node u with the appropriate unification nodes in order to calculate its status. The information of u concerns an ancestor state which has the same label as that of u. Moreover, the information of the history h_u concerns an and-subgraph whose root is that state. Since the sentential child of u, denoted as ν, is the result of unifications of labels of that and-subgraph, we should combine the new information that occurs from ν with h_u. This is achieved by defining the appropriate unification nodes as children of u. This process continues, until we meet a normal history and no other unifications of labels are necessary. Each unification child is a step closer to a normal history than its parent due to the unifications that take place.

Procedure expandUnWithUnifNodes(u)

Input: A unification node $u = \langle 1_u, h_u, \widetilde{D}_u, \mathtt{sts}_u \rangle$, where $h_u = \langle \Lambda_u, \mathbf{r}_u, \rightarrowtail_u \rangle$.

Output: A status value for u.

1 Let ν be the sentential child of u.

2 **foreach** $(\langle \Lambda_0, r_0, \rightarrowtail_0 \rangle \in hybrid(u, \nu))$ **do**

3      $h := \mathtt{filterHist}(1_u, \mathtt{defConciseHist}(1_u, \langle \Lambda_u \cup \Lambda_0, \mathbf{r}_u, \rightarrowtail_u \cup \rightarrowtail_0 \rangle))$

4   **foreach** $(h' \in Det(h))$ **do**

5   Define the node $u' = \langle 1_{u'}, h_{u'}, \widetilde{D}_{u'}, \mathtt{sts}_{u'} \rangle$: $1_{u'} := 1_u$, $h_{u'} := h'$,
           $\widetilde{D}_{u'} := \widetilde{D}_u \cup \{\nu' \in \mathtt{dependency}(u, \nu) \mid 1_{\nu'} \neq 1_u\}$, $\mathtt{sts}_{u'} := \perp$

6         $\mathtt{constructTableau}(u, \perp, u')$

7 **return** $\left(\bigcup_{(u,u_0) \in E} H_{u_0}, \bigcup_{(u,u_0) \in E} D_{u_0} \right)$

Theorem 1 (Soundness, Completeness, Complexity). *A formula φ is satisfiable iff the procedure call* isSat(φ) *returns true. The algorithm runs in double exponential time in the general case, but, in the case of iteration-free formulas, it runs in single exponential time. (see [16] for proofs).*

An Example of a Tableau (see Fig. 1). Sentential nodes are presented within a rectangle, whereas unification nodes are not restricted to some shape. Partial nodes are presented within dashed rectangles. Backward edges are depicted as dashed arrows, whereas cyclic edges as dotted arrows. Assuming the steps of

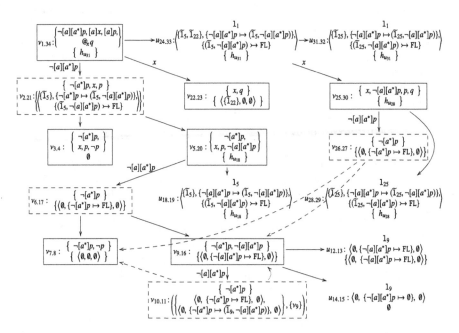

Fig. 1. The tableau for the satisfiable set of formulas $\{\neg[a][a^*]p, [a]x, [a]p, @_x q\}$

the algorithm to be numbered, and each step being either about creating a node, or defining the status of a node, we write $v_{i.j}$ for the node which becomes created at step i and gets its status defined at step j. For any node $v_{i.j}$, we simply refer to it by writing v_i and if it is sentential, we refer to its label as 1_i. We present only the set of formulas of a label without its reduction function. The reachability function of a history is represented as a set of mappings (e.g. $\{\varphi \mapsto (1, \psi), \chi \mapsto \mathrm{FL}, \dots\}$) and the fulfillment relation as a set of appropriate related values, e.g. $\{(\widetilde{1}_1, \psi_1) \rightarrowtail (\widetilde{1}_2, \psi_2), (\widetilde{1}_2, \psi_2) \rightarrowtail \mathrm{FL}, \dots\}$. Finally, we omit the dependency sets of the nodes when they are the empty set.

The tableau of Fig. 1 concerns the satisfiable set of formulas $\{\neg[a][a^*]p, [a]x,$ $[a]p, @_x q\}$. All the states remain in the cache set from the moment that they are created to the end of the construction of the tableau. Notice how the states v_7 and v_9 are reused. The eventuality $\neg[a][a^*]p$ is fulfilled through the nodes v_1, v_2, v_5, v_6 and v_7 (see also v_9, v_{10} and v_7). The only bad loop that is formed is for $\neg[a][a^*]p$, between v_9 and v_{10} (notice that $D_{v_{10}} = \{v_9\}$), and it is detected by the cyclic history of u_{14}. The satisfaction statement $@_x q$ of v_1 leads to the definition of v_{22}. So, the nominal x occurs in states v_5 and v_{22} and thus, the unification node u_{24} merges them into v_{25}. For more examples, we refer the reader to [16].

4   Conclusions and Further Work

We have presented a novel tableau-based satisfiability algorithm for HPDL@ and we have given all the necessary details that can lead to an implementation. It defines a variant of an and-or graph, as for each non-leaf state, there are the appropriate unification nodes which take care of the nominal labels of a non-normal history. The algorithm detects unfulfilled eventualities on-the-fly and unifies labels based on the history of a unification node (either implicitly through defConciseHist or explicitly through unify). Definitions 3 and 2 enclose the usual static rules in a single one, so that world cycles of eventualities are avoided.

Partial caching ensures the termination of the algorithm and restricts the expansion of a tableau more effectively. The status of a sentential node represents the necessary information so that its reuse is possible. A history is a data structure which holds information for an appropriate and-subgraph of a tableau. Each state is available for possible reuse until the status of one of its dependency nodes (if it has any) is defined. After that moment, it cannot be reused as it is considered out of date. Our algorithm runs in double exponential time. However, in the case of iteration-free formulas, loops are not formed. All the states are reused the whole time and thus, it works in single exponential time.

Besides the iteration-free formulas, thanks to partial caching, the algorithm has the potential to achieve acceptable performance. All the nodes of a loop are reused until the status of their dependency node is defined. So, if loop-nodes do not reappear after that moment, the algorithm runs in exponential time. Now, suppose that there are only loops of sentential nodes in which their dependency nodes are not dependent on any node. Since the dependency nodes are reused the whole time, even if a state of a loop is recreated, the initial loop cannot be re-formed and its newly redefined states remain in the cache set. Therefore, such loops do not seem to be a problem. Of course, further work is required to address how the algorithm behaves in practice through an experimental evaluation.

To the best of our knowledge, it is the first deterministic tableau-based satisfiability algorithm for HPDL@ which defines a variant of an and-or graph, works on-the-fly and exploits the (partial) caching of nodes.

To make the algorithm optimal, we should ensure that it has the ability to reuse all the saturated sentential nodes the whole time. To achieve this, we should devise an update mechanism for the loop dependencies so that the cached states remain up to date. Dependencies are created due to loops, in which the statuses of ancestor nodes have not been calculated yet. Eventually, the status of such a dependency node is calculated. To reuse the nodes which are dependent on it, we should somehow recalculate their statuses by considering this new status. Such update mechanisms have been used in the algorithm of [10] for PDL. Further work is required to extend our approach to incorporate such mechanisms.

Acknowledgments. I would like to thank Prof. Chrysafis Hartonas for helpful comments and suggestions on an earlier version of this paper. I would also like to thank the anonymous reviewers for their constructive comments on the paper.

References

1. Areces, C., Blackburn, P., Marx, M.: The computational complexity of hybrid temporal logics. Logic J. IGPL **8**(5), 653–679 (2000)
2. Areces, C., ten Cate, B.: Hybrid logics. In: Blackburn, P., Benthem, J.V., Wolter, F. (eds.) Handbook of Modal Logic, pp. 821–868. Elsevier, Amsterdam (2007)
3. Bolander, T., Blackburn, P.: Termination for hybrid tableaus. J. Logic Comput. **17**(3), 517–554 (2007)
4. Braüner, T.: Hybrid Logic and its Proof-Theory. Springer, Heidelberg (2011). doi:10.1007/978-94-007-0002-4
5. Fischer, M.J., Ladner, R.E.: Propositional dynamic logic of regular programs. J. Comput. Syst. Sci. **18**(2), 194–211 (1979)
6. Giacomo, G.D., Massacci, F.: Combining deduction and model checking into tableaux and algorithms for converse-PDL. Inf. Comput. **162**, 117–137 (2000)
7. Goré, R.: And-or tableaux for fixpoint logics with converse: LTL, CTL, PDL and CPDL. In: Demri, S., Kapur, D., Weidenbach, C. (eds.) IJCAR 2014. LNCS, vol. 8562, pp. 26–45. Springer, Cham (2014). doi:10.1007/978-3-319-08587-6_3
8. Goré, R., Kupke, C., Pattinson, D., Schröder, L.: Global caching for coalgebraic description logics. In: Giesl, J., Hähnle, R. (eds.) IJCAR 2010. LNCS, vol. 6173, pp. 46–60. Springer, Heidelberg (2010). doi:10.1007/978-3-642-14203-1_5
9. Goré, R., Nguyen, L.A.: Exptime tableaux for ALC using sound global caching. J. Autom. Reason. **50**(4), 355–381 (2013)
10. Goré, R., Widmann, F.: An optimal on-the-fly tableau-based decision procedure for PDL-satisfiability. In: Schmidt, R.A. (ed.) CADE 2009. LNCS, vol. 5663, pp. 437–452. Springer, Heidelberg (2009). doi:10.1007/978-3-642-02959-2_32

11. Goré, R., Widmann, F.: Optimal and cut-free tableaux for propositional dynamic logic with converse. In: Giesl, J., Hähnle, R. (eds.) IJCAR 2010. LNCS, vol. 6173, pp. 225–239. Springer, Heidelberg (2010). doi:10.1007/978-3-642-14203-1_20
12. Harel, D., Kozen, D., Tiuryn, J.: Dynamic Logic. MIT Press, Cambridge (2000)
13. Hoffmann, G.: Lightweight hybrid tableaux. J. Appl. Log. **8**(4), 397–408 (2010)
14. Kaminski, M., Schneider, T., Smolka, G.: Correctness and worst-case optimality of Pratt-style decision procedures for modal and hybrid logics. In: Brünnler, K., Metcalfe, G. (eds.) TABLEAUX 2011. LNCS, vol. 6793, pp. 196–210. Springer, Heidelberg (2011). doi:10.1007/978-3-642-22119-4_16
15. Kaminski, M., Smolka, G.: A goal-directed decision procedure for hybrid PDL. J. Autom. Reason. **52**(4), 407–450 (2014)
16. Kritsimallis, A.: Tableaux with partial caching for hybrid PDL with satisfaction statements (ext. ver.) (2017). https://www.academia.edu/32581641/Tableaux_with_Partial_Caching_for_Hybrid_PDL_with_Satisfaction_Statements
17. Nguyen, L.A.: Exptime tableaux with global state caching for the description logic SHIO. Neurocomputing **146**, 249–263 (2014)
18. Nguyen, L.A., Golińska-Pilarek, J.: An exptime tableau method for dealing with nominals and qualified number restrictions in deciding the description logic SHOQ. Fundamenta Informaticae **135**(4), 433–449 (2014)
19. Nguyen, L.A., Szałas, A.: An optimal tableau decision procedure for converse-PDL. In: KSE 2009, pp. 207–214. IEEE (2009)
20. Passy, S., Tinchev, T.: PDL with data constants. Inf. Process. Lett. **20**, 35–41 (1985)
21. Passy, S., Tinchev, T.: An essay in combinatory dynamic logic. Inf. Comput. **93**(2), 263–332 (1991)
22. Pratt, V.R.: Models of program logics. In: Proceedings of 20th Symposium on Foundations of Computer Science, pp. 115–122. IEEE (1979)
23. Pratt, V.R.: A near-optimal method for reasoning about action. J. Comput. Syst. Sci. **20**(2), 231–254 (1980)
24. Prior, A.: Past, Present and Future. Oxford University Press, Oxford (1967)
25. Tzakova, M.: Tableau calculi for hybrid logics. In: Murray, N.V. (ed.) TABLEAUX 1999. LNCS, vol. 1617, pp. 278–292. Springer, Heidelberg (1999). doi:10.1007/3-540-48754-9_24

PTrie: Data Structure for Compressing and Storing Sets via Prefix Sharing

Peter Gjøl Jensen, Kim Guldstrand Larsen, and Jiří Srba$^{(\boxtimes)}$

Department of Computer Science, Aalborg University,
Selma Lagerlöfs Vej 300, 9220 Aalborg East, Denmark
srba@cs.aau.dk

Abstract. Sets and their efficient implementation are fundamental in all of computer science, including model checking, where sets are used as the basic data structure for storing (encodings of) states during a state-space exploration. In the quest for fast and memory efficient methods for manipulating large sets, we present a novel data structure called PTrie for storing sets of binary strings of arbitrary length. The PTrie data structure distinguishes itself by compressing the stored elements while sharing the desirable key characteristics with conventional hash-based implementations, namely fast insertion and lookup operations. We provide the theoretical foundation of PTries, prove the correctness of their operations and conduct empirical studies analysing the performance of PTries for dealing with randomly generated binary strings as well as for state-space exploration of a large collection of Petri net models from the 2016 edition of the Model Checking Contest (MCC'16). We experimentally document that with a modest overhead in running time, a truly significant space-reduction can be achieved. Lastly, we provide an efficient implementation of the PTrie data structure under the GPL version 3 license, so that the technology is made available for memory-intensive applications such as model-checking tools.

1 Introduction

Formal verification techniques are being increasingly employed in many different industrial applications, including both hardware and software systems. In the hardware industry such techniques have been adopted by most of the major leading companies and a widespread adoption in the software industry is under way. Formal techniques have become essential for certain safety-critical applications for example in the avionics and aerospace industry but also in other areas—like the development of operating systems, control systems for railways and numerous other applications. The performance of the respective verification tools depends to a large extent on fast and memory efficient implementations of the underlying data structures used in the verification algorithms. This is in particular due to the state-space explosion problem that all modern model checkers must deal with. Such tools are not only constrained by the time requirements but also by the physical limitations like the amount of memory resources of the hardware that the implementation is targeted for.

© Springer International Publishing AG 2017
D.V. Hung and D. Kapur (Eds.): ICTAC 2017, LNCS 10580, pp. 248–265, 2017.
DOI: 10.1007/978-3-319-67729-3_15

A common data structure used in model checking and many other applications is a set. We revisit the state-of-the-art implementation approaches for storing sets that offer the basic operations of inserting an element to the set, removing an element from the set and a membership check. This simple set interface is sufficient for the applications in many explicit model checkers, while the symbolic approaches may require more complex operations like intersection and union that are, however, more expensive in implementation. In order to compete with the foremost hash-based approaches for storing sets, we develop a particular tree-based representation of a set called PTrie that is optimized both for speed and memory. PTrie is designed for storing binary strings of arbitrary length but via binary encoding/decoding techniques it can be used as a general set-implementation. An early implementation of PTrie was briefly mentioned in a tool paper by Jensen et al. [15], indicating encouraging performance results. Since then the data structure was further developed, extensively tested and matured so that it became competitive with the industrial leading implementations.

Although generic data structures for sets already exist in the standard-library of C++, Google's `google::dense_hash_set` (and `google::sparse_hash_set`) implementations perform significantly faster (or have a smaller memory footprint) than other reasonable alternatives as documented e.g. in [22,23]. PTrie are designed as an almost general replacement of such library implementations and yield a sensible trade off between time and space consumption by utilizing the inherent prefix-sharing whenever beneficial. The main characteristic of the structure is the partial (lazy) construction of the trie—hence the name Partial Trie (PTrie)—that is optimized for storing a large number of binary strings of varying size. At the same time the PTrie data structure utilizes the prefix-sharing of the binary strings, often resulting in significant compression of the stored data, sometime up to 70% compared to the Google's hash-based implementation . In the present paper, we formally define the syntax and semantics of PTries, give the algorithms for the interface operations, prove their correctness and provide an open-source implementation that is thoroughly tested against other approaches.

Related Work. While tries were introduced already in the 1960's [11], their primary focus was on reducing search time in large sets of text-strings. Different variants of tries have been developed during the years, such as Radix tree [12,18] designed for storing more than single characters on edges or trie-based hashmaps for both the sequential and concurrent setting [1,19]. Our work differs by having a very conservative approach to the expansion of the trie in order to achieve both speed and overall memory reductions. Notably, the burst tries [13] do not make use of a B-Tree-style pointer scheme and do not enforce removal of the prefix, resulting in an overhead in memory-consumption and not reduction as in PTries. The HAT-tries [1] enforce the use of hashes for elements in buckets, which is not necessary in our data structure. Moreover, neither [13] nor [1] provide a formal definition of their algorithms or the semantics, and they do not present the delete-operation (or "inverse burst"), which we provide. Also Bagwells work on HAMT [2] is mostly using trie-structures in combination with hashes of data and comes with added memory-footprint rather than memory reduction. In our experiments, we compare the PTrie performance only with Google's dense-hash/sparsehash implementations as other popular trie libraries [5,20,25] are not competitive with Google hash libraries for the model checking application domain that relies on fast and memory efficient implementation of sets.

Various forms of trees (Red/Black trees, binary trees, heaps) are conventionally also used for implementing sets and map-like data structures but such implementations are generally regarded inferior in terms of performance [6,7]. Binary Decision Diagrams (BDD) [3] are another efficient way of storing binary strings, however with a very high average computational cost (as documented e.g. in [15]) for the basic single-element operations such as insert and delete.

In the domain of model-checking, Laarman et al. [17] introduced a tree-style compressing data-structure for multi-core model checking, a method that compresses inserted data on-the-fly by utilizing sub-string sharing between integer strings, encoded into a tree structure. A similar technique has been used by the tool DIVINE [21], leading to great memory reductions, however, at the cost of performance. While both papers demonstrate promising results, we argue that these works are orthogonal as they both rely on efficient map and set implementations. Furthermore, these methods come with a number of restrictions making them less suitable as general set and map implementations. Other model checking specific compression-techniques like *Delta*-compression [9] have been proposed but suffer from even a greater impact on running-time as well as lacking general applicability. The explicit-state model checker LoLa [24] implements a basic prefix sharing scheme for the state-compression, but has yet to provide this as a stand-alone library with accompanying benchmarks and does not include the essential performance enhancements used in PTrie.

2   Definition of PTrie

Let $\mathcal{B} = \{0, 1\}$ be a binary alphabet and let $\mathcal{B}^*$ be the set of all binary strings over $\mathcal{B}$ where ϵ is the empty string. If $w = b_1 b_2 \ldots b_n$ and $w' = b'_1 b'_2 \ldots b'_m$ then $w \circ w' = b_1 b_2 \ldots b_n b'_1 b'_2 \ldots b'_m$ is the concatenation of the two strings (we shall often write just ww' instead of $w \circ w'$). For a binary string $w = b_1 b_2 \ldots b_n$, the length of w is defined as $|w| = n$ where by definition $|\epsilon| = 0$, and we use the substring notation $w_{[i,j]}$ where $1 \leq i, j \leq n$ such that $w_{[i,j]} = b_i b_{i+1} \ldots b_j$ if $i \leq j$ and $w_{[i,j]} = \epsilon$ if $i > j$.

Let $\mathcal{B}^n$ be the set of all binary strings of length n and let $\Theta^n = \{ww' \mid w \in \mathcal{B}^*, w' \in \{\bullet\}^*, |ww'| = n\}$ be the set of all extended binary strings of length n, i.e. binary strings that can be suffixed with a sequence of wild characters $\bullet$. The semantics of an extended binary string w is the set of all binary strings it represents $[\![w]\!]$ and it is inductively defined as follows (where $b \in \mathcal{B} \cup \{\bullet\}$ and $w \in (\mathcal{B} \cup \{\bullet\})^*$).

$$\llbracket \epsilon \rrbracket = \{\epsilon\}$$

$$\llbracket b \circ w \rrbracket = \begin{cases} \{b \circ w' \mid w' \in \llbracket w \rrbracket\} & \text{if } b \in \mathcal{B} \\ \{0 \circ w', 1 \circ w' \mid w' \in \llbracket w \rrbracket\} & \text{if } b = \bullet \end{cases}$$

In the rest of this paper, we assume an implicitly given integer constant $\iota > 0$ called the byte size and an integer constant $\kappa \geq 2$ called the bucket size.

Definition 1 (PTrie Syntax). *A PTrie is a tuple* $\mathbb{P} = (F, L, E, \top, \lambda, \beta)$ *where*

1. F *is a finite set of forwarding vertices,*
2. L *is a finite set of leaf vertices such that* $F \cap L = \emptyset$,
3. $E \subseteq F \times (F \cup L)$ *is a finite set of edges such that* $(F \cup L, E)$ *is a tree,*
4. $\top \in F$ *is the root vertex of the tree* $(F \cup L, E)$,
5. $\lambda : E \to \Theta^\iota$ *is a labeling function assigning an extended binary string of length* ι *to each edge such that*
   (a) $\llbracket \lambda(u, v) \rrbracket \cap \llbracket \lambda(u, v') \rrbracket = \emptyset$ *for all* $(u, v), (u, v') \in E$ *where* $v \neq v'$, *and*
   (b) $\lambda(u, v) \in \mathcal{B}^\iota$ *for all* $(u, v) \in E$ *where* $v \in F$,
6. $\beta : L \cup F \to 2^{\mathcal{B}^*}$ *is a bucket function such that*
   (a) $0 < |\beta(u)| \leq \kappa$ *for all* $u \in L$,
   (b) $|w| \geq \iota$ *for all* $w \in \beta(u)$ *where* $u \in L$,
   (c) $w_{[1,\iota]} \in \llbracket \lambda(u, v) \rrbracket$ *for all* $w \in \beta(v)$ *where* $(u, v) \in E$ *and* $v \in L$, *and*
   (d) $|w| < \iota$ *for all* $u \in F$ *and all* $w \in \beta(u)$.

A PTrie example is given in Fig. 1a. We note particularly the difference between forwarding and leaf vertices. The bucket at a forwarding vertex contains the suffix of the string to be appended to the labels on the path from the root to the vertex (for example vertex c contains the bucket with the suffixes $\{1, 00\}$ that represent the strings $010 \circ 1$ and $010 \circ 00$). However, the bucket at a leaf vertex must first specify the concrete binary string that matches the extended binary string on its incoming edge, followed by the suffix of the string (for example the vertex b represents the strings 111 and $111 \circ 0$ as the first three bits of each string in the bucket of b must match the extended binary string $11\bullet$).

Before we introduce the main algorithms of the data structure, let us formally define the semantics of a PTrie as a set of strings that the PTrie represents.

Definition 2 (PTrie Semantics). *Let* $\mathbb{P} = (F, L, E, \top, \lambda, \beta)$ *be a PTrie. The semantics of* $\mathbb{P}$, *denoted by* $\llbracket \mathbb{P} \rrbracket \subseteq \mathcal{B}^*$, *is defined inductively as follows in the height of the tree so that* $\llbracket \mathbb{P} \rrbracket = \llbracket \top \rrbracket$ *and*

$$\llbracket u \in L \rrbracket = \beta(u)$$

$$\llbracket u \in F \rrbracket = \beta(u) \cup \bigcup_{(u,v) \in E,\ v \in F} \{\lambda(u, v) \circ w \mid w \in \llbracket v \rrbracket\} \cup \bigcup_{(u,v) \in E,\ v \in L} \llbracket v \rrbracket .$$

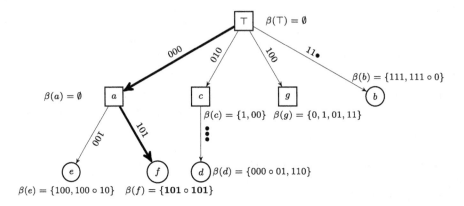

(a) A PTrie $\mathbb{P} = (F, L, E, \top, \lambda, \beta)$ with byte size $\iota = 3$ and maximal bucket size $\kappa = 2$ containing the binary strings $[\![\mathbb{P}]\!] = \{000 \circ 100, 000 \circ 100 \circ 10, 000 \circ 101 \circ 101, 010 \circ 1, 010 \circ 00, 010 \circ 000 \circ 01, 010 \circ 110, 100 \circ 0, 100 \circ 1, 100 \circ 01, 100 \circ 11, 111, 111 \circ 0\}$. Squares indicate forwarding vertices and circles indicate leaf-vertices. We let the labeling (λ) be implicitly indicated by the labeling on the edges. The path and suffix of the binary string $000 \circ 101 \circ 101$ is highlighted.

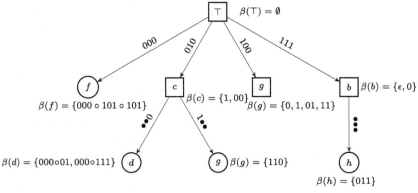

(b) The PTrie from Figure 1a after inserting $\{010 \circ 000 \circ 111, 111 \circ 011\}$ and removing $\{000 \circ 100, 000 \circ 100 \circ 10\}$.

Fig. 1. Running example

3   Operations on PTrie

Let us assume a given PTrie $\mathbb{P} = (F, L, E, \top, \lambda, \beta)$ and a binary string w. We shall now explain the algorithms for the basic set operations

- $\texttt{Member}(\mathbb{P}, w)$ for checking the existence of w in $\mathbb{P}$,
- $\texttt{Insert}(\mathbb{P}, w)$ for adding w into $\mathbb{P}$, and
- $\texttt{Delete}(\mathbb{P}, w)$ for removing w from $\mathbb{P}$.

The algorithms will use the following functions for manipulating PTries: $\text{Find}(\mathbb{P}, u, w)$ for searching from the vertex u for the binary string w, $\text{Split}(\mathbb{P}, v)$ for subdividing a vertex once its bucket size becomes larger than κ, and its inverse $\text{Merge}(\mathbb{P}, v)$ for reducing the size of the PTrie by merging two vertices. We also define the parent function (used by the Split and Merge algorithms) as $P : F \cup L \to F$ such that $P(v) = u$ where $u \in V$ is the unique vertex such that $(u, v) \in E$ and by agreement $P(\top) = \top$.

3.1   Member Algorithm

The algorithm for checking whether a binary string is already stored in a PTrie is presented in Algorithm 2 which is based on Algorithm 1 that searches for the presence of a binary string in a PTrie. This algorithm is also used for the insertion and deletion algorithms.

Algorithm 1 implements a search from a given vertex u following a given binary string as long as possible, until either a leaf-vertex is reached or no further

---

Algorithm 1. $\text{Find}(\mathbb{P}, u, w)$

Data: A PTrie $\mathbb{P} = (F, L, E, \top, \lambda, \beta)$, a vertex $u \in V$ and a binary string w
Result: (v, w') where w' is a suffix of w that cannot be any further matched by
a (unique) path starting from u and labeled with the longest possible
prefix of w and $v \in V$ is the vertex where this mismatch happens

1 **begin**
2   **if** $|w| < \iota$ **then**
3 | **return** (u, w)
4    $E_u = \{(u, v) \in E \mid w_{[1,\iota]} \in [\![\lambda(u, v)]\!]\}$;
5   **if** $E_u = \emptyset$ **then**
6 | **return** (u, w)
7   **else**
8   Let $\{(u, v)\} = E_u$ // note that $|E_u| \le 1$ due to Definition 1, case 5a
9   **if** $v \in L$ **then**
10 | **return** (v, w)
11   **else**
12 | **return** $\text{Find}(\mathbb{P}, v, w_{[\iota+1,|w|]})$

Algorithm 2. $\text{Member}(\mathbb{P}, w)$

Data: A PTrie $\mathbb{P} = (F, L, E, \top, \lambda, \beta)$ and a binary string w
Result: tt if $w \in [\![\mathbb{P}]\!]$, else ff

1 **begin**
2    $(v, w') \leftarrow \text{Find}(\mathbb{P}, \top, w)$;
3   **if** $w' \in \beta(v)$ **then**
4 | **return** tt
5   **else**
6 | **return** ff

match is possible and the algorithm returns the reached vertex and the suffix of the string w that could not be uniquely matched in the PTrie. This algorithm closely mimics the inductive definition of the semantics of PTrie in Definition 2.

Theorem 1. *Algorithm 2 run on an input PTrie $\mathbb{P}$ and a binary string w terminates and returns tt if and only if $w \in [\![\mathbb{P}]\!]$.*

3.2 Insert Algorithm

We shall now focus on inserting a binary string w into a PTrie $\mathbb{P}$ as described in Algorithm 3. We start by matching the prefix of w from the root of the PTrie (line 2) to the vertex v from which we cannot follow the prefix of w any further. Either the vertex v is a forwarding vertex and if the unmatched suffix w' of w is shorter than ι, we insert it into the bucket of v at line 8 and we are done. If w' is on the other hand longer than ι, we need to create a new leaf vertex u and

---

Algorithm 3. Insert$(\mathbb{P}, w)$

Data: A PTrie $\mathbb{P} = (F, L, E, \top, \lambda, \beta)$ and a binary string w
Result: $\mathbb{P}'$ where $[\![\mathbb{P}']\!] = [\![\mathbb{P}]\!] \cup \{w\}$ and $\mathbb{P}'$ satisfies all conditions of Definition 1.

1 **begin**
2 $\quad$ $(v, w') \leftarrow$ Find$(\mathbb{P}, \top, w)$;
3 $\quad$ **if** $w' \in \beta(v)$ **then**
4 $\quad\quad$ | $\quad$ **return** $\mathbb{P}$
5 $\quad$ **else**
6 $\quad\quad$ **if** $v \in F$ **then**
7 $\quad\quad\quad$ **if** $|w'| < \iota$ **then**
8 $\quad\quad\quad\quad$ | $\quad$ $\beta(v) \leftarrow \beta(v) \cup \{w'\}$;
9 $\quad\quad\quad\quad$ | $\quad$ **return** $(F, L, E, \top, \lambda, \beta)$
10 $\quad\quad\quad$ **else**
11 $\quad\quad\quad\quad$ $\ell \leftarrow$
$$\underset{\ell' \in \Theta^\iota \text{ where } w'_{[1, \iota]} \in [\![\ell']\!]}{\operatorname{argmax}} \begin{cases} 0 & \text{if } \exists u \in F \cup L \text{ s.t. } [\![\ell']\!] \cap [\![\lambda(v, u)]\!] \neq \emptyset \\ |[\![\ell']\!]| & \text{otherwise} \end{cases}$$
12 $\quad\quad\quad\quad$ Make a fresh leaf vertex u;
13 $\quad\quad\quad\quad$ $L \leftarrow L \cup \{u\}$;
14 $\quad\quad\quad\quad$ $E \leftarrow E \cup \{(v, u)\}$;
15 $\quad\quad\quad\quad$ $\lambda(v, u) \leftarrow \ell$;
16 $\quad\quad\quad\quad$ $\beta(u) \leftarrow \{w'\}$;
17 $\quad\quad\quad\quad$ **return** $(F, L, E, \top, \lambda, \beta)$
18 $\quad\quad$ **else**
19 $\quad\quad\quad$ $\beta(v) \leftarrow \beta(v) \cup \{w'\}$;
20 $\quad\quad\quad$ **if** $|\beta(v)| \leq \kappa$ **then**
21 $\quad\quad\quad\quad$ | $\quad$ **return** $(F, L, E, \top, \lambda, \beta)$
22 $\quad\quad\quad$ **else**
23 $\quad\quad\quad\quad$ | $\quad$ **return** Split$((F, L, E, \top, \lambda, \beta), v)$

Algorithm 4. $\mathtt{Split}(\mathbb{P}, v)$

Data: A PTrie $\mathbb{P} = (F, L, E, \top, \lambda, \beta)$ and a vertex $v \in L$ such that $\beta(v) > \kappa$.
Result: $\mathbb{P}'$ such that $[\![\mathbb{P}]\!] = [\![\mathbb{P}']\!]$ and $\mathbb{P}'$ satisfies all conditions of Definition 1

```
 1  begin
 2  │   if |[[λ(P(v), v)]]| = 1 then
 3  │   │   F ← F ∪ {v}; L ← L \ {v};
 4  │   │   β(v) ← {w[ι+1,|w|] | w ∈ β(v) and |w| < 2ι};
 5  │   │   B ← {w[ι+1,|w|] | w ∈ β(v) and |w| ≥ 2ι};
 6  │   │   if B = ∅ then
 7  │   │   │   return (F, L, E, ⊤, λ, β)
 8  │   │   else
 9  │   │   │   Make a fresh leaf vertex u;
10  │   │   │   L ← L ∪ {u}; E ← E ∪ {(v, u)}; λ(v, u) ← •ι; β(u) ← B;
11  │   │   │   if |β(u)| ≤ κ then
12  │   │   │   │   return (F, L, E, ⊤, λ, β)
13  │   │   │   else
14  │   │   │   │   return Split((F, L, E, ⊤, λ, β), u)
15  │   else
16  │   │   Let w ∘ •^m = λ(P(v), v) such that w ∈ {0, 1}* and m > 0.
17  │   │   ℓ₀ ← w0 ∘ •^{m−1}; ℓ₁ ← w1 ∘ •^{m−1};
18  │   │   B₀ = {w ∈ β(v) | w[1,ι] ∈ [[ℓ₀]]}; B₁ = {w ∈ β(v) | w[1,ι] ∈ [[ℓ₁]]};
19  │   │   if B₀ ≠ ∅ and B₁ ≠ ∅ then
20  │   │   │   Make a fresh leaf vertex u;
21  │   │   │   L ← L ∪ {u}, E ← E ∪ {(P(v), u)};
22  │   │   │   λ(P(v), v) ← ℓ₀; λ(P(v), u) ← ℓ₁;
23  │   │   │   β(v) ← B₀; β(u) ← B₁;
24  │   │   │   return (F, L, E, ⊤, λ, β)
25  │   │   else
26  │   │   │   if B₀ ≠ ∅ then
27  │   │   │   │   λ(P(v), v) ← ℓ₀;
28  │   │   │   else
29  │   │   │   │   λ(P(v), v) ← ℓ₁;
30  │   │   │   return Split((F, L, E, ⊤, λ, β), v)
```

---

store w' in its bucket at line 16. The point is to label the edge (v, u) with the most general and non-conflicting label ℓ selected at line 11. In the second case where v is a leaf vertex, we add the suffix w' of w into the bucket at line 19 and should the size of the bucket exceed the maximum size κ, we call the function $\mathtt{Split}$ at line 23 to balance the PTrie.

An example of inserting two strings is given in Fig. 1b. The insertion of the string $010 \circ 000$ causes the creation of the sibling g for the vertex d and splitting of the label $\bullet\bullet\bullet$ into $0\bullet\bullet$ and $1\bullet\bullet$. The insertion of $111 \circ 011$ implies that the leaf vertex b turns into a forwarding vertex while we create a fresh leaf vertex h and adjust the buckets accordingly.

Theorem 2. *Algorithm 3 run on an input PTrie $\mathbb{P}$ and a binary string w terminates and returns a PTrie $\mathbb{P}'$ such that $[\![\mathbb{P}']\!] = [\![\mathbb{P}]\!] \cup \{w\}$.*

3.3   Delete Algorithm

We here discuss the algorithm for removing a binary string w from a PTrie $\mathbb{P}$ as described in Algorithm 5. As with the insertion algorithm, the `Delete` algorithm may call the function `Merge` defined in Algorithm 6—a function that attempts to revert divisions previously made by the `Split` algorithm.

Algorithm 5. `Delete`$(\mathbb{P}, w)$

Data: A PTrie $\mathbb{P} = (F, L, E, \top, \lambda, \beta)$ and a binary string w
Result: $\mathbb{P}'$ where $[\![\mathbb{P}']\!] = [\![\mathbb{P}]\!] \setminus \{w\}$ and $\mathbb{P}'$ satisfies all conditions of Definition 1

```
 1 begin
 2  |    (v, w') ← Find(P, ⊤, w);
 3  |    if w' ∉ β(v) then
 4  |    |    return P
 5  |    else
 6  |    |    β(v) ← β(v) \ {w'};
 7  |    |    if v ∈ F then
 8  |    |    |    if v has no children then
 9  |    |    |    |    if v = ⊤ then
10  |    |    |    |    |    return (F, L, E, ⊤, λ, β)
11  |    |    |    |    if |β(v)| > κ then
12  |    |    |    |    |    return (F, L, E, ⊤, λ, β)
13  |    |    |    |    L ← L ∪ {v}; F ← F \ {v};
14  |    |    |    |    β(v) ← {λ(P(v), v) ∘ w | w ∈ β(v)};
15  |    |    |    |    return Merge((F, L, E, ⊤, λ, β), v)
16  |    |    |    else
17  |    |    |    |    if v has exactly one child u and u ∈ L then
18  |    |    |    |    |    return Merge((F, L, E, ⊤, λ, β), u)
19  |    |    |    |    else
20  |    |    |    |    |    return (F, L, E, ⊤, λ, β)
21  |    |    else
22  |    |    |    return Merge((F, L, E, ⊤, λ, β), v)
```

Initially we try to match the prefix of w to a unique path from the root of the PTrie (line 2 of `Delete`) and we let v be the vertex reached at the end of this prefix and w' be the unmatched suffix of w. If w did not exist in the PTrie, we return the unaltered PTrie at line 4. Otherwise we remove w' from the bucket of v. Either $v \in L$, and we attempt to reduce the PTrie (line 22), or we are in the more complex situation where $v \in F$. If $v \in F$ and v has no children (as illustrated by vertex g in Fig. 1a) then we can turn v into a leaf node (line 13) and attempt to reduce the size of the PTrie (line 15). However, as $\top$ has to stay in F, we return $\mathbb{P}$ if $v = \top$ (line 10). If $|\beta(v)| > \kappa$ then turning v into a leaf-node would violate condition 6a in Definition 1 and we therefore return the PTrie as it is (line 12). If $v \in F$ and v has only a single child such that this child is not a forwarding vertex, and merging v with its child will not violate condition 6a

---

Algorithm 6. $\mathtt{Merge}(\mathbb{P}, v)$

Data: A PTrie $\mathbb{P} = (F, L, E, \top, \lambda, \beta)$ and a vertex $v \in L$
Result: $\mathbb{P}'$ s.t. $[\![\mathbb{P}]\!] = [\![\mathbb{P}']\!]$ and $\mathbb{P}'$ satisfies all conditions of Definition 1

1 **begin**
2   **if** $\lambda(P(v), v) = \bullet^\iota$ **then**
3   **if** $|\beta(v)| = 0$ *and* $|\beta(P(v))| > \kappa$ **then**
4           $E \leftarrow E \setminus \{(P(v), v)\}$; $L \leftarrow L \setminus \{v\}$;
5   **return** $(F, L, E, \top, \lambda, \beta)$
6   **if** $P(v) = \top$ **then**
7   **return** $\mathbb{P}$
8   **else**
9           $u \leftarrow P(v)$; $\ell \leftarrow \lambda(u, v)$;
10   **if** $|\beta(v)| + |\beta(u)| \leq \kappa$ **then**
11              $E \leftarrow (E \cup \{(P(u), v)\}) \setminus \{(P(u), u), (u, v)\}$; $F \leftarrow F \setminus \{u\}$;
12              $\lambda(P(u), v) \leftarrow \ell$;
13              $\beta(v) \leftarrow \{\ell \circ w \mid w \in \beta(v) \cup \beta(u)\}$;
14   **return** $\mathtt{Merge}((F, L, E, \top, \lambda, \beta), v)$
15   **else**
16   **return** $(F, L, E, \top, \lambda, \beta)$
17   **else**
18   Let $b_1 \ldots b_n \bullet^m = \lambda(P(v), v)$;
19        $\ell \leftarrow b_1 \ldots b_{n-1} \bullet^{m+1}$;
20        $V \leftarrow \{(P(v), u) \in E \mid u \neq v$ and $[\![\lambda(P(v), u)]\!] \cap [\![\ell]\!] \neq \emptyset\}$;
21   **if** $V = \emptyset$ **then**
22           $\lambda(P(v), v) \leftarrow \ell$;
23   **return** $\mathtt{Merge}((F, L, E, \top, \lambda, \beta), v)$
24   **else**
25   **if** $V = \{u\}$ *for some* $u \in L$ *and* $|\beta(v)| + |\beta(u)| \leq \kappa$ **then**
26              $\lambda(P(v), v) \leftarrow \ell$;
27              $\beta(v) \leftarrow \beta(v) \cup \beta(u)$;
28              $E \leftarrow E \setminus \{(P(u), u)\}$; $L \leftarrow L \setminus \{u\}$;
29   **return** $\mathtt{Merge}((F, L, E, \top, \lambda, \beta), v)$
30   **else**
31   **return** $\mathbb{P}$

---

in Definition 1, then we also attempt to merge (line 18). Otherwise just return PTrie without further modifications (line 20).

An example of removing two different strings from our running example is presented in Fig. 1b. The removal causes the leaf vertex e to get an empty bucket implying that it gets removed. This change in turn propagates to the vertex a that is also removed and its bucket content is merged with that of f.

Theorem 3. *Algorithm 5 given a PTrie $\mathbb{P}$ and a binary string w terminates and returns a PTrie $\mathbb{P}'$ such that $[\![\mathbb{P}']\!] = [\![\mathbb{P}]\!] \setminus \{w\}$.*

4   Implementation

The PTrie interface is implemented as an open source C++ library and it is available at https://github.com/petergjoel/ptrie under the GPL version 3 license. Apart from the implementation of all the basic set operations on PTries as described in this paper (implemented in `ptrie::set`), two other flavors of PTries exist: one providing unique and non-changing identifiers for inserted elements (`ptrie::stable_set`) and one providing the functionality of a map, combined with non-changing identifiers (`ptrie::map`)[1]. The source code provides further documentation and information.

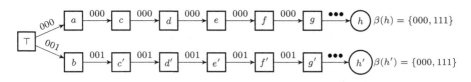

Fig. 2. A worst-case scenario for PTries with $\iota = 3$ and $\kappa = 2$ containing 4 binary strings $\{000 \circ 000 \circ 000 \circ 000 \circ 000 \circ 000 \circ 000, 000 \circ 000 \circ 000 \circ 000 \circ 000 \circ 000 \circ 111, 100 \circ 100 \circ 100 \circ 100 \circ 100 \circ 100 \circ 000, 100 \circ 100 \circ 100 \circ 100 \circ 100 \circ 100 \circ 111\}$

Let us now settle some implementation details. We currently use the bucket size $\kappa = 64$ and the byte size $\iota = 8$, following conventions for standard byte-sizes. As modern architectures do not support addressing nor allocation of memory areas of less than a single byte, our implementation of PTries allows only the insertion of binary strings with bit-lengths that are a multiple of ι. Furthermore, to avoid frequent splits and re-merging of PTries, the `Delete` and `Merge` algorithms initiate the balancing of PTrie only once the buckets become smaller than $\frac{\kappa}{3}$, as opposed to the constant κ used in the pseudocode. The experimental evaluations point towards a slightly worse memory utilization at the exchange of less frequent re-balancing of the PTrie.

Regarding the memory for storing vertices of a PTrie, forwarding vertices are implemented as directly indexed tables with 64-bit indexes and with some additional book-keeping information they occupy 2064 bytes. Leaf vertices are, on the other hand, lightweight constructions taking up only 16 bytes. The current implementation of PTrie prefixes all inserted binary strings with their length (using two additional bytes). In our experience, such an addition generally improves the performance and reduces memory-consumption. Moreover, as we aim at making the PTries fast, the speed optimization can occasionally imply an increased memory consumption for some very specific sets of binary strings, as demonstrated in Fig. 2, where just a few strings create a long sequence of memory-demanding forwarding vertices. This implies that long, almost similar, binary strings which differ only at the beginning and at the end will make the PTrie perform badly in terms of memory.

---

[1] Both these extension come with a smaller overhead in run-time and memory. Also, currently neither of these extensions support `Delete`.

Hence, depending on the specific application domain, the concrete encoding of the states into binary strings can have an effect on the PTrie performance. As a heuristic attempt to improve prefix-sharing of Petri net markings (an experiment discussed in detail in the next section), we first statically order places in the models by the number of incoming and outgoing arcs. Each such marking is then encoded according to a number of schemes in order to minimize its length. The schemes all fall in one of three categories: either only non-empty places are stored (with the least amount of bits), or a bit-vector is used to represent non-empty places in the fixed ordering of places, or we use a combination of the two previous schemes. To determine which way a marking was encoded, we prefix the encoding with a 8-bit header describing the exact encoding scheme that is employed. Details of the encoding-scheme can be found at https://bit.ly/AlignedEncodercpp.

5   Experimental Evaluation

We conducted two series of experiments comparing our PTrie implementation against `google::sparse_hash_set` and `google::dense_hash_set` by Google[2], generally regarded as the state-of-the-art [22,23] space-efficient and time-efficient, respectively, implementations of sets based on hashing. We employ `jemalloc` [10] for memory allocation and `MurmurHash64A`[3] as hash-function for the hash-map implementations. In our evaluation we omit the `std::unordered_set` implementation from the standard library of `C++14` as it was consistently outperformed by the Google implementations (see [22,23] for further benchmarks).

In the first round of experiments, we test the speed and memory requirements of insertion, deletion and lookups, simulating a workload using pseudo-random 64-bit integers (with the same seed so that the same sequence of numbers is inserted/deleted/checked in all test setups). In the second round of experiments, we modify the verification-tool `verifypn` [14][4] that is distributed as a part of the Petri net verification tool TAPAAL [4,8], and we conduct an exhaustive exploration of the full state-space of large Petri net models used at the MCC'16 competition [16]. All experiments were conducted on AMD Opteron 6376 Processors and limited to 120 GB of RAM and 4 days of computation.

5.1   Simulated Workload

We conduct three sets of experiments called *Insert*, *Insert+50%Delete* and *Insert+50%Member*, all scaled by the number 2^E of pseudorandomly generated and inserted elements into the set implementation. In the *Insert* experiment, we iteratively insert 2^E binary numbers encoded as 64-bit unsigned integers.

---

[2] Both available at https://github.com/sparsehash/sparsehash.

[3] Available at https://github.com/aappleby/smhasher/wiki/MurmurHash2.

[4] Available at https://code.launchpad.net/verifypn.

In the *Insert+50%Delete* and *Insert+50%Member* experiments, after each insertion, we choose with 50% probability whether to execute a `Delete` or `Member` operation, respectively. In *Insert+50%Delete*, we randomly draw for deletion an element that was previously inserted, but we do not check whether the element was already removed or not. This implies that with 33% probability it tries to remove a nonexisting element. In *Insert+50%Member*, we randomly select an element for which we do an `Member` operation, such that about one half of the existence checks are with a positive answer.

Table 1. Time in seconds for the simulated workload experiments

E	ptrie	dense	sparse	ptrie/dense	ptrie/sparse
Insert					
28	437.2	386.0	569.1	113%	77%
29	869.0	757.1	1111.3	115%	78%
30	1749.2	1540.2	2326.7	114%	75%
31	3572.0	3081.7	4785.6	116%	75%
32	7184.6	6126.6	9963.6	117%	72%
Average	2762.4	2378.3	3751.2	115%	75%
Insert+50%Delete					
28	751.5	744.1	742.7	101%	101%
29	1516.8	1494.3	1461.9	102%	104%
30	3038.5	3032.1	2997.8	100%	101%
31	6392.3	5837.4	6150.1	110%	104%
32	13356.1	11701.0	13115.5	114%	102%
Average	5011.1	4561.8	4893.6	105%	102%
Insert+50%Member					
28	709.6	591.2	771.0	120%	92%
29	1468.4	1219.3	1583.8	120%	93%
30	2829.1	2363.0	3195.4	120%	89%
31	5839.8	4707.6	6597.3	124%	89%
32	12244.2	9473.2	13676.5	129%	90%
Average	4618.2	3670.8	5164.8	123%	90%

The results measuring the speed of operations are presented in Table 1. For pure insertions, PTries are on average about 15% slower than dense_hash but 25% faster than sparse_hash. When we add deletions, PTries are only about 5% slower than dense_hash and essentially comparable with sparse_hash (on average just 2% slower). In the last experiment where we add frequent queries on the presence of a string in the set, dense_hash becomes 23% faster but on the other hand PTries are by 10% faster than sparse_hash. In summary, sparse_hash is in general slower or equal in speed with PTrie, while dense_hash is the fastest of the three data structures.

However, we can see in Table 2 a significant reduction of the memory-footprint in all of the experiments (*Insert+50%Member* is not included as its memory usage is identical with pure inserts). PTries deliver about 70% of the memory reduction compared to dense_hash and between 42–57% reduction compared to sparse_hash (depending on whether deletions are included or not).

In conclusion, PTrie is the most memory efficient data structure that is faster or at worst equal in speed with sparse_hash. The fastest set implementation is dense_hash, however, at the cost of a large memory overhead. We remark that the drop in relative memory-reduction in the *Insert* experiment when $E = 32$ is due to the creation of a large number of forwarding vertices—this occurs with high probability for truly random strings when E is a multiple of 8.

Table 2. Memory in megabyte for the simulated workload experiments

E	ptrie	dense	sparse	ptrie/dense	ptrie/sparse
Insert and *Insert+50%Member*					
28	2033.6	6151.7	4239.6	33%	48%
29	3197.6	12295.7	8455.9	26%	38%
30	6115.7	24583.7	16923.0	25%	36%
31	10827.6	49159.7	33908.2	22%	32%
32	37839.6	98311.7	67757.7	39%	56%
Average	12002.8	38100.5	26256.9	29%	42%
Insert+50%Delete					
28	1935.8	6157.7	3032.3	31%	64%
29	3383.8	12301.6	5966.5	28%	57%
30	6960.7	24589.6	12057.8	28%	58%
31	13488.9	49165.6	24914.0	27%	54%
32	37493.6	98317.6	68195.0	38%	55%
Average	12652.6	38106.4	22833.1	31%	57%

5.2 Real Workload by Petri Net Model Checking

In order to test the PTrie performance on a realistic scenario, we integrate PTrie as a part of a Petri net model checker. We replace the state-storage of the verification algorithm used by verifypn with the respective set implementations (by using an encoding of Petri net markings to binary strings as discussed in the implementation section). We then conduct an exhaustive state-space search on the P/T nets from the MCC'16 competition. To reduce the impact of auxiliary datastructures used by the algorithm, we conduct the search with two different search-strategies (breadth first and depth first), and we report the minimum of the memory and time-consumption from either of these searches. We consider in total 94 Petri nets with a nontrival but feasible state-space size. More concretely, we selected all nets with more than 10^6 and less than 10^{10} reachable markings. Out of these 94 nets, PTrie-based variant completed 89 test-cases, ran out of memory on 4 models and timed out on a single instance. The dense_hash-based model checker completed only a subset of the test-cases solved by PTrie and exceeded the memory-bound for additional 9 nets. A similar performance was achieved by sparse_hash that also completed only a subset of problems solved by PTrie but exceeded the memory for 7 additional nets. In the summary tables we consider so only 80 state-space searches that were completed by all three set-implementations.

In Table 3 we can see that PTries are on average as fast as the fastest hash-map implementation via dense_hash with only a 3% overhead on average, while PTries provide significant 14% speedup compared to sparse_hash. There seems to be no correlation between the number of states/markings (equivalent to the number of insert operations) and the relative performance achieved. With respect to memory usage, the experiments confirm the effectiveness of PTrie as

Table 3. Time in seconds for the 5 best, 5 median and 5 worst Petri net models, ordered by the performance of ptrie relative to dense_hash. Legend for the models: a = Angiogenesis-PT-05, b = PolyORBNT-PT-S05J20, c = Diffusion2D-PT-D05N010, d = SmallOperatingSystem-PT-MT0128DC0032, e = SmallOperatingSystem-PT-MT0 128DC0064, f = ARMCacheCoherence-PT-none, g = TCPcondis-PT-05, h = Auto Flight-PT-01b, i = SimpleLoadBal-PT-10j = ResAllocation-PT-R020C002, k = Param ProductionCell-PT-5, l = ParamProductionCell-PT-0, m = SwimmingPool-PT-04, n = SwimmingPool-PT-03 and o = IOTPpurchase-PT-C05M04P03D02.

Model	ptrie	dense	sparse	ptrie/dense	ptrie/sparse	10^6 states	10^6 operations
a	408.7	517.8	680.5	79%	60%	42.7	486.9
b	12882.8	15888.9	19163.1	81%	67%	693.8	2151.2
c	2337.9	2839.3	3693.7	82%	63%	131.1	5553.7
d	244.6	292.3	526.6	84%	46%	113.3	863.5
e	589.2	693.6	1141.2	85%	52%	261.2	2010.6
f	69451.0	68601.0	70879.3	101%	98%	320.6	22339.6
g	16.4	16.1	20.6	102%	79%	3.0	24.9
h	318.7	312.8	389.7	102%	82%	48.9	354.4
i	5011.5	4917.2	5812.8	102%	86%	406.0	3051.2
j	69.5	67.9	78.3	102%	89%	11.5	66.8
k	25.7	20.4	21.3	126%	121%	1.7	6.7
l	41.4	32.8	33.8	126%	123%	2.8	13.2
m	439.9	345.7	647.9	127%	68%	164.4	1047.5
n	78.3	60.9	112.4	129%	70%	32.2	199.3
o	263.9	163.6	185.2	161%	143%	17.4	108.4
Avg	4608.4	4482.2	5380.0	103%	86%	289.3	3195.2

Table 4. Memory in megabytes for the 5 best, 5 median and 5 worst Petri net models, ordered by the perforamce of PTrie relative to sparse_hash. Legend for the models: a = DNAwalker-PT-06track28RL, b = DNAwalker-PT-04track28LL, c = DNA walker-PT-07track28RR, d = DNAwalker-PT-05track28LR, e = DNAwalker-PT-12ring LLLarge, f = Kanban-PT-0010, g = BridgeAndVehicles-PT-V50P50N20, h = Bridge AndVehicles-PT-V50P20N10, i = BridgeAndVehicles-PT-V50P50N10, j = AutoFlight-PT-05a, k = ParamProductionCell-PT-0, l = IOTPpurchase-PT-C05M04P03D02, m = ParamProductionCell-PT-5, n = ParamProductionCell-PT-3 and o = Param ProductionCell-PT-4.

Model	ptrie	dense	sparse	ptrie/dense	ptrie/sparse	10^6 states	10^6 operations
a	2815.6	16481.6	15063.5	17%	19%	435.3	2983.9
b	2817.6	16481.5	15063.6	17%	19%	432.9	2961.9
c	2855.6	16481.6	15063.6	17%	19%	432.9	2961.9
d	2883.6	16481.6	15063.6	18%	19%	435.3	2983.9
e	14707.6	65901.4	60223.4	22%	24%	1885.4	15271.5
f	16579.6	35751.6	33971.6	46%	49%	1005.9	12032.2
g	21283.5	44344.2	43515.5	48%	49%	896.3	3363.7
h	7539.6	20667.6	15373.6	37%	49%	347.6	1271.7
i	7541.6	20667.5	15375.5	37%	49%	347.6	1271.7
j	1463.6	5203.6	2965.6	28%	49%	68.2	1286.2
k	133.7	169.6	129.6	79%	103%	2.8	13.2
l	879.7	1303.6	763.6	68%	115%	17.4	108.4
m	105.7	91.6	81.6	115%	130%	1.7	6.7
n	93.6	87.5	71.6	107%	131%	1.5	5.9
o	147.7	169.6	111.6	87%	132%	2.4	9.8
Avg	5150.6	13339.3	11056.9	39%	47%	289.3	3195.2

seen in Table 4. In general we observe a significant memory footprint reduction by up to 81% compared to sparse_hash and on average by 53%. The reductions in the case of dense_hash are as expected even higher. We can notice that higher relative memory reduction occurs when we use PTries for models with a larger number of reachable states/markings, confirming that PTries are particularly beneficial for memory demanding applications like model checking. We can observe that for some instances of prefix-sharing, PTries are particularly effective as demonstrated by the "DNAwalker"-cases (using less than 7 bytes per stored marking versus 36 for sparse_hash), while ineffective for the "ParamProductionCell"-cases (using more than 64 bytes per marking versus 49 for sparse_hash). Here we experience the situation described in Fig. 2 caused by the ordering of places in the binary encoding of markings and by the fact that there is large number of places where the number of tokens hardly ever changes during the computation.

6   Conclusion

We presented PTrie, a novel data structure for compressing sets of binary strings while providing fast operations for element addition/removal and containment checks. Compared to the state-of-the-art alternatives that either trade memory savings for time (`google::sparse_hash_set`), or focus on optimizing the speed of operations (`google::dense_hash_set`), our data structure improves the performance of `sparse_hash` both in terms of memory as well as time. Compared to `dense_hash`, we are on average 5–23% slower on random strings, while only 3% slower when storing strings coming from a real application domain, and at the same time we provide 60–70% of memory reduction.

In the future work, we plan to provide an efficient parallelization of the PTries for the use in multi-core architectures, and extend the set of basic operators with intersection, union and difference. Even though these additional operations are not necessary for explicit model checking applications, they may find other application domains and tree-based design of PTries seems to be suitable for this purpose. Finally, a research of tree-walking algorithms for PTries, facilitating complex searches through the elements of the set, are of high interest too.

Acknowledgements. We acknowledge the support from Sino-Danish Basic Research Center IDEA4CPS, the Innovation Fund Denmark center DiCyPS, and the ERC Advanced Grant LASSO. The third author is partially affiliated with FI MU in Brno.

References

1. Askitis, N., Sinha, R.: HAT-trie: a cache-conscious trie-based data structure for strings. In: Proceedings of the Thirtieth Australasian Conference on Computer Science, vol. 62, pp. 97–105. Australian Computer Society Inc. (2007)
2. Bagwell, P.: Ideal hash trees. Es Grands Champs, vol. 1195 (2001)
3. Bryant, R.E.: Graph-based algorithms for Boolean function manipulation. IEEE Trans. Comput. **C–35**(8), 677–691 (1986)
4. Byg, J., Jørgensen, K.Y., Srba, J.: TAPAAL: editor, simulator and verifier of timed-arc petri nets. In: Liu, Z., Ravn, A.P. (eds.) ATVA 2009. LNCS, vol. 5799, pp. 84–89. Springer, Heidelberg (2009). doi:10.1007/978-3-642-04761-9_7
5. Jones, D.C.: HAT-trie implementation. https://github.com/dcjones/hat-trie. Accessed 19 Apr 2017
6. cplusplus.com. C++ map implementation reference. http://www.cplusplus.com/reference/map/map/. Accessed 20 Jan 2017
7. cplusplus.com. C++ set implementation reference. http://www.cplusplus.com/reference/set/set/. Accessed 20 Jan 2017
8. David, A., Jacobsen, L., Jacobsen, M., Jørgensen, K.Y., Møller, M.H., Srba, J.: TAPAAL 2.0: integrated development environment for timed-arc petri nets. In: Flanagan, C., König, B. (eds.) TACAS 2012. LNCS, vol. 7214, pp. 492–497. Springer, Heidelberg (2012). doi:10.1007/978-3-642-28756-5_36
9. Evangelista, S., Pradat-Peyre, J.-F.: Memory efficient state space storage in explicit software model checking. In: Godefroid, P. (ed.) SPIN 2005. LNCS, vol. 3639, pp. 43–57. Springer, Heidelberg (2005). doi:10.1007/11537328_7

10. Evans, J.: A scalable concurrent malloc (3) implementation for FreeBSD. In: Proceedings of the BSDCan Conference Ottawa (2006)

11. Fredkin, E.: Trie memory. Commun. ACM **3**(9), 490–499 (1960)

12. Gwehenberger, G.: Anwendung einer binären verweiskettenmethode beim aufbau von listen/use of a binary tree structure for processing files. IT Inf. Technol. **10**(1–6), 223–226 (1968)

13. Heinz, S., Zobel, J., Williams, H.E.: Burst tries: a fast, efficient data structure for string keys. ACM Trans. Inf. Syst. **20**, 192–223 (2002)

14. Jensen, J.F., Nielsen, T., Oestergaard, L.K., Srba, J.: TAPAAL and reachability analysis of P/T nets. In: Koutny, M., Desel, J., Kleijn, J. (eds.) Transactions on Petri Nets and Other Models of Concurrency XI. LNCS, vol. 9930, pp. 307–318. Springer, Heidelberg (2016). doi:10.1007/978-3-662-53401-4_16

15. Jensen, P.G., Larsen, K.G., Srba, J., Sørensen, M.G., Taankvist, J.H.: Memory efficient data structures for explicit verification of timed systems. In: Badger, J.M., Rozier, K.Y. (eds.) NFM 2014. LNCS, vol. 8430, pp. 307–312. Springer, Cham (2014). doi:10.1007/978-3-319-06200-6_26

16. Kordon, F., Garavel, H., Hillah, L.M., Hulin-Hubard, F., Chiardo, G., Hamez, A., Jezequel, L., Miner, A., Meijer, J., Paviot-Adet, E., Racordon, D., Rodriguez, C., Rohr, C., Srba, J., Thierry-Mieg, Y., Trinh, G., Wolf, K.: Complete Results for the 2016 Edition of the Model Checking Contest, June 2016. http://mcc.lip6.fr/2016/results.php

17. Laarman, A., van de Pol, J., Weber, M.: Parallel recursive state compression for free. In: Groce, A., Musuvathi, M. (eds.) SPIN 2011. LNCS, vol. 6823, pp. 38–56. Springer, Heidelberg (2011). doi:10.1007/978-3-642-22306-8_4

18. Morrison, D.R.: Patriciapractical algorithm to retrieve information coded in alphanumeric. J. ACM (JACM) **15**(4), 514–534 (1968)

19. Prokopec, A., Bronson, N.G., Bagwell, P., Odersky, M.: Concurrent tries with efficient non-blocking snapshots. ACM SIGPLAN Not. **47**(8), 151–160 (2012). ACM

20. Renaud, M.: Trie (aka. prefix tree). https://github.com/m-renaud/trie. Accessed 19 Apr 2017

21. Ročkai, P., Štill, V., Barnat, J.: Techniques for memory-efficient model checking of C and C++ code. In: Calinescu, R., Rumpe, B. (eds.) SEFM 2015. LNCS, vol. 9276, pp. 268–282. Springer, Cham (2015). doi:10.1007/978-3-319-22969-0_19

22. Timonk. Big memory, part 3.5: Google sparsehash! (2011). https://research.neustar.biz/2011/11/27/big-memory-part-3-5-google-sparsehash/. Accessed 20 Jan 2017

23. Welch, N.: Hash table benchmarks. http://incise.org/hash-table-benchmarks.html. Accessed 20 Jan 2017

24. Wolf, K.: Running LoLA 2.0 in a model checking competition. In: Koutny, M., Desel, J., Kleijn, J. (eds.) Transactions on Petri Nets and Other Models of Concurrency XI. LNCS, vol. 9930, pp. 274–285. Springer, Heidelberg (2016). doi:10.1007/978-3-662-53401-4_13

25. Yang, J.: An implementation of two-trie and tail-trie using double array. https://github.com/jianingy/libtrie. Accessed 19 Apr 2017

Security

Inferring Secrets by Guided Experiments

Quoc Huy Do$^{(\boxtimes)}$, Richard Bubel, and Reiner Hähnle

Department of Computer Science, TU Darmstadt, Darmstadt, Germany
{do,bubel,haehnle}@cs.tu-darmstadt.de

Abstract. A program has secure information flow if it does not leak any secret information to publicly observable output. A large number of static and dynamic analyses have been devised to check programs for secure information flow. In this paper, we present an algorithm that can carry out a systematic and efficient attack to automatically extract secrets from an insecure program. The algorithm combines static analysis and dynamic execution. The attacker strategy learns from past experiments and chooses as its next attack one that promises maximal knowledge gain about the secret. The idea is to provide the software developer with concrete information about the severity of an information leakage.

Keywords: Information flow · Symbolic execution · Static analysis

1 Introduction

Information flow security is concerned with the development of methods that ensure that programs do not leak secret information, i.e., that it is not possible to learn secret information by looking at publicly accessible output.

To ensure that programs have secure information flow relative to a given information flow policy, a large number of static analyses have been devised (see [22] for a survey). Most of these approaches are *qualitative*, in the sense that they try to establish that a program is secure and they reject programs as insecure otherwise. In case of a leak (even if allowed by a given declassification policy) they do not provide details about how much information is leaked. *Quantitative* information flow analysis [1–3,14,20,23] complements qualitative analyses by measuring the amount of leaked information. Developers can use this feedback to decide whether the leakage is acceptable or not.

Our aim is to support detection and comprehension of information flow leaks during software development. In previous work [8] we presented an approach to generate demonstrator code for leakages in the form of failing tests. These tests could be examined and debugged by a developer to fix the leak. The generated tests merely demonstrated that a program does not respect a given information flow policy, but it was not possible to extract actual secrets. Extracting a secret or at least narrowing down the number of possible values of a secret information helps in two ways: (i) the software developer obtains additional information about the nature of the leak and (ii) it becomes easier to judge the severity of a leak and to assign its fix an appropriate priority.

© Springer International Publishing AG 2017
D.V. Hung and D. Kapur (Eds.): ICTAC 2017, LNCS 10580, pp. 269–287, 2017.
DOI: 10.1007/978-3-319-67729-3_16

The work presented in this paper applies techniques developed for quantified information flow analysis to guide the systematic creation of an (as small as possible) set of experiments/attacks to be conducted to gain maximal knowledge about a secret. The set of experiments is built incrementally. New experiments are added only if they are non-redundant and lead to a "maximal" knowledge gain. This sets our approach apart from previous work [3,14,20] that uses a random set of experiments (or simply states the existence of such a set), i.e. we are able to obtain a tighter characterisation of secrets than before.

We introduce a novel approach for automatic generation of a "good" experiment set to exploit information flow leaks. The main contributions are: (i) an algorithm that combines static analysis and dynamic analysis. Symbolic execution is used to statically analyse a program's behaviour, to compute path conditions and symbolic states. Based on this information, knowledge about a secret is incrementally increased by devising knowledge-maximizing experiments that in turn refine the static analysis results. These experiments are obtained by (ii) maximizing information leakage relative to metrics that *depend on public input*. The result of our algorithm is a (iii) logical characterisation of a secret. Hence, a model finder can be used to extract the remaining candidates for the secret, and in the best case, the secret itself as the only remaining model.

The paper is structured as follows: In Sect. 2 we give the necessary background to make the paper self-contained. Section 3 is about our approach and its design. Section 4 describes the generation of the input values for the experiments with a focus on efficiency. An experimental evaluation is presented in Sect. 5. We finish with related work (Sect. 6) and conclusions/future work (Sect. 7).

2   Background

The programming language used throughout the paper is a simple, deterministic and imperative language with global variables of a 32-bit integer type (we denote their domain with $\mathbb{Z}_{32}$). We consider here only programs where termination is guaranteed for all inputs. Our actual implementation supports a rich subset of sequential Java, including method calls, objects with integer fields, and integer-typed arrays (see Sect. 5.1).

In the remaining paper we use p to denote a program and $Var = \{x_1, \ldots, x_n\}$ to denote an ordered set of all program variables occurring in p.

2.1   Characterization of Insecurity Using Symbolic Execution

Symbolic execution (SE) is a versatile static analysis technique [13]. SE "runs" a program with symbolic (input) values instead of concrete ones.

Example 1. The program in Listing 1.1 uses l, h as program variables. For values of l below 100, the computed value stored in l represents the result of comparing the initial values of l and h, where l is assigned 3, 0, −3 for l being equal, less than, and greater than h, respectively. For values of l of 100 and above, the value 2 is assigned to l.

Starting SE at line 1 in an initial state where l and h have symbolic input values l_0 and h_0, respectively (short: $l : l_0$, $h : h_0$) causes a split into two SE paths. The first branch deals with the case where the *branch condition* $l_0 < 100$ holds and the second branch with the complementary case. We continue symbolic execution on the first branch with the **if**-statement in line 2. This causes another split with branch conditions $l_0 \doteq h_0$ and $l_0 \neq h_0$. Continuing again with the first branch, we symbolically execute the assignment of value 3 to l in line 3.   □

Symbolic execution creates an SE tree representing all possible concrete execution paths. Each node corresponds to a code location and contains the symbolic state at that point: a mapping from program variables to their symbolic value and a path condition. The *path condition* is the conjunction of all branch conditions up to the current point of execution. The initial state of any execution path through a node with path condition pc must necessarily satisfy pc.

Path conditions and symbolic values are always expressed relative to the initial symbolic values present in the initial symbolic state. In the following, instead of introducing a new constant symbol v_0 to refer to the initial value of a program variable v, we simply use the program variable v itself. This means program variables occurring in path conditions and symbolic values refer always to their initial value.

Listing 1.1. Running example

```
1  if (l < 100) {
2    if (l == h)
3      l = 3;
4    else
5      if (l < h) l = 0;
6      else l = -3;
7  } else l = 2;
```

We use SET_p to refer to the SE tree of program p and N_p to refer to the number of symbolic execution paths of SET_p. For each leaf node of an SE path i ($1 \leq i \leq N_p$) the corresponding path condition is denoted with pc_i and the symbolic value of variable $v \in Var$ in the final state of path i is denoted with the expression f_i^v. Later we need to express symbolic values or path conditions over a different variable signature: Let $V = \{x_1, \ldots, x_n\}$, $V' = \{x'_1, \ldots, x'_n\}$ be ordered, disjoint sets of program variables with the same cardinality; we write $pc_i[V'/V]$, meaning that each x_i in pc_i has been replaced by x'_i. In case of two disjoint variables sets V_1, V_2 we write $pc_i[V'_1, V'_2 \,/\, V_1, V_2]$ instead of $pc_i[V'_1/V_1][V'_2/V_2]$. Similar for the symbolic values f_i^v.

There are several approaches to deal with loops and recursive method calls in SE to achieve a finite SE tree. We follow the approach presented in [11], which uses specifications, namely, method contracts and loop invariants. In case of sound and complete specifications this approach is fully precise. In case of incomplete specifications, completeness (but not soundness) is sacrificed. In brief, the effect of loops and method calls is encoded as part of the path condition and the introduction of fresh symbolic values.

The approach presented in this paper extends our previous work [8] in which SE is used to compute path conditions and the final symbolic values of program variables to obtain a logic characterisation of insecurity. We recapture the most important ideas: Let L, H be a partitioning of Var. The noninterference policy $H \not\rightarrow L$ forbids any information flow from the initial value of high (confidential/secret) program variables H to low (public) variables L. In [7] self-composition is used as a means to formalize, in terms of a logic formula, whether or not a program is secure relative to a given noninterference policy. The negation of such a *security formula* is true for insecure programs, i.e. any model of the negated formula describes a pair of program runs that leak information. We use this idea as follows: Given two SE paths i and j with path conditions pc_i, pc_j and final symbolic values f_i^v, f_j^v, $v \in Var$. The *insecurity formula*

$$Leak(i,j) \equiv (\bigwedge_{v \in L} v \doteq v') \wedge pc_i \wedge (pc_j[\mathit{Var'}/\mathit{Var}]) \wedge \bigvee_{v \in L} f_i^v \neq (f_j^{v'}[\mathit{Var'}/\mathit{Var}]) \quad (1)$$

has a model (an assignment of values to program variables satisfying (1)) if there are two program runs, one taking path i and the other one path j ($i = j$ possible), that end in final states differing in the value of at least one low variable, even though their initial states coincided on the low input. Our target programs are deterministic, hence, this can only be the case if the value of high variables influenced the final value of the low variables. To check whether a program is insecure, we compare all pairs of symbolic execution paths:

$$\bigvee_{1 \leq i \leq j \leq N_p} Leak(i,j) \quad (2)$$

An SE path that contributes to an information leak is called a *risky path*. The set of all risky paths is denoted by $Risk$. Details on how to support other information flow policies than noninterference can be found in [8].

2.2   Quantitative Information Flow Analysis

We recall some measures for quantifying information leaks [3,15,23,25]. Given a program p and a noninterference policy $H \not\rightarrow L$, let $O \subseteq L$ (usually: $O = L$) be a subset of low variables whose value can be observed by an attacker after termination of p. We assume that before running p, the attacker knows about the values of low variables (or can even manipulate them); and that the initial values of variables in H and L are independent (i.e. from an attacker's perspective knowledge about L does not entail any knowledge about H).

Let $\mathbb{L}, \mathbb{H}$ denote the finite sets of all possible values of L and H, e.g., for two unrestricted integer program variables $H = \{h_1, h_2\}$, $\mathbb{H}$ is the Cartesian product $\mathbb{Z}_{32} \times \mathbb{Z}_{32}$ of their domain. Similarly, let $\mathbb{O}$ be the set of all possible output values of O. Let the function $\mathbb{O}_p : \mathbb{L} \rightarrow 2^{\mathbb{O}}$ that computes the set of all possible output values of O for a given low input be defined as follows: $\mathbb{O}_p : \bar{l} \mapsto \{\bar{o} \mid \bar{o} \text{ final values of } O \text{ after executing } p(\bar{l}, \bar{h}), \text{ for each } \bar{h} \in \mathbb{H}\}$.

Each low input value $\bar{l}$ defines a random variable $O_{out}(\bar{l})$ corresponding to the observed output values in the set $\mathbb{O}_p(\bar{l})$ after running program p with fixed low level input $\bar{l}$. We denote with $O_{out}(L)$ the function from $\mathbb{L}$ to the space of random variables as defined above. The random variables corresponding to the initial values of H are denoted with H_{in}.

Conventionally, the amount of information that is leaked from H to O can be measured by quantifying the amount of unknown information about H's value (the secret) w.r.t. the attacker before running the program (the attacker's initial uncertainty about the secret) and after observing the output value of O (the attacker's remaining uncertainty about the secret). Then we have:

$$\text{information leaked} = \text{initial uncertainty} \quad - \quad \text{remaining uncertainty}$$

To measure uncertainty different notions of entropy are in use, for instance, Shannon entropy [5,21], min entropy [23], and guessing entropy [3,15]. To quantify information leakage, we adapt the definition given in [25].

Given random variables X, Y with sample spaces $\mathbb{X}$ and $\mathbb{Y}$, respectively. The *Shannon entropy* of X is defined as $\mathcal{H}(X) = -\sum_{x \in \mathbb{X}} P(X = x) \log(P(X = x))$. The *conditional Shannon entropy* of X given Y is defined as

$$\mathcal{H}(X|Y) = \sum_{y \in \mathbb{Y}} P(Y = y) \sum_{x \in \mathbb{X}} P(X = x | Y = y) \log(P(X = x | Y = y))$$

Intuitively, $\mathcal{H}(X)$ is the average number of bits required to encode the values of X and $\mathcal{H}(X|Y = y)$ quantifies the average number of bits needed to describe the outcome of X under the condition that the value of Y is known.

Shannon entropy and its conditional variant are used to quantify information leakage as follows: the initial uncertainty of the attacker about the input value of H is interpreted as Shannon entropy of H_{in}, while the remaining uncertainty of the attacker about H_{in} when $O_{out}(L)$ is known is interpreted as conditional entropy. Then information leakage can be computed as $\text{ShEL}_p(L) = \mathcal{H}(H_{in}) - \mathcal{H}(H_{in}|O_{out}(L))$ that is the *mutual information* of H_{in} and $O_{out}(L)$.

While Shannon entropy is a natural approach to quantify leakage, it fails to reflect the vulnerability that high values might be guessed correctly in a single try. Consider the two programs

$$p_1 \equiv \textbf{if } (\texttt{h\%8==0}) \texttt{l=h } \textbf{else } \texttt{l=1}), \qquad p_2 \equiv \texttt{l=h\&0777}$$

taken from [23]. Using Shannon entropy, the mutual information leakage of program p_1 is smaller than that of p_2, i.e., p_1 is considered to be more secure than p_2. However, the risk of leaking the complete value of H in a single run is significantly higher for p_1 than for p_2. Smith [23] proposed *min entropy* as an alternative metric to address this problem. Min entropy $\mathcal{H}_\infty(X)$ of a random variable X equals $-\log \mathcal{V}(X)$ where $\mathcal{V}(X) = \max_{x \in \mathbb{X}} P(X = x)$. Intuitively, the min entropy of a random variable X represents the highest probability that X can be guessed in a single try. Using min entropy to measure information leakage is similar to Shannon entropy: the initial uncertainty is interpreted as min entropy of H_{in} and the remaining uncertainty is the conditional min entropy of H_{in} given O_{out}.

The final leakage metric considered in this paper is guessing entropy. Intuitively, the *guessing entropy* of a random variable X is the average number of questions of the kind: "Is the value of X equal to x?" that are needed to infer the value of X. The derivation of the computation of the guessing entropy-based leakage is similar to the previous ones. Details of min and guessing entropy-based leakage can be found in the technical report [9].

3   Automatic Inference of a Program's Secrets

This section describes our attacker model and presents the core logic of our algorithm to automatically infer a program's secrets.

3.1   Attacker Model and Overview

We assume that the attacker knows the source code and can run the program multiple times to observe public outputs. The notation p, L, H, etc. is as above.

Figure 1 shows an overview of our approach. First, the source code is analysed statically by symbolic execution to identify execution paths, called risky paths, that might cause information leakage (directly or indirectly). Based on this analysis a number of experiments are performed to infer the secret. An experiment is a program run with concrete input

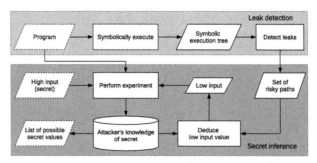

Fig. 1. Structure of the algorithm to infer secrets

together with the outcome. To perform an experiment the algorithm selects suitable low input based on knowledge about risky execution paths and knowledge accumulated in previous runs. The algorithm terminates when one of the following conditions holds: (i) all secrets have been inferred unambiguously; (ii) it can be determined that no new knowledge can be inferred; (iii) a specified limit of concrete program runs is reached.

We assume that high variables are not modified by or in between runs. We use $\overline{h}_s \in \mathbb{H}$ to refer to a secret, i.e.. concrete (to us unknown) values of H.

3.2   Knowledge Representation of High Input

We fix a program p, a noninterference policy $H \not\rightarrow L$, and a set $O \subseteq L$ of observable low variables. The concrete value sets $\mathbb{L}, \mathbb{H}, \mathbb{O}_p(\cdot)$ are as before. To gain knowledge about a secret, a series of experiments is performed.

Definition 1. *A pair* $\langle \overline{l}, \overline{o} \rangle_{\overline{h}_s}$ *with* $\overline{l} \in \mathbb{L}$, $\overline{o} \in \mathbb{O}_p(\overline{l})$ *is called an* experiment *for* p *and* $\overline{h}_s$ *denoting the high input value used in the run. As long as it is clear from the context, we omit the subscript* $\overline{h}_s$.

Let $E = \{\langle \bar{l}_j, \bar{o}_j \rangle \mid 1 \leq j \leq m\}$ be a set of experiments for a program p. Symbolic execution of p yields a precise logical description of all reachable final states, see Sect. 2. Recall that N_p is the number of all feasible (i.e., with satisfiable path condition) symbolic execution paths. For each symbolic execution path i, we obtain its path condition pc_i and the final symbolic values f_i^v of any program variable v. Let O' be an ordered set of fresh program variables such that for any $v \in O$ there is a corresponding $v' \in O'$ and the cardinality of O and O' is equal, i.e. $|O| = |O'|$. The formula

$$Info(L, H, O') = \bigvee_{1 \leq i \leq N_p} InfoPath_i(L, H, O') \tag{3}$$

where $InfoPath_i(L, H, O') = pc_i \wedge \bigwedge_{v' \in O'} v' = f_i^v$ "records" the information about final values contained in a symbolic execution path. It is true whenever the variables in L, H, O' are assigned values $\bar{l}$, $\bar{h}$, $\bar{o}$ such that executing p in an initial state $\langle \bar{l}, \bar{h} \rangle$ terminates in a final state where the variables in O have values $\bar{o}$. For a concrete experiment $\langle \bar{l}, \bar{o} \rangle$ formula (3) is instantiated to

$$Info_{\langle \bar{l}, \bar{o} \rangle}(H) = Info(\bar{l}, H, \bar{o}) = Info(L, H, O')[\bar{l}, \bar{o}/L, O'] \tag{4}$$

This formula is true at the time of running the experiment, because (i) the taken execution path must be contained in one of the symbolic execution paths, and (ii) the observed output values must be equal to those obtained by evaluating the symbolic values with the concrete initial values of the low and high variables.

We write $Info_{\langle \bar{l}, \bar{o} \rangle}(H)$ to emphasize that the truth value of the formula only depends on the assignment of concrete values to the program variables in H. The formula $Info_{\langle \bar{l}, \bar{o} \rangle}(H)$ constrains the possible high values and can be seen as the information about $\bar{h}_s$ that can be learned from experiment $\langle \bar{l}, \bar{o} \rangle$. The *knowledge* about $\bar{h}_s$ gained from all experiments in a set E is then

$$K^E(H) = K^\emptyset(H) \wedge \bigwedge_{\langle \bar{l}, \bar{o} \rangle \in E} Info_{\langle \bar{l}, \bar{o} \rangle}(H) \tag{5}$$

where $K^\emptyset(H)$ is the *initial knowledge* about $\bar{h}_s$ that is known before performing any experiment, for example, domain restrictions. If nothing is known about $\bar{h}_s$, then the initial knowledge $K^\emptyset(H)$ is simply *true*. The set of all models of $K^E(H)$ contains by construction also the actual secret $\bar{h}_s$ (a simple inductive argument with base case that $K^\emptyset(H)$ is satisfied by $\bar{h}_s$).

We want to design a set of experiments that reduces, as much as possible, the number of possible concrete values for H that satisfy (5). The smaller this number is, the more we succeeded to narrow down the possible values for the secret. In particular, if only one possible value remains, we know the secret.

Some notation: the set of all values of a variable set X that satisfy a formula $\varphi(X)$ is denoted by $Sat(\varphi)$. Hence, $Sat(K^E(H))$ is the set of all values of H that satisfy $K^E(H)$. As usual we use $|S|$ to denote the cardinality of a set S.

Data: p: program to be attacked (with the high input already set); noninterference policy
$H \not\to L$; $O \subseteq L$: observable low variables; $K^0(H)$: initial knowledge about H; $maxE$:
maximum number of experiments
Result: $K^E(H)$: the accumulated knowledge about H obtained by executing the
experiments E

$E \leftarrow \emptyset$;
$K \leftarrow K^0(H)$;
while $|E| < maxE$ **do**
    $(\bar{l}, leakage) \leftarrow findLowInput(E, K)$;
    if $leakage > 0$ **then**
        execute p with low input $\bar{l}$;
        $\bar{o} \leftarrow$ values of O when p terminates;
        $E \leftarrow E \cup \langle \bar{l}, \bar{o} \rangle$;
        $K \leftarrow K \wedge Info_{\langle \bar{l}, \bar{o} \rangle}(H)$;
        if $|Sat_H(K)| = 1$ **then**
           | exit while;
        end
    else
        | exit while;
    end
end

Algorithm 1. Secret inference

Example 2. Consider again the program from Listing 1.1 with 1 as low variable
and h as high variable. Assume the value of h is 10. Initially, the knowledge
about the value of h is its domain $-2^{31} \leq h < 2^{31}$.

Given two experiment sets $X = \{\langle 5, 0 \rangle, \langle 3, 0 \rangle, \langle 8, 0 \rangle\}$, $Y = \{\langle 5, 0 \rangle, \langle 17, -1 \rangle\}$.
The knowledge about the secret input value of h that can be gained from X and
Y is $K^X(\{h\}) = 8 < h < 2^{31}$ and $K^Y(\{h\}) = 5 < h < 17$, respectively. Even
though $|X| > |Y|$, it is the case that $|Sat(K^Y(\{h\}))| \ll |Sat(K^X(\{h\}))|$, hence
the knowledge about the secret value of h obtained from Y is higher than the
one obtained from X. □

We want to accumulate maximal knowledge about a secret with as few experiments as possible. In particular, we do not want to perform experiments that
do not create any knowledge gain. Avoiding redundant experiments is essential
to achieve performance.

Definition 2. *An experiment* $\langle \bar{l}, \bar{o} \rangle$ *is called* redundant *for* $K^E(H)$ *if the following holds:* $\forall \bar{h}.(K^E(\bar{h}) \to Info_{\langle \bar{l}, \bar{o} \rangle}(\bar{h}))$.

A redundant experiment $\langle \bar{l}, \bar{o} \rangle$ gains no new information about a secret $\bar{h}_s$
for knowledge $K^E(H)$, because $K^E(\bar{h}) \wedge Info_{\langle \bar{l}, \bar{o} \rangle}(\bar{h}) \equiv K^E(\bar{h})$.

3.3 Algorithm for Inferring High Input

Algorithm 1 implements the core of our approach. The result is a logical formula
that represents the accumulated knowledge about the high variables the algorithm was able to infer. The result can be used as input to an SMT solver or
another model finder to compute concrete models representing possible secrets.

Algorithm 1 receives as input the program p, the symbolic execution result
for p, i.e. p's SE tree together with all path conditions and symbolic values in the

final symbolic execution state, the attacker's initial knowledge, etc. In particular, the formula $Info_{\langle \bar{l}, \bar{o} \rangle}(H)$ can be computed.

First, the set of already performed experiments E is initialized with the empty set and the accumulated knowledge K is initialized with the initial knowledge of the attacker. At the beginning of each loop iteration K contains the accumulated knowledge of all experiments executed up to now, i.e. $K = K^E(H)$. In the first loop statement the low input $\bar{l}$ for a new experiment is determined by method $findLowInput(E, K)$ based on the set of experiments E and the knowledge K accumulated so far. That method returns also a measure of the leakage expected to be observed by executing p with the provided low input. The method returns 0 as leakage only if all low input values would result in redundant experiments. In its most basic implementation the method returns simply random values and a positive value for leakage. We discuss more refined implementations in Sect. 4.

If the expected leakage is positive (i.e. something new can be learned), program p is executed with the computed low input $\bar{l}$ and the set of experiments is extended by the pair $\langle \bar{l}, \bar{o} \rangle$ where $\bar{o}$ are the values of the observable variables when p terminates. In the next step we update the accumulated knowledge by adding the conjunct $Info_{\langle \bar{l}, \bar{o} \rangle}(H)$. Afterwards, we check whether the accumulated knowledge uniquely determines the values of the high variables. If this is the case we know the exact secret and return. Otherwise, we enter another loop iteration until the maximal number of experiments $maxE$ is reached. If the expected leakage is zero, no useful low input can be found and the algorithm terminates.

4   Finding Optimal Low Input

We aim to provide a more useful implementation of method $findLowInput(E)$ than the trivial one sketched above. The main purpose of the method is to determine optimal low input values that lead to a maximal gain of knowledge about the values of the high variables. We use the security metrics discussed in Sect. 2.2 to guide this process and show how these can be effectively computed by employing symbolic execution and parametric model counting. We refer to the technical report [9] for all proofs of theorems.

4.1   Risky Paths and Reachable Paths

We start with a set of experiments E $(|E| = m)$ and the accumulated knowledge about the high variables in form of the logic formula $K^E(H)$. We assume the initial knowledge about secret $K^\emptyset(H)$ is correct ($\bar{h}_s$ satisfies $K^\emptyset(H)$), hence $\bar{h}_s$ also satisfies $K^E(H)$. Our aim is to find the low level input $\bar{l}_{m+1}$ for a new experiment that is most promising for maximal knowledge gain. Next we show how to avoid generation of low input that would lead to a redundant experiment.

A *risky path* is a symbolic execution path which might contribute to an information leakage (see Sect. 2.1).

Definition 3. *Let p be a program and N_p be the number of all symbolic paths of p. A symbolic path i ($1 \leq i \leq N_p$) is called a* risky path *for a noninterference* *policy $H \nrightarrow O$ iff $\exists k.(1 \leq k \leq N_p \wedge Leak(i,k))$ is satisfiable. The set of all risky paths of p is denoted with $Risk$.*

The set of risky paths gives rise to a condition for redundant experiments. If a given low input never leads to the execution of a risky path, then it does not contribute to an information leakage and thus the experiment is redundant. The following theorem characterizes this intuition formally:

Theorem 1. *$InRisk(L)$ denotes the formula $\exists \overline{h}.(K^E(\overline{h}) \wedge \bigwedge_{i \notin Risk} \neg pc_i[\overline{h} / H])$. If for some $\overline{l} \in \mathbb{L}$ the formula $InRisk(\overline{l})$ is false then the experiment $\langle \overline{l}, \overline{o} \rangle$ is redundant for $K^E(H)$.*

Example 3. The SE tree of the program in Listing 1.1 has four paths with path conditions $pc_1 = 1 < 100 \wedge 1 = h$, $pc_2 = 1 < 100 \wedge 1 < h$, $pc_3 = 1 < 100 \wedge 1 > h$ and $pc_4 = 1 \geq 100$. The set of risky paths is $Risk = \{1, 2, 3\}$. The fourth path is not a risky path as it does not contribute to any leak. We have $InRisk(\{1\}) = \exists h. \neg(1 \geq 100) \equiv 1 < 100$ indicating that only low input values less than 100 may lead to any information gain.   □

Definition 4. *An SE path i is called a reachable path for $K^E(H)$ iff the following formula is satisfiable:*

$$K^E(H) \wedge pc_i \tag{6}$$

R^E denotes the set of all reachable paths for $K^E(H)$.

Example 4. (Example 3 cont'd) Assume the initial knowledge about the value of h is $-2^{31} \leq h < 2^{31}$ and the secret value of h is 1000. We execute the program in Listing 1.1 with $1 = 98$. The execution terminates in a state where 1 has been set to 0. Using this experiment, we obtain as accumulated knowledge about h: $-2^{31} \leq h < 2^{31} \wedge ((98 = h \wedge 3 = 0) \vee (98 < h \wedge 0 = 0) \vee (98 > h \wedge -3 = 0))$ $\equiv 98 < h < 2^{31}$. With this knowledge about h, the risky path 3 becomes unreachable because the formula $98 < h < 2^{31} \wedge 1 < 100 \wedge 1 > h$ is unsatisfiable. □

Theorem 2. *For all experiments $\langle \overline{l}, \overline{o} \rangle$, it holds that $K^E(H) \wedge Info_{\langle \overline{l}, \overline{o} \rangle}(H) \equiv K^E(H) \wedge \bigvee_{i \in R^E} InfoPath_i(\overline{l}, H, \overline{o})$.*

Theorem 2 shows that all unreachable paths can be ignored while constructing the knowledge about $\overline{h}_s$. Moreover, it allows us to consider only reachable paths when deducing optimal low input, which we explain in the next sections.

4.2   Quantifying Leakage by Symbolic Execution

We denote the number of assignments of values to the variables in H that satisfy $K^E(H)$ by $S_E = |Sat(K^E(H))|$. We assume that the actual value of H satisfies $K^E(H)$, i.e. $K^E(H)$ is correct.

Definition 5. *For a formula g, let V be the set of all program variables occurring in g and let $V = X \dot\cup Y$ be a partitioning. Function $C_X[Y](g)$ is called parametric counting function iff it returns the number of assignments to the variables of X that satisfy g (i.e. the number of models) as a function of Y.*

Example 5. Given $V = \{1, h\}$ and $g = 0 \le h < 100 \wedge h \ge 1 \wedge 0 \le 1 < 100$. Then the number of models of h satisfying g depends on 1 and can be determined for any value of 1 satisfying $0 \le 1 < 100$ by $C_{\{h\}}[\{1\}](g) = 100 - 1$.   □

We want to extend the experiment set E by adding a new experiment $\langle \bar{l}, \bar{o} \rangle$ such that the observable leakage (knowledge gain on high variables) is as high as possible. The following theorem provides an iterative method to compute the different leakage measures from Sect. 2.2 based on counting the models of $K^E(H)$.

Theorem 3. *Let E be an experiment set and $K^E(H)$ the knowledge about the high variables. If the probability distribution of the values for H is uniform, the Shannon entropy-based $\mathtt{ShEL_p}(L)$, the min entropy-based $\mathtt{MEL_p}(L)$, and the guessing entropy-based $\mathtt{GEL_p}(L)$ leakages can be computed as follows:*

$$\mathtt{ShEL_p}(L) = log(S_E) - \frac{1}{S_E} \sum_{\bar{o} \in \mathbb{O}_p(L)} \left(C_H[L](g(L, H, \bar{o})) log(C_H[L](g(L, H, \bar{o}))) \right)$$

$$\mathtt{GEL_p}(L) = \frac{S_E + 1}{2} - \frac{1}{2S_E} \sum_{\bar{o} \in \mathbb{O}_p(L)} \left(C_H[L](g(L, H, \bar{o}))(C_H[L](g(L, H, \bar{o})) + 1) \right)$$

$$\mathtt{MEL_p}(L) = log(C_{O'}[L](\exists \bar{h}.g(L, \bar{h}, O')))   \qquad (O' \text{ as defined in Sect. 3.2})$$

where $g(L, H, O) = K^E(H) \wedge InRisk(L) \wedge \bigvee_{i \in R^E} InfoPath_i(L, H, O)$.

Intuitively, the theorem states that given the current stage of the experiment with $K^E(H)$ providing the initial uncertainty, the theorem expresses a characterization of leakages by observing the low outputs.

When pc_i and the symbolic observable output values $\overline{f}_i^O$ are linear expressions over integers, the computation of $C_H[L](\ldots)$ and $C_{O'}[L](\ldots)$ can be reduced to counting the number of integer points in parametric and non-parametric polytopes for which efficient approaches (and tools) exist [24].

4.3   Method *findLowInput*

Algorithm 2 shows detailed pseudo code of method *findLowInput*. It computes the optimal low input values for a given leakage metric together with the computed leakage. First, the set of reachable paths R^E is determined by checking the reachability of all paths using formula (6). If no reachable paths exist or all reachable paths are not risky, the algorithm exits and returns 0 as leakage value (in that case the low input values are irrelevant). Otherwise, the optimal low input values for the leakage metric are computed.

Data: Set of performed experiments E, current knowledge $K^E(H)$
Result: $(\bar{l}, leakage)$: optimal low input value and corresponding leakage
$R^E \leftarrow findAllReachablePaths(K^E(H))$;
if $|R^E| > 0 \land R^E \cap Risk \neq \emptyset$ **then**
    $QLeak(L) \leftarrow$ appropriately instantiated entropy formula;
    $\bar{l} \leftarrow findL2Maximize(QLeak(L))$;
    if $\bar{l} = null$ **then**
        | $\bar{l} \leftarrow$ random value that does not appear in E;
    end
    $leakage \leftarrow QLeak(\bar{l})$;
else
    $\bar{l} \leftarrow null$;
    $leakage \leftarrow 0$;
end

Algorithm 2. Implementation of method $findLowInput$

Here $QLeak(L)$ is one of $\mathtt{ShEL_p}(L)$, $\mathtt{GEL_p}(L)$, $\mathtt{MEL_p}(L)$ according to the chosen security metric. The low input values are determined by solving the optimization problem: $argmax_{\bar{l} \in \mathbb{L}} QLeak(\bar{l})$. In case of $\mathtt{ShEL_p}(L)$ and $\mathtt{GEL_p}(L)$ this is equivalent to minimizing the sum expression in the corresponding formula of Theorem 3.

4.4 Choosing a Suitable Security Metric

Choosing the right security metric for a given program plays an important role for finding optimal low input values. The choice influences the computational complexity of the optimization problem as well as the quality of the found low input. It turns out that computing the Shannon and guessing entropy-based metrics is significantly more expensive than the min entropy-based metric. The reason is that min entropy-based leakage merely requires to estimate the *cardinality* of the observable output values, while the two others require to *enumerate* each possible output value (but can find better low level input).

Consequently, the Shannon and guessing entropy-based leakage metrics are only feasible for programs whose observable output (i) either depends only on the chosen SE path, but not on the actual values of the low or high variables (i.e. each SE path assigns only constant values to the observable variables); (ii) or the output values depend only on the low input (i.e. for a specific concrete low input, their concrete value can be determined by evaluating the corresponding symbolic value f). For all other programs, determining the possible concrete output values is too expensive in practice. We illustrate (for space reasons only for case (i) described above) how the Shannon and guessing entropy-based leakage metrics can be used.

Let i be a reachable path with path condition pc_i and symbolic output values $\overline{f_i^O}$. By assumption (i), the symbolic values in $\overline{f_i^O}$ are constants (i.e. independent of any program variables), so they can be evaluated to concrete values $\bar{o}_i$. We may assume that the output values for all SE paths $i \neq j$ differ, hence $\bar{o}_i \neq \bar{o}_j$ (otherwise, paths i, j are merged into one with path condition $pc_i \lor pc_j$). Further, $\mathbb{O}_p(L) = \{\bar{o}_i | i \in R^E\}$, because we only consider reachable paths. Hence, we can conclude that for all $i, j \in R^E$ with $i \neq j$ the formula $InfoPath_i(L, H, \bar{o}_j)$ is equivalent to false and $InfoPath_i(L, H, \bar{o}_i)$ simplifies to pc_i. We use this to simplify the definition of g in Theorem 3 to $g(L, H, \overline{o}_i) \equiv K^E(H) \wedge pc_i$. The computation of $\mathrm{ShEL_p}(L)$ and $\mathrm{GEL_p}(L)$ becomes now significantly cheaper, because the cardinality of the set of possible observable outputs is bound by the number of reachable paths and only path conditions need to be considered.

Example 6. (Example 3 Cont'd) For our running example we already identified the set of risky paths as $Risk = \{1, 2, 3\}$ and obtained $InRisk(1) = 1 < 100$. A closer inspection of the program reveals the following: as long as our only knowledge about h is that its value is within an interval $[a, b]$ then choosing the arithmetic middle $\frac{b+a}{2}$ for the input value of 1 is the best choice.

The initial knowledge about h is that its value is between -2^{31} and $2^{31} - 1$, hence, the best choice is 0 or -1. We show that the solution computed *automatically* by our algorithm reaches the same conclusion. To avoid redundant experiments, we know already that 1 must be chosen such that $1 < 100 (= InRisk(1))$. Let φ denote $-2^{31} \leq h < 2^{31} \wedge 1 < 100$. From the symbolic output values, we obtain $\mathbb{O}_{\{1\}} \subseteq \{3, 0, -3\}$ and:

$$g(1, h, 3) = \varphi \wedge h = 1 \qquad g(1, h, 0) = \varphi \wedge h > 1 \qquad g(1, h, -3) = \varphi \wedge h < 1$$
$$g(1, h, 1') = \varphi \wedge \left((1 = h \wedge 1' = 3) \vee (1 < h \wedge 1' = 0) \vee (1 > h \wedge 1' = -3)\right)$$

where $1'$ is a new program variable representing the final value of 1. Model counting (we used the tool Barvinok [24]) yields the following functions:

$$C_{\{h\}}[1](g(1, h, 3)) = \begin{cases} 1, & \text{if} - 2^{31} \leq 1 < 100 \\ 0, & \text{otherwise} \end{cases}$$

$$C_{\{h\}}[1](g(1, h, 0)) = \begin{cases} 2^{31} - 1 - 1, & \text{if} - 2^{31} \leq 1 < 100 \\ 0, & \text{if } 1 \geq 100 \\ 2^{32}, & \text{otherwise} \end{cases}$$

$$C_{\{h\}}[1](g(1, h, -3)) = \begin{cases} 2^{31} + 1, & \text{if} - 2^{31} \leq 1 < 100 \\ 0, & \text{otherwise} \end{cases}$$

$$C_{\{1'\}}[1](\exists h.g(1, h, 1')) = \begin{cases} 3, & \text{if} - 2^{31} < 1 < 100 \\ 2, & \text{if } 1 = -2^{31} \\ 1, & \text{otherwise} \end{cases}$$

From the final function we see that the maximum leakage measured by the min entropy-based metric is $log\ 3$ for all values of low input in the range $(-2^{31}, 100)$. This restricts the choice of a suitable value for 1 only slightly. Computation of the maximal leakage for the Shannon and guessing entropy-based metrics requires more effort. Using the optimizers *Bonmin* and *Couenne*[1] with the first three functions, we get as result $1 = 0$ which meets our intuition.

---

[1] www.coin-or.org/Bonmin and projects.coin-or.org/Couenne.

Listing 1.2. Listing 1.1 with specification annotations

```
1  public class RelaxPC {
2    public int l; cprivate int h;
3    /*! l | h ; !*/
4    /*@ requires -2147483648 <= h && h < 2147483648; @*/
5    public void check(){
6      if (l < 100) { ... } ...
7    }
8  }
```

Moreover, the maximum Shannon entropy leakage when choosing l = 0 is approximately 1, i.e. 1 bit of h is revealed. For this program, the Shannon and guessing entropy-based metrics perform significantly better than the min entropy-based metric. The latters' successive application generates a series of experiments that performs binary search to uncover the secret.   □

5   Implementation and Experiments

5.1   Implementation

We implemented the approach described above on top of the KEG tool [8]. KEG is used to create failing tests for insecure Java programs. The information flow policy specification is provided in terms of source code annotations. KEG supports noninterference and delimited information release policies. For loops and (recursive) methods KEG supports loop invariants and method contracts. Beside primitive types, object types are also supported.

   Listing 1.2 shows the annotated Java code from Listing 1.1. Line 3 contains a class level specification that forbids any information flow from the high variable h to the low variable l. The check method's precondition in line 4 specifies the initial knowledge about h. The program is given to our tool which performs the analysis explained in the previous sections and illustrated in Fig. 1. Our implementation supports the computations described in Sect. 4 and outputs the corresponding optimisation problems as AMPL [10] specifications. This makes it possible to use any optimizer supporting the AMPL format. Currently, KEG uses a combination of two open source optimizers, *Bonmin* and *Couenne*, as well as the commercial optimizer *Local Solver* [4]. For model counting we use Barvinok [24]. The latter only supports counting for parametric polytopes, which restricts the use of the secret inference feature to programs with linear path condition and symbolic output expressions. This restriction does not affect KEG's other features, including leak detection and leak demonstrator generation.

5.2   Experiments

For the running example, KEG detects an information flow leak for the specified noninterference policy. In case the high variable has a value greater than 99, KEG stops after one experiment and returns $99 < h < 2147483648$ as the accumulated knowledge, which is all that can be learned. However, if h is less or equal than 99, KEG automatically extracts the exact value of h after only 31 experiments when using the Shannon or guessing entropy-based metric.

In addition, we evaluated our approach on a sample of insecure programs under the assumption that for any program the attacker knows nothing about the secret except that it is a 32 bit integer. Loop specifications and method contracts are supplied for programs containing unbounded loops and recursive method invocations. The tool has been configured to terminate its attack when it was either able to infer the values of the high variables, the maximum achievable knowledge has been reached, or the number of experiments exceeded the limit of 32. The evaluation was performed on an Intel Core i5-480M processor with 4GB RAM and Ubuntu 14.04 LTS. The results are shown in Table 1.

Table 1. Case study statistics

File name	#SP/RP	High input	Shannon entropy		Min entropy		Guessing entropy	
			#RB/E	T(s)	#RB/E	T(s)	#RB/E	T(s)
PassChecker	2/2	2135451222	0/32	159	0/32	13.3	0/32	139.3
RelaxPC	4/3	-1208665253	32/31	31.7	1/32	6.9	32/31	29.4
MultiLows	6/3	395444738	32/20	22.6	1/32	7.5	32/22	24.3
ODependL	4/3	-13484756	1/1	0.9	1/1	0.2	1/1	0.3
ODependL	4/3	95464630	32/31	29.8	1/32	6.7	32/31	29.6
ODependLH	6/5	-941087637	n/a	n/a	32/1	0.7	n/a	n/a
ODependLH	6/5	23269332	n/a	n/a	1/1	0.7	n/a	n/a
LoopPlus	3/2	-552256949	n/a	n/a	1/1	0.2	n/a	n/a
LoopPlus	3/2	1707132530	n/a	n/a	32/1	1.3	n/a	n/a
EWallet	3/2	692935244	n/a	n/a	21/32	10.1	n/a	n/a

#(SP/RP): nr of **S**ymbolic **P**aths/**R**isky **P**aths
#(RB/E): nr of **R**evealed **B**its/necessary **E**xperiments   T(s): Time for experiments (seconds)
(available at www.se.tu-darmstadt.de/research/projects/albia/download/secret-inferring/)

Discussion. Table 1 shows that using min entropy to guide experiment generation is in most cases the fastest option, but it lags often behind the other entropies regarding the amount of inferred information, because it considers merely the number of output values. The Shannon and guessing entropy-based metrics can only be used for analysing the programs *PassChecker*, *RelaxPC*, *MultiLows*, and *ODependL*, because only those fall into the class of programs characterized in Sect. 4.4. For these programs (exception *PassChecker*) the Shannon and guessing entropy-based metrics turn out to be very effective. Both reveal almost 1 bit per experiment.

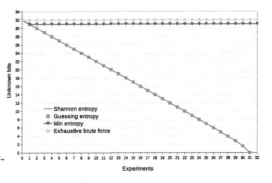

Fig. 2. Bits revealed per experiment

Figure 2 compares for program *RelaxPC* the number of bits revealed after each experiment for each of the supported metrics and with a simple exhaustive brute force attack (the latter could be lucky and hit the secret in one of the first 32 attempts). For this program we can see that in case of the min entropy-based metric the first experiment (which chose 0 as low level input) manages to reveal about one bit of information, namely that the secret's value is below 0 and stalls afterwards. The reason is that under the assumption of a uniform distribution the min entropy-based metric considers any possible choice of l between -2^{31} and 99 to be equally good. Consequently, the min entropy-based metric does not perform significantly better than a brute force attack. The Shannon and guessing entropy-based metrics perform best, extracting almost one bit per experiment and reveal the complete secret after 31 steps.

The program *PassChecker* is a simple password checker, leaking only whether the given input is equal to the secret or not. The amount of leakage does not depend on the low input and all entropy-based approaches perform equally bad as random experiments or exhaustive brute-force attacks.

For programs whose observable output depends on high variables (*ODependLH*, *LoopPlus* and *EWallet*), Shannon and guessing entropy are practically infeasible as the range of observable values is too large. However, min entropy is still applicable and quite effective, as it leads to the generation of low input for paths on which the observable output depends on the high input. Observe that *LoopPlus* and *EWallet* contain unbounded loops and recursive method calls.

The programs *ODependL*, *ODependLH* and *LoopPlus* witness the fact that successful secret inference may also depend on the values of high variables. The reason is that in these programs the high variable influences the taken symbolic execution path and the final output values, which renders the set of reachable paths value-dependent on high variables. Hence, the quality of the generated experiments depends as well on the high variables.

6   Related Work

An information-theoretic model for an adaptive side-channel attack is proposed in [15]. The idea of the attacker strategy is to choose at each step the query that minimizes the remaining entropy. This is achieved by enumerating all possible queries to choose the best one, which is rather expensive. In contrast our approach quantifies the potential leakage as a function of low input, and hence, we can use efficient available optimizers to find the optimal input value.

Pasareanu et al. [19] propose a non-adaptive side-channel attack to find low input that maximizes the amount of leaked information. In contrast to our approach, only path conditions are considered, but not symbolic states. Hence, they cannot measure leakage caused by explicit information flow. The authors of [12] define a *quantitative policy* which specifies an upper bound for permitted information leakage. The model checker CBMC is used to generate low input that triggers a violation of the policy. Both of [12,19] use channel capacity, that is measured via the number of possible observable output values, as their leakage metric. Thus their generated low input is often not the optimal one: for example, in case of Listing 1.2, we are able to generate a sequence of low inputs for 1, each of which extracts nearly 1 bit of information, allowing to find the exact secret after 31 experiments. Their approach can only return a single, *arbitrary* input for $1 \in (-2^{31}, 100)$, hence, using it for an attack would not perform better than brute force. Both approaches require a bound on the number of loop iterations or the recursion depth, whereas we can deal with unbounded loops and recursion.

Low input as a parameter of quantitative information flow (QIF) analysis is also addressed in [18,25]. In [25], the authors only analyze the bounding problem of QIF for low input, but do not provide a method to determine a bound for the leakage and they do not discuss how to find the input maximizing the leakage.

In [14] a precise quantitative information flow analysis based on calculating cardinalities of equivalence classes is presented. The author assumes an optimally chosen set of experiments, but does not describe how to construct such a set.

The authors of [6] model attacker knowledge as a probability distribution of the secret and show how to update such knowledge after each experiment. In [3], the authors briefly discuss the correlation between the set of experiments and the attacker's knowledge. However, none of these papers describes how to construct an optimal experiment set that maximizes the leakage. Other approaches in quantitative information flow [16,17,20] do not address low input in their analyses and consider only channel capacity with the same drawbacks as discussed earlier.

7 Conclusion and Future Work

We presented an approach and a tool to automatically infer secrets leaked by an information flow-insecure program. It features a novel, adaptive algorithm that (i) combines static and dynamic analysis, (ii) uses leakage metrics that *depend on low input* (which, to the best of our knowledge, sets it apart from any existing work) to guide experiment generation and (iii) provides a logic characterisation of the search space for the secret that can be put into a model finder to extract the secrets. The approach can deal with programs containing unbounded loops and recursive methods. The viability of the method has been demonstrated with a number of representative benchmark programs that clearly illustrate its potential and its current limitations. The latter are mainly derived from restrictions in current parametric model counting tools so that any progress in this area will directly benefit our approach as well. We plan to integrate specification generation techniques to reduce the need for user-provided annotations such as loop invariants. We will also look at non-uniform distributions of secret values.

References

1. Alvim, M., Chatzikokolakis, K., Palamidessi, C., Smith, G.: Measuring information leakage using generalized gain functions. In: 2012 IEEE 25th Computer Security Foundations Symposium (CSF), pp. 265–279, June 2012

2. Alvim, M.S., Scedrov, A., Schneider, F.B.: When not all bits are equal: worth-based information flow. In: Abadi, M., Kremer, S. (eds.) POST 2014. LNCS, vol. 8414, pp. 120–139. Springer, Heidelberg (2014). doi:10.1007/978-3-642-54792-8_7

3. Backes, M., Kopf, B., Rybalchenko, A.: Automatic discovery and quantification of information leaks. In: 30th Symposium on Security and Privacy, pp. 141–153 (2009)

4. Benoist, T., Estellon, B., Gardi, F., Megel, R., Nouioua, K.: Localsolver 1.x: a black-box local-search solver for 0–1 programming. 4OR **9**, 299–316 (2011)

5. Clark, D., Hunt, S., Malacaria, P.: A static analysis for quantifying information flow in a simple imperative language. J. Comput. Secur. **15**(3), 321–371 (2007)

6. Clarkson, M.R., Myers, A.C., Schneider, F.B.: Quantifying information flow with beliefs. J. Comput. Secur. **17**(5), 655–701 (2009)

7. Darvas, Á., Hähnle, R., Sands, D.: A theorem proving approach to analysis of secure information flow. In: Hutter, D., Ullmann, M. (eds.) SPC 2005. LNCS, vol. 3450, pp. 193–209. Springer, Heidelberg (2005). doi:10.1007/978-3-540-32004-3_20

8. Do, Q.H., Bubel, R., Hähnle, R.: Exploit generation for information flow leaks in object-oriented programs. In: Federrath, H., Gollmann, D. (eds.) ICT Systems Security and Privacy Protection. IFIPAICT, vol. 455. Springer, Cham (2015). doi:10.1007/978-3-319-18467-8_27

9. Do, Q.H., Bubel, R., Hähnle, R.: Inferring secrets by guided experiments. Technical report, TU Darmstadt (2017)

10. Gay, D.M.: The AMPL modeling language: an aid to formulating and solving optimization problems. In: Al-Baali, M., Grandinetti, L., Purnama, A. (eds.) Numerical Analysis and Optimization. PROMS, vol. 134. Springer, Cham (2015). doi:10.1007/978-3-319-17689-5_5

11. Hentschel, M., Hähnle, R., Bubel, R.: Visualizing unbounded symbolic execution. In: Seidl, M., Tillmann, N. (eds.) TAP 2014. LNCS, vol. 8570, pp. 82–98. Springer, Cham (2014). doi:10.1007/978-3-319-09099-3_7

12. Heusser, J., Malacaria, P.: Quantifying information leaks in software. In: Proceedings of the 26th Annual Computer Security Applications Conference, pp. 261–269. ACM (2010)

13. King, J.C.: Symbolic execution and program testing. Commun. ACM **19**(7), 385–394 (1976)

14. Klebanov, V.: Precise quantitative information flow analysis–a symbolic approach. Theor. Comput. Sci. **538**, 124–139 (2014)

15. Köpf, B., Basin, D.: An information-theoretic model for adaptive side-channel attacks. In: Proceedings of the 14th ACM Conference on Computer and Communications Security, CCS 2007, pp. 286–296. ACM (2007)

16. Malacaria, P., Chen, H.: Lagrange multipliers and maximum information leakage in different observational models. In: Proceedings of the 3rd ACM SIGPLAN Workshop on Programming Languages and Analysis for Security, pp. 135–146. ACM (2008)

17. Meng, Z., Smith, G.: Calculating bounds on information leakage using two-bit patterns. In: Proceedings of the ACM SIGPLAN 6th Workshop on Programming Languages, Analysis for Security, PLAS 2011, pp. 1:1–1:12. ACM (2011)

18. Ngo, T.M., Huisman, M.: Quantitative security analysis for programs with low input and noisy output. In: Jürjens, J., Piessens, F., Bielova, N. (eds.) ESSoS 2014. LNCS, vol. 8364, pp. 77–94. Springer, Cham (2014). doi:10.1007/978-3-319-04897-0_6

19. Pasareanu, C.S., Phan, Q., Malacaria, P.: Multi-run side-channel analysis using symbolic execution and Max-SMT. In: IEEE 29th Computer Security Foundations Symposium, CSF 2016, pp. 387–400. IEEE Computer Society (2016)
20. Phan, Q.-S., Malacaria, P., Tkachuk, O., Păsăreanu, C.S.: Symbolic quantitative information flow. SIGSOFT Softw. Eng. Notes **37**(6), 1–5 (2012)
21. Robling Denning, D.E.: Cryptography and Data Security. Addison-Wesley, Boston (1982)
22. Sabelfeld, A., Sands, D.: Declassification: dimensions and principles. J. Comput. Secur. **17**(5), 517–548 (2009)
23. Smith, G.: On the foundations of quantitative information flow. In: de Alfaro, L. (ed.) FoSSaCS 2009. LNCS, vol. 5504, pp. 288–302. Springer, Heidelberg (2009). doi:10.1007/978-3-642-00596-1_21
24. Verdoolaege, S., Seghir, R., Beyls, K., Loechner, V., Bruynooghe, M.: Counting integer points in parametric polytopes using Barvinok's rational functions. Algorithmica **48**(1), 37–66 (2007)
25. Yasuoka, H., Terauchi, T.: On bounding problems of quantitative information flow. J. Comput. Secur. **19**(6), 1029–1082 (2011)

ECBC: A High Performance Educational Certificate Blockchain with Efficient Query

Yuqin Xu[1], Shangli Zhao[1], Lanju Kong[1], Yongqing Zheng[1,2],
Shidong Zhang[1], and Qingzhong Li[1(✉)]

[1] School of Computer Science and Technology, Shandong University,
Jinan, China
xuyuqin_sdu@163.com, jnzsl163@126.com,
{klj,zyq,zsd,Lqz}@sdu.edu.cn
[2] Dareway Software Co., Ltd., Jinan, China

Abstract. Currently, most digital infrastructures for educational certificate management cannot guarantee data security and system trust. Using blockchain can solve this problem. However, there are still some defects with the existing blockchains that cannot be applied. Most of them are dependent on tokens, and limited by throughput and latency, moreover, no one can support certificate query with precise and high efficiency. In order to solve these problems, this paper presents educational certificate blockchain (ECBC) which can support low latency and high throughput, and provide a method to speed up queries. To reduce latency and increase throughput, consensus mechanism of ECBC uses the cooperation of peers to create blocks in place of the competition. ECBC builds a tree structure (MPT-Chain) which can not only provide an efficient query for a transaction, but also support historical transactions query of an account. MPT-Chain only needs short time to update and can speed up block verification. In addition, ECBC is designed with transaction format to protect user's privacy. The experiment shows that ECBC has better performance of throughput and latency, supporting quick query.

Keywords: Consensus mechanism · Blockchain scalability · Quick query

1 Introduction

The certificate is a manifestation of student's learning ability, it helps students to find a satisfactory job, of course, it can prevent us from getting a job if we provide a forged certificate. However, the validation process for certificates is lengthy and complex, which makes it possible to forge [1]. Therefore, it is imperative to establish a reliable digital infrastructure for certificates. In China, the website XueXinWang [2], as a certificate digital infrastructure, provides a lot of convenience. For example, it verifies the authenticity of the certificate quickly. But it also has many shortcomings, using central storage to save data cannot guarantee data security, under attack; the data may be lost, altered or leaked. In addition, the centralized system cannot guarantee system trust.

D.V. Hung and D. Kapur (Eds.): ICTAC 2017, LNCS 10580, pp. 288–304, 2017.
DOI: 10.1007/978-3-319-67729-3_17

Blockchain can guarantee data security and solve the problem of system trust [3] which is first raised in bitcoin [3, 4]. So using blockchain to achieve certificate system for the management of certificates will be reliable, safe and trustworthy. However, the existing blockchain for the management of certificates still show many shortcomings.

First of all, the existing blockchains are mostly dependent on tokens, but the certificates management does not require tokens. Secondly, consensus mechanisms (e.g. POW) waste a lot of computing resources, in addition, its throughput and latency cannot meet the requirements of certificate system [5, 6]. Thirdly, storing data transparently will lead to the disclosure of personal privacy [7]. Finally, only the ethereum [8] provides an index structure called MPT can achieve a quick query for the latest status of account, but cannot support the efficient query for history transactions of an account [9]. Querying the history records of a certificate holder is very important, because people always want to be able to query a person's education experience.

Based on the discussion above, this paper proposes an educational certificate blockchain (ECBC) to manage educational certificates. In order to improve performance, consensus mechanism does not need peer to compete to calculate the block's link value. The link value of the block needs to be generated by the cooperation of peers, and no one can know the link value of the block in advance. ECBC has the following advantages that it avoids waste of computing resources, has no fork, does not depend on tokens, and can meet the requirements of throughput and latency.

ECBC treats the issuance or revocation of a certificate as a transaction, which will be written into the blockchain, and designs transaction format to prevent privacy leaks. The privacy data of users is encrypted, which ensures that even if someone maliciously obtains the blockchain data, it is not possible to obtain users' information. Using Patricia tree [10] can quickly locate query results. Merkle tree [11, 12] is used to ensure that data accepted from others is not corrupt and not replaced, and even can check that others do not spoof or publish false data. Based on these, ECBC combines the features of Patricia tree and merkle tree, constructing a tree structure (MPT-Chain) to speed up query and ensure the correctness of query results in a distributed network.

In order to support querying history records efficiently, MPT-Chain extends the leaf nodes so that the leaf nodes can store the logical relationship of the account transaction chain. In addition, the node of MPT-Chain stores intermediate value for merkle root calculation, which can be used to speed up the MPT-Chain update and block verification.

The main contributions of this paper are as follows:

1. A consensus mechanism is proposed for blockchain, without bifurcation, and achieves high throughput and low latency.
2. This paper proposes a tree structure (MPT-CHAIN), which takes little time to update, supports query account transaction chain and speeds up block verification.

The remainder of the paper is organized as follows: Sect. 2 introduces related work which had done lots of work for certificate management and the performance of blockchain. In Sect. 3, educational certificate blockchain architecture is introduced. Section 4 describes consensus mechanism for creating blocks in detail. Section 5 introduces the MPT-Chain of ECBC. And Sect. 6 shows efficiency analysis and experiments.

2 Related Works

Prior to us, the Massachusetts Institute of Technology Media Laboratory (MIT Media Lab) has been noted problems of the existing digital infrastructures for educational certificate. They tried to use blockchain to solve the problem of system trust and data security, and designed a set of tools to display and validate educational certificates [1]. The overall design of the certificate architecture is simple. When the issuer signs an educational certificate, its hash value would be stored in the bitcoin's blockchain.

It is undeniable that the MIT Media Lab's solution can solve the problem of data security and system trust, but the educational certificate stored in the bitcoin's blockchain, which makes certificates administration more complex and relies on tokens. Bitcoin development has been severely constrained by its throughput and latency, the low performance is fatal for certificates management [6, 13].

In Bitcoin, the way that a transaction actually works "under the hood" is that it consumes a collection of objects called unspent transaction outputs ("UTXOs") created by one or more previous transactions, and then produces one or more new UTXOs, which can then be consumed by future transactions. A user's balance is thus not stored as a number; rather, it can be computed as the total sum of the denominations of UTXOs that they own [14].

UTXOs are stateless, and so are not well-suited to applications more complex than asset issuance and transfer that are generally stateful, such as various kinds of smart contracts. It would be very difficult to understand the logical relationship between transactions, because the relationship between the user and transactions is confused in UTXO model if we treat a transaction as the issuance or cancellation of a certificate.

The use of certificates is frequent in the certificate management process. But there is no strategy can support efficient query in bitcoin. Traversing data is not feasible, which will be more and more slowly while data increasing. The recent rise of the Ethereum to do some of this work, but for the management of certificates is not enough. They put forward an account model which can manage transactions better than UTXO model. Besides, Ethereum sets up three index trees (MPT) to speed up query, one for getting transaction, and one for getting account's balance, the remaining one is for receipt. All of them are for latest state of account, cannot support to find transaction chain of an account. But querying the history records of a certificate holder is very important.

3 ECBC Architecture

In this section, Educational Certificate Blockchain Architecture is introduced. ECBC uses blockchain to organize schools, regulators, students, and employers. It facilitates the review of the certificate data by the regulatory authority and also protects the security of certificate data and improves system trust.

The p2p-based educational certificate network consists of peers and entities:

Definition 1. Peer. Peer represents schools and regulators. It is versatile can be involved in creating blocks in the network. Each peer has an identity authentication, can use public key for encrypting messages and private key for signing blocks. It can ensure the security of message and blocks cannot be forged.

Definition 2. Quorum. Quorum refers to a peer who has the right to participate in the consensus process. The consensus mechanism of ECBC will dynamically will dynamically select some peers to become quorums which can generate blocks through cooperative consensus algorithms.

Definition 3. Entity. Entity represents students, and employers. ECBC provides light client for entities to verify and query the certificate, some entities are the holder of educational certificates, can get public and private key to protect user privacy. Entity can submit query request, and verify the correctness of the query results through block header.

Peers use consensus mechanism presented in this paper to generate a block, its basic structure is shown in Fig. 1. The block structure consists of a block header and a number of transactions. The block header includes link value of previous block, the link value of this block, the creator, the block height, the timestamp and the merkle root of MPT-Chain. The link value of the block is created in the peers' consensus process by all the peers' cooperation. Each block (except the genesis block) contains the link value of the previous block, thus forming a blockchain. In addition, the merkle root of MPT-Chain can guarantee the correctness of query results and the consistency of MPT-Chain in the network.

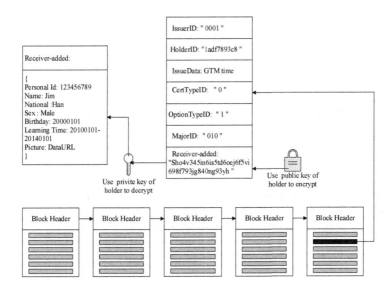

Fig. 1. ECBC architecture

The issuance or revocation of a certificate as a transaction will be written into blockchain, which is initiated by an issuer (such as school). Transaction format is designed in accordance with open badges specification [15], which includes IssuerID that can represent the issuer, and holderID can anonymously identify the certificate holder, the major, the type of certificate, the type of operation, the encrypted information concerning the privacy data, and the timestamp. The Operation Type is used to indicate whether the certificate was issued or revoked, because the data for the blockchain can only append. Blockchain as a distributed ledger, its data is open and transparent, which requires us to protect personal privacy [16]. Asymmetric encryption algorithm can guarantee data privacy, but also can cause the transaction cannot be verified. Therefore, we will use the asymmetric encryption algorithm encrypts the part of the transaction data which is related to user privacy, but does not affect the transaction verification, such as personal ID, name, date of birth, learning time, personal photos and so on.

4   Consensus Mechanism of ECBC

In this section, we will describe consensus mechanism of ECBC in detail. ECBC is a permission chain; the peer who wants to into the network must have permission. Each peer represents a trustworthy organizations or units, of course, we cannot rule out these peers which may become Byzantium peer. In bitcoin, the peers can join unlimited, which may lead to high possibility of byzantine peers [5, 6]. Therefore, the fault tolerance of POW is 51% of all the peers. The joining of peers must be permitted and peers' credibility is high, this characteristic for designing a consensus mechanism has brought different view. We reduce the fault tolerance of the network to one-third, and design a consensus mechanism which is scalable, high efficient, while ensures security and credibility. Creating block is a process of rotary, so we only describe a round of creation.

4.1   Dynamic Quorums

In order to ensure block creation secure and reliable, each block wants to take effect should reach a consensus by all the peers in the network. However, the number of peers in the network is increasing. All the peers are involved in consensus process, which is a waste of computing resources. So we select some peers called quorums to reach a consensus, but fixed quorums may cause security problems. For avoiding the occurrence of this phenomenon, we dynamically pick out quorums. Use computing power (P), and the number of times who had been as quorum (T) to calculate peer's comprehensive value (C_V). Calculation formula of C_V is as follows:

$$C\_V = P/\sqrt{T} \tag{1}$$

To ensure that quorum is changed dynamically, the number of times who had been as quorum is used as a limiting factor. Suppose the number of peers in the network is $N(N = 3f + 1)$, where f represents the number of Byzantine nodes that may exist in the network. Sort the peers from big to small according to C_V, select the first $2f + 1$ of this sequence to be quorum. The time complexity of this algorithm is $O(N * \log(N))$, time overhead is negligible for ECBC.

Quorums selected will reach a consensus on a block. A round of consensus process may create a block or may not. After a round of consensus process, the number of consensus round increases affirmatively and the block height may not. Each consensus round will correspond to a set of quorums that called view, when a round of consensus process ends, due to changes in T, resulting in view change.

4.2   Cooperation Consensus Algorithm

Cooperation consensus algorithm does not depend on computing power of the peer, but requires quorums to work together. It can be divided into three steps: The first step is quorums reach a consensus for the block's link value; the second step is to select primary peer which can create block in this round; the third step is quorums vote for block created by the primary peer.

In first step, each quorum generates a random number, and uses its private key to sign the random number, then sends it to others. When a quorum receives all the random numbers from other, using random numbers, the merkle root of transactions in the block, the link value of previous block and time stamp calculate hash value as the link value of this block. Link value is used to guarantee that block is not easily falsified. If anyone wants to modify any transaction value in the block, all previous blocks' link value need to be changed accordingly.

If the random number sent to others by the quorum is inconsistent, the link value will be different for different quorum. This phenomenon will lead to multiple primary peers in a consensus process, will also be multiple blocks. So this consensus process is no doubt a failure. Byzantine peers pay a small price can lead to a significant increase in the failure rate of consensus. To prevent such attacks, it is necessary to check the random number when the quorum receives a random number. The quorum packaged all random numbers into a set, and then broadcast it to others. All the quorum check random numbers by the set, if the one is not the same, the random number generator will be removed from quorums.

And then, select a quorum as primary peer to create block through random numbers. The primary peer is selected by the average of all the random numbers, whose random number is closest to the average and it broadcasted random number in the earliest time will be selected as primary peer. The primary peer can construct block and broadcast it to all the peers in the network. Constructing a complete block consists of packing the transaction into the block and calculating the MPT-Chain's merkle root in the block header. The calculation of merkle root will be highlighted in the next section.

When a quorum receives the block by the primary peer, and then verifies the correctness of the block, including the index root, transactions, block height, merkle root of MPT-Chain and then vote for the block. If a block can get votes more than half of the total number of quorum, which is $f + 1$. Then this block can be written in the blockchain, the height of blockchain and consensus round increases. Otherwise, consensus round increases.

Algorithm 1   Cooperation Consensus Algorithm

Input: quorums
Output: block
1: Each quorum generates a random number
2: Send random number with signature to others
3: **If** (the number of random numbers had been received =
the number of quorums)
4:Check random numbers
5:Calculate block's link value
6:    **Go to line 13**
7: **End if**
8: **Else if** (time out && don't receive the random number
)
9:    The quorum removed
10:   the number of quorum = the number of quorum -1
11:    **Go to line 3**
12: **End if**
13: Select primary peer to create block and then broadcast
14: **If**(time out && no block by primary peer)
15:    **Go to line 26**
16:**End if**
17:**Else if** (verify block == true)
18:    Vote
19:**End if**
20: **If** (the number of vote = f +1)
21:    write block into blockchain
22:    block height = block height +1
23:    round = round +1
24:**End if**
25: **Else**
26:    round = round +1
27:**End else**

Considering that information may be lost in the process of transmission or quorum failure (such as earthquake and other natural disasters), which will cause messages cannot be transferred. We set time threshold to prevent such situations. If the waiting time is more than time threshold and others still does not receive the random number, block or vote by the quorum, we can come to the conclusion that the quorum cannot communicate. In order to prevent the infinite wait for random number in the consensus process, the quorum cannot communicate should be removing from quorums. When the block and enough votes cannot receive until waiting time is more than time threshold, the consensus process will be failure.

4.3   Basic Properties of Cooperation Consensus

Given that cooperation consensus is a new blockchain creation rule, it is imperative to first show that all peers eventually adopt or accept a certain block uniformly. For any block B, we define C_B is the creator of block B. The definition ψ_B is the time of B when it was first accepted or abandoned. In addition, $H(\psi_B)$ is defined as the height of blockchain when the time is ψ_B.

Proposition 1.1. (The Convergence of History). $P_r(\psi_B < \infty) = 1$. In other words, every block is eventually either fully abandoned or fully adopted.

To prove the proposition, we make use of the following claim.

Claim 1.2. $\forall(\psi_B) < \infty$. For any block B, ψ_B is always less than infinity.

Proof. It can be seen from the algorithm of Cooperative consensus that the growth speed of educational certificate block chain is mainly influences by network delay. Let D be the delay diameter of the network. Assume that block B is either adopted or abandoned by all peers when time is Ψ_B. That is to say, at time Ψ_B, block B has votes which are not more than half of the quorums and a round of cooperation consensus has not ended. All peers in consensus network will continue to wait until the block receives votes more than half of the quorums, or the waiting time exceeds the time threshold. The time threshold is set to eliminate that a round of consensus cannot reach the termination of the state caused by the network delay.

Proof of Proposition 1.1. If $\psi_B = \infty$ then there are no new blocks added to blockchain. The probability of this case must be zero. As by Claim 1.2 we know that $\forall(\psi_B)$ is finite.

Proposition 1.3. (Resilience from 50% attacks). The 50% attack here is for the consensus network. If C_B is a byzantine peer and block B contains illegal transactions, When this round of consensus for block B is completed, $H(\psi_B)$ is not incremented. That is, all peers will abandon block B, the 50% attack initiated by the byzantine peer is a failure.

Proof. In consensus network, the upper bound of the number of byzantine peers is f, and the total number of peers is 2f + 1. If a byzantine peer becomes the primary peer construct block B and join all the byzantine peers in the network together to cheat. The maximum number of votes that block B can get is f, but the block that wants to join into blockchain must obtain votes at least f + 1. However, for a block that cannot pass validation, it is not possible to get votes that exceed f + 1. Therefore, we can conclude that in consensus network, 50% attacks which initiated by the byzantine peer always fail.

5   MPT-Chain of ECBC

ECBC not only solves the problem of data security and system trust, but also provides users with efficient query services. With the block height increasing, the number of transactions is also growing rapidly. The speed of linear query cannot meet user's requirement. This paper proposes a tree structure called MPT-Chain to speed up query, which combines the features of Patricia tree and merkle tree. MPT-Chain can ensure the consistency of distributed index and the correctness of query results.

Using Patricia tree as index can quickly locate the user's query results. And the update of Patricia tree does not need to spend too much computing resources, just need to modify the leaf node. Still, if primary peer broadcast index along with the block, huge data transmission may block the network. If the peers using transactions build index locally, this may cause the byzantine peer to return the wrong query result. Traversing data set is an only way to verifying the result.

Merkle tree is used to ensure that the data accepted from others is not corrupt and replaced, and can check that others do not spoof or publish false data. The merkle proof it provides is the basis of SPV (simple pay verification) [18], which can support the validation of the data in the light client. Based on these, this paper combines merkle tree and Patricia tree, constructs MPT-Chain which makes ECBC can guarantee the consistency of indexes in the distributed network and the correctness of query results.

5.1 Node Structure of MPT-Chain

MPT-Chain is a tree structure which contains four different types of nodes. The node structure is shown in Fig. 2. The structure of the root node consists of two parts: branch pointer and value. Branch pointer stores the pointer point to the branch node. Value field stores merkle root of the MPT-Chain, which stored in the block header will be changed when creates a block. The branch node is a list, its length is 17. HolderID in hexadecimal encoding format is used as search key, so all the branch node has 16 keys for storing the child pointer. The key in the branch node lists all possibilities of character, which reduces the trouble of dynamic updates. When search path reaches this branch node, the index number of the key represents the value of the search code. The value field of branch node stores merkle root of the merkle tree when taking the branch node as the root. Starting from the leaf node, calculated layer-by-layer until it reaches the branch node, stored merkle hash calculated in the value field.

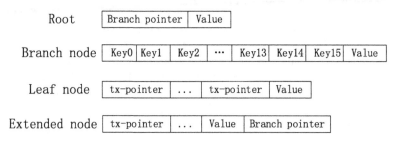

Fig. 2. Node structure of MPT-Chain

The leaf node is a list that can be dynamically changed in length. It consists of two parts: tx-pointer and value. The tx-pointer stores the pointer point to the transaction that can dynamically append when the holderID related transactions are increasing. The leaf node will add a new tx-pointer when a new transaction of the holderID is written into blockchain. The value field stored in leaf node is a hash that can be calculated by constructing the merkle tree of the transactions, which is pointed by tx-pointer in the leaf node. An extended node is an extension of a leaf node. It is used to solve the problems when a holderID encoding is a prefix for others, extend the leaf node of the holderID to an extended node in order to extend the encoding. When a leaf node extends to an extended node, the leaf node needs to be added a field to store the branch pointer. The value field stored in leaf node is a hash that can be calculated by the hash of the transaction pointed by tx-pointer and the value of the branch node pointed by branch pointer.

The value field in the branch node, the leaf node and the extended node is intermediate value of the merkle root. When primary node creates a new block, it needs to update the MPT-Chain; the update process will require the recalculation of the value field of the MPT-Chain's nodes. So the node of MPT-Chain stores intermediate value of the merkle root, which will be reused when the branch is not updated and can prevent the waste of computing resources. In addition, it can also shorten the block creation time.

5.2   The Example of MPT-Chain Structure

Users can query the certificates by holderID, and check the personal information by decrypting the Receiver-added information to confirm whether the owner of the certificate is consistent with the person who provides holderID. It is inspired by a zero-knowledge proof [17]. The requirement of users for the query is different, such as some users may only need to query a certificate, and some users may query all the holder's certificates.

The MPT implemented by the Ethereum is only the latest state query. It cannot support the history transactions of account. And with the application of blockchain in many fields, the index structure that can only retrieve the latest state will not meet the requirement of query and verification. Therefore, this paper proposes a MPT-Chain based on node structure which is extended from MPT. The leaf node of MPT-Chain contains multiple tx-points. These pointers will point to all transactions related to holderID, which constitute the holderID's transaction chain. Based on above, the tree structure proposed by this paper calls MPT-Chain.

Table 1. Example of transactions

Transaction	0	1	2	3	4
IssuerID	0001	0231	0032	0671	0001
HolderID	0517	89ca7f	05173	4a22f	0517
IssueData	20130601	20160601	20160601	20160601	20160607
CertTypeID	1	2	1	1	2
OptionTypeID	0	0	0	0	0
MajorID	001	022	402	013	001
Receiver-added	Ciphertext	Ciphertext	Ciphertext	Ciphertext	Ciphertext

In ECBC, holderID is an anonymous id that does not map the real world, and uniquely identifies a certificate holder. This paper builds the MPT-Chain to speed up query by using holderID as the search key. For ease of understanding, we have listed five educational certificate transactions that are shown in Table 1 and given the structure of MPT-Chain in Fig. 3. MPT-Chain stores the pointer of transaction in the tx-pointer of the leaf nodes. When using holderID to query, MT-Chain reads the holderID bit by bit and matches holderID starting from the root to the leaf node or the extended node.

Figure 3 use gray to represent the search path by using holderID in Table 1, and shows a tx-pointer that points to a transaction in the blockchain. It is assumed that the transactions in Table 1 exist in the blockchain in a graphical way. According to the data in Table 1, transaction 0 is a pre-transaction for transaction 4, the logical relationship can be learned by the structure of the leaf nodes or extended nodes, which is the difference between the MPT of ethereum. In addition, the latest Merkle root of MPT-Chain is also stored in the block header of the latest block; this relationship is expressed in Fig. 3 using dashed lines.

The update of MPT-Chain and the calculation of its Merkle root will affect the verification time of the block, thus affecting the transaction throughput. So, this paper chooses Patricia tree to speed up query, because as the data increases, the update of Patricia tree takes less time. Moreover, the value field of the branch node, the leaf node, and the extended node in MPT-Chain, which can be re-used in the calculation process, in order to shorten the block validation time.

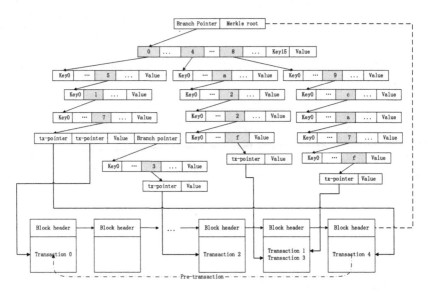

Fig. 3. MPT-Chain structure

When the primary peer starts creating a block, it first determines which transactions are stored in this block, and then updates the MPT-Chain based on these transactions to compute merkle root. After that, the primary peer stores merkle root of MPT-Chain in the block header. The primary peer broadcasts the block created to the network, other peers receive the block and check it. The other peers need to check the correctness of the transactions contained in the block and the data in the block header, including the calculation of merkle root for MPT-Chain. Using the transactions contained in the block to update MPT-Chain stored locally, calculate merkle root, compared it to the merkle root stored in block that is created by primary peer.

6 Efficiency Analysis and Experimental

This section discusses efficiency from the point of throughput, network delay and information transmission, and the theoretical analysis is proved by the experimental results.

The primary measure of ECBC's scalability is the number of transactions per second (TPS). The TPS is the rate of growth of the blockchain, multiplied by the size of blocks, and divided by the average size of a transaction. Thus,

$$\text{TPS}(\lambda, b) = \lambda \cdot b \cdot K \tag{2}$$

ECBC is a chain without fork, so block creation rate is the rate of growth of the blockchain defined as λ, b is the size of blocks and K is the average number of transactions per KB.

6.1 Delay and the Size of Blocks

As we have already seen, the delay in the network is a highly significant factor that impacts the rate of creation block. A measurement study which was recently presented by Decker and Wattenhofer [19] addresses the issue. They have set up a node on the Bitcoin network that connected to as many accessible nodes as possible. Since each such node announces new blocks to its neighbours, it is possible to record these events and estimate the time it takes blocks to propagate.

The experiment of Decker and Wattenhofer depicts this linear effect quite clearly. The interesting point is that the linear dependence on the block size, which is characteristic of a single link, also holds in aggregate for the entire network [19]. This paper adopts a linear model of the delay:

$$D_{50\%}(b) = D_{prop} + D_{bw} \cdot b \tag{3}$$

The time it takes to get to 50% of the network's peers is quite accurately described by the best fit of such a linear relation to the data. Notice that D_{prop} is a measure of aggregate propagation delay, and D_{bw} is an aggregate measure in units of seconds per KB. The fit parameters are: D_{prop} is 1.8 s, and D_{bw} is 0.066 s per KB.

Through the above analysis, we can conclude that the growth rate of the chain is mainly affected by the network delay and the block size. We get $\lambda = \lambda(D, b)$, D is used to represent the network delay. From the experimental results of Decker and

Wattenhofer, we find that, in the ideal case, the network delay is proportional to the size of the transmitted data, that is $D = D(b)$, so we conclude that $\lambda = \lambda(b)$.

In the ECBC, a round of consensus, the three types of information needs to be transmitted between peers, which include random number, block and vote. The size of random number and vote is small, the network delay caused by random number and vote is smaller than block, so we can draw a conclusion that TPS most depends on the block size.

6.2 Estimate of the Achievable TPS

In ECBC, JSON format is used to build transactions. By testing, the value of K is about 16. The next important thing is that we need to do a measure with network delay and block size. In ECBC, after a round of consensus, it does not always create block which can be added to the blockchain. Maybe, this round of the consensus is futile. If a round of consensus time is too long, but the result is futile. There is no gain for increasing the throughput, on the other hand, this phenomenon reduces throughput. Therefore, we make a trade-off between transaction latency and block size. The block size we select is 200 KB, and set the time threshold for the consensus process. Time threshold for the random number and the vote is 2 s, the block's time threshold is 20 s.

In theory, the growth rate of the block is about 1/16 block per second when the network is in good condition, so TPS $\approx$ 200 if K = 16 and b = 200. This value is the theoretical estimate by using Decker and Wattenhofer's experimental data. Moreover, the experiment in this paper verifies the theoretical data by constructing an actual network environment. The peers in ECBC need permission to enter and the number of peers relative to the bitcoin is less than bitcoin which peers from the world and can be arbitrarily joined.

6.3 Experimental Results

At present, relatively mature blockchain technology has been open source which is convenience for our work, and we would like to appreciate these generous researchers and developers. Refer to some of the mature open source code, such as ethereum and hyperledger [20], some of the blockchain common technology which has been implemented is also applicable in ECBC. Such as network communication, signature, encryption and so on. Their contributions help us reduce our workload and speed up validation of theory this paper proposed.

ECBC learns membership management service module from hyperledger and achieves a peer who want to join needs to be allowed by network. Block data and MPT-Chain use levelDB to store, which is an efficient key-value database. This paper tested with 5, 50, 100, and 200 peers when we examined transaction latency and throughput of ECBC. In the case of good network conditions, we confirmed our theoretical analysis through experimental data. Hardware configuration of the peer is the same. The server is E5620 @ 2.40 GHz, 24 GB of memory, CentOS operating system, and Gigabit Ethernet directly between the peers.

The experimental data used in this paper is more than 1.6 million transactions from more than 500 blocks in ECBC. We compare creation time of block and transactions throughput with Bitcoin, which is significantly better than Bitcoin. Figure 4 shows transactions throughput, it can reach three hundred per second. Statistics show that the number of graduates is about 7 million in 2016 China, the throughput of ECBC is able to meet the requirements of certificates management. Figure 5 indicates creation time of block. According to the experimental data, we can see that transaction latency is about 10 s that entities can bear.

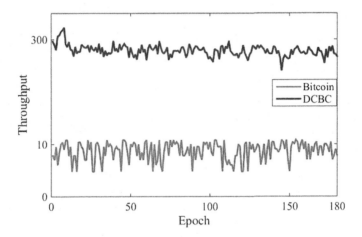

Fig. 4. Transaction throughput

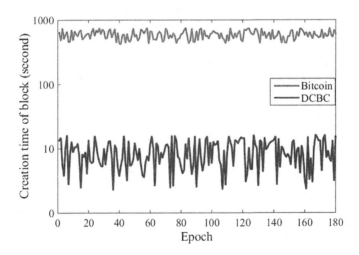

Fig. 5. Creation time of block

It is no doubt that MPT-Chain can speed up the query. But like other indexes, MPT-Chain also needs extra storage space. But it makes the query more efficient, which allows us to ignore the storage space occupied. Moreover, the storage resource is much cheaper than the computing resources. In Sect. 5.2, the MPT-Chain structure can support the holderID-based transaction query. However, its structure is not only available for accurate query, but also for range query. For example, select bachelor's degree certificates issued by a school. The above example can construct a composite search code (<IssuerID, CertTypeID>) and establish MPT-Chain based on the composite search code.

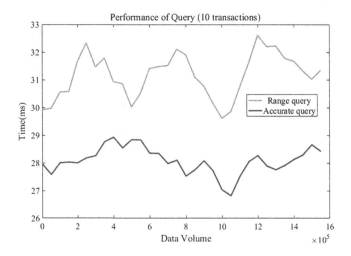

Fig. 6. Query time of MPT-Chain (10 transactions)

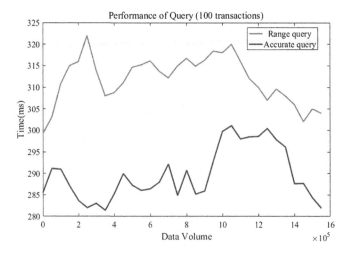

Fig. 7. Query time of MPT-Chain (100 transactions)

The experiment uses more than 1.6 million transactions to prove the efficiency of MPT-Chain, not only tests the accurate query efficiency based on holderID, but also builds multiple composite search keys (e.g. <IssuerID, CertTypeID>) to test the range query efficiency. Range query can be used for regulatory and statistical data. This paper uses multiple query statements to count the query time and calculate the average of query time. Figures 6 and 7 show the accurate query (e.g. select the historical transactions by holderID) and range query time respectively, when the query returns 10 transactions and 100 transactions. According to the experimental data, when using MPT-Chain as the query index, the query time is a millisecond-level user can tolerate.

MPT-Chain can speed up block validation because it stores intermediate values for calculating merkle root. The validation process of block needs to verify the correctness of the merkle root; the intermediate values can be reused. This paper also proves that MPT-Chain can speed up block validation by experiment; the update speed of MPT-Chain is faster than MPT. Moreover, when using account model, verification of the transaction may need to rely on the historical transaction of the account. Meanwhile, the contribution of MPT-Chain to the transaction throughput will become even greater, because of the high efficiency query of history record.

Through the above experimental results, we believe that the ECBC proposed in this paper can be applied to educational certificate management as a digital infrastructure. It not only can meet the requirements of delay and throughput, and supports millisecond query time for providing more convenient and efficient service. Therefore, we believe that, ECBC is a quiet useful educational certificate infrastructure, its application for real life can bring convenience to people's lives.

7   Conclusions

This paper had proposed an educational certificate blockchain, called ECBC, which can be used as an educational certificate infrastructure. It is permission chain that realized data security, system trust and provides management and query service for educational certificate. ECBC has a high throughput and low latency that can meet the needs of educational certificate management in real-world and has designed transaction format to protect personal privacy. The query index is called MPT-CHAIN, which can support high efficiency query, speed up block verification, and takes short time to update. We had proved our theoretical analysis and the feasibility of ECBC by using experimental data. In conclusion, it is believed ECBC proposed in this paper is a practical blockchain application which can be used as digital infrastructure to manage educational certificates and provide better service for user. Of course, our theory can not only be applied to the educational certificate. It can be applied to more fields, for example, proof of identity, proof of professional qualifications. The more areas to provide services are also what we are expanding.

Acknowledgment. This work is partially supported by National Key Research and Development Plan No. 2016YFB1000602, the Science and Technology Development Plan Project of Shandong Province No. 2016GGX101034, TaiShan Industrial Experts Programme of Shandong Province No. tscy20160404.

References

1. MIT Media Lab, educational certificates. http://certificates.media.mit.edu/
2. China Higher Educational Student Information Network (XueXinwang). http://www.chsi.com.cn/
3. Nakamoto, S.: Bitcoin: a peer-to-peer electronic cash system. Consulted (2009)
4. Bitcoin wiki. Scalability (2015). https://en.bitcoin.it/wiki/Scalability
5. Eyal, I., Gencer, A.E., Sirer, E.G, Renesse, R.V.: Bitcoin-NG: a scalable blockchain protocol (2015). http://arxiv.org/abs/1510.02037
6. Luu, L., Narayanan, V., Baweja, K., Zheng, C., Gilbert, S., Saxena, P.: SCP: a computationally-scalable Byzantine consensus protocol for blockchains. Cryptology ePrint Archive, Report 2015/1168
7. Zyskind, G., Nathan, O., Pentland, A.: Decentralizing privacy: using blockchain to protect personal data. In: Security and Privacy Workshops, pp. 180–184. IEEE (2015)
8. Ethereum Project. https://www.ethereum.org/
9. Ethereum MPT. https://github.com/ethereum/wiki/wiki/Patricia-Tree
10. Jiang, J.: Implementing the PATRICIA data structure for compression algorithms with finite size dictionaries. In: International Conference on Data Transmission - Advances in Modem and Isdn Technology and Applications, pp. 123–127. IEEE Xplore (1992)
11. Dan, W., Sirer, E.G.: Optimal parameter selection for efficient memory integrity verification using Merkle hash trees. In: IEEE International Symposium on Network Computing and Applications, pp. 383–388 (2004)
12. Jakobsson, M., Leighton, T., Micali, S., Szydlo, M.: Fractal Merkle tree representation and traversal. In: Joye, M. (ed.) CT-RSA 2003. LNCS, vol. 2612, pp. 314–326. Springer, Heidelberg (2003). doi:10.1007/3-540-36563-X_21
13. Sompolinsky, Y., Zohar, A.: Accelerating Bitcoin's transaction processing. Fast money grows on trees, not chains. In: Financial Cryptography, Puerto Rico (2015)
14. Thoughts on UTXOs by Vitalik Buterin, Co-Founder of Ethereum. https://medium.com/@ConsenSys/thoughts-on-utxo-by-vitalik-buterin-2bb782c67e53
15. Open Badges Specification. https://openbadges.org/
16. Yves-Alexandre, D.M., Erez, S., Samuel, S.W., Alex, S.P.: openPDS: protecting the privacy of metadata through safeanswers. PLoS ONE 9(7), e98790 (2014)
17. Rackoff, C., Simon, D.R.: Non-interactive zero-knowledge proof of knowledge and chosen ciphertext attack. In: Feigenbaum, J. (ed.) CRYPTO 1991. LNCS, vol. 576, pp. 433–444. Springer, Heidelberg (1992). doi:10.1007/3-540-46766-1_35
18. Gervais, A., Capkun, S., Karame, G.O., et al.: On the privacy provisions of Bloom filters in lightweight bitcoin clients. In: ACM Computer Security Applications Conference, pp. 326–335. ACM (2014)
19. Decker, C., Wattenhofer, R.: Information propagation in the Bitcoin network. In: 13th IEEE International Conference on Peer-to-Peer Computing (P2P), Trento, Italy, September 2013
20. IBM Hyperledger Project. https://www.hyperledger.org/

Author Index

Printed in the United States
By Bookmasters